The Movie Mom's Guide to Family Movies

The Movie Mom's Guide to Family Movies

◆

2nd Edition

*A PARENTS' GUIDE TO MORE THAN
500 MOVIES ON VIDEO
FOR KIDS AGES 2 TO 18*

Nell Minow

[handwritten inscription: To always - Gorgeous - Deborah - with always love — G GGs forever! Nell]

iUniverse, Inc.
New York Lincoln Shanghai

The Movie Mom's Guide to Family Movies
2nd Edition

iUniverse, Inc.

For information address:
iUniverse, Inc.
2021 Pine Lake Road, Suite 100
Lincoln, NE 68512
www.iuniverse.com

ISBN: 0-595-32095-3

Printed in the United States of America

In this book, I salute the leading men of the classic movies:
The acrobatic ebullience of Cary Grant in Holiday;
the quiet integrity of Gregory Peck in To Kill a Mockingbird;
the poetic sweetness of Gary Cooper in Ball of Fire;
the irresistible rascality of Clark Gable in It Happened One Night;
the elegant tenderness of William Powell in I Love You Again;
the literate discernment of Jimmy Stewart in The Philadelphia Story;
the impeccable grace of Fred Astaire in Shall We Dance?;
the athletic exuberance of Gene Kelly in It's Always Fair Weather,
the courage and loyalty of Humphrey Bogart in To Have and Have Not;
the optimistic resilience of Mickey Mouse in The Band Concert;
the legal skills of Spencer Tracy in Adam's Rib and Inherit the Wind;
the heartbreaking sensitivity of James Dean in East of Eden;
the inspirational persuasiveness of Robert Preston in The Music Man;
the romantic patience of Buster Keaton in The General;
the strength and commitment of John Wayne in The Quiet Man; and
the anarchic irreverence of all of the Marx brothers.

This book is for David, my own leading man, who is all of that and more.

Contents

PART II: MOVIES ABOUT GROWING UP

Acknowledgements

The best part of writing a book is the chance to thank the people who are most dear to me. This book would not have been possible without Judy Viorst, who provided inspiration, encouragement, and her agent. Bob Lescher guided it through its original publication, along with Rachel Klayman, a perceptive and talented editor. Sally Waters and Gabriel London provided dedicated assistance with research and fact-checking, and the encyclopedic Jody Neblett cheerfully answered the most esoteric movie trivia questions. My dear friends Alyssa Machold and Julia Riesenberg provide indispensable back-up for my website and delightful companionship at screenings.

Thanks to my young movie fan friends, especially Claire, Julia, and Nora Riesenberg, Harrison and Samuel Fahn, Sophie and Teddy Klein, Jackson Marlette, Sam, Toby, Theo, and Chas Leiss, Sam, Nell, and Noah Norman, Claire, John Patrick, and Elizabeth Adams, Alex, Zach, and Claire Prosperi, Alex, Claire, and Mary Ben Apatoff, Lorenzo Acciai, Mira Singer, Mary Bingham, William and Emily Stephen, Laura and Katy Rosen, Amaya and Walker Whitworth, Simon O'Sullivan, Ben and Maggie Schaffzin, and Andrew Thomson.

Thanks to editors Lilah Lohr at the Chicago Tribune and Chris Collins at USA Today who always make my columns better and let me take the credit. Thanks to all my friends at the radio stations across the US and Canada who make it so much fun to talk about the movies on the air every week.

Thanks to my beloved friend and partner, Bob Monks, whose influence is on every page, and to all of our colleagues at The Corporate Library, who graciously supported this frolic and detour from the world of corporate governance.

There is a special kinship among those who watch great movies together, and there is an even more special kinship among those who share the truly atrocious ones. Thanks to my generous, wise, and always-cherished movie critic friends, especially Arch Campbell, Tim Gordon, Willie Waffle, James Hill, Bill Henry, Cynthia Fuchs, Jim Judy, Dave Cuozzo, Eric Childress, Herb Kane, Mike Clark, Jay Carr, Gary Arnold, Christian Toto, Dann Gire, Nick DiGilio, Steven Hunter, Jane Horwitz, David Edelstein, Jeffrey Lyles, Elias Savada, Michael O'Sullivan, Jeanette Catsoulis, and Desson Thomson. You make even the bad movies fun just by being there and your insights enrich my appreciation for the great ones.

Movie viewing is not always a pleasure, but movie-going is, thanks to Sara Taylor, Dan Maloney, and all the folks at Allied. So is writing about what I see, thanks to Liz Perle, Jim Steyer, all the folks at Common Sense Media, and Sal Taylor, Harry Medved, and all the folks at Yahoo Movies.

Thanks and love to my mishpocha, the family who feel like friends and the friends who feel like family: Kathy and Andrew Stephen, Kristie Miller, Deborah Davidson, Tom Dunkel, all the Caplins, Vicki Apatoff, Adam Frankel, David Drew, Stuart Brotman, Deborah Baughman, Jennie Fahn, Leonard and Bobbi Starr, John Adams, Shannon Hackett, Matt and Danny Ornstein, Henry Geller, Sandy and Ellen Twaddell, Elyse Pine, Will Fertman, Beth Young, Nadine Prosperi, Kathy Schultz, Patty Marx, Toby Kent, Steve Friess, Faith Falkner, Steve Wallman, Jim Richter, Sheldon Seigel, Tommy Gardner, Larry Bergreen, Bill Pedersen, Michael Kinsley, Jeff Sonnenfeld, Alan Kahn, Rosemary Brown, Ellen Burka, Gail Ifshin, Jamie Heard, Alexandra Lajoux, Steve Lawrence, Victoria and Joe Klein, Jon Friedman, Helena Han, Laurence and Celia Beasley, Sophie L'Hélias, Judy Pomeranz, Kayla Gillan, Jesse Norman and Kate Bingham, Jeanne Patterson, Nancy Altman, Kit Bingham and Sarah Kavenaugh, Jane Leavy, Duncan Clark, T.L. Hawkins, Terry Savage, Renée Crown, Paula Trienens, Elaine Levis, Ann Yerger, Cynthea Riesenberg, Parvané Hashemi, Sarah Teslik, Caroline Mayer, Isabel Contreras, and all the Renaissancers. I am always grateful for my wonderful sisters, Martha and Mary, and for all the fabulous Minows, Apatoffs, Browns, Tierneys, Frankels, Resnicks, Greenes, and Baskins.

Thanks especially to my mother, who told me when a really great movie was going to be on *The Late Show* and then stayed up and watched it with me. Thanks especially to my dad, who left my sisters and mom at home to take me to see *Around the World in 80 Days* and *The Wonderful World of the Brothers Grimm*. Thanks to Fran Apatoff, who taught me to look for the poetry in everything, even in the movies. Thanks to those I miss every day, especially Bill Apatoff, Stan Frankel, Beth Tierney, and Burton Minow. Thanks to two very special girls, Lauren Webster and Alison Anthes. Thanks to my children, Ben and Rachel Apatoff, who never forgot to cheer for me.

Thanks most of all to my husband, David Apatoff, still and forever the best person I know.

Notes to the Reader

- When the title of a movie appears in boldface, this means it is discussed in another part of the book. Reviews of many of the movies mentioned in the book and many others are available online at http://movies.yahoo. com/moviemom or http://www.moviemom.com

- Running times are approximate because different versions of movies are sometimes available.

- The abbreviation NR stands for Not Rated and indicates that a movie was not submitted to the MPAA for a rating.

- I love to hear from readers and I welcome comments, suggestions and questions at moviemom@moviemom.com

INTRODUCTION

"I know *Cliffhanger* is rated R, but it's only for violence, not for sex, Dad!"

The boy in the video store added that all his friends had seen it and said it was no worse than several other gruesome titles he had already seen. His father sighed and gave in.

This kind of exchange goes on in just about every family. The same technology that has enabled us to have a range of entertainment broader than anyone could have imagined has created tough challenges for families. Too often parents end up grabbing videos from the "Just Released" shelf or watching the same ones over and over. This electronic baby-sitting has nothing to do with engaging the mind or heart. Instead, we use it as something of a video pause button, parking kids in front of a numbing cavalcade of explosions and jump cuts. The messages of these movies are never consciously considered, yet they sink in. Too often, parents feel unable to impose any kind of control.

In 1961, when I was nine years old, my father, Newton Minow, made headlines around the world (and ultimately became a Trivial Pursuit answer) by calling television a "vast wasteland." As President Kennedy's new, thirty-five-year-old Chairman of the Federal Communications Commission, he was the first person ever to hold that position to tell the National Association of Broadcasters that he would not allow their licenses to be renewed unless they met their obligation to serve the public interest. He has been fighting for better television ever since. He and my mother did their best to teach their three children to think critically about what we saw on television, and they were always looking for movies and television shows we could watch together and talk about afterward. They never hesitated to tell us that we were not allowed to watch something they considered inappropriate. Most important, they made me think very hard about what I was watching.

My parents both love movies, and I always have, too, even as a very small child. When I was sixteen, the last week of my sophomore year in high school, I came down with a very bad case of mononucleosis, and was confined to bed for the entire summer. My eyes were infected, which made it difficult for me to read, so my mother allowed me the unprecedented privilege of having a television set

1

in my bedroom. While my friends were off at camp and the beach, I spent an entire summer watching movies on our small black-and-white television set. This was long before the days of cable and the VCR, so I was pretty much stuck with whatever came on. It was a great education in the movies of the 1940s and 1950s, and when I got better I began to read books (and later take classes) about film history and criticism. I kept watching every movie I could.

All of this paid off years later, when I had two small children on a rainy vacation. We had made cookies, worked on puzzles, and played board games and were all looking for something new. I sat them down on the sofa and said, "Some mothers can do sports, and some can do craft projects. I am not one of those moms. On the other hand, there is one thing I can do better than any other mother. I can do a MomFest!" Once I explained that this meant a movie festival, they were delighted. Every day we watched a movie and did a related project. We saw **1776** and took the train to Philadelphia to see where it all took place. We saw *State Fair* and visited a county fair. We saw **The King and I** and looked up the history of Thailand in the encyclopedia and made Thai puppets. The MomFest was such a success that it became an annual tradition.

Knowing a lot about movies also helped me find movies that related to my children's interests. Probably my greatest challenge was on the day when my son wanted a movie about boxing and my daughter wanted a musical. I remembered the Gene Kelly musical *It's Always Fair Weather* has a song with the names of every heavyweight champion in it, and both of my children got a big kick out of it. Sharing my favorites with the kids was like seeing them for the first time. I tried to teach them what my parents had taught me about thinking critically about what we watched and I tried to protect them from inappropriate material.

Unfortunately, in that respect I had a tougher challenge than my parents did. When I was a child parents could sit their children down in front of the television set confident that what they saw might be boring or even dumb, but that the most dangerous thing they might see would be tobacco commercials. Violence was confined to a few cowboy shoot-outs. Sex was just about nonexistent: Rob and Laura Petrie slept in twin beds, Lucy was not allowed to use the word "pregnant," and Jeannie's harem pants had to cover her belly button. When we came home from school, we watched *The Mickey Mouse Club*. Today's kids can come home from school and watch television talk shows with topics like, "Men who have sex with their babysitters"; "I don't know which of my lovers is the father of my child"; and "My mother is a stripper." Early evening sitcoms have jokes about wife swapping and premature ejaculation. Cable television shows naked people having sex and hardcore pornography is available to anyone with a computer.

We baby boomers spent afternoons speculating on the lyrics to "Louie Louie"; today's kids hear teenage girls sing about "cameltoes" and Eminem sing about wanting to kill women. The average child spends 15,000 hours in front of a television set by age fifteen, 4,000 more hours than in school, far more than he or she spends with parents. Nowhere is really safe. I took my kids to see a G-rated movie and sat through a coming attraction in which a woman said to a man, "I am going to give you lots of sex." I do not advocate a return to the repression and ignorance of the past. This is not a healthy situation for kids either. It is so pervasive that parents feel overwhelmed.

Yet it is still possible to protect kids from the media onslaught, to find videos that exercise the mind and spirit and bring families closer together. Classic movies that once were available only on scratchy prints in art houses or shot through with commercials on the "Late Late Show" now appear in video stores, public libraries, and mail-order houses, pristine new prints, as timeless as Rembrandts. Films that enchant, inspire, thrill, even teach, are there for parents who know where to look.

It can be a challenge, once you have found these movies, to get kids to watch them. Children love the familiar. That's why they want to hear the same books over and over when they are small and see the same videos (or almost-carbon-copy sequels) over and over when they are bigger. Mental exercise, like physical exercise, is not as easy as watching a movie that is, to use Frank Lloyd Wright's description of television, "chewing gum for the eyes."

Furthermore, the style of moviemaking has changed, so that older movies can at first seem unfamiliar and slow-moving. Kids accustomed to movies like *X-Men* or **Finding Nemo** or even television shows like *Sesame Street* are used to kaleidoscopic images and nonstop action.

Be patient and persistent. Just as important as their exposure to wonderful stories, beautifully presented, is the stretching kids have to do to adjust to quieter, subtler storytelling. Although introducing these movies to today's children can be a challenge, it can be done, and it is worth the effort.

ENCOURAGING KIDS AND TEENS TO WATCH OLDER MOVIES

Entice them. Get children curious and interested before the movie begins. Tell them what the challenge or conflict is in the movie, but don't tell them how it turns out. "This is a movie about a girl who dreams of owning the fastest and most beautiful horse in the world." "This is a movie about a teacher who goes to a country far from home to teach the children of a king." Children are also curious about the movies that were their parents' (and grandparents') favorites when they were young.

Engage them. Movies should not be background noise for whatever else they happen to be doing. If they wander off, bicker, or start to play with toys, turn off the television set and tell them they can see the movie when they are ready to watch. Stretch their attention spans. Don't let them zone out between explosions and car chases.

Challenge them. Make sure that every movie they see is one you genuinely feel is worth the two hours it takes away from books, music, talking with you and with each other, homework, creating something, or helping around the house. Be aware that older movies are more slowly paced, and some children will complain that black-and-white movies are boring. Just reply with a slight tone of regret that you are sorry to have made a mistake in thinking they were old enough for these movies, and maybe they can try again next year, and that for now they can go to their rooms and read or draw while you watch it.

Challenge them to challenge the film, as well. Make sure they are thinking about what is happening. Ask them what they would do if they were in that situation. Ask why the character is behaving that way. Ask them what the people who made the movie wanted them to think about the characters, and how they can tell. How does the movie spring its surprises? How does it make you feel the suspense? This not only teaches them about narrative and point of view, it also helps to teach them critical thinking.

Prepare them. No matter how bright and well-educated a child is, a child under age twelve is unlikely to be able to follow and understand and truly enjoy a full-length movie's plot, especially one set in another time or place, without some kind of preparation. This is another reason children like to watch the same movie over and over; each viewing allows them to understand it better.

Give children a general overview to make sure they understand the situation, the issues, and the characters. If they ask questions, give them more details, but don't tell them how it turns out. Instead, say: "That's just what the guy in the movie is trying to decide! Watch to see what he does!" Sometimes, with younger children, it helps to read together a book on the same or a related subject. With musicals, it helps to listen to the music a few times before seeing the movie; it usually sparks kids' curiosity, too. Sometimes a classic movie will seem like a cliché to children who have seen the imitations. There is no way to make a John Ford Western seem new to a child who has already seen a dozen shoot-'em-ups. It can be fun to tell them that this movie was so popular, it was copied over and over again. Let them try to catch the original inspiration and see if they can figure out why it had such an impact.

Connect with them. Pick a movie that relates to the child's interests or experiences in some way. If you have visited (or plan to visit) New York City, try *On the Town*, in which three sailors have only one day to see the city. If the child loves baseball, try *The Pride of the Yankees* or *The Rookie*. Many classic children's books have been made into movies. Children who have read **The Secret Garden, Little Women, Anne of Green Gables, The Diary of Anne Frank, Tuck Everlasting**, or **The Phantom Tollbooth**, will especially enjoy the movie versions. A child who has learned about Abraham Lincoln, Thomas Edison, Malcolm X, Charles Lindbergh, or Helen Keller in school can see movies about their lives.

Children also love movies that feature a child as a major character. Try *The Little Princess, Heidi*, **The Canterville Ghost**, *Oliver!, Annie, Lassie Comes Home*, or **The Prince and the Pauper**.

Everyone watches **A Christmas Carol, Miracle on 34th Street**, and **It's a Wonderful Life** at Christmas, but other holidays have movies, too. For example: *1776* for the Fourth of July, *The Long Walk Home* or *Boycott* for Martin Luther King Day, *I Remember Mama* for Mother's Day, *Life with Father* or **To Kill a Mockingbird** for Father's Day, *The Pajama Game* or **Norma Rae** for Labor Day *and Sergeant York* or *To Hell and Back* for Memorial Day.

If a child likes a particular genre (Westerns, pirates, detective stories, adventure), seek out movies in that category. Some children get attached to particular actors and will want to see all of their films. One movie can lead to a related one: **The Wizard of Oz** to *The Wiz*, **West Side Story** to **Romeo and Juliet**, **Rudy** to *Knute Rockne, All American*. Movies can teach a child about the careers or backgrounds of family members or friends. A child dealing with challenges like courage, loss, growing up, moving, confidence, or tolerance can find them easier to talk about (or even think about) after seeing them in a movie.

Warn them. Older movies do have the advantage of telling their stories without the kind of language, violence, or nudity that led to the development of the rating system in the late 1960s. The disadvantage is that they sometimes reflect assumptions or attitudes that are insensitive or even offensive by today's standards, particularly in their treatment of women and minorities.

This creates an important opportunity for discussions with children about those attitudes, about the history they were a part of and the history since, and, most importantly, about being able to identify prejudice and its impact, to make sure it is eradicated.

Protect them. Examine the ratings carefully and make sure the movie is suitable for children before you bring it home. Never rely on the information on the box, which is designed to sell, not inform. One mother brought home *Sirens* for her 12-year-old son, not realizing that most of the movie features three naked women discussing sex very explicitly, because the box made it look like something from *Masterpiece Theatre*. Many parents have allowed their children to see *The Good Son* or the *Ace Ventura* movies because they seemed like children's movies. They are not. If you are watching a movie with the children and decide it is not appropriate, turn it off. This has nothing to do with how smart or sophisticated they are for their ages; it has to do with your communicating to them your views on what is appropriate. Showing it to them implies your endorsement. It is very tough, in this era, to protect children from inappropriate material, but they will appreciate every effort, if not now, later.

Join them. Sharing a movie with your children shows them you are not putting them in front of the television set to give yourself a break; you are sharing something with them that you think is worthwhile. It gives you the chance to assess their reactions, answer their questions, model critical responses, and tell them what you think of characters or issues. Even a movie with some inappropriate material can have some value if it prompts a discussion about the objectionable behavior. It gives you a chance to point out aspects of your past ("I used to dress like that!"; "You see, all airplanes had propellers!") or places you have been. It gives you a chance to talk about values without sounding as though you are preaching to them.

Best of all, it gives you a chance to win the Grand National Steeplechase with Velvet, save King Richard with Robin Hood, learn to communicate with Helen Keller, and climb the Alps with Heidi. You'll fall in love with the movies along with your children, and the movies will be a part of your shared experience and frame of reference that you will always treasure.

WHAT THIS BOOK IS (AND IS NOT)

This is not a book of movies "for kids." It is a book of movies for families with children from ages two through eighteen to watch together, to use as a starting point for discussions of values, feelings, and consequences, to provide a common experience, to share something that will be fun for everyone. Although most of these films can be watched by children and older kids without adults present, they are selected because they are family films, not just "kids' films."

This is not a book of movie reviews, or of film criticism. Reviews are written to give you enough information so you can decide if you want to see the movie, without giving away so much information that you don't need to see it. Film criticism, like literary criticism, usually assumes that you have seen the movie and want to explore some additional insights, and often assumes or gives away important details. A review of **Citizen Kane** won't tell you what Rosebud is, but criticism will.

This book has a different purpose. All of the movies I recommend are "good" in some sense, meaning that they are worth watching. While many of the films in this book are classics that no one should grow up—or be a grown-up—without seeing, some others are selected less for inherent artistic merit than for the likelihood that they will be enjoyed by families and provide a good starting point for discussions of issues. These write-ups are designed to give you the information you need to determine whether this film suits your values and the interests and needs of your child.

This book is also not intended to compete with encyclopedias that have thousands of thumbnail sketches to give you just enough information to jog your memory about whether you have seen a particular film or give you some sense of whether you might like it. Those books are great (I especially like Leonard Maltin's), but they do not provide the information that a parent needs to decide whether a particular movie is appropriate for a particular child or teenager. For that reason, I do include "spoilers" in many write-ups, meaning that I let you know how the movie comes out. Only you know how your child will react to plot developments like the death of one of the characters. "Happier" endings may also raise concerns. Many children will be delighted when the parents get back together in **The Parent Trap**. Some children, who are still having problems dealing with divorce in their own families, may find it upsetting. So I try to alert parents to anything in the movie that could create problems for a child.

Most important, this is a supplement, not a substitute, for moral instruction by parents. They learn from you, and from your example, not from stories you tell them. This book can only illuminate and supplement that example by exposing them to stories and situations to compare to their own experience, that allow them to imagine how they might react, to better understand the reactions of others.

You are their moral teacher, and not just when you talk to them about values, but every waking moment. There is no movie that can teach a child the importance of integrity when a parent says, "You don't need to buy pencils; I'll bring some home from the office"; or, "Tell the man you are only ten so we can get a discount"; or, "If we don't get a new car, people will think we are worthless"; or, "Good thing no one saw me scrape that parked car! Let's leave now before anyone comes." You can show them a dozen movies about tolerance, but it means nothing if you have never entertained friends from other races or religions in your home. There is no movie that can teach children about the dangers of substance abuse or disrespect or violence if they live in a home where that behavior is accepted.

This book is not a lesson plan. The discussion and question sections included for each of the main entries are not intended to make every family viewing session into a seminar. Rather, they are intended to give parents an idea of the issues raised by the movie so that parents can decide whether it is one that is appropriate for a particular child at a particular stage, based on the issues he or she is dealing with. Sometimes they can be used to get children interested before the movie. More important, they can provide a starting point for talking about what you have seen.

It is likely that parents will think of better questions on their own; it is inevitable that children will. The most important thing is for families to watch together so that parents can see how their children react, so children can see how their parents react, so that the movies are something to think about instead of something to put one's mind on hold.

Many of the movies have full-length write-ups. The rest have briefer descriptions, including notes about any areas of special sensitivity or connections to particular interests or to other movies. Many more movies are included in my website (http://movies.yahoo.com/moviemom), which also covers current releases. A shorter write-up does not mean that the film is less good or less important or less instructive; it just means that it was less complex, or that it illustrated issues included in the discussion of another film.

The longer write-ups include details of the plot, a discussion of topics raised, bullets detailing any profanity, nudity/sexual references, alcohol/drug abuse, violence/scariness, or tolerance/diversity issues, questions that could be prompted by the movie, "connections" and activities. For movies aimed at younger children, the activities are usually connected to some aspect of the movie (i.e., "Find Thailand on a map" after watching **The King and I**). For movies likely to be viewed by middle school or high school kids, the connections are more likely to be other movies featuring the same performers or director, or with related themes. The "connections" tend to be a little of everything, including some of my favorite bits of film trivia.

This is a book of family movies, so it does not include movies kids like that are just about impossible for parents to sit through, like the Pokemon series. Regretfully, I have left out all but a few subtitled films, because they do not lend themselves well to family viewing.

If I have left out your family's favorite movie, it was probably for lack of time, space, or availability; send me an email at moviemom@moviemom.com so I can include it in the next edition.

HOW THIS BOOK IS ORGANIZED

The movies listed in this book are organized by themes, in two sections. The first part contains value-related themes like Honesty and Integrity, Tolerance and Making Moral Choices.

The second part contains themes relating to "growing up," movies about issues that all kids must learn how to handle. It includes movies about evaluating priorities and risks in making choices, about issues like ambition, competition, and money. It also includes movies illustrating different kinds of families, and has a section focusing on the special challenges faced by teenagers.

On my website, I have many of these and suggested "just for fun" movies, with movies for every holiday and season, and the best in musicals, fantasies, comedies, romance, adventure, and mystery and suspense, plus movies to watch on rainy or snowy days, or when a child (or a parent) is sick in bed.

TALKING WITH KIDS ABOUT WHAT THEY WATCH

Watching Movies with a Young Child

Movies can provide a wonderful opportunity to help young children in their development, particularly in understanding emotions. Ask them about the characters ("Is she happy or sad?"; "Is he angry or frightened?") and encourage them to talk with you about what the characters are feeling. Movies can also help children develop empathy by teaching them to understand and even identify with the perspective of others.

One of the great advantages of watching a movie with children is their freshness of perspective. They don't know that if an orphan boy meets a rich man whose beloved child was once mysteriously kidnapped, chances are he will turn out to be that child. They don't know it's corny, or a cliché. Never allow anyone (including an older sibling) to make them feel dumb for being surprised by what happens. Enjoy the freshness it brings to your own appreciation of the film, and encourage them to begin to recognize patterns.

Watching Movies with an Older Child

School-age kids are ready to identify more complex patterns and predict consequences. Teach them that every story is like a mystery, and that as they watch, they should ask why each character and each event is in the story, and what they add to the narrative or the atmosphere. If the difference between story and life is editing, why were these characters and events chosen to illustrate this story? What makes it a story?

Normally, the hero is changed at the end of a story; he or she learns something or loses something. Teach kids to look for this, and try to understand what writers call the "arc" of the story. Tell them about Chekhov's comment that "if there is a gun on the mantelpiece in Act I, it should be fired by the end of Act III." Ask them to use indicators like that to predict what will happen, and to comment on the characters' behavior, on consequences, and on the reactions of other characters.

Ask them to summarize the movie, an excellent mental challenge. Anyone who has ever spent time with eleven-year-olds knows that they love to tell you the entire movie, scene by scene. To help them learn organization and communication skills, teach them to pick the most important parts to tell someone unfamiliar with the story. Kids at this age love to share movies with their friends and it can be fun to have a group of families share a monthly movie and discussion.

Almost every movie falls into one or more of the following thirteen plot patterns. Kids ages ten and up enjoy learning to recognize them and categorize the movies they see.

- **Road movies**. People who start out not knowing or even disliking each other learn to respect, like, and even love each other, often while traveling together to accomplish some goal (examples: **The Wizard of Oz, Toy Story, It Happened One Night**). Sometimes it is a group of diverse people who must confront some challenge together. Another variation features people who are somehow connected but have not seen each other for a while or do not know each other well, like family members or former classmates.

- **The reluctant hero**. A cynic or a callow youth discovers or rediscovers the hero within. These movies often provide a chance to observe moral judgments and choices (examples: **Casablanca, Star Wars, The Matrix**).

- **Fish out of water**. Someone outside our culture or society throws our cultural assumptions and personal foibles into stark relief by highlighting a fresh perspective (examples: **The Gods Must Be Crazy, The Jungle Book, King of Hearts**).

- **Boy who cried wolf**. People who don't tell the truth have to deal with the consequences. This theme is often found in romantic movies (examples: **Alice Adams, Daddy Long Legs**), and it is also very popular in comedies (example: **Mrs. Doubtfire**).

- **Cat in the Hat**. An ordinary person's life is disrupted by a wacky but exciting and lovable outsider, revealing to the ordinary person how much more there is to life (examples: **Bringing Up Baby, Ball of Fire**).

- **Rise and fall**. A character with ambition and vision (and, usually, good intentions) achieves success, and then wants too much or forgets his original purpose. This popular theme goes back to the ancient Greek dramas and myths, where it was called "hubris," a human's attempt to be like the gods (examples: **All the King's Men, Citizen Kane**).

- **Growing up and family stories**. One or more young people come of age, learning sometimes painful lessons about loss and responsibility. This is often combined with one of the other plot patterns (examples: **Little Women, I Remember Mama, The Yearling**).

- **Redemption**. People who have lost their self-respect or integrity find it. People who never had it develop it (examples: **Bad Day at Black Rock**; Doc Holliday in *Gunfight at the OK Corral* and other versions of the same story). We often see the hero overcoming a tragic flaw—or learning his lesson but being felled by the flaw (example: **The Gunfighter**).

- **Triumph of the underdog.** Someone no one believes in, who does not believe in him/herself, grows, learns, and achieves an all-but-impossible goal (examples: **Rocky, Rudy, Seabiscuit**, and countless movies about ragamuffin sports teams, as well as **The Solid Gold Cadillac, Erin Brockovich**, and **Mr. Smith Goes to Washington**).

- **Boy meets girl**; boy loses girl; boy gets girl. This, of course, is the classic romance (examples: *On the Town*, **My Big Fat Greek Wedding, His Girl Friday**).

- **The quest for the MacGuffin.** "MacGuffin" was Alfred Hitchcock's word for whatever it is that the hero and heroine are so eager to get. These movies involve a search for treasure, solving a mystery, or saving the world. Sometimes the hero is a professional (examples: James Bond movies; *The Thin Man*), but more often, the hero is an ordinary person thrust into terror and intrigue and called upon to exercise extraordinary courage and skill (examples: **Raiders of the Lost Ark**; most Hitchcock movies).

- **Biography.** These movies allow us a peek into the life of an interesting or unusual person. They often include elements from the underdog or coming-of-age genre as well (examples: **The Spirit of St. Louis, Young Tom Edison, Abe Lincoln in Illinois, The Great White Hope, The Rookie**).

- **Explosion movie.** Then there are movies with lots of explosions. Something in the impact of hot weather on brain cells seems to require everyone to attend at least one of these each year (example: **Independence Day**).

Some good questions to ask intermediate and middle school kids: With so few plots used over and over, what makes the difference between a good and a bad movie? What does the main character learn? What problem does he solve? What does he lose? What does he gain?

Watching Movies with a Teenager

Surprisingly, teens are a lot like toddlers. Both are going through stages in which oppositional behavior is a temporary substitute for genuine independence. Just as a toddler's brain is optimally constructed to be able to absorb information, a teenager's is optimally constructed to absorb rules of interaction and behavior. For the first time, they are looking outside the family for guidance on how to behave, and they learn a lot from the movies. Like toddlers, they are more comfortable talking about what is going on with the characters on-screen than they are talking about themselves. So movies can be an important way to help you connect with them about issues like communication, values, priorities, and evaluating risk.

Teens are busy and often prefer to go to movies with their friends, but parents should continue to impose limits (just because your child is over thirteen does not mean that any PG-13 movie is appropriate), get a sense of what movies they are watching, and do their best to watch with them as often as possible. Child development specialists encourage parents to have "floor time" with toddlers, to get down on their level and let them lead the play. For parents of teens, the equivalent of floor time is letting them pick the movies you watch together part of the time (within your own guidelines for appropriateness), maybe taking turns. Watch the movies they love, without criticism, as a way to connect with them. Teens love to express their views of morality, and so they may be willing to talk with you about issues raised by the movies.

WARNING: SOME MOVIES ARE NOT WHAT THEY SEEM

It is almost impossible to appreciate just how damaging today's movies can, be. Movies today are not just different in content, they are also more readily available. Kids may not be able to buy tickets to R-rated movies in a theater, but they can see R-rated movies playing on the screens at the video store, or at home on cable or the VCR.

It is hard for adults to think of this kind of material from the perspective of a child, because we have something they do not: context, based on our experience. In *Four Weddings and a Funeral*, for example, a couple has sex after perhaps two dozen words of conversation, and she describes her thirty-one other lovers before they decide that they are deeply in love. Adults may find the movie witty, charming, and fairly tongue-in-cheek, rather than sordid. We know that the world does not really work that way, but a twelve-year-old, or even a seventeen-year-old, is likely to view it in much more literal terms.

When parents in the 1990s were growing up, it was unthinkable for heroes and heroines to engage in casual sex; now it is assumed in movies that any two people who feel warmly toward each other will sleep together. If parents bring their children to a popular romantic comedy like *While You Were Sleeping*, they will see a prolonged (and presumably humorous) reference to a missing testicle as well a number of sexual references. *The Truth About Cats and Dogs* has an extended phone-sex sequence. As delightful as these movies are, or, indeed, because they are so delightful, they can teach our kids lessons we do not want them to learn, especially if parents are uncomfortable discussing their own values.

Kids (and parents) often grab videos based on the titles or packaging, and the teens behind the video store counters are not much help. Just because the title or cast makes it appear to be acceptable does not mean that it is. Beware of movies like *Kindergarten Cop* (explicit violence, bedroom scene, and a genuinely kinky villain), *Problem Child* (crude and gross, and the sequel is even worse), *Killer Klowns From Outer Space* (violent and scary—the Klowns drink blood), the Ace Ventura movies (numerous sexual references), *Bebe's Kids* (animated but not for kids, very raunchy), and *The Good Son* (a thriller with Macaulay Culkin playing a murderous child). *The Brady Bunch Movie* may be based on a thoroughly G-rated television series, but the movie is rated PG-13 for innuendo. The Eddie Murphy version of *The Nutty Professor* is rated PG-13, and has very explicit sexual humor—for example: "Your mother is so fat that after I had sex with her, I rolled over twice and was still on top of her".

Nor is it safe to assume that you can't go wrong with a comedy. Movies made by Jim Carrey, the Zuckers (the *Airplane!* and *Naked Gun* movies) Mel Brooks (*Robin Hood: Men in Tights,*) the Mike Meyers Austin Powers series, and their "slob comedy" imitators are filled with extremely raunchy and scatological references, and should be screened by parents before allowing kids to watch them.

Movies are often marketed to the broadest possible audience. Be careful of promotional tie-ins (like fast-food giveaways) designed for young children advertising movies that may not be appropriate for them. Big media conglomerates do a lot of cross-promotions that may be deceptive. For example, when the *Legally Blonde* movies were released, the company that produced them came out with a series of books directed at ten-to-thirteen-year-olds, even though the movies were rated PG-13 for raunchy humor. Television cartoons based on *The Mask* and *Beetlejuice* are directed at a much younger audience than the movies that inspired them.

Beware of knockoffs. Low-budget producers market videos in packaging designed to be easily confused with popular movies. A documentary about the Apollo 13 mission was repackaged to look like the Tom Hanks movie, and *Gordy* (the bad talking pig movie) was repackaged to look like **Babe** (the good talking pig movie). *Happily Ever After* was designed to look like a Disney sequel to *Snow White*, instead of the inferior Filmation Studios production that it is. Very often a dreadful movie that features a rising star in a walk-on will be repackaged to make it look as though he or she had the leading role. Read the box carefully and check it out before bringing it home.

That applies to quoted reviews as well. There are a number of critics who will give a rave to anything in order to publicize their names. Keep in mind that the box is designed to sell the product, and read everything on it with a critical eye.

MOVIES ON TELEVISION: PROS AND CONS

It's almost always best to watch a movie in a theater. There is something about sitting there, in the dark, popcorn on your lap, that lets you give yourself to the movie in a way you cannot at home, with the laundry and the telephone close at hand. On television, scenes are cut, sound tracks are changed, and movies are almost always shown with the sides of the picture cut off, to fit the television screen. If you watch **Seven Brides for Seven Brothers** on television, you may only see five brothers dancing. (The rare exceptions are movies that are designated Letter-Box, shown with dark strips on the top and bottom to preserve the "aspect ratio" of the theatrical release.)

There is one advantage to seeing movies on television. The Disney Channel and the broadcast networks will cut objectionable material before showing a film, and in some cases, this may make an otherwise acceptable film with one or two unacceptable scenes suitable for family viewing. Airlines do this as well, so be aware that a movie that was appropriate in any of these venues may be quite different if you rent or buy it at a video store. Families who would like to get "airplane versions" of theatrical releases can now do so. They can order special adapted videos from cleanfilms.com or use software from clearplay.com to show regular DVDs but skip over inappropriate material.

WHAT CHILDREN LEARN FROM WHAT THEY WATCH

The main debate that rages about the effect of television and movie viewing on children revolves around what it teaches children about violence and sex. While this debate captures much of the attention, it is by no means the only question parents should think about when they consider what to allow their children to watch.

In fact, the debate can be made much simpler for parents when we move away from the cause-and-effect studies of violence and sex on the screen into a broader review of the impact of what kids watch. Violence and sex aside, television and movies provide characters that teach children about actions, motives, consequences, and character; overall, how to act in the adult world. In many ways, it has been shown that the characters a child meets on the screen simply become part of the "environment" in which he or she grows up, as powerful a character and role model as the people the child sees at home and in school.

A child's developmental capacity for abstraction is a crucial factor in appreciating his or her capacity to understand a movie. A related but separate factor is the child's capacity for moral reasoning. Jean Piaget discovered that children younger than eight or nine had trouble judging people on their intentions. Rather, when read hypothetical stories, younger children would judge people on the final outcome of their actions. One story concerned a boy who broke a cookie jar while helping his mother clean the kitchen. The other was about a boy who stole a cookie when his mother was not looking, but did not break the cookie jar. Before the developmental shift at around age eight or nine, children almost always saw the child who broke the cookie jar as the one who did something wrong. They were far less inclined to take into account a character's intentions than the ten- and eleven-year-olds were. Once children begin to understand motives and consequences, it is safer for them to see more sophisticated programs and movies.

The same susceptibility of children to the negative effects of television and movies means that, conversely, the right kind of material can have very positive effects on children. Programs like *Sesame Street*, *Barney & Friends*, *The Puzzle Place*, and *Mister Rogers' Neighborhood* have taught many children not just numbers and letters but also problem-solving, tolerance, and interpersonal skills. In one experiment to test Mister Rogers' effectiveness, preschool children were observed in a classroom for twelve days. They were observed for four days without television, four days during which they watched Mister Rogers' Neighborhood or another less positive show, and for four days after. The children who watched were found to have significant increases in positive social behavior and in total social contacts, and the positive social behaviors were maintained during the follow-up days when the children were no longer viewing the program. As former Federal Communications Commissioner Nicholas Johnson said, "All television is educational. The only question is what we are learning from it."

SENSITIVITY TO GENDER AND DIVERSITY ISSUES

Social attitudes toward women and minorities have changed dramatically over the past few decades. Although I have tried to flag instances of sensitivity (or insensitivity) to issues of gender, race, religion, or nationality, I have not tried to judge movies made decades ago by today's standards. So, unless otherwise noted, it is fair to assume that any movie more than thirty years old will have a cast that is all white (and all physically able, and all of some undefined Christian religion) and that women (if any) will be relegated to the jobs of secretary, teacher, or nurse and will wait to be rescued by the hero.

For example, in the otherwise charming Shirley Temple movie, *Poor Little Rich Girl*, a black railroad porter is respectfully but stereotypically portrayed, but her father says to another character, "That's white of you." In the Disney animated movie *Peter Pan* (originally released in 1953), the song "What Makes the Red Man Red" now seems embarrassingly racist and sexist. I have also pointed out movies that display sensitivity to these issues. The boxing classic *Body and Soul* is a rare example of a movie made before 1960 (indeed, it is rare in any movie of any era) that treats a black character with both equality and dignity. Even in that movie, however, he dies tragically.

For some reason, the films of the 1950s and early 1960s were far worse in terms of the portrayal of women than earlier movies, which featured dozens of feisty heroines played by Rosalind Russell, Bette Davis, Katharine Hepburn, Joan Crawford, and Barbara Stanwyck. I have noted dialogue or plot developments that seem especially egregious (e.g., "Girls can't do that;" or "You're so much smarter than I am"). The Women Worth Watching, chapter offers a more extended discussion of the issue of role models for adolescent girls and suggests ways to work with them to discern the messages in movies and find heroines they can be inspired by.

It is beyond the scope of this book to mention every moment in every movie that is insensitive to gender or diversity issues, or even racist or sexist. One of the reasons it is so important for parents to watch movies with their children is so that they can point out that in the days these movies were made (in our parents' childhoods, and even in our own), opportunities were very limited ("Look! There is not one kid in that classroom who is not white!"; "There isn't one woman doctor in that hospital. Isn't that strange?"). It is absolutely essential to the development of a child's critical thinking skills as well as to his or her tolerance and appreciation for diversity that we challenge the portrayal of American life in the movies we watch and teach our children to challenge it as well.

A FEW WORDS ABOUT TASTE

Profanity and Obscene Language

If it were up to me, I would not want my children to see any movie that contains language I don't want them to use. Any parent knows it is much more difficult to teach children that certain words are not permitted in the house if you then show them a movie where even the good guys use those words.

Why is such language in the movies at all? The first reason is the one your mother always told you: lack of imagination. Even today, when we are less easily shocked, four-letter words provide an easy thrill. The second reason is more cynical: It sells tickets. A four-letter word is an easy way to get a PG or PG-13 rating, crucial for getting sixteen-year-olds to buy tickets for repeated showings. This point is addressed explicitly in the underrated *Last Action Hero*, where the young hero uses a magic ticket to step into the latest movie featuring his favorite star, played by Arnold Schwarzenegger. At one point, trying to convince the action hero that he is just a character in a movie, he shows him a piece of paper and asks him to say the word on it aloud. Schwarzenegger refuses. "You see?" the kid says triumphantly. "You can't say it, because this is a PG-13 movie!" The distributors of the lovely **Fly Away Home** literally insisted that a four-letter word be added so that the movie would avoid a G rating, telling the director that kids will not go to a G-rated movie except for a Disney cartoon.

A movie from a more innocent era that addresses the issue of profanity is the original *Angels in the Outfield* (1951). Baseball manager Paul Douglas cannot receive the help of the angels for his team unless he cleans up his behavior and his language. His use of profanity is amusingly left to the imagination. He must find a whole new vocabulary for expressing his feelings about the acuteness of the umpire's vision, and he ends up using Shakespeare as a guide. In **A Christmas Story**, the little boy's father is described as an artist of profanity, but the actual words are muffled. When the boy himself uses one four-letter word (never spoken aloud), he is punished.

The fact is that most modern movies use language we do not permit in our homes. Even the adorable G-rated Babe uses the term "butt-head." Many movies reflect the modem tolerance for terms like "bullshit" and "damn," and many otherwise worthwhile movies contain even stronger language. Even more troubling is the use of non-profane epithets to get around the ratings. For some reason, the traditional four-letter words relating to sex and excretory functions are factored into the ratings while insults like "vomit-breath" or "butt-head" are not, despite the fact that most families are no more comfortable with them than they are with the old favorites. The Austin Powers movies are a particularly vivid example. Despite jokes about every possible sexual and excretory function, the movie gets a PG-13 rating because the characters use the made-up word "frickin'". I have done my best to alert parents to the type of language used in the movies in this book with "mild expletives" referring to the kind of language routinely heard in public or, increasingly these days, on broadcast television.

Although older movies do not contain these words, they often include words that are considered unacceptable in today's society—usually racial terms, and usually not intended to be demeaning or insulting, as when Ingrid Bergman calls Dooley Wilson "boy" before she asks him to play "As Time Goes By" in **Casablanca**. I have tried to alert parents about the use of these kinds of terms as well.

I find the best way to handle this issue is to tell my children that I think they are old enough to hear this language without imitating it, and that if I find out otherwise, I will stop letting them see movies until they are.

Alcohol and Drug Abuse

I am concerned about the way alcohol is used in movies. I am especially concerned about movies where people react to stress by reaching for a drink (for some reason, this is particularly prevalent in movies made in the 1950s and 1960s), or movies where people become drunk without any adverse consequences. If drunken behavior is portrayed as funny or even fun, I question whether the movie is appropriate for children. Illegal drug use without consequences can also make a movie inappropriate. In the case of an otherwise worthwhile movie like **Field of Dreams**, where there is a reference to past drug use, I have included the movie but alerted parents to the reference so they can make their own decision about its appropriateness and be prepared to discuss it if they decide that the movie is one they want their children to see. Some of the movies about teenagers include alcohol use; it is worthwhile for parents and teens to view these films together to share their views. Similarly, many movies directed at teens show smoking as a badge of coolness and independence. Parents should make sure kids are aware of the subtle marketing efforts included in product placements and movie tie-ins.

Sex and Sexual Behavior

When it comes to sex, I am more concerned with the values shown in the movies than I am with the body parts. It isn't that I am entirely comfortable with nudity in movies seen by children and teenagers; it is that I am far more uncomfortable with behavior that gives viewers a dangerously inaccurate idea about sex—especially casual sex—and its consequences. In an otherwise innocuous movie of the "slob comedy" genre, *Revenge of the Nerds*, there is some behavior that is deeply disturbing, especially since it is presented in a comic context. First, a group of unattractive girls are matched up with unattractive nerds, who happily have sex with the girls and then never see them again. Later in the movie, one of the male leads has sex with a campus beauty queen by wearing a mask so that she thinks he is her boyfriend. When she discovers she has been tricked, she is delighted. It turns out that the nerd is so much more expert a lover than her boyfriend that she immediately becomes his girlfriend.

All of this may seem trivial from an adult perspective. We are so thoroughly aware of the reality of sexual behavior and politics that it is almost impossible to understand what it is like to view this material from the more limited and literal perspective of a child or teen. I am not saying that a thirteen-year-old who sees this movie will inevitably conclude it is all right to trick a woman into having sex, but a scene like this is incorporated in an adolescent's sexual values, influencing notions of what is appropriate.

Someone once said that well over 95 percent of the sex shown in movies is of people who are having sex with each other for the first time. I have no idea how this data was compiled, but it is very hard to think of a counter-example. The only one that comes to mind is the famous scene in *Don't Look Now*, legendary for its eroticism in part because it involves a couple who so clearly are deeply intimate and have profound knowledge of each other and a history together.

A Martian trying to understand American sexual behavior from a study of our movies would conclude that everybody has sex with everybody else, but only once, and that it is always magnificent that one time. In sexual terms, a child is a Martian. Thanks to the luxury of the latency period, children come upon the whole notion of sex overpoweringly as they enter adolescence. They may be able to recite the facts about where babies come from at age seven or eight, but that is a long way from being able to understand sexual desire, much less passion and the risks of intimacy. When a twelve-year-old says that she thinks you have a baby every time you have sex, it is not because she does not understand all of the factors that go into procreation; it is because she is still not quite sure why people would have sex other than to have babies. In the 1950s, girls were encouraged to seem to know less about sex than they really did; these days, they are encouraged to seem to know more. As shown in films like **Smooth Talk**, that can be very dangerous.

Today's children, tragically, learn about AIDS before they learn about sex. So often they are terrified of this powerful desire that makes people take such terrible risks and suffer such dire consequences. When an eleven-year-old says that men can't have sex with each other because there is "no place to put it," he is not asking for a diagram; he is asking for some more time to grow up before dealing with the details.

Yet all around us, and especially in the movies, people seem to be having exciting, wonderful, completely fulfilling sex with each other all the time. This is a message that is hard for parents to compete with. Few even try, either because they don't know how or because they mistake superficial sexual precocity for genuine understanding.

A movie that might otherwise be fun for kids, like *The Cutting Edge*, begins with the leading man waking up with a woman whose name he does not quite recall. This is presented simply as evidence of his charming disorganization, like being late to the Olympic hockey match. Later, frustrated sexually and otherwise by his spoiled ice-skating partner, he goes off for a weekend with the specific goal (apparently successful) of having sex with anyone he can find. This is portrayed sympathetically—what else should anyone expect? Because there are no bare breasts in this movie, it gets a PG rating. I think this portrayal of sexuality is inappropriate for children, and even for teenagers. *Love Actually* is rated R for language and comic nudity as a shy couple make polite conversation while they pose as nude stand-ins. Yet based on the behavior of the people in the movie, I think it is far more appropriate for teenagers than smarmy PG-13 movies like *My Boss's Daughter* or *A Guy Thing*.

The often delightful *Clueless*, a huge hit among young teenagers, also has a disturbingly casual attitude toward sex. The heroine and her friend are virgins, but the friend airily explains that she takes care of her boyfriend's sexual needs in other ways. The heroine impulsively decides to have sex with a boy she has just met (ultimately she does not, not because either of them makes a mature decision to wait but because he is gay).

There are two movies that do attempt to portray teenage sex honestly. Despite the movies' considerable other limitations (like poor scripts and uneven performances), parents might want to watch them with their adolescents to begin a discussion of sexual values. In *Little Darlings*, summer campers Tatum O'Neal and

Kristy McNichol make a bet over who will be the first to lose her virginity. It is a dreadful concept, and the movie is not very good, but the scene in which McNichol is reacting to her first sexual experience is very real. She says, "I feel so lonely," and, "God, it was so personal—like you could see right through me." She clearly regrets having been so casual about sex, and about herself. She later finds out that all of the girls at camp lied about being sexually experienced, because they were ashamed to tell the truth.

The other movie is *Fast Times at Ridgemont High*, loosely based on the real-life experiences of writer-director Cameron Crowe (*Almost Famous*), then a young journalist, who enrolled in high school, pretending to be a teenager. Like *Porky's* and other teenage sexual farces, the kids in this movie are obsessed by sex, but in *Fast Times*, as in *Little Darlings*, a girl (Jennifer Jason Leigh) is disappointed and embarrassed after her first sexual encounter. I do not recommend this movie, however. Parents should know that there is also a boy in the movie who is perpetually stoned (played by Sean Penn, one of many outstanding young actors who appear), and this is portrayed as kind of lovable and charming. In addition, one of the other young girls in the movie (Phoebe Cates) is a sexual sophisticate, also portrayed as an admirable quality in a teenager.

Every generation insists that it faces an entirely new world that the previous generation cannot begin to understand. In this case, on this subject, they are right. When I was eleven, driving cross-country with my parents, we stopped in a small town that had one theater. I remember very well my parents asking the woman in the box office whether the movie *Island of Love* was okay for children, and I remember her answer: "It doesn't have anything you don't see in the papers." I asked my mother what that meant, and she said that sometimes newspaper ads showed girls in their underwear. The movie, a romantic farce, did have a character who became pregnant without being married (this was supposed to be funny), though, it was presented so mildly that I did not realize it until I saw the movie again as an adult.

When I was in high school, I went to one of the smarmiest movies ever made (with my boyfriend's parents!), *The Impossible Years*. The entire plot revolved around a middle-aged psychology professor's obsession with whether his daughter had had sex with her hippie-ish boyfriend. There are two points to make about this miserable so-called comedy. First, she had not had sex with the boyfriend; at the end it turned out that instead she had had sex with the father's hip young colleague, but only after they secretly had gotten married. Second, to give you some idea of how it rates according to today's standards, this movie is rated G.

Today, movies about drag queens are considered suitable for all ages, and television sitcom reruns on during the "family hour" feature Peg Bundy's complaints and insults about her husband's sexual performance. Even family shows, like *Everybody Loves Raymond* and *The Bernie Mac Show* depend on children's sexually precocious wisecracks for many of their laughs. Today's children know what Kobe Bryant was accused of, why Bill Clinton was impeached, why some Catholic priests are in trouble, and what "Queer Eye on the Straight Guy" means. In the 1960s, episode after episode of *That Girl* reiterated that Ann Marie (Marlo Thomas) was saving herself for her wedding night. In today's television shows, fiction and nonfiction, it is a rare teenager who has not had sex, and in today's movies, every warm moment between a man and a woman is consummated sexually.

We used to watch *The Mickey Mouse Club* after school, while our moms gave us Twinkies and milk. Many of today's kids come home to empty houses and watch sleazy afternoon talk shows, where teenagers brag about how many people they have slept with. Or they turn on cable, or rent videos, or log online for even worse. Somewhere, in this sensory overload, we must help our children find values that will help them treat themselves and others with respect.

Violence and Gore

As with sexual references and alcohol, the issue of violence/gore is one of context. Seeing a man shot on a battlefield is entirely different from seeing the same man shot in his own home by a professional hit man, or seeing a child slapped by an adult. Even the battlefield scene could be portrayed a number of different ways, depending on whether the man was on "our" side or the enemy's, and on whether the director and screenwriter were making an action movie or an antiwar movie.

There are many different kinds of violence. Wile E. Coyote always emerges unscathed from his perpetual catastrophes. There are the guts-on-the-floor special effects of *Scream*. In "action" (i.e., cartoon-style) violence, many punches are thrown but no one gets seriously hurt. Someone may get shot, but we never see blood spurting from the wound. Movies like the *Home Alone* series distort the consequences of violence with wildly exaggerated "comic" bobby traps that thwart the bad guys without real harm. By importing cartoon conventions to live action they make it seem more believable for children.

Individual family members of all ages will have different interests in and tolerance for violence. Many kids enjoy this kind of fantasy violence (and imitate it), but should be warned that it is just pretend. More disturbing are more explicit violence, unprovoked violence, violence with sadistic undertones, and violence directed toward children. Movies featuring this kind of violence are not included in this book. A few movies showing more realistic violence (like *Glory*, a Civil War movie) are included. One of the biggest problems caused by violence in films and the "if it bleeds, it leads" school of local television news broadcasts is the completely unrealistic picture of the world it creates. Surveys show that kids believe that the crime rate and especially the rate of violent crime is many times higher than it actually is. Make sure children and teens compare what they see to the real statistics, and that they recognize the real consequences of violence.

HOW TO TALK TO CHILDREN AND TEENAGERS ABOUT MORALITY AND VALUES

The rules and goals you establish for your children, even basics like wearing seat belts, not going off with strangers, not taking drugs, not having promiscuous sex (or any sex outside of marriage, if those are your values), have to be presented in a moral context or they have no meaning. Most important, there is no more powerful teacher than your own behavior.

One way to set an example for your child is to be explicit in your own moral choices and the processes you use to evaluate them. "Oh, the clerk gave me too much change. I can't keep that. Let's go back and return it to her." Or, "Someone at work wants me to tell him something that I promised to keep secret, but of course I can't do that." Or, "One of our neighbors made a racist joke. I had to tell him I don't find that acceptable." Invite them to make the decisions with you. "I found this wallet on the street. What do you think I should do with it?"

Parents should also be explicit about views on the choices and behavior of others. "I'm glad that politician is going to jail. That's what he deserves for taking that bribe." Or, "I have never felt the same about that man since he told me how he cheated on his taxes." Or, "I don't respect the way she treats her husband, criticizing him in front of other people." Or, "That man spends a lot of money on his boat, but never gives a penny to charity." Or, "I hated seeing that kid smoking cigarettes. What a stupid choice." You do not need to send a message that violation of the rules makes someone a bad person; but it does mean that violation of the rules is a bad moral choice. Explain the ways you evaluate the political candidates, what you like and respect about your friends, family, and colleagues, what you are proud of in your own life, and how you decide which issues are most important to you. There is nothing that makes more of an impression on a child than hearing (or overhearing) you telling someone else about something they did right.

Movies illustrate every possible kind of choice and lesson that can be imagined. They show us characters resolving conflicts about money, love, work, community, and friendship. Again, it helps to provide a context for discussion of these issues if parents are explicit about their own choices ("I could make more money, in that job, but it would take too much time away from the family"), the choices of others ("I really respect the way she has gone back to school because she loves learning new things"), and the choices of the people on the screen ("Why do you think Robin Hood decided to oppose Prince John? Why did the other nobles decide to support him?").

THE MOVIE MOM'S FREQUENTLY ASKED QUESTIONS

These are the questions parents most often ask me.

Is there really a problem, or are you overreacting?

Literally thousands of studies show that kids are harmed by premature exposure to portrayals of sex, violence, substance abuse, and other inappropriate material. They become desensitized and get a distorted view of adult life. As one college student said to me, "My parents pretty much let me watch anything I wanted. At the time I thought it was great, but now I'm sorry. I feel like someone took something from me that I wish I'd been able to keep longer." I was surprised to find that not one of the young people I interviewed while researching this book thought his or her parents had been protective enough.

The boomer generation is in something of a bind. We rebelled against repression, but forgot there is a difference between repression and protection, and we threw out the babies with the bathwater. I am not saying we should repress a child's natural curiosity about adult issues and concerns; on the contrary. Some movies provide an exceptionally good context for initiating discussions on these issues. Others, however, do not, and parents can need some help in establishing limits.

Why does it matter? It's only a movie.

Movies are our sagas, our myths, our touchstones, our collective cultural heritage. They illuminate and shape our culture, and they transmit it as well. Think back to when you fell in love: the movies you went to together, the movies you discovered that only the two of you appreciated or hated in just the right way. Think of the way that movies create a cultural language for us: Bogart telling the cop that the Maltese falcon is "the stuff that dreams are made of"; Claude Rains saying, "Round up the usual suspects," or, "I'm shocked…shocked to find gambling going on in Casablanca"; Gene Kelly singing in the rain; Vivien Leigh as Scarlett O'Hara, saying, "As God is my witness, I'll never be hungry again!"; or Orson Welles murmuring "Rosebud" as he drops the snow globe.

Movies are one important way that we teach ourselves and our children cultural norms. Movies give kids their first exposure to the world outside the family and school. How do we behave with the opposite sex? How do we behave in the workplace? How do we behave when our parents are not there to tell us what to do?

Movies give our children their first glimpse of these worlds, teaching how a couple moves closer to show their attraction, then how a woman holds her head when she wants to be kissed; how people evaluate risk and set their priorities; how people make decisions about work; how people follow their dreams and how they react when they fail.

More than 40 percent of children in America today grow up in families that have no particular religious affiliation. This means that unless families sit down together on a regular basis to talk about values, there is no one place where children go to learn moral lessons and confront ethical dilemmas. Thus, they are going to get it from television and the movies, whether you like it or not. You can either play a part in that process or not, but it will happen.

Movies show us the modem equivalent of parables or Aesop's Fables. Characters confront moral dilemmas, they evaluate risk, establish priorities, adapt to change, learn important lessons, overcome loss and fear, grapple with responsibility, face consequences, solve problems, and find redemption, and in doing so, they teach your child how to do those things as well. They provide a superb opportunity for family discussions of values and feelings.

There are advantages to using movies to initiate discussions about these issues. Like parables and fables, stories told to us through movies have the power of distance. For kids, especially for very young kids and teens, it can be much easier to talk about what is going on with the people on the screen than it is to talk about what is going on inside them. The difference between movies and life is that life doesn't have to make sense. Movies do, and thus they give us a manageable starting point for a discussion of the most sensitive and painful topics.

Do you ever lighten up?

Of course I do. I love to watch movies just for fun with my family, and this book includes lots of these movies. There is no activity that brings a family closer together than sharing laughter, and I believe that the importance of laughter is one of the most essential family values. Sharing a movie comedy is great fun, and favorite moments often become a part of the family's own set of in-jokes. As **Sullivan's Travels** reminds us, "There's a lot to be said for making people laugh…It isn't much, but it's better than nothing in this cock-eyed caravan." As Sullivan himself realizes, those who laugh are not disrespectful of real problems; it is in some cases the kindest and wisest response to them.

Laughter provides essential perspective. One of the sweetest family moments on screen is the end of **A Christmas Story,** when the family's reaction to their hilariously bizarre Christmas dinner is not disappointment or blame, but laughter. Genuine humor is the highest level of emotional and mental functioning. If you can get the joke, especially when it is on you, you can handle anything.

For some reason, people are much more sensitive about their sense of humor than any other attribute. We don't take it personally if someone likes chocolate when we like vanilla, but for some reason we do take it personally when we like the Marx Brothers and someone else likes the Three Stooges. Try to avoid these kinds of debates within the family. Instead, talk more generally, especially with older kids, about what makes something funny.

There is a very fine line between comedy and tragedy, with both encompassing the same kinds of events: mistakes, misunderstandings, near misses, and embarrassing mishaps. The difference between comedy and tragedy is that in comedy the characters get a second chance. In a tragedy, Romeo doesn't get the message and, thinking Juliet is dead, he kills himself. In a romantic comedy, he would get the message just in time. In a screwball comedy, she would not have gotten the message that she was supposed to take the potion in the first place, and would be racing around trying to find him. In a fantasy comedy, she would have taken the wrong potion and turned into a purple monkey with feathers. In a slapstick comedy, she would have taken the wrong potion, and it would have made her sneeze every time someone sat down. In any of those, it all would work out all right in the end.

One of the reasons we love comedy is its reassuring sense that no matter how many times Moe bonks Curly, no matter how many times Baby the leopard escapes, no matter how many people squeeze into Groucho's stateroom, everything will turn out all right. A fall that hurts someone isn't funny, but a fall that doesn't hurt is. The bombastic Clarence Day of **Life With Father** is funny, but the tyrannical father in *The Barretts of Wimpole Street* is not. The cowardly milquetoast in *Fancy Pants* is funny, but the cowardly milquetoasts in **High Noon** are not. The greed is comic in **It's a Mad Mad Mad Mad World;** it is tragic in **The Treasure of the Sierra Madre.** The direst circumstances often inspire the wildest comedy, as we see in movies like *The Great Dictator, Arsenic and Old Lace,* and **Dr. Strangelove**. See if your family can figure out what makes the difference; how the director, screenwriter, actors, and composer set the mood for laughter instead of tension or tears.

Another reason we love comedy is that it is inherently subversive, questioning our assumptions, our standards, and our sacred cows. Movies like *The Great Dictator* and *To Be or Not to Be* took on Hitler much more aggressively than any pre-WWII dramas did. Humor allows a movie like **Some Like It Hot** to make humorous references to cross-dressing and impotence long before they were considered appropriate subjects for serious movies. Two movies addressing the perils of the Cold War arms race were made in 1964. It was the comedy (**Dr. Strangelove**) that had the greatest impact and the most enduring appeal, not the drama (*Fail-safe*).

Talk to the family about what makes something funny. Humorist Christopher Cerf has identified what he calls the "joke-oid," often found on television sit-coms. They have the rhythm of a joke (often the classic three-count), and the language of a joke (as Walter Matthau explains, courtesy of Neil Simon, in *The Sunshine Boys,* words with a letter "k" are funnier than words without), they have the element of surprise, and there is laughter on the sound track, but they are not actually funny. In real humor, the element of surprise usually comes from making you see something from an angle you hadn't considered, whether it is, "What's black and white and red all over?" or a sophisticated political cartoon. Often in "joke-oids" this element comes not from an insightful surprise but from mere incongruities, like insults or precocious comments about sex from small children, elderly people, or someone otherwise relatively powerless. Getting kids to recognize this distinction is a step in the right direction, because they will learn about critical listening, and because they will then begin to insist on better.

They should watch critically as well. Many comic actors and comedians (the classic vaudeville distinction is that "A comic does funny things; a comedian does things funny") have exceptional physical grace and timing that is an essential part of their humor. Bob Hope was a boxer. Buster Keaton and Cary Grant were acrobats. W. C. Fields began as a juggler. When Fields saw *The Great Dictator,* he announced with jealous fury that Chaplin was "a ballet dancer." Today, Steve Martin and Jim Carrey are extraordinary physical comedians. In comedy, even more than in drama, precise timing is essential, and this is never clearer than when we watch Stan Laurel, Buster Keaton, Charlie Chaplin, or Jacques Tati.

It is a great joy to watch the development of humor in children as they grow. There is the low humor of the potty-training period, and the laughter at the misfortunes of others. Then there is this wonderful moment when they are around seven, when they first really understand that a word can have more than one meaning, and they spend a year asking you riddles. By then, some of them will begin to think up wisecracks, not to be rude or sarcastic, or even cynical, just to show that they don't take themselves or the world too seriously. Others will need a bit more time. Others may need a lot more time. Maybe those are the ones who need these movies the most.

How do you determine whether a child is old enough for a particular movie?

As any parent knows, this is a very complex issue. The key is whether the child is ready from a developmental standpoint. No matter how intelligent he or she is, a child follows a path of comprehension-development that is directly related to age. Age-based development matters above all else, even intelligence, in a child's comprehension of the messages of movies and television. So it really does not make sense for a parent to say, "It says ages five and up, but my child is very bright, so she can watch even though she is only three." A three-year-old might be so bright that he can read at the second-grade level, but that does not necessarily mean that he can follow a story line that involves changes in time and location, or one that turns on some characters knowing a secret that others do not.

Children are less cynical than adolescents and adults are about what they see, more prone to confuse important issues raised by what they view, less able to see actions in light of motives and consequences, more apt to confuse fantasy and reality, and more ready to accept screen characters as behavior models. As a result, children are more vulnerable to the potential negative messages in what they watch, including violence and other inappropriate behavior.

The nature of film and television lies in fast-paced action and cuts that are difficult for young children to follow, often causing them to miss the consequences and motives that are central in understanding and analyzing actions. In one study, kindergartners, second, fifth, and eighth graders were shown an edited version of an aggressive television program. Afterward, they were asked to recount the plot, their understanding of the main characters' motives, and the consequences of the main characters' actions. Kindergartners typically remembered only the aggressive actions and didn't mention any motives or consequences.

However, older children associated consequences first, then motives, and finally the full complex of motives and consequences as they described aggressive action. Thus, younger children are prone to see actions such as violence as stand-alone deeds. Children are more likely than adolescents or adults to act on violence they witness on the screen if it is portrayed as rewarding (which it often is). By watching violence or other aggressive behavior with an underdeveloped ability to see the relevant painful consequences or reasoned motives, children get a distorted impression of what actions mean in the real world.

A definitive shift in viewing sophistication generally occurs around the age of nine. For example, before the age of nine, children tend not to understand the difference between a television program and the commercials that interrupt it. This is made even more difficult by programs that are essentially half-hour-long commercials for action figures and other toys, such as Mighty Morphin Power Rangers.

The MPAA ratings (G, PG, PG-13, R, and NC-17) are based on a fairly narrow definition of "objectionable material" rather than on age-appropriateness, so they are not necessarily a good guide. The ratings are formulaic, based on particular body parts, words, and the amount of blood and guts, rather than on situations. In this book, each listing specifies the ages that are most likely to appreciate and enjoy the movie, but that is just a starting point as there is no substitute for a parent's judgment about a particular child. I have not recommended any full-length features for kids under four. While most kids under four will find one or more features they like, these are exceptions.

In general, very young children are not developmentally ready to appreciate a full-length story, and will tend to watch a feature as a collection of unconnected pieces, drawing on their own limited knowledge of the world to help them figure it out. For example, my son, then about four, seemed to have an unusual amount of trouble following a simple "good guys/bad guys" plot in a Disney movie. Finally, just before the end, he said in utter astonishment, "You mean the bad guy drives the big car?" At that point, his passion for vehicles of all kinds was so overwhelming that it was simply impossible for him to believe that a bad guy would have a great car.

My recommendation is that preschoolers watch material designed for that age group. As with kids of any age, I recommend that viewing of television or videos be strictly limited. The important "work" of the preschool years is the development of interpersonal skills and imagination, and that is best accomplished away from television. While movies and television can stimulate daydreams, studies show they can depress creative imagination by providing a plethora of ready-made mental pictures, sounds, and actions that can later be called up at will. This store of knowledge seems to hurt abilities integral to creative imagination such as the ability to dissociate oneself from existing information, a reflective style of thinking, sustained effort, and the peace and quiet necessary to give a matter careful thought.

For school-age children and teens, a parent's primary concerns are likely to be sex, violence, and scariness. There, the MPAA ratings are a starting point (especially since they now explain the basis for the rating: e.g., Titanic is rated PG-13 for "disaster-related peril and violence, nudity, sensuality and brief language"), though they cannot always be counted on. Context is crucial. There is a big difference between a character having a glass of wine at dinner and drunkenness used for comic effect. Keep in mind also that there is a big difference between sexual references concerning an exploitative relationship and one concerning two people committed to one another. In this book, I make distinctions between sexual and other material that seems to me disturbing and material that seems innocuous. The information is there so that parents can decide for themselves what is appropriate, based on their own values and their knowledge of their child.

How do you determine if a movie is too scary or too upsetting for kids?

It is simply impossible to predict the reaction of any child under age five. One almost three-year-old I know was so terrified when she saw the Disney version of Cinderella that she talked about it constantly for weeks. What scared her? Not the wicked stepmother and not the mean stepsisters. It was Lucifer the cat, who preyed on Cinderella's friends, the mice.

My niece Alexandra, a very smart, funny, tough kid who is not easily scared, showed me the ultimate folly of trying to predict how scary a movie will be for a child. When she was about four, her mother took her to see Bambi, with a favorite toy, a box of candy, and a seat by the exit in case the movie became too upsetting. Her mother even spoke to several friends ahead of time, so that she knew exactly what the scary parts were (Bambi's mother getting shot and the forest fire) and when they occurred. Alex did just fine through both, and her mother was breathing a sigh of relief when, just before the movie ended, Alex burst into tears, crying, "Where's Bambi? Where's Bambi?" As her mother assured her, Bambi was right there on the screen. To Alex, though, it did not look or sound like Bambi. He was now a young stag. "That's not Bambi! Bambi has the white spots on his back!" Nothing her mother could say would change Alex's mind. At that age, she was barely able to understand that children become adults, and Bambi appeared so different (and sounded so different because his voice had changed) that she was simply unable to comprehend it was the same character.

Very young kids react in ways we cannot predict because their fears tend to focus on a part of the story that is more understandable to them. It is better to err on the side of caution and keep them away from movies that may scare them, especially those that feature major characters in peril, menacing bad guys, or the death of any character.

By the time children are older, they will have a sense of what they can handle and may be able to talk about something they find upsetting. Just as some kids love roller coasters and some would rather die than go near them, some kids enjoy grisly movies, some like intense suspense, some love crashes, explosions, and shoot-'em-ups, and some never like them, even as adults. Always respect a child's choices about what he or she does not want to see, and do not hesitate to impose limits that you feel are appropriate on what he or she does want to see.

My child got scared. Now what do I do?

First, respect the child's fears. Never say that what they think is scary is not scary for them. That does not mean you should admit that it scares you, too (even if it does). Someone has to be the grown-up, and the thing about being a parent is that it has to be you. You cannot always protect a child from getting scared, but you can teach your child some important skills for dealing with fear.

There are some excellent books to read together. My favorite is Annie Stories by Doris Brett. Brett created these stories to help her own child deal with nightmares, starting school, loss, scary animals, and other childhood fears. She explains how parents can adapt the stories for their own children. Young children also love *There's a Nightmare in My Closet* by Mercer Mayer, *Go Away, Big Green Monster*, by Ed Emberly, and *There's a Monster Under My Bed* by James Howe.

Teach children to take some action that will help them feel more powerful than what they fear. Remind them they can always turn off the VCR, DVD player, and television if something upsets them, and make sure they know how to do it. If it makes them feel better, they can put the video on a high shelf or in a locked box or somewhere else safely out of reach. Some parents have had success using a spray bottle filled with water to "spray away" bad dreams. Encourage kids to use their imagination: "Can you draw me a picture showing you putting Lucifer the cat in jail?" "Can you sing me a song about what you will do to the bad guy?" "If you had magical powers, what spell would you cast on Cruella De Vil?"

What do I say when my child says, "Everyone but me has seen it?" Won't I harm his/her social standing?

We don't raise kids by lowest common denominator. One of the greatest gifts you can give your kids is the lesson that appeals based on what everyone else does never work. Parents who are susceptible to such appeals teach kids that they can justify their behavior by saying, "Everyone else smokes pot (or shoplifts, or has sex) and everyone else will think I'm a dork if I don't." If you hold firm, your kids may not agree with you, but they will understand that you love them enough to establish limits to protect them. Most important, of course, is that it is crucial to set an example for your kids. If they see you doing what everyone else does, they will think that is the right way to decide what to do.

If other kids' parents permit their kids to see inappropriate films, we feel sorry for them, but we don't sink down to their level. Teach your kids that cultivating an expression (and a feeling) of smug superiority when other people try to make you feel bad for not doing something you shouldn't be doing anyway is a wonderful skill to develop, and now is a great time to start. You can use some of the movies in this book to provide excellent examples of individuals who do the right thing despite peer pressure (**12 Angry Men, Erin Brockovich, Remember the Titans**, or **High Noon**, for example).

What do I do when my child goes to someone else's house?

The complaints I hear most often are from parents who tell me how careful they are, only to find that their six-year-old has seen *Dumb and Dumber* or their twelve-year-old has seen *Pulp Fiction* at someone else's house. The only way to prevent that is to talk to the parents hosting your child ahead of time and say, "My child is not allowed to watch television or videos. Will that be a problem for you?" If a parent replies, "Oh, that's a shame, because we were hoping to make popcorn and watch **Babe**," you can say, "Oh, just this once," and show your flexibility and good judgment. Or, you can take on the challenge of approving in advance whatever they intend to show the kids. It is always wise to establish clear and firm limits when your child visits friends or when a baby-sitter takes charge in your own home.

Is it okay if the objectionable material is just "over their head"?

No. Item number one in the job description of being a kid is trying to figure out everything, and they don't distinguish between the stuff we want them to figure out and the stuff we don't. That wonderful natural curiosity and persistence that enables them to learn language and understand the notion of gravity and figure out how many times they can ask us for something after being put to bed, before we get angry does not discriminate. They will puzzle about whatever they do not understand until they figure it out, and when it comes to sexual values, a little information (or misinformation) can be very disturbing.

Even when they think they do understand, it is no better. A twelve-year old who told me that *Clueless* is her favorite movie and that she has seen it more than thirty times repeated to me a joke she particularly liked, where a high school-aged character says she can't play tennis because her plastic surgeon "doesn't want her to do anything where balls might fly at [her] face." The heroine's comeback is, "There goes your social life." The twelve-year-old thought that was funny because if the girl could not play tennis, she would not have a social life-in other words, the insult was that tennis was the only social life she was likely to have. She will continue to repeat that "joke" until someone tells her what it is really about. Imagine how she will feel.

Many young kids have seen the Ace Ventura movies. Five minutes into the first one, a woman client asks Ace if he would prefer to be paid in cash or by having her pull down his zipper. He then gets oral sex-off camera, but we see his facial contortions. At the end of the movie, a woman's dress is torn off, and it turns out she has a penis (a *Crying Game* joke). In the sequel, there is a prolonged masturbation sequence and a joke about a gorilla raping a person. Will six-year-olds "get" this humor?, No, but on some level it will register, and it will teach them concepts of sex and sexual values for which they have no context, and that therefore may be very disturbing.

What are the best movies to watch in the car?

Don't watch movies in the car. Don't listen to music with earphones. For today's busy families, which seldom find time to sit down for family dinners at which everyone can talk to each other and listen to each other, the car is the only place left where families are really together for sustained periods of time.

Parents and children are captive audiences for each other, and the car can be an ideal place to teach the essential life skills of conversation, contemplation and compromise. Then there is that other essential life skill: the ability to occupy one-self. What do we teach our kids when we let them think that they can't amuse themselves—or us—for even a half-hour ride to a ballgame? When we let them think that we have so little to say to them or to show them that we have to use videos to keep them occupied? How can the subtler attractions of ethnic neigh-borhoods, interesting architecture, funny signs, regional flavor or cows on a hill-side hope to win a tug of war with Jim Carrey or Austin Powers?

Yes, a video can be a welcome respite on a long trip, and families can even use the DVD player to show movies that relate to the place they are headed or movies that lead to a discussion of characters and choices. In most cases, though, families should be careful to avoid the parallel isolation of headphones and use travel time wisely. An argument about what to listen to on the radio can be more valuable than the artificial peace and quiet of yet another viewing of **The Lion King**. Time spent with the family—even playing license-plate bingo—can be pretty magical, too.

How do I get my children to talk to me about what they see?

Watch with them. Listen to their questions, but first let them try to answer them by asking them, "What do you think?" Model the behavior you are looking for by commenting on the action yourself: "Wow, she looks happy!"; "Why do you think he decided to do that?" Vote on a rating for the movie afterward, or get the kids to pretend to give reviews at the dinner table, explaining to someone who has never seen the movie what was good or bad about it.

What if my children say old movies are boring?

Kids (and adults) tend to use television more to numb their thoughts than to engage them. Studies show that while adults think of watching television as relax-ing for themselves and their kids, it is quite the opposite. What it is instead is superficially anesthetizing, providing us with the illusion of relaxation, but in reality it jazzes us up. We can see that by the way we tend to click the remote from show to show.

Kids who grow up putting their minds on hold this way will look for more dangerous ways to zone out in the future. Make sure they learn that watching should be active exercise for their minds and spirits. It is essential to make sure they learn the difference between pleasure and happiness, both from the way that you and they use and watch movies and from the characters and stories themselves. There is a big difference between fun and distraction, and the way you use entertainment in your home is an important way to teach that to your children.

Sometimes kids who have been saturated in media need to be "detoxed" before they can begin to learn about watching a movie with the intellect and the heart instead of numbingly mainlining it into the pleasure center. The best thing to do for these kids is to go cold turkey, with a week (or more) of no television or video games. (It is harder on the parents than the kids, but it can be done.) After that, make it clear there is to be no television watching unless chores and homework are done, and make sure whatever they plan to watch is genuinely worthwhile. Even the best movies on video should not be the "default protocol" in the house.

It is important, too, not to make a particular rating a badge of maturity. Otherwise, kids want to see R-rated movies just because they are not allowed to, because it will make them feel grown up. They reject G-rated movies as babyish. One day when my son was about five, he asked me how old my grandmother was. "Almost ninety," I replied. "Wow," he said. "I'll bet she can go to any movie she wants to!" Make sure kids know that the ratings are just one of the factors you consider in making the decision about whether a particular movie is appropriate.

How do I find the movies in this book?

Begin at your local public library, which may have the movies or be able to get them for you. Netflix.com is a wonderful source for everything on DVD, and out-of-print movies on video and DVD show up on EBay all the time.

My child wants to watch the same movie over and over, as much as two or three times a day. What do I do?

Many parents have this problem. In some cases, children re-watch movies to help them understand the story. In others, like a security blanket or a favorite toy, a particular video becomes almost a "transitional object" for some children, especially when they are facing some unusual stress, either from external sources (family changes, illness, starting preschool) or internal (going through some developmental stage). I recommend respecting a child's attachment, but imposing limits, such as watching the movie no more than once a day and then only if there is time. This stage will pass. For some kids, it returns at the next huge developmental leap in the early teen years. As everything seems to be unfamiliar to adolescents, even themselves, the predictability and familiarity of a favorite movie becomes even more appealing, especially when friends share the connection to the film as well.

Why do teenagers like to watch such grisly movies?

For kids and teens, movies can serve as the training wheels for social skills that are still unsteady. Movies with very intense action can be a bonding experience, a way to blow off some steam, a way to feel a little bit out of control while knowing it is all pretend, and of course an excuse to grab on to each other.

Why is it that in most movies featuring a child in the lead role, the child is missing one or both parents?

This is often much more troubling for parents than for kids, though some children will ask what happened to Heidi's parents or Dorothy's parents or become upset when the parents are killed in **The Witches** and *James and the Giant Peach*. Even in movies where the child has loving parents, they are physically separated for the course of the movie, as in **Home Alone**, *Peter Pan*, and **Pinocchio**.

Adults who watch these films and are at a stage of life when they have reason to be concerned about losing their own parents are sometimes upset at this consistent theme and wonder if there is some sort of maliciousness behind it. There isn't. Parents are missing in children's films for three reasons. First, it is very hard to place a child in the middle of the action if a parent is there to protect and warn him. It removes most of the narrative momentum. Second, it is impossible to inject romance into a movie about a child. Third, a single parent provides the potential for a romantic happy ending to appeal to a broader audience.

How did this all happen? Why are movies so different now from the ones that I watched as a child?

The idea of appealing to a larger audience with sex and violence is not new. Some of the movies of the late silent and early talkie eras were quite frank. Responding to objections from moviegoers and the threat of some kind of censorship, the movie industry developed the Production Code, adopted in 1934. It required that evildoers be punished and prohibited plotlines like interracial romances and the portrayal of clergymen as comic characters or villains. The restrictions on sex and language were very explicit (there was a memorable fuss over whether Rhett Butler would be permitted to use the word "damn" in **Gone With the Wind**), but the rules about violence were more general, essentially requiring that it be in "good taste."

These rules remained in effect until the mid-1960s, when they were amended and then abandoned in favor of the rating system in use today. Similarly, television's National Association of Broadcasters adopted a standards and practices code in 1952 that lasted until the 1980s, when government concerns about anti-trust (and competition from cable) intervened. The television ratings system adopted in 1997 is designed to work with a V-chip, which are included in new televisions and enable a parent to limit inappropriate programs.

Now, let's go to the movies!

Part I

MOVIES ABOUT VALUES

1

DUTY AND RESPONSIBILITY

"Duty is a very personal thing. It is what comes from knowing the need to take action and not just a need to urge others to do something."
MOTHER TERESA

These days there is a lot of emphasis on doing whatever makes us feel good and a reluctance to expect others to feel obligated, which makes duty a rather neglected virtue. These movies give us examples of thoughtful people making principled choices because of a sense of responsibility to others.

Ice Age

2002, 81 min, PG, 6 and up.
Dir: Chris Wedge. Dennis Leary, Ray Romano, John Leguizamo
PLOT: "Ice Age" is a clever, funny, and touching story of an unlikely trio of animals who band together to return a human baby to his family.

The story is set when glaciers covered much of the earth, 20,000 years ago. As all of the other animals migrate south in search of food, three characters are moving in the opposite direction. They are a wooly mammoth named Manny (voice of Ray Romano), a sloth named Sid (John Leguizamo), and a saber tooth tiger named Diego (Dennis Leary). In classic road movie fashion, they don't like or trust each other very much at the beginning and the journey becomes a psychological one as they share experiences and confidences that make them see each other—and themselves—very differently.

DISCUSSION: This does not reach the level of **Shrek** for wit, there is no romance to keep the grown-ups happy, and the plot has no surprises, but it is told with terrific energy, imagination, visual invention, and humor and it moves along very quickly. Interestingly, the three lead voices are provided by performers who began as stand-up comics rather than actors. Their voices are edgy and distinctive, perfectly matched with their characters.

The computer animation is truly magnificent, from the majestic ice-covered mountains to the acorn treasure toted around by a hilarious squirrel who shows up over and over again in the travels of our heroes. The texture of the fur and feathers, the glint of the sun on ice, and soft sparkle of the snowflakes falling at night are perfectly rendered. The pristine settings convey a sense of vastness and promise that will make grown-up viewers pause to think about whether civilization has been all that civilized. All ages will enjoy the facial expressions, body language and—I have to say it—performances of the ice age mammals, so vivid and so true that you may forget that they are pixels, not people.

PROFANITY: None.
NUDITY/SEXUAL REFERENCES: A character makes a skeptical comment about "mating for life." Mild diaper humor.
ALCOHOL/DRUG ABUSE: None.
VIOLENCE/SCARINESS: Characters face peril several times throughout the movie. The mother of a young child is killed (off-screen) saving the child's life. Another character recalls the death of his family. While it is fairly mild on the "Bambi" scale, the issues of human hunting of animals, animal predators, and extinction are raised.
TOLERANCE/DIVERSITY ISSUES: A metaphorical theme of the movie.
QUESTIONS FOR FAMILIES:

• Why was it so important for Manny to return the baby, even though the humans had hunted his herd?

• How did that help to heal some of Manny's sadness?

• Why did Diego change his mind about Manny? Why did Manny change his mind about Sid? Was it because of something Sid did or because of something Manny learned about himself, or both?

• What is different about the way that Diego and Manny react to human attacks?

CONNECTIONS: Families who enjoy this movie will enjoy learning more about the real Ice Age, and should visit a local natural history museum. They should take a look at pictures of the real cave paintings from that era to see paintings of mammoths and saber tooth tigers by people who really saw them. Families with younger children will also enjoy the *Land Before Time* series of videos and Disney's *Dinosaur.*

It's a Wonderful Life

1946, 129 min, NR, b&w, 10 and up
Dir: Frank Capra. Jimmy Stewart, Donna Reed, Lionel Barrymore, Henry Travers
PLOT: George Bailey (Jimmy Stewart) has had a tough time. All he ever wanted was to leave his hometown of Bedford Falls and his family's business, Bailey Building and Loan, to travel the world free of responsibility. He has stayed on out of his sense of duty to his family and his community, and it has become too much for him. Everything he has worked for is about to unravel, and he is even considering suicide.

Clarence, his guardian angel (Henry Travers), materializes and reviews George's life up to that moment. Growing up, George was a good boy. When he saw that the pharmacist he worked for was so distraught over the death of his son, that he mixed poison in the medicine, George refused to deliver it. Before the pharmacist understood what he was doing, he boxed George's ear, leaving him hearing-impaired. George saved his brother, Harry, in a sledding accident. He gave up his dream trip so his father could use that money to send Harry to college. Harry becomes a war hero, but George stayed at home, ineligible to serve because of his deaf ear. After their father dies, George runs Bailey Building and Loan, waiting for Harry to come home.

When the Building and Loan is in trouble, George uses the money for his honeymoon to save it. Harry gets another job, and George stays on. George's foolish Uncle Billy has lost several thousand dollars of the company's money, and it looks like the business will have to be taken over by the wicked Mr. Potter (Lionel Barrymore), who cares only about money and power.

Clarence, afraid George might jump into the river, jumps in himself, and George dives in to rescue him. When George says he wishes he had never been born, Clarence shows him what Bedford Falls would have been like without him. The pharmacist would have become a vagrant after losing his job for poisoning someone with the wrong medication. Harry would have died, and so would all of the sailors he saved during the war. George's wife, Mary (Donna Reed), would have become a terrified and lonely woman. Potter would own the town.

George sees that he has had a wonderful life after all. He races home to his family, where the whole town has gathered to replace the missing money and remind him that he's the richest man they know.

DISCUSSION: The head of production at RKO Studios found the story of this movie in a Christmas card and had it made into a script. Of all the films they worked on, this perennial Christmas classic was the favorite of both its star, Jimmy Stewart, and its director, Frank Capra. For both of them, it was their first movie following service in WWII, and it said much about what they had been fighting for.

It features not only the famous "Capra-corn," (Capra's own term for his sentimental stories) but also Capra's other trademark: vivid character portraits from the bit players. In the scene where the people are taking their money out of the Building and Loan, Ellen Corby (later, Grandma Walton on the TV series) almost gives you the story of her life in the way she asks whether she can take only what she needs.

It is very difficult to know how far our duty extends to those around us. Today George would be called an "enabler" because of the way he keeps his alcoholic uncle on the payroll. George keeps taking care of everyone because he knows he is the only one who can do it.

It is a very healthy exercise for each of us to think about what we would see if someone were to show us the effect we have had on those around us. George is far from perfect. He is angry, even bitter, at not being able to follow his dream. He is not able to share his fear of not being able to keep it all together for his family. It keeps him alone, no matter how loving and devoted his family. This may be why suicide seems an option for him. Like George, we would all like to have our contributions recognized. This movie reminds us that we would all like to have made contributions worthy of this recognition.

PROFANITY: None.
NUDITY/SEXUAL REFERENCES: Oblique references to Violet as something of a party girl; Mary stuck in the bushes without clothes.
ALCOHOL/DRUG ABUSE: Uncle Billy has a drinking problem.
VIOLENCE/SCARINESS: George contemplates suicide; George is hit by pharmacist.
TOLERANCE/DIVERSITY ISSUES: Without George, Mary is portrayed as a skittish spinster.
QUESTIONS FOR FAMILIES:

• Why does George seem mad at Mary when they are on the phone with Sam?

- Why does George stay in Bedford Falls?

- Why doesn't George insist that Harry keep his promise?

- Why does Mr. Potter want to destroy George's business?

CONNECTIONS: This movie has become a touchstone of American culture. Almost everyone recognizes "Every time a bell rings, an angel gets his wings." A literary newsletter is called Zuzu's Petals in honor of the flower petals from his daughter that George finds in his pocket, confirming that he is back in the Bedford Falls he knows. The creators of Sesame Street say that the names "Bert and Ernie" do not come from this film, but one can't help wondering if those two wonderful characters didn't have some subliminal impact.

The Pirates of Penzance

1983, 112 min, G, 6 and up
Dir: Wilford Leach. Kevin Mine, Linda Ronstadt, Angela Lansbury
PLOT: This is the Gilbert and Sullivan operetta about Frederic (Rex Smith), the "slave of duty." Mistakenly indentured to pirates as a child (his nanny, Ruth, having misunderstood when his parents asked that he be apprenticed to a 'pilot'), he parts from his pirate friends on his twenty-first birthday, noting regretfully that his honor and sense of duty will now require him to devote his life to vanquishing them.

No sooner is he taken in by Mabel (Linda Ronstadt), the ward of a "very model" Major General (George Rose), than he finds to his horror that technically speaking he has not yet reached the age of majority. Because he was born on leap day, February twenty-ninth, he has lived twenty-one years, but has had only five birthdays. He must remain a pirate until he has celebrated twenty-one birthdays, which will not occur until he is eighty-four. Therefore it is his duty to remain a pirate. Meanwhile, according to Mabel, it is the duty of the local constabulary to go fight the pirates, even though they are likely to be killed. Despite all of this duty, and despite the tenderhearted pirates' unwillingness to fight anyone who is weaker than they are, or anyone who is an orphan (or claims to be), after some glorious musical numbers, all is happily resolved.

DISCUSSION: Even young children can become big fans of Gilbert and Sullivan's delicious humor and gorgeous melodies, but it may take some preparation. Play the music for them a few times before you watch the movie (most public libraries have the music on tapes or CDs) and tell them the main outline of the plot to prepare them. Explain that it was the custom in those days to apprentice children so that they had to work until they turned twenty-one, as portrayed more dramatically in **Johnny Tremain** and **Oliver!**. Make sure they understand that Gilbert and Sullivan enjoyed making fun of some of the silly things they saw going on around them.

This movie can provide the basis for a gentle inquiry into the issue of duty. Frederic is torn between two duties: one to the pirates, to whom he owes his energies until he reaches the age of majority (and for whom he has great affection), and one to his sense of honor, which is opposed to their violation of the law. What should he do?

PROFANITY: None.
NUDITY/SEXUAL REFERENCES: None.
ALCOHOL/DRUG ABUSE: None.
VIOLENCE/SCARINESS: None.
TOLERANCE/DIVERSITY ISSUES: None.
QUESTIONS FOR FAMILIES:

• Do you remember the last leap year? When is the next leap year? Why do we have a leap year? Would you like to have your birthday on February twenty-ninth?

• How do the Pirate King and the Major General figure out their misunderstanding about the word "orphan"?

• Why is Frederic called "a slave of duty"? How does he decide what his duty is? What about the policemen? What do they think their duty is?

• Why do they keep singing that they are going, and then not go?

• Can you sing as fast as the Major General?

CONNECTIONS: Note Angela Lansbury (of **National Velvet** and TV's *Murder, She Wrote*) as Ruth. Kids might also like to listen to the music of Linda Ronstadt, who plays Mabel, especially her wonderful CD for children, Dedicated to the One I Love. Children might also enjoy a rather odd but engaging video of another Gilbert and Sullivan classic, *The Mikado*, featuring Eric Idle of Monty Python.
ACTIVITIES: Most communities have live productions of Gilbert and Sullivan plays in schools or local theaters. Try to find one (especially *The Mikado* or *H.M.S. Pinafore*) and take the children to it (prepare them by playing the music

for them first). Have them try to write a song about what they are most proud of about themselves, like the Major General does.

Roman Holiday

1953, 119 min, NR, b&w, 8 and up
Dir: William Wyler. Audrey Hepburn, Gregory Peck, Eddie Albert
PLOT: Princess Anne (Audrey Hepburn) stops in Rome in the middle of an exhausting goodwill tour. Overcome with the restrictions that govern every moment of her life, she becomes very upset and says she cannot stand it anymore. She is given something to help her sleep, but as soon as her guardians leave, she slips out of the hotel to wander around on her own. She falls asleep and is found by Joe (Gregory Peck), a reporter about to lose his job. At first he does not recognize her, but when he realizes who she is, he knows the story of her escapade would save his job and make his career. He arranges for his photographer friend, Irving (Eddie Albert), to come along as they explore the city. They have a wonderful time, but as they begin to fall in love, Anne realizes she must go back, and Joe realizes he cannot betray her by writing the story.

The next morning, as she appears before a large group of reporters, he hands her an envelope containing all of Irving's pictures of their day together, and she departs from her careful diplomacy to say that Rome was her favorite city on the tour.
DISCUSSION: The movie seems almost quaint today, because neither journalists nor princesses seem to think much about duty these days. In addition to the many delights of its story and its stars (Audrey Hepburn's luminous appearance in her first major role won an Oscar), this movie provides an opportunity for a discussion of duty, loyalty, and priorities.

PROFANITY: None.
NUDITY/SEXUAL REFERENCES: None.
ALCOHOL/DRUG ABUSE: None.
VIOLENCE/SCARINESS: A minor scuffle.
TOLERANCE/DIVERSITY ISSUES: None.
QUESTIONS FOR FAMILIES:

- Why was it so important that Anne behave so strictly?

- What made Joe change his mind about the story?

- What made Anne go back?

• When Anne has a chance for freedom, she first eats ice cream and has her hair cut. What would you do?

CONNECTIONS: Fleeing a life that is pampered yet restrictive is a popular theme in movies, possibly because we are reassured to see that people of wealth and position are not as "free" as we are. In his autobiography, director Frank Capra said it was this theme that led to the success of **It Happened One Night**. The character played by Claudette Colbert was just a spoiled rich girl in the original story. By changing the script to have her run away from an overly protective father because she is longing for a taste of real life, Capra made her sympathetic not just to traveling companion Clark Gable, but also to the audience. Teenagers and their parents might be interested to know that the story for **Roman Holiday** is credited to Ian McLellan Hunter, who won an Oscar for it. He was actually a "front" for distinguished writer Dalton Trumbo, blacklisted from Hollywood during the McCarthy era, who won another Oscar for *The Brave One* screenplay written under a pseudonym during this period. This experience may have influenced his messages about duty in this story. John Dighton and Ben Hecht (uncredited) also worked on the screenplay.

A Thousand Clowns

1965, 118 min, NR, b&w, high school age
Dir: Fred Coe. Jason Robards, Barbara Harris, Martin Balsam, William Daniels, Barry Gordon
PLOT: Murray Burns (Jason Robards) is a free spirit, whimsical and spontaneous. He has quit his job as a writer for a silly kids' television show; in fact, he has quit the entire world of work and spends his days making wisecracks and doing whatever strikes him at the moment. His twelve-year old nephew, Nick (Barry Gordon), reads him the want ads and tries to persuade him to go back to work, but Murray sees work as hypocritical and soul-destroying. Murray has taken care of Nick since he was five, and they love each other very deeply, though Murray's parenting style is so casual that the child does not even have a name. "Nick" is just the most recent of the dozens of names he has tried out over the years.

Two social workers visit Murray, explaining that they are evaluating him to determine whether he is providing a suitable home for Nick. Albert Amundson (William Daniels) is stiff and formal, but Sandy Markowitz (Barbara Harris) is very warm and sympathetic. When she and Albert argue over the case, he dismisses her and leaves. It turns out she and Albert were engaged, and she is very upset about the collapse of both her personal and professional plans. Murray cheers her up, they go out together to enjoy some of his favorite haunts, and she spends the night.

The next day, Sandy explains that Murray has to get a job immediately if he wants to keep Nick. His brother, Arnold (Martin Balsam), arranges for some interviews. Meanwhile, Sandy is redecorating the apartment, getting rid of the odd knickknacks and putting up chintz curtains.

Murray cannot bring himself to accept any of the jobs. Nick, Arnold, and Sandy are all deeply disappointed that Murray has failed. When Murray's former boss, the demanding Leo of the Chuckles the Clown show (Gene Saks), comes to offer Murray his old job, Nick begs him not to accept, because it is a humiliating return to everything he hates. Murray takes the job.

DISCUSSION: Murray, like everyone else, must find a way to balance the need for compromise with the importance of personal integrity. Teenagers identify readily with Murray because he has an adolescent's easy contempt for the hypocrisy and burdens of society, and especially for having to deal with those who accept those burdens and are therefore lacking in wit, or sensitivity, or appreciation of irony. When asked to return to reality, he replies, "I'll only go as a tourist." He also appeals because as an adult, he has no parents to make him conform.

In addition to its wit and the appeal of its characters, one of this movie's strengths is the way it shows that a certain amount of compromise is necessary to have the things that matter most to us. Murray could decide never to work again and spend all of his days playing the banjo and watching ocean liners depart if he is willing to lose Nick. When he realizes how much he needs Nick, he realizes he will do whatever is necessary to keep him.

Murray describes Nick as a "forty-year-old midget named Max." Nick has had to become precociously mature. (Gordon's exceptional performance shows us the child inside the precocity.) The fact is that no one avoids responsibility without imposing its costs on someone else. This is another reason for Murray to change.

The other great strength of the movie is the way it presents all of the points of view and all of the characters with sympathy. Albert easily could have been a stock character created simply to act as a straight man for Murray's "I am much more hip and sensitive than you will ever be" humor. In a deeply affecting moment, Albert confesses he regrets that he is not "one of the warm people," and envies Murray's ability to be so relaxed and likable. Leo is certainly obnoxiously needy and self-absorbed, but insecure and clearly also envious of Murray's self-assurance.

Murray's brother, Arnold, understands his responsibility to himself and his family to mean he has had to give up some of the wild anarchy of his youth. He responds to Murray's criticism by explaining he does not have the luxury of that life anymore, and he feels good about the choices he has made, and about his "talent for surrender." It isn't that he is less sensitive than Murray, less aware of the "quiet desperation" of the working world; it is that he realizes that accepting and coping with that world is what he has to do.

PROFANITY: None.
NUDITY/SEXUAL REFERENCES: Murray and Sandy spend the night together the day they meet (and have an awkward conversation the next morning); it is clear that Murray does this often, as Nick has a routine for packing his things and going somewhere else to sleep. Nick has a "doll" whose breasts ("boobies") light up. Discussion of Nick's illegitimacy, and his mother's promiscuity.
ALCOHOL/DRUG ABUSE: None.
VIOLENCE/SCARINESS: None.
TOLERANCE/DIVERSITY ISSUES: Issues of tolerance of those with different outlooks. Sandy sees her role in the relationship in very traditional terms. When Murray fails to get a job, her reaction centers on what it says about his feelings for her rather than about its importance to Murray and Nick ("That means I have had no effect on you at all!").
QUESTIONS FOR FAMILIES:

* What can you tell about Nick from the names he has picked?

* What do you think about what Albert said about not being "one of the warm people"? How do you get to be "one of the warm people"?

* What did Arnold mean about the "talent for surrender"?

* Would you like to live with someone like Murray? Why?

* Do you agree with Murray's decision to go back to work for Leo?

CONNECTIONS: The theme of responsibility for those who depend on you is explored in a different context in **To Have and Have Not**, as Humphrey Bogart claims to have no strings but finds himself tied to sidekick Walter Brennan. In that movie, acknowledging that sense of connection enables him to develop a relationship with Lauren Bacall and also find a sense of connection to his community, and therefore a willingness to fight to protect it. It is also a part of **The Magnificent Seven**, when O'Reilly tells the boys that their fathers are braver than he is. Martin Balsam won an Oscar for his performance as Arnold Burns.

You can see William Daniels as the "obnoxious and disliked" John Adams in *1776*. He also appeared in the television program *St. Elsewhere* and as the voice of KITT the car in the television series *Knight Rider*.

SEE ALSO:

Casablanca At first, Rick says, "I stick my neck out for nobody." He later becomes someone who believes that his problems do not "amount to a hill of beans" in comparison to the importance of working to fight fascism, and he ends up sticking his neck out quite a lot.

Judgment at Nuremberg This movie, and the real-life trials that inspired it, pose this question: When orders from your superior are fundamentally immoral, and failure to follow orders risks death for you and your family, what is your duty?

Now, Voyager Two people who love each other deeply resolve to stay apart because it is best for a child they both love.

2

HONESTY AND INTEGRITY

"An honest man's the noblest work of God."
ALEXANDER POPE

Even though most movies feature at least one character telling at least one lie, it is hard to find a good illustration of the importance of honesty. One of the most popular movie plots has a character tell a lie, then fall in love with the person he/she lied to, then deal with the problem of telling the truth without losing the trust of the person he/she loves, Usually the loved one finds out the truth just as our hero/heroine was about to come clean, and it takes the third act of the movie to straighten it all out in time for the big clinch. This is a popular dramatic (and comic) structure because allowing the audience to know something a character does not know automatically provides a lot of narrative energy and audience interest.

This classic plotline is not so much about telling the truth as it is about issues of intimacy, the lie merely a metaphor for the overarching issue of the conflicts we face in wanting to be known and loved for our true selves but being wary of the risk. We ask ourselves: "What if I do let him/her know me and he/she rejects me? Maybe it is better if they just reject this false image I put up to protect myself instead." Although these stories may enable parents to begin to discuss the importance of honesty, they do not really address the central issue of integrity.

The movies in this chapter present those issues more directly. Of course, the classic is **Pinocchio**. For over a century its unforgettable graphic depiction has aided parents in talking to very young children about the importance of telling the truth. In **These Three**, an impetuous lie told by a young girl destroys the lives of her teachers and her own grandmother. In both of these stories, characters lie to protect themselves from getting in trouble. In **The Fallen Idol**, one of the tensest suspense dramas of all time, a child innocently lies to try to protect his dearest friend, only to get him more deeply into trouble. These films illustrate the incentives for—and the consequences of—dishonesty.

Some movies give us heroes who illustrate the importance of integrity by insisting on telling the truth, even under the worst kind of pressure to lie. In **Citizen Kane**, Jedediah gives up his job and his lifelong friend by telling the truth. In **Mr. Smith Goes to Washington**, Jefferson Smith tells the truth until his voice gives out, and his honesty so shames Senator Paine that he admits his corruption. Laura Partridge in **The Solid Gold Cadillac** topples the management of a major corporation by telling the truth to the shareholders. In **The Nasty Girl**, based on a true story, a young German woman insists on uncovering the truth about her community's complicity with the Nazis during World War II, despite the most horrible reprisals.

These provide a basis for a discussion of the challenge of integrity, and the risks and consequences of failing to attain it. Movies like **The Man Who Shot Liberty Valance** and **Keeper of the Flame** require us to think about what happens "when the legend becomes the fact" and it may be better for people to believe something that may not be true.

The Man Who Shot Liberty Valance

1962, 123 min, NR, b&w, 10 and up
Dir: John Ford. John Wayne, Jimmy Stewart, Lee Marvin, Vera Miles
PLOT: An aging and distinguished senator, Ransom Stoddard (Jimmy Stewart), returns to the sleepy Western town of Shinbone to attend the funeral of an old friend, Tom Donathan (John Wayne). In a flashback, Senator Stoddard recounts the early days of the Wild West when Shinbone was new and Stoddard first came to town as a young lawyer. There, he met Donathan, a tough, two-fisted, sharpshooting wrangler. Stoddard and Donathan have very different views about how to tame the West. Stoddard sets out to practice law and teach classes, while Donathan runs a ranch outside of town. In particular, the two differ about how to deal with the vile and depraved criminal, Liberty Valance (Lee Marvin), who terrorizes the town.

Both men's beliefs are sorely tested. Stoddard, who believes in nonviolence, education, and the rule of law, buys a gun to face Liberty Valance in the street. Donathan, the only man in town bigger and tougher than Liberty Valance, finds that the old ways of doing things will no longer work as civilization comes to Shinbone. There are no easy answers and a number of surprises as Stoddard and Donathan fight Liberty Valance, clash among themselves, and compete for the affections of the beautiful waitress Halley (Vera Miles).

DISCUSSION: This movie has enough gunfire, excitement, and humor to hold restless young viewers spellbound. Yet, in a very accessible and relevant way, it deals with problems of identity and civilian courage: When Liberty Valance challenges Stoddard to a gunfight on Main Street, should Stoddard leave town or defend his beliefs with a gun? Where do you turn when the town marshal responsible for law and order is a bumbling oaf who lives in fear of the criminals? Stoddard believes that "education is the basis for law and order," and holds classes trying to teach cowboys to read and write, but Donathan maintains (with some justification) "when force threatens, talk is no good anymore." Stoddard and Donathan embody different notions of what it means to be a man; Stoddard wears an apron and waits on tables to pay for his room and board until he is humiliated by Liberty Valance. Donathan steps in and protects Stoddard in one of the great "tough guy" confrontation scenes of Western films. Yet, Stoddard manages to salvage his own dignity and masculinity with his pacifism.

The struggle between Stoddard and Donathan is played out against a backdrop of the same, larger struggle for the soul of the country. As towns become more settled and the structures required to support them become more complex, law and order grapples with the Wild West, cattle barons clash with farmers, and statehood advocates clash with those supporting open territory. Early elections are portrayed with humor and insight, but underneath it all remains Donathan's deadly serious admonition: "votes won't stand up against guns."

A parallel struggle takes place in the competition for the affections of Halley. When Donathan gives her a cactus rose, Stoddard asks whether she has ever seen a "real rose." Stoddard offers her reading and writing and exposure to the larger world outside. Donathan offers her rough love in the Wild West, where her roots and heart are. Which one will she choose? Will she come to regret it?

PROFANITY: None.
NUDITY/SEXUAL REFERENCES: None.
ALCOHOL/DRUG ABUSE: The editor of the town newspaper is a drunk who gives long speeches when inebriated. Several scenes in saloons.
VIOLENCE/SCARINESS: In addition to standard gunfight scenes, younger children might be frightened by two or three short scenes in which Liberty Valance demonstrates his vicious nature by beating up innocent people.
TOLERANCE/DIVERSITY ISSUES: Donathan has a black ranch hand whom he treats well but refers to as "my boy, Pompy." In Stoddard's classroom, he calls on Pompy to explain Thomas Jefferson's lines about all men being created equal.

In a bar, the bartender tries to refuse service to Pompy and incurs Donathan's wrath.

QUESTIONS FOR FAMILIES:

- Who was a greater force for good, Donathan or Stoddard? Or are both kinds of people necessary?

- Who ended up happier? Who was more successful, and why?

- Why did it matter who was the one who shot Liberty Valance?

- In light of its title, who was the movie about?

- Did Halley make the right choice? Did she think so?

- What do you think the editor meant when he said, "When the legend becomes the fact, print the legend"? How does that relate to way the characters in the movie are portrayed?

CONNECTIONS: There is an excellent documentary about director John Ford, called *The Man Who Shot The Man Who Shot Liberty Valance*. Ford was the great cinematic poet of the West, and his movies *She Wore a Yellow Ribbon*, *Stagecoach*, and *The Searchers* helped to define the American image of the West and of the American spirit.

Pinocchio

1940, 88 min, NR, 6 and up
Dir: Ben Sharpsteen, Hamilton Luske. Voices of Dickie Jones, Cliff Edwards
PLOT: Gepetto is a wood-carver who lives with his cat, Figaro, and his fish, Cleo, and dreams of having a child of his own to love. When he wishes on a star, the Blue Fairy comes to his workshop to make his little wooden puppet come to life. She tells the puppet, Pinocchio, that if he can prove himself brave, unselfish, and able to tell right from wrong, he will become a real, live boy. She appoints Jiminy Cricket as his conscience.

Gepetto is overjoyed with Pinocchio. The next day, on the way to school, Pinocchio meets con men Honest John and Gideon, who promise Pinocchio fame and fortune on the stage. He ignores Jiminy's warning and goes with them. They sell Pinocchio to the evil Stromboli, who puts Pinocchio in his puppet show and locks him in a cage. The Blue Fairy finds him and asks for an explanation, and as he lies to her, his wooden nose grows longer and longer. She helps him escape and tells him to do better.

Pinocchio listens to Honest John again and goes to Pleasure Island, where boys can do anything they like. The boys behave so foolishly that they turn into donkeys and are sold. Pinocchio grows a donkey's ears and tail, but Jiminy rescues him before the transformation is complete. They go back to Gepetto's workshop only to find that Gepetto has gone to search for them and has been swallowed by Monstro the whale. Pinocchio and Jimmy go to rescue Gepetto and are swallowed by Monstro, too. Inside the great whale they light a fire, causing Monstro to sneeze, which propels them out of the whale's mouth. They get away, but Monstro follows, smashing their raft. Pinocchio saves Gepetto, at the cost of his own life. Back in the workshop, the Blue Fairy arrives, saying that Pinocchio has proved himself worthy and can now be a real boy. For Jimmy there is a gold badge that reads "OFFICIAL CONSCIENCE."

DISCUSSION: This is the most gorgeous, splendid, and fully realized of all of the classic Disney animated films, the high point of painstakingly hand-painted animation, before the use of photocopiers and computers. Every detail is brilliantly executed, from the intricate clocks in Gepetto's workshop to the foam on the waves as Monstro thrashes the water. It also has one of Disney's finest scores, featuring "When You Wish Upon a Star," which has become the Disney theme song. "I've Got No Strings," "Give a Little Whistle," and "An Actor's Life for Me" are also memorable.

Pinocchio is a natural for the first discussions with children about telling the truth (especially admitting a mistake) and not talking to strangers. Talk to them, too, about how to find their own conscience and listen to it as if it were Jimmy Cricket. The trip to Pleasure Island may also lead to a discussion of why things that feel like fun may be harmful, and the difference between fun and happiness.

PROFANITY: None.
NUDITY/SEXUAL REFERENCES: None.
ALCOHOL/DRUG ABUSE: The boys smoke cigars and drink on Pleasure Island.
VIOLENCE/SCARINESS: The scenes with Monstro are scary.
TOLERANCE/DIVERSITY ISSUES: None.
QUESTIONS FOR FAMILIES:

• Why does Pinocchio listen to Honest John and Gideon?

• Why does Lampwick turn into a donkey before Pinocchio does?

• If you were going to wish upon a star, what would you wish?

CONNECTIONS: The Faerie Tale Theater version of the story is also worth seeing. The idea of "becoming real" is also the theme of the classic children's story, *The Velveteen Rabbit*, which is read by Meryl Streep in the Rabbit Ears production. The book, by Carlo Collodi, is also worthwhile.

These Three

1936, 93 min, NR, b&w, 12 and up
Dir: William Wyler. Miriam Hopkins, Merle Oberon, Joel McCrea
PLOT: Martha Dobie (Miriam Hopkins) and Karen Wright (Merle Oberon) are close friends who run a girls' school with the help of Martha's foolish and pretentious Aunt Lily. One of the students, Mary Tilford (Bonita Granville), is selfish and cruel. To protect herself from being disciplined, she tells her grandmother she saw Martha in a compromising position with Dr. Joseph Cardin (Joel McCrea), Karen's fiancé. Mary blackmails another girl, Rosalie Wells, into supporting her story. Mary's grandmother withdraws her from the school and informs the other parents that it is an improper environment. The school is ruined. Martha and Karen try to bring a libel action, but they lose. Too late, Mrs. Tilford finds out that Mary lied. She goes to see Martha and Karen to offer to pay any damages they will accept and to offer her humblest apologies, but Martha and Karen know nothing anyone can do can make up for all they have lost.
DISCUSSION: There is no better depiction of the destructiveness of a lie than this movie. A selfish and impetuous girl tells a lie to distract attention from her own transgressions and ruins the lives of at least four people: Martha, Karen, Joe, and her own grandmother. Kids find this movie especially interesting because it takes place in a school and the chief villain is a child, who is responsible for the downfall of all of the powerful adults in her life. It also presents an interesting ethical dilemma for Rosalie, who does not want to lie but who feels she must protect herself from getting in trouble for stealing a bracelet. The impact of the lie on Martha and Karen, not only in the way they see the world but in the way they see each other and Joe, is depicted with insight and sensitivity.

An interesting element of the story is that the lie reveals an underlying truth. Martha is in love with Joe, as revealed in a very moving scene in which the exhausted doctor falls asleep while they are talking, and she allows her feelings for him to show while he cannot be aware of them. Mary's ability to manipulate others suggests she was aware of the vulnerability created by this undercurrent of feeling when she decided on this particular lie to tell.

PROFANITY: None.
NUDITY/SEXUAL REFERENCES: Mary's charge that Joe and Martha were sexually intimate is considered shocking in a way hard to understand for today's kids.
ALCOHOL/DRUG ABUSE: None.
VIOLENCE/SCARINESS: None.
TOLERANCE/DIVERSITY ISSUES: None.
QUESTIONS FOR FAMILIES:

- Why did Mary tell the lie? Why did Rosalie?

- How did the lie make Karen and Martha feel differently about each other? About Joe?

- What should Mrs. Tilford do for Karen and Martha when she finds out that Mary lied?

- How should Mary be punished?

- In most movies, the person who does something wrong feels bad about it by the end of the movie. That is not the case in this movie. Why?

CONNECTIONS: Lillian Hellman adapted her play *The Children's Hour* for the screen, making one major change. In the play, Mary's charge was that Martha and Karen were lesbians. This was considered much too shocking for the movies in 1936, so it was changed to an allegation of heterosexual sex between two people who were unmarried. The same director did a remake in 1961 restoring the original plot. Despite fine performances by Audrey Hepburn, Shirley MacLaine, Fay Bainter (nominated for an Oscar as Mrs. Tilford), James Garner, and Miriam Hopkins (the original Martha) as Aunt Lily, it is heavy-handed and not as effective as the original. Oddly, today that version seems even more dated than the first, due to increased openness about homosexuality. Parents also should know the remake has a much more somber ending, with Martha committing suicide and Joe and Karen splitting up.

Older kids may want to see another movie based on one of Hellman's plays, **The Little Foxes**, in which family members lie, scheme, steal, and worse. They may also want to read Hellman's memoirs, *Pentimento* (which provided the basis for the movie Julia) and *Scoundrel Time*. In light of the theme of these three, it is interesting to examine the charges that Hellman lied in these supposed works of nonfiction, most memorably by Mary McCarthy, who said that "every word is a lie, including the 'ands' and the 'thes.'"

CHEATERS

2000, 108 min, R, 14 and up, Dir: John Stockwell, Jeff Daniels, Jena Malone
In this movie based on a true story, an underdog team from inner-city Steinmetz high school in Chicago triumphs over the kids from the swanky school for rich kids and the whole city rejoices over the Rocky-like victory until it turned out that the Steinmetz team cheated. They got copies of the questions. They justified their cheating by saying that it was just leveling the playing field, making up for their lack of facilities, resources, and support. The movie puts their actions into context as they are criticized by the head of the school board (a convicted tax cheat), and sympathizes with the unfairness of the system, but is very clear about the ethical violations of the teacher and the students and the corrosive impact that cheating had on the team.

THE FALLEN IDOL

1948, 94 min, NR, b&w, 12 and up
Dir: Carol Reed. Ralph Richardson, Bobby Henrey
This tense thriller is about a young boy, the son of the French ambassador to England, whose only friend is the family's butler, Baines (Ralph Richardson). The boy adores Baines and only dimly understands that Baines is in love with a woman other than his shrewish wife. When the wife is accidentally killed, the boy, projecting his own dislike and fear of Mrs. Baines, believes Baines must have been responsible. He lies to protect Baines, but inadvertently implicates him instead, and when he tells the truth, no one listens to him.

THE NASTY GIRL

1990, 92 min, PG-13, subtitled, mature high schoolers Dir: Michael Verhoeven. Lena Stolze
This German movie is the true story of a young girl who, inspired by a prize for her historical essay, decided to write another, called "My Hometown in the Third Reich." She expected to find evidence of her community's resistance to the Nazis, as she had always been told. As she examined the evidence, she learned on the contrary, people in her community, many still there in prominent positions, had

aided Hitler. Despite every effort to stop her, interfering with her ability to get the records of the era from the library, threats, harassment, and even assault of the young woman and her family, she spent ten years documenting the truth. NOTE: Contains nudity and sexual explicitness and should be previewed by parents before being viewed by teens. The surreal tone of parts of the movie may seem peculiar to viewers accustomed to more traditional and straightforward storytelling.

THE STING

1973, 129 min, PG, 10 and up
Dir: George Roy Hill. Paul Newman, Robert Redford, Robert Shaw
One way a movie gets us to side with people who break the law is to have them steal from people who are even worse. This story of an elaborate con game reunited Paul Newman and Robert Redford with their **Butch Cassidy and the Sundance Kid** director and won seven Oscars, including Best Picture, Director, Screenplay, and Musical Score. In 1936, a small-time con man named Johnny Hooker (Redford) makes the mistake of conning an employee of big-time hoodlum Doyle Lonnegan (Robert Shaw). Lonnegan retaliates by killing Hooker's, partner. With Lonnegan's men and a corrupt sheriff chasing after him, Hooker escapes to Chicago to find Henry Gondorff, a legendary "grifter" con man. Hooker asks for his help in avenging his partner's death, which requires a deliciously elaborate series of scams to get Lonnegan's money and keep Hooker safe. NOTE: Redford spends the night with a woman he has just met; violence.

SEE ALSO:
The Emperor's New Clothes All three versions of classic fairy tale are about the pressures to lie and the power of telling the truth, with a child as the triumphant truth-teller.
Keeper of the Flame The widow of a beloved statesman must decide whether it is better to allow him to continue to be seen as a hero or to be honest about his hidden fascist agenda.
The Solid Gold Cadillac A woman discovers the power of asking honest questions when she topples the corrupt management of a large corporation.

3

EMPATHY AND COMPASSION

"If you want others to be happy, practice compassion.
If you want to be happy, practice compassion."
THE DALAI LAMA

If we are not careful, movies can deaden our sense of empathy. The average child sees 4,000 murders a year on television, and it is natural to respond by becoming less sensitive. Movies also give us a wonderful opportunity to develop our ability to understand the feelings, perspectives, and challenges of others. Every time we watch, we are caught up in the lives and concerns of the characters. As we talk about them afterward and try to understand their motives and their choices, we are developing our empathy and insight. That leads to compassion.

Movies are superb on empathy for individuals. They do less well in terms of different cultures and races, and tend to promote a sense of "us and them" by portraying nonwhite cultures as exotic people who are backward, even childish. Or they are portrayed as magical, existing for the sole purpose of bringing insight, authenticity, or redemption to white people. It is important to be sensitive to this in viewing movies with children and to make sure they see films that acknowledge the cultures and traditions of people other than white Americans. These issues are sometimes well-presented in movies specifically dealing with bigotry and intolerance.

Empathy is necessary for cooperation, and it is cooperation that really makes a difference. It is important to point out that being sensitive to others' feelings is not enough; what matters is action.

The Gods Must Be Crazy

1981, 109 min, PG, 6 and up
Dir: Jamie Uys. N!xau, Jamie Uys, Sandra Prinsloo, Marius Weyers
PLOT: Botswana Bushmen are gentle and generous, "the most contented people in the world." They have "no crime, no punishment, no laws, no rulers, no judges." They have no concept of individual ownership, because there is nothing to own. When a pilot flying overhead drops an empty Coke bottle on them, for the first time they see something new, and something that only one person can have at a time, "something that they could not share because there was only one of it." So, for the first time, they experience selfishness and jealousy. This unique item is so interesting that suddenly "everybody needed it most of the time." A man named Xi (N!xau) says the gods must have been crazy to send them this awful thing, and he will take it to the end of the world and throw it off.

Meanwhile, in "civilization," a botched coup results in several deaths on both sides. Journalist Kate Thompson (Sandra Prinsloo), decides she cannot stand city life anymore and quits her job to become a teacher out in the bush. The only car available to go meet her has no brakes and is impossible to start. The reverend (director and scriptwriter Jamie Uys) is afraid to drive it, so he sends scientist Andrew Steyn (Marius Weyers), who is very bashful around women.

Kate and Andrew have a number of mishaps and misunderstandings on the way back. When they run into Xi and the rebel forces, the result is chaos, but it all ends happily.

DISCUSSION: This gentle, low-budget comedy set a record for the highest-grossing foreign film in U.S. history. In addition to some wonderful slapstick (including a jeep that gets strung up in a tree), it has a lot to teach us about other cultures, about ourselves, and about empathy. Children are, after all, strangers to our culture, trying to understand it and learn its rules. They can identify with Xi as he tries to figure out the odd behavior of the people he meets, because, like anyone else exposed to a new situation, he makes very logical conclusions based on the limited information and experience he has. When he picks up the odd "stick" he sees, and the man runs away, he thinks it is because the man saw the evil Coke bottle; Xi does not know that the "stick" is a rifle. His amazement at seeing the trappings of modern life, the Coke bottle, motorized vehicles, Andrew's pipe, the clothes that "looked as if they were made with cobwebs," all help us see our world instead of taking it for granted.

Notice in the first interaction between Kate and Xi, they each conclude the other is "rude." Each culture thinks the other can't "speak"; to each, the language of the other sounds like chattering noises and clicks. There is further confusion because the Botswanas shake their head to mean "yes" instead of "no." Our assumptions of what is beautiful are questioned: Xi thinks the blond, blue-eyed Kate is very ugly.

In Xi's society, there is no word for "guilt." There is no concept of individual "ownership." The Bushmen apologize to an animal before killing it for food. This movie provides a wonderful opportunity to talk about some of our "civilization's" underlying principles, and the way knowing about other cultures gives us a chance to look at things differently, and to determine what is inherently human, what we have created, and why.

PROFANITY: None.
NUDITY/SEXUAL REFERENCES: The Bushmen are nearly nude. Various mishaps lead Kate to conclude that Andrew is trying to make a rather aggressive pass at her. Several of the gags result in Kate's being out in her underwear and very embarrassed, as a way of showing one of the sharp contrasts between the "civilized" and "uncivilized" people in the story.
ALCOHOL/DRUG ABUSE: Andrew smokes a pipe.
VIOLENCE/SCARINESS: Machine-gun shooting; main characters in peril.
TOLERANCE/DIVERSITY ISSUES: A major theme of the movie.
QUESTIONS FOR FAMILIES:

- How many differences can you find between Xi's culture and ours? In what ways do you think Xi's is better? In what ways is ours better?

- In Xi's culture, "they never punish a child or even speak harshly to it, so of course their children are well-behaved." Do you think these two things go together?

- Can you imagine a culture without ownership or guilt?

- Why does Xi think Kate is rude? Why does she think he is rude?

- Why does Andrew have such a hard time making a good impression on Kate? Have you ever felt that way? Why does she change her mind about him?

CONNECTIONS: The sequel, *The Gods Must Be Crazy II*, is not very good. **The Jungle Book** is another "fish out of water" story, though Mowgli is not a part of an established culture, as Xi is here. A more dramatic (and tragic) treatment of some of these themes is in an Australian movie, *Walkabout* (for mature teens), in which two white children, abandoned in the outback, are saved by an Aborigine boy.

ACTIVITIES: Kids can try to write or act out a story about what would happen if Xi came to their house. They might be amused to see how the actor's name is spelled; the "!" in N!xaus's name stands for a clicking sound.

Monsters, Inc.

2001, 93 min., G, 6 and up
Dir: Peter Docter, David Silverman, Lee Unkrich. John Goodman, Billy Crystal
PLOT: It turns out, according to this movie by the "Toy Story" folks at Pixar, that monsters are more afraid of children than children are of monsters. Monsters need to collect the screams of children to fuel their world, and children are getting so hard to scare that the monsters are suffering from rolling blackouts. What can they do? Top scarer John "Sully" Sullivan (voice of John Goodman) and rival Randall Boggs (voice of Steve Buscemi) work as hard as they can to break the scream-collection record. When Randall inadvertently lets a human child into the monster world, the monsters find out what being scared is really like.

Sully and his sidekick, Mike Wazowski (voice of Billy Crystal) are just a couple of nice guys proud of their work trying to do their jobs (except for filing the paperwork, which Mike never seems to get to). When Boo (voice of Mary Gibbs) sees Sully, she runs after him, shouting "Kitty!" At first, Sully is scared of her, but then he gets to know her and they become good friends. He develops empathy for her, and knows that he has to help her get back home.

DISCUSSION: This movie is utterly delightful. It should be put in the dictionary to illustrate the word, "adorable." It has the same delicious mixture of heart, humor, and technical wizardry that made *A Bug's Life* and the two **Toy Story** movies into instant classics. Like Jim Henson, who decided to make his "Sesame Street" characters monsters so that children would never be afraid of monsters again, the people behind this movie have created monsters that even the shyest child will find completely un-scary. In fact, kids may decide that multiple heads, removable eyes and hair made from snakes are kind of cute.

PROFANITY: None.
NUDITY/SEXUAL REFERENCES: Mild potty humor.
ALCOHOL/DRUG ABUSE: None.
VIOLENCE/SCARINESS: Characters in peril. Mildly scary scene with biohazard workers.

TOLERANCE/DIVERSITY ISSUES: A metaphorical theme of the movie. Strong female characters, but all of the "scarers" are male.
QUESTIONS FOR FAMILIES:

- Why were the monsters so scared of children?

- Why were the children scared of monsters?

- Why is Randall so jealous of Sully?

CONNECTIONS: There are lots of terrific DVD extras, including background info, a music video, ideas that never made it onto the screen, and a game. You'll also get a sneak peek at next summer's animated feature. Families who enjoy this movie will also enjoy *The Adventures of Elmo in Grouchland* and the **Toy Story** movies.

The Philadelphia Story

1940, 112 min, NR, b&w, 10 and up
Dir: George Cukor. Katharine Hepburn, Cary Grant, Jimmy Stewart
PLOT: Tracy Lord (Katharine Hepburn), the daughter of an upper-class Philadelphia family, is preparing for her wedding when her ex-husband, C. K. Dexter Haven (Cary Grant), appears with a reporter, Macauley (Mike) Connor (Jimmy Stewart), and a photographer, Elizabeth (Liz) Imbrie (Ruth Hussey). Though Tracy loathes publicity, she agrees to let them stay so their magazine will not publish a story about her father's affair with a Broadway dancer, which would humiliate her family. Tracy's fiancé, George Kittridge (John Howard), a "man of the people" who hopes for a political career, is pleased to have them there. Her father, who was not invited to the wedding, returns, putting further pressure on the family to appear as though everything is all right.

At first, Tracy and her young sister, Dinah (Virginia Weidler), behave outrageously to shock Mike and Liz. Tracy softens when she reads Mike's book of short stories and discovers they have a lot in common. She is hurt when he rejects her offer of help, and even more hurt when Dexter tells her she acts like a "goddess," rigid, unforgiving, and without compassion. She is hurt further when he says she does not have an understanding heart, and she feels oddly betrayed when her mother forgives him.

That night, at the prenuptial party, Tracy deliberately gets drunk. She and Mike have a romantic moonlight swim, and when he carries her back to the house, George and Dexter are waiting for them. The next morning, she is hung over and does not remember what happened the night before. George assumes she and Mike had an affair and insists on an apology and a pledge that she will never drink again. She turns him down, saying she knows she would disappoint him. Mike offers to marry her, but she turns him down, too, because "Liz wouldn't like it." She goes in to tell the guests the wedding has been called off, but Dexter tells her to tell them she will marry him again instead. As her father prepares to escort her down the aisle, she tells him she feels "like a human being." DISCUSSION: One of the glossiest romances ever made, with splendid dialogue and three of the greatest movie stars ever, this film is a pure pleasure to watch. At the beginning of the movie Tracy is rigid and judgmental, but only because she thinks it is the way to make sure she will never be hurt again. She tells her mother they both "picked the wrong first husbands," and she is sure that this time, in marrying someone who is the opposite of Dexter in every way, she will make up for her past mistakes.

Tracy likes to be in control. She insists on preventing her father from coming to her wedding and even renames her sister. In her first conversation with George in the movie she has to be gently reminded that their home together will be "ours," not "mine." If she cannot prevent reporters from covering her wedding, she will behave outlandishly to give herself control over the story, making sure they cannot have access to the real Tracy or the real family situation. So, she impulsively introduces her uncle as "Father."

When Tracy is moved by Mike's writing, she admits that she, too, understands what it's like to put on a tough veneer to protect a vulnerable spirit. It is Mike who is able to give Tracy back a vision of herself as "lit from within," enabling her to accept her own faults and those of others. It enables her to accept her own feelings, too, and realize it is Dexter she has loved all along. It was really herself she was hardest on. Forgiving herself frees her to feel compassion for others.

PROFANITY: None.
NUDITY/SEXUAL REFERENCES: Very mild, by today's standards, with references to Mr. Lord's affair with a dancer; an off-screen nude swim; George's assumption that Tracy and Mike slept together. Uncle Willie's pinches would be classified today as sexual harassment. Note Mike's famous line that "there are rules about that" in explaining why he did not sleep with a willing Tracy because she was "the better" for alcohol.

ALCOHOL/DRUG ABUSE: Tracy and Mike get very drunk (and have terrible hangovers); references to Dexter's past alcohol problem (which he calls his "deep and gorgeous thirst").
VIOLENCE/SCARINESS: Dexter shoves Tracy in a brief prologue and punches Mike. TOLERANCE/DIVERSITY ISSUES: Class issues.
QUESTIONS FOR FAMILIES:

- Why does Tracy want to marry George? Why does George want to marry Tracy?

- Why was it hard for Tracy to see George's stuffiness? Why do they feel differently about publicity?

- How does Tracy make Mike and Liz uncomfortable? How does Mike make Tracy uncomfortable?

- What does Tracy learn from her father? From Mike? From Dexter?

- Why does Tracy want George to think better of her than she did of herself? What is the meaning of Mike's quote about "with the rich and mighty, always a little patience?"

CONNECTIONS: Hepburn and Cary Grant appear together in **Holiday** (also directed by Cukor and based on a play by Barry adapted by Donald Ogden Stewart) and **Bringing Up Baby**. Jimmy Stewart won a Best Actor Oscar for his performance, and Donald Ogden Stewart won one for his screenplay, a deft improvement over the already excellent play. There was a musical remake in 1956 called *High Society*, with Grace Kelly, Frank Sinatra, and Bing Crosby. Despite top talent and songs by Cole Porter (including "True Love"), it is not in the same class.

The Prince and the Pauper

1937, 120 min, NR, b&w, 6 and up
Dir: William Keighley. Errol Flynn, Claude Raines, Billy and Bobby Mauch
PLOT: The heir to the throne of England is young Prince Edward, son of Henry VIII (Bobby Mauch). He meets a beggar boy (Billy Mauch) who looks exactly like him, and they decide to trade places so that each can find out what it feels like to live the life of the other.
They exchange clothes. Through a mistake, the prince is thrown out of the castle grounds, and no one believes him when he tells them who he is. He makes many

discoveries about the world outside the castle, the most disturbing being the poverty of some of his subjects, and the most terrifying the realization that his enemies inside the court have discovered his secret and are hoping to kill him, and make Tom Canty, the beggar boy, their pawn.

He finds a defender, Miles Hendon (Errol Flynn), who at first befriends him because he feels sorry for him, and then realizes the boy really is Edward, now the king, because Henry VIII has died. With the help of Miles, Edward makes it back just in time to prevent Tom from being crowned King, and takes the position himself, with the greater understanding he gained from trying life as Tom Canty.

DISCUSSION: This exciting story, based on the book by Mark Twain, has a lot of appeal because we get to experience the fantasy of feeling what it would be like to be royalty. We get to think about what our lives would seem like if a prince or princess took over from us for a day or two.

The young prince had not had a chance to develop compassion because he had simply not been aware of the realities of poverty and abuse until he went out into the world without the protection of his position. Edward has to find out how to prove his worth to people who are not impressed by his title, power, or wealth, and how to solve his problems on his own.

The young pauper develops understanding as well when he masquerades as the prince, learning that even wealth and power cannot prevent loss or loneliness or protect him from the wickedness of others. Both boys learn that rich and poor people can be lonely and afraid, but that both can also find true friends.

PROFANITY: None.
NUDITY/SEXUAL REFERENCES: None.
ALCOHOL/DRUG ABUSE: None.
VIOLENCE/SCARINESS: Sword fights.
TOLERANCE/DIVERSITY ISSUES: Class issues.
QUESTIONS FOR FAMILIES:

• How will Edward do a better job as king than he would have if he had not had this experience?

• Compare Edward to Chulalongkorn, who becomes King of Siam at the end of **The King and I**. How are their relationships with their fathers alike or different? How are their plans for ruling alike or different?

• Who would you change places with if you could?

CONNECTIONS: The movie was remade for television by Walt Disney, with one boy playing both parts, using the same special effects used in both versions of **The Parent Trap**. Miles was played by dashing Guy Williams, star of the "Zorro" television series, and the video is well worth seeing if the original is not available. In 1990, Disney made an animated version, starring Mickey Mouse, and it is delightful. Older children might like to see some of the movies featuring Edward's father, Henry VIII, such as **A Man for All Seasons** and *Anne of the Thousand Days*.

ACTIVITIES: Look up Prince Edward in an encyclopedia to find out about his brief reign, and about the long and influential reign of his half sister, Queen Elizabeth I. Older children who are good readers might like to read the book by Mark Twain.

Some Like It Hot

1959, 119 min, NR, b&w, 10 and up
Dir: Billy Wilder. Marilyn Monroe, Tony Curtis, Jack Lemmon, Joe E. Brown, George Raft

PLOT: In the first moments of the movie, what appears to be a hearse turns out to be carrying bootleg liquor, and we are prepared for a movie in which nothing will be what it seems and nothing will be treated very seriously. It is the 1920s, during Prohibition, and Joe (Tony Curtis) and Jerry (Jack Lemmon) are two musicians who play in a speakeasy. When they accidentally witness the Saint Valentine's Day massacre of a group of bootleggers by Spats Columbo (George Raft) and his mob, they have to hide out. So they accept a job with a band on its way to Florida. It is an all-girl band, so they dress as women, calling themselves "Josephine" and "Daphne."

On the train, they meet the rest of the band, including lead singer Sugar Kane (Marilyn Monroe). Both men are very attracted to her. She quickly becomes friends with "Daphne," and they have a late-night pajama party. When they get to Florida, Joe adopts yet another disguise, this time as a wealthy bachelor. Meanwhile, Osgood (Joe E. Brown), a really wealthy bachelor, is interested in "Daphne." Joe gets "Daphne" to distract Osgood so he can use Osgood's yacht for a date with Sugar.

Meanwhile, Spats and his gang arrive at the hotel for a conference with other gang leaders that results in even more bloodshed. Joe realizes that he does not want to mislead Sugar anymore and sends her a diamond bracelet (from Osgood) and a farewell note. Seeing her sadness, he is overcome and kisses her, forgetting that he is dressed as Josephine. She runs after them, and joins Joe, Jerry, and Osgood as they escape on Osgood's boat.

DISCUSSION: This is one of the wildest farces ever filmed, but it has a lot of heart as well, with brilliant performances by all three stars. Monroe is heartbreakingly vulnerable as Sugar, explaining that she always gets "the fuzzy end of the lollypop." Joe must become someone else in order to learn the truth about Sugar (who would never have confided in a man) and about himself (as he sees the consequences of his exploitive behavior and feels what it is like to have men try to force their attentions on him). Jerry, hilariously, turns out to be as suggestible as a woman as he was as a man. As himself, he ends up going along with whatever Joe tells him. In women's clothes, he starts to think of himself as a woman. The scene where he tells Joe that he and Osgood are engaged is a classic. Jerry and Joe both learn to consider the feelings of others when they realize how it feels to be treated as objects.

PROFANITY: None.

NUDITY/SEXUAL REFERENCES: Oblique and lighthearted references to everything from transvestism to impotence.

ALCOHOL/DRUG ABUSE: Sugar drinks when she is unhappy.

VIOLENCE/SCARINESS: Off-screen gangland slaying; characters in peril.

TOLERANCE/DIVERSITY ISSUES: A theme of the movie.

QUESTIONS FOR FAMILIES:

• How does Joe change, and what makes him change?

• What does he learn from being dressed as a woman?

• How do Joe and Jerry react differently to dressing as women?

• How does Sugar behave differently with "Junior" and "Josephine"?

CONNECTIONS: Other movies with male characters disguising themselves as women include the venerable *Charlie's Aunt*, filmed seven times, including a musical version with Ray Bolger, and *Tootsie*, with Dustin Hoffman (rated PG, but with mature themes). Curtis and Lemmon also appeared together in **The Great Race**. George Raft engagingly spoofs his tough-guy performances in 1930s gangster movies, even repeating his coin-flipping habit from *Scarface*. This movie was selected as the funniest of all time by the American Film Institute. Families who enjoy this movie should also watch some of the others on the top 100 list.

EMMA

1996, 111 min, PG, 8 and up
Dir: Douglas McGrath. Gwyneth Paltrow, Jeremy Northam
Emma (Gwyneth Paltrow) is a beautiful and wealthy young woman whose attempts to "help" others cause more trouble than good. She tries to elevate an awkward girl (Toni Collette) to the upper classes, preventing her marriage to the farmer she loves and encouraging her to try to win a snobbish clergyman. She learns she has completely misread (and disrupted) the romantic intentions of at least four people and finally, when she thoughtlessly insults a silly but well-meaning lady (Sophie Thompson), she begins to learn how to be truly sensitive to others. When Jane Austen was writing this book, she predicted she was creating a character no one would like, but it is impossible not to like Emma, despite her disastrous attempts to arrange the lives of everyone around her.

THE EMPEROR'S NEW GROOVE

2001, 78 min, G, 5 and up
Dir: Mark Dindal. David Spade, Eartha Kitt, John Goodman
A spoiled emperor named Kuzco, (hilariously voiced by David Spade with his trademark snarky self-absorption) dismisses his advisor Yzma (voiced somewhere between a purr and a growl by Ertha Kitt and looking like an Erte fashion design drawn with a skritchy pen). She decides to poison him. Her dim but muscular sidekick Kronk (voiced by Patrick Warburton, *Seinfeld*'s Puddy) accidentally gives Kuzco the wrong potion, and instead of being killed, he is turned into a llama. Kuzco needs to get help from a peasant named Pacha (voice of John Goodman) to get his body and his kingdom back. Their adventures almost approach Indiana Jones scale as they go over a rushing waterfall (with sharp rocks at the bottom), get covered with scorpions, cornered by jaguars, and chased by Yzma and Kronk. Kuzco has to learn a lot about empathy, including an understanding of how unhappy he was when he thought only of himself, before he can become human.

FREAKY FRIDAY

2003, 93 min, PG-13, 10 and up
Dir: Mark Waters. Jamie Leigh Curtis, Lindsay Lohan
Curtis is Tess, a compassionate therapist and a loving, if harried mother of two children (there is a cute moment as she loads her pager, cell phone, and PDA into her purse). Lohan is her daughter Anna, and like most 15-year-olds, she thinks

that she has both too much of her mother's attention (when it comes to telling her what to do) and not enough (when it comes to knowing what is important to her, which she should just be able to intuit, since Anna does not really want to tell her anything). When the two of them get into an argument at a Chinese restaurant, the owner's mother gives them magic fortune cookies. The next morning, they wake up as each other. While they figure out how to return to their own bodies, each has to spend the day living the other's life.

That means that Tess has to cope with high school, including a teacher with a grudge, a former friend-turned rival, a guy Anna has a crush on, and a big exam. Anna has some fun with her mother's credit cards but then has to cope with patients and a television appearance promoting her mother's new book. Both start to understand the pressure of the schedule conflict that is at the center of their conflict with each other. The rehearsal dinner before the wedding is at the same time as an important audition for Anna's rock band.

CONNECTIONS: This is the third movie based on the popular book by Mary Rodgers, daughter of composer Richard Rodgers (**The Sound of Music**). The G-rated 1976 version with Barbara Harris and Jodie Foster is delightful and families will have fun comparing the two to see what has (and has not) changed over the years.

SEE ALSO:

Gentleman's Agreement A reporter pretends to be Jewish to investigate anti-Semitism.

A Little Princess Every material possession is taken from Sara, and yet she continues to feel empathy for others and tries to help them.

Mr. Deeds Goes to Town Deeds's empathy for the poor farmers, and empathy from Babe and the judge for Deeds are the turning points in the movie.

4

COURAGE

"The chief activity of courage is not so much attacking as enduring, or standing one's ground against dangers."
SAINT THOMAS AQUINAS

Movies almost always have heroes, and heroes are almost always courageous. Think of Indiana Jones in **Raiders of the Lost Ark**, entering the booby-trapped cave, racing from poisoned darts, then confessing that he is terrified of snakes (and later facing thousands of them in the buried tomb).

In comedies, we see cowards. Bob Hope and Woody Allen are two archetypal examples. In Westerns, adventure sagas, mysteries, sword and sorcery epics, and war movies, we see the most thrilling depictions of physical courage. It is important to talk to children about the other kinds of courage. Movies give us that chance with examples of moral courage, as when Sir Thomas More stands up to the King in **A Man for All Seasons** or the Washington Post takes on the President in **All the President's Men**. As Adlai Stevenson said, "It is often easier to fight for principles than to live up to them." The best films show that courage is never easy, and even the bravest people get scared. It is a lot of fun to watch a movie hero run toward the guys who are shooting at him, but it is these other films that give us a chance to think and talk about what courage really means.

Invasion of the Body Snatchers

1956, 80 min, NR, b&w, 12 and up
Dir: Don Siegel. Kevin McCarthy, Dana Wynter, Carolyn Jones
PLOT: Dr. Miles Bissell (Kevin McCarthy), under restraint and being evaluated for possible commitment to a mental hospital, insists he is not crazy and tells the admitting doctors his story.

Called home early from a medical conference because a number of patients wanted to see him urgently, he finds that all have canceled their appointments. A small boy insists that his mother is not really his mother, and a woman insists that her uncle is not really her uncle. He looks and sounds like him, and has all of the uncle's memories, but he seems emotionless. It turns out that many people in the town have made similar complaints.

Becky (Dana Wynter), an old girlfriend of Miles's, is back in town, newly divorced. Miles and Becky are called to the home of friends, Jack (King Donovan) and Theodora (Carolyn Jones), who found a mysterious body in a pod in their greenhouse. It grows to resemble Jack as the night goes on, even down to the cut he had received that evening on his palm. Miles fears for Becky and runs to her house. In her basement, he finds a huge pod with a Becky-duplicate growing inside. He runs to her bedroom to wake her up, and they call the police. Everywhere they turn for help, they find people have been taken over by emotionless pod duplicates who complete the final possession when the humans are asleep.

Becky and Miles hide out in his office. They see trucks filled with pods going off in all directions. At last Jack comes, and they are relieved until they realize that he, too, has been replaced by a pod. He has brought the others with him, telling Miles, "You're reborn into an untroubled world." "Where everyone's the same?" "Exactly."

Miles races to the highway, begging anyone to stop and help him. He is brought to the mental hospital. The doctors conclude he is insane until they hear of an accident involving a truck filled with mysterious pods. As the movie ends, they are calling for help.

DISCUSSION: This has been called the most frightening film ever made. What makes it so scary is the absence of special effects and disgusting-looking aliens. The enemy is within those we trust and rely on most. The slow realization of the ultimate horror—complete annihilation of the individual personality and ability to feel—in everyone around Miles and Becky and finally in Becky herself, is genuinely terrifying.

People have argued about the political meaning of this movie since it was made. Some believe the emotionless pod people were supposed to represent the Communists. Others argue the opposite, concluding the references to conformity mean the movie is a criticism of Joe McCarthy and those who were threatened by any challenges to their way of thinking. In that light, it can be compared to **High Noon**, made four years earlier. Its appeal is enduring because it can serve as a metaphor for whatever pressures for conformity exist at the time we view it.

Miles says to Becky, "In my practice, I've seen how people have allowed their humanity to drain away, only it happened slowly and not all at once. They didn't seem to mind. All of us, a little bit, we harden our hearts, grow callous. Only when we have to fight to stay human do we realize how precious it is to us, how dear, as you are to me." One of the pod people says, "Love, desire, ambition, faith; without them, life is so simple, believe me." The pod people have "no feelings, only the instinct to survive," but Becky says, "I don't want a world without love or grief or beauty; I'd rather die." It is precisely this ability to feel that makes her so precious to Miles. (It also gives them away when, trying to pass as one of the pod people, she can't help crying out as she sees a dog run in front of a truck.)

Note that today's kids will not understand that the reference to "Reno" means that Becky was just divorced. The need to use an operator to make a long distance call will also be a surprise to them.

PROFANITY: None.
NUDITY/SEXUAL REFERENCES: None.
ALCOHOL/DRUG ABUSE: Social drinking.
VIOLENCE/SCARINESS: No violence or gore, but very scary.
TOLERANCE/DIVERSITY ISSUES: The importance of respecting individual differences is a subtext of the movie, though everyone in the movie is white and middle class.
QUESTIONS FOR FAMILIES:

- The pod people believe survival is more important than feelings, but Becky says she would rather die than live without feelings. Why does Becky include "grief" as one of the feelings she would rather die without?

- What does Miles mean when he says he has seen people let their humanity drain away?

- When do people have to "fight to stay human"? When this movie was made, it did not have the prologue (which lets you know right away he is going to get away from Santa Mira) or the epilogue (which assures you the invaders will be beaten). Do you think it is better with those additions?

- What does this movie say about the pressure to conform?

CONNECTIONS: This movie seems to get remade about once every twenty years, and each version reflects something of its specific era. The 1978 version (rated PG) was directed by Philip Kaufman (**The Right Stuff**) and features Donald Sutherland and Brooke Adams. Watch for Kevin McCarthy and director Don Siegel from the original in brief appearances. In 1994, another version, this time called *Body Snatchers* (and rated R) was released. This version is less a political analogy than a reflection of a teenager's conflicts over identity and separation.

Carolyn Jones, who plays Teddy, later played Morticia in television's *The Addams Family*. If Becky's cousin looks vaguely familiar to older viewers, it is because actress Virginia Christine went on to play "Mrs. Olson" in the long-running series of Folger's coffee commercials. She also appeared as Katharine Hepburn's bigoted business partner in **Guess Who's Coming to Dinner**. The eerie music is by Carmen Dragon, father of "the Captain" of the musical group the Captain and Tennille.

A Little Princess

1995, 97 min, G, 6 and up
Dir. Alfonso Cuaron. Liesel Matthews, Eleanor Bron
PLOT: Sara Crewe is brought to Miss Minchin's boarding school by her adored father, and promises to be "a good soldier" and be brave about staying there without him. She is the brightest girl in the school, with exquisite manners, but her odd fancies and her father's lavish provisions for her make the other girls uncomfortable or jealous. Her only friend in the school is Ermengarde, a pudgy girl who has trouble with her lessons and is very grateful for Sara's attentions. Sara also befriends Becky, a scullery maid.

Captain Crewe is missing in action. Miss Minchin takes everything from Sara and has her stay on at the school as a servant, living in an attic next to Becky. She continues to think of herself as "a good soldier," and tries to imagine she is a princess undergoing a trial to keep her spirits up despite deprivation and abuse. One night, while she is sleeping, her little attic is transformed into a comfortable bower with delicious food. She shares it with her friends. It comes from the gentleman across the street. It turns out that he has been befriending her father, not knowing that he was a close friend of his late son. Sara goes to thank him, and her father, seeing her, regains his memory. Sara leaves the school, taking Becky with her.

DISCUSSION: Unlike Cedric in *Little Lord Fauntleroy*, Sara Crewe cannot be accused of being perfect, though she is not as deliciously unlikable as Mary in *A Secret Garden*. It takes her a long time to lose her temper and snap at Ermengarde, but she does. She almost gives up hope, but she is determined to hold on to her courage to live up to her image of her father and her father's hopes for her. Her imagination is an important source of solace for her, and in a sense she is a stand-in for the author herself when she uses it to create stories for her friends.

This is also a wonderful movie to use for a discussion of empathy and compassion. Although Sara is desperately hungry, she gives almost all her food to a beggar child who is even hungrier. Note the way that her compassion inspires others: The baker who watches her give the buns to the beggar child is so moved that she gives the child a home.

PROFANITY: None.
NUDITY/SEXUAL REFERENCES: None.
ALCOHOL/DRUG ABUSE: None.
VIOLENCE/SCARINESS: None.
TOLERANCE/DIVERSITY ISSUES: Tolerance of individual differences.
QUESTIONS FOR FAMILIES:

- Why do many of the girls in the school dislike Sara?

- Why was she ashamed when the little boy gave her a coin?

- Why did she decide to give the buns to the beggar girl? What impact did that have on the baker?

- Why was Miss Minchin so mean? What should she have done when she got the news that Sara's father was missing?

CONNECTIONS: There are three filmed versions of this story. This version is sumptuously filmed, with gorgeous images. The time and location were changed to WWI-era New York, and the plot is changed to keep Sara's father alive. To make the story more acceptable for contemporary children, Becky, who is black, leaves with Sara, not to be her maid, as in the book, but to be her adopted sister. Sara democratically says that all girls are princesses.

The version that is most faithful to the book is the BBC miniseries, which is available on video and is my own favorite. There is also a version with Shirley Temple, in which, she spends much of the movie looking through veterans' hospitals for her father, wounded in WWI, finally finding him.

The Magnificent Seven

1960, 126 min, NR, 8 and up
Dir: John Sturges. Steve McQueen, Yul Brynner, James Coburn, Charles Bronson, Eli Wallach

PLOT: Farmers in a small Mexican village are being robbed by Calvera (Eli Wallach), a bandit, who takes all of their crops to feed his men. The village wise man advises the farmers to buy guns.

The farmers ask Chris (Yul Brynner) to help them buy guns. He agrees instead to help them try to find someone who can defend them. The first candidate is Chico (Horst Buchholz), who is "very young and very proud." Chris rejects him, explaining that "The graveyards are full of boys who were very young and very proud." The next candidate is Harry (Brad Dexter), an old friend who insists that if Chris is involved, there must be a lot of money in it somewhere. Chris offers Vin (Steve McQueen) the job, but he refuses at first, saying that the fee "wouldn't even pay for my bullets." Still, Vin is drawn to being a gunman "for the competition." The farmer asks, "With whom does he compete?" Chris answers, "Himself." Vin agrees to join them.

They find O'Reilly (Charles Bronson) chopping wood for food. Britt (James Coburn) is challenged to prove that he can outdraw a gun with a knife. He proves it without saying a word. Lee (Robert Vaughn), a laconic southerner, says, "I'll have the money before I go." He is on the run and needs it to pay off the people who have been hiding him. The six ride off together. Chico follows them. Now there are seven.

They arrive at the small farm village, where the farmers are afraid of them. They begin to prepare the villagers, teaching them to shoot and building new walls. Chico finds Petra, one of the girls the villagers have hidden because they were afraid to let the gunmen near them. O'Reilly tells the gunmen they have been given all the food in the village, so they share it with the villagers.

Calvera comes into the town. There is a gunfight, and Calvera retreats. As the villagers celebrate, Calvera returns. Snipers shoot at the town. The villagers and the gunmen go to their battle positions. Chris kills all the snipers, but Calvera comes back again. The seven are vastly outnumbered, and Calvera is desperate. He will fight to the finish. Some of the villagers want to give up. Chris says he will kill the first man who even so much as whispers about giving up, but some of the gunmen are thinking about it, too. Calvera traps the gunmen, with the help of the frightened villagers. He will let them go, with food and water and even their guns. "I know you won't use those guns against me. No one is crazy enough to make the same mistake twice." Chico wants to fight, but Chris knocks his gun away. They retreat.

Outside the town, they debate going back. They know they will all most likely be killed, but they go back. There is one last massive shoot-out. Chris shoots Calvera, who says as he dies, "A place like this, why? A man like you, why?"

With the village safe, Chris, Vin, and Chico ride off, but Chico returns. His place is in the village. He goes back to Petra and takes off his gun belt. Chris says, "The old man was right. Only the farmers won. We lost. We'll always lose." As Chris and Vin ride off, the boys are tending O'Reilly's grave, just as they promised.

DISCUSSION: The Western is American mythology, and this one features many of the archetypal characters and issues. The gunmen are tough, cool outsiders, their speeches brief and ironic. They know they have more in common with Calvera than they do with the villagers they are protecting. Their skills are necessary to make it safe for the villagers, but once it is safe, the villagers will be relieved to see them go. Although they know that a quiet life is not for them, that Vin could never be a "crackerjack" grocery clerk, a part of them yearns for that kind of life, which is what makes it so important for them to protect it.

O'Reilly spanks the boy who says his father is a coward. "You think I'm brave because I carry a gun. Your fathers are much braver because they carry responsibilities.... This responsibility is like a big rock that weighs a ton. It bends and it twists them until it buries them under the ground.... I have never had this kind of courage." This movie gives families an opportunity to talk about different kinds of courage, and about the commitment to honor that ultimately places Calvera and the seven on opposite sides.

You can see this in an exchange between Chris and Vin: "We took a contract." "Not the kind any court would enforce." "That's just the kind you have to keep." There is also a scene in which Chico asks, "Your gun has got you everything you have, isn't that true?" and the gunmen answer with an evenhanded assessment of what the gun has gotten for them. Vin: "Yeah, sure, everything. After a while you can call bartenders and Ferro dealers by their first name, maybe two hundred of them. Rented rooms you've stayed in, maybe five hundred. Meals you've eaten in hash houses, maybe one thousand. Home, none. Wife, none. Kids, none. Prospects, zero. Suppose I left anything out?" Chris: "Yeah. Places you are tied down to, none. People with a hold on you, none. Men you step aside for, none." Lee: "Insults swallowed, none. Enemies, none." Chris: "No enemies?" Lee: "Alive." One of the movie's greatest strengths is the way that each of the gunmen has his own history and destiny. Lee is particularly interesting, as he understands now only he can see his skill is less than it was, but soon others will see it and he will be vulnerable. His nightmares belie his efforts to appear fearless.

Calvera says to Chris, "We're in the same business...Can men of our profession worry about things like [farmers]? It may even be sacrilegious. If God did not want them sheared, he would not have made them sheep." The seven are different. A farmer tells Vin that the feeling he had when Calvera's men ran away was a feeling worth dying for. "Have you ever felt like that?" "Not for a long time." "I envy you." Vin later tells Chris that both of them have made a gunman's worst mistake in caring about the villagers. He knows it is this very feeling that is worth dying for, and that he no longer has to envy anyone.

PROFANITY: None.
NUDITY/SEXUAL REFERENCES: The farmers hide the young women because they are afraid the gunmen will molest them.
ALCOHOL/DRUG ABUSE: None.
VIOLENCE/SCARINESS: Shoot-outs.
TOLERANCE/DIVERSITY ISSUES: The villagers are Mexican, and the gunmen are Anglo except for Chico and O'Reilly.

QUESTIONS FOR KIDS:

• Many different kinds of courage are depicted and discussed in this movie. How many did you see?

• What are the answers to Calvera's questions: "A place like this, why? A man like you, why?"

• The gunmen each had different reasons for being there. What were they?

• What did Vin mean when he said he did it for the competition?

• Do any of the gunmen regret their choices? How can you tell? Why did Chris lie to Harry?

• What did Calvera mean when he said that if God did not want them sheared, he would not have made them sheep?

• How does the music help tell the story?

CONNECTIONS: **The Magnificent Seven** is a remake of a brilliant Japanese movie called *The Seven Samurai*, which is well worth making an effort to see. Virtually the entire cast can be seen in other outstanding movies. Brynner, of course, is best known for his Oscar-winning performance in **The King and I**. McQueen starred in **The Great Escape** and *The Reivers*. The score, one of the most memorable in the history of movies (thanks in part to its use in Marlboro ads) was composed by Hollywood veteran Elmer Bernstein, whose compositions have been featured in movies that include **Ben-Hur, The World of Henry Orient,** *The Blues Brothers,* **Airplane!** and *Stripes.*

The Red Badge of Courage

1951, 70 min, NR, b&w, 12 and up
Dir: John Huston. Audie Murphy, Andy Devine, Bill Mauldin
PLOT: During the Civil War, a young Union soldier named Henry Fleming (Audie Murphy) worries that he will embarrass himself by being a coward, afraid of getting the "red badge"—a wound in battle. At first, he does run away, but returns to his battalion, lying about where he has been and pretending to have been wounded. He goes into battle the next day and loses himself in the fury of the moment, charging into the fray without regard to his safety. After the battle is over (with another group getting the credit, though Henry is personally recognized by the colonel), Henry knows that he can fight, but feels his spirit reaching out for the sunlight and the birds' singing, "images of peace."
DISCUSSION: Based on the book by Stephen Crane, this is as much a story of the battle within Henry as of the battles without. At first he feels isolated, "alone in space," the only one who is afraid. What frightens him is not the battle itself, but how he will respond to it. To him, it appears that his comrades are "so sure of their courage." He is so scared that he cannot admit it. His friend Jim confesses that "I am, afraid too, a mite," but Henry insists that he is sick of drill and looking forward to battle.

When he runs from battle, he feels "betrayed." His worry is how his fellow soldiers will react. He envies the wounded, who have their "red badge of courage." He swears to help his friend Jim, who has been wounded, but is helpless when Jim collapses and dies. When he returns to the camp, he says he fought in another section of the battle and is relieved that they believe him. "He had performed his mistakes in the dark. So he was still a man." His view of "manhood" is still dependent on the way he is seen by others.

Ater he loses "every sense but his sense of hate" in the next day's battle, Henry is sure enough of his own manhood to confess to Wilson that he had run to safety the day before (though not to tell him the complete truth). When Wilson tells him that he ran, too, until the captain ordered him back, Henry says confession is good for the soul.

The stark black-and-white cinematography, by Harold Rosson, recalls the images of the Matthew Brady photographs of Civil War soldiers and perfectly matches the mood of the story.

PROFANITY: None.
NUDITY/SEXUAL REFERENCES: None.
ALCOHOL/DRUG ABUSE: None.
VIOLENCE/SCARINESS: Intense battle scenes; some characters killed and wounded.
TOLERANCE/DIVERSITY ISSUES: Definition of "manhood."
QUESTIONS FOR FAMILIES:

- What does Henry think constitutes "manhood"? How does that change over the course of the movie?

- What do we learn from the scene where the general promises to eat with all the different platoons?

- How do the different characters react differently to the dangers of battle? Which do the authors of the book and screenplay approve of most? Do you agree?

CONNECTIONS: Compare this to the antiwar classic about the young German WWI soldier, *All Quiet on the Western Front*, brilliantly filmed in 1930 (and winner of the Oscar for Best Picture), and remade for television in 1979, with Richard Thomas, who, coincidentally, appeared in the television remake of **The Red Badge of Courage** as well. High school students may also appreciate *Captain Newman, M.D.*, a comedy-drama based on the Leo Rosten novel about an Army psychiatrist who must take those sensitive enough to be deeply disturbed by war and heal them so they can be sent back to battle. They should also read *Catch 22*, the classic book about the insanity of war.

Henry is played by Audie Murphy, the most highly decorated American soldier of WWII, who knew a great deal about courage and battles. His autobiography, *To Hell and Back*, was made into a movie with himself in the lead role. Another expert on war is cartoonist Bill Mauldin, who plays Wilson. Mauldin created the WWII soldier characters Willie and Joe. A book called *Picture*, by Lillian Ross, documents the making of this movie, which included its own offscreen battles. Director John Huston (**The African Queen, The Maltese Falcon, The Treasure of the Sierra Madre**) also wrote the screenplay.

ACTIVITIES: Older students may want to read Stephen Crane's book, which was written when he was only twenty-two years old and had never seen a battle. He was also the author of some poetry that has a lot of appeal to teenagers. Mature viewers might appreciate the award-winning *Cold Mountain*, about a deserter from the Confederate Army, and the movie, starring Jude Law and Nicole Kidman.

THE CANTERVILLE GHOST

1944, 96 min, NR, b&w, 6 and up
Dir. Jules Dassin. Robert Young, Margaret O'Brien, Charles Laughton
An American soldier (Robert Young) named Cuffy is billeted at the castle of six-year-old Lady Jessica de Canterville (Margaret O'Brien). The ghost of her cowardly ancestor (Charles Laughton) is destined by a curse to haunt the castle until one of his descendants demonstrates bravery. Cuffy (who turns out to be a distant relative) and Lady Jessica triumph over their fears to discover the courage inside them. There is also a nice discussion of noblesse oblige and the duty of those to whom much has been given to give much back to the community.

SEE ALSO:
High Noon Told that a man he put in jail is coming back to kill him, a just-retired marshal must decide whether to run or stay to fight, and keep safe the people who have refused to help him.
The Nasty Girl A young woman persists in uncovering the truth about her neighbors' complicity in Nazi war crimes, despite threats, insults, and abuse.

5

COURTESY

Of Courtesy—it is much less
Than courage or heart or holiness; Yet in my walks it seems to me
That the Grace of God is in Courtesy.
HILLAIRE BELLOC

Courtesy is a neglected virtue, often dismissed as old-fashioned or even hypocritical, but courtesy is crucial, requiring us to be sensitive to the feelings of others and to show respect for them and for ourselves. This is particularly important because so many of today's movies seem to depict lack of courtesy as somehow brave, honest, or funny. The movies in this chapter teach us that being treated with courtesy or acting courteously can be a transforming experience.

Babe

1995, 92 min, G, 4 and up
Dir: Chris Noonan. James Cromwell
PLOT: "This is a tale about an unprejudiced heart, and how it changed our valley forever." So begins this lovely story about a pig who lives his dream (and saves his life) by learning to herd sheep. Farmer Hoggett (James Cromwell) wins the little pig at a fair. Back at his farm, Babe is adopted by Fly, the sheepdog, who treats him like one of her puppies. Babe learns the ways of the farm and the barnyard and is very distressed to hear from Maa, the sheep, that she thinks Fly is cruel, and even more distressed to learn from Ferdinand, the duck, that humans eat animals.

Babe gets in trouble when he goes into the house to help Ferdinand. They are scheduled to be slaughtered for Christmas dinner. Both he and Ferdinand escape the knife when another duck is killed instead. Hoggett calls Babe a "watch pig" when Babe alerts him to some thieves who make off with some of the herd. He thus earns the privilege of going with Fly and her spouse, Rex, to guard the sheep.

At first, Babe tries to herd the sheep as Rex and Fly do, threatening them and bit-ing them on the legs. Maa tells him to ask them nicely, and when he does, they comply. Rex is furious and fights with Fly. With Rex tied up and sedated and Fly injured, Babe becomes a "sheep pig."

Maa is killed by a wolf, and Hoggett, blaming Babe, decides to shoot him. Fly, desperate to save Babe, talks to the sheep for the first time to ask them to help Babe by telling her what really happened to Maa. Hoggett discovers the truth and unloads his gun.

The jealous cat tells Babe that the other animals are laughing at him and he is going to be eaten. Hoggett now believes in Babe and brings him inside the house, nursing him. Hoggett enters Babe into a competition at the fair, submitting him as the best sheepdog. At first, the sheep at the fair won't listen to Babe, but when Rex finds out the sheep password (by promising to be kind and respectful to sheep in the future), Babe uses it, along with his unique style of courteous friend-liness, to manage the sheep so brilliantly that he wins the competition.

DISCUSSION: This movie is a delight for the eye, heart, and spirit. Hoggett's small farm is a picturesque ideal of country life. The screenplay is witty without being cynical and tender without being soppy. The combination of real animals, animation, and puppetry is flawless, down to the tiny Greek chorus made up of mice, who chirp about the "Pig of Destiny."

It deals very well with many important issues. Babe and some of the other characters make mistakes, some serious, when they draw conclusions from insuf-ficient information. Ferdinand thinks the Hoggetts like his "crowing" in the morning. Babe thinks the "shiny tube" (gun) produces food. The sheep call all dogs "wolves." The pigs think they are going to "pig paradise." Hoggett thinks Babe killed Maa. It can be very useful to discuss wrong judgments you or your children have made, and how to tell if you have enough information to draw the right conclusion.

The movie is really a tale of two "unprejudiced hearts." Hoggett's belief in Babe is contrasted with Mrs. Hoggett's hysteria at the thought of having him in the competition. Babe treats all species as friends, while they show a great deal of prejudice toward each other and against him. The sheep say the dogs (whom they call wolves) are ignorant, and the dogs say the sheep are stupid. There is a great deal of jockeying for status, as determined by the affection and approval of "the boss" (the Hoggetts).

It is also the story of a dream, as Babe dreams of being useful in a way that will be more important than any value he could have as food.

The movie provides an opportunity for the discussion of some other issues as well. Rex and the cat both behave badly because of jealousy. Rex is also very sensitive about his hearing loss and, in one of the movie's most touching moments, confesses that he cannot hear for the first time when he asks the sheep for their password so he can help Babe. There are issues of trust (Babe has to decide who to trust when he is learning how the faint works and what the relationships are) and loyalty (the animals' to Hoggett; Babe's to the sheep, to Hoggett, and to Ferdinand, for whom he breaks the rule about not entering the house). There is the issue of honesty, as Hoggett commits some lies of omission in filling out the entry form (the movie makes it clear that he would not lie if the entry specified "dog"). There is the importance of kindness: Hoggett's to Babe, Fly's to Babe, Babe's to the sheep, and ultimately Rex's to Babe and how it transforms both the giver and the recipient.

PROFANITY: None (Babe uses the word "butt-heads," which is actually rather apt when applied, as it is here, to sheep!).
NUDITY/SEXUAL REFERENCES: Oblique reference to male dog being "snipped" and its effect on his ability to breed.
ALCOHOL/DRUG ABUSE: None.
VIOLENCE/SCARINESS: The issue of animal slaughter for food is dealt with very directly. Babe is alone because his family was slaughtered for food. Ferdinand says, darkly, "Christmas means carnage." It at first appears Babe's friend Ferdinand has been killed for Christmas dinner, but it later turns out it was another duck.
TOLERANCE/DIVERSITY ISSUES: A theme of the movie.
QUESTIONS FOR FAMILIES:

- Why does Babe feel differently about the sheep than Fly and Rex do?

- How does Babe decide what to believe (and whom to believe)?

- Why is the cat so mean to Babe?

- Why is Rex so angry at Babe? What makes Rex change his mind? How will Rex get along with the sheep, now that he has had to ask for their help and promise not to bite?

- Why is Babe so polite to the sheep? Why does that matter to them?

CONNECTIONS: Children may recognize "The Dance of the Hours" music from Fantasia. Children who enjoy this movie will also enjoy that other barnyard classic, *Charlotte's Web*, by E. B. White, which every family should read aloud at least once. Like Babe, it is the story of a pig's fight to be more than bacon and pork chops (these movies may create more vegetarians than Bambi). The animated movie version, with Debbie Reynolds as Charlotte, lacks White's beautiful language, but is a pleasant diversion.

ACTIVITIES: Children who enjoy this movie might like to visit a petting zoo or farm.

My Fair Lady

1964, 170 min, NR, 6 an up
Dir: George Cukor. Rex Harrison, Audrey Hepburn, Wilfrid Hyde-White
PLOT: On a rainy night in Covent Garden, Professor Henry Higgins (Rex Harrison) meets Colonel Pickering (Wilfrid Hyde-White), a fellow linguistics scholar, as he is correctly identifying accents of all those around him. Offhandedly commenting that in England people are defined by their accents, Higgins says he could even teach a poor Cockney flower girl to speak like a lady. The next day, the flower girl (Audrey Hepburn) comes to see him to offer to pay Higgins for language lessons. She wants to be "a lady in a flower shop," and that requires a more bourgeois accent and manner.

Higgins says he can do better, even teach her to speak and act like a lady of wealth and breeding, well enough to fool everyone at an upcoming ball. Pickering makes him a bet, and they agree. Eliza is overwhelmed, but her hope for something more out of life, and the kindness of Colonel Pickering, and the promise of chocolates, persuade her to stay.

Her father, dustman Alfred Doolittle (Stanley Holloway), arrives, looking for a handout. Higgins, charmed by Doolittle's cheerful amorality, gives him some money and jokingly recommends him to an American philanthropist as an astute social thinker.

Higgins and Pickering work Eliza very hard and finally think she is ready for a trial run. They bring her to the ultra-elegant Ascot races, where her uncertain veneer of refinement and her irrepressible directness appeal to Freddie Eynsford-Hill (Jeremy Brett), a poor, unskilled, but impeccably upper-class gentleman.

Meanwhile, the American philanthropist has died, leaving a substantial amount of money to Doolittle, based on Higgins's recommendation. Understanding money requires a level of respectability he had thus far happily ignored (as described in the song "With a Little Bit of Luck"), he agrees to marry his long-time companion.

After much more work, Eliza is ready for the ball, a vision of grace and beauty. She is the belle of the ball, enchanting even the prince, and speaking with such exquisite diction and manners that Higgins's rival declares she must be Hungarian royalty. Back at Higgins's home, the men are exultant over "their" success. They ignore Eliza, and she leaves, hurt. She goes to Higgins's mother, and when Higgins realizes how much he misses her and comes after her, she explains she wanted to be seen as a person. He tells her he is relieved; that now she is showing independence, he does not need to feel responsible for her. She has nowhere to go; those with upper-class bearing (like Freddie) are not employable. Higgins and Eliza cannot come to an agreement, but finally she returns to his house, and with the question "Eliza, where the devil are my slippers?" he lets her know how much he has missed her.

DISCUSSION: This musical was based on *Pygmalion*, written in 1912 by George Bernard Shaw. In this era, and in this country, it is hard to imagine how genuinely revolutionary it was for Shaw to say that the only difference between the classes was accent and demeanor. It is worth discussing the way that language and accent defined people in this era, and asking children about the conclusions people draw from accents today.

This story has its parallels to Cinderella: It has its climax at a ball, which the heroine attends in borrowed finery. Higgins and Pickering are far from fairy god-fathers. Their interest is not in rewarding Eliza for a virtuous life; they want to show off their own achievement and play something of a joke on high society. Higgins is not a prince. In a way, he reveals the princess inside of Eliza, though he never intended to. He never even took the time to imagine it to be possible.

One of Shaw's most important insights in this story is of the role of courtesy, and the different characters' ideas of its importance provide an excellent opportunity for discussion. Pickering's treating Eliza like a lady has as much to do with her becoming one as all of the training about diction and appropriate topics for conversation. As she says, he treats a flower girl like a duchess. When she says Higgins treats a duchess like a flower girl, Higgins says "the great thing" is to treat everyone the same way. That may be, but Pickering is able to treat everyone (even Eliza at her Cockney-est) with equal courtesy, instead of equal brusqueness. Mrs. Higgins is also courteous to everyone (with the possible exception of her son); her concern over having Eliza at Ascot is at least as much for Eliza's comfort as her own.

PROFANITY: Eliza shocks everyone at the Ascot races by saying, "Move your blooming arse!" (In the play, she says, "Not bloody likely," considered not shocking enough by the time the musical was written.)

NUDITY/SEXUAL REFERENCES: Very mild references (Eliza's parents not married, question about suitability of Eliza staying with the men).

ALCOHOL/DRUG ABUSE: Liquor is used to celebrate triumph; Mr. Doolittle happily drinks a great deal.

VIOLENCE/SCARINESS: None.

TOLERANCE/DIVERSITY ISSUES: Class issues are a theme of the movie.

QUESTIONS FOR FAMILIES:

• Eliza says Pickering treats a flower girl like a lady, and Higgins treats a lady like a flower girl. Higgins says what is important is treating everyone exactly the same. What do you think about this?

• Eliza sings "I Could Have Danced All Night," but she also sings "Just You Wait." Why does she feel so differently about Higgins at different points in her lessons?

• What does Higgins mean when he says the English don't teach their children how to speak?

• Do you know people who have accents? How do accents change the way people react to those who have them? Can you imitate different accents?

CONNECTIONS: See the play *Pygmalion*, on which this musical was based. There is an excellent movie version, with an Oscar-winning screenplay by Shaw himself, starring one of Shaw's favorite actresses, Wendy Hiller. Note that in the Afterword to the play, Shaw makes it very clear that Eliza marries Freddie, but in both filmed versions, the strong implication is that Eliza and Higgins become romantically involved.

Fans of *Sherlock Holmes* on PBS will enjoy a young Jeremy Brett as Freddie (his songs and Hepburn's were sung by others).

To Kill a Mockingbird

1962, 129 min, NR, b&w, 10 and up

Dir: Robert Mulligan. Gregory Peck, Robert Duvall, Brock Peters

PLOT: The story is about prejudice and injustice, seen through the eyes of a little girl, the daughter of a lawyer who defends a black man against a trumped-up rape charge in 1930s Georgia. The lawyer, Atticus Finch (Gregory Peck), is the essence of quiet dignity, integrity, and courtesy. His efforts to teach his son and daughter the values he believes in, which the community they live in does not always honor, are moving and inspiring.

Scout (Mary Badham), her brother Jem (Philip Alford), and their friend, Dill (John Megna), are fascinated by the stories about Arthur "Boo" Radley (Robert Duvall), the man who lives in the house next door and has not been seen in many years. They have heard that he stabbed his father with a pair of scissors and that he comes out at night to peer in people's windows. They dare each other to make contact with him, and once manage to run all the way to his porch, where they are terrified by an ominous shadow and run off by Boo's father's shotgun.

Their father, Atticus, has been appointed to defend Tom Robinson (Brock Peters), who has been charged with raping Mayella Ewell (Collin Wilcox). Atticus asks Scout not to fight with the children who call him a "nigger-lover." He tells Mayella's father, Bob (James Anderson), that he intends to give Tom the best possible defense. When members of the town come to jail to lynch Tom, Scout's arrival and her friendly greeting to the father of her classmate dissipates the crowd's hostility.

At the trial, Atticus shows that Mayella's injuries indicate a left-handed assailant, but Tom's left arm is useless, having been injured years before in a cotton gin. Bob Ewell, though, is left-handed, supporting Atticus's implication that Ewell is the culprit. Though it is clear that Tom is innocent, he is convicted. Though Atticus promises an appeal, Tom is killed trying to escape.

Still, Bob Ewell is furious and swears revenge. He attacks Jem and Scout, but they are rescued by Boo Radley, who carries Jem home, stays to see that he is all right, and walks back to his house with Scout without saying a word.

DISCUSSION: The sense of time and place in this movie is extraordinary—not just the time in history, but the time in the lives of the little girl and her brother. In addition to the power of the story and the appeal of the characters, this is one of the best movies about childhood ever made.

There is a great deal of emphasis in the movie on courtesy and sensitivity to the feelings of others. In the first scene, Atticus tells Scout not to embarrass a client named Walter Cunningham when he comes by to drop off some food as payment for legal services. Later, when Scout brings Walter, Jr., home for lunch, she is told not to say anything when he pours syrup all over his food. Atticus treats mean old Mrs. Dubose with gallantry, disarming her. Atticus's courtesy in cross-examining Mayella Ewell is so unfamiliar to her that she assumes it is some new sort of insult. The black people in the courtroom balcony stand as a courtesy to Atticus. Sheriff Heck Tate explains why the official record will show Bob Ewell fell on his knife. He wants to protect Boo "with his shy ways" from the well-meaning gratitude (and curiosity) of the "good ladies" of the town.

Of course, a central theme of the movie is racism. By virtue of their slovenly way of life and contempt for society, the Ewells would have been at the bottom of the town's social strata, except for the conviction that any black person was less worthy of respect than any white person. The word of a white person with a terrible reputation would automatically outweigh the word of any black person, no matter what his record was for honesty. The movie makes it clear that the deciding factors in Tom Robinson's conviction were the community's uneasiness and embarrassment over two of his statements: that Mayella tried to hug and kiss him, and that he felt sorry for her. Both of those statements struck at the very foundations of the community's sense of appropriate behavior, possibly because the foundation was already cracked. These statements made it much more difficult for the community to deny that blacks were capable of seeing themselves and being seen by whites as appealing or even superior, and that made it necessary to get rid of Tom.

It is also worthwhile to examine the structure of this story. Unlike, for example, **Destry Rides Again**, which has a very tight and linear construction, or **Meet Me in St. Louis**, which is just a series of separate incidents, this Oscar-winning screenplay is a magnificent example of a story that appears episodic and yet whose parts all turn out to be essential not just to the mood but to the theme and climax. This is even truer in the book. Both book and movie also do a superb job of presenting the story from the perspective of the child, but with the insight of the adult.

PROFANITY: None.
NUDITY/SEXUAL REFERENCES: The plot centers on a rape trial; no explicit language.
ALCOHOL/DRUG ABUSE: None.
VIOLENCE/SCARINESS: Scary expedition to Radley house; suspense over threatened lynching; children in peril.
TOLERANCE/DIVERSITY ISSUES: A theme of the movie.
QUESTIONS FOR FAMILIES:

• How can you tell Tom is innocent? Why does the jury vote to convict him?

• Why does everyone get upset when Tom says he felt sorry for Mayella?

• Why does Mr. Cunningham change his mind about lynching Tom?

- Why is the incident about Atticus shooting the mad dog in the movie? What does it tell us about Atticus and about his relationship with his children?

- Why do the people in the balcony stand and tell Scout, Jem, and Dill to stand as Atticus leaves the courtroom?

- Why is courtesy so important to Atticus? How is that shown?

CONNECTIONS: This movie is based on the outstanding book by Harper Lee, strongly recommended as a read-aloud before seeing the movie. Although they learn about Martin Luther King, Jr., and other civil rights leaders in school, children and teenagers who see this movie may be unaware of the open bigotry of that era. They should go to the library for more information, and see documentaries like the two *Eyes on the Prize* series and dramas like **The Long Walk Home**, Ghosts of Mississippi, and **The Autobiography of Miss Jane Pittman**.

ACTIVITIES: The character of Dill is based on Lee's childhood friend, Truman Capote, whose story of his childhood, *A Christmas Memory*, is also well worth reading aloud. It was beautifully filmed with Geraldine Page and was remade for television starring Patty Duke.

TO SIR, WITH LOVE

1967, 105 min, NR, mature high schoolers
Dir: James Clavell. Sidney Poitier, Judy Geeson, Lulu
Released the same year as **Up the Down Staircase**, this is also the story of a new teacher in an inner-city school, although this time the city is London and the teacher is Mark Thackeray (Sidney Poitier). An outsider by virtue of his country (West Indies) more than his color, Poitier becomes impatient with the insolence and narrow-mindedness of his students and imposes his own set of rules, foremost of which is courtesy to him and to each other. At first, they are embarrassed and awkward, as though they don't want to believe they could deserve such treatment. The other teachers make it quite clear they don't think the students deserve it. Soon the exaggerated sarcasm of "Miss Dare" and "Sir" falls away, and we see a superb example of the transforming nature of being treated with respect and treating others with respect, too.

CONNECTIONS: Judy Geeson, who plays Pamela Dare, was an occasional guest star on the television show *Mad About You* as the Buchmans' English neighbor.

6

FAIRNESS AND JUSTICE

"Injustice anywhere is a threat to justice everywhere."
THE REVEREND DR. MARTIN LUTHER KING, JR.

Any high school English teacher will tell you the first requirement for a story is conflict. The challenge for the storyteller, whether a writer or a filmmaker, is to involve us in that conflict. As a result, many movies present us with issues of fairness and justice. Many of them do so directly, by taking us into the courtroom. Because every lawsuit represents a conflict, every one is automatically a story, staged as though it was a play, with the lawyers and witnesses the clients, and the jury the very important audience.

Because the opposing sides often take extreme positions and use colorful language and creative approaches to persuade the judge and jury, it is hard to watch a lawsuit without feeling strongly about the outcome, even though we may change our minds more than once as we hear both sides. There are a number of outstanding movies that feature courtroom battles at the center of the story.

Compare, for example, two courtroom dramas, **Miracle on 34th Street** and **Inherit the Wind**. They could not be more opposite in tone. One is a delightful fantasy-comedy, almost a fairy tale, and the other is a very serious play, based on a real case argued by the foremost lawyers of their time, and dealing with issues that are still the subject of bitter controversy today. Yet in a very real sense, both are about the same question. Both are about how we know what we know, and whether it will be based on what we can prove or what we know through faith. Do we listen to our heads or our hearts? Do we believe what we are told, or do we challenge conventional wisdom, asking questions and evaluating the evidence?

The two films deal with the theme in sharply contrasting ways. Both include consideration of issues like relevance and probity of evidence to help decide the case. One crucial element in common is that in both the decision is strongly, even definitively, influenced by political considerations. Both have judges whose political advisers tell them how to decide the cases. Both have characters who are confronted with their rigidity, though one is rigidly committed to faith and one to rationality, but the cases have very different conclusions. In both, the side representing the filmmaker's point of view puts his opposition on the stand (in one case, the opposing counsel himself; in the other, the opposing counsel's son and namesake). One movie comes out in favor of empiricism, and the other in favor of faith. Yet in both cases, the resolution is one most of the audience will find highly satisfying. Watching these movies can lead to a discussion not just of the issues they pose, but also of point of view and tone in storytelling.

Some movies use the judicial system to show its fairness, while others show how it can be subverted. Some show its complexity and its limits, as when the side who won the war judges the side that lost in Judgment at Nuremberg. Other movies depict people trying to devise their own systems of justice, either because the system has failed or because they are so removed from it that they have no alternative. Then there are also movies that lead us to consider larger notions of fairness, like those concerning issues of bigotry and equality, wealth and poverty, or war and peace. These movies make us think about the injustice of our world and give us an opportunity to think and talk with each other about how it happens and how we can make it better.

Amistad

1997, 152 min, R, high school age
Dir: Steven Spielberg. Anthony Hopkins, Djimon Hounsou, Matthew McConaughey, Morgan Freeman, Nigel Hawthorne
PLOT: In 1839, a group of Africans sold into slavery were being transported to the United States on a Spanish ship. Off the coast of Cuba, they escaped from their shackles and attacked the crew, leaving two crew members alive to take them back to Africa. The Spanish sailors tricked the Africans and sailed up the coast of the United States until an American naval ship off the coast of Connecticut captured them. The Africans were brought into court to determine their fate. They were claimed as property ("like livestock") by both the Spanish crew and by the American captors.

Roger Baldwin (Matthew McConaughey), a property lawyer, persuades abolitionists Theodore Joadson (Morgan Freeman) and Lewis Tappan (Stellan Skarsgard) that he has a theory that will help the Africans. He argues that it is not a property case at all. The law provides that only the child slaves can be a slave. Since the Africans were not born slaves they are free, and their actions were merely self-defense in aid of restoring their freedom. If Baldwin can prove that they were born as free people in Africa, and not, as their captors alleged, slaves in the West Indies, they would not be considered property; they would be considered human beings.

The trial attracts the attention of President Martin Van Buren (Nigel Hawthorne), who is in the midst of a campaign for re-election and very aware that he will need the support of Southern voters to win. He is under additional pressure from the eleven-year-old queen of Spain, Isabella II, and her ambassador, who raise claims on behalf of the Spanish fleet. When the judge and jury appear sympathetic to the Africans, Van Buren arranges for a new judge to hear the case without a jury.

Meanwhile, the Africans try to understand what is going on around them. Baldwin and Joadson are able to find a man who speaks Mende, the language of Cinque (Djimon Hounsou) and some of the other Africans. They win in court and the government appeals. Former President John Quincy Adams (Anthony Hopkins) represents them before the U.S. Supreme Court, where seven of the nine justices are slaveholders. In a moving and eloquent argument, he persuades the justices (with one dissenter) that the Africans were free, and that if they had been white, they would have been called heroes for rebelling against those who tried to take that freedom away.

DISCUSSION: Adams explains that in court the one with the best story wins. Indeed, we hear many different stories in the course of the movie as each character tries to explain why his view is the right one. In the first courtroom scene we hear several different "stories" about what happens to the Africans. All of those stories assume that the Africans are property; the only question being whose property they are. Interestingly, as "property," they cannot be charged with murder or theft. One cannot be both property and capable of forming criminal intent. The only issue before the court is where the Africans will go and not the question of homicide.

As Baldwin begins to tell Joadson and Tappan his story of the case, we see them slowly becoming aware of what had always been obvious to us. The Africans cannot be property. They were free, in which case their actions were not only honorable but heroic, in the same category as America's founding fathers, whose rebellion is central to our own story about who we are as Americans. Despite the attempts of Van Buren to subvert the legal system established just decades before, the essential commitment to freedom is so much a part of the story that, at least in this one brief moment, justice triumphed. Adams, the son of the second President, made that his story.

PROFANITY: None.
NUDITY/SEXUAL REFERENCES: Slaves are nude in brief scenes.
ALCOHOL/DRUG ABUSE: None.
VIOLENCE/SCARINESS: Very violent opening scene with slave uprising and other violent scenes in flashbacks (including whipping, beating, and drowning) and when the slave fortress is liberated (including shooting).
TOLERANCE/DIVERSITY ISSUES: A theme of the movie.
QUESTIONS FOR FAMILIES:

• Why was it important to prove where the Africans were from?

• What was Calhoun's justification for slavery?

• Why does Tappan say that the death of the Africans may help the cause of abolition more than their freedom?

• Why does Spielberg organize his story as he does, taking the audience from the confrontation to the courtroom and only later providing the background about the capture of the Africans?

• What does it mean that there is no Mende word for "should"?

CONNECTIONS: Chief Justice Storey is portrayed by real-life former Supreme Court Justice Harry Blackmun.

Anatomy of a Murder

1959, 160 min, NR, b&w, 12 and up
Dir: Otto Preminger. Jimmy Stewart, Ben Gazzara, Arthur O'Connell, George C. Scott, Lee Remick, Eve Arden
PLOT: This classic courtroom drama was written by a lawyer (later a judge), based on one of his own cases, and the judge is played by a real life lawyer-judge, Joseph Welch. That lends this story of a murder trial some extra authenticity, and the dazzling performances and electrically-charged direction make it unforgettable.
    Frederick Manion, an Aimy lieutenant (Ben Gazzara), is on trial for murder for shooting Barney Quill, the owner of a bar. Paul Biegler (Jimmy Stewart), a former district attorney returning to law practice after losing his bid for reelection, agrees to defend him. Manion says he killed Quill because he raped Man-

ion's wife, Laura (Lee Remick). With a strong hint from Biegler, Manion says he must have been crazy.

Biegler, aided by legal research by an old friend with a drinking problem (Arthur O'Connell) and his loyal secretary (Eve Arden), puts together a defense strategy based on a ruling by another court in the state that "irresistible impulse" is a defense to a murder charge. All they must do is prove that it was irresistible impulse for Manion to shoot Quill. Manion is acquitted, but another "irresistible impulse" causes him to leave town without paying his bill.

DISCUSSION: The use of precedent, the role of the expert witness, the advice to Laura about how to appear for her testimony, the evidentiary rulings, the cross-examination, and the acknowledgment by Biegler that the jury can never "disregard" what they have heard are all real-life legal details that are also compelling drama. The courtroom presentation is almost a play within a play, as we see when Biegler tells Laura how to dress for her testimony as though he was directing her in a part. There is a great deal of moral complexity as well. Biegler never seems interested in the issue of Manion's guilt or culpability; all he cares about is winning the case (and beating the man who defeated him at the polls). Yet there is morality and redemption in the movie in the dedication to the law and to at least some form of truth and fairness.

PROFANITY: None.
NUDITY/SEXUAL REFERENCES: Frank discussion of the rape.
ALCOHOL/DRUG ABUSE: Manion and his wife drink a lot; McCarthy has a drinking problem.
VIOLENCE/SCARINESS: Off-screen rape and murder.
TOLERANCE/DIVERSITY ISSUES: None.
QUESTIONS FOR FAMILIES:

- What does the title tell us? Is it a murder if the jury finds that it isn't?

- How did Paul get Manion to say that he must have been crazy without telling him to say it?

- Should Manion have gone to jail? What is the relevance to his culpability or credibility of whether Laura was in fact raped or not? Shouldn't the issue be what he believed, since his defense was insanity?

- How does the filmmaker make you want Paul to win? How could he make you want Manion to be convicted?

• What do you think of the ending? What is that supposed to show us?

CONNECTIONS: Joseph Welch, who plays the judge, was a real American hero, the man who put a stop to Joseph McCarthy. Try to watch the footage of his famous confrontation of McCarthy, where he asked, "Have you no shame?" It might lead you to watch *Tail Gunner Joe*, a made-for-television movie about McCarthy's life.

ACTIVITIES: Read Stephen Becker's novel *A Covenant with Death*, which has a similar tone and some of the same themes.

Inherit the Wind

1960, 127 min, NR, b&w, 10 to adult
Dir: Stanley Kramer. Spencer Tracy, Fredric March, Gene Kelly
PLOT: In the famous Scopes "monkey" trial, three-time presidential candidate and Wilson administration Secretary of State William Jennings Bryan argued that Darwin's theory of evolution should not be taught to high school, students. Clarence Darrow, the most renowned trial lawyer in American history, argued that it should. In this movie, the names and some of the facts are changed, but some of the dialogue is taken from the transcripts of the real Scopes trial.

At first, some of the town leaders are concerned that the trial will be bad for the town, but when they hear that Matthew Harrison Brady (Fredric March playing the character based on William Jennings Bryan) has volunteered to come to Hillsboro to prosecute the case, they decide to accept. The merits of the law aside, Brady's presence will "fill up the town like a rain barrel in a thunderstorm," which is good for business. Bertram Cates will be defended by Henry Drummond (Spencer Tracy as the character based on Clarence Darrow).

One of the first people to arrive is E. K. Hornbeck (Gene Kelly as a reporter, based on acidic newspaper correspondent H. L. Mencken), whose newspaper is paying Drummond's fee.

At the trial, Drummond tries to present a series of distinguished scientists to testify in favor of Cates. Brady objects; their testimony is not relevant to the issue of whether Cates violated the law. The judge agrees. Drummond is so furious that he asks for permission to withdraw from the case. Cates won't let him cross-examine Brady's witness, Cates's own girlfriend, Rachel, and the judge won't let Drummond present his own. For him, the issue is not whether Cates violated the law, but whether the law violates a larger law. "I warn you that a wicked law, like cholera, destroys everyone it touches, its upholders as well as its offenders."

Drummond says, "What I need is a miracle." Kelly sardonically hands him the Bible. "Here's a whole bag full, courtesy of Matthew Harrison Brady." For Drummond, the Bible does provide the answer. The next morning, Drummond calls Brady to the witness stand as "one of the world's foremost experts on the Bible and its teachings." Drummond says that he thinks one thing is holy: "The individual human mind. In a child's power to master the multiplication table there is more sanctity than in all your shouted 'Amens!' 'Holy Holies!' and 'Hosannas!' An idea is a greater monument than a cathedral. the advance of man's knowledge is a greater miracle than all the sticks turned to snakes or the parting of the waters…The Bible is a good book, but it is not the only book…How do you know God didn't speak to Charles Darwin?"

Drummond keeps pressing Brady on how he knows what he knows. When Brady finally says in frustration that God tells him what to support, the crowd for the first time turns against him, frightened by his arrogance and fervor. Brady is beside himself.

The next day, the mayor warns the judge that the lieutenant governor wants the publicity to "simmer down." Elections are coming. The jury finds Cates guilty, but the judge imposes only a token fine, one hundred dollars. Brady wants to make a speech, but the judge adjourns the trial and the crowd leaves. It has been too much for him. He collapses, and shortly after he dies. Drummond is deeply saddened. "A giant once lived in that body, but Matthew Brady got lost because he looked for God too high up and too far away." Hornbeck looks at Drummond and says, "You're just as religious as he was." Drummond holds both books, the Bible and Darwin's, one in each hand, then puts them together and walks out of the courtroom.

DISCUSSION: In 1925, the two greatest lawyers in America went to court to argue what was called the trial of the century. It wasn't about a famous person like Martha Stewart, or a famous crime like Lorena Bobbitt's or Jeffrey Dahmer's. It wasn't even one of the cases that changed American life, about abortion or desegregation. It was the Scopes trial, a case about how we decide what we teach our children in school. At the heart of the case, though, was a fight about how we know what is true. Do we listen to our heads or our hearts? Do we believe what we are told, or do we insist on asking questions and evaluating the evidence?

As in any courtroom drama, the question of fairness arises over and over, but in this case it both surrounds and exemplifies the core issue of the case. How do we know what is true? If that depends, in some sense, on making it a "fair trial," what does that mean? How do we make a trial fair?

Note the issue of jury selection. A juror who says, "I believe in the holy word of God, and I believe in Matthew Harrison Brady" is excused. Apparently, even in a case that challenges the right of teachers and students to question the Bible, some notion of fairness requires the issue be judged by a juror who has a more open mind. Drummond objects to the fact that Brady is addressed in court by the honorary title of Colonel, just bestowed on him by the town. He believes it adds more weight to Brady's comments and lends him a greater aura of respect and authority. How is it resolved? Surprisingly, not by addressing both attorneys as "Mr.," but by bestowing the same honorific on Drummond, albeit temporarily. Drummond asks that a sign outside the courtroom with the exhortation READ YOUR BIBLE should either be removed or be augmented with a sign telling people to READ YOUR DARWIN. The sign is removed.

The trial is about keeping one kind of information out of the classroom, but, as in any trial, a significant amount of time is spent keeping certain kinds of information out of the courtroom, and it is very interesting to contrast the justification for excluding information raised in both contexts. In science, all information is evaluated on the basis of its accuracy and relevance; in law, these are also important. For example, the scientific testimony Drummond wants to present is excluded for reasons of relevance; whatever the scientists have to say is judged to have no relation to the issue of whether or not Cates violated the law.

There are concerns besides accuracy and relevance. Some of the challenges to information in the courtroom relate to fairness, as with Drummond's request that prayer meetings not be announced by the judge for fear it will prejudice the jury. Another example is the objection to certain testimony as "hearsay," the staple of any courtroom drama. The legal system has determined that hearsay (reporting on what someone else said) is just not reliable enough to be used in court, with certain narrow exceptions. In other words, the likelihood that it will help us find out the truth is outweighed by the likelihood that it will be inaccurate and lead us to the wrong conclusions.

Sometimes a lawyer will object to something a witness or the opposing lawyer has said, and the judge will tell the jury to pretend they didn't hear it, as happens here when Brady refers to Cates as having "gone astray." Of course, the jury can't really forget about it (as Jimmy Stewart notably acknowledges in Anatomy of a Murder, a courtroom drama actually written by a lawyer), but the point is they can be reminded not to rely on it in coming to a decision. Finally, some information is kept out of the courtroom because Cates won't let Drummond cross-examine Rachel. He decides he would rather go to jail than see her put through that difficult experience. Some things are more important than the truth, even to him.

Drummond is not permitted to read from Darwin in order to be able to ask Brady about it during the trial. Just as it is considered too dangerous and inflammatory for the students to hear, it is too dangerous for the jury, and perhaps even the members of the community in the courtroom, to hear. Drummond cannot put Darwin on trial; his only alternative is to put the refusal to consider Darwin on trial, and he does that in his cross-examination of Brady.

In this movie about skepticism, science, and faith, Drummond does have faith in one thing. He believes in the ability of the human mind to think, to question, and to know. When he is examining one of Cates's students during the trial, he asks, "Did you believe everything Mr. Cates told you?" When the boy answers, "I don't know, I gotta think about it," Drummond responds, "Good for you! Good for you!" Drummond is not there on behalf of Darwin; he is there on behalf of open-mindedness. It is not Drummond who is the nonbeliever in this case; it is Hombeck, the most cynical of newspapermen.

What does Brady believe in? Brady is not there on behalf of the Bible or even faith as much as he is on behalf of a narrow and rigid view that prizes certainty above anything else. His world is composed of platitudes and facile retorts. He is described by Hornbeck as "the only man I know who can strut sitting down." When Drummond shows him a fossil determined by geologists to be millions of years old, Brady says he is "more interested in the Rock of Ages than in the age of rocks." When Drummond questions Brady, he shows just how easy that kind of faith is to crack, and how devastating the consequences are when it does. Drummond demonstrates his method of finding the answers is able to prove one fact—that Brady's faith is superficial, based on fear, not strength. As Mrs. Brady says to Rachel, "Maybe it meant too much to him."

It may be said the filmmakers stacked the deck, and presented the story less than completely evenhandedly. It is clear throughout whose side they are on. A courtroom must be fair and objective; a movie can seldom get away with that without being static and a little boring. Just as Cates/Scopes had ideas he wanted to teach his students, and Brady/Bryan and Drummond/Darrow had ideas they wanted to persuade the jury about, the writers and director of this movie had their story, too, their own version of what they thought was true, and like each of the characters and their real-life counterparts, they did their best to persuade their audience. Their audience's challenge is to do their best to determine what the truth really is.

PROFANITY: In keeping with his character as something of a heretic, Drummond uses some mild language, at one point censoring himself when he is about to say "damn."
NUDITY/SEXUAL REFERENCES: None.
ALCOHOL/DRUG ABUSE: None.
VIOLENCE/SCARINESS: Threats by crowd.
TOLERANCE/DIVERSITY ISSUES: None, beyond an accurate, historical representation of traditional notions of "a woman's place."
QUESTIONS FOR FAMILIES:

- Who won this case? Brady, who was able to persuade the jury to convict Cates, or Drummond, whose view ultimately prevailed?

- Both Drummond and Brady say, at different points in the case, that all they are interested in is the truth. Is that right? Do they mean different things when they use the word "truth"?

- Who should decide which version of the facts is taught to children: parents, teachers, or lawmakers?

- How do we know what is the best way to find the truth: the Brady way (to have faith) or the Drummond way (to question)? Which is each good for? Which is each bad for? What truth does the Drummond method show about Brady?

- In this movie, Drummond acknowledges that Cates broke the law, but argues it is a bad law and should not be enforced. Should a jury do that? Under what circumstances?

CONNECTIONS: This movie features three of the most talented and versatile actors in Hollywood history. All three were superb in dramatic or comedic roles, and of course Kelly is a legend for his dancing in a series of magnificent MGM musicals. It might be special fun to compare the two versions of *Dr. Jekyll and Mr. Hyde*, one with March (1932) and one with Tracy (1941). Fans of the early episodes of *Bewitched* will recognize Dick York (Cates) as the original Darrin Stephens (1964–69), and fans of TV's *The Rockford Files* will recognize Noah Beery, Jr. (Stebbens), as Jim Rockford's father, Rocky.

The director, Stanley Kramer, made a number of movies about political and social controversies, including **Judgment at Nuremberg** and **Guess Who's**

Coming to Dinner (both with Tracy) and *On the Beach*, about people in Australia waiting to die after nuclear bombs have destroyed everything else.

ACTIVITIES: High school students can do research on controversies over the curriculum in local schools. They may also want to learn something about Darwin and his theories, or something about Clarence Darrow's colorful career.

The Ox-Bow Incident

1943, 75 min, NR, b&w, 10 and up
Dir: William Wellman. Henry Fonda, Dana Andrews
PLOT: Two drifters, Gil Carter (Henry Fonda) and Art Croft (Harry Morgan), ride into a small town in Nevada in 1885. A rumor spreads that a well-liked cattle rancher named Kinkaid has been killed by rustlers, and the people in the town make up a posse to go after them. A shopkeeper named Davies (Harry Davenport) tries to stop them, warning, "We want to act in a reasoned and legitimate manner and not like a lawless mob." The judge asks them not to act in "this same spirit of lawlessness that begot this foul crime." His pomposity and equivocation ("Of course, you can't flinch from what you believe to be your duty, but certainly you don't want to act hastily") are unpersuasive. He reminds them that the sheriff is away, and his deputy has no legal authority to deputize others. He does, anyway. One of the group jeeringly invites Sparks (Leigh Whipper), a black handyman and preacher, to come along, telling him that praying will be needed, and he gently replies that they are "accidentally right," and he will go with them.

Some in the group are going along to revenge the death of their friend. Some go because they are bored and looking for excitement. Some are frustrated with the delays and "lawyer's tricks" of the legal system. One man is just a bully who enjoys feeling powerful at others' expense. A former Confederate major longs to be a leader again and to teach his son to be a man, "which I haven't been able to do." Carter and Croft go along in part because when they resist, suspicion falls on them.

As the group is about to give up, they find three men traveling with cattle that belonged to Kinkaid. Donald Martin (Dana Andrews) says that he has bought the cattle, but they do not have a bill of sale, and one of them has Kinkaid's gun, which he says he found. This is enough for the group, who sentence the three men, by a vote of twenty-one to seven, to be hanged immediately. Martin asks for a trial or for a delay while his story is checked out, and when the major turns him down, he asks that the other two men, a Mexican (Anthony Quinn) and a feeble-minded old man (Francis Ford), be allowed to go free. All the mob will grant him is a reprieve until dawn so that he may write a farewell letter to his wife.

Martin gives the letter to Davies, who begs to read it aloud in hopes that it will make the mob understand that Martin is innocent, but Martin refuses. The men are hanged. The major's son cannot bring himself to hit the horse out from under one of the condemned man, so the major strikes him and orders one of the other men to finish the job. Sparks kneels by the men to pray for them.

On the way back to town, the mob meets up with the sheriff, who tells them that Kinkaid has not been killed and will recover. Furthermore, the sheriff caught the men who shot him. When he hears what the mob has done, the sheriff says, "The Lord better have mercy on you. You won't get it from me." The major, in disgrace, kills himself. The rest raise $500 for Martin's widow. Carter reads aloud Martin's letter about conscience and the law, and then he and Croft leave town to deliver the letter and the money to Martin's widow.

DISCUSSION: This film was made at a time when lynchings were still going on in the United States. The Tuskegee Institute documented nearly 2,000 from 1882 to 1943. Lynchings took place in every state, and although victims were of all races, the vast majority were black. The subject was so controversial that this film was not released until almost two years after it was filmed.

While lynchings have been all but eradicated in this country, the lesson of this movie that ordinary, moral persons can be induced to commit acts of terrible cruelty and injustice is still valid. This is not a wild-eyed mob acting out of hysteria. This is a combination of revenge, boredom, cruelty, cowardice, moral weakness, demagoguery, and irrationality overcoming humanity and fairness.

Compare this movie to *Stagecoach*, in which a sheriff in the Wild West combines traditional legal procedures with very rough ad hoc notions of "justice," giving the Ringo Kid the opportunity for a shoot-out with the men who killed his family.

PROFANITY: None.
NUDITY/SEXUAL REFERENCES: Very oblique reference to Carter's past relationship with a young woman they meet on the road.
ALCOHOL/DRUG ABUSE: Drinking.
VIOLENCE/SCARINESS: Major strikes his son; a hanging and a suicide, both off camera.
TOLERANCE/DIVERSITY ISSUES: Sparks is the only person of faith in the movie; his deferential manner of speaking to whites is typical of the period.

QUESTIONS FOR FAMILIES:

- Why was it so easy for these people to abandon the legal system's way of handling questions of guilt and innocence?

- What is the evidence convincing the crowd the men are guilty? How would that evidence be treated in court?

- Why is it important that the people in the mob have so many different reasons for going along?

- What does Martin mean about all consciences being part of one big conscience? Do you think he was right?

CONNECTIONS: The book, by Walter Van Tilburg Clark, is worth reading for high school students. *Fury*, with Spencer Tracy, is a powerful film about lynching in a more contemporary setting. There are also references to lynching in some of the movies set in the early Civil Rights era, like **The Autobiography of Miss Jane Pittman**. Compare this community to the one in **High Noon**, where the people in the town would not act. In **The Ox-Bow Incident**, they are too willing to act, with disastrous consequences. Compare it, too, to **Lord of the Flies** on the issue of the disintegration of concepts of fairness and equality in a mob setting.

12 Angry Men

1959, 95 min, NR, b&w, 10 and up
Dir: Sidney Lumet. Henry Fonda, Lee J. Cobb, Ed Begley, Martin Balsam, Jack Klugman, Jack Warden
PLOT: Twelve jurors, hot and tired after a six-day murder trial, file into the jury room. They begin with a vote—eleven vote for a guilty verdict, but one (Henry Fonda), juror number eight, votes to acquit. The others are impatient, and there are mutters of "there's always one." Juror number eight says he is not convinced the boy, accused of killing his father, is innocent, but he believes they owe him more than one quick vote. They should talk about it before they find him guilty, which means an automatic sentence of death.

We never hear the men's names, but we learn a great deal about them as they deliberate. The boy admitted arguing with his father. He admitted buying a switchblade with a distinctive handle, exactly like the one the man was stabbed with. One witness says she saw the boy stab his father with the knife in the brief moment when an El train sped by the window. Another witness says he heard a body fall to the floor and then saw the boy run out of the apartment. The boy says he wasn't there, that he went to a movie, though on that night he could not remember the name of the movie or any of the details. He said the knife must have fallen out of his pocket.

After an hour, juror number eight says they should vote again, and if the eleven are still in favor of a guilty verdict, he will vote with them. Then another juror changes his vote, and they continue to debate. They examine each piece of evidence, each word of testimony carefully. They examine themselves, uncovering prejudices and blind spots that interfere with their ability to be impartial. One by one, each finds a flaw in the evidence that persuades him of the boy's innocence.

DISCUSSION: The men are impatient to come to a conclusion not just because they are hot and tired, but also because they are uncomfortable sentencing a boy to death. They want it to be easy and clear-cut, and they want it to be quick, so they do not have to think too hard about what they are doing. Juror number eight's most difficult challenge is to get each of them to think independently and objectively about the evidence. One of the last jurors to change his mind is the ultra-logical juror number four (E. G. Marshall). When a new fact is introduced calling the logic of his calculations into question, he is willing to change his vote. For most of the others, the issue is emotional as well as logical. Families should try to identify the way each juror brings his background, personal or professional, into the deliberations. In some cases, that background provides insight that was helpful, as when juror number five (Jack Klugman) speaks of his experiences growing up in a slum. In others, the background is an obstacle that has to be overcome, as in the bigotry of juror number ten (Ed Begley) or the displaced anger of juror number three (Lee J. Cobb).

Notice in particular the way that juror number eight listens to everyone else, even when it does not relate to the case, as when the foreman tells him about the time his big game was rained out. Compare that to the energy juror number three devotes to refusing to listen, and to juror number seven's (Jack Warden) constant efforts to deflect or push away any engagement, intellectual or emotional, with wisecracks. Juror number seven's use of humor is in sharp contrast to that of some of the others, like juror number eleven, who use humor to make a point, to take the discussion further, as in the comment about the use of proper English. This is also an outstanding example of different approaches to problem-solving, an especially important subject for family discussion.

PROFANITY: None.
NUDITY/SEXUAL REFERENCES: None.
ALCOHOL/DRUG ABUSE: None.
VIOLENCE/SCARINESS: Tense, but not violent.
TOLERANCE/DIVERSITY ISSUES: A theme of the movie.
QUESTIONS FOR FAMILIES:

• What would have happened if juror number eight had not been on the jury?

• Why didn't they use their names during the deliberation (or in the credits), and why did two of them introduce themselves before they left the court-house?

• Why do you think juror number three's son won't see him? How did that affect his judgment?

• Why do we have juries, instead of just letting the judge decide every case? Why do we have twelve, and not fewer or more?

• Does this movie make you feel better or worse about the jury system? How will it affect you when you serve on a jury?

CONNECTIONS: This film includes outstanding character actors Martin Balsam, Ed Begley (both Oscar-winners for other performances), E. G. Marshall (from television's *The Defenders*), Jack Klugman (from televison's *The Odd Couple* and *Quincy*), and Jack Warden (Harry Rosenfeld in **All the President's Men**). One of the best books ever written about filmmaking is Sidney Lumet's *Making Movies*, which includes a fascinating explanation of the making of this, his first feature film. Watch the way he uses camera angles to create different impressions within the confines of the one-room set. The movie was remade for cable television in 1997, starring Jack Lemmon and George C. Scott, also very worthwhile.

ACTIVITIES: Talk to the family about your own service on a jury, or, if you have not had the chance to serve, see if someone else they know can tell them what it was like. Take them to sit in on a trial, or pick one suitable for them to watch on Court TV. Ask them how they would handle serving on a jury deciding the outcome of the Kobe Bryant or Martha Stewart cases or some other trial in the news.

The Winslow Boy

1948, 117 min, NR, b&w, 10 and up
Dir: Anthony Asquith. Robert Donat, Margaret Leighton
LOT: This is the story of a real court case that was, in its, day, almost as notorious as the Dreyfus affair. In 1912, a fourteen-year-old boy was "sacked" (expelled) from a naval academy school for stealing a five shilling postal order (worth less than a dollar). At enormous cost—financial, emotional, and personal—the family challenges this decision until, granted a special right to have a barrister (Robert Donat) present their evidence in court, Ronnie Winslow is exonerated.
DISCUSSION: Ronnie Winslow was kicked out of school without a chance to review the evidence against him or get any kind of hearing. The school refused to permit his father to see the evidence, and the government prohibited any kind of challenge, arguing that to permit people to sue a government agency would create a dangerous precedent. Ronnie's father insists on pursuing it with the help of the country's top barrister (trial lawyer). The issue of what is "fair" is presented from several different perspectives.
As the case drags on, Ronnie's brother must leave school and get a job, and his sister's engagement is broken. Ronnie's father and sister never waver in their support of his right to a hearing to establish his honesty. The members of the family (including the erstwhile fiancé) and Sir Robert react to the situation differently, which reveals the character as well as the perspective of each one.
Families should discuss the ways that Ronnie's family decided to make considerable sacrifices to support his exoneration, as well as Sir Robert's comment that his goal was "right," rather than "justice."

PROFANITY: None.
NUDITY/SEXUAL REFERENCES: None.
ALCOHOL/DRUG ABUSE: None.
VIOLENCE/SCARINESS: None.
TOLERANCE/DIVERSITY ISSUES: Ronnie's sister, Catherine, is a suffragist, though she explains more than once she is not "militant." (When Sir Robert tells her it's a lost cause, she replies, "How little you know women.") A female reporter says that she expects people to be surprised when they find a woman journalist, then she conforms to stereotype by acting like a fluttery scatterbrain.

QUESTIONS FOR FAMILIES:

• Were you surprised when Sir Robert agreed to represent Ronnie and, after questioning him, said he was innocent? How do you think that he made up his mind?

• Sir Robert admits some of what he does is more like putting on a play than arguing a case. When does he do that?

• What can you tell about John by the way he reacts to Ronnie's dismissal from school? What do the scenes in the music hall add to the movie?

• Ronnie's sister tells Sir Robert that she and her father have different goals. What are they? What do they tell you about each of the characters?

• Everyone in the Winslow family made enormous sacrifices to pursue the case. How would your family evaluate their options in such a case?

CONNECTIONS: The movie was remade in 1999 by David Mamet, starring Nigel Hawthorne as Mr. Winslow and Jeremy Northam as Sir Robert Morton.
ACTIVITIES: The issue of who has the right to sue the government is still an important one. Look up the Magna Carta (which is referred to in the movie) in an encyclopedia to see how the question was first raised in Britain, and look up "sovereign immunity" to find out how it has been addressed in the United States. The issue of children's rights is also a continuing controversy. Young people will like to read about *Tinker v. the School Board of Des Moines*, in which the Supreme Court upheld the right of a high school student to exercise free speech by wearing a black armband to protest the Vietnam War, and *In re Gault*, in which the Court found that children and teenagers had a right to the same fair treatment as adults, despite arguments that these rights were suspended for their "protection."

Judgment at Nuremberg

1961, 178 min, NR, b&w, high schoolers
Dir: Stanley Kramer. Spencer Tracy, Burt Lancaster, Maximilian Schell
PLOT: One of the most fascinating explorations of moral choices in history was the Nuremberg trials that followed World War II. When this movie begins, the trials of the highest-ranking war criminals are over, and the men now on trial are the judges who abandoned their sworn commitment to truth and justice to follow the orders of Hitler and provide legal authority for his atrocities. Spencer Tracy plays the American judge assigned to preside over the trial of his German

counterparts, one of whom is portrayed by Burt Lancaster. Richard Widmark plays the prosecuting attorney, and Maximilian Schell (who won an Oscar) plays the lawyer for the defense.

The judges say that they were "just following orders," and that if they had done anything else they would have been imprisoned or killed. Tracy must confront his own moral dilemma when he is pressured to be lenient with the judges to protect American political interests. Though he has some reason to be especially sensitive on this point, having lost a reelection to his position in America, he insists on issuing a judgment based on upholding "justice, truth, and the value of a single human being."

Every family with teenagers should make an effort to watch this film together, to talk about the history involved and how to evaluate the necessity for disobeying orders, even at the direst risk to oneself and one's family. NOTE: The movie includes description and explicit documentary footage of concentration camp atrocities.

CONNECTIONS: There are many excellent books to read about the Holocaust and the Nuremberg trials, including *Night*, by Elie Wiesel, and *Ordinary Men*, by Christopher R. Browning. **Schindler's List**, and the play *The Andersonville Trial*, by Saul Levitt (about a Civil War prison camp), raise related issues. Harvard Law School professor Martha L. Minow's book *Between Vengeance and Forgiveness* discusses the ways that the world legal systems have responded to genocide in cases including Rwanda and South Africa.

WITNESS FOR THE PROSECUTION

1957, 114 min, NR, b&w, 10 and up
Dir: Billy Wilder. Tyrone Power, Marlene Dietrich, Charles Laughton
Handsome and likable Leonard Vole (Tyrone Power), accused of killing his wealthy benefactor, is defended by a choleric barrister (Charles Laughton) in this Agatha Christie courtroom classic that raises many questions of fairness and justice. Marlene Dietrich plays the enigmatic Mrs. Vole, and Elsa Lanchester (Laughton's wife) plays the barrister's fluttery nurse.

7

HELPING OTHERS

*"The best of alms is that which the right hand giveth,
and the left hand knoweth it not."*
MUHAMMAD

Compassion and empathy are important, but they are not enough. Those feelings must be translated into action that makes a difference. In these films, characters try several different ways of helping others, and sometimes find that it takes more than enthusiasm and good intentions. The first challenge is to understand what the problem is. As the movie director hero finds in **Sullivan's Travels**, the poor people he wants to help are more grateful for funny movies than they would be for the turgid dramas he wanted to make to show his sensitivity to their suffering. Major Barbara learns that handouts at the mission are not as helpful to people as jobs.

It is also important to help others in a way that preserves, or better yet enhances, their sense of dignity. These films show us that helping others and being able to accept help ourselves give our lives meaning and resonance, and help our spirits grow and deepen.

Bells Are Ringing

1960, 127 min, NR, 6 and up
Dir. Vincente Minnelli. Judy Holliday, Dean Martin
PLOT: Ella Peterson (Judy Holliday) works for an answering service. Her job is to "take and deliver messages" to the clients, but she can't help trying to solve their problems, too. Shy in person, over the phone she plays Santa Claus for one mother who wants help persuading her son to eat his spinach, prescribes a mustard plaster for an opera singer with a chest cold, and provides motherly advice to Jeffrey Moss (Dean Martin), a playwright who is struggling with his first solo effort following a split with his longtime partner. She has a crush on Jeffrey and

113

says they have a "perfect relationship," where "I can't see him, he can't see me, he thinks that I am eighty-three." When he oversleeps on the day of an important appointment, she goes to his apartment to make sure he wakes up, intending to leave before he sees her. He does see her, and she makes up a different name and identity for herself and stays to help him get his work done. He falls in love with her. Ella also visits two other clients, an out-of-work actor and a dentist who wants to be a songwriter. Based on what she has learned from her other clients, she gives them advice about how to get jobs and disappears before they can ask who she is.

In the meantime, Ella's cousin, Sue (Jean Stapleton), the owner of the answering service, has a new boyfriend, Otto (Eddie Foy, Jr.), who tells her she is accepting record orders for him when she is really placing illegal bets. Two detectives are following Ella to investigate the answering service as a possible call-girl operation. Ella agonizes over how to tell Jeffrey that she is not "Melisande Scott" but just the answering service operator he calls "Ma." All of this is resolved as the dentist, the actor, Jeffrey, the detectives, and the bookie show up at Ella's office, and everyone lives happily ever after, even Otto, whose arrest saves him from a worse fate at the hands of mobsters.

DISCUSSION: In these days of Voicemail and answering machines, it is a good idea to begin by explaining to children what an answering service is. They may also find it hard to understand the "Drop a Name" scene, in which Ella is taught how to succeed at a snobbish party by acting as though she knows anyone who is famous. It is unlikely they will recognize any of the names in the song, other than Lassie.

The movie begins with a "commercial" for Susansaphone, amusingly followed by a scene that shows that the real operation is far less elegant than portrayed in the ad. The story and the music are wonderful (including the standards "Just in Time" and "The Party's Over"), and there are a lot of good issues to talk about with children, including the importance of being yourself, dealing with feelings of shyness and inadequacy, and the way a person can transform the lives of others with a sympathetic ear and the willingness to get involved.

PROFANITY: None.
NUDITY/SEXUAL REFERENCES: Suspicion that the answering service is a call-girl operation.
ALCOHOL/DRUG ABUSE: Jeffrey drinks (off camera) to avoid having to work on his own.
VIOLENCE/SCARINESS: None.

TOLERANCE/DIVERSITY ISSUES: None.
QUESTIONS FOR FAMILIES:

- Why does Ella find it easier to talk to people on the phone than in person?

- Why is Jeffrey afraid to work on his play?

- What does Ella do to help Blake and Dr. Kitchell?

- What makes Ella so special? Do you know anyone who helps people the way she does?

CONNECTIONS: Jean Stapleton of TV's *All in the Family* plays Ella's cousin, Sue. Frank Gorshin (The Riddler on television's *Batman*) plays Blake Barton (a parody of 1950s actors who liked to imitate Marlon Brando by mumbling their lines). Eddie Foy, Jr.'s, real-life show-business family was portrayed in the movie *The Seven Little Foys*, starring Bob Hope as vaudevillian Eddie Foy, Sr. You can also see Foy, Jr. playing his own father in *Yankee Doodle Dandy* and *Wilson*. Ella's disastrous blind date in the beginning of the movie is with her real-life love, jazz great Gerry Mulligan.
ACTIVITIES: See if the kids can learn the cha-cha along with Ella. Try to come up with names that might fit in the song "Drop That Name" if it were written today.

Finding Nemo

Dir: Andrew Stanton, Lee Unkrich. Albert Brooks, Ellen DeGeneres, Willem Dafoe
PLOT: Marlin (voice of Albert Brooks) is a fond but nervous and overprotective clown fish. A predator ate his wife and all but one of their eggs. The surviving egg becomes his son Nemo (voice of Alexander Gould), and when it is time to start school, Nemo is excited, but Marlin is very fearful.

Nemo has an under-developed fin. Marlin has done a good job of making Nemo feel confident and unselfconscious. They call it his "lucky fin." It still makes Marlin a little more anxious about protecting Nemo, and it still makes Nemo a little more anxious about proving that he can take care of himself.

On his first day of school, Nemo swims too far from the others and is captured by a deep sea diver, a dentist who keeps fish in his office aquarium. Marlin must go literally to the end of the ocean to find his son and bring him home.

So, in the tradition and spirit of stories from *The Odyssey* to **The Wizard of Oz**, Marlin takes a journey that will introduce him to extraordinary characters and teach him a great deal about the world and even more about himself. He meets up with Dory (voice of Ellen DeGeneres), a cheerful blue tang who has a problem with short-term memory loss. They search for Nemo together, despite stinging jellyfish, exploding mines, and creatures with many, many, many, many teeth.

Meanwhile, Nemo has made some very good friends in the dentist's aquarium, including a tough Tiger Fish (voice of Willem Dafoe) who helps him plan an escape before the dentist can give Nemo to his careless eight-year-old niece, whose record with fish portends a short lifespan.

DISCUSSION: Pixar Studios may have the most advanced animation technology in the world, but they never forget what matters most in a movie: story, characters, imagination, and heart. "Finding Nemo" has it all.

It is an epic journey filled with adventure and discovery encompassing the grandest sweep of ocean vastness and the smallest longing of the heart.

The movie is a visual feast. The play of light on the water is breathtaking. The characters imagined by Pixar in **Monsters, Inc.** were fabulously inventive, but they have nothing on the even more fabulously inventive Mother Nature. This movie will make an ichthyologist out of anyone, because all of the characters are based on real-life ocean species, each one more marvelous than the one before. While preserving their essential "fishy-ness," Pixar and the talented people providing the voices have also made them each wonderfully expressive, and it seems only fair to say that they create performances as full and varied as have ever been on screen.

There are terrifying-looking creatures, but one of the movie's best jokes is that even the sharks are so friendly that in an AA-style program, they keep reminding each other that "we don't eat our friends." There really are no bad guys in this movie—the danger comes from a child's thoughtlessness and from natural perils. The movie has no angry, jealous, greedy, or murderous villains as in most traditional Disney animated films.

Another strength of the movie is the way it handles Nemo's disability, frankly but matter-of-factly. Best of all is the way it addresses questions that are literally at the heart of the parent-child relationship, giving everyone in the audience something to relate to and learn from.

PROFANITY: None.
NUDITY/SEXUAL REFERENCES: Mild potty humor.

ALCOHOL/DRUG ABUSE: None.

VIOLENCE/SCARINESS: Parents should know that even though there are no traditional bad guys in this movie, there are still some very scary moments, including creatures with zillions of sharp teeth, an apparent death of a major character, and many tense scenes with characters in peril. At the beginning of the movie, Marlin's wife and all but one of their eggs are eaten by a predator. It is off-screen, but might upset some viewers.

TOLERANCE/DIVERSITY ISSUES: The issue of Nemo's stunted fin is handled exceptionally well.

QUESTIONS FOR FAMILIES:

• How can parents balance their wish to protect their children from being hurt (physically or emotionally) with the need to let them grow up and learn how to take care of themselves?

• How does Marlin help Nemo handle his "lucky fin?" Everyone has different abilities that make some things easier for each of us to do than for most people and some things harder. How do you know what your abilities are, and what do you do to make the most of them?

CONNECTIONS: The DVD has some marvelous extras, including commentary, deleted scenes, and Pixar's first-ever short feature, *Knick-Knack*. It shows how far the technology has advanced, but it also shows that Pixar's sense of fun was there right at the beginning.

Families who enjoy this movie will also enjoy the other Pixar films, *A Bug's Life*, the **Toy Story** movies, and **Monsters Inc**. They will appreciate other movies with underwater scenes, including Disney's *The Little Mermaid*, **Pinocchio**, *Bedknobs and Broomsticks*, and the magnificent **Yellow Submarine**, with innovative animation, a witty and touching script, and, of course, glorious music from the Beatles. Families with younger children will enjoy reading *The Runaway Bunny*, and families with older children will enjoy *Amazing Fish* from the outstanding Eyewitness series.

Holes

2003, 117 min. PG, 10 and up.
Dir: Andrew Davis. Shia LaBeouf, Sigourney Weaver, Patricia Arquette, John Voight

PLOT: Adapted by Louis Sacher from his Newbery award-winning book, this is the story of Stanley Yelnats (Shia LaBeouf), whose name is the same backwards and forwards, a palindrome. Stanley is wrongfully accused of stealing a very valuable pair of sneakers and sentenced to a juvenile facility in the desert. Each boy there is required to dig a five-foot-deep hole every day. They are told it is to help them develop character, but could it be that the Warden (Sigourney Weaver) is looking for something that just might be buried in the endless stretch of sand that once was Green Lake?

We cannot understand the answer to that question until we learn the stories of Stanley's pig-stealing great-great grandfather, who was cursed by a gypsy, and of the notorious outlaw of the Old West, Kissin' Kate Barlow, who left lipstick kiss prints on the faces of the men she killed.

These two stories are interwoven with Stanley's, providing counterpoint and illumination.

DISCUSSION: Author Louis Sacher (who appears briefly as a man who is going bald) adapted his own story, and it retains all of the complexity and understated, offbeat charm of the book. The adult actors are excellent, especially Patricia Arquette and Dulé Hill, but the kids are the center of the story, and they handle it beautifully. Khleo Thomas is wonderfully engaging as Zero.

In sharp contrast to most movies directed at 10–15-year-olds (come to think of it, to most movies of any kind), "Holes" respects the intelligence of its audience. It is even willing to challenge them, and that makes it a movie for everyone in the family to treasure. **Holes** is also a good story to introduce young readers to the idea that the setting of a story can tell you something about the characters. Green Lake appears in very different form in the three stories. What does that tell you about what is going on with the people in the stories?

Parents should know that the movie deals frankly with some very serious issues, including racism, injustice, and the sometimes tragic consequences of poor choices.

PROFANITY: Strong language for a PG.
NUDITY/SEXUAL REFERENCES: None.
ALCOHOL/DRUG ABUSE: Character drinks and smokes.
VIOLENCE/SCARINESS: Characters are in intense peril and some are killed. There is a gross wound and a character throws up on screen. A character commits suicide. The boys at Green Lake are not beaten, but they are treated very badly and do not always treat each other very well.
TOLERANCE/DIVERSITY ISSUES: There are very devoted and loyal interracial relationships, including one that ends tragically due to prejudice.

QUESTIONS FOR FAMILIES:

• Families who see this movie should talk about its themes of fate and choice. What actions in the movie seem to have been decided by fate (or a curse) and what were decided by the characters?

• How much of our present is influenced by or determined by the past?

• There are even more connections between the three stories than you see at first. How many can you find?

• If you pay close attention, there is something significant about when the boys use their real names and when they use their tough nicknames. What does that tell you?

• Why doesn't Stanley tell the truth in his letter to his mother?

• How is Stanley different at the end of the movie?

CONNECTIONS: Families who enjoy this movie will also enjoy **Willie Wonka and the Chocolate Factory** and **Tuck Everlasting**. They should read the book and the companion volume, **Stanley Yelnats' Survival Guide to Camp Green Lake**, as well as Sacher's other terrific books, including those about the Wayside School.

Lilies of the Field

1963, 93 min., NR, b&w, 10 to adult
Dir. Ralph Nelson. Sidney Poitier, Lilia Skala, Stanley Adams
PLOT: Homer Smith (Sidney Poitier), a black itinerant handyman driving through the Arizona desert, stops at a farm to ask for some water. The farm is the home of a small group of nuns, recent refugees from Eastern Europe. He stays on to do some work for them, but resists when the flinty Mother Superior (Lilia Skala) wants him to build a chapel, especially when it is clear that they are not going to pay him. "I ain't no contractor. I don't need all that work," he says.

Ultimately, for his own reasons, the chapel becomes his dream, too. The skepticism and prejudice of the local builder makes him want to prove himself. He tells Mother Maria, "All my life, I wanted to really build something, you know? Well, maybe, if I had an education, I would have been an architect or even an engineer and throw the Golden Gate Bridge across San Francisco Bay. And even maybe build a rocket ship to Venus or something." As fiercely independent as

Mother Maria, he wants to do it himself, but he learns how to accept the help of the community and to become their leader. When the chapel is complete, he writes his name in the cement in the bell tower and drives on.

DISCUSSION: When this movie was made in the midst of the early 1960s civil rights battles for integration and tolerance, a black man in the leading role made it seem that the movie was about race. Now, more than thirty years later, we see that race is just one of many differences the characters must understand in order to be able to work together. A black Baptist, a group of nuns who have just escaped from East Germany, a Mexican-American atheist, a group of Mexican-American Catholics, and an Irish priest find themselves building a chapel together in the Arizona desert. Until Smith takes over, it is like the Tower of Babel, but with his leadership they all work together as a community.

More important than the cultural and religious differences between Smith and Mother Maria are their temperaments and personalities, especially their insistence on independence, a theme throughout this movie. Both are fiercely independent and refuse to accept help, and both, in this story, learn to do so. Smith, who puts a sign saying DON'T TOUCH ANYTHING on the bricks, finally accepts the help of the members of the community when they begin handing him bricks. At first he sulks, but when it becomes clear that they need him, he takes over. Mother Maria refuses to acknowledge his contribution, saying, "I thank Him. You couldn't help yourself." When she criticizes him for bringing candy to the nuns, Smith says to her, "You are very large on religion and all of that, but you don't even know how to accept a gift from somebody without making him feel small." As he is getting ready to go, he says, "Sank you," gently mocking her accent, and as she corrects him, showing off the English he has helped her improve, she says, "Thank you," and they both realize that she is acknowledging his contribution.

PROFANITY: None.

NUDITY/SEXUAL REFERENCES: None.

ALCOHOL/DRUG ABUSE: The priest has an (off-screen) drinking problem. Smith has an off-screen escapade that leaves him hung over and is hung over again the night after the fiesta celebrating the completion of the chapel.

VIOLENCE/SCARINESS: None.

TOLERANCE/DIVERSITY ISSUES: The issue of race is sensitively handled in this movie. Smith, teaching the nuns to speak English, uses his own skin to illustrate the word "black." Ashton, the local builder, calls Smith "boy," prompting Smith to prove himself to Ashton, to the nuns, and to himself. Later on, Ashton humbly asks "Mr. Smith" to come back to work for him. Without Smith's leadership, the chapel becomes something of a Tower of Babel, with all of the different cultures and languages spoken by the members of the community. Once he takes over, they all work together cooperatively.

QUESTIONS FOR FAMILIES:

• In what ways are Mother Maria and Homer alike?

• In what ways are they different?

• What did the chapel mean to each of them?

• How will Homer's life be different from now on?

CONNECTIONS: Poitier, the first black movie star to play leading roles, became the first black man to win an Oscar for his performance in this movie. A made-for-television movie sequel, *Christmas Lilies of the Field*, starred Billy Dee Williams.

Magnificent Obsession

1954, 108 min, NR, 10 and up
Dir. Douglas Sirk. Rock Hudson, Jane Wyman, Agnes Moorehead
PLOT: Bob Merrick (Rock Hudson), a careless playboy, is injured in an accident, and critical medical equipment is used to save his life, making it unavailable to save the life of a beloved doctor. The doctor's widow, Helen Phillips (Jane Wyman), discovers that the doctor left no money, but she receives mysterious messages from many people he had helped by lending them money. He never had allowed them to pay him back because "it wasn't used up yet."
Bob inadvertently causes an accident that blinds Helen. Overcome with guilt, he meets an artist who explains the doctor's secret, his "magnificent obsession." He had devoted his life to helping others, with two requirements: It must be a secret, and he must not be repaid. Instead, he had urged them to pass it along by helping someone else the same way. Bob finds this foolish. Using another name, he befriends Helen, and they fall in love. He begins to see the satisfaction in helping others. He returns to the medical studies he had abandoned and is able to develop an operation to restore Helen's sight.
DISCUSSION: This is by no means a good movie in terms of its literary qualities. Though gorgeously produced, it is a shameless, if irresistible, potboiler. For someone young enough not to know how corny and melodramatic it is, it can be

very affecting, and the point it makes about finding meaning in life through helping others without any repayment, and without boosting one's reputation, is very
worthwhile.

PROFANITY: None.
NUDITY/SEXUAL REFERENCES: None.
ALCOHOL/DRUG ABUSE: Social drinking; references to Bob's drinking too
much in his playboy days.
VIOLENCE/SCARINESS: Helen hit by car.
TOLERANCE/DIVERSITY ISSUES: None.
QUESTIONS FOR FAMILIES:

- What did the doctor mean when he told the people he helped, that he hadn't
  "used it up yet"?

- Why was it important that they were not allowed to tell anyone?

- Why was it important that they were not allowed to pay him back?

- Why could Bob show his real self to Helen only after she was blind?

CONNECTIONS: This is a remake of a 1935 version starring Robert Taylor
and Irene Dunne, based on a novel by Lloyd C. Douglas, whose books includes
The Robe. Jewish philosopher Moses Maimonides created a hierarchy of charity,
with the lowest level a contribution in which the donor and the recipient know
each other, and the highest level the creation of a society in which charity is no
longer necessary. His emphasis on the dignity of the recipient and the genuineness of the charity from the donor (without expectation of thanks or reward) fits
well with this movie. The idea of finding cheer, fulfillment, and happiness
through helping others is a part of many religions and philosophies.

Mr. Deeds Goes to Town

1936, 115 min, NR, b&w, 10 and up
Dir: Frank Capra. Gary Cooper, Jean Arthur
PLOT: Longfellow Deeds (Gary Cooper), of Mandrake Falls, Vermont, is a quiet
bachelor who writes rhymes for birthday cards and plays the tuba for concentra-
tion. Informed that he has inherited twenty million dollars, he goes to New York
City to collect it.

Swarms of people come after him to try to get some of the money, but the only one he will talk to is Babe Bennett (Jean Arthur), who attracts his attention by fainting. She tells him she is an unemployed secretary, but in reality she is a tough journalist out for a good story. He has a lot of fun feeding doughnuts to hungry cab horses and chasing fire engines. When some snooty poets make fun of his rhymes, he says, "I know I must look funny to you. Maybe if you came to Mandrake Falls, you'd look just as funny to us.... But nobody'd laugh at you and make you ridiculous 'cause that wouldn't be good manners." He tells Bennett his impressions of the city, explaining that the wealthy people in New York "work so hard at living, they forget how to live...They've created a lot of grand palaces, but they forgot about the noblemen to put in them."

Bennett writes a newspaper story making fun of him, calling him "The Cinderella man," and he becomes a figure of ridicule. She realizes she has fallen in love with him, with his innate goodness and sincerity and his ability to have fun.

Heartbroken by her betrayal, and disgusted with life as a wealthy man, Deeds makes plans to give the money away to help poor farmers. Unscrupulous relatives take him to court, arguing he is not competent and they should have control of the money.

He is too miserable to defend himself. Bennett persuades him that she loves him and he must try. The judge concludes, "In my opinion, you are not only sane, you are the sanest man who ever walked into this courtroom."

DISCUSSION: This is one of Frank Capra's populist classics, and its Depression-era sensibility is still appealing. Finding meaning in life through helping others is well-presented, as are the issues of what makes people important (Deeds says, "All famous people aren't big people"). The public policy issue of how much help we give to those "who can't make the hill on high" is something teenagers with an interest in politics might like to pursue.

The issue of the role of the press is even timelier now, as public figures and even private ones are considered fair game. More important, and more relevant to young people, especially teenagers, is the issue of cynicism as a mode of approaching the world. Bennett says, "He's got a lot of goodness, Mabel. Do you know what that means? No, of course you don't. We've forgotten. We're all too busy being smart alecks." That's a good description of teenagers who put on a cynical demeanor to protect themselves from being vulnerable. A thoughtful journalist once said that a reporter's responsibility was to be skeptical without being cynical, and that statement is a good way to open a discussion of this issue. Deeds's statement that "It's easy to make fun of someone if you don't care how much you hurt 'em" is also something for kids to think about.

It is also worthwhile to consider how the same facts can be interpreted differently. Deeds plays the tuba, feeds doughnuts to horses, and wants to give money away. Those actions can be seen as foolish (as portrayed in Bennett's newspaper), crazy (as portrayed by the lawyer), or endearing (as portrayed by Cooper and Capra). What does that tell us about being careful to challenge "spin"?

PROFANITY: None.
NUDITY/SEXUAL REFERENCES: None.
ALCOHOL/DRUG ABUSE: Deeds gets drunk (which is one of the charges against his competency).
VIOLENCE/SCARINESS: Deeds punches some people.
TOLERANCE/DIVERSITY ISSUES: Tolerance for different kinds of people, especially those in need.
QUESTIONS FOR FAMILIES:

• Why did Babe Bennett's editor want her to make fun of Deeds?

• What do you do to help you concentrate?

• If Mr. Deeds inherited the money today, what group do you think he would give it to?

• What would you do if you inherited twenty million dollars?

CONNECTIONS: This movie popularized two words: "doodle" and "pixilated." As Deeds points out, doodling is highly individual. A dreadful 2002 remake starring Adam Sandler is not worth watching.
ACTIVITIES: Let the kids "doodle" while watching the movie, and see what they come up with. They might also like to try making up some words of their own.

Sullivan's Travels

1941, 91 min, NR, b&w, 10 and up
Dir: Preston Sturges. Joel McCrea, Veronica Lake
PLOT: "Sully" Sullivan (Joel McCrea) is a successful director of silly comedies, including Ants in Your Pants and Hey, Hey in the Hayloft. The studio wants him to make more, but he wants to make a movie with a serious message about The Depression and man's inhumanity to man. He plans on calling it *O Brother, Where Art Thou?* When he lists all the things that are wrong with the world, the

studio executive replies, "Maybe they'd like to forget that." His own butler advises him that "the subject is not an interesting one. The poor know all about poverty, and only the morbid rich find the subject glamorous…. It is to be stayed away from, even for the purpose of study. It is to be shunned." Sullivan is determined. Before he can make the movie, he has to see what life is like as a "bum." His first efforts fail, as the luxurious studio trailer follows him around. He meets "the Girl" (Veronica Lake), a would-be actress, and she persuades him to let her go with him, dressed as a boy, and they start over again.

This time he discovers the sadness and lack of dignity among the homeless. Before he can go back home, he and the Girl are separated, and he is hit on the head, becomes disoriented, and loses his memory. He punches a railroad guard and is sentenced to six years on a chain gang. Meanwhile, the hobo who has stolen his shoes is killed and, through the studio identification card sewn into the shoes, is identified as Sullivan. One night, the prisoners are taken to a small church, where they see a Mickey Mouse cartoon. Sullivan realizes the joy laughter gives to these men who have nothing else.

When Sullivan regains his memory, he gets out of jail by "confessing" to his own murder so he can contact his lawyer and be properly identified. He goes home to find that his wife has remarried, leaving him free to marry the Girl. He resolves to make more funny movies, because he realizes that is the best way for him to help the world, concluding, "There's a lot to be said for making people laugh. Did you know that's all that some people have? It isn't much, but it's better than nothing in this cock-eyed caravan."

DISCUSSION: Sensitive teenagers often make the mistake of thinking they cannot care deeply and still find things funny, or that those around them cannot appreciate their pain and still find anything funny, even something that has no relation to the situation they are struggling with. This movie makes it clear that laughter and insight go together, that humor is never an insult to a serious situation, indeed that humor can be the highest form of awareness and perception, and that making people laugh can be a good way to help them. Sullivan himself is funny, with his pretensions and his misguided attempts to find out what poverty is like.

PROFANITY: None.
NUDITY/SEXUAL REFERENCES: Mild references to casting couch and to adultery.
ALCOHOL/DRUG ABUSE: None.

VIOLENCE/SCARINESS: Fighting; a hobo is killed; Sullivan is sent to jail.
TOLERANCE/DIVERSITY ISSUES: Class issues are a subtext.
QUESTIONS FOR FAMILIES:

- Why does Sullivan want to make a different kind of movie?

- Why don't the studio executives want him to? How do they try to persuade him?

- What is the difference between the ways that the two servants try to find out how Sullivan can board the train? Why does the second one work?

- What does the Girl mean when she says, "The nice thing about buying food for a man is that you don't have to laugh at his jokes"?

- What does Sullivan learn from the Mickey Mouse cartoon?

- Do you think this is the kind of movie Sullivan would make when he gets back to the studio?

CONNECTIONS: Woody Allen echoed the sentiments of this movie when he had aliens inform his character in *Stardust Memories* (very mature material), "You want to help humanity? Write funnier jokes!" In *No Time for Comedy*, Jimmy Stewart plays a character somewhat like Sully, the author of a series of very successful comedies on Broadway, starring his wife, played by Rosalind Russell. In his case, another woman persuades him that he is too sensitive and important to write comedies, and with her "inspiration" he writes a serious play that is a disaster. Poet W. H. Auden said it best: "The funniest mortals and the kindest/are most aware of the baffle of being/don't kid themselves our care is consolable/but believe that a laugh is less heartless than tears."

Screenwriter/director Preston Sturges described the movie this way: "Bit by bit I took everything away from (Sullivan)—health, fortune, name, pride, and liberty. When I got down to there, I found he still had one thing left: the ability to laugh. So, as a purveyor of laughs, he regained the dignity of his profession and returned to Hollywood to make laughter."

Sturges himself was one of Hollywood's best "purveyors of laughs," with a unique combination of satire and slapstick enabling him to get away with angrier and even more savage messages than any other director of his time. In 1944, for example, when all of America was patriotically starry-eyed, he attacked hero worship and war heroes in *Hail the Conquering Hero*. His satire skewered the rich

(*Easy Living*, *The Lady Eve*, *The Palm Beach Story*) and the not-so-rich (*Christmas in July*, *The Miracle of Morgan's Creek*), the clever (*The Great McGinty*), and the not-so-clever (*Christmas in July*), the honest (*The Lady Eve*) and the not-so-honest (*The Lady Eve* again), and, always, anyone with any pretensions. In his best movies, including this one, he allowed his characters to learn something and, in learning, achieve intimacy.

SEE ALSO:

Awakenings A doctor who tries to help patients no one thought could be helped has to question whether it was the right thing to do when his efforts result in only a brief improvement.

Hello, Dolly! Dolly finds a way to help everyone around her discover their dreams and then make them come true.

Major Barbara A central theme of the movie is the best-meaning most moral and most effective-way to help people who need it.

White Christmas The issue of finding a way to help a general without hurting his pride is sensitively handled.

8

RESPECT

*"The greatest good you can do for another is not just to
share your riches but to reveal to him his own."*
BENJAMIN DISRAELI

Like education, respect has a transformational effect. Over and over, movies show us being treated with respect makes people feel differently about themselves and about the people around them. Interestingly, respect for oneself and respect for others are closely linked. Some films show us characters so transformed by respect that they are able to allow themselves to fall in love and to feel worthy of being loved. In some cases, the characters find they have been worthy of respect all along; in others, they change their behavior to earn it and find more meaningful changes in themselves than they had hoped. Courtesy is linked to this value because it implies respect for others.

Bus Stop

1956, 96 min, NP, b&w, 10 and up
Dir: Joshua Logan. Marilyn Monroe, Don Murray, Arthur O'Connell, Hope Lange
PLOT: Bo (Don Murray) is a rough cowboy who comes to the city for the first time with his worldlier friend, Virgil (Arthur O'Connell), to compete in a rodeo. They meet Cherie (Marilyn Monroe), a good-hearted girl who sings and hustles drinks in a saloon. Cherie's casual affection persuades Bo that she is the one he wants to marry, and he carries her off, without her permission, on the bus.

The roads are snowed in, and they get stuck at a bus stop. Bo will not listen when Cherie insists she is not going with him. With the help of the others at the bus stop, she persuades him that he cannot make her marry him. Then it emerges that she is afraid she cannot live up to the vision he has of her. She has had "many boyfriends." He is crushed at first but, after talking to Virgil, tells her that since he has never had any girlfriends, they balance each other out. After a gentle kiss, she tells him she would go anywhere with him. He wraps her in his warm coat and puts her back on the bus, at first objecting when Virgil says he is not going with them because it is time for him to move on, but finally accepting it. He does not need Virgil to take care of him anymore; he has to take care of Cherie.

DISCUSSION: This is probably Marilyn Monroe's finest performance as a dramatic actor. The way she sings "That Old Black Magic" tells us a lot about Cherie's dreams of herself as a singer, and Monroe has the courage to make Cherie a far less talented performer than Monroe was herself. In her dealings with Bo, Cherie insists on her right to make her own choices, but Monroe also lets us see how much she longs to be loved the way Bo wants to love her, how much she wants to deserve it.

The movie also shows nicely the way that people must allow themselves to be vulnerable by being honest in order to be known and loved. Bo adds to his natural bluster because he does not want to let Cherie see how panicked he is by his overwhelming feelings for her. He longs to be close to her, but is afraid she won't want to be with him if he lets her see he is not always strong and confident. He finds out she responds to his vulnerability because it is honest, because it allows her to play an equal role, and because she wants to be needed. Cherie fears she does not deserve the level of devotion he offers. When he is willing to love her after hearing what she is ashamed of, she can allow herself to love him.

PROFANITY: Mild.
NUDITY/SEXUAL REFERENCES: References to Cherie's past (subtle by today's standards).
ALCOHOL/DRUG ABUSE: Drinking in a bar.
VIOLENCE/SCARINESS: Fistfight.
TOLERANCE/DIVERSITY ISSUES: Tolerance of differences.
QUESTIONS FOR FAMILIES:

- Why is Bo so insistent on making Cherie come with him? Why doesn't he listen to her?

- How can you tell she has mixed feelings about him? What are they?

- What purpose do the other characters in the movie serve?

- What makes Cherie change her mind?

- What does it show us when Bo gives Cherie his coat?

• Why does Virgil decide to leave Bo?

CONNECTIONS: The movie is based on a play by William Inge, author of **Splendor in the Grass**. Older students might like to read the play, which takes place entirely at the bus stop, to see how it was expanded and adapted for the screen.

Captains Courageous

1937, 116 min, NR, b&w, 7 and up
Dir: Victor Fleming. Spencer Tracy, Freddie Bartholomew, Lionel Barrymore, Melvyn Douglas, Mickey Rooney
PLOT: Harvey Cheyne (Freddie Bartholomew) is a spoiled rich boy who thinks the way to succeed is to be a bully and a show-off. He tries to buy his way to success at boarding school. His father (Melvyn Douglas), preoccupied and indulgent, believes that Harvey is thriving at school. When Harvey gets in trouble at school, Mr. Cheyne takes him on an ocean liner to Europe. Harvey tries to show off to the other children onboard and bets that he can drink six sodas. He succeeds but, feeling sick, he falls overboard. He is not heard by anyone on the ship, but he is rescued by Manuel (Spencer Tracy), one of a crew of Portuguese fishermen. No matter how much Harvey tries to bribe or threaten the sailors, they tell him they cannot take him back until they complete their fishing expedition.

Harvey finds he wants their approval and learns he can only get it on their terms, which means competent, responsible, hard work. The other fishermen ignore or belittle him, but Manuel, feeling responsible for the "fish" he caught, befriends Harvey. As Harvey works to gain Manuel's respect, Manuel pays him the compliment of inviting him to share his dory, the first person to be invited since Manuel's father died. On the way home, as they race a rival ship, Manuel is in an accident, Knowing he will die, he says good-bye to Harvey, who is heartbroken. Later, back home, Harvey's father goes with him to the memorial service, and together they throw memorial rings of flowers into the water. As they drift out to sea, the rings intertwine.
DISCUSSION: This is an exciting and touching story. There is always something very satisfying about seeing a spoiled brat get his comeuppance (see also *The Magnificent Ambersons* and *Private Benjamin*). What is shown especially well here is the way that with Manuel, Harvey for the first time learns to respect others and himself. It is clear how unhappy, even desperate, Harvey is at school and on the ocean liner. He wants to be respected and liked but has no idea of how to go about it because no one has been there to teach him. As soon as he meets some-

one who is willing to tell him what he must do, he is eager to learn and is thrilled with the results. This movie shows that work is good for the spirit, that spoiled kids are unhappy (an astonishing concept for children), and that making friends is a skill that can and must be learned.

PROFANITY: None.
NUDITY/SEXUAL REFERENCES: None.
ALCOHOL/DRUG ABUSE: None.
VIOLENCE/SCARINESS: An accident that kills Manuel.
TOLERANCE/DIVERSITY ISSUES: None.
QUESTIONS FOR KIDS:

• What does Harvey try to do to get other kids to like him? Why doesn't it work? Have you ever seen a person behave that way? What did you do?

• Who does Harvey like? Why?

• Why does Manuel's approval mean so much to Harvey?

• Why does Manuel talk to Harvey when no one else will?

• What does it mean when Manuel invites Harvey to share his dory? What does Harvey learn from Manuel? Do you think Harvey's relationship with his father will change? How?

• Will Harvey have to teach his father anything? What?

CONNECTIONS: This movie has an outstanding cast, featuring some of MGM's finest actors. Freddie Bartholomew was one of the most popular child stars in film history. He appears here with Mickey Rooney, who was the most popular star of any age in Hollywood from 1939–41. They also appeared together in *Little Lord Fauntleroy*. Spencer Tracy won the first of his Academy Awards for his performance as Manuel, an uncharacteristic performance for an actor who did not like to use accents or makeup to create a character. The following year, he won again for his portrayal of Father Flanagan in *Boys Town*, also starring Mickey Rooney. Lionel Barrymore, brother of movie stars John and Ethel, was one of MGM's most reliable character actors. Families will enjoy his performance in *On Borrowed Time* as the grandfather who traps Death in a tree, and in **You Can't Take It With You** as the patriarch of the lovably nutty Sycamore family. Of course, he also plays the evil Mr. Potter in **It's a Wonderful**

Life, in the wheelchair to which he was confined for the last fifteen years of his life. The director, Victor Fleming, went on to direct **The Wizard of Oz** and **Gone With the Wind**. The movie is based on a book by Rudyard Kipling, the author of *The Jungle Book* and the *Just-So Stories*.

Johnny Belinda

1948, 103 min, NR, b&w, 12 and up
Dir: Jean Negulesco. Jane Wyman, Lew Ayres
PLOT: Belinda (Jane Wyman) lives with her father and aunt on a farm on an island off the coast of Nova Scotia. Her father, Black McDonald, is hard and angry. He resents Belinda because her mother died when she was born, and he treats her like an animal because she is deaf and mute. People in the town refer to her as "the dummy." Dr. Robert Richardson (Lew Ayres) teaches Belinda to communicate through sign language, and for the first time, her sweet and loving personality emerges. She is raped by Locky McCormick, a drunken brute, and becomes pregnant. The baby is named Johnny Belinda.

Everyone assumes that Robert is the father, and he must leave the community. Belinda's father finds out Locky was responsible and confronts him. Locky kills Black, making it look like an accident. When Locky's wife cannot have children, he wants Belinda's baby, knowing it is the only child he will ever have. The people in the town believe that Belinda cannot take care of the baby and decide to take it away from her.

Locky goes to Belinda's house and tries to take the baby, but she thinks he means to harm him. Trying to protect herself and the baby, she kills Locky. She is charged with murder. It looks as though she will be convicted, until Locky's widow comes forward and tells the truth. The community understands that even though Belinda cannot speak, she is loving, devoted, brave, and intelligent. Robert returns to be with Belinda and her child.

DISCUSSION: Jane Wyman spoke of trying to achieve an "anticipation light" when she was preparing for this role, the look of interest and attention she saw in deaf people who were trying to understand what hearing people were trying to communicate. See if the kids can recognize this look and even try to create it themselves. They also may want to wear earplugs, as Wyman did, to help adjust her reactions to those of someone who does not respond to auditory cues and signals.

This movie does a good job of showing that learning a little bit can make a person hungry to learn more, and that having even one person believe in someone can make that person feel capable of achieving anything. The key themes of this movie, recognizing the humanity in those who are different and the impact that having that humanity recognized has on people and everyone around them, are well worth discussing.

Some kids may want to know more about rape as well, and this provides an opportunity to discuss it as a crime of power and aggression rather than of sex. Young girls often misunderstand and worry about somehow sending a signal that invites rape. It is important to make sure they understand, as shown in this movie, rapists are not accepting an invitation and, on the contrary, it is the idea of overpowering someone who does not want to consent to sex that is exciting to them.

PROFANITY: None.
NUDITY/SEXUAL REFERENCES: Belinda is raped.
ALCOHOL/DRUG ABUSE: Locky is drunk when he rapes Belinda.
VIOLENCE/SCARINESS: The rape scene is sensitively handled, but still scary.
TOLERANCE/DIVERSITY Issues: A theme of the movie.
QUESTIONS FOR FAMILIES:

- Why is Belinda's father so hard on her?

- How much do you think Belinda understands before she learns sign language? How can you tell?

- What makes her decide to be more aware of her appearance?

- Why does Aggie change in the way she treats Belinda? What does she mean when she says their family may fight with each other, but they support each other when any one of them needs it?

- How is this movie similar to **The Miracle Worker**? How is it different?

- Why does Locky's widow decide to tell the truth?

- Why does the ability to communicate make such a difference in the way people see Belinda?

CONNECTIONS: The defense attorney is played by Alan Napier, later Alfred on television's *Batman* series.
ACTIVITIES: Belinda learns American Sign Language, rather than the more laborious finger-spelling that Annie Sullivan teaches to Helen Keller in **The Miracle Worker**, because Belinda can see. Most libraries have good books or videos

to teach beginning sign language, and children and teenagers will enjoy learning some of the, signs.

IT SHOULD HAPPEN TO YOU

1954, 87 min, NR, b&w, 8 and up
Dir: George Cukor. Judy Holliday, Jack Lemmon
Judy Holliday plays a young woman who feels so thoroughly ignored by the world that she spends every penny she has left to have her name put on a billboard. Somehow this manages to turn her into a celebrity. All of a sudden, she is treated with great respect by a range of people who want things from her, which changes the way she thinks about herself. She ends up having to choose between the glamorous life (with Peter Lawford) and a quieter existence (with a documentary filmmaker played by Jack Lemmon, in his very appealing debut performance).

SEE ALSO:
Funny Girl Both Fanny and Nick have problems with self-esteem that ultimately make it impossible for them to stay together.

9

TOLERANCE

*"Human diversity makes tolerance more than a virtue;
it makes it a requirement for survival."*
RENE DUBOS

Movies reflect our society. Most have careless, insensitive, or even overtly bigoted portrayals of everyone who is not white, vaguely Protestant, and male. The best we can do is try to be alert enough to teach our children to be aware of the subtle messages these movies send. It is especially important, as I have tried to point out through this book, to encourage kids to compare the way that minorities and women are portrayed (and the way they are simply omitted) in films of the 1930s, 40s, and 50s with those of more recent times. Young people today are lucky enough to find it hard to understand the explicit prejudice demonstrated by the characters in these movies, as well as by the filmmakers themselves. They need to understand these movies are time capsules enabling us to get a glimpse of the wounds for which they may be able to see only the scars. It is essential for parents to make certain that all children receive a broad exposure to stories and characters from a variety of cultures, through series like Rabbit Ears's *We All Have Tales* and HBO's *Happily Ever After*. We are fortunate, too, that contemporary movies offer a broader assortment of heroes and heroines than in any time in movie history, but we are still far from equality.

Some movies explicitly reflect the painful grappling with issues of race, religion, class, nationality, disability, and gender discrimination our nation has faced since its earliest days. The films in this chapter all provide starting points for family discussions of tolerance and prejudice. Some present the issue metaphorically. Some portray real-life conflicts. Some explore the reasons for prejudice, which include ignorance, displaced anger, fear, and a need to feel superior and powerful stemming from insecurity and self-hatred. Some show that even people who mean well can perpetuate the devastating effects of bigotry. Mature high school students may appreciate movies depicting the devastating self-hatred that can result from living in a bigoted world.

Adam's Rib

1949, 101 min, NR, b&w, 10 and up
Dir: George Cukor. Spencer Tracy, Katharine Hepburn
PLOT: Doris Attinger (Judy Holliday) shoots her husband, Warren (Tom Ewell), in the middle of a tryst with Beryl Craighn (Jean Hagan). He is wounded in the shoulder, and Adam Bonner (Spencer Tracy), of the district attorney's office, is assigned to prosecute Mrs. Attinger.

Adam's wife, Amanda (Katharine Hepburn), also a lawyer, thinks it is unfair that Doris has been charged. She believes there is a double standard tougher on women than on men and therefore social prejudices will cause Doris to be convicted of a crime for which a man would go free. She becomes Doris's defense lawyer over Adam's strong objection. She refuses to let Doris plead guilty, intending to turn the case into an argument over equal rights.

At first, Adam and Amanda are able to keep their court battle out of their relationship. It soon becomes personal. Amanda brings in witnesses to show women can do anything men can do, and even has a circus strong-woman lift Adam in the courtroom. Adam moves out of their apartment.

Amanda's argument to the jury asks them to think of the case as if Doris were the faithful husband who found his wife in a compromising position with a predatory playboy. Adam tells the jury that anyone who shoots at another person should be punished. The jury is persuaded by Amanda, and Doris is acquitted.

That night, Amanda shares a drink with her neighbor, composer Kip Lurie (David Wayne), who has a crush on her. Adam bursts in and points a gun at them, saying the decision of the jury proves he has a right to use it. Amanda cries out no one has that right. Adam, gratified she has accepted his argument, puts the nozzle of the gun in his mouth and, as Amanda screams, bites off the end. It is licorice.

The next day, Adam and Amanda meet in their lawyer's office to talk about their separation. Amanda is touched when she sees tears in Adam's eyes, and they leave together. That night, Adam explains he can turn on the "waterworks" whenever he wants to. Amanda says this proves there is very little difference between men and women, and Adam reminds her of the French saying "Vive la différence!" which means, "Hurray for that difference!"

DISCUSSION: Adam and Amanda agree men and women should be treated equally. Adam believes anyone—male or female—who shoots at someone else should be prosecuted. Amanda believes as long as men go free for that crime, women should, too. In keeping with the movie's theme of equality, each wins and each loses. Amanda wins the court case, but loses on the overall point by agreeing "no one has the right" to shoot someone, no matter what the provocation. Adam loses the court case, but wins overall.

It will be hard for children (or even their parents) to imagine how revolutionary this movie was half a century ago. Many of those who watched this movie when it came out could remember when women did not have the right to vote. It would be more than a decade before women would have a legal right to equal treatment in the workplace. The idea of a woman's ability to have the same professional achievements as a man was still something that had to be proven in court in a romantic comedy. It was a long way from being taken seriously. Yet Adam and Amanda are a completely believable couple who have worked out a partnership of equals making them both very happy.

PROFANITY: None.
NUDITY/SEXUAL REFERENCES: References to infidelity.
ALCOHOL/DRUG ABUSE: Social drinking.
VIOLENCE/SCARINESS: Doris shoots Warren; Adam threatens Kip and Amanda with what they think is a real gun.
TOLERANCE/DIVERSITY ISSUES: A theme of the movie.
QUESTIONS FOR FAMILIES:

• What do Adam and Amanda disagree about? What do they agree on?

• Who is right?

• Who do the filmmakers think is right?

CONNECTIONS: Jean Hagan (**Singin' in the Rain**), Tom Ewell; David Wayne; and Judy Holliday (**Bells Are Ringing** and **Born Yesterday**) all made their debuts in this movie. The song Kip writes, "Farewell, Amanda," is by Cole Porter. For a brilliant analysis of this movie, see the book *The Pursuit of Happiness*, by Stanley Cavell.

The Bingo Long Traveling All-Stars & Motor Kings

1976, 110 min, PG, 12 and up
Dir. John Badham. James Earl Jones, Billy Dee Williams, Richard Pryor

PLOT: Leon (James Earl Jones) and Bingo (Billy Dee Williams) are two of the brightest stars of baseball's Negro National League, during segregation. Unhappy with their treatment by the owners of the teams, they join together to establish their own team, to be owned by the players, so they can "control the means of production." Other players join them, including Charlie Snow (Richard Pryor), who insists he will be able to join the white league by pretending to be Cuban, and Esquire Joe Calloway (Stan Shaw), a shy young player.

Told by a local promoter they have to be in show business as well as baseball to attract paying customers, they become adept at flamboyant entrances and razzle-dazzle. The Negro National League's owners decide to shut them out and will not allow their teams to play with them. So the All-Stars start to play white teams, using humor and humility to keep racial tensions under control. The Negro National League's owners get even tougher, stealing the All-Stars's money and attacking Charlie, who is badly hurt. Paying for Charlie's hospital stay all but bankrupts the team, and Bingo ends up stealing a car. Leon cannot work that way, so he quits.

The Negro National League's owners make them an offer to play one game. If the All-Stars win, they can join the league on their own terms. If they lose, all the players have to go back to their old teams. Just to make sure they will win, the owners lock up Leon, but he escapes in time to hit the winning run out of the park.

Their jubilation becomes bittersweet when Esquire Joe brings them some news. He has been invited to play for a white team. Bingo and Leon know that the era of the Negro National League is coming to an end.

DISCUSSION: Parents should be aware that there is some material they may consider inappropriate even for older children, in this movie, including sexual references and strong racial epithets. For many parents, that will be outweighed by its rare and sympathetic look at a part of baseball and American history.

In addition to the issues of racism and the contest for control between the owners and the players, it is worth pointing out the extraordinary loyalty of most of the players to each other and discussing Bingo's decision to steal a car and Leon's reaction.

PROFANITY: Some, especially racial epithets (used mostly by black characters).
NUDITY/SEXUAL REFERENCES: Scenes of characters (dressed or covered) in bed with women (including one in bed with the team owner, with the implication that it is a condition of employment); some locker room comments.
ALCOHOL/DRUG ABUSE: Drinking.

VIOLENCE/SCARINESS: One character is pushed around by thugs; another is badly cut; a chase scene.

TOLERANCE/DIVERSITY Issues: Racial tolerance is a theme of the movie; bias against the woman owner.

QUESTIONS FOR FAMILIES:

• What did "controlling the means of production" refer to? Where does that term come from?

• Why did Bingo lie about getting concession money to hand out to the players? Why was it important that Esquire Joe was an equal partner from the first day? Why did the promoter tell them they had to understand they were in "show business" as well as baseball?

• How did Bingo justify stealing the car?

CONNECTIONS: Jones plays a character based on Josh Gibson, the only baseball player ever—black or white—to hit a ball out of the park in Yankee Stadium. Williams's character is based on Satchel Paige. The screenplay is based on a novel by William Brashler. The PBS series *Baseball*, by Ken Burns, provides some of the history of the Negro National League. *Soul of the Game* (also known as *Baseball in Black and White*), a more historically accurate drama about the careers of Gibson and Paige, and their hopes of playing the role given to Jackie Robinson as the first black man to play in the major leagues, was produced by HBO in 1996. Jackie Robinson played himself in *The Jackie Robinson Story*.

Director John Badham (who also directed *Saturday Night Fever* and **War-Games**) is the brother of Mary Badham, who played Scout in **To Kill a Mockingbird**.

ACTIVITIES: A nonfiction book called *Josh and Satch: The Life and Times of Josh Gibson and Satchel Paige*, by John B. Holway, describes their lives and careers. Every family should take a look at Paige's famous rules for living, available in many collections of quotations and anthologies.

The Defiant Ones

1958, 97, min, NR, b&w, 12 and up
Dir. Stanley Kramer. Tony Curtis, Sidney Poitier
PLOT: Two convicts shackled together, one black (Sidney Poitier as Cullen), one white (Tony Curtis as Jackson), must overcome their hostility to work together when they escape from a chain gang. When we first see them, they are about to

get into a fistfight as they are being transported with other prisoners in a truck. When Jackson pulls back his fist to hit Cullen, it swings Cullen's fist along with it.

At first, after they escape, they try to break the chain with rocks, Jackson calling Cullen "boy," and Cullen saying, "No more 'yassah boss'" each time he smashes the rock down. They realize they cannot break the chain. Though Jackson wants to go South, Cullen knows that is too risky for him. "Get off my back! I ain't married to you! What do I care?" Jackson has no choice. He can't drag Cullen, and until the shackle is broken, they have to go together.

They go through a river to throw the dogs off their trail, and Cullen is almost swept away. When Cullen thanks Jackson for pulling him out, Jackson says, "I didn't pull you out. I kept you from pulling me in."

When they sneak into a town at night, Cullen puts dirt on Jackson's face to make it harder to see them. They are captured, and the men in the town organize a lynching party, sending the women and children home. At first, Jackson tries to save them both, then, desperate, he says, "You can't lynch me! I'm a white man!" They are freed by a man whose scar on his wrist shows that he was once a chain-gang convict, too.

Now Cullen is bitter and angry. They start to have the fight they have promised each other, until a boy appears and points a gun at them. Working together, they knock the gun away from him, and he falls, hitting his head on a rock. He is unconscious. Jackson wants to run, but Cullen insists they make sure the boy is all right. When the boy comes to, he runs to Jackson for protection; he fears Cullen because he is black. They go to the boy's home, and his mother (Cara Williams) gives them food. She is clearly attracted to Jackson, and is a bit surprised and almost amused when he insists that she feed Cullen as well. They remove the chain, and Jackson collapses from his infection. She nurses him all night, and they talk about their feelings of loneliness and their longing to get away.

The next morning, she tells Cullen his best route is through the swamp, and she and Jackson plan to travel as husband and wife. After Cullen leaves, she confesses that she has sent Cullen to certain death to make sure he won't lead anyone to them. Jackson cannot stay with her. As he leaves, the boy shoots him in the shoulder. He catches up with Cullen. Cullen makes it onto the train and reaches for Jackson but, in trying to pull him on, they both fall off, tumbling back down. Cullen holds the wounded Jackson and sings softly to him as the sheriff walks over to them.

DISCUSSION: It is impossible to recreate the pre-Civil Rights era atmosphere making this movie appear to be so radical when it was released, but it is worthwhile for kids to see how accepted and casual racism was, from calling Cullen "boy" to lynching, only a few decades ago. They also may be interested in hearing that chain gangs have been reinstated recently in one state, after several years in which they were banned.

This movie is exceptionally well-constructed, making it especially well-suited for discussion with teenagers, who can trace the development of the relationship between Jackson and Cullen from the beginning, where their fight causes the accident that allows them to escape, to their first discussion about themselves and the crimes they committed, to their wordless cooperation in disarming the boy, to the decision by each of them to sacrifice a chance at freedom to help the other.

PROFANITY: None.
NUDITY/SEXUAL REFERENCES: Implication that Jackson and the woman sleep together.
ALCOHOL/DRUG ABUSE: None.
VIOLENCE/SCARINESS: Tension; some fighting.
TOLERANCE/DIVERSITY ISSUES: A theme of the movie (includes racial slurs and epithets).
QUESTIONS FOR FAMILIES:

- Cullen and Jackson share some details of their lives before prison. In what way were they similar? In what way were they different? What is different about their views of the world, and about what they want from life?

- What can you tell about their relationship from what they call each other?

- Why do they still "feel" chained, even after the chain is broken? Why does Jackson go after Cullen to save him? Why does Cullen risk falling off the train for Jackson?

- What do the screenwriters and director want to show you with the scenes of the posse? With the treatment of the dogs, compared to the treatment of the prisoners? With the attitude of the sheriff? With the music?

CONNECTIONS: Other movies featuring chain gangs include *Cool Hand Luke*, **Sullivan's Travels**, and *I Am a Fugitive from a Chain Gang*.
Carl "Alfalfa" Switzer of *Our Gang* plays Angus, television star Claude Akins plays Mack, and Lon Chaney, Jr., plays Big Sam, the man who sets them free.

Screenwriter Nedrick Young was billed under a pseudonym because he was blacklisted.

Enemy Mine

1985, 108 min, PG-13, 12 and up
Dir: Wolfgang Petersen. Dennis Quaid, Louis Gosset, Jr.
PLOT: One hundred years in the future, a war is going on between humans and aliens called Dracs, so far from Earth that the humans fighting can barely remember it. In an aerial battle, two aircraft are shot down over a deserted planet. The only survivors are Davidge (Dennis Quaid) and Jerry (Louis Gossett, Jr.). Enemies at first (Jerry captures Davidge), they begin to depend on one another for survival. They learn each other's language and customs. Jerry saves Davidge's life. When Davidge asks why, he replies, "I like to see another face, even your ugly one." They ultimately develop respect and even affection for one another.

Davidge explores the planet to find evidence only of scavengers, human thieves who enslave the Dracs and use them to mine ore. He returns to find that Jerry is pregnant; Dracs are both male and female. Jerry dies in childbirth, and Davidge raises the baby, named Zammis, with great tenderness.

The scavengers return and capture the Drac child. Davidge is shot trying to rescue him and is brought back to a space station for burial. He comes to and steals a plane to go back to get Zammis. He rescues Zammis with the help of the Drac slaves and his colleagues from the spaceship, who followed him to provide support. He is able to fulfill his promise to Jerry to take Zammis home and sing the song of his lineage before all the Dracs.

DISCUSSION: The war going on all around them loses its meaning very quickly when it is just two creatures on an inhospitable planet who need each other to survive. At first sworn enemies because they have been trained to be so by their cultures, these two individuals have a more personal hatred: It was their fury in battle over seeing friends killed that led to the reckless behavior that stranded them. They try to hold on to their identities as soldiers at war. When it becomes clear they must depend on each other to survive, they overcome their prejudices and ultimately develop respect and affection for each other. They also learn respect for one another's culture, as is poignantly demonstrated when Davidge responds to Zammis's wish to be a human instead of a Drac.

PROFANITY: Some.
NUDITY/SEXUAL REFERENCES: None.
ALCOHOL/DRUG ABUSE: None.

VIOLENCE/SCARINESS: Jerry and Davidge in peril; space-age shooting; Drac slaves whipped and beaten; evidence that slaves have been killed and eaten by scavengers.

TOLERANCE/DIVERSITY ISSUES: A theme of the movie.

QUESTIONS FOR FAMILIES:

- Why were the humans and Dracs fighting? Who was right? Why do you think so?

- What surprised Jerry and Davidge most about each other? How were they alike?

- How were they different? How did they change? Why was Zammis so important to Davidge?

- What do you think about the importance of lineage to Dracs? What does it tell you about their culture?

CONNECTIONS: This story is similar to *Robinson Crusoe on Mars* as well as other stories of people from different cultures being forced to cooperate, developing respect and ultimately affection for one another. Louis Gossett, Jr., won an Oscar in the R-rated *An Officer and a Gentleman*. Always an actor of arresting presence and focus, his performance in this movie is particularly impressive, given the challenges of conveying an alien creature with both male and female elements while his face is completely covered.

ACTIVITIES: The Drac culture's focus on lineage is a good way to begin a discussion of family history with your children. Compare the comfort Jerry draws in being able to name his ancestors and his pride in his heritage with Davidge's "thin" history of a grandfather who might have been a farmer and a grandmother who was a good cook. Ask children what they would say if a Drac asked about their lineage, and tell them stories about your family.

Fiddler on the Roof

1971, 181 min, G, 6 and up
Dir: Norman Jewison. Topol, Molly Picon, Paul Michael Glaser
PLOT: Tevye (Topol), a poor milkman; his wife, Golde; and their five daughters live in a small Jewish community in rural Russia. They are bound by tradition, which decrees all aspects of their lives. Each of his daughters presents Tevye with a new challenge. The oldest one, Tzeitel, wants to pick the person she marries,

not the wealthy widower Lazar Wolf, whom her parents and the matchmaker have chosen, but the poor tailor Motel, whom she loves.

Tevye approves and, by faking a message from a dream, gets Golde to agree, too. The second daughter tests him further by telling him she will marry Pertchik, a student with revolutionary ideas, whether Tevye approves or not. He accepts the marriage, but when his third daughter, Chava, falls in love with a man who is not Jewish, Tevye cannot accept it. They get married, and he refuses to speak to them.

Anti-Semitism is growing, and Cossacks ride through the town destroying everything they can. The residents sadly make plans to leave, hoping their traditions will continue to sustain them. Tevye says, "God be with you" to Chava before they go.

DISCUSSION: This is one of the all-time great Broadway musicals, with a score filled with standards ("Sunrise, Sunset"; "If I Were a Rich Man"; "To Life"; "Matchmaker, Matchmaker"). It will have special meaning for the descendents of the Eastern European Jewish immigrants it depicts, but will resonate for anyone whose parents came to the United States to find something better for their families. The themes are universal—keeping a family together in a world that often tries to tear it apart and maintaining traditions while adapting to changing circumstances.

PROFANITY: None.
NUDITY/SEXUAL REFERENCES: None.
ALCOHOL/DRUG ABUSE: Social drinking.
VIOLENCE/SCARINESS: Pogrom.
TOLERANCE/DIVERSITY ISSUES: A theme of the movie.
QUESTIONS FOR FAMILIES:

- What does the song "Tradition" tell you about the community?

- How do Tzeitel and Motel persuade Tevye to let them get married? How does Tevye persuade Golde?

- Why can't he accept Fyedka? Does Tevye's reaction to Fyedka show any less prejudice than that which Fyedka's people show the Jews?

- What traditions are important to your family? How is that different from your grandparents or great-grandparents? How do traditions change? How do we know when it is time to change? What does the title refer to?

CONNECTIONS: Pertchik is played by Paul Michael Glaser of the television show *Starsky and Hutch*, now a director. Younger kids will enjoy **An American Tail**, a Steven Spielberg animated feature about an immigrant Jewish family (of mice).

Gentleman's Agreement

1947, 118 min, NR, b&w, 10 and up
Dir: Elia Kazan. Gregory Peck, Dorothy McGuire, Celeste Holm, John Garfield
PLOT: Journalist Phil Green (Gregory Peck) is a feature writer for a magazine assigned to do a story on anti-Semitism. He has a hard time coming up with an approach until he remembers the success of previous articles when he went "undercover." He decides to find out what anti-Semitism is like from the inside by letting people think he is Jewish.

After his secretary (June Havoc) tells him she could not get a job at the magazine until she changed her name, he sends identical letters applying for jobs and making hotel reservations, one signed with a neutral name, one with a "Jewish-sounding" name. The difference in the responses shocks him. Even more shocking is the reaction of Kathy (Dorothy McGuire), the editor's niece, the woman he is beginning to love. Phil says, "I've come to see that lots of nice people who aren't [anti-Semites]—people who despise it and deplore it and protest their innocence—help it along and then wonder why it grows…That's the biggest discovery I've made about this whole business, Kathy, the good people, the nice people." His friend, Anne (Celeste Holm), says, "The Krays everywhere are afraid of getting the gate from their little groups of nice people. They make little clucking sounds of disapproval, but they want you and Uncle John to stand up and yell and take sides and fight. But do they fight? Oh, no!"

Phil's support through all of this comes from his wise, strong mother (Anne Revere), his oldest friend, Dave (John Garfield), a Jewish former GI, and Anne. His story is published and opens up a deeper dialogue. Kathy confronts her own weakness in opposing bigotry and helps Dave and his family move to the restricted area where she has a home.
DISCUSSION: This movie, an Oscar-winner for best picture and director, is dated now, but that is part of what makes it so interesting. Young people today will find it hard to imagine that there was a time within the lives of their parents and grandparents when laws in some areas prohibited the sale of property to Jews and blacks. (Explain to them that the term "gentleman's agreement" referred to an implicit agreement by people in the community where there were no such laws.) Perhaps what is most dated is the way the movie finally pulls its punch by

allowing Phil to end up with Kathy instead of Anne. The Motion Picture Academy showed its support for Anne by giving an Oscar to Celeste Holm.

The central message of Gentleman's Agreement—that the greatest injury comes from people who think the right things but are afraid or unwilling to act on their views—is still valid. Kathy tells Phil she felt sick when she heard a bigoted joke, but admits she didn't say anything about it. Anne says, "Kathy and Harry and all of them…think they've fought the good fight for democracy in this country. They haven't got the guts to take the step from talking to action. One little action on one little front. Sure, I know it's not the whole answer, but it's got to start somewhere. And it's got to be with action, not pamphlets, not even with your series. It's got to be with people—nice people, rich people, poor people, big and little people."

PROFANITY: None.
NUDITY/SEXUAL REFERENCES: None.
ALCOHOL/DRUG ABUSE: None.
VIOLENCE/SCARINESS: None.
TOLERANCE/DIVERSITY ISSUES: A theme of the movie.
QUESTIONS FOR FAMILIES:

• What do you think of Phil's "angle" on the story? What did that enable him to find out that he would not have otherwise discovered? Who was it hardest on?

• What was wrong with Kathy's response when Tommy was taunted by anti-Semitic kids?

• What do you think Kathy would have to do to help Dave?

• What is better today? What is worse?

• Why are people so surprised when Phil says he is Jewish? How is he different from what they expected?

• What kind of prejudice have you seen or experienced?

• Did you ever hear someone tell a bigoted joke, as Kathy did? How did you react? How do we make sure that "nice people" do more than talk?

CONNECTIONS: Anne Revere, who also appears in **National Velvet** and *Body and Soul*, turns in another memorable performance as a mother with great strength and wisdom. Ironically, shortly after this movie was made, she was blacklisted, an example of exactly the kind of prejudice the movie was trying to abolish. Phil's secretary, Miss Wales, is played by June Havoc, the real-life "Baby June" who was Gypsy Rose Lee's older sister. Their life together is portrayed in *Gypsy*. You can see her perform a brief dance in *Brewster's Millions*.

John Howard Griffin, a reporter inspired by this fictional account, went a step further and had his skin darkened to find out what it was like to be black. His book, *Black Like Me*, was made into a movie in 1964. More recently, a black Harvard Law School graduate named Lawrence Otis got a job as a busboy (he was not permitted to be a waiter) in an all-white country club in the same area in which the fictional Kathy in this movie lived. He wrote an essay about his experiences (included in his book *Member of the Club: Reflections on Life in a Racially Polarized World*) showing the approach author Laura Z. Hobson created for Phil Green can still give us insight into the hypocrisies and failures of "nice people."

Glory

1989, 12 min, R, 14 and up
Dir. Edward Zwick. Denzel Washington, Matthew Broderick, Morgan Freeman, Cary Elwes
PLOT: This is the deeply moving story of the first black battalion of the Civil War, led by Robert Gould Shaw (Matthew Broderick), the twenty-five-year-old son of abolitionists. Shaw, already a wounded veteran of battle, volunteers to lead the battalion. The Confederate army announces they will immediately enslave any captured blacks and execute any wearing a uniform of the North. Nevertheless, the men stay, even when they are offered a chance for a discharge. They include Trip (Denzel Washington), a tough and bitter runaway slave who endures a brutal beating when he goes AWOL to get some much-needed boots; the bookish Searles (Andre Braugher); and Rawlins (Morgan Freeman), whose wisdom and courage result in his becoming one of the first black noncommissioned officers.

They are told they will be paid less than the white soldiers, and they protest. Shaw and his fellow officers join in the protest by refusing their own pay. The blacks are not permitted to fight. Instead, they are assigned menial tasks and told to loot the captured villages. One of the other white officers assigned to a black battalion says this is an ideal assignment for blacks. Shaw does everything he can to have his men treated with respect, finally blackmailing a superior officer into giving them a chance to go into battle. Their performance is outstanding, and they are next assigned an impossible mission, against overwhelming odds. Most of them are killed and buried together with the white officers in a common grave.

DISCUSSION. The performance of the black soldiers encouraged the Union generals to recruit more, which may have been responsible for keeping this nation united. The black soldiers are asked to fight with greater risk (worse conditions and immediate death if caught by the Confederates) and less money, under the command of people who treat them with contempt. Although theoretically fighting for the freedom of the slaves, most of the white Union soldiers are racist bigots who do not even want to give the soldiers guns, arguing that they are "little monkey children" who will drop the guns and run under fire. Even Shaw has to be persuaded that the black soldiers can fight. Once he is, he is tortured, as all commanding officers are, by the thought of sending such brave and capable men into battle.

This is an outstanding film, one of the best ever made about war in general, insightful about the most devastating war in American history in particular, and simply about the human spirit. Like *Cry Freedom* and *The Long Walk Home*, this film was criticized for presenting the black story through white eyes. We can hope very much someone will tell the story through the eyes of the black soldiers themselves, but this movie is very meaningful on its own terms. Based in part on the letters written by Shaw, the movie is partly his story as well. He and his fellow officer Cabot Forbes (Cary Elwes) have a lot to learn from these soldiers. So do the viewers, which should include every American.

PROFANITY: None.
NUDITY/SEXUAL REFERENCES: None.
ALCOHOL/DRUG ABUSE: Some drinking.
VIOLENCE/SCARINESS: Very powerful and bloody battle scenes.
TOLERANCE/DIVERSITY ISSUES: A theme of the movie.
QUESTIONS FOR FAMILIES:

• Who changes the most in this movie? Why?

• Why was equality such a difficult idea during a war that was supposed to be about equality?

• What is the meaning of the title?

CONNECTIONS: Denzel Washington won an Oscar for his performance, and another should have gone to Freeman, who is unforgettable as Rawlins. The music is performed by the Boys Choir of Harlem.

ACTIVITIES: Check an encyclopedia to read about the controversy following President Truman's order to integrate the troops after World War II. Older teens may be interested in reading Shaw's letters in *Blue-Eyed Child of Fortune: The Civil War Letters of Colonel Robert Gould Shaw*, edited by Russell Duncan, Peter Burchard's book *One Gallant Rush*, or Lincoln Kirstein's *Lay This Laurel*, all sources for the screenplay.

In the Heat of the Night

1967, 109 min, NR, 14 and up
Dir: Norman Jewison. Sidney Poitier, Rod Steiger, Warren Oates, Lee Grant
PLOT: Virgil Tibbs (Sidney Poitier) is waiting in a train station in Sparta, Mississippi, when he is picked up by the local police on suspicion of murder. A wealthy developer was found dead, and the police assume that Tibbs is the culprit because he was unfamiliar and black. The officers and their chief, Sheriff Gillespie (Rod Steiger), are embarrassed to learn that Tibbs is in fact a police detective from Philadelphia, an expert in homicide in town to visit family. Although his supervisor encourages him to stay to help solve the crime, Tibbs is eager to go, and Gillespie is eager to have him leave. The murder victim's widow (Lee Grant) insists he stay because it is clear to her he knows what he is doing. Gillespie agrees; if Tibbs succeeds, the local police will get the credit. If he fails, it will be his fault.

As they work together, Tibbs and Gillespie must both look beyond their prejudices. Gillespie sees Tibbs's competence and expertise. Tibbs sees that, underneath his superficial bigotry, Gillespie is an honest policeman with a strong sense of fairness. They pursue a number of leads that turn out to be wrong but that teach them more about their own prejudices and about the town and its people, ultimately leading them to the real killer.
DISCUSSION: This is a brilliant film in every respect, including writing, directing, and acting. Though the quantity and quality of racism may have changed in this country, the film does not seem dated, partly because it has a universal quality. Anyone who has ever felt underestimated will find great satisfaction as Tibbs proves his expertise; anyone who has ever felt disrespect will feel great pleasure when Gillespie makes fun of the name Virgil and asks, "What do they call you, boy?" only to be told, "They call me MISTER Tibbs!" (Indeed, this became the name of the movie's sequel.)

In **To Kill a Mockingbird**, the black man's worst sin is to admit he felt sorry for the poor white girl. In this movie, there is a similar scene, when Tibbs, trying to make a connection with Gillespie, says Gillespie is lonely, which makes

Gillespie furious. It is one thing for Gillespie to give Tibbs respect; it is another to accept his pity. This shows how securely bigotry rests on the need to feel superior to someone.

PROFANITY: Some, including racial epithets.
NUDITY/SEXUAL REFERENCES: Dolores Purdy accuses policeman of getting her pregnant and describes their encounter; some discussion of the way men peek into her window when she walks around in the nude; reference to (illegal) abortion.
ALCOHOL/DRUG ABUSE: Some drinking.
VIOLENCE/SCARINESS: Mostly implied or off-screen. Wealthy bigot slaps Tibbs, who slaps him back. Autopsy scene.
TOLERANCE/DIVERSITY ISSUES: A theme of the movie.
QUESTIONS FOR FAMILIES:

• Tibbs and Gillespie make a number of wrong starts on the way to finding the murderer. What leads them to each of them? What do they learn from each other helping them go in the right direction?

• Why does Dolores Purdy lie about the man who made her pregnant?

• What makes Tibbs and Gillespie feel differently about each other?

• How have things changed since the time of this movie? What made those changes happen?

CONNECTIONS: Kids should read about this era, including *Eyes on the Prize* by Juan Williams to understand how recently such blatant bigotry was not only permitted but accepted. This movie won five Oscars, including Best Picture and Actor (Rod Steiger).

Remember the Titans

2000, 113 min, PG, 8 and up
Dir: Boaz Yakin. Denzel Washington, Will Patton, Kip Pardue, Wood Harris
PLOT: This movie about the real-life integration of a Virginia high school football teem teeters on the brink of cliché and stereotype but manages to come down on the side of archetype, thanks to a sure script, solid direction, and another sensational performance by Denzel Washington.

It was not until 1971, seventeen years after the *Brown v. Board of Education* decision, that black students came to T.C. Williams High School in Alexandria Virginia. Every other team in that football-loving district was still segregated. The white T.C. Williams players were confronted with not only a whole new set of black players, but a black coach, Herman Boone (Washington). In a matter of a few weeks, Boone has to make them into a team, and it has to be a winning team, because the school board is looking for any reason to fire him so they can reinstate Coach Yoast (Will Patton), now demoted to assistant.

This is the kind of movie that begins with all the characters attending a funeral under a bright autumn sun and then takes us back to where it all began. This is the kind of movie in which people say things like, "Is this even about football anymore or is it just about you?" and where the supreme bonding moment is when everyone sings Motown songs together. In other words, no surprises here. If everyone hadn't achieved a sense of brotherhood that transcended race and it hadn't all turned out pretty well, Disney would not have made a movie about it. That just leaves us free to enjoy the movie's appealing characters and special moments, and that is just fine. There is a reason for the classic structure of the sports movie—we like to watch raw recruits learn honor and loyalty out there on the field when it's done right, and here it is done very nicely.

DISCUSSION: Washington is, as ever, that rarest of pleasures, equally an actor and a movie star. His power to mesmerize and inspire as a performer works perfectly with his role as a coach who can capture the attention and loyalty of these teen-age boys. Boone is so secure in himself that he can devote all of his energy to the team, so he inspires them by example.

Boone loves football because the football field is the one place where only what is inside the players matters—talent, loyalty, hard work, integrity. He is a man who has faced racism with dignity and self-confidence, not bitterness. He also loves football because it provides a constructive outlet for his emotions. He tells the team that football is "about controlling that anger, harnessing that aggression to achieve perfection."

Boone takes the boys to a college near Gettysburg for training. It is impossible to say which is the tougher workout for the team, the physical challenges of drills and practices or the emotional challenge of overcoming a lifetime of anger and prejudice. He takes them to the Gettysburg battlefield and tells them that "Fifty thousand men died on this same field fighting the same battle we are still fighting today...If we don't come together right now on this hallowed ground, we too will be destroyed."

There is another battlefield waiting for them when they get back to school. The team has a number of tough moments on and off the field. So do the coaches. As Boone reminds them, in mythology the titans were even greater than the gods. Like all great coaches, Boone and Yoast teach the team that they have it within themselves to be great as well. They also realize that they get as much from the boys as the boys get from them.

PROFANITY: Some strong language, including racist comments.
NUDITY/SEXUAL REFERENCES: Some locker room talk. When the boys refer to a long-haired teammate as a "fruitcake," he responds by kissing one of them on the mouth.
ALCOHOL/DRUG ABUSE: None.
VIOLENCE/SCARINESS: A major character is critically injured in a car accident. There are some scuffles and threats of more serious violence.
TOLERANCE/DIVERSITY ISSUES: A theme of the movie.
QUESTIONS FOR FAMILIES:

- Boone and Yoast have different ideas about how to motivate the team. Which is right?

- Who inspires you to do your best, and how do they do it?

- Boone may criticize a player's performance on the field in front of the others, but that he never lets the team know that he is helping one member with his schoolwork. Why is that?

- Why do the boys show respect and affection by insulting each other?

- Why does Yoast stay on as assistant coach, despite the blow to his pride, and why does he relinquish his chance to be in the Hall of Fame?

CONNECTIONS: Parents may want to share their recollections of the civil rights era in light of the players' experience in not being allowed to eat at a restaurant. The movie focuses on racism, but it also deals with other kinds of prejudice. See if the kids in the family notice the prejudice against the boy with long hair or Boone's patronizing attitude toward Yoast's football-loving daughter.

Families who enjoy this movie will enjoy *Brian's Song*, the true (and very sad) story of the first racially mixed roommates in the NFL, Gale Sayers and Brian Piccolo.

The Russians Are Coming! The Russians Are Coming!

1966, 126 min, NR, 6 and up

Din Norman Jewison. Alan Arkin, Carl Reiner, Eva Marie Saint, Jonathan Winters, Brian Keith

PLOT: A Russian submarine crew, curious about the United States, accidentally gets too close to the shore and gets stuck on a sandbar near an island off the coast of New England. Lieutenant Rozanov (Alan Arkin) and a small group of sailors are assigned to go onshore as unobtrusively as possible to find a boat they can use to free the submarine. They stop at the house of Walt Whittaker (Carl Reiner), a writer on vacation, whose family is getting ready to go back home to the mainland. Unable to persuade Walt that they are friendly Norwegians, they confess they are Russians and take him into town, leaving Kolchin (John Phillip Law) with the Whitaker family. Most of the Americans, certain they are being attacked, react with complete hysteria. The Russian captain becomes angry and is about to attack for real when both sides have to stop and work together to rescue a child.

DISCUSSION: Today's children may find it hard to understand just how revolutionary this Cold War comedy seemed when it was first released. It still stands up well as both delicious slapstick and social commentary.

PROFANITY: None.

NUDITY/SEXUAL REFERENCES: None.

ALCOHOL/DRUG ABUSE: None.

VIOLENCE/SCARINESS: Child in peril on church steeple.

TOLERANCE/DIVERSITY ISSUES: The theme is tolerance of political/cultural diversity.

QUESTIONS FOR FAMILIES:

• Why were the Russians and Americans so scared of each other? What made them less afraid?

• Who in the town reacted the most rationally?

• How would you react if it were your family the sailors came to first?

• Is there a country that could scare Americans today the way the Russians did when this movie was made?

CONNECTIONS: This movie is based on a book by Nathaniel Benchley, son of humorist Robert Benchley (in many movies, including *The Major and the Minor*) and father of Peter Benchley (author of *Jaws*). The screenplay was written by William Rose, also the author of **It's a Mad Mad Mad Mad World** and *The Secret of Santa Vittoria* as well as the more serious **Guess Who's Coming to Dinner**.

School Ties

1992, 107 min, PG-13, 12 and up
Dir: Robert Mandel. Brendan Fraser, Amy Locane, Peter Donat, Chris O'Donnell, Matt Damon
PLOT: David Green (Brendan Fraser), a Jewish boy from Scranton, gets an athletic scholarship to an affluent (and all-WASP) boy's prep school in the mid-1950s. He keeps his religion a secret, enduring casual anti-Semitic remarks and playing football on Rosh Hashanah. Dillon (Matt Damon), initially friendly, becomes bitter when David replaces him as quarterback and dates the girl he likes (Amy Locane). Dillon finds out that David is Jewish, gets the other students to harass him, and ultimately frames him in a cheating incident. Although the school honor society votes against David, based on bigotry, Dillon's roommate tells the headmaster the truth, and Dillon is expelled. The headmaster advises David to forget the incident and suggests that David may wish to leave to avoid embarrassment. David says that he will stay on as a constant reminder. "You used me for football; I'll use you to get into Harvard."
DISCUSSION: This movie is, in a way, more effective than the much more prestigious **Gentleman's Agreement**. The prejudice is explicit (a swastika is painted in David's room), and sounds even more chilling coming from such fresh-faced and attractive young people. The most moving exchange in the movie is when Dillon tells David he envies him because "If you get what you want, you'll deserve it, and if you don't, you'll manage. You don't have to live up to anyone's expectation. You are who you are. That's what really draws people to you, David; it's not because you're the cool quarterback." The movie is smart enough to allow that envy is the real motivation for Dillon's behavior, with anti-Semitism just an excuse.
Like **Dead Poet's Society**, this film also addresses the burden of expectations the young men face. One has a breakdown after a French teacher takes him apart in class.

PROFANITY: Very rough locker-room language.

NUDITY/SEXUAL REFERENCES: Nudity in dorm showers; ugly reference to a girl's alleged promiscuity used as an insult to her brother.

ALCOHOL/DRUG ABUSE: David's secret revealed by drunken alum.

VIOLENCE/SCARINESS: None.

TOLERANCE/DIVERSITY ISSUES: A theme of the movie.

QUESTIONS FOR FAMILIES:

- What would have been different if David had told everyone he was Jewish on the first day of school?

- Compare David's playing on Rosh Hashanah to Eric Liddell's refusal to run on the Sabbath in **Chariots of Fire** (and real-life baseball great Sandy Koufax's refusal to play in the World Series on Yom Kippur).

- What are the reasons the boys use to support their prejudice?

- In movies about prejudice, sometimes viewers feel the main character is too perfect, not allowed to have any faults. Is that the case in this movie?

- What do you think about what the boys did to the French professor? Was it fair? Did they accomplish what they wanted to?

CONNECTIONS: Dillon is played by Matt Damon, who went on to co-write and star in *Good Will Hunting*. Chris O'Donnell, who plays David's roommate, went on to star with Al Pacino in *Scent of a Woman* and played Robin in *Batman Forever* and *Batman and Robin*. The headmaster is played by Peter Donat, son of Robert Donat, who played a much more understanding headmaster in **Goodbye, Mr. Chips**.

Skin Game

1971, 102 min, PG, 10 and up

Dir. Peter Bogart. James Garner, Louis Gossett, Jr., Edward Asner, Susan Clark

PLOT: Quincy (James Garner) and Jason (Louis Gossett, Jr.) are con men who travel through slave territory in the pre-Civil War era. Quincy "sells" Jason, and then they escape together with the money. Jason, who has been free all his life, is increasingly resentful about the humiliation of even pretending to be a slave. Quincy is sympathetic, but mildly reminds him, "You're the color people are buying this year."

Jason agrees to one more sale and persuades Quincy to buy Naomi, a lovely young woman who is to be auctioned off. John Brown (Royal Dano) disrupts the action and frees all the slaves. Many of them are later captured by the cruel slave trader Plunkett (Edward Asner), including Naomi. Plunkett manages to buy Jason and chain him so he cannot escape. Plunkett sells Jason and Naomi to Mr. Calloway, who responds to Jason's claims that he is a free man by having him whipped.

Quincy and Ginger (Susan Clark), a fellow con artist, look everywhere for Jason. In the meantime, Jason must learn how to behave like a slave. Calloway keeps African slaves, purchased illegally, on his farm as well. Jason befriends them, and they think of him as their leader, even though they speak no English. When Jason and Ginger arrive, Jason insists they must arrange for the departure of Naomi and the Africans as well. Quincy is discovered to be a fraud and is whipped. Jason kills Plunkett. They all escape to Mexico. Jason stays with the Africans, and Quincy and Ginger go out West.

DISCUSSION: The lighthearted story of the clever con artists is nicely combined with sensitively handled themes of the effect of bigotry and slavery on the human spirit. Both Jason and Quincy are con men who find it easy to diminish everyone else as marks for them to steal from. This allows them to avoid thinking too hard about slavery, except as something to exploit for easy money. Quincy in particular cannot allow himself to see the big picture and acts as though his treating of Jason as an equal should be enough. When Quincy finds Jason at Calloway's farm, he tries to soothe him by saying Jason has had worse experiences, but Jason replies firmly slavery is the worst. As Jason points out, he and Quincy may be as alike as brothers, but the one difference means one of them can sell a human being and the other can only be sold. After his experience of what it really means to be black in America, he cannot go back to his old life or indeed to America at all.

Interestingly, Jason's initial reaction to the Africans can be called bigoted. He is terrified of them and runs away, yelling that they are cannibals. Quincy at first calls them "savages." By then, Jason knows they are men, like himself, far from home.

PROFANITY: Mild.
NUDITY/SEXUAL REFERENCES: Quincy and Ginger share a bathtub (off screen) and a bed; Ginger uses sex to get what she wants.
ALCOHOL/DRUG ABUSE: None.

VIOLENCE/SCARINESS: Off-screen whippings; some fistfights; Plunkett is shot.

TOLERANCE/DIVERSITY ISSUES: A theme of the movie.

QUESTIONS FOR FAMILIES:

- When did Quincy show his loyalty to Jason? When did he show insensitivity?

- Why was Naomi's master selling her? What lets you know how he felt about it?

- Why was the way Jason spoke so important?

- What were the rules for being a slave that Jason had to learn?

CONNECTIONS: The plot of this movie recalls an "auction" by famed antislavery leader Henry Ward Beecher (brother of Harriet Beecher Stowe, who wrote Uncle Tom's Cabin). It is described in a brief essay by Mrs. Beecher called "The Day Mr. Beecher Sold Slaves in Plymouth Pulpit," which originally ran in the Ladies Home Journal and is well worth reading. Beecher used the "auction" to buy the slaves' freedom, but also to demonstrate the inhumanity of selling human beings.

The movie was remade for television as *Sidekicks*, with Gossett and Larry Hagman.

Though listed as "Pierre Marton," the co-scriptwriter was Peter Stone (**Charade, 1776**).

John Brown is played by longtime character actor Royal Dano, who appeared as the Tattered Man in **The Red Badge of Courage**, as Carey in **The 7 Faces of Dr. Lao**, and as the man who delivered the bad news to the test pilots' families in **The Right Stuff**. Louis Gossett, Jr., also starred in **Enemy Mine**. Plunkett is played by Edward Asner, later on television as Lou Grant.

ACTIVITIES: Look up real-life abolitionist John Brown in an encyclopedia and compare his tactics to the nonviolent approaches of Gandhi and Dr. Martin Luther King, Jr.

West Side Story

1961, 151 min, NR, 10 and up
Dir: Robert Wise and Jerome Robbins. Natalie Wood, Richard Beymer, Rita Moreno, George Chakiris, Russ Tamblyn

PLOT: Modeled on *Romeo and Juliet*, this movie puts the star-crossed lovers in two warring gangs in the slums of New York. The opening dance number brings us up-to-date. The Sharks (Puerto Ricans) and the Jets (Anglos) have blown up a series of petty insults and turf disputes into a war over who will rule the territory. The leader of the jets, Riff (Russ Tamblyn), goes to see his best friend, Tony (Richard Beymer), the former leader of the gang. Riff asks Tony to come to the dance that night to support him as he negotiates fight terms with Bernardo (George Chakiris), the leader of the Jets. Tony has outgrown the gang and wants more from life, but he and Riff are friends "womb to tomb," so he agrees to go.

Meanwhile, Bernardo's sister Maria, just arrived in the United States, is getting ready for the dance, begging to have her dress cut just a little lower. Bernardo's girlfriend, Anita (Rita Moreno), watches over her protectively. At the dance, well-meaning Mr. Hand tries to get the teenagers to mix with each other, but tensions are high. As each side dances furiously, everything seems to stop for Tony and Maria, who see each other and are transformed.

Bernardo is furious when he sees them together and he takes Maria home. That night, Tony visits her, and they declare their love for each other. She asks him to make sure there is no fighting, and he agrees. At the "war council" he persuades them to make it a fistfight only and he feels successful. Maria wants him to make sure there is no fighting of any kind, so he agrees to try to stop them. Things get out of control, and Bernardo kills Riff with a knife. Tony, overcome with grief and guilt, grabs the knife and kills Bernardo.

Running from the police and the Jets, Tony finds Maria. They dream of a place where they could always be safe and together. Anita agrees to take a message to Tony, but when the Jets harass her, she angrily tells them that Maria is dead. Blinded by grief, he stumbles out into the night and is shot by one of the Sharks. Maria holds him as he dies, and together, the Sharks and Jets carry him away.

DISCUSSION: The story retains its power, but the gangs are endearingly tame to us now. Can it be that once there were gangs who fought only with fists and knives?

This is a good opportunity to explore the reasons why people fight. Anita says the boys fight like they dance, "Like they have to get rid of something, quick." According to her, they are getting rid of "too much feeling." Young people understand that idea and may like to talk about what "too much feeling" feels like to them. The music and dances in this movie do as much to tell the story as the dialogue and plot, and they illustrate this idea especially well.

One important difference between this movie and Romeo and Juliet is that in Shakespeare's play, the older generation plays an important role. In **West Side**

Story, the few adults who appear are ineffectual and tangential, like Mr. Hand (John Astin), who thinks he can get the kids to be friends by having them dance together. Listen to the lopsided music-box song he plays for them and see what a good job it does of expressing both what he is trying to accomplish and how hopeless it is.

Of course, this is an important movie to use in talking about prejudice. See if you can get kids to watch carefully enough to figure out why the Sharks and Jets resent and mistrust each other.

PROFANITY: In 1960s fashion, they invented substitutes; words like "buggin'" are used to suggest four-letter words.
NUDITY/SEXUAL REFERENCES: Implication that Maria and Tony sleep together; threatened sexual attack on Anita.
ALCOHOL/DRUG ABUSE: Reference in a song to drug use; lots of cigarettes.
VIOLENCE/SCARINESS: Gang fights with knives.
TOLERANCE/DIVERSITY ISSUES: The theme of the movie.
QUESTIONS FOR FAMILIES:

- If you were going to adapt the story of Romeo and Juliet today, what groups would the boy and girl come from?

- Listen to the song "America," with the Sharks and their girlfriends disagreeing about whether America has been good or bad to them. Which side do you agree with? Are they both right? Why?

- In the song "Tonight," both sides sing, "Well, they began it!" Have you ever seen people act that way?

- One of the boys tells Doc, "You was never my age." What does he mean? Do all teenagers feel like that at times?

- Listen to the song "There's a Place for Us." Have you ever dreamed of a special place where you could always be safe? What would it be like?

- Tony has to decide how he can be loyal to his friend and loyal to Maria. Why is that hard? Who else in the movie has to make a decision about loyalty?

- If you could talk to Tony and Maria, what would you tell them to do?

CONNECTIONS: This is a great double feature with **Romeo and Juliet** or the 1997 version, **William Shakespeare's Romeo + Juliet**. It is fun to see how much of the movie's structure is taken from the play. In both, the lovers see each other at a party and are immediately overcome. In both, the boy comes to see the girl later that night. Juliet speaks to Romeo from a balcony. Maria speaks to Tony from a fire escape. Romeo and Tony are both pulled back into the fight due to the deaths of their friends. In both movies, tragedy results from missed messages.

Moreno and Chakiris both won Oscars for their performances, two of the ten won by this movie, including Best Picture. The brilliant music and lyrics are by Leonard Bernstein and Stephen Sondheim.

GUESS WHO'S COMING TO DINNER

1967, 108 min, NR, 10 and up
Dir: Stanley Kramer. Spencer Tracy, Katharine Hepburn, Sidney Poitier
A liberal white newspaperman (Spencer Tracy) and his wife (Katharine Hepburn) must confront their hypocrisy when their daughter (Katharine Houghton) announces she is going to marry a black doctor (Sidney Poitier). This is worth watching as something of a period piece, but also for Tracy's brilliant performance (his last) as a man who wants to protect his daughter from the problems she will face, but who also wants her to experience the happiness of a life spent with someone she really loves.
CONNECTIONS: Hepburn's daughter is played by her real-life niece, Katharine Houghton.

THE LONG WALK HOME

1990, 97 min, PG, 10 and up
Dir: Richard Pearce. Sissy Spacek, Whoopi Goldberg
This is the story of the Montgomery, Alabama, bus boycott, seen through the eyes of a white child as she watches her privileged suburban mother, Miriam Thompson (Sissy Spacek), struggle to reconcile the clash between the comfort of her home life and the comfort of her conscience. At first, Miriam gives the housekeeper, Odessa Cotter (Whoopi Goldberg), a ride to work because it is the only way she can get there to do the housework. Miriam comes to understand that she has to drive her and help the other boycotters, because segregation is not right, and she must do so publicly, no matter the cost to her way of life. There are a few stories about this era from the perspective of the black community (mostly made-for-television movies instead of theatrical releases), and more of them are needed. This movie's depiction of the struggle with racism (and, in subtext, feminism) in the white community is also a part of the story that deserves to be told.

THE SNEETCHES

(in *The Cat in the Hat* and *Dr. Seuss on the Loose*) 1960, 50 min, 3 and up
The classic Seuss story about prejudice (the star-bellied Sneetches and the plain-bellied Sneetches each think they are the best, even when a machine removes the stars from the star-bellies and puts them on the plain-bellies) is included on this tape, along with *Green Eggs and Ham* and *The Zax*.

SEE ALSO:
Amazing Grace and Other Stories A little black girl triumphs over prejudice to play Peter Pan in the school play, teaching everyone that her dreams are bigger than anyone's attempt to limit them.
Bad Day at Black Rock Spencer Tracy plays a man who must confront prejudice against outsiders, the disabled, and the Japanese in a small Western town.
Johnny Belinda A young deaf woman overcomes prejudice when she is taught to communicate with sign language.
The King and I A British teacher and a Siamese king learn to appreciate each other's cultures, and she helps him impress British diplomats who are inclined to see Asians as barbarians.
A League of Their Own While the baseball players were off fighting in WWII, the baseball owners sponsored a league of women players, and the women showed they had the courage, the heart, and the skill to play and attract an audience.
The Learning Tree A young black boy must keep his ideals even though he's surrounded by bigotry.
Mask A young boy whose illness results in enlarged and distended facial features teaches those around him that his loving heart and fine intellect are what matter.
The Phantom Tollbooth Neighboring kings feud over which is more important, numbers or words, and learn to appreciate the importance of both.
A Raisin in the Sun Lorraine Hansberry's classic play is about a black family trying to move into a white neighborhood, despite the prejudice of their new neighbors and their own fears.
To Kill a Mockingbird A white Southern lawyer defends a black man in this story of teaching children to be tolerant despite a culture of racism and intolerance.

10

LOYALTY

"We must not confuse dissent with disloyalty."
EDWARD R. MURROW

Loyalty is more than blind devotion. Keep in mind that for every good guy in a movie, there is a bad guy who also has very loyal supporters. They most often demonstrate their loyalty by agreeing with their leader and doing whatever he asks, primarily because one of the hallmarks of the movie bad guy is that he insists on absolute obedience. Heroes, however, demonstrate a more thoughtful and complex form of loyalty. Whether it is based on admiration for an individual or devotion to a cause, true loyalty requires a willingness to put the interests of others ahead of oneself and to do whatever is necessary to protect the people and the ideals that have earned loyalty.

As viewers, our own loyalties can surprise us because part of the filmmaker's art is to capture our loyalty for the star. We tend to side with whomever in the movie provides the point of view, whether the character is the cop or the robber. Some movies succeed by taking advantage of our tendency to side with the typical hero, as in **Stalag 17**. Like Sefton's fellow prisoners, we dislike him because he is a cynical loner and we share their surprise and confusion when we find that the real traitor is someone else.

It is not a coincidence that three movies sharply depicting the challenges of loyalty are set onboard ships, closed communities in which men must make careful decisions about where their loyalty lies. The main issues to consider in viewing these different illustrations of loyalty are these: How do I determine where my loyalty lies, and how is that loyalty best demonstrated?

The Adventures of Robin Hood

1938, 102 min, NR, 6 and up
Dir. Michael Curtiz and William Keighley. Errol Flynn, Olivia de Havilland, Claude Rains, Basil Rathbone, Alan Hale
PLOT: Errol Flynn is the definitive Robin Hood in this glorious Technicolor version of the classic story, one of the most thrillingly entertaining films of all time.

King Richard the Lion-Hearted, off fighting in the Crusades, has been captured and held for ransom. His unscrupulous brother John (Claude Rains) schemes to make sure Richard never returns, so he can take over as king. All of the knights offer their support but one, Sir Robin of Locksley (Flynn), who vows to raise the ransom money himself. He and his followers use Sherwood Forest as cover so they can steal from the rich and powerful to help the poor and raise the ransom money. They capture a group of travelers that includes the Sheriff of Nottingham (Melville Cooper), Sir Guy of Gisbourne (Basil Rathbone), and the lovely Maid Marian (Olivia de Havilland), the King's ward. Marian is at first scornful, but when she learns that Robin and his men are loyal to Richard, and sees how the Normans have abused the Saxons, she becomes sympathetic.

In order to capture Robin, the Sheriff plans an archery contest, with the prize to be awarded by Marian. They know Robin will not be able to resist. He enters in disguise, but his superb skill reveals his identity, and he is caught and put in the dungeon. With the help of his men and Marian, however, he is rescued in time to help save Richard from John's plot to have him assassinated.

DISCUSSION: In this story, Robin is the only one of the knights to stay loyal to Richard. Though he is a Norman, he is willing to lose everything he has to protect the poor Saxons. His loyalty is not limited to his own people; rather, he sees everyone who behaves justly as his people. "It's injustice I hate, not the Normans," he tells Marian.

Robin is not only the world's greatest archer and a master swashbuckler. He has a complex and multi-layered character, revealed in his interactions with Marian and with his men. He has a strong and clear sense of fairness and honor. He is always respectful of those who deserve it, including the peasants. He is confident and direct, but also unpretentious and even irreverent. When he tells Marian that her manners are not as pretty as her looks, Prince John laughs that this is quite a contrast to Sir Guy, whose feelings for Marian leave him tongue-tied. In the scene where he meets Little John, Robin fights him for the right to cross the river first, just for the fun of it. When Little John wins, tossing him into the water,

Robin is delighted. "I love a man that can best me!" Robin is not especially concerned with goodness or piety; he even steals food from Friar Tuck. With the poor and weak, he is gentle and considerate and he is, above all, loyal. When he finds that the people who appear to be traveling monks are loyal to Richard, he says he will only take half of what they have. At the end, when the king asks him what he wants as a reward, all he asks for is amnesty for his men.

This is also a good movie to use for a discussion of what makes a leader. Robin's confidence in himself inspires the confidence of others. In one of history's finest pairings of actor and role, Errol Flynn brings his own assurance, grace, and passionate enjoyment to a part that added courage, integrity, and lively dialogue, creating one of the screen's greatest heroes.

PROFANITY: None.
NUDITY/SEXUAL REFERENCES: None.
ALCOHOL/DRUG ABUSE: None.
VIOLENCE/SCARINESS: Sword fights (including the famous one on the stairs in the castle); battles with arrows; etc.
TOLERANCE/DIVERSITY ISSUES: None.
QUESTIONS FOR FAMILIES:

• Why does Robin stay loyal to King Richard?

• How does Marian learn that Robin is not just a thief?

• What do you learn about Robin from his meeting with Little John?

• What makes the men want to follow him?

• What makes someone a leader?

CONNECTIONS: This is the ultimate version of one of the most classic and enduring stories of all children's literature, flawless in every respect, from performances to art direction to the unforgettably rousing score to the gorgeous jewel-like Technicolor.
The director, Michael Curtiz (brought in due to studio concerns over original director William Keighley), was also the director of another classic, **Casablanca**. The stirring music is by Erich Wolfgang Korngold, one of Hollywood's greatest composers. Flynn and de Havilland made nine movies together, including *Captain Blood* (the ultimate swashbuckler) and *They Died With Their Boots On*, a completely inaccurate but very exciting portrayal of the battle of Little Bighorn.

There are at least fourteen other movies about Robin Hood, not counting silent movies. Younger children may enjoy the 1973 Disney animated retelling of the story, with animals as all of the characters and some good songs by Roger Miller. Some of the other versions are all right (including the passable 1952 Disney live-action version, *The Story of Robin Hood and His Merrie Men*, with Richard Todd), but children should not be allowed to see the 1991 Kevin Costner movie (*Robin Hood: Prince of Thieves*). Although it has some exciting moments, the plot is a dreadful mishmash, with some truly disgusting violence and behavior that is ugly to the point of kinkiness ("Who told you that you could cover yourself?" snaps Alan Rickman as the Sheriff of Nottingham to the naked young woman in his bed when they are interrupted by his henchmen with a message). I don't recommend the Mel Brooks parody *Robin Hood: Men in Tights*, either. A couple of funny moments are surrounded by dozens of tasteless jokes about chastity belts and other sexual and scatological references.

ACTIVITIES: Children who like this movie will enjoy the book by Howard Pyle (try to get an edition with Pyle's magnificent illustrations). Older children and teenagers might like to know more about this era and these characters. *Ivanhoe* tells the story of another group who stayed loyal to King Richard; if you watch carefully, you will see a character called Locksley who is based on the same historical figure as Robin Hood. For a movie that shows the earlier lives of both King Richard and his brother John, see *The Lion in Winter*, with Peter O'Toole as Henry II and Katharine Hepburn as Eleanor of Aquitaine, their parents. Anthony Hopkins plays Richard. A thin and sad movie about Robin Hood's later years is *Robin and Marian* (written by James Goldman, also the author of *The Lion in Winter*), starring Sean Connery and Audrey Hepburn.

The Caine Mutiny

1954, 125 min, NR, 12 and up
Dir: Edward Dmytryk. Humphrey Bogart, Van Johnson, Fred MacMurray, Jose Ferrer
PLOT: The USS Caine is a minesweeper-destroyer during WWII. The people assigned to it feel far from the "real war." The story is told through the eyes of Ensign Willie Keith (Robert Francis), who does not like working with the Caine's captain and is hoping for better when a new captain is assigned.

The new man is Captain Queeg (Humphrey Bogart), career Navy, in contrast to the rest of the officers, who enlisted or were drafted for the war. He is rigid and formal and explains he expects people to go "by the book." "You may tell the crew that there are four ways of doing things aboard ship: the right way, the wrong way, the Navy way, and my way. They do things my way and we'll get along."

Keith and his colleagues, sophisticated writer Keefer (Fred MacMurray) and thoughtful, responsible Maryk (Van Johnson), contemptuous of Queeg's poor seamanship, finally take over when the ship nearly founders in a typhoon.

At Maryk's court-martial, his defense counsel, Lieutenant Greenwald (Jose Ferrer), cross-examines Queeg intensely, causing the captain to reveal his instability. Greenwald refuses to join the others in celebration. He arrives at their party drunk and furious, telling them they had no right to judge, much less destroy, a man who was doing the dirty work of defending America. He tosses a glass of champagne in the face of the man he blames the most: Keefer.

DISCUSSION: This is a gripping story, with a brilliant performance by Humphrey Bogart as Queeg. His testimony at the court-martial is one of the most memorable scenes ever filmed. What gives the movie its lasting resonance is the complexity of its resolution. It dares to be more than a simple good guys versus bad guys story, with the smart guys triumphing over someone who is weaker than they are.

Talk to children about the role of each of the main characters. Keith is there as the representative of the audience; the story is told through his eyes. Maryk at first supports Queeg, but is persuaded by Keefer that Queeg is not only incompetent but dangerously unstable. Keefer may be persuasive, but when the time comes, and Maryk is on trial, Keefer does not back Maryk up. At the celebration following the trial, Maryk says, "I didn't think you'd have the guts to come," and Keefer replies, "I didn't have the guts not to."

Queeg is there to represent those who must perform the tasks others consider beneath them. He puts a great deal of pressure on himself and on those around him, saying, "Substandard performance is not permitted to exist; that I warn you." He finds it impossible to ask for help directly, at best saying, "A command is a lonely job. Sometimes a captain of a ship needs help." His officers could have responded, but chose not to. This drives Queeg further into rigidity as he seeks to prove to them and to himself he does not need their help.

PROFANITY: None.
NUDITY/SEXUAL REFERENCES: None.
ALCOHOL/DRUG ABUSE: Some drinking; Greenwald gets drunk.
VIOLENCE/SCARINESS: Tension on the ship and at the trial.
TOLERANCE/DIVERSITY ISSUES: None.

QUESTIONS FOR FAMILIES:

- How does Willie's relationship with his girlfriend contribute to your understanding of Willie and of the main story?

- Why were the strawberries so important to Queeg?

- If Keefer had not been on the ship, what would Maryk have done differently? Why didn't the officers respond to Queeg when he asked for help?

- Why was Greenwald so angry with Keefer?

CONNECTIONS: The Pulitzer Prize-winning novel by Herman Wouk is worth reading. Compare this movie to *A Few Good Men*, a contemporary exploration of some of the same issues, though without the courage to pursue the problems it raises. As in **The Caine Mutiny**, the climax of *A Few Good Men* is the cross-examination of a high-ranking officer. Both movies focus on the conflict between those who must become "grotesque," as Jack Nicholson's character in A Few Good Men admits, in the cause of protecting those who have the luxury of making fine distinctions.

Viewers should note, as the prologue to **The Caine Mutiny** points out, that in reality there has never been a mutiny on a U.S. ship.

Dead Man Walking

1995, 122 min, R, mature high school ages
Dir: Tim Robbins. Susan Sarandon, Sean Penn
PLOT: Sister Helen Prejean, a Louisiana nun, works in an inner-city neighborhood. She receives a letter from Matthew Poncelet, a prisoner sentenced to death for raping a young woman and murdering her and her boyfriend. Poncelet is hoping Sister Helen will help him with his appeal.

He is hard to like, hostile, ignorant, defiantly expecting and inviting the disapproval of others. He insists it was his friend who was responsible for the rape and murders. He parrots the bigotry of the Aryan Nation prisoners, extinguishing any possibility of clemency. He tries to distance himself from Sister Helen, insisting they have nothing in common and even making a clumsy pass at her. She listens patiently, never judging him but never losing sight of the truth as her faith reveals it to her. She quietly tells him they do have something in common: They both live among the poor. She tries to get him to talk to her: "Death is breathing down your neck, and you're playing your little man-on-the-make games." She does not try to convert him. She just wants him to accept responsibility for what he has done and she wants him to see that he is loved. Both goals are connected, as he must acknowledge his crimes in order to feel he can be loved in spite of them.

Sister Helen struggles to find the best way for her to live up to her commitment as a person of faith. She is aware the families of Matthew's victims have suffered deeply and she wants very much to support them. When they make it clear providing support to Matthew is unacceptable to them, she grieves for the pain she causes them, but accepts the consequences of her choice to do what she can for him.

DISCUSSION: This is a very rare movie depicting a person of faith who is not foolish, corrupt, or one-dimensional. Sister Helen's faith is a source of strength and a guide for her. Yet she struggles with her loyalty to her friends, who are hurt by her support of a bigot, a rapist, and a killer. She wants to provide support for the families of his victims, but realizes her connection to Matthew can only give them pain. We see Sister Helen with her family and we see her enjoy a quiet laugh with another nun over the irony of the plans to bury Matthew in a plot adjoining a nun who would have been disconcerted by the thought of spending eternity next to a man. This helps us understand that Sister Helen is not a saint but a human being, struggling to do the best she can, as we do, and as Matthew does.

The struggle is often about loyalty. Sister Helen believes she owes loyalty to Matthew, to the victims and their families, to her own family, to her fellow nuns and her friends, and ultimately to Jesus. The way she thinks about these issues and the choices she makes are deeply moving. So is the impact on Matthew of unconditional love.

Tim Robbins, who wrote and directed the movie, refuses to make any easy emotional appeals. Like Sister Helen, he sees and sympathizes with both sides, and the issue of the death penalty is raised with sensitivity and respect.

PROFANITY: Strong language.
NUDITY/SEXUAL REFERENCES: References and depiction in flashback to a brutal rape.
ALCOHOL/DRUG ABUSE: References to alcohol and drug abuse; smoking.
VIOLENCE/SCARINESS: Rape and murder depicted in flashback; execution portrayed tastefully but frankly.
TOLERANCE/DIVERSITY ISSUES: Racist statements made by Matthew; objection by Sister Jean's black friends to her work with Matthew.

QUESTIONS FOR FAMILIES:

- Why does Sister Jean befriend a man who has committed such a horrible crime?

- Why doesn't she try to convert him?

- How does her faith help her make decisions?

- What do we learn from the scene with Matthew's family? From the scene with Sister Helen's family?

- Why is it important for Matthew to acknowledge what he has done before he dies?

CONNECTIONS: Susan Sarandon won an Oscar for this performance. The director-screenwriter, Tim Robbins, is her longtime companion.
ACTIVITIES: Read the book, by Sister Helen Prejean.

Julia

1977, 118 min, PG, high school age
Dir: Fred Zinnemann. Jane Fonda, Vanessa Redgrave, Jason Robards, Maximilian Schell
PLOT: Lillian and Julia are close friends as young girls, spending a lot of time together and sharing their dreams. When they grow up, Lillian (Jane Fonda) becomes a playwright with the help of her lover, writer Dashiell Hammett (Jason Robards).

Julia (Vanessa Redgrave), always deeply concerned with justice and improving conditions for those less fortunate, becomes involved with the resistance movement in pre-WWII Europe. They see each other again when Lillian visits Julia in a Viennese hospital after she is injured in a student uprising. Julia mysteriously disappears from the hospital, and Lillian waits for a message. Ultimately, a message comes through a man named Johann (Maximilian Schell), who asks Lillian to help Julia by bringing American currency into Germany to be used to rescue victims of the Nazis. Lillian is terrified, but brings the money to Julia. Their meeting in a small German cafe is brief and guarded, but meaningful. Lillian is concerned about Julia's health (she lost a leg in the Viennese hospital and looks worn down), but Julia still glows with passion, with affection for Lillian, and with tenderness for her child, named Lily, living in France for safety. Later, after Julia is killed, Lillian tries to find Lily but is unable to overcome obstacles from bureaucrats and Julia's own family.

DISCUSSION: Families will want to discuss the contrast between Julia's deep and unswerving commitment to fighting the Nazis, Lillian's struggles to make a contribution despite her fears, and the blasé indifference of many of the other characters. They may also want to compare the impact of Lillian's and Julia's ways of fighting the Nazis. Julia becomes deeply and personally involved, at the greatest possible personal risk.

Although it is not covered in the movie, in reality Lillian Hellman, perhaps influenced by Julia, made a contribution by writing an influential play (later a movie), *Watch on the Rhine*, one of the first strong public anti-Nazi statements.

PROFANITY: Mild.

NUDITY/SEXUAL REFERENCES: Brief reference to brother-sister incest; a character suggests that Lillian and Julia had a lesbian relationship; an unmarried couple lives together.

ALCOHOL/DRUG ABUSE: A lot of drinking and smoking.

VIOLENCE/SCARINESS: Tension; characters in peril; character injured and later killed (off-screen).

TOLERANCE/DIVERSITY ISSUES: The two central characters are independent, strong, capable women, committed to their work. Hammett, a successful writer, is very supportive of Lillian's efforts to write a play.

QUESTIONS FOR FAMILIES:

- How are Julia and Lillian alike? How are they different?

- How did Julia and her family influence one another?

- How was Dashiell Hammett most helpful to Lillian?

- What was Julia's most important influence on Lillian?

CONNECTIONS: The movie is based on a story in *Pentimento*, a memoir by Lillian Hellman, author of **The Children's Hour** and **The Little Foxes**. The book has been criticized as self-serving and inaccurate, and that debate itself became the subject of a play by Nora Ephron called *Imaginary Friends*.

Jason Robards portrays Hellman's longtime lover, Dashiell Hammett, author of **The Maltese Falcon** and **The Thin Man**. Hammett wrote the screenplay for

Watch on the Rhine, which starred Paul Lukas and Bette Davis as a German man and his American wife who bring the message of early Nazi atrocities to America.

Redgrave and Robards won Oscars for **Julia**, as did screenwriter Alvin Sargent. Meryl Streep makes her movie debut with a brief appearance in the bar scene. Zinnemann also directed **High Noon** and **A Man for All Seasons**.

Mister Roberts

1955, 123 min, NR, 12 and up
Dir: John Ford and Mervyn LeRoy. Henry Fonda, Jack Lemmon, William Powell, James Cagney
PLOT: Mister Roberts (Henry Fonda) is the second-ranking officer on a WWII supply ship, The Reluctant. He is restless, feeling he is "sailing from tedium to apathy and back again, with an occasional side trip to monotony" and wants desperately to serve in the "real war," in combat. He continually petitions for a transfer, but the despotic captain (James Cagney) refuses to approve the petition. Ensign Pulver (Jack Lemmon), the ship's morale officer, does his best to avoid work and stay out of the captain's way. Doc (William Powell) is the ship's weary doctor, philosopher, and when called for, moonshiner.

Roberts does his best to protect the crew from the petty tyrannies of the captain. They ignore a direct order from the captain to put their shirts back on in the scalding heat, and obey only when Roberts issues the order. This disrespect and lack of control makes the captain furious. He tells Roberts he will only give the crew the long-overdue shore leave they want if Roberts will stop applying for a transfer and cooperate with his orders. Roberts agrees.

The crew has a deliriously sybaritic shore leave, but when they return, they are disappointed by Roberts's new attitude and lose their respect for him. It is only when they overhear the captain, furiously yelling at Roberts for throwing his beloved palm tree overboard that they understand what he has done for them. "They forge not only another request for a transfer, but also the captain's approval, and the transfer order comes in.

Pulver gets Roberts's job. The captain gets two new palm trees. Pulver and Doc find out Roberts has been killed in action. Doc gives Roberts's last letter to the crew, and Pulver goes to confront the captain.

DISCUSSION: Roberts's last letter says, "I've discovered, Doc, the unseen enemy of this war is the boredom that eventually becomes a faith and, therefore, a terrible sort of suicide, and I know all the ones who refuse to surrender to it are the strongest of all." That is true in peacetime as in war, and in a way parallels the exchange between Drummond and Brady in Inherit the Wind: "Do you ever think about what you do think about?" The energy it takes to fight inertia in thinking and acting is one of the crucial messages of this film. Doc thinks. Pulver plans. He is almost a comic variation on Hamlet as he brags about his elaborate schemes. Roberts acts. It isn't until he leaves that he learns he had been active all along, even in combat. His combat was fighting the surrender he writes about.

Another important aspect of the movie is the issue of obeying orders and following rules. Notice the way that Pulver, Doc, and Roberts use small rebellions to feel more independent and alive. They are all loyal to the war effort, to each other, and to the men, but not always loyal to the system (with the captain as its representative). This willingness to be subversive is another way of fighting mental and emotional inertia.

It is ironic the very qualities that make Roberts want to leave, make him indispensable to the captain. Those qualities are his willingness to approach all tasks, even the delivery of toilet paper and toothpaste, with energy and integrity. Pulver, on the other hand, just wants the easiest and most risk-free life he can maneuver for himself, at least until Roberts is killed, and he understands there are greater risks than the risk of challenging the captain. Maybe, too, trying to live up to Roberts's example is a way to keep his friend alive and close.

PROFANITY: Mild.
NUDITY/SEXUAL REFERENCES: Much conversation about peering with a telescope into the nurses' quarters; some talk about getting nurses to go out on dates, etc.
ALCOHOL/DRUG ABUSE: Drinking (including making their own liquor).
VIOLENCE/SCARINESS: Tension rather than scariness; off-screen death of major character in battle.
TOLERANCE/DIVERSITY ISSUES: Women treated as sex objects.
QUESTIONS FOR FAMILIES:

- Why did the captain resent Roberts so much?

- Why did Roberts throw the palm tree overboard?

- How is this movie like **The Caine Mutiny** and how is it different?

CONNECTIONS: Co-playwright Thomas Heggen was one of two successful young authors whose work was influenced by service in WWII, and who died young. Their lives were explored in *Ross and Tom: Two American Tragedies*, by

John Leggett. There is a pallid sequel (with a couple of nice moments) called *Ensign Pulver*, starring Robert Walker, Jr. and Burl Ives.

Mutiny on the Bounty

1935, 131 min, NR, b&w, 8 and up
Dir: Frank Lloyd. Clark Gable, Charles Laughton, Franchot Tone
PLOT: This movie, based on a true story, begins in 1787, when the British ship The Bounty sets sail from Portsmouth to Tahiti under the leadership of Captain Bligh (Charles Laughton) and First Mate Fletcher Christian (Clark Gable). Bligh is demanding to the point of cruelty, imposing harsh punishment for minor infractions of the rules. He says of the crew, "They respect one law—fear." Bligh also profits at the expense of the men, sending some of the provisions of cheese to his home before sailing and reporting it as stolen by the men. The crew has a blissful sojourn in Tahiti. Christian and some of the other sailors have romances with the native women.

Back at sea, Bligh becomes even more brutally capricious. He orders sick men to stay on duty and has others whipped for drinking water. He orders the ship's doctor to the deck to witness a flogging, even though he is very ill. When the doctor dies from the effort, Christian takes over the command, announcing he is in charge of the ship. He will not permit the men to harm Bligh, but puts him, with three sailors loyal to him, in a boat with food, water, a sextant, and some tools. When Bligh says, "You're taking my ship?" Christian replies, "The King's ship, and you're not fit to command." Bligh warns that he will get back to England, and that Christian will "hang from the highest yardarm in the British fleet."

Christian takes the ship back to Tahiti. After forty-nine days, Bligh's boat arrives in the Dutch East Indies, and he gets a ship to go after the mutineers. By this time, the mutineers have settled on Pitcairn Island; Bligh captures them and takes them back to England for a court-martial. Although they present evidence of his brutality, the crew is sentenced to death, even Roger Byam, who had remained loyal to Bligh (and is later pardoned by the king). Bligh is exonerated by the tribunal, but is an outcast among his peers.
DISCUSSION: The question of loyalty is especially compelling in the context of the armed services, with its clearly established hierarchy. It is possibly most compelling in a naval context because sailors live in isolated communities when they are at sea. Christian and the others are literally sworn to be loyal and obedient to their superiors.

Christian has nowhere to go to report his concerns about Bligh, nowhere to seek advice or ask for a transfer, no way to avoid the constant confrontation between Bligh and the men, between what he is asked to do and what he feels is right. We see every step he is asked to take, every unjust action he must tolerate, beginning with Bligh's theft of the cheese. Christian will countenance this violation because of his larger duty of obedience, because Bligh may be a bad man but he is an effective captain, and possibly because Christian wants to keep his job. At a certain point, he must draw the line, even at the risk of his own life and the lives of the crew. That risk is outweighed by what he perceives as a greater risk from Bligh's treatment.

Christian's loyalty to the men becomes more powerful than his loyalty to Bligh. We see this same phenomenon in **The Adventures of Robin Hood** and in other dramas of mutiny or near-mutiny, as in **Mister Roberts** and **The Caine Mutiny**.

Christian draws yet another line in his treatment of Bligh, preventing another crew member from shooting him and ensuring that Bligh has a chance of piloting his boat to shore (which he in fact did, and which is still regarded as an extraordinary feat of seamanship).

PROFANITY: None.
NUDITY/SEXUAL REFERENCES: None.
ALCOHOL/DRUG ABUSE: Some drinking.
VIOLENCE/SCARINESS: Abuse of sailors; death of ship's doctor.
TOLERANCE/DIVERSITY ISSUES: Sailors have romances with native women.
QUESTIONS FOR FAMILIES:

- Compare this movie to **The Caine Mutiny**. How are the situations alike and how are they different?

- What should an officer do about a superior officer who is a bad man but an effective leader?

- Why did Christian take The Bounty back to Tahiti instead of England? What does that tell you about the motive for the mutiny? Were you surprised by the outcome of the trial? Why is obedience and order so especially important onboard a ship?

CONNECTIONS: The facts of this famous case are still in dispute. Bligh made a persuasive case in his memoirs that the real reason for the mutiny was that the crew "has assured themselves of a happier life among the Tahitians than they could possibly have in England, which, joined to some female connections, has most likely been the leading cause of the whole business." Bligh went on to a distinguished career (despite another mutiny during his service as the governor of New South Wales) and achieved the rank of vice admiral.

The story has been filmed twice more: in 1962, with Marlon Brando as Christian and Trevor Howard as Bligh, and in 1984, with Mel Gibson as Christian and Anthony Hopkins as Bligh (called *The Bounty*). Each has a different viewpoint on the relationship and the issues of loyalty, based on the perspective of the writer and director and the approach of the actors, and it is fascinating to compare them. Gable's Christian is a vigorous man of action who cannot contain himself any longer; Brando's version is introspective, almost like Hamlet, until he finally must act; Gibson's is more of an everyman, acting out of some deeply felt notion of decency.

Another mutiny drama, *Crimson Tide* (rated R for language), made in 1995, is based more on policy issues, though the dispute is strongly rooted in principle on both sides. When a message to fire a missile on Russia is followed by a garbled message that may have rescinded the order, Denzel Washington, representing the young, idealistic "new Navy," wants to wait, while Gene Hackman, representing the traditional, by-the-book "old Navy," wants to fire. In a somewhat unsatisfying but undeniably correct conclusion, they are told they were both right and both wrong.

To Have and Have Not

1944, 100 min, NR, b&w, 10 and up
Dir: Howard Hawks. Humphrey Bogart, Lauren Bacall, Walter Brennan
PLOT: Harry (Humphrey Bogart) and his drink-addled friend, Eddie (Walter Brennan), make a living taking tourists out in their fishing boat in Martinique, during the early days of World War II. They meet "Slim" (Lauren Bacall), a beautiful woman whose insolent, tough demeanor does not conceal her sense of honor. Harry is asked by his friend Gerard to take his boat out to pick up a leader of the underground, and Harry refuses. When asked, "What are your sympathies?" he replies, "Minding my own business." He does not want to get involved or take a risk for any cause. He agrees to do it when Slim tells him she wants to go home but does not have enough money.

Harry picks up Paul de Bursac and his wife, Helene, and gets them back to Martinique, but Paul is shot. Helene is angry with Harry at first, but is impressed with his courage and his care for her husband's wound.

The Nazis come looking for the de Bursacs and, when Harry will not tell them anything, they arrest Eddie. Harry realizes he does care about Eddie and Slim and he cannot avoid fighting the Nazis anymore. He finds a way to leave and take both of them with him, knowing that they must join the fight.

DISCUSSION: This is a classic, with crackling dialogue (including Bacall's famous lesson on whistling), an exciting story, wonderful characters, and a lot of heart. In a way, it is a variation on **Casablanca** (made two years earlier), only this time, Rick goes off with Ilsa instead of with Captain Renault (in real life, too—Bogart met the nineteen-year-old Bacall on the set of this movie, and they married soon after). Like Casablanca, it presents a cool, tough, independent hero with a fight he cannot walk away from.

Harry tries to explain his views in relativistic terms, saying, "You save France. I'll save my boat," and telling Slim, "You ought to pick on somebody to steal from who doesn't owe me money." As Slim points out, he does have "strings" attached, and ultimately he realizes he cannot limit his sense of commitment.

PROFANITY: None.
NUDITY/SEXUAL REFERENCES: Very mild.
ALCOHOL/DRUG ABUSE: Eddie is an alcoholic (and in today's terms, Harry and Slim are enablers); much action takes place in a bar.
VIOLENCE/SCARINESS: Suspense; some fighting and gunplay.
TOLERANCE/DIVERSITY ISSUES: Reference to "colored man" in song.
QUESTIONS FOR FAMILIES:

• Why do you think Harry is friends with Eddie?

• What does it tell us that Slim is the only one who answers Eddie's question about the dead bee "correctly"?

• Why does Harry tell Slim to walk around him? How does she bring that up later to show him he was wrong?

• What changes Harry's mind? Paul says that for Harry "the word 'failure' does not even exist." Is that right? What evidence in the movie supports your answer?

CONNECTIONS: Cricket is played by composer Hoagy Carmichael, whose songs include the Oscar-winner "In the Cool, Cool, Cool of the Evening." Listen to some of his music, possibly Willie Nelson's recording of "Stardust" (or any other recording—it is possibly the most recorded song of all time) and Ray Charles's "Georgia on My Mind." Carmichael also appears in **The Best Years of Our Lives**.

Howard Hawks said this movie was the result of his boast to Ernest Hemingway he could make a movie from Hemingway's "worst" novel. Not much in the movie comes from the novel. Co-scriptwriters Jules Furthman and William Faulkner wrote what today would be called a "back story" for the characters in the novel, about what happened to the characters leading them to the place where the book begins. According to Pauline Kael, "the novel's ending was used to polish off John Huston's film version of Maxwell Anderson's dreary play *Key Largo*; the novel's plot was used for another movie, *The Breaking Point*, directed by Michael Curtiz, in 1950; and the short story *One Trip Across*, which Hemingway had expanded into To Have and Have Not, was used for an Audie Murphy movie, *The Gun Runners*, directed by Don Siegel, in 1958."

Bacall's debut in this movie made her an instant star, despite the fact that her famous sultry "look" (looking up while holding her head down) was just her attempt to control her shaking from nervousness. Bogart and Bacall made three more movies together, *The Big Sleep, Key Largo*, and *Dark Passage*.

ACTIVITIES: Find Martinique on a map and read about the Vichy and the French resistance. Very thoughtful teenagers who want to know more should see *The Sorrow and the Pity*, about Nazi-occupied France.

SEE ALSO:

Breaking Away Four friends just out of high school provide support for each other.

Captain Blood Blood, a doctor, risks losing his life by treating a wounded rebel. He explains his loyalty is to his fellow man, not to the king.

Spartacus The leader of a slave rebellion demonstrates deep loyalty to fellow slaves, and they give their lives to protect him.

Stand by Me An author reminisces about the loyalty of his childhood friends.

11

EDUCATION

*"The library is the temple of learning, and
learning has liberated more people than all the wars in history."*
CARL ROWAN

After the novelty wears off, just about the time that homework begins to seem tedious, young students start to wonder what the point is of going to school, and how anything having to do with x's and y's or spelling or history can ever have any relevance to their lives, which they confidently assume will consist of work on computers with calculators and spellcheckers and CD-ROM reference materials. That is where these movies come in, because they do a good job of illustrating the transformation of both mind and spirit that comes from learning.

Sometimes the hero or heroine is driven by curiosity and a longing for something more. In other cases it takes a teacher to motivate the quest by giving a student a glimpse of a wider world or just by showing him he can learn. Several "All work and no play makes Jack a dull boy" movies provide a delightful counterpoint, with characters who spend too much time on serious things finding out that laughter and music are just as important.

Born Yesterday

1950, 103 min, NR, b&w, 10 and up
Dir: George Cukor. Judy Holliday, Broderick Crawford, William Holden
PLOT: Harry Brock (Broderick Crawford), a loud, vulgar, thuggish man, has made a fortune in "junk" and hopes to make a bigger one if he can get some favorable legislation passed. So he comes to Washington with his fulltime lawyer, Jim Devery (Howard St. John), a once-great legal mind now dissipated through alcohol and small corruptions; his cousin Eddie, a glorified gofer; and his girlfriend, Billie Dawn (Judy Holliday), a bored ex-showgirl.

When they meet Norval Hedges, the senator they have paid off to help them, Billie's lack of sophistication is an embarrassment, so Harry hires Paul Verrall (William Holden), a local reporter, to "educate" her. Paul agrees because he hopes to find out enough to expose Harry and because he likes Billie, who may not be sophisticated but who is refreshingly direct. She agrees, even though she suspects it may be smarter not to be smart, because she has "a yen" for Paul.

Billie surprises Paul and herself (and Harry) by becoming genuinely interested in what she is learning. She develops a great deal of respect for the democratic ideal and a growing horror at the abuse of that ideal by Harry and Senator Hedges. She also develops so much healthy self-respect she can no longer continue as Harry's companion. She and Paul fall in love. Harry is hurt and jealous. To make things more complicated, on paper she controls much of his company due to a tax and liability dodge concocted to protect Harry when it was assumed Billie would always sign whatever was put in front of her. She agrees to sign the company back to him, a little at a time, if he will agree to behave himself in the future, and she and Paul go off together.

DISCUSSION: This is a delightful comedy that includes real messages, not just about democracy and integrity, but about the transformational aspect of learning, the importance of believing in yourself and being with people who believe in you.

At some level, Billie has been in denial. She was not proud of her life and she knew she was not living up to the ideals her father had raised her to have. She knew if she ever thought about it, she could not stay. Yet she did stay, because she thought she knew what she wanted. Like Drummond cross-examining Brady in **Inherit the Wind**, Paul asks Billie to "think about what [she] thinks about," to question her assumptions. True to the spirit of what he is teaching her, he listens thoughtfully when she questions his assumptions and he realizes that he has been writing too ponderously and pretentiously. He helps her find the power within herself; like Alice in Wonderland, she defeats the enemy by simply calling him by name.

PROFANITY: None.
NUDITY/SEXUAL REFERENCES: Harry and Billie live together without being married (considered shocking when the movie was made); oblique references, the most explicit of which is "If he don't come across, I don't come across."
ALCOHOL/DRUG ABUSE: Devery has a drinking problem that is either the reason for his downfall or an attempt to forget it or both.
VIOLENCE/SCARINESS: Harry slaps Billie.

TOLERANCE/DIVERSITY ISSUES: Billie is not expected by Harry or by herself to be able to think for herself.

QUESTIONS FOR FAMILIES:

• Compare this story to **My Fair Lady,** in which a teacher and a student learn a great deal from each other. Or is it more like *Sleeping Beauty,* with the "princess" awakened by ideas instead of by a kiss?

• Why do people like Devery and Hedges behave the way they do?

• Why is Harry such a bully?

CONNECTIONS: Mature high school students might enjoy *Never on Sunday,* a variation of this story involving a Greek lady of the evening and a naive scholar. In that case, he learns more from her than she learns from him.

Born Yesterday was remade in 1993 with Melanie Griffith, Don Johnson, and John Goodman. It is not nearly as good, but it is watchable and provides an interesting and perceptive update on some aspects of the original. Its best scene has Paul teaching Billie a set of all-purpose answers to any question that can be asked at a Washington cocktail party. In another scene, Billie teaches a group of high-powered Washingtonians a song celebrating the Amendments to the Constitution, set to the tune of "The Twelve Days of Christmas," not a bad mnemonic!

Judy Holliday, who won an Oscar for this performance, can also be seen in **Bells are Ringing, The Solid Gold Cadillac, Adam's Rib,** and **It Should Happen to You.**

ACTIVITIES: Try reading some of the books that Paul assigns to Billie and talking about how the ideas she read about changed her mind about her own life and the way she saw the people around her. Every family should visit Washington to see the Capitol Building, the Library of Congress, the Smithsonian, and the White House.

The Corn Is Green

1945, 114 min, NR, b&w, 10 and up Dir: Irving Rapper. Bette Davis, John Dall
PLOT: Miss Moffat (Bette Davis), an educated and very independent woman, arrives in a small Welsh mining village in 1895 to live in a house she inherited and start a school for the miners' children. She is told, "Down here, they're only children until they're twelve. Then they are sent away to the mine and are old men in a week."

None of the children can read or write, and few know any English at all. She persuades Miss Ronberry (Mildred Dunnock) and Mr. Jones (Rhys Williams) to help her, but the local landowner, called "the Squire" (Nigel Bruce), and the owners of the mine are opposed and do everything they can to stop her. She is about to give up when she sees an essay by Morgan Evans (John Dall), a young mine worker, that shows a real gift. She tells him he is "clever," which makes him "want to get more clever."

They work together for two years, but she does not realize he is becoming resentful and impatient. His friends make fun of him for learning and call him the schoolmistress's dog. He quits. Later, when Mr. Jones persuades him to come back, Miss Moffat prepares him for Oxford and even uses "soft soap and curtsying" to persuade the Squire to recommend him. He wins a scholarship. Bessie, the dishonest and slatternly daughter of Miss Moffat's housekeeper, is pregnant with Morgan's child. Miss Moffat adopts the child so that Morgan will be able to go to Oxford. She tells him his duty is to the world. Then she tells herself, "You mustn't be clumsy this time," and resolves to be more sensitive in raising Morgan's child than she was with him.

DISCUSSION: This movie is an adaptation of a play by Emlyn Williams, who was actually saved from the coal mines by an understanding teacher. It has a lot of parallels to **My Fair Lady** and **Born Yesterday**, which also deal with intense teacher-student relationships that transform the lives of both. Like Billie Dawn and Eliza Doolittle, Morgan is excited and disturbed by the way learning changes him; he panics at the thought of losing everything familiar to him (including ignorance), and he gets angry and impatient. Eliza would understand Morgan's telling Miss Moffat, "I don't want to be thankful to no strange woman." Like Henry Higgins, Miss Moffat does not want thanks.

Miss Moffat is different because of her reason for teaching Morgan. She responds to his spirit and his potential in that first essay. Perhaps because she responds so strongly, she stays very distant from him, admitting she knows every part of his brain, but does not know him at all. She cares for him deeply. The contrast between her spirited response to the Squire when he prevents her from using the barn for a school and her "soft soap and curtsying" to get him to help Morgan shows how far she is willing to go.

Ultimately, she takes on Morgan's child, knowing it means she will never see him again, because both of them believe the child will be better off if the break is permanent.

Also worth discussing: the consequences of careless sexual involvement, the idea that there may be something more important to some women than getting married (especially in that era, when married women had so little say over what happened to them), and Bessie's statement that she only had sex with Morgan to spite Miss Moffat.

PROFANITY: None.
NUDITY/SEXUAL REFERENCES: Bessie becomes pregnant out of wedlock with Morgan's child.
ALCOHOL/DRUG ABUSE: Morgan drinks, and says the liquor gave him the courage to speak.
VIOLENCE/SCARINESS: None.
TOLERANCE/DIVERSITY ISSUES: Class issues.
QUESTIONS FOR FAMILIES:

• Why didn't the Squire want the Welsh children to learn?

• Why did the miners make Morgan feel bad about learning?

• Why did telling Morgan he was clever make him want to learn more? Why did Bessie's telling him he was clever have a different effect?

• What did Miss Moffat mean by "soft soap and curtsying" and how did she use them? How did she feel about using them?

• Why was Morgan so angry about having to be grateful?

CONNECTIONS: The real-life Morgan Evans, Emlyn Williams, became a playwright and actor and can be seen in **Major Barbara** as Snobby Price. The Squire is played by Nigel Bruce, best known as Dr. Watson in the American-made series of Sherlock Holmes' movies. Bessie's mother belongs to a group like the one Sister Sarah belongs to in **Guys and Dolls**, or Major Barbara does in the film of the same name.
ACTIVITIES: A good book about this part of the world is *On the Black Hills*, by Bruce Chatwin, and there are some outstanding books about the history of coal miners in many different parts of the world.

EDUCATING RITA

1983, 110 min, PG 13, mature high age
Dir: Lewis Gilbert. Michael Caine, Julie Walters
An uneducated girl from the lower class comes to see a burned-out professor, who has forgotten what the books he teaches ever meant to him, to ask him to help

her pass the exams she needs to get into college. Her unpretentious joy in what she reads and her undiluted awe of him as the caretaker of wisdom make him excited about teaching. He fears, though, she will lose her honest, unaffected, very direct responses to literature. He also knows as she becomes better educated she will discover his limitations. Michael Caine and Julie Walters (re-creating the role she originated on the stage) are both outstanding. NOTE: Strong language and a suicide attempt.

MALCOLM X

1992, 194 min, PG-13, high school age
Dir: Spike Lee. Denzel Washington, Angela Bassett, Al Freeman, Jr.
As a child, Malcolm Little (Denzel Washington) saw his home burned and his minister father killed by racists. He becomes a street hustler and is sent to prison for theft. A fellow prisoner teaches him about Elijah Muhammad, but also about self-respect and the exhilaration and power that come from learning. He sheds his last name, the symbol of slave owners, becoming Malcolm X. When he is released from prison, he joins Elijah Muhammad as a Black Muslim minister.

Malcolm X becomes a brilliant and charismatic leader. He attracts a lot of support and a lot of controversy. Outspoken and angry, he insists that whites are responsible for the evil imposed on American blacks, and they cannot be part of any solution. He encourages his followers to become independent and self-sufficient. When asked for a comment on President Kennedy's assassination, he can only say obliquely that the "chickens have come home to roost." Significantly, he continues to learn and grow. His wife, Betty, nourishes his tender side. He makes a pilgrimage to Mecca and learns people of all races can share a spiritual bond. He discovers his hero, Elijah Muhammad, has not always held himself to the standard he preaches. Shortly after he confronts Elijah Muhammad, Malcolm X is assassinated.

This is a thoughtful, complex, brilliant movie, with a galvanizing performance by Denzel Washington. He makes the intellectual passion and the essential integrity of Malcolm X heartbreakingly touching. There is no better illustration of the transformative power of learning. It changes not just the way he sees the world, but the way he sees himself.

SEE ALSO:
Stand and Deliver A group of inner-city students learns calculus and self-respect from an inspiring teacher

To Sir With Love A group of lower-class students learn to respect themselves and each other from an inspiring teacher.

12

PEACE (AND WAR)

"You may not be interested in war, but war is interested in you."
LEON TROTSKY

In movies, as in life, we see very mixed signals about the role of violence. Almost everyone would agree violence is not a good way to resolve conflicts. Yet the powerful pull of violence continues to make violent movies among the most popular and lucrative. It is astonishing how often a movie features a hero who opposes violence but who must ultimately use it.

These resolutions are undeniably satisfying. We have the best of both worlds: We get to identify with a hero who is on the right side, and we get to see him hit or shoot someone who "deserves it." In children's films like *Ferdinand the Bull* and *The Reluctant Dragon*, we see (anthropomorphic) heroes who successfully avoid violence. In films for older kids and adults, we rarely see anyone walk away from the big fight, especially a hero.

Some thoughtful movies show us the painful distance between those who are capable of and willing to engage in violence and those they must protect. Others show us the consequences of a life of violence or that even the best intentions can have tragic consequences when violence erupts.

Movies do a less ambiguous job of opposing violence on the largest scale and a number of movies point out the insanity of war, some by taking us into battle. Others demonstrate the irony of war by setting the story in medical units that repair the ravages of war and send the men back into battle. Movies like **The Day the Earth Stood Still** and **20,000 Leagues Under the Sea** raise the question of the threat or use of violence to prevent greater violence through war. **War Games** reminds us "the only way to win is not to play," and **Gulliver's Travels** reminds us how trivial issues that incite violence often are. Ask kids to compare movies made during WWII with those made after it was over to see how the perspective shifts and becomes more complex. The two versions of **Henry V**, one made in wartime and one in peacetime, provide fascinating contrasts.

The use of violence, like other moral choices, is depicted in many forms. In **High Noon**, Will Kane, having made a commitment to his new Quaker bride, at first tries to run away from the threat of violence. His sense of honor and his commitment to the community (far greater, it turns out, than theirs to him), require him to turn around. In **On the Waterfront**, Terry's triumph is not in hitting anyone (he is grossly outnumbered); it is in surviving being hit. His determination and resilience are an inspiration to the dockworkers.

These films provide an opportunity to get past the comic book concepts of violence promoted by *Grand Theft Auto*, *The Matrix*, and *X-Men*, and to begin to talk about when, if ever, violence is justified, and what the consequences are.

The Day the Earth Stood Still

1951, 93 min, NR, b&w, 8 and up
Dir: Robert Wise. Michael Rennie, Patricia Neal, Sam Jaffe
PLOT: A spaceship lands in Washington, D.C., near the Washington Monument. Surrounded by army troops, a door opens, and Klaatu steps out, looking like an elegant human male. A nervous soldier shoots at Klaatu, and his robotlike companion, Gort, shoots back.

Klaatu is taken to a hospital but escapes and finds a place to stay in a boardinghouse run by widow Helen Benson (Patricia Neal). He gets to know Helen and her son, Bobby, and he and Bobby go to visit a distinguished scientist (Sam Jaffe) so Klaatu can deliver his message about the risk the earth faces from its aggressive development of weapons, jeopardizing not just the planet but the entire solar system and the universe.

Klaatu wants to find a peaceful way to deliver his message, so he shuts down all power sources on the planet, except for hospitals and other essential systems. Worried he will be attacked again, Klaatu tells Helen the secret code to prevent Gort from attacking to protect him from harm: "Klaatu berrada nikto." Klaatu is shot and killed, and Helen delivers the message just in time. Gort brings Klaatu back to the spaceship and revives him. Klaatu speaks to the people, telling the assembled scientists they must ensure peace, and that Gort and his fellow robots will be on guard to destroy the earth if they cannot find a way.
DISCUSSION: Although this is very much a movie of the Cold War era, the "duck and cover" years when children practiced air raid drills in schools, its themes are eternal, especially for children. In addition to the themes of nonviolent conflict resolution (possibly easier for today's children to discuss in the context of this 1951 movie), there is the larger theme of making friends with those who may appear at first to be different.

PROFANITY: None.
NUDITY/SEXUAL REFERENCES: None.
ALCOHOL/DRUG ABUSE: None.
VIOLENCE/SCARINESS: Some sci-fi shooting; Klaatu gets hurt.
TOLERANCE/DIVERSITY ISSUES: A theme of the movie.
QUESTIONS FOR FAMILIES:

- Why did some people want to kill Klaatu? Why did some want to try to talk to him instead?

- This movie was made only six years after the first atomic bombs were used to end WWII. Why is it important to know this to understand the movie? What is different now? What is the same?

- How does this compare to other movies about the importance of stopping wars, and how does it compare to other movies about visitors from other planets?

- If you could meet Klaatu, what would you say?

CONNECTIONS: A more obscure movie with a similar theme is *The Next Voice You Hear*, a 1950 film directed by William Wellman. This time it is God who tells everyone on Earth (over the radio), including costar Nancy Reagan, that it is time to stop all war forever.

Destry Rides Again

1939, 94 min, NR, b&w, 8 and up
Dir. George Marshall. Jimmy Stewart, Marlene Dietrich, Brian Donlevy, Charles Winninger
PLOT: Bottleneck is a rough Western town. Most of the action takes place in the Last Chance Saloon, presided over by hostess-showgirl Frenchy (Marlene Dietrich) and town boss Kent (Brian Donlevy). As the movie opens, Kent is in a poker game with his cronies and a blissful sucker named Claggett, crowing over his good luck. Frenchy comes in, encourages him to bet everything he has and, when he has put the deed to his ranch on the table, spills coffee on him, allowing for a switch of the cards. Kent wins and now has all the land he needs to impose a fee on cattle driven through that part of the country.

Claggett asks Sheriff Keogh for help. Keogh goes to Kent and is killed. Kent announces that Keogh has been called out of town permanently. He says Judge

Slade, the mayor (Samuel S. Hinds), will appoint a new sheriff. Slade appoints the town drunk, Washington "Wash" Dimsdale (Charles Winninger). Wash, once deputy to the famous Sheriff Tom Destry, swears he will give up drinking for the job. He will also bring Tom Destry, Jr., to town to help him.

Destry (Jimmy Stewart) arrives by stagecoach. In contrast to tough fellow passenger Jack Tyndall, he appears to be meek, even foolish. Wash, furious and humiliated, tells Destry to leave. Destry tells Wash that his famous father's guns didn't protect him because he was shot in the back. Destry doesn't think that is the way to solve the town's troubles. "You shoot it out with 'em and for some reason or other—I don't know why—they look like heroes. But you put 'em behind bars and they look little and cheap, the way they oughta' look." Wash swears him in.

Destry stops some marauders by showing his accuracy with a gun. When Claggett and his family are barricaded on their ranch in a shoot-out with Kent, Destry insists they leave. Kent has the deed and the legal right to the ranch. Destry promises he will get their ranch back if they give him time. Destry knows he has to prove that Kent killed Keogh. He talks to Frenchy, who lets it slip that Keogh was "taken care of."

With the help of Boris (Mischa Auer), a Russian immigrant called "Callahan" by everyone because he married a widow by that name, Destry finds Keogh's body and arrests Kent henchman Bugs Watson. Kent thinks he has nothing to fear, with the corrupt mayor acting as town magistrate, but Destry has arranged for a federal judge to hear the case. When Kent hears that, he decides to kill Wash and Destry. Frenchy sends for Destry, to protect him, but when he hears shots, he runs to find Wash, who is dying. Destry comforts Wash, saying that like his father, Wash was shot in the back. "They didn't dare face him, either." Wash dies peacefully.

Destry straps on his father's guns. With Tyndall's help, he goes to the saloon. Frenchy has brought the women of the town in to stop the fight. She sees Kent taking aim at Destry, tries to warn him, then blocks the bullet herself, wipes off her lipstick for a kiss, then dies in his arms. Destry shoots Kent. As the movie ends, the town is peaceful (except for the battling Callahans). Destry is the idol of the young Claggett boy and much admired by Tyndall's sister as well.

DISCUSSION: Like Shenandoah (also starring Stewart), High Noon, and Friendly Persuasion, this movie gives us a hero opposed to fighting who reaches a point where no alternative is possible. It provides a good opportunity for a discussion of how we decide on methods of conflict resolution, and what we do when they fail. It is also a good starting point for a discussion of how people change when they get a glimpse of what they might be. Destry sees what Frenchy might be, what she is under her "mask," telling her, "I'll bet you've got a lovely face under all that paint. Why don't you wipe it off someday and have a good look—figure out how you can live up to it." He reminds her she can be however she wishes, whenever she decides to. He also appreciates Wash and gives Boris a role that enables him to develop enough self-respect to insist he be called by his own name.

Older children who enjoy a more literary approach to movies might appreciate the exceptionally tight narrative of this story, the way each incident not only tells you something about the characters (and tells the characters about each other) but also moves the story along.

PROFANITY: None.
NUDITY/SEXUAL REFERENCES: None.
ALCOHOLDRUG ABUSE: A lot of drinking in the bar; "manliness" measured by what a man drinks; Wash is the town drunk who reforms when he becomes sheriff.
VIOLENCE/SCARINESS: Gunfights, fistfights; two lead characters killed.
TOLERANCE/DIVERSITY ISSUES: Clara (played by Lillian Yarbo) is portrayed as a stereotyped movie black maid. Interestingly, as often happens with African-American characters in movies of this era, her comments are always accurate, though the other characters pay no attention to her. The word "nigger" is used in a song sung by an extra in the final scene.
QUESTIONS FOR FAMILIES:

- Why does Destry like to pretend the stories he tells are from a friend?

- Why do the people think that Destry is not strong or tough at first? Was that a good basis for that conclusion? What changes their minds?

- Destry is determined not to use his guns "the old way" but to use the law "the new way." Does he fail? Why or why not?

- How can you tell when you have no alternative but to use force? What did Destry say to Frenchy that made her want to be different?

CONNECTIONS: This movie was filmed once before with Tom Mix and remade as *Destry* with WWII war hero Audie Murphy and again as *Frenchie* with Shelley Winters. Jimmy Stewart and Samuel S. Hinds (a real-life lawyer here playing a judge) also appeared together in *It's a Wonderful Life* as George Bailey and his father.

ACTIVITIES: Look up the definition of "bottleneck" in a dictionary. Look at a bottle to discover how that term was derived. Why was that a good name for the town in this movie?

Dr. Strangelove or: How I Learned to Stop Worrying and Love the Bomb

1964, 93 min, b&w, NR, high schoolers
Dir: Stanley Kubrick. Peter Sellers, George C. Scott, Sterling Hayden
PLOT: In this blackest of black comedies, a Duck Soup for the Cold War era, a rogue American general named Jack D. Ripper (Sterling Hayden) goes mad and sends planes to drop nuclear bombs on the Soviet Union. He cuts off all communication to the base, and only he knows the three-letter code to cancel the attack.

The mild-mannered president of the United States (Peter Sellers) and Captain Mandrake, a highly civilized British officer (Sellers again), are no match for the bloodthirsty General Buck Turgidson (George C. Scott) and the demented Dr. Strangelove (Sellers again!), a former Nazi expert on nuclear weapons whose prosthetic arm gets out of control, giving a "Heil, Hitler" salute and even trying to choke him. Turgidson's view is that America should take advantage of the accidental initiation of war to fight to the finish and establish American supremacy. Mandrake is unable to trick Ripper into revealing the code, but after Ripper commits suicide, following his explanation that fluoridation is a Communist plot, Mandrake figures it out. He is almost prevented from revealing it, however, when the suspicious Colonel "Bat" Guano (Keenan Wynn) arrives in search of Ripper, and then when it turns out that no one has change for the pay phone. At the last minute, the correct code is sent, but an enterprising American pilot insists on carrying out the mission. The Americans spend their last moments designing a post-nuclear world, where the few remaining people live in mine shafts, with ten women (selected for their fertility and appeal) for every man. The Soviet ambassador thinks this is an outstanding idea, but Turgidson still worries that the Soviets might have more mine shafts than the Americans.

DISCUSSION: Teens who view this movie may need some background to understand the sense of helpless peril of the Cold War years. More importantly, they may need some preparation to understand the nature of black comedy, and some may find it very disturbing, particularly the unconventional ending, in which the world is annihilated. This can be a good way to initiate discussions about the nature of war and peace (begin with Ripper's quote from Clemenceau about war's being too important to be left to the generals), and about the best ways of ensuring an enduring peace.

PROFANITY: None.
NUDITY/SEXUAL REFERENCES: Many references, mostly euphemistic, beginning with a suggestive opening shot of one plane refueling another. The imagery (and to a lesser extent, the dialogue) create a link between men's sexual impulse and their interest in war. Buck and his secretary (who is wearing a bikini) are clearly having an affair, and the men are delighted with the idea that in a post-nuclear world they will be obligated to impregnate many women.
ALCOHOL/DRUG ABUSE: Soviet leader reported to be drunk.
VIOLENCE/SCARINESS: It is a comedy about nuclear war; in addition to the mushroom clouds and reports of planes being shot down, there is an off-camera suicide.
TOLERANCE/DIVERSITY ISSUES: All the people in power are white males; women are sex objects (part of the satire).
QUESTIONS FOR FAMILIES:

- What do you think of making fun of issues like madness and nuclear destruction? Does it make you feel more or less comfortable about the possibility of nuclear war?

- If the movie were to be made today, what details would be changed? Who would the nuclear threat come from?

- Who should decide when to initiate nuclear warfare?

CONNECTIONS: The same issues are addressed in a serious dramatic context in *Fail-Safe*, released the same year. Some of the same issues of control of the war machinery are raised by **WarGames** and even by **Independence Day** (which has an explicit reference to this movie in Randy Quaid's attack on the alien spaceship). See **Thirteen Days** and *The Fog of War* for more background on this era and these issues.
ACTIVITIES: Teens should see if they can find out what the current state of nuclear disarmament is and what the current issues are.

Ferdinand the Bull

1938, 29 min, NR, 4 and up
(in Willie the Operatic Whale video) Dir: Dick Rickard

PLOT: The classic story by Munro Leaf and Robert Lawson is about the bull who did not want to fight. Even when he was very young, Ferdinand did not play with the others, butting heads. He just wanted to sit quietly and smell the flowers. When some men come looking for bulls for a bullfight, the others race around, trying to look fierce, but Ferdinand sits quietly. Unfortunately, he sits on a bee, gets stung, and charges the men, making them think he is the fiercest of all. They take him to the bullfight, but instead of fighting, he just smells the flowers thrown to the matador. The matador does everything he can think of to get Ferdinand to fight, and becomes so upset that he bursts into tears. "So they had to take Ferdinand home. And for all I know, he is sitting there still, under his cork tree, smelling the flowers. He is very happy."

NOTE: This volume of the Walt Disney Mini Classic series includes three short cartoons about being different. I strongly recommend that you skip the first one, in which a whale sings opera. Children will not be especially interested and will not get most of the jokes (for example, the whale wears clown makeup when he sings Pagliacci). Furthermore, the whale is rather blithely killed off at the end, with the narrator noting that he is still singing in heaven. Children (and indeed, grown-ups) may find it hard to draw much comfort from this, especially since the whalers who harpoon him suffer no adverse consequences or remorse.

The third cartoon, Lambert the Sheepish Lion, is a pleasant ugly duckling tale about a lion cub mistakenly delivered (by a stork) to a ewe. She and Lambert love each other, but the lambs make fun of him because he can't baaa or butt heads. One night, while the lambs are asleep, a wolf approaches the flock. Lambert is frightened at first, but the lion in him rises to the occasion and he scares the wolf away.

DISCUSSION: Ferdinand the Bull is a great movie to use to talk with children about nonviolence and about how happy Ferdinand is, even though he is different. Lambert the Sheepish Lion deals with the second issue as well. Note that in both, loving mothers appreciate their children and put no pressure on them to conform.

PROFANITY: None.
NUDITY/SEXUAL REFERENCES: None.
ALCOHOL/DRUG ABUSE: None.
VIOLENCE/SCARINESS: None. Ferdinand is about as anti-violent a story as has ever been written.
TOLERANCE/DIVERSITY ISSUES: The theme of all three cartoons is accepting those who are different.

QUESTIONS FOR FAMILIES:

- Why doesn't Ferdinand want to fight like the other bulls?

- How does he feel about being different? How can you tell?

- How does Lambert feel about being different?

- Do you ever feel different?

- Do students at your school tease people who are different? Why?

CONNECTIONS: All children should read Ferdinand the Bull. They might also enjoy other stories about outsiders, like *The Ugly Duckling*, *Rudolph the Red-Nosed Reindeer*, and *Stuart Little*.

The Ferdinand the Bull cartoon has a Disney inside-joke. The matador is none other than Walt Disney himself.

Gulliver's Travels

1939, 74 min, NR, 6 and up Dir: David Fleischer
PLOT: The most famous episode of Jonathan Swift's classic satire is the visit of shipwrecked sailor Lemuel Gulliver to Lilliput, where no one is more than six inches tall. In this animated version, Gulliver is washed ashore, discovered by Gabby, the town crier, and captured by the Lilliputians. Their king had just been celebrating the engagement of his daughter to a neighboring prince, when a dispute over which nation's song would be played at the wedding results in a broken engagement and a declaration of war. Gulliver persuades the Lilliputians he wants to be their friend. The king knows having a giant on his side will keep them safe. Three silly spies for the other king try to get rid of Gulliver, but Gulliver, realizing the prince and princess love each other, stops the fighting on both sides and brings them together, singing both songs in a duet.
DISCUSSION: Brothers Max and David Fleischer were Disney's major competition in the early days of animation. Although they did not come close to Disney's standards for visual artistry, they made some cartoons that stand up very well (including the Betty Boop, Popeye, and Koko the Clown series). This is the better of their two full-length features, released just after Disney's *Snow White*. The use of the rotoscope (to draw over footage of real actors) for Gulliver and the prince and princess makes them seem a little out of keeping with the more "cartoony" characters like Gabby, the spies, and the king, but the story is strong, and

there is some very funny slapstick as the Lilliputians use block and tackle to tie Gulliver up and transport him to the castle.

As in the book where the controversies were over heel heights on shoes and how to break an egg, the movie makes fun of trivial political disputes. Children can discuss why the Lilliputians were afraid of Gulliver, what the kings should have done about the dispute over the songs, and how Gulliver made his decision about how to resolve it.

PROFANITY: None.
NUDITY/SEXUAL REFERENCES: None.
ALCOHOL/DRUG ABUSE: None.
VIOLENCE/SCARINESS: Storm at sea; fistfights; war stopped by Gulliver.
TOLERANCE/DIVERSITY ISSUES: A theme of the story is tolerance, which in this version is represented by a war over which song will be played at the wedding of the prince and princess.
QUESTIONS FOR FAMILIES:

• Would you like to visit Lilliput? What would you do?

• Why did the two kings fight about the songs? What would you tell them to do? How did Gulliiver decide what he should do?

• This movie is only about one chapter in the real book about Gulliver. In the next part of the book, he visits a place where he is as small as the Lilliputians are to him. Which one would you like better?

CONNECTIONS: Young people who like this movie will enjoy finding out about Gulliver's other travels. A live-action 1960 version, *The 3 Worlds of Gulliver*, is very watchable and far superior to the 1977 version. In 1996, a good made-for-television miniseries version (now available on video) starred Ted Danson. Teenagers may appreciate the satire in the book by Swift.

King of Hearts

1966, 101 min, NR, high school age
Dir: Philippe De Broca. Alan Bates, Genevieve Bujold
PLOT: Retreating WWI German troops leave a bomb in a small French village, set to explode a munitions storehouse at midnight. Word is sent to the British troops by a barber-spy, who is shot by German soldiers before he can say where the bomb is hidden. The colonel of a Scottish regiment selects Charles Plumpick

(Alan Bates) to dismantle the bomb because he is fluent in French, in spite of the fact the gentle ornithologist knows nothing about explosives.

When he arrives, the town has been evacuated, and the only inhabitants are the residents of the local "lunatic asylum" and the circus animals they have freed. The inmates are happily dressing up in outlandish costumes and acting out their delusions. Plumpick is both frustrated and enchanted by them, and tries to make them understand they are in danger as they crown him their "King of Hearts." He tries to get them to leave the town, but they won't go, telling him, "It's too dangerous. You won't believe how wicked they are out there!"

German soldiers arrive to check on the bombs, but are chased away by the inmates, playing with the tanks. Scottish soldiers arrive to check on Charles, but they are scared away by the animals and strange behavior of everyone they meet. Charles falls in love with Coquelicot (Genevieve Bujold). At the last minute, he figures out the secret of the bomb and saves the town.

Charles's regiment arrives and celebrates with the inmates, whom they take to be the town's residents. The next morning, as the soldiers are leaving, the inmates grab Charles and take him away. The German troops arrive, and in the ensuing battle all of the soldiers on both sides are killed. The town's residents return, and the inmates go back to the asylum.

Charles and his pigeon are given medals, but he cannot go back to war. In the last scene he stands nude, holding a birdcage, at the gate of the asylum, waiting to be let in.

DISCUSSION: The "mad" people in this movie are those who are harmless, tolerant, happy, and generous. The "sane" people are those who fight suicidal battles, give medals to a bird, and mistake fireworks for gunfire.

The theme of outsiders (whether mentally ill, mentally or physically disabled, or from a different culture) as more astute than the rest of us is an enduring one. It has special appeal for teenagers who often feel they are outside adult society. They are reassured by the portrayal of someone else who feels that way, too. For that reason, movies like **King of Hearts**, *Harold and Maude*, and **A Thousand Clowns** are college-town perennials.

Of course, the people in this movie bear no resemblance to those with real mental illnesses. These are fantasy lunatics, more childlike than troubled, designed to create a contrast to the real madness of the war. The "madness" of the soldiers is also exaggerated to make the point. The three Scot soldiers are so eager they run off before they know their assignment. The soldiers are unable to perceive the people in the town are "lunatics," but they conclude Charles is mad.

Charles is in the middle. Repeatedly hit on the head, he is in a daze throughout the movie. Frustrated and helpless, he finally gets angry at the lunatics for making him care about them, but ultimately he joins them.

PROFANITY: None.
NUDITY/SEXUAL REFERENCES: Reference to whores, cuckold, and brothel; Coquelicot asks Charles to make love to her; madam sitting in bed with general tells him her girls will have babies to make soldiers for him; brief nudity (rear) in final scene.
ALCOHOL/DRUG ABUSE: Some drinking.
VIOLENCE/SCARINESS: Barber is shot; pigeon is shot; firing line; battle in which all of the soldiers are killed.
TOLERANCE/DIVERSITY ISSUES: The "mad" people are tolerant and do not even see the kinds of distinctions that the "sane" people are killing each other over.
QUESTIONS FOR FAMILIES:

- In this movie, the "mad" people act "sane," and the "sane" people act "mad." Can you give some examples?

- Is war always "insane" in some way?

- Will Charles stay in the lunatic asylum?

- Why is the mental hospital called an "asylum"?

- Charles says, "I don't need anyone," and Coquelicot replies, "Yes, you do." Does he? How can you tell?

CONNECTIONS: Other movies that depict the insanity of war include *Catch-22*, *M*A*S*H*, and *Oh, What a Lovely War*.

Shane

1953, 118 min, NR, 8 and up
Dir: George Stevens. Alan Ladd, Van Heflin, Jean Arthur, Jack Palance, Brandon de Wilde
PLOT: Shane is an old-fashioned Western about a battle of wills between homesteaders trying to plant crops and cattle ranchers trying to graze cattle on the open range. Shane (Alan Ladd), a reformed gunfighter trying to escape his past, rides into town and immediately gets caught up in the dispute. The homesteaders

initially mistake Shane for one of the hired guns of the Stryker family, who dominate the cattle ranchers. Shane soon bonds with a farmer named Joe (Van Heflin) and becomes a protector for the whole beleaguered community of homesteaders.

Stryker first tries to buy out the stubborn farmers but when that does not work, he tries to drive them away by force. He increases the pressure, finally bringing in a hired killer named Wilson (Jack Palance). Joe feels it is his responsibility to go to town for the final confrontation with Stryker, but Shane recognizes that this is not a job for a farmer. It is a job for a man with Shane's skills, a professional. Shane knocks Joe unconscious so that "nobody can blame him for not keeping that date," then deliberately walks into the trap set for Joe. Shane vanquishes the bad guys, then leaves town for good, acknowledging that he can't settle down: "There's no going back for me."

DISCUSSION: By today's standards, Shane seems riddled with clichés. This is the movie where the hero walks into a bar and orders "soda pop," only to be heckled by the grimy, bearded bad guys; this is the movie where the womenfolk wail, "We'd all be better off if there were no guns in this valley," while their menfolk go off to fight battles of honor; this is the movie where the homesteader gives an impassioned speech about how he won't be driven off his land because "our roots are here"; this is the movie where villains in black hats gang up on the hero in a fistfight, or shoot in the back. This movie may not have invented these archetypes, but it helped define them.

Yet these wooden and obvious stereotypes help frame the issues in ways that make them more accessible. How do people behave when "the law is a three-day ride from here"? What is true strength and what is weakness? When is violence justified? Joe's son, Little Joey, provides a child's-eye view of frontier justice as he observes how different men behave. He is proud of his father, but dazzled by Shane. He asks his father, "Can you whip Shane?" "Can Shane shoot better than you?" Little Joey emulates Shane, and asks for shooting lessons. He begins to define masculinity in Shane's terms and is disappointed when Shane does not fight the men who make fun of him for ordering a soda. Joe's wife, Marion (Jean Arthur), is not immune to his appeal. Joe understands this, telling Marion, "I been slow, but I see things…I know if anything happened to me, you'd be taken care of better than I could myself."

Shane, of course, remains heroic but remote, feeling deeply but recognizing that "there is no living with a killing. It's a brand that sticks." Stryker's position is portrayed with some sympathy, as he explains how he came to this spot many years ago, facing death to tame it and make it safe, only to be followed by "squatters" who dam up all the rivers and fence in the grazing land. The movie has enough complexity so that children can recognize that there are genuine tensions to be resolved and hard decisions to be made, but ultimately it makes no secret about what is right and what is wrong.

Like ranchers and farmers, the community builders and the outsiders both serve different but necessary functions that coexist uncomfortably at best. It is very rare that anyone can become an insider after living successfully as an outsider. A rare example is when Dana Andrews as Fred in **The Best Years of Our Lives** learns that just as the bomber planes he used to fly in can be made into homes, he can learn peacetime skills. More often, we see people like Shane, or Johnny Ringo in **The Gunfighter**, trapped by the choices they have made. It is worth talking about how people make choices that put them in one category or the other, and the consequences that follow.

PROFANITY: None.
NUDITY/SEXUAL REFERENCES: Stryker suggests that Shane stays on at Joe's ranch because he has designs on Marion.
ALCOHOL/DRUG ABUSE: Drinking as a sign of manliness.
VIOLENCE/SCARINESS: Gunfights; characters in peril.
TOLERANCE/DIVERSITY ISSUES: Tensions between farmers and ranchers.
QUESTIONS FOR FAMILIES:

- Why did Shane leave at the end? Why didn't he settle down and become a farmer?

- What makes Joey admire Shane? When does he change his mind? How will he feel about Shane when he grows up?

- Why did Stryker resort to violence? Was there another way to resolve the conflict between the farmers and the ranchers?

- Who is right? The farmers, the cattle ranchers, or Shane? Can you find ways that each of them is right and each is wrong?

- What disputes about land use are going on in your community? How are they resolved?

- What will Shane do next?

CONNECTIONS: This movie explores many of the classic themes also found in stories about knights, war movies, and crime dramas, particularly the irony of the community's need for an outsider who can by definition never be a part of them, and the longing of each for what the other has. Like Johnny Ringo in **The Gunfighter** (though for a different reason), Shane finds he cannot hang up his guns and become like Joe. Like Destry in **Destry Rides Again**, and Will in **High Noon**, Shane finds that there are some problems that can only be resolved with guns.

Shane was the only Western directed by George Stevens, and it is interesting to compare it with some of the classic by veteran directors John Ford and Howard Hawks. Stevens was attracted to stories about outsiders, and he does a superb job of evoking the longing of the outsider for the society he helps make possible in this film, creating a sense of connection between Shane and the Starretts, but always showing that he can never be a part of what they are building.

Palance, who has only twelve lines in this film, became something of an icon of Western menace, a role that he parodied with great enthusiasm and affection in *City Slickers*, which brought him an Oscar. Warren Beatty says that the sound of the shots in this movie was so far superior to those in any other that he used the same technique in *Bonnie and Clyde*. Though the movie was nominated for several Oscars, including Best Picture, it won only for Cinematography, which is ironic because the footage was converted to wide-screen after it was shot, and lost some of its original composition and color.

Watch for Nancy Kulp (Miss Hathaway on television's *The Beverly Hillbillies*) as Mrs. Howell.

ACTIVITIES: Kids will enjoy the classic book by Jack Shaefer, as well as some of his others like *Old Ramon*, a Newberry Honor book.

Thirteen Days

2000, min, PG-13, 13 and up.
Dir: Roger Donaldson. Kevin Costner, Bruce Greenwood, Dylan Baker.
PLOT: For once the tag line has it just right: "You'll never know how close we came."

It may seem like a movie script, but it really happened. American planes took photos of Soviet missiles in Cuba, a "massively destabilizing move." If they had been armed, they could have wiped out most of the mainland US population in five minutes. President John F. Kennedy had written a book while he was in college about the failure of England to respond to German aggression when it still might have been possible to prevent World War II. He had also made his own mistake, a bad one, by responding too aggressively at the Bay of Pigs. Advisors like Dean Acheson and the military urged him to bomb the sites. Adlai Stevenson says, "One of us in the room should be a coward," and he asks the President to come up with a diplomatic solution. Kennedy knows better than to fight the last war, but he is not sure how to fight the next one.

There is no time spent on introductions or exposition, giving the story a sense of immediacy and urgency. It will leave audiences reminding themselves that we are still here, so it must have turned out all right. The President and his advisors argue about what to do ("Bombing them sure would feel good!"), interrupted by "just as usual" events to avoid letting the press or the Soviets suspect that anything was going on. When President Kennedy tells Chicago Mayor Daley that he "wouldn't miss this event for the world," we appreciate the literal meaning of his words.

DISCUSSION: Producer Kevin Costner plays a real person, Kennedy staffer Kenny O'Donnell, but the character combines the roles and actions of several people and essentially exists to help tell the story as efficiently as possible. Most of the time, he blends in with a large, capable cast of character actors (though he seems to make himself too important in a pep talk scene and at the end there is a sort of "Three Musketeers" shot that seems inappropriate).

This is an outstanding movie, with much for families to talk about. Parents and grandparents should tell children any memories they may have of the Cuban missile crisis. Families should also talk about what we do when we have hard choices to make, how we evaluate the alternatives and who we go to for advice. President Kennedy and his brother, his closest advisor, listen to advice from experts, but, as the President says, "There is something immoral about abandoning your own judgment." At the end of the day, he realizes that "there's no wise old men; there's just us."

PROFANITY: Brief strong language.
NUDITY/SEXUAL REFERENCES: None.
ALCOHOL/DRUG ABUSE:
VIOLENCE/SCARINESS: Extremely tense situations, sad death.
TOLERANCE/DIVERSITY ISSUES: None.
QUESTIONS FOR FAMILIES:

• Why does Kenny O'Donnell say that the only word in politics is "loyalty?"

• Why did the Soviets send a message through a reporter instead of using diplomatic channels? Why was it important for Adlai Stevenson to make a strong statement at the UN?

• Why did they ignore the second letter from Kruschev? How did that change things?

• What must someone do in order to direct soldiers to take actions that may get them killed? Who told the truth and who lied? Why?

CONNECTIONS: Families who enjoy this movie will also enjoy "Air Force One" and some of the books and documentaries about President Kennedy and his brother, Robert Kennedy. They should also see the magnificent 2003 documentary about Robert McNamara, *The Fog of War* to hear his recollections of this era. The DVD is packed with extras that are genuinely thrilling, from commentary by the real-life participants to a copy of the shooting script.

20,000 Leagues Under the Sea

1954, 127 min, NR, 8 and up
Dir: Richard Fleischer. Kirk Douglas, James Mason, Paul Lukas, Peter Lorre
PLOT: This is the Disney version of the Jules Verne novel that predicted the invention of the submarine. It begins with sailors reporting a "shipkiller" monster with one eye "like a lighthouse," and "breath like a furnace." Professor Aronax (Paul Lukas) and his aide, Conseil (Peter Lorre), go looking for it on behalf of the government. When their ship is sunk by the "monster," only the two of them and a harpooner named Ned (Kirk Douglas) are saved. They find the "monster" is really a submarine, the creation of Captain Nemo (James Mason). At first, he orders Ned and Conseil to be thrown back into the sea, but when the professor insists on joining them, Nemo allows all three of them to stay onboard, saying, "I found out what I wanted to know."

Nemo is a very cultured man, serving gourmet meals (entirely made of ingredients from the sea) and playing Bach on a pipe organ. As he admits, he is not a civilized man. Disgusted with humanity's destructive impulses, he refuses to share his inventions and discoveries with the world because he fears they will be used in war. Instead, he uses his submarine to blow up ships that are aiding in a war effort. He shows the professor people gathering explosive materials for weapons, and explains he once worked there, too. Then he sinks the ship carrying those explosives so they cannot be used in war. Ned is furious: "Those were sailors, like me." The professor calls Nemo a murderer and a hypocrite, but Nemo answers, "They are the assassins, the dealers in death. I am the avenger." Ned goes on land and is chased back to the submarine by natives. Nemo flips a switch to give the natives electrical charges sending the natives back to the shore.

Ned and Conseil used their time on land to send notes in bottles with the directions to Nemo's home base. When they return, the navy is there. Nemo blows up the submarine, rather than give it to those who might use it for war. Only the professor, Conseil, and Ned escape.

DISCUSSION: Some of the conflict in this story stems from the fact that its characters value very different things. The professor values science. Ned values life. Nemo values independence. When Nemo is attacked by the squid, Ned saves his life. Afterward, Nemo asks why, and Ned says, "That's a good question" and goes off to get drunk. There are a lot of good issues here about the use and abuse of technology. Nemo (and Verne) were right; when the submarine was developed, it was used for destructive purposes.

PROFANITY: None.
NUDITY/SEXUAL REFERENCES: None.
ALCOHOL/DRUG ABUSE: Ned gets drunk after he saves Nemo's life.
VIOLENCE/SCARINESS: A fight with squid; sinking ships; explosions. Ned and Conseil hit each other, which somehow seals their friendship.
TOLERANCE/DIVERSITY ISSUES: None.
QUESTIONS FOR FAMILIES:

- Jules Verne created a submarine long before scientists and engineers were able to make one work in real life. What invention can you think of that would make an exciting story?

- Nemo tries to stop people from destroying each other, but in order to do that, he destroys many people, too. Is that his only alternative?

- Nemo has several different motivations, including hate, revenge, and a wish for peace. How do you see each of these elements in him?

- Nemo likes being undersea because he can make his own rules. Could he do that today anywhere? Why or why not?

- Why does Ned save Nemo? Would Nemo have saved Ned?

CONNECTIONS: This movie has terrific underwater shots and Oscar-winning special effects. Students who are interested in submarines will also enjoy **Yellow Submarine**, *Operation Petticoat* (a 1959 comedy about U.S. Army nurses stuck on a submarine with Cary Grant and Tony Curtis), *The Hunt for Red October*, a Tom Clancy story about a defecting Soviet submarine commander, and *Crimson*

Tide (rated R), in which Gene Hackman and Denzel Washington must decide whether to use nuclear weapons when they are cut off from communication with their commanding officers.

ACTIVITIES: Verne wrote this book before the invention of the submarine. Look at some pictures of early submarines and try some experiments to see how one submerges and rises. Try to make a periscope with mirrors. At Disneyland and Disney World's Magic Kingdom you can take a short trip on the Nautilus.

Parents probably won't be able to persuade children to try any of the underwater delicacies Nemo serves in the movie (like sauté of unborn octopus), but you may be able to get them to try some seafood to get a sense of what the characters in the movie ate.

See if they recognize the music Nemo plays on the organ. It also appears in **Fantasia**. If they like it, find a recording of some other Bach organ music.

War Games

1983, 110 min, PG, 10 and up
Dir: John Badham. Matthew Broderick, Ally Sheedy, Dabney Coleman
PLOT: When a test reveals soldiers are reluctant to follow orders to launch missiles capable of massive destruction, the U.S. Defense Department creates an automatic system to launch missiles when the United States is attacked, without any possibility of human interference. Meanwhile, a teenage boy named David (Matthew Broderick) is at home, fooling around with his computer, trying to tap into the computer of a software manufacturer to try out their new games. He accidentally connects to the Defense Department instead and he "plays" something called "Global Thermonuclear War," showing it to his friend Jennifer (Ally Sheedy).

The Defense Department thinks he is a serious hacker and they come to get him. He realizes he has accidentally set in motion an unstoppable series of commands that will lead to a real thermonuclear war. David and Jennifer escape to seek out the scientist who designed the program, now a recluse. They bring him back and manage to figure out a way to teach the computer not to undertake an initiative that will leave no one a winner, concluding "the only winning move is not to play."

DISCUSSION: Time has caught up with the technology of this movie, and using modems to connect computers is no longer as astonishing as it was when this movie was made, but it is still an exciting story and an important issue.

PROFANITY: Mild.
NUDITY/SEXUAL REFERENCES: None.
ALCOHOL/DRUG ABUSE: None.
VIOLENCE/SCARINESS: Tension and suspense; overall anti-violence message.
TOLERANCE/DIVERSITY ISSUES: None.
QUESTIONS FOR FAMILIES:

- If it is true humans will hesitate before launching nuclear missiles, is that a good thing or a bad thing?

- What can we do to make sure the right decision is made?

- What are the risks, now that the technology David had is so widespread?

CONNECTIONS: This was, at the time it was filmed, the most expensive set ever built. Ironically, the "computer graphics" on the screens were created by old-fashioned animation, at that time a more advanced and flexible technology than computer design.

ACTIVITIES: Mathematically inclined kids might like to learn some elementary game theory, like the prisoner's dilemma, in which the simplest strategy of cooperation beats all of the complicated challenges. (See *The Evolution of Cooperation*, by Robert Axelrod.)

SEE ALSO:
Friendly Persuasion A theme of this movie is the response of people committed to nonviolence when others are fighting a war to protect their ideals and their lives and property.
The Gods Must Be Crazy The gentleness of the movie's bushman hero contrasts with the violence of the "civilized" world.
The Man Who Shot Liberty Valance A man who believes in the law finds out the law has its limits in the face of violence.

13

MAKING MORAL CHOICES

"Reason deceives us; conscience, never."
JEAN JACQUES ROUSSEAU

Even more important than talking to young people about values like integrity and responsibility is talking with them about the challenges of applying those values and the consequences of the choices we make. It is one thing to make kids understand it is wrong to steal; it is another to give them the tools they need to resist when their friends suggest shoplifting some candy from the store and it seems to them their reputation depends on doing it. Moral dilemmas are rarely presented to us unambiguously. A child may understand it is wrong to cheat but may see things differently when he is desperate for the good grade his parents expect. Movies can be especially helpful in illustrating the complexity and difficulty of making these choices and in giving us a chance to see the consequences.

The most interesting moral dilemmas (and therefore the most dramatic) are those that are complex. Often this is a function of two important but clashing values. In **High Noon**, a man must weigh his commitment to his wife against his commitment to the community, a community that seems to have no commitment to him. His wife must weigh her opposition to violence against her love for her husband. In **A Doll's House**, a young wife must decide whether or not she should commit forgery in order to obtain the money she needs to save her husband's life. In **Major Barbara**, a woman who has devoted her life to helping others must decide whether she can ethically accept funding from people who have made their money by harming or exploiting the very people she wants to help. In **Friendly Persuasion**, a family devoted to peace must decide what to do when their neighbors are risking their lives to protect them. In **Judgment at Nuremberg**, the issue is the culpability of Nazi judges for following Nazi law, after their country has lost the war. In political movies like **All the King's Men**, **Advise & Consent**, **State of the Union**, and **The Best Man**, characters must evaluate a number of small moral compromises against the opportunity to do great good. It is not coincidental that none of these politicians gets what he dreamed of.

We see characters giving their lives for moral reasons, perhaps most heartbreakingly in **Spartacus**, where 6,000 slaves give their lives rather than betray their leader to the Romans. In **A Man for All Seasons**, Thomas More gives his life rather than lie about what he believes. Others give up their careers, as in **Mutiny on the Bounty**, or someone they care about (**The Maltese Falcon**) or a way of life (**The Adventures of Robin Hood, The Long Walk Home**). Movies like **These Three** and **Fail-Safe** show characters who must try to make up for the wreckage left by the bad choices of others.

Younger children may be especially interested in movies showing children and other characters they can identify with, like **Pinocchio, Willie Wonka and the Chocolate Factory**, and **Tuck Everlasting**.

Older kids will find interesting the movies that show careful calibration of moral choices. In movies like **The Scarlet and the Black, A Man for All Seasons**, and **Schindler's List**, characters make decisions about how far they can go in pursuit of a moral imperative. In **The Scarlet and the Black**, the priest says he will help prisoners escape but he will not help destroy anyone, even the Nazis. In **A Man for All Seasons**, More says he will stay silent, and thus avoid having to compromise himself with a lie. In **Schindler's List**, Schindler never tries to save anyone else, but puts everything he has into saving the people on his "list." In contrast, look at the unsuccessful efforts of both of the leading characters in **Quiz Show** to calibrate their choices by making distinctions that do not hold up. Charles Van Doren tells himself at first that he is not really cheating if they only give him the questions and he researches the answers. Then he tells himself it doesn't matter because he is getting young people excited about learning. Dick Goodwin tells himself he can protect Van Doren from the hearings because the real bad guys are the people at the network. Part of what makes these four films so compelling is that all of the stories are true.

Many movies have particularly good examples of the consequences of decisions that seem quite small when they are made. For example, in **All My Sons**, a man's decision to make extra money by cheating on the specifications of airplane parts (and then framing his partner) has devastating consequences for the next generation. Small compromises by characters in **All the King's Men, The Apartment**, and **State of the Union**, become serious corruptions. In **The Apartment, On the Waterfront**, and **All My Sons**, we see how choices that seem easy to a character when considered as abstractions seem very different when they directly affect people he knows. In **Norma Rae**, what makes the character decide to act is simply learning she can.

These are especially important points to make to help students learn how to think about the choices they face. The movies in this section all show us characters who are confronted with a choice and who must bring their sense of morality to bear in deciding what to do. Not all of them make the right choices, though some later change their minds. These kinds of films are especially important to watch as a family, to talk about how the choices are presented, how they are evaluated, and what the impact is on the people who make the choices and the people they care about.

All the President's Men

1976, 138 min, PG, 12 and up
Dir: Alan J. Pakula. Robert Redford, Dustin Hoffman, Jason Robards
PLOT: Based on the real-life story of the two reporters who would not give up on the story of the Watergate break-in, this is as gripping as any detective novel. Bob Woodward (Robert Redford), a junior reporter for the Washington Post, is sent to cover a small-time break-in of the office of the Democratic National Committee (located in the Watergate office building). He works with Carl Bernstein (Dustin Hoffman), another reporter, to find, after tediously painstaking research, that it is just part of a complex pattern of corruption in President Nixon's reelection campaign.
DISCUSSION: Star Redford was so intent on authenticity, he even flew actual garbage from the Washington Post wastepaper baskets out to the set. The movie does a good job of showing how much of the work of the reporters was dull persistence, and it also does a good job of showing us what went into the decisions of editor Ben Bradlee (Jason Robards in an Oscar-winning performance) and (off-screen) publisher Katherine Graham about what they needed in terms of proof in order to be able to publish the story.

There is an interesting range of moral choices and calibrations. The famous "Deep Throat" (Hal Holbrook), still unidentified, is someone from the inside who will not allow himself to be identified or even quoted, but is willing to confirm what the reporters are able to find elsewhere. Most memorably, he tells them to "follow the money."

Others involved in the scandal, both in the corruption and in its cover-up, must decide what to do and how much to disclose. One key development is the decision made by someone identified only as "the bookkeeper" (Jane Alexander) to talk to Bernstein. The participants must also deal with the consequences of their choices. Donald Segretti (Robert Walden) manages to evoke sympathy when what began as juvenile pranks leave him in disgrace. Woodward and Bernstein also make mistakes and must deal with the consequences.

As the movie ends, in 1972, Nixon is reelected, and it seems to the reporters that their work has had no impact at all. Students who view this film may need some context in order to understand it, and will want to know what else happened before Nixon resigned in August of 1974.

PROFANITY: Some strong language.
NUDITY/SEXUAL REFERENCES: Epithets.
ALCOHOL/DRUG ABUSE: None.
VIOLENCE/SCARINESS: None.
TOLERANCE/DIVERSITY ISSUES: None.
QUESTIONS FOR FAMILIES:

• Why were Woodward and Bernstein the only reporters interested in the story? Why did they insist on two sources before they would publish anything?

• What were Donald Segretti's "dirty tricks"? How was he different from Sloan? From the bookkeeper? From "Deep Throat"?

• One of the people portrayed in the movie later testified before the Watergate Committee that he had "lost his moral compass." What does that mean? How does something like that happen?

CONNECTIONS: Look for future Oscar-winner F. Murray Abraham (**Amadeus**) as an arresting officer. *The Final Days* is a made-for-television sequel, based on Woodward and Bernstein's follow-up book. For more on this era, see *Nixon*, with Anthony Hopkins, and Nixon's famous "Checkers" speech, available on video. An odd little movie, *Nasty Habits*, is an allegory of Watergate, set in a convent, with Glenda Jackson as a Nixonian nun.

ACTIVITIES: The book this movie was based on is not much fun to read, with more reporting than analysis. Older kids who want to know more can read *Breach of Faith*, by Theodore White, or the books written by participants like Judge Sirica, John Dean, and H. R. Haldeman (whose diaries are available on CD-ROM).

The Chocolate War

1988, 103 min, R, mature high-school age
Dir: Keith Gordon. John Glover, Ilan Mitchell-Smith, Wally Ward
PLOT: While Jerry Renault (Ilan Mitchell-Smith), a freshman at Trinity Prep boys' school, is belittled by the football coach, two boys, Archie (Wally Ward) and Orbie (Doug Hutchison), sit high up in the stands watching them. Archie determines the "assignments" to be given to those boys selected for the school's elite club, the Vigils, and Orbie is the club's secretary. Jerry, whose mother has recently died, is selected for an assignment.

At home, Jerry's father is remote, still overcome by grief. In school, teacher Brother Leon (John Glover) is tough and imperious. He brutally berates an outstanding student, and then tells him, "You passed the toughest test of all—you were true to yourself."
Brother Leon tells Archie the boys have to sell 20,000 boxes of chocolates for their annual fund-raiser, twice the number from previous years, and at twice the price, to help ensure he will become headmaster. He won't refer to the Vigils by name, but acknowledges Archie's "influence." Each boy must sell fifty boxes. All of the other boys agree, but Jerry refuses. Brother Leon says selling is voluntary ("that is the glory of Trinity"), but tells the class that "the true sons of Trinity can pick up your chocolates in the gym. The rest—I pity you."

It turns out that refusing to sell the chocolates was the "assignment" given to Jerry to prove his worth to the Vigils. Even after the time period of the assignment expires, he continues to refuse to participate, despite harassment by the other boys. It gives him a feeling of strength and independence, not just from Brother Leon, but from the Vigils as well. Brother Leon says that sales are poor because the boys have become "infected" by Jerry. Brother Leon tells Archie that "if the sale goes down the drain, you and the Vigils go down the drain. We all go down the drain together."

The Vigils decide to make the chocolate sale a success by making it popular. The head of the Vigils tells Archie his position depends on his making his plan work.
At last, all of the chocolates are sold, except for Jerry's quota. Archie arranges an assembly, with a raffle; the prize is the chance to select the punches in a boxing match between Jerry and a tough boy named Janza. Archie has to take Janza's place, and Jerry beats him. Jerry says, "I should have just sold the chocolates, played their game, anyway." Archie is now secretary, and Orbie has taken over assignments for the Vigils.

DISCUSSION: Mature teenagers, especially fans of the popular book by Robert Cormier, will appreciate this dark story, a kind of *Dangerous Liaisons* for teenagers. Archie says that "people are two things, greedy and cruel," and devises his plans to take advantage of those qualities.

Although the story is exaggerated for satiric effect, much of it will seem true to teenagers, who often feel a heightened sense of proportion. The movie shows us some of Jerry's dreams or fantasies, which add to the surreal and claustrophobic feeling of the movie.

The movie provides a good basis for a discussion of the different ways that people get other people to do what they want, the exercise of power, and the ways that power is maintained and lost. The interaction between Brother Leon and Archie is especially interesting because of their uneasy interdependence. As powerful as both of them seem, they ultimately lose their power without much of a struggle.

PROFANITY: Very strong language, the reason for the R rating.
NUDITY/SEXUAL REFERENCES: References to masturbation; (false) accusation of homosexuality used to taunt Jerry.
ALCOHOL/DRUG ABUSE: Smoking by teens.
VIOLENCE/SCARINESS: Jerry is beat up by a gang of smaller kids; a boxing match at the end; blackmail, harassment, and other emotional violence.
TOLERANCE/DIVERSITY ISSUES: All of the boys are white and Christian; some issues of tolerance of individual differences.
QUESTIONS FOR FAMILIES:

- What are the tools that Archie uses to maintain and exercise power? What tools does Brother Leon use?

- How can anyone or any group decide to make something "popular" and "cool," as Archie does with the chocolate sale?

- Why does Archie tell Janza to "use the queer pitch" on Jerry?

- Why do we see Archie holding an impaled butterfly when he talks to Janza on the phone? Why does Jerry tell the girl she was right?

- What is the significance of the Vigils's marble test for the person who gives the assignments?

CONNECTIONS: Read the book by Robert Cormier, and his other popular novel, *I Am the Cheese* (filmed in 1983). Compare this story to other books and movies about power struggles in a school context, including **Lord of the Flies**, **School Ties**, and, for mature high school and college students, *The Lords of Discipline* (1983, rated R), the surrealistic *if...*(1968, rated R), and one of its inspirations, the French film *Zero for Conduct* (1933).

Friendly Persuasion

1956, 140 min, NR, 8 and up
Dir: William Wyler. Gary Cooper, Dorothy McGuire, Anthony Perkins
PLOT: This is the story of the Birdwells, a loving Quaker family in the midst of the Civil War. Eliza (Dorothy McGuire), a devout woman, is the moral center of the family. Jess (Gary Cooper) is a thoughtful man, not as strict as Eliza on prohibitions like music and racing his horse, but with a strong commitment to his principles. Their children are Joshua (Anthony Perkins), a sensitive young man who opposes violence but feels he must join the soldiers; Mattie (Phyllis Love), who falls in love with Gord, a neighbor who is a Union soldier; and Young Jess (Richard Eyer), a boy who is fascinated with the talk of war and battles.

A Union soldier comes to the Quaker prayer meeting to ask the men to join the army. They tell him they cannot engage in violence under any circumstances. "We are opposed to slavery, but do not think it right to kill one man to free another." Even when the soldier points out this means others will be dying to protect their lives and property, no one will support him.

The Confederate army approaches, and Joshua and Enoch, a freed slave who works on the Birdwells's farm, decide to join the Union. Eliza does everything she can to keep Joshua from going, even telling him that in doing so he will not only reject what he has learned in church but he will reject her, too. Jess says Joshua has to make up his own mind. "I'm just his father, Eliza. I'm not his conscience. A man's life ain't worth a hill of beans unless he lives up to his own conscience. I've got to give Josh that chance." Joshua prays for guidance and leaves to join the army the next morning. At first Eliza won't respond, but then she runs after him to wish him well.

As the war gets closer, Jess and Eliza refuse to run away from their farm as others are doing. When Josh's horse comes back without him, Jess goes looking for him. He finds his good friend Sam mortally wounded by a sniper. When the sniper shoots at Jess, too, Jess takes his gun away but will not harm him; he tells the sniper, "Go on, get! I'll not harm thee." Josh is wounded and deeply upset because he killed a Confederate soldier. Jess brings him home.

In the meantime, the Confederates ride onto the farm, and in keeping with her faith, Eliza welcomes them and gives them all her food, but when one of the soldiers goes after her beloved pet goose, she whacks him with the broom, amusing her children and leaving herself disconcerted and embarrassed. Jess and Josh return, and the family goes off to church together to continue to do their best to match their faith to their times.

DISCUSSION: This is an exceptional depiction of a loving family, particularly for the way that Jess and Eliza work together on resolving their conflicts. They listen to each other with enormous respect and deep affection. Jess does his best to go along with Eliza's stricter views on observance, because in his heart he believes she is right. Nevertheless, he cannot keep himself from trying to have his horse beat Sam's as they go to church on Sunday, and he decides to buy an organ knowing she will object. In fact, he doesn't even tell her about it. She is shocked when it arrives and says she forbids it, to which he replies mildly, "When thee asks or suggests, I am like putty in thy hands, but when thee forbids, thee is barking up the wrong tree." Having said if the organ goes into the house, she will not stay there, she goes off to sleep in the barn. He does not object but he goes out to the barn to spend the night with her. They reconcile and find a way to compromise.

All this provides a counterpoint to more serious questions of faith and conscience. In the beginning, when the Union soldier asks the Quakers if any of them will join him, one man stands up to say nothing could ever make him fight. Later, when his barn is burned, he is the first to take up a gun. Even Eliza, able to offer hospitality to the same men who may have just been shooting at her son, finds herself overcome when one of them captures her beloved pet goose.

Jess is willing to admit the answer is not so simple. All he asks is "the will of God be revealed to us and we be given the strength to follow his will." He understands the difficulty of finding the right answer for himself and for Joshua. He resolves it for himself in his treatment of the sniper, and he respects Joshua and the issues involved enough to let Joshua make his own choice.

The movie is a rare one in which someone makes a moral choice through prayer, which many families will find worth emphasizing. Josh, who was able to respond without violence to the thugs at the fair, decides he cannot benefit from risks taken by others unless he is willing to take them, too. He cries in battle, but he shoots.

The issue of how someone committed to nonviolence responds to a violent world is thoughtfully raised by this movie.

PROFANITY: None.

NUDITY/SEXUAL REFERENCES: None.

ALCOHOL/DRUG ABUSE: None.

VIOLENCE/SCARINESS: Sam killed by sniper; Jess shot at: Gord and Josh wounded (off-screen).

TOLERANCE/DIVERSITY ISSUES: Tolerance of religious differences is a theme of the movie.

QUESTIONS FOR FAMILIES:

- How is the religious service in the movie similar or different from what you have experienced?

- How was the faith of the characters tested in this movie? What did they learn from the test?

- How should people who are opposed to violence respond to violence when it is directed against them? When it is directed against others?

CONNECTIONS: The screenplay was written by Michael Wilson, who received no screen credit because he was blacklisted during the "Red Scare." His involvement makes the issues of conscience raised in the book even more poignant. The book on which the movie is based, by Jessamyn West (a Quaker, and a cousin of Richard Nixon), is well worth reading.

Cooper faces some of the same issues (and has a Society of Friends bride) in **High Noon**. *Shenandoah*, with Jimmy Stewart as the father of a large family who tries to keep his sons out of the Civil War, raises some of the same themes without the religious context. It later became a successful Broadway musical.

ACTIVITIES: Take your child to a meeting (religious service) of the Society of Friends, which they prefer to the term "Quaker".

The Gunfighter

1950, 84 min, NR, b&w, 10 and up

Dir: Henry King. Gregory Peck, Karl Malden

PLOT: Jimmy Ringo (Gregory Peck) is the fastest gun who ever lived, which makes him a target for every young man who wants to prove himself. On his way to Cayenne, Ringo stops in a bar. A "young squirt" taunts him, and Ringo makes every possible effort to placate him, asking the young man's friends to make him stop, but finally he pulls his gun on Ringo, who kills him. Even though everyone saw it was in self-defense, the witnesses tell him to move on. The dead man had three brothers, and "they won't care who drew first."

The three brothers come after Ringo, but he is waiting for them and he takes their guns and sends their horses back to town, telling them to go back on foot, but he knows they will probably follow him instead, and once he gets to Cayenne, he will only have a brief time to do what he has in mind.

He gets to Cayenne and is surprised and pleased to find his old friend Mark Strett (Millard Mitchell) as the sheriff. Mark tells him he will have to leave; even though Ringo does not want any trouble and has not committed any crimes, trouble will come looking for him, as there are too many young men who will risk everything to be able to claim the credit for killing Ringo. Ringo wants to see his wife, Peggy, and their child. Mark knows where they are but won't say. He does agree to ask Peggy if she will see Ringo, and tells Ringo to stay put, under the care of the sympathetic bartender (Karl Malden).

Ringo stays quietly in the corner. Every one of the boys in town plays hooky to peer in at him through the saloon window. The local "squirt," hot-headed Hunt Bromley (Skip Homeier), comes after him. Ringo scares him off with a bluff. Jerry is across the street with a rifle pointed out the window, sure Ringo must be the one who killed his son. The three brothers have found horses and guns and are approaching fast.

Peggy at first refuses to see him. She finally agrees, and when he says he wants to settle down in a place where no one knows him, she says if he can do that for a year, she will join him. He spends some time with his son and prepares to leave, happy at the thought of his new life. Hunt is waiting for him and shoots him in the back.

As Ringo dies, he says he drew first. He doesn't want Hunt hanged. He wants him to suffer as he has suffered, knowing wherever he goes, there will be someone who wants to be known as the man who shot the man who shot Ringo.

DISCUSSION: This is really a Western version of the story of King Midas. Ringo's wish came true, but at a terrible price. There was a time when he could think of nothing finer, nothing manlier, than being known as the fastest gun in the West. We see a glimmer of that again when he asks what Jimmy (who does not know Ringo is his father) thinks of him. When he hears that Jimmy admires Wyatt Earp, he can't help telling the boy he is far tougher than Earp. Yet now Ringo is tired. He knows every moment he will have to watch for someone trying to kill him (as happens throughout this movie), and someday someone will be a little less tired (or, as happens, a little less honorable) than he is.

It provides a good opportunity for a discussion of notions of manhood and courage, along the lines of the moving speech by Charles Bronson in **The Magnificent Seven**. Ringo would trade all of his fame for the chance to live with his family, as shown most poignantly when he shares a drink with a young rancher. Ringo is more successful with his intelligence than his speed. He is able to avoid shoot-outs with the brothers, with Jerry, and in the first encounter with Hunt. He arranges to have money paid to Peggy without giving away their connection, and thinks of a plausible reason to tell Jimmy why he wanted to see him so he doesn't have to tell him the truth. His innate decency and sense of justice are shown in his dealings with Jerry, his dreams for a life with Peggy, and especially in the scene in which he talks to the ladies of the town, when they do not know who he is. His pleasure in being able to have a moment's interaction with people who are not terrified, angry, or trying to shoot him is very moving.

This is also a good movie about the consequences of our choices. There are so many movies about redemption and triumph it is automatically branded an "adult Western" when a gunfighter doesn't shoot the bad guy and ride off into the sunset. Unlike Alan in *The Petrified Forest*, who dies to help someone else, or *Butch Cassidy and the Sundance Kid*, whose deaths at the end of the movie only brighten their legend, Ringo chooses to tarnish his legend as he dies, to curse Hunt to the same fate that he suffered, and possibly also to give little boys and young squirts less reason to try to be like him.

PROFANITY: None.
NUDITY/SEXUAL REFERENCES: None.
ALCOHOL/DRUG ABUSE: Much of the action takes place in bars, and there is a lot of drinking.
VIOLENCE/SCARINESS: Gunfights.
TOLERANCE/DIVERSITY ISSUES: None.
QUESTIONS FOR FAMILIES:

- Why does every town have a "young squirt" who wants to prove he is faster than Ringo?

- Why doesn't Mark carry a gun?

- Why does Ringo insist that he drew on Hunt?

- Why was Mark able to get away and start over, when Ringo and Buck were not?

- Why does Peggy call herself "Mrs. Ringo" at the end?

CONNECTIONS: One of the three brothers who come after Ringo was played by Alan Hale, Jr., who went on to play the Captain in the television show *Gilligan's Island*, and was the son of Alan Hale, who played Little John in **The Adventures of Robin Hood**.

Compare Ringo's final decision to the one made by Jimmy Cagney in *Angels with Dirty Faces*. A tough criminal on death row, he is asked by his lifelong friend, a priest, to go to his death a coward, so that the boys who look up to him will not want to follow his example.

Guys and Dolls

1955, 150 min, NR, 8 and up
Dir: Joseph L. Mankiewicz. Marlon Brando, Frank Sinatra, Jean Simmons, Vivian Blaine
PLOT: The story takes place among the small-time underworld characters of New York City. Nathan Detroit (Frank Sinatra) runs a "floating crap game" (held in a different place each time) providing entertainment and bankrolls many members of the community. His problem is that he can't find a place to have the next game. The only place available wants $1,000 up front, and he does not have it. Furthermore, his (very) long-term fiancée, Adelaide (Vivian Blaine), a showgirl, is so distressed over his failure to marry her that she has developed a psychosomatic cold.

Trying to get the money he needs, Nathan makes a bet with Sky (as in willing to bet sky-high) Masterson (Marlon Brando). After Brando brags he can get any "doll" to go out with him, Nathan challenges him to ask Sarah Brown (Jean Simmons), the local mission worker. Sky persuades Sarah to go to Havana for dinner, and after he spikes her drink with liquor, they have a wonderful time, and she starts to fall in love with him.

When they get back, however, she finds that the crap game was held in the mission and feels betrayed. In order to persuade her that his intentions are honorable, Sky rolls the dice in the crap game against the "souls" of the other players, and when he wins, they must all go to a meeting at the mission, the two couples get married, and everyone lives happily ever after.
DISCUSSION: This musical classic, based on the stories of Damon Runyon, is a lot of fun, despite the fact that two of the leads are not singers and none of them can dance. Even so, Brando and Simmons do surprisingly well, especially in the

scenes set in Havana, and the movie is brash and splashy enough to be thoroughly entertaining.

Themes worth discussing include honesty in relationships and in competition (Harry the Horse cheats and threatens the other players) and how people decide whether to align themselves with (or between) the two extremes presented by the mission workers and the grifters and gamblers.

PROFANITY: None.
NUDITY/SEXUAL REFERENCES: Very oblique reference to the face of the hotel clerk when an unmarried couple checks in; "Take Back Your Mink" is a song about a girl who accepts a lot of gifts from a man but is not "one of those girls."
ALCOHOL/DRUG ABUSE: Sky gets Sarah drunk in Havana by arranging for her drink to be spiked with liquor.
VIOLENCE/SCARINESS: None.
TOLERANCE/DIVERSITY ISSUES: Portrayal of Adelaide as hopelessly waiting to marry Nathan would earn her a spot on the Oprah show today.
QUESTIONS FOR FAMILIES:

• Adelaide says she has developed a cold from waiting for Nathan to marry her. How do people get physically sick from unhappiness or worry?

• What is the meaning of Sky's father's advice about the deck of cards? Is that good advice?

• Who changes the most in this movie? How can you tell?

CONNECTIONS: Other movies based on Runyon's colorful characters include *Little Miss Marker* (four versions, including *Sorrowful Jones*, and *Forty Pounds of Trouble*. The best one has the original title and stars Shirley Temple; the later version of that title has a nice performance by Walter Matthau, but is otherwise tedious). Additional movies based on Runyon stories are *Lady for a Day* (remade with Bette Davis as *Pocketful of Miracles*), *The Lemon Drop Kid* (also filmed twice, with the Bob Hope version the better one), and a very sad movie starring Lucille Ball and Henry Fonda called *The Big Street*.
ACTIVITIES: Young people who like this movie may enjoy reading (or having read aloud to them) some of Damon Runyon's stories, especially "Butch Minds the Baby."

High Noon

1952, 84 min, NR, b&w, 10 and up
Dir: Fred Zinnemann. Gary Cooper, Grace Kelly, Lloyd Bridges, Katy Jurado
PLOT: Marshall Will Kane (Gary Cooper) marries Amy (Grace Kelly) and turns
in his badge. She is a Quaker, and he has promised her to hang up his gun and
become a shopkeeper. They get word that Frank Miller is coming to town on the
noon train. Kane arrested Miller and sent him to jail, and Miller swore he would
come back to kill him.
Will and Amy leave town quickly. He cannot run away, so he turns around. He
knows they will never be safe; wherever they go, Miller will follow them. He has a
duty to the town. Their new marshal will not be arriving until the next day.
    Will seeks help from everyone, finally going to church, where services are in
session. He is turned down, over and over again. Amy says she will leave on the
noon train. Will's former deputy, Harvey (Lloyd Bridges), refuses to help because
he is resentful that Will did not recommend him as the new marshal. Will's
former girlfriend, Helen Ramirez (Katy Jurado), now Harvey's girlfriend, will not
help him, either. She sells her business and leaves town. Others say it is not their
problem, or tell him to run, for the town's good as well as his own. The previous
marshal, Will's mentor, says he can't use a gun anymore. The one man who had
promised to help backs out when he finds out no one else will join them. The
only others who offer to help are a disabled man and a young boy. Will must face
Miller and his three henchmen alone.
    At noon, Frank Miller gets off the train. The four men come into town. Will
is able to defeat them, with Amy's unexpected help. As the townsfolk gather, Will
throws his badge in the dust, and they drive away.
DISCUSSION: This outstanding drama ticks by in real time, only eighty-four
tense minutes long. Will gets the message about Frank Miller at 10:40, and we
feel the same time pressure he does as he tries to find someone to help him. We
see and hear clocks throughout the movie, and as noon approaches, the clock
looms larger and larger, the pendulum swinging like an executioner's ax. In the
brilliant score by Dimitri Tiomkin, the sound of the beat suggests both the train's
approach and the passage of time.
    This is like a grown-up "Little Red Hen" story. Will cannot find anyone to
help him protect the town. Everyone seems to think it is someone else's problem
(or fault). Teenagers may be interested to know that many people consider this
film an analogy for the political problems of the McCarthy era. It was written
during the height of the Hollywood "Red Scare." After completing this screen-

play, Carl Foreman, an "unfriendly witness" before the House Un-American Activities Committee, was blacklisted. This unforgettable drama of a man who will not run from his enemy, or his own fears, transcends all times and circumstances.

PROFANITY: None.
NUDITY/SEXUAL REFERENCES: None.
ALCOHOL/DRUG ABUSE: Drinking in a bar; bad guys drink.
VIOLENCE/SCARINESS: Shoot-out.
TOLERANCE/DIVERSITY ISSUES: Women are exceptionally intelligent and respected compared to other movies of the era. Helen speaks of the prejudice she faced as a Mexican woman, and Amy listens sympathetically.
QUESTIONS FOR FAMILIES:

• Everyone seems to have a different reason for not helping Will. How many can you identify? Which reasons seem the best to you? Which seem the worst? What makes Amy change her mind?

• Why does Will throw his badge in the dirt?

• Do you think Carl Foreman, the screenwriter, chose the name "Will" for any special reason?

• How do you decide when to stay and fight and when to run? How do you evaluate the risks? What should the law be?

CONNECTIONS: This movie was the first attempt at an "adult" Western, its stark black-and-white images a contrast to the gorgeous vistas in the Westerns of John Ford and Howard Hawks. It was included in the first group of films named to the National Film Registry, established by the Library of Congress to identify films "culturally, historically, or esthetically important."

It won Oscars for Cooper, best editing, best score, and best song (lyrics by Ned Washington, sung by Tex Ritter). It has had tremendous influence and has inspired many imitations and variations. *Outland*, starring Sean Connery (and rated R), is a not very good attempt to transfer this plot to outer space. *Three O'clock High* moves it to a high school, with a new student challenged by the school bully. Despite some directorial pyrotechnics, it is not very good, either. *The Principal* has another **High Noon**-style confrontation in a school, but this time it is the title character who must show his mettle. *The Baltimore Bullet* moves the confrontation to a pool hall.

Major Barbara

1941, 135 min, NR, b&w, 10 and up
Dir: Gabriel Pascal, Harold French, David Lean. Wendy Hiller, Rex Harrison, Robert Morley
PLOT: Major Barbara (Wendy Hiller) is a member of a mission devoted to saving souls and she promotes temperance, nonviolence, and socialism. Adolphus Cusins (Rex Harrison), a classics professor, falls in love with her, but before she accepts his proposal she insists he must meet her family. He is surprised to find out she is the daughter of a wealthy industrialist.

Her father, Andrew Undershaft (Robert Morley), a munitions manufacturer, returns to the family after an absence of many years. He tries to convert Barbara to his views by presenting her with an ethical dilemma: Will she accept large contributions to her mission from the makers of munitions and liquor, the very things she opposes? She cannot, and is disillusioned but understanding when her superior accepts the funds, reasoning that despite their source, the money will do some good.

Barbara visits the munitions factory and sees she can do more to help those in need by running a business than by preaching. It does not mean much when someone accepts her views in order to get food and shelter, but if she can persuade people simply by the force of her ideas, those are converts worth having. Furthermore, she can aid the poor by providing good jobs, good wages, and good benefits. Her father says that being a millionaire is his religion. Christianity is Barbara's religion, but she will pursue it through capitalism.

DISCUSSION: More directly political than *Pygmalion* (and the musical version, **My Fair Lady**), this provides a good opportunity for a discussion of what is now termed "corporate social responsibility," and the role of the government, the church, and the corporation in meeting society's needs.

PROFANITY: None.
NUDITY/SEXUAL REFERENCES: None.
ALCOHOL/DRUG ABUSE: References to alcohol abuse.
VIOLENCE/SCARINESS: None.
TOLERANCE/DIVERSITY ISSUES: Class issues.
QUESTIONS FOR FAMILIES:

- How socially responsible should corporations be? How should they balance the interests of employees, customers, shareholders, suppliers, and the community?

- Who is in a better position to help society: government, religion, or business? Which kinds of help are each uniquely able to provide?

CONNECTIONS: Robert Morley, age thirty-two when this movie was made, was only four years older than the actress who played his daughter. A very young Deborah Kerr appears as Jenny Hill, and Emlyn Williams, author of the autobiographical **The Corn Is Green**, appears as Snobby Price. Wendy Hiller, picked by Shaw himself to appear in this movie and Pygmalion, also appears in **A Man for All Seasons** and *Murder on the Orient Express*.

Playwright and co-screenwriter Shaw was one of the twentieth century's most brilliant writers, well-known as a dramatist, essayist, critic, and social reformer. He was awarded the Nobel Prize for Literature in 1925. His play, Pygmalion (also filmed with Wendy Hiller) became the musical My Fair Lady. Among the many pleasures of his work are the superb female characters, strong, intelligent, and principled.

ACTIVITIES: Teenagers may want to read or even act out some of Shaw's other plays, including *The Man of Destiny*, *Misalliance*, *Caesar and Cleopatra*, and *Arms and the Man*, and will also enjoy his essays and criticism.

The Maltese Falcon

1941, 100 min, NR, b&w, 10 and up
Dir: John Huston. Humphrey Bogart, Mary Astor, Sidney Greenstreet, Peter Lorre
PLOT: Sam Spade (Humphrey Bogart) is a private detective. A woman who says her name is Ruth Wonderly (Mary Astor) comes to see him, asking for help in finding her sister. Sam sends his partner, Miles Archer (Jerome Cowan), to follow her when she meets Floyd Thursby, the man she thinks her sister is with, and both Archer and Thursby are killed. It turns out the woman has given him a false name. She is really Brigid O'Shaughnessy, and it turns out it is not her sister she is seeking but a small, jeweled statue of a falcon and she is mixed up with some people who will do anything to get it.

One of those people is Joel Cairo (Peter Lorre), who comes to see Sam to insist—with a gun—that he be allowed to search Sam's office to see if the falcon is there. Sam is not at all intimidated by Joel, but allows him to search. Also after the statue is Mr. Gutman, "the fat man" (Sidney Greenstreet), with his "gunsel," Wilmer. They alternately threaten and attempt to bribe Sam while Brigid appeals to his protective nature and his heart., but Sam turns them all over to the police, including Brigid, whom he loves.

DISCUSSION: One of the most interesting aspects of this classic movie is the way that Sam Spade thinks through the moral dilemmas. When he is deciding whether to tell the police about Brigid, he is very explicit about weighing every aspect of his choices. It is not an easy decision for him; he has no moral absolutes. On the one hand, he loves her, and he did not think much of his partner. On the other, he does not trust her, he does not think she trusts him, and he knows they could not go on together, each waiting to betray or be betrayed. He also has some pride; he says when your partner is killed, you are supposed to "do something." While it may be good for business not to appear too ethical, it is bad for business to allow a partner in a detective firm to get killed without responding. If he turns her over to the police, he loses her. If he does not, he loses a part of himself, his own brand of integrity.

When this movie was made, moviegoers were used to cool, debonair detectives (like Philo Vance and Nick Charles, both played by William Powell), a sort of cross between Sherlock Holmes and Fred Astaire. Sam Spade, created by Dashiell Hammett based on his experiences as a detective, was a modern-day version of the cowboy, a loner with his own sense of honor.

This was the first movie directed by John Huston, who also wrote the screenplay, but he was already a master. Watch the two scenes where Sam goes to talk to Gutman, and see how the camera angles in the first scene lead the viewer to suspect that Sam's drink is spiked (it isn't), and then how different angles are used in the second scene to make the viewer confident it won't be (it is).

PROFANITY: None.
NUDITY/SEXUAL REFERENCES: None.
ALCOHOL/DRUG ABUSE: Some drinking.
VIOLENCE/SCARINESS: Some suspense, scuffles, threats of violence.
TOLERANCE/DIVERSITY ISSUES: Subtle prejudice against less-than-macho Joel Cairo and Wilmer, who (in the mildest 1940s terms) the movie implies are gay; implication that Spade was having an affair with Archer's wife.
QUESTIONS FOR FAMILIES:

• What does Sam mean when he says the statue is "the stuff dreams are made of"?

• Where is Sam faced with moral conflicts? How does he resolve them? What are his reasons?

CONNECTIONS: Note the director's father, Walter Huston, in an un-credited brief appearance as Captain Jacobi. Jerome Cowan, who appears briefly as Miles Archer, plays the prosecuting attorney who tries to prove that Kris Kringle is not Santa Claus in **Miracle on 34th Street**. Bogart appeared as a similarly tough detective, Philip Marlowe, in *The Big Sleep*, based on the novel by Raymond Chandler. The books by Hammett and Chandler are well worth reading.

A Man for All Seasons

1966, 120 min, NR, 10 and up
Dir: Fred Zinnemann. Paul Scofield, Wendy Hiller, Robert Shaw, John Hurt, Orson Welles
PLOT: The Lord Chancellor, Sir Thomas More (Paul Scofield), is a man of great principle and a devout Catholic in the time of King Henry VIII. The king wants to dissolve his marriage to the queen (a Spanish princess and the widow of his late brother) so that he can marry Anne Boleyn. All around him, courtiers and politicians plot to use this development to their advantage, or at least to hold on to their positions, given the conflict between the Church's position that marriage is indissoluble and the king's that it must be dissolved. For More, the choice is clear, and God comes before the king. Because of More's incorruptible reputation, his support is crucial. Every possible form of persuasion and coercion is attempted. More will refrain from opposing it explicitly but he will not make any affirmative statement on behalf of the divorce. More will not lend his allegiance to the new church headed by the king.

Finally, having lost his position, his fortune, his reputation (on false charges), and his liberty, More is sentenced to death. He accepts it with grace and faith, forgiving the executioner.

DISCUSSION: This is an outstanding (and brilliantly filmed) study of a man who is faced with a harrowingly difficult moral choice. The choice remains clear to him, even at great cost not just to himself but to his family. Yet within his clear moral imperative, he does calibrate. His conscience does not require him to work against or even speak out against the divorce; he need only keep silent.

PROFANITY: None.
NUDITY/SEXUAL REFERENCES: None.
ALCOHOL/DRUG ABUSE: Some drinking.
VIOLENCE/SCARINESS: Non-explicit execution scene.
TOLERANCE/DIVERSITY ISSUES: None.

QUESTIONS FOR FAMILIES:

* What does the title mean?

* The same director made **High Noon**. Do you see any similarities?

* What would you consider in deciding what to do if you were More?

* What other characters in history can you think of who sustained such a commitment to a moral principle?

CONNECTIONS: This movie won six Oscars, including Best Picture, Director, and Actor.

Children and teens should read some of the books about this period and see if they can find reproductions of the paintings by Hans Holbein of the real-life characters. They may want to watch some of the many other movies about this era as well. As history shows, the marriage that led to the establishment of the Church of England did not last. *Anne of the Thousand Days* tells the story of the relationship of Henry VIII and Anne Boleyn, including, from a different perspective, some of the events of **A Man for All Seasons**. A British miniseries, *The Six Wives of Henry VIII*, devotes one episode to each wife, and is more historically accurate and very well done. Henry VIII is such a colorful figure he appeared in several movies, including the classic *The Private Life of Henry VIII* with Charles Laughton. His death appears in the (completely fictional) **Prince and the Pauper**, and his daughter with Anne Boleyn, Queen Elizabeth I, is featured in several movies, including *The Private Lives of Elizabeth and Essex* (with Bette Davis and Errol Flynn), *Mary, Queen of Scots* (with Glenda Jackson as Elizabeth), *Mary of Scotland* (with Katharine Hepburn as Mary and Florence Eldridge as Elizabeth), and *Elizabeth* (with Cate Blanchett).

Mr. Smith Goes to Washington

1939, 129 min, NR, b&w, 8 and up
Dir: Frank Capra. Jimmy Stewart, Jean Arthur, Claude Rains
PLOT: Naive Jefferson Smith (Jimmy Stewart) is sent to Washington to serve the remaining term of a senator who has died. The governor (Guy Kibbee) and a businessman, Jim Taylor (Edward Arnold), believe that Smith, the leader of a Boy Scouts-type organization called the Boy Rangers, will do whatever he is told by senior Senator Joseph Paine (Claude Rains), a friend of his late father, who

was an idealistic newspaper editor. Paine approves of the appointment: "A young patriot turned loose in our nation's capital—I can handle him."

At first, Smith is such a hopeless rube that he is an embarrassment. The cynical press ridicules him. He is daunted by jaded staffers Diz Moore (Thomas Mitchell) and Saunders (Jean Arthur) and reduced to stumbling incoherence by Paine's sophisticated daughter (Astrid Allwyn). A visit to the Lincoln Memorial reminds him of what he hopes to accomplish and he returns to the Senate to promote his dream, a national camp for boys. Saunders begins to soften when he tells her what he believes: "Liberty is too precious a thing to be buried in books." She acknowledges her own idealistic roots as the daughter of a doctor who treated patients who could not pay, that idealism now buried under the practicality that resulted from her having to go to work at sixteen because her family had no money. "Why don't you go home?" she asks. "You're halfway decent."

Saunders warns him Paine is corrupt, that he is promoting unnecessary legislation that will benefit Taylor. Smith goes to see Paine and is crushed to learn Saunders was right. Paine tries to explain it is just a compromise. "It's a question of, give and take. You have to play by the rules—compromise—you have to leave your ideals outside the door with your rubbers." Smith promises to expose Paine, but Paine moves quickly and makes it appear it is Smith who is corrupt. He presents a forged deed showing Smith is the owner of the land for the proposed camp and will therefore profit from the legislation.

Smith is ready to quit, but Saunders explains he can filibuster on the floor of the Senate and keep speaking while his mother and friends get out the real story. While Smith holds the floor, his Boy Rangers print up and try to distribute their own newspaper. Taylor's henchmen stop them. After speaking for twenty-three hours, Smith sees all of the letters and telegrams are against him. He looks over at Paine. "I guess this is just another lost cause, Mr. Paine. All you people don't know about the lost causes. Mr. Paine does. He said once they were the only causes worth fighting for. And he fought for them once, for the only reason that any man ever fights for them. Because of just one plain simple rule, 'Love thy neighbor.' And in this world today, full of hatred, a man who knows that one rule has a great trust."

He vows to go on, but collapses from fatigue. Paine, overwhelmed with shame, runs into the cloakroom and tries to kill himself, confessing he was the one who was corrupt.

DISCUSSION: Frank Capra was to movies what Norman Rockwell was to illustration; he gave us a vision of our national identity that never ignored the challenges we face, although it was idealistic about our ability to meet them. This movie, made on the brink of World War II, was criticized for its portrayal of dishonesty and cynicism in Washington. Ultimately, it was recognized for the very patriotic and loyal statement that it is.

PROFANITY: None.
NUDITY/SEXUAL REFERENCES: None.
ALCOHOL/DRUG ABUSE: Diz, the press secretary, is a heavy drinker.
VIOLENCF/SCARINESS: None.
TOLERANCE/DIVERSITY ISSUES: None.
QUESTIONS FOR FAMILIES:

- Paine tells Smith he has to learn to compromise. Is that wrong? How could Smith tell this was not compromise, but corruption?

- Watch the scene where the press meets the new senator for the first time. People today often criticize the press for being unfair or too mean to politicians. Do you think they are unfair? Are they too mean? Why does the press like to make fun of politicians?

- What makes Saunders change her mind about Smith?

CONNECTIONS: It is hard to imagine a time when Jimmy Stewart was not a major star, but this is the movie that made him one. He was a perfect choice for the shy, young idealist. Capra selected cowboy actor Harry Carey to play the vice president, who presides over the Senate during Smith's filibuster. His look of weather-beaten integrity perfectly suited the part, and contrasted well with Rains's suave urbanity.
ACTIVITIES: Families should visit the Washington locations featured in the movie, the Lincoln Memorial and the U.S. Capitol building to be inspired the way Smith was. Those who can't get to Washington might enjoy taking a look at today's Congressional proceedings on C-SPAN and comparing them to those portrayed in the movie.

On the Waterfront

1954, 108 min, NR, b&w, high school age
Dir: Elia Kazan. Marlon Brando, Rod Steiger, Lee J. Cobb, Eva Marie Saint, Karl Malden
PLOT: Based on a true story (with a less satisfying conclusion), this is the story of the men who had the courage to stand up to the corrupt longshoremen's union.

The union is controlled by Johnny Friendly (Lee J. Cobb). He and his men decide who will work each day, which means they get paid off by the men and by the ship owners who rely on the union to unload their goods. "Everything moves in and out, we take our cut," Johnny brags. One of Johnny's top aides is Charley Malloy (Rod Steiger), whose brother Terry (Marlon Brando), a former prize-fighter, is treated almost like a mascot by Johnny. He gives Terry errands to run and makes sure he gets the easiest and most lucrative work assignments. Terry keeps pigeons on the roof of his apartment building and is a hero to the local boys.

As the movie begins, Joey Doyle, who dared to speak out about the corruption, is killed by Johnny's thugs. Terry had unwittingly helped to set Joey up, and he is distressed. "Too much Marquess of Queensberry, it softens him up," Charley explains, telling Johnny that Terry's exposure to the rules of fair fighting in boxing have made him idealistic. Joey's sister Edie (Eva Marie Saint) tells local priest Father Barry (Karl Malden) he has to get out of the church to help them; "Saints don't hide in churches." Father Barry invites the longshoremen to the church to talk about what is going on. Charley tells Terry to go to the meeting to keep tabs on who is being disloyal. At the meeting, one man explains that "everyone on the dock is D&D—deaf and dumb." Everyone knows if he speaks out, or even notices too much, he will not be allowed to work; he may even be killed, as Joey was. Thugs break up the meeting. Terry escapes with Edie. Dugan (Pat Henning) agrees to talk, and Father Barry agrees to support him. Dugan is killed, too.

Terry and Edie fall in love. Johnny tells Charley to make sure Terry does not tell the crime commission about his activities, because if he lets Terry tell the truth, everyone will do it, and he'll be "just another fellow." At first Charley resists, but Johnny makes it clear that if Charley can't stop Terry, Johnny will get someone else to take care of him. So Charley finds Terry, and they talk, in the back seat of a cab. Terry tells Charley he hates being a bum instead of a "contender" for a boxing title. He says Charley should not have made him take a dive in the boxing ring, a "one-way ticket to palookaville." Charley lets Terry go, and then Charley is killed by Johnny's thugs. Terry is overcome with grief and swears he will get Johnny. Father Barry persuades him the way to do it is to testify, and Terry does, while Johnny stares at him from across the room.

No one will talk to Terry. The boys who once worshipped him kill all of his pigeons. Down on the dock, at first Johnny wins, putting everyone to work except for Terry. When Terry calls him out, they have a furious battle as the longshoremen watch. Terry is badly hurt. When Johnny tells them to go back to work, they refuse, saying they are waiting for Terry to lead them to work. Father Barry whispers to Terry that "Johnny's laying odds you won't get up." Father Barry and Edie help him up, and he walks slowly to the dock, Johnny shouts, but everyone ignores him.

DISCUSSION: This movie contrasts two conflicting ways of looking at the world and especially at responsibility. Edie and Father Barry see a world in which people have an obligation to protect and support each other. Johnny sees the world as a place where what matters is taking as much as you can. Terry is somewhere in the middle, with his kindness to the Golden Warriors and his pigeons on the one side and his willingness to take what Johnny's way of life has to offer on the other. Then Joey is killed, and Terry meets Edie.

In part, Terry falls in love not just with Edie but with the vision of another life Edie represents. At first, when she asks, "Shouldn't everybody care about everybody else?" he calls her a "fruitcake" and says that his philosophy of life is, "Do it to him before he does it to you...Everybody's got a racket." He tells her, "I'd like to help, but there's nothing I can do." Like Edie, Terry is inspired to fight back by the death of his brother. When he tells Charley, "You should have looked after me," he is acknowledging the obligation brothers have for each other. He should have looked out for Charley, too.

After Terry testifies, Edie tells him to leave town, asking, "Are they taking chances for you?" Terry tells her he's not a bum, and that means he must stay. Fighting Johnny, Terry finds a way out of "palookaville."

This movie also raises some important issues about the nature of power. At the beginning, Johnny seems very powerful, and power matters more to him than money, but it is clear the choices he makes to protect that power, more than any action taken by anyone else, are the beginning of the end. As he orders people to be killed, even Charley, his own close associate, begins to appear desperate. The men who will kick back a few dollars and stay "D&D" about corruption will not stand for that level of violence and uncertainty.

PROFANITY: None.
NUDITY/SEXUAL REFERENCES: None.
ALCOHOL/DRUG ABUSE: Alcohol in tavern. Terry takes Edie for her first beer, which makes her a little giddy.
VIOLENCE/SCARINESS: Fighting; menacing thugs; Charley's body hung on a fence to intimidate Terry.
TOLERANCE/DIVERSITY ISSUES: None.

QUESTIONS FOR FAMILIES:

- Joey's jacket is worn by three different characters in this movie. What do you think that means?

- Why do you think the director does not let you hear the conversation when Terry tells Edie about his role in Joey's death?

- Edie admits she is in love with Terry, but still wants him to leave. Why? What do you think of Edie's ideas about what makes people "mean and difficult"? Do you think that applies to Johnny?

- How does Johnny get power? How does he lose it?

- If Johnny had not killed Charley, would Terry have testified against him?

CONNECTIONS: The music is by Leonard Bernstein, composer of **West Side Story**. This movie won eight Oscars, including Best Picture, Best Director, Best Supporting Actress, and Best Screenplay. Steiger, Malden, and Cobb were all nominated as well.

Quiz Show

1994, 133 min, PG-13, 12 and up
Dir: Robert Redford. Ralph Fiennes, Paul Scofield, John Turturro, Rob Morrow
PLOT: This true story takes place in the early days of television. One of the most popular and successful program formats was the quiz show, in which contestants competed for huge cash prizes by answering questions. Charles Van Doren (played by Ralph Fiennes) was a member of one of America's most distinguished literary families, and he became an immensely popular contestant on Twenty-One. When it turned out the quiz shows were fixed, and contestants were supplied with the answers by the shows' producers, Van Doren became the symbol of betrayal.

In this film, Van Doren is contrasted with Herb Stempel (John Turturro) and with Congressional staff investigator Dick Goodwin (Rob Morrow), Stempel, a Jewish man from Brooklyn with "a face for radio" is bitter over being pushed aside for the impeccably WASP-y Columbia University professor. Goodwin shares the Jewish outsider's background with Stempel, and the Ivy League polish (as he frequently mentions, he was first in his class at Harvard Law School) with Van Doren. Dazzled by Van Doren, Goodwin does not want to believe that he, like Stempel, participated in the fraud. When he finds out that Van Doren did,

Goodwin tries to protect him from being discovered. He wants to bring the real culprits, the network executives, to light. When the hearings are held, however, the Congressmen's cozy relationships with the network executives prevent any tough questions from being asked. The producer takes the blame.

Eight years later, the producer was back in television. Stempel became a bureaucrat. Van Doren, forced to leave Columbia, lives very privately, working for Encyclopedia Britannica. Goodwin went to work for President Kennedy and later wrote highly respected books.

DISCUSSION: This is an outstanding drama that provides an excellent opportunity for examining the way that people make moral choices. Stempel cheats because he wants to be accepted and respected, and because he believes that is the way the world works. Nevertheless, he is outraged and bitter when he finds he has been cheated and the producer has no intention of living up to his promise to find him a job in television. It is important to note that his decision to tell the truth was based on vengeance, not on taking responsibility for a moral failure.

When first presented with the option of cheating, Van Doren reflects ("I'm just wondering what Kant would make of this"), and then refuses. Indeed, he concludes this is just a test of his suitability, and one that he has passed. Once on the program, however, he is given a question he had answered correctly in the interview. He knows the answer, but he also knows it is not a legitimate competition for him to answer it. (He does not know that Stempel has agreed to fail.) At that moment, what is he thinking? What moral calculus goes through his mind? Is this the decision to cheat, or is that a separate decision, later?

In the movie's most painful scene, Van Doren must tell his father what he has done. At first, Van Doren makes some distinctions between being given the questions, so he can get the answers on his own, and being given the answers, but in his heart he knows both are equally wrong.

Why, then, did he do it? The movie suggests it was in part a way to establish himself as independently successful, out of the shadow of his family. He enjoyed the fame and the money. He argues no one is being hurt by it. Goodwin, on the other hand, sees it is wrong, and never for a moment hesitates, when the producer tries to buy him off. Yet, as Goodwin's wife points out, he makes his own moral compromises when he tries to protect Van Doren. In part he does it because he is after those he considers the real culprits. In part he does it because he likes Van Doren, and because as much as he takes pride in being first in his class at Harvard, some part of him still thinks the Van Dorens are better than he is.

PROFANITY: Some.
NUDITY/SEXUAL REFERENCES: None.
ALCOHOL/DRUG ABUSE: Social drinking and smoking.
VIOLENCE/SCARINESS: None.
TOLERANCE/DIVERSITY ISSUES: Issue of prejudice based on class and religion.
QUESTIONS FOR FAMILIES:

• Why did Stempel agree to cheat? Why did he tell the truth to the investigators? Why did Van Doren cheat?

• What were some of the feelings Van Doren had about his parents? How can you tell?

• In what ways was Goodwin like Stempel? In what ways was he like Van Doren? Why was Goodwin intimidated by the Van Dorens?

• Who was responsible for the "quiz show scandals"? Was the outcome fair? Who should have been punished, and how?

CONNECTIONS: Goodwin's account of the story can be found in his book *Remembering America: A Voice from the 60s*. *Champagne for Caesar*, a light satiric comedy on the same subject, was produced in 1950, several years before the events portrayed in this movie. It is very funny, with outstanding performances by Ronald Colman as the unbeatable professor-contestant, and Celeste Holm as the femme fatale brought in to shake his concentration. The question they find to stump him with is a lulu!

Van Doren's father is played by Paul Scofield, who appeared as Sir Thomas More in **A Man for All Seasons**. Goodwin's wife is played by future Oscar-winner Mira Sorvino.

The Scarlet and the Black

1983, 155 min, NR, 10 and up
Dir: Jerry London. Gregory Peck, Christopher Plummer
PLOT: Gregory Peck plays Monsignor Hugh O'Flaherty in this true story of WWII Rome. The Vatican had diplomatic neutrality, which meant no one within its borders could be arrested. O'Flaherty used the Vatican as a base of operations to save thousands of Allied POWs in a long, elaborate, and deadly game of cat and mouse with German Colonel Herbert Kappler (Christopher Plummer).

As Italy is falling to the Allies, Kappler knows the war is over. He seeks out O'Flaherty, his bitterest enemy, to ask a favor: to draw on the same resources he used to help the POWs escape to get Kappler's family to Switzerland. Kappler does not find out until he is being interrogated by the Allies that his family is safe, and he protects O'Flaherty from charges of collaboration by refusing to give any information about his operation, even though it would have shortened his sentence.

DISCUSSION: This movie presents us with an assortment of characters who each try to do what they believe is best to protect the values they care about. O'Flaherty and his colleagues decide all they can do is rescue and protect; they cannot undertake or even aid anti-German activities like espionage or sabotage. A fellow priest who does become involved in these activities is captured and executed. Kappler genuinely loves his family and loves Rome. His sense of honor is clear in the sacrifice he makes to protect O'Flaherty. He is brutal only in capitulation to the orders of his superiors.

The Pope preserves what politicians call "deniability" by not permitting himself to know much about what O'Flaherty is doing. Though he warns he will not be able to protect him when the Germans come, the Pope refuses to turn him over to them. The British emissary says he cannot help, even though the captured men are his own soldiers, explaining, "My strictest duty is to do nothing which might compromise the neutrality of the Vatican State or His Holiness the Pope." His aide, however, is one of the most important participants in O'Flaherty's efforts. This is an outstanding story of true personal moral courage and redemption, with a conclusion that is deeply moving.

PROFANITY: None.
NUDITY/SEXUAL REFERENCES: None.
ALCOHOL/DRUG ABUSE: None.
VIOLENCE/SCARINESS: Tense situations; some war casualties.
TOLERANCE/DIVERSITY ISSUES: None.
QUESTIONS FOR FAMILIES:

- Were O'Flaherty and Kappler alike in any ways? How?

- Why wouldn't O'Flaherty do more to fight the Germans?

- Why did O'Flaherty help Kappler's family?

- Were you surprised by the ending?

CONNECTIONS: Plummer appeared as a man who fled from the Nazis in **The Sound of Music**, another true story, and Peck appeared as a Nazi in the fantasy *The Boys From Brazil*. O'Flaherty's decision to help the prisoners but not to enter into the fight is similar to that made by Jess in **Friendly Persuasion**.

Spartacus

1960, 198 min, PG-13, high school age
Dir: Stanley Kubrick. Kirk Douglas, Laurence Olivier, Tony Curtis, Jean Simmons, Peter Ustinov, Charles Laughton
PLOT: Spartacus (Kirk Douglas) is a slave in the Roman Empire, about seventy years before the birth of Christ. A rebellious and proud man, he is sentenced to death for biting a guard but rescued by Biatius (Peter Ustinov), who buys him and takes him to his school for training and selling gladiators. Slave women are provided to the men as rewards. Varinia (Jean Simmons), a British slave, is given to Spartacus. He is awestruck by her grace and beauty, but when he sees that Biatius is watching them, he screams, "I am not an animal!" and will not touch her.

Crassus (Laurence Olivier), a Roman dignitary, visits Biatius's home with two spoiled and decadent women who insist on seeing a fight to the death. Spartacus is paired with Draba (Woody Strode), an Ethiopian who fights with net and trident. Draba corners Spartacus but refuses to kill him and instead rushes toward Crassus, who slits his throat. Crassus buys Varinia, and when a guard taunts Spartacus about her, Spartacus kills him and leads the other slaves in a revolt.

They escape to the countryside, and other slaves join them as they make progress toward the sea, where they hope to escape. Varinia and Antoninus (Tony Curtis), a slave singer and magician, escape from Crassus and join the slaves. The Romans send troops to capture them, but the slaves defeat them, sending back the message all they want is the freedom to return to their homes. Crassus uses the slave revolt to gain political power by promising "order" if he is given complete control. When he is successful, triumphing over his political rival, Gracchus (Charles Laughton), he cuts off the slaves' access to ships, and surrounds them with troops. Many are killed on both sides, and the slaves are recaptured. Crassus promises them their lives if they will just give him Spartacus. As Spartacus is about to step forward, each of the slaves cries out, "I am Spartacus!" The Romans crucify them all except for Spartacus and Antoninus, lining the Appian Way with 6,000 crucifixes.

Crassus takes Varinia and her new baby back to his home. If he can win her affection, it will represent the ultimate triumph over Spartacus. Spartacus and Antoninus are ordered to fight to the death, with the survivor to be crucified.

Each tries to kill the other, to save him from the slow death of crucifixion. Spartacus is successful, killing Antoninus out of love and mercy, and then he is crucified. Before he dies, he is able to see Varinia and his son, now both free, thanks to Gracchus.

DISCUSSION: This epic saga of the price of freedom is thrilling to watch, the struggles of conscience as gripping as the brilliantly staged battle scenes. When we first see Spartacus, he strikes out at an oppressor almost reflexively. He does not care that the consequence is death; as he later says, for a slave death is only a release from pain.

His life is spared when he is purchased by Biatius. His training as a gladiator gives him his first chance to form bonds with fellow slaves. His exposure to the guards and to the degenerate women from Rome, who insist on watching muscular men kill each other, shows him that power is not based on worth. When he shouts, "I am not an animal!" he is saying it to himself as much as to Biatius. When he strikes out again, he is armed not only with the fighting skills he has learned, but also with an ability to lead, founded in a new sense of entitlement to freedom.

The characters in this movie are especially vivid and interesting. Varinia has a wonderful grace and a rare humor, which adds warmth to her character. She is able to shield her emotional self from the abuse she is forced to endure without deadening her feelings. Gracchus conveys the essential decency of a man who has made many compromises, political and spiritual.

Both the author of the book and the screenwriter were blacklisted during the McCarthy era, and families should discuss how that influenced their approach to the story. Students may also be interested to know this was among the most popular movies shown in the former Soviet Union, and should consider what it was that appealed to the Communists.

PROFANITY: None.
NUDITY/SEXUAL REFERENCES: Implied nudity; slave women are treated as commodities, provided to male slaves as a reward; implication of homosexual advances by Crassus to Antoninus.
ALCOHOL/DRUG ABUSE: None.
VIOLENCE/SCARINESS: Very intense battle scenes, fights, crucifixions; also (off-screen) suicide.
TOLERANCE/DIVERSITY ISSUES: A theme of the movie.

QUESTIONS FOR FAMILIES:

- Why was it important for the Romans to spread the rumor Spartacus was of noble birth?

- What did Biatius mean when he said he had found his dignity? How was he changed?

- What did it mean when Gracchus responded that "dignity shortens life even more quickly than disease"?

- Why did Crassus say he was more concerned about killing the legend than killing the man?

- Why did all of the slaves claim to be Spartacus?

CONNECTIONS: The movie cuts back and forth between the speeches given by Crassus and Spartacus to inspire their followers. Compare the speeches to each other, and to the most famous such speech in literature, Henry V's "we few, we happy few" speech, delivered by Olivier (who also played Crassus) in the 1945 version of *Henry V*, and delivered with a very different interpretation by Kenneth Branagh in the 1989 version. The sense of community and loyalty of the slaves is reminiscent of similar scenes in **The Adventures of Robin Hood**.

This was the first screen credit for scriptwriter Dalton Trumbo after he was jailed for refusing to cooperate with Senator Joseph McCarthy's House UnAmerican Activities Committee, though he wrote under other names during that period and even won two Oscars for best screenplay under other names.

Peter Ustinov won an Oscar for his performance as the slave dealer who runs the gladiator school. He is a rare actor who is able to keep his character as interesting after becoming more virtuous as he was before.

All of the performances are outstanding. Jean Simmons can also be seen in Guys and Dolls and Great Expectations. Charles Laughton can be seen in Witness for the Prosecution and Advise & Consent. The movie also won Oscars for art direction, costume design, and cinematography.

In 1991, an expanded version of the film was released, which shows restored scenes that had been cut for the original release, including a bathing scene with Crassus and Antoninus with an implication of sexual interest. Because the original sound track was not available and Olivier was dead, his voice was dubbed by Anthony Hopkins.

ACTIVITIES: Students who like this movie might enjoy the novel by Howard Fast, also the author of a novel about the American Revolution, *April Morning*.

Titanic

1997, 195 min, PG-13, 12 and up
Dir: James Cameron. Leonardo DiCaprio, Kate Winslet, Billy Zane, Kathy Bates, Gloria Stuart
PLOT: This blockbuster movie is the winner of eleven Oscars including Best Picture and Best Director and is on its way to becoming the highest grossing movie of all time. The real-life disaster serves as the backdrop to a fictional tragic love story between Rose (Kate Winslet), an upper class (though impoverished) girl and Jack (Leonardo DiCaprio), a lower class (though artistic) boy who won the ticket in a poker game.
DISCUSSION: Classic Greek tragedies explored the theme of hubris as human characters dared to take on the attributes of the gods only to find their hopes crushed. This is a real-life story of hubris, as the ship declared to be "unsinkable" (and therefore not equipped with lifeboats for the majority of the passengers) sank on its maiden voyage from England to the United States.

The movie raises important questions about choices faced by the characters, as we see a wide range of behavior from the most honorable to the most despicable. The captain (whose decision to try to break a speed record contributed to the disaster) and the ship's designer (whose plan for additional lifeboats was abandoned because it made the decks look too cluttered), go down with the ship, but the owner and Rose's greedy and snobbish fiancé survive. Molly Brown (dubbed "Unsinkable" for her bravery that night) tries to persuade the other passengers in the lifeboats to go back for the rest. They refuse, knowing there is no way to rescue them without losing their own lives. They wait to be picked up by another ship, listening to the shrieks of the others until they are all gone.

Many parents have wondered about the appeal of this movie to young teens, especially teen-aged girls. The answer is that in addition to the charm of its young stars, it is an almost perfect adolescent fantasy for girls. Rose is an ideal heroine, rebelling against her mother's snobbishness and insistence that she marry for money. Jack is an ideal romantic hero-sensitive, brave, honorable, completely devoted, and (very important for young girls) not aggressive. She has all of the power in the relationship. She makes the decision to become involved, and he is struck all but dumb when she insists on posing nude. Furthermore, if he is not quite androgynous, he is not exactly bursting with testosterone either, and, even more important, ultimately, he is not around. As with so many other fantasies of the perfect romance, from Heathcliff and Cathy in Wuthering Heights to Rick and Ilsa in Casablanca, the characters have all the pleasures of the romantic dream with no risk of having to actually build a life with anyone. It is interesting that the glimpses we get of Rose's life after the Titanic show her alone, though we meet her granddaughter and hear her refer to her husband. Parents can have some very good discussions with teens about this movie by listening carefully and respectfully when they explain why it is important to them, as this is a crucial stage in their developing understanding of the adult world.

Parents should know the movie features brief nudity (as Rose poses for Jack) and the suggestion of sex (in a steamy car). A much more serious concern is the tragedy itself, with hundreds of frozen dead bodies floating in the water, which may be upsetting or even terrifying for some young people.

PROFANITY: Several swear words.
NUDITY/SEXUAL REFERENCES: Rose poses nude for Jack. They have sex in a car (nothing shown).
ALCOHOL/DRUG ABUSE: Social drinking.
VIOLENCE/SCARINESS: Very scary and sad scenes as the ship is sinking; Rose's fiancé shoots at Rose and Jack.
TOLERANCE/DIVERSITY ISSUES: Rose rebels against the limited opportunities for women; class issues.
QUESTIONS FOR FAMILIES:

- Who was to blame for the ship's sinking?

- Was there a way to prevent at least some of the deaths?

- What new rules were made as a result of the Titanic disaster?

- Why was telling Rose what to do so important to her mother and to Cal?

CONNECTIONS: There are a number of other fictional and documentary moves about the Titanic, including *A Night to Remember* and the IMAX film *Titanica*.

ALL MY SONS

1948, 94 min, NR, b&w, 12 and up
Dir: Irving Reis. Burt Lancaster, Edward G. Robinson

Based on the play by Arthur Miller, this is the story of the second generation's attempt to grapple with the consequences of corruption and lack of accountability of their parents. A soldier named Chris Keller (Burt Lancaster) returns from WWII to discover that his father (Edward G. Robinson) sold defective airplane parts to the U.S. Air Force. When it was discovered, he framed his partner, George Deever (Howard Duff), who was sent to jail. Keller's mother (Mady Christians) is in denial about her husband's activities and cannot accept the death of her other son in the war. With the help of Deever's daughter, Keller insists that everyone acknowledge the truth.

THE APARTMENT

1960, 125 min, NR, b&w, mature high school age
Dir: Billy Wilder. Jack Lemmon, Shirley MacLaine, Fred MacMurray
This Oscar-winner for Best Picture, Screenplay, and Director is a biting comedy and a tender romance. A bachelor named Baxter (Jack Lemmon), whose career advancement depends on his willingness to permit senior executives to use his apartment for their assignations with their girlfriends, agrees, at first, and is delighted with his promotion. Then he finds out one of the girlfriends is Miss Kubelik, the elevator operator he adores (Shirley Maclaine). When she tries to kill herself in his apartment after the boss (Fred MacMurray) tells her he won't marry her, Baxter takes care of her and comes to the realization he can no longer be a part of a corrupt system. Baxter feels differently about his choices when he sees the impact they have on someone he cares about, and Miss Kubelik's decision to have the affair with the boss leads her to lose her sense of self-worth. Making the decision to change makes it possible for them to go on together in a relationship of trust and respect.

AU REVOIR. LES ENFANTS (GOOD-BYE, CHILDREN)

1987, 103 min, PG, 12 and up
Dir: Louis Malle. Gaspard Manesse, Raphael Fejto
(French with subtitles)
This is the autobiographical story of the director's friendship with a young Jewish boy, Bonnet, at a Catholic boarding school during WWII's occupied France. The kind Fathers at the school are hiding Bonnet (Raphael Fejto) and two other boys from the Nazis. From the beginning, Julien (Gaspard Manesse) is curious about Bonnet, and takes it upon himself to discover his true identity which has been hidden from the children. In an unthinking moment, Julien inadvertently permits this knowledge to reveal Bonnet's identity to Nazi soldiers. The movie beau-

tifully balances the beauty of childhood friendships with the realities of war and the Nazi occupation. It thoughtfully addresses religion, friendship, bravery, responsibility and loss.

NOTE: This movie does not have a happy ending. It depicts what happened to millions of Jews during the Nazi reign and the overwhelming guilt felt by a boy who was only dimly able to comprehend the meaning and consequences of anti-Semitism. Other parental concerns include the tension when the boys are lost; the cook's drinking problem; smoking by older boys; and the boys' discussion of sex, including examination of dirty postcards.

THE DEVIL AND DANIEL WEBSTER

1941, 85 min, NR, b&w, 10 and up
Dir: William Dieterle. Walter Huston
There can be no starker or more literal moral choice than the one presented to Faust—shall a man sell his soul, whatever the price? In Stephen Vincent Benét's famous story, a New Hampshire farmer sells his soul to the devil and when the devil comes to collect, the father has legendary orator Daniel Webster argue his case.

This version is visually striking, with outstanding performances by Edward Arnold as Webster and Walter Huston as "Mr. Scratch" (the devil).
CONNECTIONS: This version is also known as *All That Money Can Buy*. A 2001 remake starred Anthony Hopkins as Webster and Jennifer Love Hewitt as the Devil. Other representations of Faustian themes include the musical comedy *Damn Yankees*, the brilliant *Alias Nick Beal*, and, for mature teens and adults, the wickedly funny original version of *Bedazzled*. Benét also wrote the story that was the basis for *Seven Brides for Seven Brothers*.
ACTIVITIES: The Benét story is fun to read aloud, and kids will also enjoy the poetry of his brother, William Rose Benét.

KEEPER OF THE FLAME

1942, 100 min, NR, b&w, 12 and up
Dir: George Cukor. Spencer Tracy, Katharine Hepburn
The performances of Spencer Tracy and Katharine Hepburn are the highlights of this talky movie about a reporter who visits the widow of a great statesman only to find that he was secretly the head of a fascist organization plotting to overthrow the government. Though it is somewhat dated, the rise of the militia movement makes it relevant again, and the moral issue of whether it will better

further the principles of freedom and democracy to allow people to continue to believe in the man or to expose him is still worth debating.

SCHINDLER'S LIST

1993, 195 min, R, b&w, mature high schoolers
Dir: Steven Spielberg. Liam Neeson, Ralph Fiennes
This Oscar winner for Best Picture, Director, and Adapted Screenplay stars Liam Neeson as Oskar Schindler. He was a profiteer who loved luxury, but who became one of the great heroes of WWII when he saved a group of Jews by claiming they were essential for his "munitions factory," which never produced a usable shell. By focusing on one tiny group of people who were saved, this brilliant film is able to present a more searing picture of the insanity and butchery of the Holocaust that might otherwise be unbearable. Schindler and Goeth (Ralph Fiennes), the commander of the concentration camp, are mesmerizing in their utterly different reactions to the most horrifying circumstances, showing us that everyone has the potential to be either—or both.
NOTE: The movie includes depictions of concentration camp brutality and atrocities.

THE SURE THING

1985, 94 min, PG-13, mature high school age
Dir: Rob Reiner. John Cusack, Daphne Zuniga
An East Coast college student (John Cusack) is assured by a friend that "a sure thing" is waiting for him in California, a beautiful girl guaranteed to be willing to have sex with him, with no strings attached. He and a classmate (Daphne Zuniga), who is on her way to see her boyfriend, get a ride west with a relentlessly cheerful couple, but they argue so much the couple throws them out and they have to find a way to get to California together. By the end of the trip, they trust and respect each other so much that Cusack turns down the "sure thing." The setup may be a movie cliché, but it is well-handled, with lead characters who are believably awkward (rare in movies) and believably intelligent (even more rare). This is a good movie to initiate a discussion of sexual pressures and values.

SEE ALSO:
Casablanca The famous last scene at the airport shows Rick able to make the moral choice, at great emotional and physical risk to himself, because he knows that he and Ilsa love each other.

Eight Men Out This sympathetic portrayal of the real-life story of the Chicago "Black Sox" shows how vulnerable people can make the wrong choices and that those who are more culpable as a moral matter are not always more culpable as a legal matter.

Judgment at Nuremberg The issue of "following orders" when the orders are immoral, but the risks of disobedience are dire, is compellingly presented.

The Man Who Shot Liberty Valance Characters confront the problem of trying to use the law to stop someone who refuses to be bound to it and the problem of using a lie to help accomplish a greater good.

PART II

MOVIES ABOUT GROWING UP

1

AMBITION

"Intelligence without ambition is a bird without wings."
C. ARCHIE DANIELSON

Movies give parents a terrific opportunity to show kids both the positive and negative consequences of ambition. One of the classic movie plots is the person with a dream who works hard to make it come true. We see that over and over again, often in the context of sports or show business but also in the context of learning, science, record-breaking or exploration. More rarely, movies address ambition in the context of politics, and even more rarely in business. These movies usually have an unhappy ending because the protagonists are defeated or corrupted by those environments.

Movies also show us the dark side of ambition, with stories of characters who sacrifice their honor or their families to achieve goals that may ultimately seem shallow to them.

There are also movies about people who struggle with another kind of ambition. They are characters who, in Joseph Campbell's famous terms, "follow their bliss." While those around them struggle for fame or money, they define success in terms of friends, family, love, learning, and creating. Perhaps most important for young people, there are movies about people their age who must fight against their own fear of failure to allow themselves to dream and to risk failure in trying to make their dreams come true.

All About Eve

1950, 138 min, NR, b&w, 12 and up
Dir: Joseph L Mankiewicz. Bette Davis, Anne Baxter, Celeste Holm, George Sanders
PLOT: Margo Charming (Bette Davis), a Broadway diva beginning to show her age, meets the young fan who stands outside the theater after every performance

245

(Anne Baxter as Eve Harrington). Taken by her devotion, humility, and hard-luck story, Margo gives Eve a job as a gofer-secretary.

At first, she is delighted, but later comes to realize Eve is ruthless and will stop at nothing to steal Margo's career, not to mention her fiancé (Gary Merrill as director Bill Simpson). Eve manipulates Margo's friends and colleagues, becomes her understudy and finally, after scheming to keep her away from the theater, goes on in her place after arranging for critics to be at her performance. She takes the starring role in a new production that would have been Margo's, and wins an award for it. By then, Margo and her friends are back together, Eve is tied to a critic who is as ambitiously manipulative as she is and, as the movie ends, she, too, meets a devoted young fan who could be another Eve.

DISCUSSION: This movie, with one of the most literate scripts ever written (by Joseph L. Mankiewicz, who also directed) is not just the finest backstage drama ever filmed, but also a compelling parable of ambition and loyalty.

Bette Davis is brilliant as Margo, bringing both the ferocity and the vulnerability of Margo to life. No one can forget her at the beginning of her party: "Fasten your seat belts, it's going to be a bumpy night." She is the first to notice Eve is not what she seems, but her friends assume it is just petty jealousy and it only makes them want to protect Eve. That is just what Eve needs to get them to do what she wants, and it almost results in the breakup not only of Margo and Bill, but also of their best friends, playwright Lloyd Richards and his wife, Karen. Ultimately, the loyalty of all four friends keeps them together. Ultimately, Eve is reined in by someone who is her equal, acidic columnist Addison De Witt (a silky George Saunders).

This is a good movie to use to discuss how to determine what actions are appropriate to realize ambition. Compare it to movies like **Rudy**, which is also about the achievement of a dream. It is not the dream that differs here as much as how it is achieved. Eve lies and has no compunction about creating misery for others, while Rudy is scrupulous about meeting every requirement and doing everything with honor and integrity. Indeed, that is part of his dream; without that, it would not mean anything. **National Velvet** is another example. Velvet bends some rules (mostly by competing in a race in which girls are not allowed to ride) and relies on faith a good deal, but has enormous integrity in defining her dream and in her treatment of others.

PROFANITY: None.
NUDITY/SEXUAL REFERENCES: None.

ALCOHOL/DRUG ABUSE: Social drinking (sometimes to excess), some "I need a drink" responses to stress.
VIOLENCE/SCARINESS: None.
TOLERANCE/DIVERSITY ISSUES: None.
QUESTIONS FOR FAMILIES:

• Who is the first one to realize Eve is not trustworthy? Who is the second? Why?

• Why don't Margo's friends believe her when she criticizes Eve?

• Why doesn't Eve tell the truth?

• Why does Addison stop Eve? Does she get what she wants?

• What do you think will happen to Phoebe?

• Do you think Margo was like Eve? Why or why not?

CONNECTIONS: All About Eve won six Academy Awards, including Best Picture, Best Supporting Actor (George Sanders), Best Screenplay, Best Direction, and Best Costume Design. There have been many other fine movies offering a glimpse of life backstage. A very serious one is *The Country Girl*, with Grace Kelly married to alcoholic former star Bing Crosby but falling in love with director William Holden. Some of the more lighthearted backstage movies include *Mother Wore Tights, There's No Business Like Show Business, Royal Wedding, Footlight Parade, Kiss Me Kate*, and *The Barkleys of Broadway*.

Joseph L. Mankiewicz and his brother Herman (coauthor of Citizen Kane) were responsible for many of the finest scripts ever produced. Don't miss Marilyn Monroe in one of her earliest appearances, as Miss Caswell.
ACTIVITIES: It might be fun for students to talk about how the theater differs from movies. Take them to a local production or get a book of plays for children from the library and help them produce one.

All the King's Men

1949, 109 min, NR, b&w, 12 and up
Dir: Robert Rossen. Broderick Crawford, Mercedes McCambridge
PLOT: This is the story of the rise and fall of a Southern politician, based on the career of Louisiana's Huey Long. Here, the politician is named Willie Stark (Broderick Crawford), and the Southern state where it takes place is never named.

Stark is a poor but honest lawyer in a small town who crusades against a corrupt political machine. Newsman Jack Burden (John Ireland) is assigned to cover his campaign. No one is interested in supporting him until some children are killed when a school built by the machine collapses. The state bosses see that he is gaining support and decide to run him for governor. They figure they can control his campaign and make certain he splits the vote so their candidate will win. He follows their instructions, delivering dull, statistics-laden speeches. Sadie Burke (Mercedes McCambridge), assigned to work with him by the machine, switches her allegiance and tells him he is being used. He gets drunk, then begins to deliver speeches with his own message, telling people he's a hick "just like all you hicks," abused like they are by the people with power. He tells them "Nobody ever helped a hick but a hick himself." He is exhilarated by the response from the voters.

He does not win, but four years later he runs again, promising to tax the rich to pay for better services for the poor. He wins and spends generously on new highways, schools, hospitals and bridges. This is accomplished through corruption and graft. At first, he insists it is the only way to accomplish what he has dreamed of for the state. He becomes caught up in the power of the position, and soon power is his goal. He becomes ruthless, forcing Burden's girlfriend, Anne (Joanne Dru), to become his mistress, blackmailing a judge (her uncle) so that he commits suicide, even having a man murdered when he won't be bought off or bullied after his daughter is killed in an accident involving Stark's stepson. Anne's brother is shattered, and shoots Stark. He is killed by Stark's bodyguards, but Stark dies, too, saying, "It could have been the whole world."

DISCUSSION: Jack Burden asks his editor, "What's so special about him?" when assigned to write about Stark. "They say he's an honest man," is the reply, and this puts him in the "man bites dog" category of newsworthiness. He is an honest man at first, motivated to study law and run for office out of a genuine desire to fight corruption and abuse of power. As Lord Acton stated so memorably, "Power corrupts, and absolute power corrupts absolutely." In allowing himself to exploit the same mechanisms he once protested, in a vain effort to use the ends to justify the means, Willie makes himself politically and spiritually vulnerable, and he does not have a trusted adviser or a moral foundation to keep him from spinning out of control.

It is interesting to watch the other characters decide how much corruption they are prepared to accept or participate in. Jack switches from being a journalist to what would now be called a specialist in "oppo" research (finding dirt on the opposing candidate). The judge agrees to support Stark, swayed in part by the "good comes out of bad" argument, but probably swayed more by the chance to be Attorney General. Still, there is a limit. When he is forbidden to prosecute a crony of Stark's, he must publicly oppose Stark. Even the prospect of blackmail will not force him to back down, only to kill himself.

This movie provides a good opportunity for a discussion of politics (and political scandals) today.

PROFANITY: None.
NUDITY/SEXUAL REFERENCES: Stark has affairs with Anne and Sadie, among others.
ALCOHOL/DRUG ABUSE: Drinking.
VIOLENCE/SCARINESS: Stark and his assailant are shot and killed.
TOLERANCE/DIVERSITY ISSUES: Class issues.
QUESTIONS FOR FAMILIES:

- What changes Stark from someone who just wants to help people to someone who is willing to do anything to get and keep power?

- Why was he unable to hold on to his ideals?

- Is it possible to accomplish what he did without making deals?

- How can you establish how far to go in compromising?

- Why did the "hicks" continue to support him, in spite of all the evidence against him?

CONNECTIONS: Read the Pulitzer Prize-winning book by Robert Penn Warren that inspired this movie, or a nonfiction examination of Long's career, such as *Huey Long*, by Thomas Harry Williams and Harry T. Williams. This movie won Oscars for Best Picture, Actor, and Supporting Actress. Ken Burns, the producer of the PBS series on the Civil War and on baseball, made an excellent documentary called *Huey Long* that is available on video. Docudramas about the colorful politician were made for TV and starred Ed Asner and John Goodman.

A Lion Is in the Streets has James Cagney as a Long-style politician. Long's equally colorful brother Earl, who became governor of Louisiana, is portrayed by Paul Newman in the R-rated *Blaze*, which focuses on his romance with stripper Blaze Starr. A similar story in a more allegorical context, with the politician Thomas Mitchell literally selling his soul to the devil (Ray Milland), is *Alias Nick Beal*. A wickedly satiric treatment of corrupt politicians is Preston Sturges's *The*

Great McGinty. Another story of the corruption of an idealist is *Citizen Kane*, covering his careers in journalism and politics.

Crawford was the son of character actress Helen Broderick, who appears in *Top Hat* and *Shall We Dance*. Tom Stark is played by John Derek, who later married a young woman named Mary Frances Collins whom he renamed Bo Derek. Ireland and Dru, who were married at the time this film was released, also appeared together in *Red River*.

Holiday

1938, 93 min, NR, b&w, 10 and up
Dir: George Cukor. Cary Grant, Katharine Hepburn, Lew Ayres
PLOT: After a whirlwind romance at a ski resort, Johnny Case (Cary Grant) is on his way to meet his new fiancée, Julia Seton (Doris Nolan). Overwhelmed by the mansion at the address she gave him, he assumes she must be on the staff, and goes to the back door to ask about her. It turns out she is the daughter of the wealthy and distinguished family that occupies the house. He is surprised and amused, and enjoys meeting Julia's sister, Linda (Katharine Hepburn), and brother, Ned (Lew Ayres). They promise to help him win over their father, who is likely to object to the engagement because Johnny is not from an upper-class wealthy family.

Johnny is a poor boy who has worked hard and done very well. Julia likes him because she sees a similarity to her grandfather, who made a fortune. She wants him to do the same, and tells him, "There's nothing more exciting than making money." Johnny, who has just taken the first vacation of his life, only wants to make enough so he can take a "holiday," to "find out why I've been working." As the movie begins, he is about to achieve that goal.

Linda thinks this is a great idea. She is something of an outsider in the family, forsaking the huge formal rooms of the mansion for one cozy place upstairs, which she calls "the only home I've got." She tries to persuade Julia and their father that Johnny is right. Even though he completes the deal giving him enough for his holiday, Johnny gives in and promises Julia to try it her way, and go to work for her father for a while. As her father presents them with a honeymoon itinerary and explains he is arranging for a house and servants for them, Johnny balks. He knows if he accepts all of this, he will never be able to walk away from it. Julia breaks the engagement, and Linda joins Johnny on his holiday.

DISCUSSION: Many students will identify with the feeling of wanting to take a holiday, to step back from daily life and study the larger picture. The idea that other things are more important than making money and living according to traditional standards of success may also have some appeal. This is a good opportunity to talk with them about what success really means, and about finding the definition within yourself instead of putting too much weight on the definitions of others. There is nothing inherently wrong with making a fortune, of course, just as there is nothing inherently wrong with not making one.

This movie has two exceptionally appealing characters in Johnny's friends the Potters, played by Jean Dixon and Edward Everett Horton. Their kindness and wisdom contrast with the superficial values of the Seton family.

PROFANITY: None.
NUDITY/SEXUAL REFERENCES: None.
ALCOHOL/DRUG ABUSE: Ned is an alcoholic, his method of coping with a life he considers intolerable.
VIOLENCE/SCARINESS: None.
TOLERANCE/DIVERSITY ISSUES: Theme of tolerating those who are different in background or aspirations.
QUESTIONS FOR FAMILIES:

- Why was it so important to Linda that she be allowed to give the engagement party?

- Why did Johnny change his mind about trying it Julia's way?

- If you were going to take a holiday, what would you do? Remember, this is more than a vacation—it is more like a journey of discovery. Where would you go? What would you hope to find?

- How do you think people decide what jobs they want to have? Ask your parents what they thought about in choosing their jobs, and whether they ever took (or wanted to take) a "holiday."

- What do you think Johnny will do at the end of his holiday?

- If Julia thought making money was exciting, why didn't she want to do it herself?

CONNECTIONS: Cary Grant began in show business as an acrobat, and you can see him show off some of that prowess in this movie. The same stars, director, author, and scriptwriter worked on another classic, **The Philadelphia Story**.

Rudy

1993, 112 min, PG, 11 and up
Dir: David Anspaugh. Sean Astin, Charles S. Dutton
PLOT: In this true story of determination and courage, a young man from a blue collar family wants to play football for Notre Dame, despite the fact he has neither the athletic nor the academic skills. Daniel "Rudy" Ruettiger (Sean Astin) is told by his family and his teachers college of any kind is out of the question for him, and he should be content with the good, steady work with his family at a steel mill. Only his best friend, Pete, believes in him, and when Pete is killed in an accident at the mill four years after their high school graduation, Rudy puts on the Notre Dame jacket Pete gave him and takes the bus to South Bend. A sympathetic priest helps him get into nearby Holy Cross Junior College, where, with the help of a shy tutor named D-Bob (John Favreau), he is able to make the grades necessary to be accepted as a transfer to Notre Dame.

The coaches make it clear he will never be good enough to play, but they accept him on the team to act as an opposing team player in practice sessions. His determination and commitment endear him to the team, and he is finally permitted to play for seven seconds of his last game, assuring him a place in the record books as having made it to the Fighting Irish.

DISCUSSION: With some reservations about the language (see Profanity section), this is a good family movie for a discussion of dreams—the importance of having them and the possibility of achieving them through persistence and commitment. Rudy is contrasted not only with the athletes who have far more ability but none of the "heart," but also with his friend Fortune (Charles S. Dutton), who reveals near the end that he was once a member of the team but quit, and has regretted it every day since.

Rudy's father is afraid of dreams; his own father lost everything in the Depression by risking all he had to have a dairy farm. He insists Notre Dame is not for people "like us." Rudy's older brother, Frank, does not want Rudy to succeed, because then he will have to confront his own failure to try for something more. Rudy's teammates want him to "tone it down a notch," not to "play every practice like it was the Super Bowl." Ultimately, his spirit and his insistence on giving everything he can every single time inspires them. Rudy becomes an indispensable part of the team, and each of his teammates goes to the coach to insist Rudy play in his place.

PROFANITY: Very strong language for a PG movie. A man calls another a "pussy," and there is a reference to "busting your balls." D-Bob's girlfriend tells him not to swear anymore.

NUDITY/SEXUAL REFERENCES: None.

ALCOHOL/DRUG ABUSE: Beer drinking. Rudy gets a little drunk, with consequences; he makes the mistake of telling the secret he had been trying to keep.

VIOLENCE/SCARINESS: Scuffle in a bar.

TOLERANCE/DIVERSITY ISSUES: Subtext of class issues.

QUESTIONS FOR FAMILIES:

- What are some of the things Rudy has to do to be able to be on the team? Which are the hardest?

- What are some of the things he had to give up?

- Which do the people who made the movie think is more important, ability or determination? How can you tell?

- Why didn't Fortune admit he left Rudy the key? How did Fortune change Rudy's mind?

- Why didn't the quarterback do what the coach said at the end of Rudy's last game?

- Why did Pete's death make Rudy decide not to wait any longer?

- Do you think determination is a talent you have to have, or can you learn it? Have you ever been determined to make something happen? What did happen?

CONNECTIONS: Ideally, this movie should be seen as a double feature with *Knute Rockne, All-American*, that other great movie about Notre Dame football. Pat O'Brien appears in the title role, and Ronald Reagan plays "the Gipper," whose deathbed request inspired the most famous motivational speech of all time, memorialized on a plaque in the Fighting Irish's locker room and read aloud by Rudy.

Rudy is played by Sean Astin, son of Patty Duke (**The Miracle Worker**) and John Astin (**West Side Story**). In real life, Rudy (who appears in a photo at the end of the movie and as a fan in the stands) had a second dream: to make a movie about his time at Notre Dame. Like the first dream, it seemed impossible, and like the first dream, he made it come true.

A good book for young children to read on this theme is *Ronald Morgan Goes to Bat*, by Patricia Reilly Giff. It is about a boy who has no athletic ability but "helps the team feel good."

SEE ALSO:
Major Barbara A young woman's ambition turns from saving souls through religion to saving them through jobs.
Mr. Deeds Goes to Town A man who suddenly becomes wealthy discovers that his ambition is helping others.
Red River A man is so consumed by ambition that he is unable to feel any kindness or tenderness, even toward those closest to him.

2

COMPETITION

"Victory is in the quality of competition, not the final score."
MIKE MARSHALL

Like ambition, competition's best and worst aspects are vividly portrayed on film. Competition is constructive when it spurs us to perform at levels we could not otherwise have reached. It can also cause people to lose sight of values that are far more important. In these days of athlete superstars who make as many headlines for bad behavior when they are not playing as for good behavior when they are, it is worth talking to young people about which kinds of competition are worthwhile and which kinds of competitors deserve to be our heroes.

Ali

2001, 159 min, R, 14 and up
Dir: Michael Man. Will Smith, Jon Voight
PLOT: Will Smith delivers a knock-out punch as Muhammed Ali in this outstanding film that follows the champ from his first heavyweight title to the "Rumble in the Jungle" when he won the title again by defeating George Foreman in Zaire.

Smith is a great choice to play Ali. Both have pretty faces and easy charm that mask the ferocity and fury that it takes to make it all the way to the top. Ali never trained harder for a fight than Smith did for this role, spending two years packing on muscle and throwing and receiving real punches in the ring. Smith perfectly captures Ali's Kentucky drawl. Like his fighting style, it can float like a butterfly and sting like a bee. Director Michael Mann strikes just the right balance between the personal and the political, setting Ali's struggles in the context of the racial conflicts of his era but never losing sight of the fact that it is one man's story.

Ali repeatedly tells those around him that he will be the champ his own way, and we see him try to figure out what that way will be. He won't be the white man's idea of a "good Negro," like Joe Louis. He will become a Muslim, let Elijah Muhammad's son be his manager and even shun his friend Malcolm X when told to. He knows that they need him more than he needs them, and he will be a Muslim his way, too. He will be more faithful to his refusal to fight than he will be to any of the women in his life. He will use the force of his personality—more powerful than any punch—to go the distance and get the title. No one can stop him.

Even limited to only 10 years in Ali's life, the story spills out of the screen, with achingly brief glimpses of some of the key characters in Ali's life. This is a double loss, because these small roles are played by some of the most brilliant and under-used actors working today, including Jeffrey Wright as Ali's photographer, LeVar Burton as Martin Luther King, Joe Morton as Ali's lawyer, and Giancarlo Esposito as Ali's father. Jon Voight struggles under far too much rubber make-up but makes a fine impression as Howard Cosell, the sportscaster who was Ali's favorite straight man and one of his truest friends. Mario van Peebles is quietly magnetic as Malcolm X, and Ron Silver marshals his intensity just right as trainer Angelo Dundee. Mykelti Williamson is jubilantly entertaining as Don King.

Mann, as always, gives us brilliantly revealing moments. Before a fight, Dundee quietly loads his pockets with first aid equipment, knowing that the brilliantly healthy and fit fighter will soon be needing it between rounds. In a heartbreaking moment Ali hugs the just-defeated Jerry Quarry. That moment even more devastating for those aware of Quarry's ultimate fate—he became severely impaired from injuries sustained in boxing matches and died at age 53. It is impossible to watch the movie without thinking of Ali's own injuries and feeling the loss of the resplendently vigorous champ he once was.

PROFANITY: Strong language
NUDITY/SEXUAL REFERENCES: Sexual situations and references, including adultery
ALCOHOL/DRUG ABUSE: Drinking and smoking
VIOLENCE/SCARINESS: Tense scenes and brutal boxing matches
TOLERANCE/DIVERSITY ISSUES: Racial and religious discrimination is a theme of the movie.

QUESTIONS FOR FAMILIES:

- Families who see this movie should talk about the conflict Ali faced when he was drafted. How did he decide what to do?

- How did he stay true to himself? What was the biggest challenge?

- When his wife told him not to trust the fight promoters who "talk black, act white, and think green," who was right?

CONNECTIONS: Families who enjoy this movie should be sure to watch the brilliant Oscar-winning documentary *When We Were Kings* to see what really went on in the Rumble in the Jungle. Smith's performance is brilliant, but it can never match the real-life champ's inimitable style. Of some additional interest is Ali's performance as himself in a mediocre film called "The Greatest."

There are many outstanding boxing films, including **Rocky**, *Raging Bull*, (for mature audiences only), *Golden Boy*, *Requiem for a Heavyweight*, and *Body and Soul* (with John Garfield and a rare screen performance by stage actor Canada Lee).

Chariots of Fire

1983, 123 min, PG, 8 and up
Dir: Hugh Hudson. Ian Charleson, Ben Cross, Nigel Havers, Ian Holm, Alice Krige
PLOT: This is the true story of two athletes who raced in the 1924 Olympics, one a privileged Jewish student at Cambridge (Ben Cross as Harold Abrahams), the other a missionary from Scotland (Ian Charleson as Eric Liddell). Wonderfully evocative of the time and place, with superb performances, the movie shows us the source of the runners' determination, for one a need to prove his worth to himself and the society that discriminates against him, for the other, a way of connecting to God.

The movie begins with the memorial service for Harold Abrahams, and then takes us back to his first day at Cambridge, just after World War I. A speaker reminds the entering class that they must achieve for themselves and for those who were lost in the war. Abrahams is a bit arrogant, but finds friends and impresses the whole university by being the first to meet a long-term challenge to race all the way around the quad within the twelve strokes of the clock at noon.

Liddell is deeply committed to missionary work, but when his sister asks him to give up running so he can return to missionary work, he explains, "I believe

God made me for a purpose. He also made me fast. And when I run, I feel His pleasure."

Abrahams is devastated when he loses to Liddell, saying he won't race unless he can win. His girlfriend reminds him he can't win unless he races. Both Abrahams and Liddell make the Olympic team. There is a crisis when Liddell's event is scheduled for a Sunday, because he will not run on the Sabbath. Lord Lindsay (Nigel Havers) graciously allows Liddell his place in a different event, "just for the pleasure of seeing you run," and both Liddell and Abrahams win their events. DISCUSSION: Both of the athletes must make difficult choices with a great deal of opposition. One uses a coach (who isn't even English), in defiance of tradition and expectations. The other resists the urging of his sister, the person he loves most, who wants him to quit racing, and defies the Prince of Wales, who wants him to race on the Sabbath.

PROFANITY: None.
NUDITY/SEXUAL REFERENCES: None.
ALCOHOL/DRUG ABUSE: None.
VIOLENCE/SCARINESS: None.
TOLERANCE/DIVERSITY ISSUES: One of the themes of the movie is the problem the Jewish athlete has in dealing with the prejudices of society. Liddell has to confront the conflict between the dictates of his religion and the requirements of the sport (including the entreaties of the heir to the throne) when he is asked to compete on the Sabbath.
QUESTIONS FOR FAMILIES:

• Why was running so important to these men?

• Was it different for different athletes?

• Why does Harold Abrahams think of quitting when he loses to Liddell? Have you ever felt that way? What did you do?

• Why doesn't Eric's sister want him to race? Why does he race despite her objections?

• Why don't the teachers at Harold Abrahams's school think it is appropriate to have a coach? Would anyone think that today?

CONNECTIONS: This movie won its own competition, with the Oscars for Best Picture, Screenplay, Costume Design, and Music.

Families who enjoy this movie will also enjoy a two-part drama made for television miniseries called *The First Olympics: Athens 1896*, about the American team entering the first modern Olympics in 1896. It features Louis Jourdan (of *Gigi*), David Caruso (of the original cast of television's *NYPD Blue*), and David Ogden Stiers (of Disney's *Beauty and the Beast*). While it does not have the resonance and meaning (or the production values) of **Chariots of Fire**, it is heartwarming, funny, exciting, and a lovely period piece. An extremely silly movie about the first modern Olympics is *It Happened in Athens*, with Jayne Mansfield and real-life Olympic athlete Bob Mathias.

Miracle is the true story of the 1980 U.S. hockey team, which astonished the world at the Olympics in Lake Placid. One of the oddest Olympic made-for-television movies, *The Golden Moment*, is the story of a romance between a Soviet gymnast and an American athlete. Curiously, it takes place at an Olympics in which, in real life, the U.S. never competed, because that was the year the U.S. protested the Soviet invasion of Afghanistan by boycotting the Moscow Olympics.

See also *Cool Runnings*, about the 1988 Jamaican bobsled team, *The Bob Mathias Story*, with the real-life decathlon champion playing himself, *The Jesse Owens Story*, with Dorian Harewood as the legendary athlete, and *Babe*, with Susan Clark as Babe Deidrickson Zaharias.

On the silly side, try *Animalympics*, an animated spoof of the Olympics with some comical moments, and the very funny *Million Dollar Legs*, with W. C. Fields as the President of Klopstockia, a country entering the Olympics. Of course Bud Greenspan's documentaries about the Olympics are always worth watching, for the stories and the personalities as much as for the athletic achievements.

The Great Race

1965, 150 min, NR, 6 and up
Dir: Blake Edwards. Tony Curtis, Jack Lemmon, Natalie Wood, Peter Falk, Keenan Wynn
PLOT: Dedicated to "Mr. Laurel and Mr. Hardy," this movie is both a spoof of and a loving tribute to the silent classics, with good guys, bad guys, romance, adventure, slapstick, music, wonderful antique cars, and the biggest pie fight in history. The opening credits are on a series of slides like those in the earliest movies, complete with cheers for the hero and boos for the villain, as though shown by a flickering old-fashioned projector that at one point appears to break down.

Always dressed in impeccable white, the Great Leslie (Tony Curtis) is a good guy so good his eyes and teeth literally twinkle. His capable mechanic and assistant is Hezekiah (Keenan Wynn). The bad guy is Professor Fate (Jack Lemmon), assisted by Max (Peter Falk). Like Wile E. Coyote, Fate concocts cartoon-like hilarious stunts to stop Leslie and they inevitably backfire. After a brief prologue, in which Fate tries to beat Leslie in breaking various speed records, literally trying to torpedo him at one point, they both enter an automobile race from New York to Paris. So does a beautiful reporter (Natalie Wood as Maggie DuBois) trying to prove she can get the story, dressed in an endless series of exquisite ensembles designed by Hollywood legend Edith Head.

The race takes them across America, through the Wild West, to a rapidly melting ice floe in the Pacific, and into a European setting that is a cross between a Victor Herbert operetta and *The Prisoner of Zenda*, where a spoiled prince happens to look exactly like Professor Fate. It takes all of the stars to foil an evil Baron (Ross Martin) who wants to use Fate to take over the throne.

DISCUSSION: This is a perfect family movie, just plain fun from beginning to end. It may also provide an opportunity for a discussion of competition and sportsmanship. At the end, Leslie deliberately loses as a gesture of devotion to Maggie DuBois. Professor Fate, after all, shows some sense of honor—apparently it is all right for him to cheat to win, but not all right to win by having Leslie refuse to compete. "You cheated! I refuse to accept!" Modern adults may wince a bit at DuBois's notion of how to attain equal opportunity. She ultimately succeeds by showing her leg to the editor, who becomes too dazed to argue further. Like **Mary Poppins**, it provides a chance to remind children to realize when their great-grandparents were children, women did not even have the right to vote.

PROFANITY: None.
NUDITY/SEXUAL REFERENCES: Fate and Max speculate mildly about Leslie's relationship with DuBois.
ALCOHOL/DRUG ABUSE: The prince has a drinking problem; Leslie frequently has champagne as evidence of his sophistication and elegance.
VIOLENCE/SCARINESS: Slapstick punches and, of course, the pie fight.
TOLERANCE/DIVERSITY ISSUES: The reporter played by Natalie Wood is something of a caricature of feminism, more committed to shocking people than to any thoughtful concept of equality. She has an unquenchable spirit, she is courageous and resilient and, of course, she is Natalie Wood, which makes her irresistible to Leslie and to us.

QUESTIONS FOR FAMILIES:

- Should Leslie have let Fate win?

- Why wasn't Fate happy when he beat Leslie?

- Why was Fate so jealous of Leslie?

- Why did DuBois want to be a reporter so badly?

CONNECTIONS: Curtis and Lemmon also appeared together in the movie selected as the American Film Institute's funniest comedy of all time, **Some Like it Hot**. Children who enjoy this movie might like to see some of the silent classics it saluted, like *Two Tars*, in which Laurel and Hardy create chaos in the middle of an enormous traffic jam. They might also enjoy *Those Magnificent Men in Their Flying Machines* or *Those Daring Young Men in Their Jaunty Jalopies*. Children who have enjoyed Ed Wynn as Uncle Albert (who "loves to laugh") in **Mary Poppins** may like to know that his son, Keenan Wynn, plays Leslie's assistant Hezekiah.

Spellbound

2002, 97 min., G, 8 and up
Dir: Jeffrey Blitz. Harry Altman, Ashley White, Nupur Lala
PLOT: This is the true story of the 1999 National Spelling Bee in Washington, D.C., and especially of eight regional winners in the competition. They are: Ashley, a black girl who lives with her mother in a housing project in the city where the competition takes place, Harry, the youngest of the group, a slightly hyper kid who impulsively answers one interviewer's question in the voice of a "musical robot," April, whose fond but mildly befuddled parents cannot quite figure out how such a ragingly focused child appeared in their house, Angela, the daughter of an illegal Mexican immigrant who still speaks no English, Ted, a loner from Missouri, Neil, the son of Indian immigrants whose intense focus—including special spelling tutors and hours-long drills—has him the second member of the family to be a regional champion, Emily, the child of privilege, who wonders if she should bring her au pair along to the competition, and Nupur, another child of Indian immigrants, whose regional title is saluted by a sign on the local Hooters that reads, "Congradulations Nupur!"

These and 240 other contestants are all 8th grade and younger. They don't quite understand what a heart-breakingly awkward and painful moment that is in their lives, but we do. As we watch these kids, girls towering over boys, more with braces than without, puberty's uneven effects everywhere, many of the kids confessing that they feel all alone in their school, we see them hold on to this mastery of words eclipsing anything an adult can do as a lifeline, or maybe a flashlight, leading them to their adult selves. There were audible gasps in the theater as each new word was given to the contestants, including hellebore, terrene, logorrhea, kirtle, clavecin, helioplankton, cabotinage, and opsimath. Half of those words are not even recognized by the spellchecker in my word processing program, but these kids, who learned how to read only a little more than half their lives ago, are able to handle an astonishing number of them. Meanwhile, some words recognizable to most college-educated adults turn out to be stumpers for the kids, sharply drawing the line between expertise and experience.

DISCUSSION: Every family should see this m-a-r-v-e-l-o-u-s movie about the national spelling bee because it is about so much more. It is about the strength of American diversity and the commitment of this country to opportunity. The eight featured competitors include three children of immigrants (one's father still speaks no English) and a wide range of ethnic and economic backgrounds. It is about ambition, dedication, and courage. It is about finding a dream that speaks to each individual. Most of all, it is about family—the opportunity to discuss the wide variation in styles of family communication and values is in itself a reason for every family with children to watch this movie together. Plus, it is one of the most genuinely thrilling, touching, and purely enjoyable movies ever made.

The movie is filled with brilliantly observed moments that illuminate the lives of the individuals but also the lives of all families and all dreamers. These kids, with their slightly old-fashioned area of expertise (this is the era of the spellchecker, after all, and as that list shows, these are not words likely to come up in conversation or even most college textbooks) have an engaging sense of adventure, affection, and wonder about words and language. One shows off her huge dictionary almost as big as she is and about to fall to pieces from use, and says she does not think she will ever part with it. Three boys talk about how they lost to Nupur in the regional bee. Ashley tells us she is a "prayer warrior" who feels like her life is a movie.

We also get to see every kind of family and a wide range of styles of communicating love and support. All the parents assure their children that they are winners no matter what happens at the national bee, but some do so more convincingly than others. Each family has its own idea of what it means to achieve success and what they think success could mean for their future. One father hires special spelling tutors and runs constant drills. Others look on all but speechless at children whose talents seem as exotic to them as though they had sprouted feathers.

PROFANITY: One brief word.
NUDITY/SEXUAL REFERENCES: None.
ALCOHOL/DRUG ABUSE: None.
VIOLENCE/SCARINESS: Tense scenes of competition.
TOLERANCE/DIVERSITY ISSUES: A theme of the movie.
QUESTIONS FOR FAMILIES:

- How do the families in the movie, especially the immigrant families and those at the lower end of the economic spectrum, see the importance of the spelling bee?

- What does it take to be a winner in any category of achievement and how do you and your family measure your own successes (and failures)?

CONNECTIONS: Families who enjoy this movie will also enjoy **Searching for Bobby Fischer**, based on a real-life child who became a chess champion.

AMADEUS

1984, 158 min, PG, 12 and up
Dir: Milos Forman. F. Murray Abraham, Tom Hulce
Antonio Salieri (F. Murray Abraham. in an Oscar-winning performance), the court composer, should have been Mozart. He followed all the rules, worked hard, and cared deeply. Music was his life. Mozart (Tom Hulce) arrives, a bawdy, bratty, foolish boy whose music could enchant the angels. Salieri, ironically the only one who understands music well enough to realize Mozart's genius, is consumed with jealousy. Teens will be interested to learn this movie was written by Peter Schaffer, a man whose twin brother Anthony Schaffer (Sleuth) was for a time the more commercially successful of the two, which surely influenced his choice of subject and his approach. NOTE: Very strong language for a PG.

ANNIE GET YOUR GUN

1957, 110 min, NR, b&w
Dir: George Sidney. Betty Hutton, Howard Keel
This big, brassy, Irving Berlin musical is based on the story of Annie Oakley, the backwoods girl who out-shot everyone and became the star of Buffalo Bill's traveling Wild West show. Annie (Betty Hutton) falls in love with sharpshooter

Frank Butler (Howard Keel) at first sight. He is attracted to her, but finds it very difficult to cope when she beats him in a shooting contest. They are both very competitive. Indeed, this movie contains the most competitive musical number of all time ("Anything You Can Do, I Can Do Better"), as well as a thunderously sexist song ("The Girl That I Marry"). Ultimately, Annie loses on purpose, to endear herself to Frank. In the recent Broadway revival, the sexist and racist material was considerably toned down.

CONNECTIONS: There is also a delightful video of a 1957 television production of this musical starring Mary Martin and John Raitt. The production values are far below current standards, but the singing is arguably even better than in the movie. Anyone who sees this musical in any form should also watch the superb Rabbit Ears video, *Annie Oakley*, which accurately points out Frank Butler was never anything but delighted by Oakley's prowess.

BRIAN'S SONG

1970, 73 min, G, 10 and up
Dir: Buzz Kulik. James Caan, Billy Dee Williams
This is the true-and heartbreaking-story of Brian Piccolo and Gale Sayers, players for the Chicago Bears, who were the first interracial roommates in pro sports, based on the memoir by Sayers. Piccolo (played by James Caan) was not as talented as Sayers (played by Billy Dee Williams), but he had enormous commitment, perseverance, and competitiveness in the most positive sense. He knew trying to beat Sayers was what made him do his best.

When Sayers was injured, Piccolo devoted himself to making sure he recovered fully, because he wanted to beat Sayers at his best, not beat him because of the injury. Piccolo, trying to motivate Sayers to exercise his injured knee, calls him "nigger" in the hopes of getting him excited. It is such a ludicrous insult that both men collapse into laughter.

Sayers comes back, Piccolo is added to the starting lineup, and all seems fine until Piccolo becomes ill. It turns out he has terminal cancer. The shy and reserved Sayers must learn to handle a devastating loss by keeping the best of Piccolo inside him.

This is a touching and inspiring film (originally made for television), with an outstanding musical score by Michel Legrand. The friendship and devotion between the two friends (and their wives) is very moving, as is the treatment of racial issues.

SEE ALSO:

Breaking Away A group of local boys in a college town resents the college students, but secretly fear they could not compete with them. They get their chance when the college's annual bicycle race is opened to outsiders for the first time.

Hoop Dreams In this documentary, two young men from poor families believe basketball stardom is their only hope for a better life.

A League of Their Own The teammate and younger sister of the star pitcher is overwhelmed by feelings of competition.

3

DREAMS AND REALITY

"Hold fast to dreams
For if dreams die
Life is a broken-winged bird that cannot fly."
LANGSTON HUGHES

Kipling advised memorably that we should strive to "dream, and not make dreams your master." Achieving that balance is a complicated challenge in real life. Movies are, after all, a sort of collective dream to those of us who sit in darkness, and so we dream along with the characters, wanting Rocky to go the distance (**Rocky**), wanting Ray Kinsella to turn his corn crop into a baseball field (**Field of Dreams**), wanting Dave Stohler and the rest of the "cutters" to get on their bicycles and beat the college boys from Indiana University (**Breaking Away**), wanting the Younger family to move into that new neighborhood so their dream doesn't dry up (**A Raisin in the Sun**), wanting Johnny Case to walk away from the house and servants (and snobbish fiancée) to find out what really matters in **Holiday**.

Some of the movies' most memorable characters are dreamers who insist on following their dreams long after any reasonable chance of achieving them seems possible. Yet sometimes those dreams are endearingly modest. Rocky just wants to go the distance. Rudy does not dream of making the winning touchdown, only of being on the field with the team. How do we form our dreams? How do we know how much we can hope for?

We love stories, too, about people who are taught how to dream, people who once had no hope of anything more than what they saw around them and who learned, in the words of Bloody Mary in *South Pacific*, that "you got to have a dream/if you don't have a dream/how you gonna have a dream come true?"

Movies also show us dreams have a price. For every Rocky whose dream brings him Adrian and a shot at the title, there is a Fanny Brice, who loses her Nicky Arnstein (**Funny Girl**). For every Ray Kinsella whose dream brings him his father, there is a Charles Foster Kane who thinks he can make some small compromises without losing the most precious part of himself (**Citizen Kane**). For every Dave Stohler who makes it across the finish line and wins for every kid who didn't have it easy, there is a Kasper Gutman and Brigid O'Shaughnessy who lie, cheat, steal and kill for a falcon that turns out to be false, described by Sam Spade as "the stuff that dreams are made of" (**The Maltese Falcon**).

Movies give us heroes whose lives are illuminated by dreams. They also give us characters who must learn when to put away the dreams shielding them from reality instead of helping them shape it. Those characters must learn J. M. Power's lesson: "The best way to make your dreams come true is to wake up."

Billy Elliot

2000, min, R (edited PG-13 version also available), 15 and up
Dir: Stephen Daldry. Jamie Bell, Julie Walters
PLOT: As two 11-year-olds walk home from school, the girl casually bounces a stick along the side of a building. The building ends and, still chatting, she keeps bouncing it along the shields held up by a line of policemen. They pay as little attention to her as she does to them. It is Thatcher-era England, 1984, and the police have come to this small mining town of Durham to keep order during the miners' strike.

The 11-year-olds are Billy Elliot (Jamie Bell) and the daughter of the local ballet teacher, Mrs. Wilkenson (Julie Walters). Billy watches the ballet class from his boxing lesson. When Mrs. Wilkenson impulsively pulls him into the class, he discovers that ballet both answers and creates a need in him that he can no more name than he can resist.

Billy lives with his father (Gary Lewis), brother, and grandmother. His mother died the year before, his grandmother is forgetful, and his father and brother are on strike. The adults are busy with their own problems, and no one has time to notice Billy other than to shout at him or swat him out of the way. So for a while he manages to switch from boxing to ballet without anyone finding out. When his father discovers what Billy has been doing, he is furious. He is sure that this means that Billy is going to be gay and sure that this would be the ultimate failure on his part. He forbids Billy to go back.

Billy has to dance, and he reminds Mrs. Wilkenson of a passion she once had for ballet. She gives him private lessons without charge, to prepare him for an audition with the London Ballet. Billy hides his ballet shoes under the mattress and hopes that no one will pay enough attention to him to figure out what he is doing, but his father does find out about the lessons and the audition, and that turns out to be a good thing for both of them.

DISCUSSION: This movie is well above average, tender, funny, and touching. Bell is extraordinary as Billy. Lewis is also first-rate as the father who makes an unbearably painful sacrifice in order to give his son the chance he never had. Be sure to notice director Stephen Daldry's real gift for visual story-telling. A chase through hanging laundry, dance lessons in a boxing ring, and the opening shot of Billy on a trampoline are images that are fresh and memorable.

PROFANITY: Constant extremely strong language.
NUDITY/SEXUAL REFERENCES: Sexual reference, childhood sex talk, a brief glimpse of bare buttocks, homophobic comments, and a cross-dressing character.
ALCOHOL/DRUG ABUSE: Drinking and smoking.
VIOLENCE/SCARINESS: Very tense and hurtful family situations. A parent hits a child and threatens another.
TOLERANCE/DIVERSITY ISSUES: A theme of the movie
QUESTIONS FOR FAMILIES:

- What should a family do when one member finds something as vitally important to him as dancing is to Billy?

- How can the stress of painful external circumstances affect the ability of family members to be kind to each other?

- Why was the strike so important to Billy's dad and brother? How was that like and not like the importance of ballet to Billy?

- Why did Mrs. Wilkenson want to help Billy?

- Why did Billy's interest in ballet make Billy's dad think he might be gay, and why was that so terrifying to him? What made him change his mind?

- Why do you think the writer put a gay character who did not have anything to do with ballet into the story?

- What does it tell us that Billy's father had never been out of Durham, and that Billy had never been to see Durham's famous cathedral?

- What do you think of Billy's dad's response when Billy says he is scared?

CONNECTIONS: Families who enjoy this movie will also enjoy **Educating Rita**, in which Julie Walters plays a lower-class university student who studies with a professor played by Michael Caine. Two popular movies with similar themes are *Brassed Off* (laid-off miners find music and meaning in a brass band competition) and *The Full Monty* (laid-off workers put on a strip show).

The question "Why do you dance?" and Billy's answer recall a similar scene in that most famous of all ballet movies, the brilliant *The Red Shoes*.

Citizen Kane

1941, 119 min, NR, b&w, 10 and up
Dir: Orson Welles. Orson Welles, Joseph Cotton, Everett Sloane
PLOT: Charles Foster Kane (Orson Welles) dies alone at Xanadu, his enormous mansion. His last word is the mysterious "Rosebud." A newsreel gives us the highlights of his life, the wealthy young man who became an influential newspaper magnate and political candidate, who married first the niece of the president and then, after a scandal that led to the end of his political career, a singer. As the lights come up in a screening room, an editor says, "It's not enough to tell us what a man did. You have to tell us who he was."

One of the reporters, Jerry Thompson, goes off to find out who Kane really was. He meets with five different figures who were important in Kane's life to try to understand the small mystery of Kane's last word and the larger mystery of the man who was capable of both integrity and corruption, and who seemed to have no sense of peace or happiness.

Thompson begins by reading the journals of millionaire Walter Parks Thatcher (George Coulouris), now dead, the trustee who oversaw Kane's early years. He explains that Kane's mother (Agnes Moorehead) was a landlady who became wealthy when a prospector who had not paid his bill left her the deed to his mine. The mine turned out to be one of the world's richest sources of silver. Mrs. Kane believed her son would do better if Thatcher, a bank executive, took charge of his education and upbringing. She wanted him far away from his bully of a father. Kane was a rebellious charge, and as soon as he reached his majority, he bought a failing newspaper, which he used to criticize Thatcher and the rest of the financial elite.

Next, Thompson speaks to Mr. Bernstein (Everett Sloane), who worked with Kane at the newspaper. He talks of Kane's high ideals, and his devotion to the individual struggling against the powerful. He also speaks of Kane's first marriage and its disintegration (shown in a stunning series of scenes set at breakfasts over the years).

He then talks to Jedediah Leland (Joseph Cotton), once Kane's best friend and the drama critic for Kane's newspaper, who tells him of Kane's second marriage, to Susan Alexander (Dorothy Commingore), a nightclub singer. Kane was determined to make her a success as an opera singer. When Leland wrote a bad review of her performance, Kane finished writing it for him, printed it, and then fired him.

Thompson visits Susan Alexander, now an alcoholic. She tells him about the isolation of her life with Kane, and her decision to leave him. Neither she nor the butler at Xanadu is able to tell Thompson anything about "Rosebud."

The viewer, however, is permitted to solve the smaller mystery of Rosebud, but the answer only proves there are never any simple answers to the complexity of the human spirit.

DISCUSSION: Young people who watch this movie can never know how revolutionary it was: Every one of its dozens of innovations, from the flashback structure to the use of sets with ceilings for additional authenticity, has become all but standard. No problem—there is time enough for students to study these aspects of the film's brilliance if they decide to learn more about film history and criticism. For their first viewing of this extraordinary work (and for purposes of a family discussion), just let them focus on the story, the dialogue, and the characters, which remain as compelling and contemporary as they were more than fifty years ago.

Like Willie Stark in **All the King's Men,** Kane begins as a populist and dies corrupt and alone, and we cannot help hoping for some explanation of how that happened, as Thompson does. Importantly, both Kane and Stark were based on real-life figures, Kane, of course on William Randolph Hearst, the almost-impossibly wealthy heir to the largest gold and silver mine in America who became a powerful publishing magnate. Kane might also have been based on Welles, only twenty-five years old when he co-wrote, directed and starred in this film, and who then spent the rest of his life coming up with one excuse or another for why he never came close to that level of achievement again.

As we see in flashback, Kane was taken from his parents when he was six, and raised by the bank, or by Thatcher, nearly as impersonal a guardian as the bank. This created an emotional neediness and a deeply conflicted view of money and power that is one factor in his downfall. As soon as he had control over his money, Kane bought the newspaper, perhaps for the same reason Welles went to work for a Hollywood studio; he said it was "the greatest electric train set any boy ever had."

A rebel by nature (as we see when he hits Thatcher with his sled, and in his glee in getting the staff to remake the paper over and over), he enjoys what H. L. Mencken referred to as the purpose of a newspaper: "To comfort the afflicted and afflict the comfortable." Afflicting the comfortable is great fun for him, especially comfortable people like Thatcher and his colleagues and his wife's uncle, the president of the United States.

Like Stark, though, Kane's taste of power makes him feel the rules do not apply to him. He begins to feel the ends justify the means. He does not just want to sway the electorate in favor of the candidate of his choice; he wants to be that candidate. As we see in a striking scene, with Kane in front of the enormous poster of his face, he loves the adulation of the crowd.

As we also see, he is drawn to Susan Alexander (whom he meets as he is on his way to sit among his late mother's effects) because she responds to the private Kane, the one who can wiggle his ears and make hand shadows. When he realizes he cannot have both Susan and public acclaim, he makes the critically wrong choice of trying to make her into a publicly acceptable figure, an opera star. Leland writes an honest review (after getting drunk for courage). Kane's last shred of integrity requires him to print the review, but he cannot bear to face Leland again.

Indeed, he cannot bear to face anyone. He retreats to Xanadu, where Susan Alexander spends her nights working on jigsaw puzzles. She cannot bear it anymore, either, and finally leaves him; he hardly notices, except to become even more isolated. That private self she responded to, and that once mattered so much to him, has become as completely inaccessible as the little house inside the snow globe that crashes to the floor when he dies.

PROFANITY: None.
NUDITY/SEXUAL REFERENCES: Scandal over Kane's affair with Susan Alexander.
ALCOHOL/DRUG ABUSE: Leland and Susan both have drinking problems.
VIOLENCE/SCARINESS: None.
TOLERANCE/DIVERSITY ISSUES: Mrs. Kane makes a mild anti-Semitic remark about Bernstein.
QUESTIONS FOR FAMILIES:

• What do you think of Kane's pledge on the first page of the newspaper?

• How do the scenes at the breakfast table tell you what is going on in Kane's first marriage?

- Why do you think he said "Rosebud"?

- Who, if anyone, in the movie is satisfied with his or her life? How can you tell?

- Why does Kane change?

CONNECTIONS: Fans of Phoebe Tyler on television's *All My Children* will enjoy seeing a young Ruth Warrick as Kane's first wife.
ACTIVITIES: It is hard to say who is the more interesting real-life character, William Randolph Hearst or Orson Welles. There are many biographies of both, and they are fascinating reading. The biographies of Hearst detail his reaction to this movie. His efforts to use his newspapers to discourage people to see the movie were just what Kane himself might have done. Everyone should make an effort to see San Simeon, the model for Xanadu, now open to the public in California.

There are also volumes of material about this movie, probably the most honored ever to be produced in Hollywood, and always at or near the top of critics' surveys on the best film ever made.

Field of Dreams

1989, 116 min, PG, 12 and up
Dir, Phil Alden Robinson. Kevin Costner, Burt Lancaster, James Earl Jones, Amy Madigan, Ray Liotta
PLOT: Ray Kinsella (Kevin Costner), who grew up in New York and went to college at Berkeley, stands in the middle of his first Iowa corn crop and hears a voice say, "If you build it, he will come." He begins to understand this means he must plow under the corn crop and build a baseball field so "Shoeless" Joe Jackson, barred from baseball since 1919 and dead for years, can play on it. Ray and his wife (Amy Madigan) know this is a crazy thing to do, but they do it. Shoeless Joe Jackson does show up, with his teammates. Jackson had been the hero of Ray's father, a former minor leaguer, with whom Ray had never been able to connect.

The voice speaks again: "Ease his pain." Ray comes to understand this refers to an iconoclastic author of the 1960s named Terrence Mann (James Earl Jones), now a recluse. Ray finds him, and together they hear the voice say, "Go the distance." This leads them back in time to find an elderly doctor (Burt Lancaster), who had a brief career in baseball but never got a chance at bat. On their way back to the farm, they find him again, as a young man, and together, they go home, just as the farm is about to be foreclosed. The doctor gets his chance at bat.

Mann gets to tell another story. Ray gets a second chance to do what he regrets not doing as a teenager, to play catch with his father.

DISCUSSION: The themes of this movie are dreams, family, and baseball. There are echoes of Ray's father throughout the movie. It begins with Ray's description of growing up, using his refusal to play baseball as his teenage rebellion, and as a way to test his father's love. Ray tells Mann his father's name was used for a character in one of Mann's books. Ray builds the field to bring back Shoeless Joe, his father's hero, the hero Ray accused of being corrupt because he knew that would hurt his father. Of course at the end, it turns out the dream all along was not bringing back the greats of baseball, but of a reconciliation with his father that was not possible before he died. "I only saw him when he was worn down by life," Ray says. His own understanding and maturity are what enable him to see his father as he really was, even before he reappears on the baseball field. Ray asks his father, "Is there a heaven?" and his father answers, "Oh, yeah. It's the place dreams come true."

PROFANITY: Some epithets.
NUDITY/SEXUAL REFERENCES: "Masturbation" used metaphorically to refer to self-involved and unproductive thinking.
ALCOHOL/DRUG USE: References to drug use, including pot and LSD.
VIOLENCE/SCARINESS: Costner threatens Jones to get him to go to the baseball game, but both know he does not really have a gun.
TOLERANCE/DIVERSITY ISSUES: None.
QUESTIONS FOR FAMILIES:

• Why doesn't Annie's brother Mark see the baseball players at first? Why is he able to see them later?

• What did Ray mean when he talked about how he needed to insult his father's hero when he was a teenager?

• How do you know when to follow a dream that seems crazy or foolish?

CONNECTIONS: Young people who watch this may want to know more about Shoeless Joe Jackson and the famous "Black Sox" scandal. *Eight Men Out*, with D. B. Sweeney as Jackson, tells this story sympathetically. The Ken Bums PBS documentary about the history of baseball also has a video devoted to the story. See also **The Bingo Long Traveling All-Stars & Motor Kings** and **The Sandlot** (both also starring Jones) and **A League of Their Own**. James Earl Jones provided the voice for Darth Vader in Star Wars.

ACTIVITIES: Take the kids to a baseball game. If they have attended major-league games, try a farm team or semipro. Help them with batting practice.

Lost Horizon

1937, 132 min (restored version), NR, b&w, 8 and up

Dir: Frank Capra. Ronald Coleman, Jane Wyatt, Sam Jaffe, Edward Everett Horton

PLOT: "Haven't you ever dreamed of a place where there was peace and security, where living was not a struggle but a lasting delight?" Such a place exists in this movie, and its name, Shangri-La, has become a synonym for utopia. As the movie begins, distinguished and brave British statesman Robert Conway (Ronald Coleman) has been sent to China to evacuate "ninety white people." He and four others just make the last plane. They are prim paleontologist Alexander P. Lovett (Edward Everett Horton), Conway's brother George (John Howard), Gloria Stone, a blonde with a racking cough (Isabel Jewell), and Henry Barnard (Thomas Mitchell), a brash businessman. Exhausted, they fall asleep and wake to discover the plane is going in the wrong direction. After stopping for more gas at what appears to be a rebel outpost, they land on a snowy mountaintop. The pilot is dead. As Conway prepares to go for help, a group of people led by Chang (H. B. Warner) arrive to rescue them. After a long, arduous climb, they arrive in Shangri-La, a place of beauty, harmony, and peace.

Conway is strangely at home there. While the others are impatient to leave, he feels both contented and curious. Conway asks Chang, "What religion do you practice here?" Chang answers their religion is moderation in all things, including virtue. "We rule with moderate strictness and are satisfied with moderate compliance." They have no police because they have no criminals. "There can be no crime when there is a sufficiency of anything." Conway wisely deduces, "There is something so simple and naive about all this I suspect there has been a shrewd guiding intelligence somewhere."

Sure enough, the first European to find Shangri-La, two hundred years before, is the man who created this utopia. Conway is permitted to meet the High Lama, and discovers it is the very same man who arrived in Shangri-La two hundred years before. Part of Shangri-La's magic is that people live a very long time. The High Lama has brought Conway there to take his place. His dream was to make Shangri-La a place where all of the beauty and culture of the world could be preserved against the prospect of greed, selfishness, and destruction and to create "a way of life based on one simple rule: Be kind."

Conway falls in love with Sondra, a teacher. It was she who read his books and knew he would be the one to lead Shangri-La. She saw his ideals, and also the emptiness he felt.

The Lama dies, telling Conway to take his place. George and Maria (Margo), the Russian girl George loves, insist on leaving. Maria tells Conway the High Lama is mad and cruel, that he lied when he said she'd arrived in 1888 and that she will age immediately if she leaves. Conway begins to have doubts, and agrees to leave with them. On their way down the mountain, Maria does become an old woman, and dies. George, mad with grief, falls off the mountain. Conway makes it down the mountain, barely alive. He then spends ten months finding his way back. As he arrives, the bells ring to welcome him home.

DISCUSSION: No one can resist the prospect of describing his or her own version of Shangri-La. As the High Lama says, "There's a wish for Shangri-La in everyone's head." The original provides a good starting point. So is the real-life Dalai Lama's statement, "My religion is very simple. My religion is kindness."

Though it has some troubling overtones by today's standards, the ideals of moderation and kindness are worth exploring with the family. Older children may be interested in talking about whether it is possible to create a society with a "sufficiency of anything" and whether there are both good and bad points of "an absence of struggle." Is it a coincidence that Shangri-La had, for example, no running water? While it may not be necessary to have running water to have a productive and creative society (look at the Renaissance), it is worth noting that Shangri-La itself produced little if any art (the children are shown singing an English song) and no scientific or technological advances.

Compare Shangri-La to the world portrayed in **The Gods Must Be Crazy**. In the latter, a real-life society based on kindness and "a sufficiency of anything" (and even more technologically rudimentary than Shangri-La) is deeply disturbed by the introduction of a Coke bottle: It is the first object in their experience that can be used or owned by one person to the exclusion of the others. Compare this movie also to *Brigadoon*, another timeless paradise found by an outsider who felt more at home there than in the real world." Compare it to Orson Welles's famous speech in *The Third Man*, comparing the achievements of the peaceful Swiss to the achievements of the turbulent Medicis.

PROFANITY: None.
NUDITY/SEXUAL REFERENCES: None (children swim without suits, nothing revealed).
ALCOHOL/DRUG ABUSE: None.
VIOLENCE/SCARINESS: Scary fall from a mountain.
TOLERANCE/DIVERSITY ISSUES: Racist undertones. As the movie begins, Conway is sent to China to evacuate "ninety white people before they are butchered in a local revolution." As he loads the plane, he says, "Be sure none of the natives get in!" Conway later reflects on the irony of saying the nonwhites "don't count." In Shangri-La, the people who are educated and in power are all white except for Chang. The servants are all natives. The High Lama speaks of a time when "the Christian ethic may be at last fulfilled." The movie is also somewhat sexist by today's standards; when Conway asks what happens when two men desire the same woman, he is told the men defer to one another, with no suggestion the woman should play a role of any kind!
QUESTIONS FOR FAMILIES:

• What was the High Lama's dream for Shangri-La? Was it different from Chang's?

• What do you think about the way Chang describes their "religion"?

• Why did Maria and George want to leave? Why did Maria lie?

• What did "Lovey" mean when he said Bernard should take off his mask?

• If you were going to collect the best examples of the world's beauty and culture, what would you pick? How would you decide?

CONNECTIONS: Fans of Rocky and Bullwinkle will recognize Edward Everett Horton as the voice in the *Fractured Fairy Tales* segment on "Rocky and His Friends." He was also a supporting actor in some of the best Astaire and Rogers films, and gave a touchingly professorial performance in **Holiday**. The author of the book on which this movie is based, James Hilton, was the author or screenwriter of a number of other movies, including *Goodbye, Mr. Chips*, *Portrait of Jennie*, *Random Harvest*, and *Camille*.

Do not waste your time on the musical remake, also called *Lost Horizon*. Even with a wonderful cast, it is unwatchably bad.
ACTIVITIES: A good book for children with a very different utopian idea is *The 21 Balloons*, by William Pene du Bois. Families might like to read about some of

the other utopian ideas people have designed, either in books or in real communities, and see how they have fared, and try to design their own Shangri-Las.

Matrix

1999, 136 min, R, 14 and up
Dir: Andy and Larry Wachowski. Keanu Reeves, Laurence Fishburne
PLOT: Keanu Reeves plays a computer programmer with a sideline as a hacker who gets mysterious messages that lead him to Morpheus (Laurence Fishburne), leader of a rag-tag group that lives aboard a rocket-style craft. It turns out that it is not 1999 but somewhere around a hundred years into the future. All of humanity has been turned into a source of energy to keep machines "alive" by what Morpheus describes as "a computer generated dream world built to keep us under control." The Matrix is a massive computer program that has the humans believing that they are still living in a world that has been destroyed. Morpheus believes that Neo is "the one" who can retake the world for the humans.

Special agents, led by Smith (Hugo Weaving) seek out Morpheus and his followers, to destroy them. This movie became a phenomenon and a cultural touchstone because of its then-revolutionary special effects, especially the "bullet time" effect that quickly became an icon and then a subject for parody (the best example is in *Shrek*). Just as important in the success of the movie is the way it addresses the nagging feeling everyone (but especially adolescents) has about whether we are truly aware of the "real" reality. It also addresses the question of destiny vs. choice. The visuals are stunning and the action sequences are electrifying, but for me the most intriguing and intelligent scene in the movie is Neo's quiet conversation about fate with a woman who is taking some cookies out of the oven.

DISCUSSION: The movie can lead to some interesting discussions about the relationship between humans and machines, and why Smith says that the first Matrix program, creating the perception of a utopia-like society, was unacceptable to the humans. Their attempt to keep the humans compliant through happiness did not work, so they had to try again with the past "reality" of a stress-filled world. There are also issues of destiny versus free will and loyalty versus self-interest. Parents should think about raising the issue of violence in movies, and the impact it has on viewers, especially impressionable or disaffected ones, as well.

The Matrix series taps into some of the most enduring themes of myth and epic, themes with special appeal for children and teenagers. The first is the chosen one with a hidden source of power. Characters from Pokemon to Harry Potter, Dorothy in Oz, Alice in Wonderland, and Clark Kent/Superman allow kids, who often feel powerless in a world of adults, to enjoy the fantasy of strength and control. Superpowers as a metaphor for adolescence are even more explicitly portrayed in 2002's mega-hit *Spider-Man* and in the *X-Men* movies.

Characters from Moses to Hamlet to Luke Skywalker to King Arthur and Rick in Casablanca exemplify another aspect of the hidden source of power—the reluctant hero who, confronted with dire circumstances, is able to call upon his capacity for greatness. This theme is immensely reassuring to teens, who can think of themselves as hopeless losers or as unappreciated superstars (or both) at any given moment. Imagining themselves in this position is more than a fantasy; it is a dress rehearsal for adulthood.

When movies like these become cultural phenomena, they also act as training wheels for the emerging social interaction of teenagers who are beginning to relate to each other in new ways. Movies are always a good way to get things started for kids at this stage because they take up a large part of the evening with an important shared experience but no need to have to talk to each other. Then, when it is over, the movie gives them a lot to talk about and a shared language in which to do it. A movie like **Matrix** has enough to fuel several evenings of conversation.

Anyone who has ever lived with a nine-year-old knows that it takes him two hours to see the movie and then it takes him two hours to tell you about the movie. They can remember every detail of what they saw, but it's still all about the trees of plot. It isn't until they get to about high school age that they begin to be able to understand in the forest of meaning, to appreciate metaphor and multiple layers of interpretation. They are still close enough to that nine-year-old self to be enchanted rather than overwhelmed by a fully-realized world with endless detail to be absorbed and memorized (other examples that inspire passions in this age group are the worlds of J.R. R. Tolkien and *Star Trek*).

This movie was made for just that developmental moment. **Matrix** screenwriter/directors Larry and Andy Wachowski have provided a wonderfully rich hodgepodge of references from classical mythology and philosophy to the New Testament, Alice in Wonderland, Karl Jung, and comic books. One of the best things about this movie is that it will lead teenagers to want to learn more about how the shadows on the wall of Plato's cave inspired some of the themes of illusion and reality and about the sources for names in the movie like Morpheus, Trinity, Niobe, Persephone, Nebuchadnezzar, and Merovingian.

The Matrix movies also address key issues for this age group. Erik Erikson brilliantly described the search for identity that is the central experience of adolescents. Each one must separate from the assumptions they have never previously challenged, including just about everything their parents ever taught them. They usually begin by becoming contrarians, reflexively rejecting everything they once accepted, to give them some breathing room while they begin to apply their developing analytical skills to come to a more thoughtful understanding.

The Matrix films present teenagers with an ideal story for this journey—along with some very cool fight scenes, special effects, and sunglasses. In the original, a man named Tom Anderson finds out that the ordinary life he thought he led, with an apartment and a job and interaction with other people, was just an illusion. In reality, machines have taken over. They use humans as their source of power, and to keep them quiescent the machines pipe the illusion of "normal" daily interaction into their minds. Given the (literally) new name of Neo, he considers whether he is indeed "the one" who can make it possible for all humans to understand reality.

The issues the Matrix movies raise of destiny and choice, consciousness, authenticity, freedom, and identity are thrilling to explore, especially for the first time. Parents may think that *Matrix* is just another silly summer explosion movie (not that there's anything wrong with that), but they should treat it—and their kids' passion for it—with sincere respect.

PROFANITY: Some very strong language.
NUDITY/SEXUAL REFERENCES: Sexual references and situations.
ALCOHOL/DRUG ABUSE: None.
VIOLENCE/SCARINESS: Frequent, intense, and graphic violence.
TOLERANCE/DIVERSITY ISSUES: Diverse characters.
QUESTIONS FOR FAMILIES:

- What did Morpheus mean when he said, "Fate, it seems, is not without a sense of irony?"

- Is it possible that humans could create machines that would "decide" to take over?

- What do the names "Morpheus," "Trinity," and "Neo" signify?

- Most important, would you choose the red pill or the blue pill, and how do we make that choice in our "real" lives?

CONNECTIONS: Families who enjoy this movie will also enjoy both *Terminator* movies and *Blade Runner*. The two sequels released in 2003 had some great special effects but did not have the power of the original.

Miracle on 34th Street

1947, 96 min, NR, b&w, 6 and up
Dir. George Seaton. Natalie Wood, Maureen O'Hara, Edmund Gwenn
PLOT: Doris Walker (Maureen O'Hara), an executive at Macy's, is responsible for the Thanksgiving Day Parade. When the Santa Claus she has hired for the parade shows up drunk, she quickly substitutes Kris Kringle (Edmund Gwenn), who is an enormous success. She hires him to serve as the store's in-house Santa. There, he is an even bigger success. He tells customers to shop elsewhere when Macy's doesn't have what they want. The employees are aghast, but it turns out to be a public relations triumph, and Macy's becomes known as "the store with a heart."

Doris has a little girl named Susan (Natalie Wood). She has decided to raise Susan without any fantasies or illusions, to help her handle "reality." Susan does not believe in Santa Claus. Kris tells her he really is Santa Claus, and when she sees him singing a song in Dutch to comfort a little girl who doesn't speak English, she begins to believe him. He teaches her how to use her imagination, so the other children will enjoy playing with her. He has the enthusiastic support of lawyer Fred Gailey (John Payne), who cares deeply for Doris and Susan.

Kris's insistence that he really is Santa Claus leads to a hearing on his mental competency. Kris is so unhappy he does not even want to assist in his defense. Doris and Susan write to let Kris know they believe in him, and a postal clerk decides to send along with it all of the letters addressed to Santa Claus as well. Fred persuades the court this is conclusive proof that the U.S. government believes Kris is Santa, and the judge rules in his favor. The next day is Christmas, and when Doris, Fred, and Susan all get what they asked for, it is clear it was Kris who made it possible.

DISCUSSION: In a way, this is the opposite of **Inherit the Wind**. Both are courtroom dramas about how we decide what is true, based on faith or based on provable fact. They have opposite conclusions, however, and the great gift of the movies is both seem right to us. (One similarity is that in both, the judges are warned they must make a decision that will have favorable political consequences.)

Doris has been hurt, and thinks she can protect herself and Susan from further hurt by not letting herself believe in anything outside themselves anymore. She finds out both she and Susan have missed a lot, not just in imagination but in the ability to trust and to allow themselves to get close to other people.

PROFANITY: None.
NUDITY/SEXUAL REFERENCES: None.
ALCOHOL/DRUG ABUSE: None.
VIOLENCE/SCARINESS: Kris bops Sawyer on the head for mistreating Albert.
TOLERANCE/DIVERSITY ISSUES: Tolerance of individual differences.
QUESTIONS FOR FAMILIES:

- Why doesn't Doris want Susan to use her imagination? Why do Kris and Fred think it is important?

- Why is it important that Kris told people to go to other stores to buy things they didn't have at Macy's?

- Why doesn't Mr. Sawyer like Kris?

- Why did Fred have Mr. Mara's son testify in the trial?

- Why doesn't Kris try harder to win the case at first? What makes him change his mind?

CONNECTIONS: Gwenn won a well-deserved Oscar, as did the screenplay. Ignore the pallid 1973 (television) and 1994 (theatrical) remakes. The original is much, much better, and the 1994 version completely ruins the courtroom denouement.

October Sky

1999, 108 min, PG, 8 and up
Dir: Joe Johnston. Jake Gyllenhaal, Chris Cooper, Laura Dern
PLOT: This is the true story of a boy from a small town who dreams of becoming a rocket scientist. In 1957 the Soviet Union launched Sputnik, the first man-made orbiting satellite. Thanks to Miss Riley (Laura Dern), a gifted teacher, Homer Hickam (Jake Gyllenhaal) and his high school friends peer up into the clear October sky over their tiny West Virginia coal mining town to see its tiny spark drift across the stars. Homer dreams of being a rocket scientist. His father, John (Chris Cooper), the mine supervisor, does not understand Homer's longing for wider horizons. Others do. Miss Riley roots for "the unlucky ones." Homer's mother who covers the kitchen wall with a mural of the seascape she longs to see. Homer's friends are glad to be a part of something new and important, and the community is proud to have a hero.

DISCUSSION: We know from the beginning where this story is going, just as we knew with **Rocky**. The triumph of the underdog is one of literature's most enduring themes. As long as it is done well, audiences are happy to go along. It is never done better than it is here. The script, the production design, and the acting are all superb. Gyllenhaal's expressive eyes show his simultaneous longing for the stars and for his father's approval. Cooper makes a role that could have been a one-dimensional tyrant multi-layered and complex, even sympathetic. Plot twists that might seem heavy-handed or melodramatic work because we know they really happened, and because these characters make us believe. We care so deeply about them that when we see real home movie footage of the real-life Homer's experiments we feel as though they are a part of our family.

Parents should use this movie to talk to kids about how Homer, not a great student and not especially strong in math, became so inspired by an idea that he begins to think in new ways. Using math and science to solve problems made it real to him, and the work involved was, like the eight-mile walk to his experimental launch site, unquestionably worth it.

PROFANITY: None.
NUDITY/SEXUAL REFERENCES: Mild boy-girl interaction.
ALCOHOL/DRUG ABUSE: Character abuses alcohol.
VIOLENCE/SCARINESS: Domestic abuse.
TOLERANCE/DIVERSITY ISSUES:
QUESTIONS FOR FAMILIES:

• Why was it hard for John to support Homer's ambitions? Why did his mother see it differently?

• Did Homer made the right choice in going to work in the mine? In leaving it?

• How do kids at your school treat the "nerds" and why?

• How are people evaluated differently in school than they are once they get out?

CONNECTIONS: Kids who enjoy this movie might also enjoy *The Corn is Green*, another true story about a boy from the coal mines who is transformed by education. Two different versions are available on video, one with Katharine Hepburn and one with Bette Davis.

Rocky

1976, 116 min, PG, 8 and up
Dir: John G. Avildsen. Sylvester Stallone, Talia Shire, Burgess Meredith, Carl Weathers
PLOT: Rocky Balboa (Sylvester Stallone) is a sweet-natured but not very bright boxer and small-time enforcer for a loan shark. He has a crush on Adrian (Talia Shire), the painfully shy sister of his friend, Paulie (Burt Young). Apollo Creed (Carl Weathers) is the heavyweight champion, whose big upcoming fight is cancelled when his opponent is injured. Creed and his promoters decide to give an unknown a shot at the title, and pick Rocky.

Rocky has never really committed to anything before, but this opportunity galvanizes him. He works with Mickey (Burgess Meredith), a demanding trainer. He takes Adrian on a date, and they fall in love. When her brother becomes furious over their relationship, she moves in with Rocky. Rocky knows he cannot beat Creed; his goal is to "go the distance," to conduct himself with class and dignity in the ring and still be standing at the end of the fight.

Apollo, sure of himself and busy marketing the fight, neglects his own training. Apollo wins, but it is a split decision. Rocky goes the distance. Surrounded by fans and the press, he bellows over and over, "Adrian!"
DISCUSSION: In Rocky's first fight, we get a glimpse of his potential. It is also clear he has failed to make a commitment to anything. Mickey wants to throw him out of the gym because he doesn't take boxing seriously enough. It is less an insult to boxing than an insult to himself. He takes pride in small things, like his pet turtles, and the fact that his nose has never been broken. When he gets the call from Apollo, he assumes he is going to be invited to be a sparring partner for the champion, the greatest honor he could imagine for himself.

Apollo's impetuous offer gives Rocky a chance to see himself differently. That offer does for him what Paul does for Billie in **Born Yesterday**, what Miss Moffat does for Morgan in **The Corn is Green**, or Obi-Wan does for Luke in **Star Wars**. Rocky has a chance to think of himself as someone who can hold his own with the world champion, and once he has that image of himself, it is just a matter of taking the steps to get there. That image also gives him the courage to risk getting close to Adrian.

Rocky also gives Adrian a chance to see herself differently. He was told when he was young he was not smart, so he should concentrate on his physical ability; she was told she was not pretty, and should concentrate on her mental ability. Each of them sees in the other what no one else did. He sees how pretty she is;

she sees how bright he is; each sees the other as lovable, as no one has before. This, as much as anything, is what allows both of them to bloom.

Rocky is realistic about his goal. He does not need to win. He just needs to demonstrate honor and dignity, and to show that he is in the same league as the champion. In order to achieve that goal, he will risk giving everything he has, risk even the small pride of an unbroken nose. He develops enough self-respect to risk public disgrace.

This is a big issue for teenagers. Adolescence has been characterized as the years in which everything centers around the prayer, "God, don't let me be embarrassed today." Rocky begins as someone afraid to give his best in case it is not good enough, and becomes someone who suspects his best is enough to achieve his goals, and is willing to test himself to find out.

It is worth taking a look at Creed as well. Like the hare in the Aesop fable, he underestimates his opponent. He is so sure of himself, and so busy working on the business side of the fight, he comes to the fight unprepared.

It is especially meaningful the action behind the scenes paralleled that in the movie. Stallone, a small-time actor, was offered a great deal of money for this script, which he wrote. He insisted instead on selling it for a negligible sum, provided he play the lead. The entire movie was made for less than $1 million. Stallone beat even longer odds than Rocky did when the movie went on to win the Oscar as Best Picture. Stallone also became only the third person in history (after Charlie Chaplin and Orson Welles) to be nominated for both Best Actor and Best Screenplay for the same film.

PROFANITY: Mild.
NUDITY/SEXUAL REFERENCES: Rocky and Adrian have (off-screen) sex and move in together; Adrian's involvement with Rocky infuriates her brother Paulie.
ALCOHOL/DRUG ABUSE: Paulie comes home drunk.
VIOLENCE/SCARINESS: Paulie becomes violent and trashes a room with a baseball bat; brutal boxing match.
TOLERANCE/DIVERSITY ISSUES: Apollo and his promoters want to pick a white unknown fighter for marketing reasons.
QUESTIONS FOR FAMILIES:

• Why did Mickey want to throw Rocky out of the gym?

• Why didn't Rocky have higher aspirations, until after he got the offer from Apollo?

- How is Apollo like the hare in the fable about the tortoise and the hare?

- Why is it so hard for Rocky and Adrian to get to know one another?

CONNECTIONS: There are four sequels, all increasingly garish and cartoon-like. They are barely more than remakes, and are only for die-hard fans.

The Rookie

2002, 127 min, G, 7 and up
Dir: John Lee Hancock. Dennis Quaid, Brian Cox
PLOT: If this hadn't really happened, Disney would have had to make it up. A high school science teacher did tell the baseball team he coached that if they won the division title he would try out for the major leagues. They did and he did and Jim Morris did become the oldest rookie in 40 years. Then, when he went in as relief pitcher in his first major league game, he struck out the first player at bat. Sometimes, life just is a Disney movie.

This story turns out to make a very nice movie indeed, thanks to not one but two irresistible underdog-with-a-dream stories, dignified-but-heartwarming direction by John Lee Hancock, and a hit-it-out-of-the-ballpark performance by Dennis Quaid.

A leisurely prologue sets the scene. After a mystical fairy tale about some nuns and wishing and rose petals, we meet a boy who lives for baseball. It is the one constant in his life as his family moves from one Army base to another around the country. When they finally find a place to stay, it is Texas, where the only game anyone cares about is football.

Fade into the present, when Morris (Quaid) is happily married, with deep roots in that same dusty Texas town. He had his shot at the big leagues, but didn't make it. We don't learn the specifics, but we see a big scar twisting around his shoulder. As he tells his son, "It's never one thing" that derails you.

Morris is the high school baseball coach, but it is still a football town, and no one pays much attention to the team. One day, Morris throws a few balls to the catcher and the team is impressed with the power of his arm. When he challenges them to try harder, they challenge him back. If he wants them to dream big, he will have to show them the way. So he promises that if they win the division title, he will try out for the major leagues.

He never expects it to work, but the boys turn into a team and they start winning games. So Morris ends up going to the try-outs, though he has to take his kids along. It turns out that despite what had always been thought to be the incontrovertible rule that pitches slow down as pitchers get older, Morris is throwing faster than ever, up to 98 miles an hour.

Well, we know what happens next. We probably even predict that at some point Morris will think about quitting but will rediscover the simple joys of base-ball by watching some kids play. We might not care too much about some dra-matic embellishments, like the awkwardly inserted reconciliation with his father and the way the minor league coach tells Morris the big news, which would be unforgivably torturous if it happened in real life. The dream is so pure and Quaid is so good that most audiences will be happy to go along.

DISCUSSION: Dreams ask a lot of us. The success of the team brings Morris a coaching offer from a bigger school. Morris can take it and give his family a more comfortable life. Or he can accept the offer to play on a minor league team, with the slim hope that he might get picked up by the major leagues. His dream asks a lot of him, but it asks a lot from his family, too, perhaps more than is fair to expect.

PROFANITY: None
NUDITY/SEXUAL REFERENCES: None
ALCOHOL/DRUG ABUSE: None
VIOLENCE/SCARINESS: Some tense family scenes
TOLERANCE/DIVERSITY ISSUES: Diverse teammates
QUESTIONS FOR FAMILIES:

• How can help those we care about try to make their dreams come true and to share the dreams of those we love?

• How did the way Morris believed in his team and the way they believed in make both their dreams come true?

• Morris's father tells him that it is "okay to think about what you want to do until it is time to do what you were meant to do." How do you know when it is time to put a dream aside?

CONNECTIONS: For some reason, there are more great movies about baseball than about any other sport. Families who enjoy this movie will also enjoy **The Sandlot**, *Rookie of the Year*, *It Happens Every Spring*, and *Angels in the Outfield*, either the 1951 or 1994 versions. Older teens and adults will also enjoy **Field of Dreams**.

THE GLASS MENAGERIE

1987, 134 min, PG, 12 and up
Dir: Paul Newman. Joanne Woodward, Karen Allen, John Malkovich
Tennessee Williams's "dream play" based on his own family is about a fragile girl
and her mother, both trapped by their dreams. Amanda (Joanne Woodward) is
determined her shy and crippled daughter, Laura (Karen Allen), can will herself
into a good job and a romance, but Laura prefers to stay home and tend to her
collection of glass animals, especially her prized unicorn. When her brother
brings a colleague home for dinner, it turns out to be the man Laura has secretly
loved since high school. The women have the chance to accept reality, but choose
not to.
CONNECTIONS: This play was also filmed in 1950, with Gertrude Lawrence
and Jane Wyman, and was produced for television in 1973, with Katharine Hepburn and Joanna Miles.

HARVEY

1950, 104 min, NR, b&w, 12 and up
Dir: Henry Koster. Jimmy Stewart, Josephine Hull
Jimmy Stewart plays the gentle, genial, and generous Elwood P. Dowd, a modest
but very friendly man who horrifies his social-climbing sister because he insists
his best friend is an invisible six-foot-high rabbit with magical powers named
Harvey. She sends him to a mental hospital, where the doctor decides he'd like to
have a Harvey, too. As with King of Hearts, this is a movie where the crazy person is saner than the sane people. Elwood explains his view of life: "My mother
always used to say to me, 'Elwood,'—she always called me Elwood, by the
way—'Elwood, in this life you must be oh, so smart or oh, so pleasant.' For years
I was smart. I recommend pleasant."
CONNECTIONS: Elwood's sister is played by Josephine Hull, who also appears
in *Arsenic and Old Lace*.

HOOP DREAMS

1994, 169 min, PG-13, 14 and up
Dir: Steve James.
Over four years, a dedicated documentary team followed the lives of two promis-
ing inner-city high school basketball players and their families, Arthur Agee and
William Gates were initially given athletic scholarships to a prestigious private
school, the one once attended by NBA star Isaiah Thomas, but Agee's scholarship

is cut off when his skills (and his height) do not meet the coach's expectations. The boys and their families dream of using their basketball skills to get to college, and then to the NBA. Where they are, even that .00005 percent chance seems a better bet than any of their other alternatives for making it out of the inner city. This extraordinary film is one of the most perceptive and involving portraits of America ever made. Its portrayal of these families and its messages about race, class, and American notions of success are unforgettable. There is heartbreak and triumph on and off the basketball court. At the end, one of Gates's friends asks, "If you get to the NBA, will you remember me?" and Gates responds, "If I don't, will you remember me?" NOTE: Mature language and themes; out-of-wedlock pregnancies; drug use.

THE PIRATE

1948, 102 min, NR, b&w, 10 and up
Dir: Vincente Minnelli. Judy Garland, Gene Kelly, Walter Slezak, the Nicholas Brothers
Manuela (Judy Garland) dreams of falling in love with a dashing pirate, so circus performer Serafin (Gene Kelly) pretends to be the pirate to win her heart. When it appears that Serafin will be sentenced to death, he must find a way to make the real pirate confess, and Manuela finds he is not what she dreamed of after all.

This musical (with songs by Cole Porter) was too satiric to be successful when it was first released, but now it has a strong following. Everyone agrees "Be a Clown" is one of the all-time great musical numbers. It is also a chance to get a rare glimpse of the dazzling Nicholas Brothers, the most astonishingly energetic dancers ever filmed.

SEE ALSO:
Chariots of Fire Two very different athletes bring their dreams of running to the Olympics.
The Music Man Professor Harold Hill, a con man, brings dreams of music to a small Iowa town and the dream of love to a local librarian.
The Never-Ending Story A young boy learns about the power of his imagination.
The Rainmaker Starbuck, a con man, brings dreams to an insecure woman and a parched community.

4

MONEY

"Money will be slave or master."
HORACE

Every possible kind of attitude toward money is reflected in the movies. We see adventure movies where people risk their lives for treasure. We see mystery and suspense movies in which people are willing to cheat, steal, and even murder for money. We see dramas in which people forego love or family for money or are about to do so when they learn their lesson. In dramas and in comedies we see people tempted by money to do things they would never have thought possible, losing sight of every value and every shred of self-respect. We see people learning that having money to spend is less important than giving to the community and having the respect of those you care about.

Parents are often reluctant to talk about money with children, either because they want to protect them from family worries about money, because they do not want children to become overly mercenary or status conscious, or because they think children do not care about it. They do. Thanks to the latency period, most children are not interested or willing to talk about sexual values until they are nearing adolescence (if then). They begin to think about money when they are very young and by age four or five are usually aware of "we can't afford it" as a reason for not getting something they want, or "it was a terrific bargain" as something to be proud of.

The family in **I Remember Mama** sits down together once a week to allocate the family resources, illustrating one method of involving the family in discussions of money and priorities. Other families may want to use movies like these to initiate more general discussions of how to develop a healthy understanding of and attitude toward money as well as a starting point for a discussion of things that are more valuable than money.

Barbershop

2003, 103 min, PG-13, 13 and up
Dir: Tim Story. Ice Cube, Cedric the Entertainer
PLOT: It all takes place on one day as Calvin (Ice Cube), under a lot of financial pressure, decides to sell his family's barbershop to the local loan shark and then spends the rest of the day trying to raise the money to buy it back. Meanwhile, two other guys from the neighborhood have stolen an ATM machine, and they spend their day hiding it from the police and trying to break it open.

That's the plot, but this movie is not about the story. It is about the characters and the community. As Calvin learns, that's what life is all about, too. The barbershop plays a central role in the life of the community, a place where people gather to exchange news and views and just enjoy each other's company. Calvin has some sense of this when he makes the loan shark promise not to change it. After the deal is done, the loan shark tells him he will keep it the same only on the outside. He plans to turn it into a "gentlemen's club."

As the day goes by, and Calvin's hopes for raising the money dim, he and the audience are treated to the pleasures of conversation will make you wish you could wander into the barbershop and join in.

Cedric the Entertainer plays Eddie, the irascible, seen-it-all-and-knows-it-all senior barber. Rap star Eve plays Terri, who seems equally concerned by her cheating boyfriend and her missing apple juice. A college student (Sean Patrick Thomas) likes to show off his knowledge and brag about his plans for the future. A two-time loser named Ricky (Michael Ealy) has been given a chance at an honest job, but he is immediately suspected in the ATM theft. A Nigerian immigrant named Dinka (Leonard Howze) is trying to learn his way in America (and let Terri know that he likes her) and a white barber (Troy Garrity) is trying to be accepted by the black employees and customers.

DISCUSSION: "Barbershop" is an unassuming ensemble comedy with a surprisingly gentle and heartfelt center. It is impossible not to be charmed by it.

Calvin sees that the barbershop is a place where people can find something to be proud of. He has given Ricky a chance at a job and he gives another young man a haircut to give him confidence for an important job interview. Ultimately, Calvin learns that the barbershop has given him something to be proud of, something he will want to pass on to the child he and his wife are expecting as it was passed on to him by his father.

It is great to see Ice Cube in a role that gives him a chance to show what a fine actor he has become. All of the performances are marvelous, with the give and take of the barbershop conversation playing like a series of great jazz riffs. The slapstick story of the ATM thieves is just a distraction (though it helps to tie things up at the end). We want to be where the characters want to be: in the barbershop.

PROFANITY: Some strong language, including racist terms.
NUDITY/SEXUAL REFERENCES: Sexual situations and bawdy references.
ALCOHOL/DRUG ABUSE: Drinking and brief drug references.
VIOLENCE/SCARINESS: Comic peril and violence.
TOLERANCE/DIVERSITY ISSUES: A theme of the movie. Some controversial remarks about the early civil rights era made by one character and objected to by the other characters.
QUESTIONS FOR FAMILIES:

- What are the places that serve as the center of your community? Where do people go to see each other and find out what is going on? Where do people go when they need a second chance? Where do they go to hang out and talk about whatever comes into their minds?

- What do you think about the way everyone treated Isaac? Was it fair? Why did he want to be there when no one seemed to want him?

- Why do you think people who heard about the movie got so upset over Eddie's comments?

CONNECTIONS: The comments made by one character about Rosa Parks may the interest of younger viewers to learn more about the people they have heard about in school. In fact, Rosa Parks was not the first person arrested for refusing to give up a seat reserved for whites, but it was her case that led to the historic Montgomery bus boycott. The discussion of her role may lead to a very worthwhile family conversation about the fact that the civil rights movement—and Ms. Parks' involvement—was far more complex and extensive than they might think after reading one of the "Rosa was tired" books developed for children. The made-for-tv movie *Boycott* with Jeffrey Wright as the Reverand Dr. Martin Luther King is outstanding.

The 2004 sequel *Barbershop 2* is also a lot of fun. People who enjoy this movie will also enjoy another movie with great scenes of people just hanging out and talking, *Diner*. They will also enjoy Ice Cube's fine performances in **Boyz N the Hood** and *Three Kings* (all for mature audiences).

Catch Me if You Can

2002, 141 min, PG-13, 12 and up
Dir: Steven Spielberg. Leonardo DiCaprio, Tom Hanks
PLOT: Leonardo DiCaprio plays Frank Abagnale, Jr. He adores his parents. His father (Christopher Walken) thinks he can always find an angle to get what he wants, and he often can. He has Frank Jr., still a teenager, pretend to be his chauffeur so that he can make an impressive showing when he tries to borrow money from a bank. Eventually his schemes catch up with him and he gets in trouble with the IRS. The family has to leave their home and Frank has to leave his prep school.

When Frank is 16, his parents get divorced and he is told to choose which one he will live with. He cannot handle it and he runs away. Like a child, he thinks he can recreate the perfect world he once thought he had. He has one very un-child-like quality, an astonishing eye for detail. Combined with the charm and panache he learned from his father, the ability to appear innocent to give him apparent credibility and, just as important, the actual youthful innocence to make him all but fearless because he just doesn't know how outrageous his scams are, he becomes one of the most successful con men in history. Before he is imprisoned in France, he manages to pass himself off as a pilot, a doctor, and a lawyer. He also manages to pass off bad checks worth over $4 million.

DISCUSSION: Steven Spielberg has made the real-life story of the youngest person ever to make the FBI's 10 Most Wanted List into a terrifically entertaining movie. It is set in the candy-colored ring-a-ding 1960's where jet pilots were glamorous and even bank tellers in big cities had a small-town belief in the honesty of someone cashing a check, especially if he had a charming smile. There is no hint of the upheavals and anguish of that era. This is the 1960's of big hair, smooth surfaces, and bikinis, fueled by martini music like Sinatra's "Come Fly With Me."

Every single element of this movie works brilliantly together and the result is as irresistible as its con man hero. The Saul Bass-inspired opening credits and Henry-Mancini-inspired John Williams score set the mood just perfectly, part period piece, part chase film, part drama. The screenplay by Jeff Nathanson (based on Abagnale's book) is as crafty as its subject and with just the right touch of heart. DiCaprio and Hanks are as good as they have ever been, and that means as good as it gets. Hanks, as the FBI agent who chases, admires, and ultimately inspires Frank, makes each moment on screen a small masterpiece, even the way he bites an éclair or hands someone a fork. DiCaprio captures us from his first moment as an awkward thirteen-year-old to his sheer pleasure in his own ability to master the adult world.

The main character is a con man who never considers the impact that his lies and scams may have or the risks he is taking. We may feel some sympathy for him, even want him to get away with it, but we know, as he does, that the money will never fill up the part of him that feels empty.

PROFANITY: Some strong language.
NUDITY/SEXUAL REFERENCES: Non-explicit sexual situations and a negotiation with a call girl. A character says that her parents refuse to see her following her out of wedlock pregnancy and abortion.
ALCOHOL/DRUG ABUSE: Drinking and smoking.
VIOLENCE/SCARINESS: Tense scenes and some peril.
TOLERANCE/DIVERSITY ISSUES: None.
QUESTIONS FOR FAMILIES:

- How do we see Frank and Hanratty feel differently about each other at different times?

- How were Frank Sr. and Hanratty like opposing father figures in Frank's life?

- What did Frank hope for in the relationship with Brenda?

CONNECTIONS: Families who enjoy this movie will also enjoy two other movies about charming con men: *Dirty Rotten Scoundrels*, **The Sting** (both with mature material) and **The Music Man**, one of the best movies ever made for people of any age.

The Treasure of the Sierra Madre

1948, 126 min, NR, b&w, 12 and up
Dir: John Huston. Humphrey Bogart, Walter Huston, Tim Holt
PLOT: Fred C. Dobbs (Humphrey Bogart) lives by panhandling in Tampico, MexicoHoward (Walter Huston), a grizzled prospector, tells Dobbs and Curtin (Tim Holt) of the thrill and the danger of hunting for and finding gold. They resolve to use their cash to get the equipment they need to go prospecting, ignoring Howard's warnings about what gold does to men. They are short of money for equipment until Dobbs wins the lottery and contributes the prize money.

It is hard going, but they work as a team. Just as Curtin and Dobbs say they will give up, Howard tells them he has found gold. They build a mine so they can refine it on the site. As they start to see the gold, they become suspicious and selfish, insisting it be meticulously divided each night. As Howard warned, they worry about hiding it from each other, and become suspicious and greedy.

When Curtin goes to town to get supplies, a man named Cody follows him back to the site. They try to get him to leave, but he insists on staying, telling them they can kill him, run him off, or take him in as a partner from that day forward, keeping for themselves everything they have collected so far. He warns if they decide to kill him, the one who does it will be in the power of the other two forever. They decide to kill him, anyway. Before they can, the bandits arrive. Cody is killed helping to fight them off. Dobbs, Curtin, and Howard read a letter from Cody's wife, saying that she hopes he comes home soon, and adds his finding gold is not important to her.

On their way back with the gold, they are stopped by local Indians, who need help with a boy rescued from drowning who hasn't regained consciousness. Howard goes with them and when he saves the boy, they insist on bringing him to their village to reward him. He goes with them, trusting the others with his share of the gold.

That night, Dobbs tells Curtin they should split his share. When Curtin refuses, Dobbs says he will kill Curtin and take it all. They cannot go to sleep because they know whoever falls asleep first will be killed by the other. Dobbs accuses Curtin of planning to take it all, and he shoots him. He starts to unravel, unable to rest, unable to decide whether to bury the body or leave it for the buzzards. He goes to move it, and it is gone. Curtin has managed to get to Howard, who treats his wounds. Dobbs is killed by the bandits, who take the hides he was carrying for camouflage and throw the sacks away, thinking they are worthless.

The bandits are captured and executed by the police as Howard and Curtin come to town. They find the empty bags as a windstorm blows the gold dust back to the mountains. It hurts less than they expected; Howard will go back to the Indians, who revere him as a healer, and Curtin will seek out Cody's wife, who knows what treasure really is.

DISCUSSION: This movie is almost an autopsy of, greed. At the beginning, Dobbs is a feckless but fundamentally decent character. When he wins in a lottery the money they need for prospecting, he contributes it freely to the venture, refusing his right to a larger share of the proceeds because he contributed more capital. He insists they are all a team. He thinks about whether all men can be corrupted by gold as Howard has said, but decides "it depends on the man." Yet even his awareness of the risk and his resolve not to let it happen are not able to save him from irrationality, paranoia, and abandonment of all moral principles.

Like the end of another Huston-Bogart movie, **The Maltese Falcon**, at the end the characters find the treasure is only "the stuff that dreams are made of." Like the end of **The Wizard of Oz**, the (remaining) characters find what they were seeking was within them all along. Howard will find the fame he was seeking among the Indians, and Curtin hopes to find his orchard with Cody's wife, contrasting the peace of the natural world with the false value of gold.

This movie includes a textbook example of projection, well worth pointing out to kids who watch it. Dobbs insists it is Curtin who wants to murder him and take all the gold, when he is really the one fantasizing about murder.

PROFANITY: None.
NUDITY/SEXUAL REFERENCES: None.
ALCOHOL/DRUG ABUSE: Dobbs and Curtin get drunk waiting for the boss to come pay them.
VIOLENCE/SCARINESS: Fistfights; shooting.
TOLERANCE/DIVERSITY ISSUES: A wide range of Mexican and American characters; Howard shows respect for the customs of the Indians.
QUESTIONS FOR FAMILIES:

- Why does Dobbs tell the man who gave him handouts he never looked at his face, only at his hands and the money?

- What makes Dobbs change? What is the evidence of his changes? Why did gold become so important to him, when he had lived without money for so long?

- Which of Cody's options would you have accepted if you were one of the three men? Why?

- What do you think of the ending? How is it different from most adventure stories?

CONNECTIONS: Director-screenwriter John Huston appears in the early part of the film as the American who gives Dobbs a handout. The director's father, distinguished matinee idol Walter Huston, was persuaded (by force, according to rumor) to play the part of Howard without his dentures. His performance earned him an Oscar for Best Supporting Actor.

Almost as interesting as the story of the movie is the story of the author of the original book, the mysterious B. Traven, who was intensely private. Huston suspected Traven's "representative," who negotiated the rights and consulted on the film, was Traven himself. A biography, *The Secret of the Sierra Madre: the Man Who Was B. Traven*, by Will Wyatt, was published in 1980.

CAN'T BUY ME LOVE

1987, 94 min, PG-13, high school age
Dir: Steve Rash. Patrick Dempsey, Amanda Peterson
Ronald Miller (Patrick Dempsey), a nerdy boy, pays the most popular girl in school $1,000 to pretend to be his girlfriend for a month so he will become popular, too. She agrees, only because she is desperate for money, but finds herself liking Ronald until the popularity goes to his head. The movie is only fair, but does have a perceptive treatment of high school social strata. Once Ronald is accepted by a popular girl, he is immediately accepted by everyone, and everything he does is automatically considered cool. NOTE: Some strong language and teen drinking, and some particularly troublesome bimbo behavior by some of the girls.
CONNECTIONS: The 2003 remake *Love Don't Cost a Thing* is not worth watching.

A HARD DAY'S NIGHT

1964, 85 min, NR, b&w, 8 and up
Dir: Richard Lester. The Beatles
The documentary style of this movie masks its tight construction, clever script, and sublime anarchy second only to the Marx brothers. A surrealistic day in the life of the most overwhelmingly popular rock group of all time, it portrays the Beatles sympathetically. Like the heroine of **It Happened One Night**, they are constantly told what to do and are smothered by all they have, while Paul's "clean" grandfather causes most of the trouble. Musical numbers include a classic song about the limits of money, "Can't Buy Me Love," and other Beatles hits like "If I Fell," "Should Have Known Better," and the title song, inspired by one of Ringo's malapropisms. Themes for discussion include the nature of fads and the problems created by success.
CONNECTIONS: See also *Help!* (more like a comedy with music, while this one is more like a musical with comedy). Kids twelve and up might enjoy *I Wanna Hold Your Hand*, about teens overcome by Beatlemania, or *That Thing You Do*, written and directed by Tom Hanks, the story of a 1960s Erie, Pennsylvania, rock group that has an unexpected hit song.

IT'S A MAD MAD MAD MAD WORLD

1963, 155 min, NR, 6 and up
Dir: Stanley Kramer. Spencer Tracy, Sid Caesar, Mickey Rooney, Ethel Merman
Every television, movie, and vaudeville comedian in Hollywood and every conceivable slapstick stunt appear in this epic comedy about a disparate group of characters racing each other and the police to find a stolen $250,000. Jimmy Durante is the thief on his way to collect his loot when his car runs off the highway and he "kicks the bucket," telling the drivers who stopped to help him only that it is buried under "a big W." They try to cooperate, but when they cannot agree on how to split the money, it is every man (and woman) for himself, and the race is on, picking up more greedy treasure seekers along the way, each of them becoming all but irrational at the prospect of getting the money. Spencer Tracy is the long-suffering police chief on the trail of the money and the people who are after it. It might be simpler to list the comic actors who do not appear in this movie than to list the ones who do, so suffice it to say that the cast includes: Mickey Rooney, Phil Silvers, Ethel Merman, Dorothy Provine, Jonathan Winters, Terry-Thomas, Arnold Stang, the Three Stooges, and Jerry Lewis. Themes worth discussing include greed, loyalty, integrity, and the importance of laughter.
CONNECTIONS: Movies with similar themes include Mel Brooks's *The Twelve Chairs* and *Rat Race*.

THE MAN THAT CORRUPTED HADLEYBURG

1980, 40 min, NR, 12 and up
Dir: Ralph Rosenblum. Robert Preston, Fred Gwynne
In this video made for the "American Short Story Collection," based on a satire by Mark Twain, a stranger (Robert Preston) comes to a town famous for the honesty of its citizens and proves they are all greedy hypocrites. The stranger has a bag of money for whoever in the town once helped a poor man with twenty dollars and some good advice. All that is necessary is for the person to identify himself by providing that advice in a sealed envelope to the town's former clergyman. It turns out the reward is a clever trap prepared by a man still bitter over his treatment in Hadleyburg years before. When he makes it possible for each of the town's leading citizens, the "Nineteeners," to claim credit for the good deed, each conspires to get the money and keep it away from all the others, until a final public confrontation shows each of them to be completely corruptible.
CONNECTIONS: Another fine adaptation of this story was produced by Global Stage (http://www.globalstage.net) in 2000.

POOR LITTLE RICH GIRL

1936, 72 min, NR, b&w, 4 and up
Dir: Irving Cummings. Shirley Temple, Alice Faye, Jack Haley
One of Shirley Temple's best movies is this story of a reverse Cinderella who finds happiness when she leaves her wealthy father and meets up with a poor but jolly family and a pair of vaudevillians. Shirley Temple plays Barbara Barry, the daughter of a wealthy widower, owner of a soap company. She is a curious and imaginative child, but very lonely due to her isolated upbringing. Waited on and fussed over, she is sent to bed after just one sneeze. Her father arranges to send her away to school, but the nanny is injured taking her there, and Barbara decides to take the opportunity to explore the world and meet people. Two vaudevillians (Jack Haley and Alice Faye) take her in and, once she joins their act, they get a job performing on the radio. Barbara does not realize their sponsor is her father's biggest rival in the soap business, Simon Peck, a cranky old man who is (of course) charmed by the little girl with the ringlets. Once her father finds her again, she paves the way for a merger of the two soap companies and her father's marriage to Peck's Secretary. NOTE: A black porter is respectfully but stereotypically portrayed; Barbara's father uses the expression "white of you."
CONNECTIONS: The secretary is played by Gloria Stuart, who was nominated for an Oscar in 1998 as Rose in Titanic. Jack Haley also appears as the Tin Woodsman in **The Wizard of Oz**.

WHAT A WAY TO GO!

1964, 111 min, NR, 8 and up
Dir: J. Lee Thompson. Shirley MacLaine, Paul Newman, Dean Martin, Gene Kelly, Dick Van Dyke, Robert Mitchum
This wild black comedy stars Shirley MacLaine as a simple young woman who wants nothing more in life than a quiet home with the man she loves. Unfortunately, she marries a series of husbands (Dick Van Dyke, Paul Newman, Gene Kelly, and Robert Mitchum) who make fortune after fortune and then die. Each marriage parodies a different style of movie, from artsy European to splashy big-budget musical. Throughout the movie, like Dorothy in Oz, she keeps trying to go "home." She finally finds happiness with a husband who makes sure she will never be troubled with money again. NOTE: Some kids will not be comfortable with black comedy, and may find the constant deaths of the husbands upsetting, but others will find it funny and will appreciate the message.

SEE ALSO:

A Christmas Carol A man who has sacrificed love and family to make money learns true riches come from giving to others.

King Midas and the Golden Touch This is the classic fairy tale about the king who loves gold so much he wishes everything he touches would turn to gold, and finds when the wish is granted, the results are not what he expected.

Mr. Deeds Goes to Town A man who inherits a fortune finds he is most fulfilled when he gives it away to help others.

Split Infinity A young girl who wants to be rich goes back in time to meet her wealthy grandfather as a young man, and together they find out money is not as important as they had thought.

5

SOLVING PROBLEMS

"Adversity introduces a man to himself."
ANONYMOUS

Most films present their protagonists with some kind of challenge, and most often it comes in the form of a change or crisis. Watching the characters respond can teach kids (and their parents) a great deal not just about the way people solve problems, but about the ways that people adapt to new and unexpected events and the kind of flexibility, confidence, and creativity that are required.

In movies, we see characters coping with everyday changes, like going to a new school, changing technology, and changing times, to the most overwhelming, like the loss of a family member or the devastation of war and genocide. Even good news creates changes that must be assimilated. Fantasy and science fiction movies show us characters confronting astonishing and even bizarre circumstances. Yet these characters employ the same skills as those facing more familiar challenges. Make sure young people see adapting successfully changes the way the characters feel about themselves.

Help children notice the methods the characters use to adapt. Some give up and accept whatever happens. Some are too inflexible to adapt to change. Some find themselves hemmed in by the choices they have made, and are unable to change, even though they want to. Some survive by trying different ways of achieving a sense of control over some concrete aspect of the situation, even a very small one. Some transfer the skills they had to the tasks before them. Some whose skills are not transferable look for another place where their skills are needed. Some adapt by using humor or by dreaming of ways to make things better or by becoming close to others in the same situation. Some ask for help through prayer, some through reading or learning a new skill or seeking help from a trusted adviser. Some work creatively and doggedly to solve the problem at hand. Others find one part of the problem they can solve. Sometimes, they stay and fight. Sometimes, they leave and start a new life somewhere else. In every case, whether explicitly or intuitively, the characters recognize the change and its consequences and determine how they will respond. The ones who triumph are those who approach challenges with spirit, integrity, self-respect, and determination.

2001: A Space Odyssey

1968, 139 min, G, 10 and up
Dir., Stanley Kubrick. Keir Dullea, Gary Lockwood
PLOT: In this science-fiction masterpiece, Stanley Kubrick tracks the odyssey of mankind, from the dawn of man 4 million years ago to the exploration of deep space. The film begins with a desolate time when our apelike predecessors led frightened and brutal lives, scrounging for food and huddling against the cold night while wild animals howled in the distance. In a few short minutes, Kubrick has spanned the epochs, depicting the origins of tribes and the miraculous morning when apes awoke and learned how to use tools. With this ability, mankind was launched on its journey to the stars. On Kubrick's time line, it is just a small next step to the exploration of the moon. From the moon, mankind heads off to Jupiter. What is triggering these immense changes? Why are humans evolving, and what is their destiny? At transforming moments along this odyssey, a mysterious black monolith appears, drawing humans ever forward. Toward what? The surprise ending to this film is legendary, and has probably inspired more late-night discussions in college dorms than any other movie.
DISCUSSION: For children twelve or older, **2001** can be a mind-boggling experience. In a series of dramatic vignettes, it introduces children to cosmic mysteries and gives them an opportunity and an incentive to grapple with issues that span the millennia, rather than dwell on their last argument over a toy. Younger children may be impressed by the drama, the special effects, and the beautiful music, but may have a hard time following the plot. In addition, they will lose patience with some of the longer segments dealing with space exploration. (The special effects used by Kubrick were revolutionary in their day, but will seem commonplace to children raised on **Star Wars** and *Star Trek: The Next Generation*). Even twelve-year olds may not appreciate the subtle references to political rivalries and intrigue on Earth, the cover-up of mysterious developments on the moon, or the more ironic aspects of the clash between man and machine (HAL the computer plaintively crying that he is afraid and that he can feel his mind going is a poignant example). In fact, the cryptic ending of the movie is famous for stumping even thoughtful adults.

Most teenagers cannot help but be swept up in this film, which stretches their minds and gives them mysteries and uncertainty instead of endings where everything is neatly tied up with a bow. As children strive to deal with the uncertainty of the ending, and fill in its gaps and illuminate its gray areas by drawing upon their own personality and sense of the world, they are on their way to appreciating greater and more mature forms of art.

PROFANITY: None.
NUDITY/SEXUAL REFERENCES: None.
ALCOHOL/DRUG ABUSE: None.
VIOLENCE/SCARINESS: Characters in peril; some are killed.
TOLERANCE/DIVERSITY ISSUES: None.
QUESTIONS FOR FAMILIES:

- Why is the moment the apes use tools a turning point?

- What does the monolith represent?

- HAL says he was made in 1992. Now that we have passed that date, how many of the film's ideas about the future seem to be accurate?

- HAL says he can "feel." What does "he" mean?

- What happens to Dave at the end? Why?

CONNECTIONS: A sequel, 2010, was made in 1984, with author Arthur Clarke appearing briefly on a park bench. It answers many of the questions raised in 2001, at least in a literal sense, but is not as satisfying as the more open-ended original. Kids who like this movie should read some of Arthur C. Clarke's science-fiction books, especially *Childhood's End*, and Isaac Asimov's *Foundation* trilogy.
ACTIVITIES: Teens may want to use the Internet to learn more about artificial intelligence and space travel.

Apollo 13

1995, 135 min, PG, 8 and up
Dir: Ron Howard. Tom Hanks, Gary Sinise, Ed Harris, Kevin Bacon, Bill Paxton
PLOT: This movie should be called "Smart and Smarter." In addition to the thrilling story, masterful performances, and impeccable technical authenticity, it

is a heartening story of the triumph of smart guys with slide rules, a relief in this era of movies about characters who triumph by being dumb. Two-time Oscar-winner Tom Hanks plays real-life astronaut-hero Jim Lovell in this true story of the mission to the moon that almost left three astronauts stranded in space when an oxygen tank exploded. Even though we know it turned out all right, even though the technical material is dense and the action is confined to a space smaller than an elevator, the tension is breathtaking as the astronauts and the mission control team in Houston try to think their way back home. Everything from duct tape to the cover of the flight manual to one of the astronaut's socks is used in this pre-MacGyver story, where mission control asks simply, "What's good on that ship?" and builds from there.

DISCUSSION: Because of the technical material and intensity of the story, it is a good idea to prepare kids beforehand by telling them what the movie is about; you also may want to reassure them, since it is a true story, that the astronauts did come home all right.

Talk to older kids about the way that Mission Control solves the problems happening thousands of miles away by recreating the conditions inside the spaceship. Point out how the adults handle the strain, sometimes losing their tempers, trying to escape blame, or blaming one another, but mostly working very well together.

Lovell and Ken Mattingly (Gary Sinise) were presented with a very tough problem when exposure to the measles led Mission Control to pull Mattingly from the mission. Lovell tries to insist that Mattingly go along, but ultimately realizes the good of the mission has to override his feelings of loyalty. Children may have their own ideas about how this should have been handled.

The legendary "Failure is not an option," said by Gene Kranz, head of Mission Control, when most people were certain the astronauts would never make it back, is worth discussing. So are the changes since you were your children's age: Note that everyone in Mission Control is a white male (and they all smoke all the time), and they are amazed a computer is small enough to fit into one room. Parents may have to explain why adults who watch the movie laugh when the engineers take out their slide rules. For modern-day kids, they are more exotic than an abacus.

PROFANITY: A couple of mild expletives.
NUDITY/SEXUAL REFERENCES: One or two oblique references, including one to "the clap."
ALCOBOL/DRUG ABUSE: Drinking at a party; smoking.

VIOLENCE/SCARINESS: Very tense; characters in peril.
TOLERANCE/DIVERSITY ISSUES: All of the professionals are white males.
QUESTIONS FOR FAMILIES:

- What does it mean to say "Failure is not an option"?

- Who in the movie is more worried about escaping blame than solving the problem?

- Describe Lovell, Mattingly, Haize, Kranz, and Swigert. What is each one's greatest strength?

CONNECTIONS: Jim Lovell's book about this expedition, originally entitled *Lost Moon*, was reissued as *Apollo 13* following the release of this film. *For All Mankind* is a good documentary about the Apollo expeditions, including this one. There is also a video documentary about this mission. Director Howard (the child star of **The Music Man**) always puts his brother Clint in his movies. Here, he plays one of the Mission Control technicians. In this film, Howard also cast his mother, who is outstanding as Mrs. Lovell, mother of the astronaut.

The Best Years of Our Lives

1946, 172 min, NR, b&w, 12 and up
Dir. William Wyler. Fredric March, Dana Andrews, Myrna Loy, Harold Russell, Teresa Wright.
PLOT: Three men are returning home from service during WWII. Fred Derry (Dana Andrews), a bombardier; Al Stephenson (Fredric March), a middle-aged foot soldier; and Homer Parrish (Harold Russell), a sailor who has lost both hands, fly back to their hometown of Boone City, excited, but a little apprehensive about beginning their postwar lives. Fred is returning to a beautiful wife, Marie (Virginia Mayo), whom he barely knows. Al is coming back to his wife, Milly (Myrna Loy), and their two children, who have grown up while he was gone. Homer is coming back to face his family and his fiancée, Wilma (Cathy O'Donnell), with hooks replacing his hands.

Each of them has a lot of adjusting to do. Al is awkward with his wife at first, and insists they go out to a bar owned by Homer's Uncle Butch (Hoagy Carmichael), where they meet Fred, who has not been able to find his wife and Homer, who wanted to get away from his parents. Al and Fred get very drunk, and Al and Milly take Fred home with them. Al's daughter, Peggy (Teresa Wright), comforts Fred when he has a nightmare about the war, and the next morning makes breakfast for him and drops him off at his apartment. After everyone leaves the Stephensons' apartment, Al and Milly reconnect to their feelings for one another. Fred finally finds Marie, who is delighted to have him home. Homer barely speaks to Wilma.

Al returns to his job at the bank, but when he approves loans to ex-servicemen who don't meet the bank's requirements for collateral, his boss is concerned. At a banquet, Al gets drunk and explains movingly that he learned in the war you have to trust people, and give them a chance, and the old rules must be changed.

Homer is still uncommunicative and withdrawn until Wilma comes to his house late one night to talk to him. He is finally able to show her the extent of his injuries, and is relieved it makes no difference to her. They set a date for the wedding.

Fred, who was a soda jerk before the war, says that is the one job he will never do again., but he finds himself back serving ice cream when he can't find anything else, until he punches a customer who insults Homer and the other ex-servicemen. Marie, who cares about nothing but fun and money, is quickly bored with him, and starts seeing other men.

Fred falls in love with Peggy, but when Al asks him not to see Peggy anymore, he decides to leave town. At the airport, he climbs into the cockpit of one of the old bomber planes, destined to be turned into scrap metal. He meets a man who is using the metal for building and asks for a job, explaining he knows nothing about it, but also knows that he is willing to learn. He is hired.

Fred is Homer's best man. At the wedding, Fred sees Peggy, and the words of the wedding service bring them together.

DISCUSSION: Although today's families will have a hard time relating to the specifics of the postwar era, the theme of adaptation to changing circumstances and the need for genuine closeness is a timeless one. The most important scene in the movie is the one in which Fred realizes he can use the same skills he used in the war, especially his ability to learn, to bring him what he is looking for.

Fred and Homer both have a hard time believing they deserve love, because each feels helpless and inadequate. Homer is afraid to risk rejection by Wilma, so he brusquely ignores her. Fred plans to leave town and never see Peggy again. Both ultimately take the risk and find the love they hoped for.

Al is also brusque and awkward with Milly at first, but by their first morning together he is ready to return to the relationship they had. Milly's description of marriage to Peggy is particularly important in this context, making it clear that "living happily ever after" requires commitment, courage, and work.

PROFANITY: None.

NUDITY/SEXUAL REFERENCES: Subtle references (by today's standards) to Marie's infidelity.

ALCOHOL/DRUG ABUSE: Al and Fred get drunk; Milly makes Al promise not to drink so much and checks what he is drinking at the wedding to make sure he is keeping his promise.

VIOLENCE/SCARINESS: Scuffle.

TOLERANCE/DIVERSITY ISSUES: Tolerance for those with disabilities is a theme of the movie, though it's dated by today's standards, as there is no suggestion that Homer can or should get a job.

QUESTIONS FOR FAMILIES:

- What were the challenges faced by each of the servicemen in adjusting to life after the war?

- Would it have been easier for Homer if his family and Wilma had talked to him about his injuries when he first came home?

- Why was it easier for Homer to talk to Fred and Al about his injuries than it was to talk to his family?

- Why was Al so awkward with Milly at first?

- What did Al mean when he talked about "collateral" at the banquet?

- Why was it important for Fred to realize he knew how to learn? How did that change the way he thought about himself?

CONNECTIONS: Harold Russell, who lost his hands in a grenade accident in training, received both a special Oscar and the Oscar for Best Supporting Actor for his performance as Homer. He did not make another movie until *Inside Moves*, in 1980. He also served as the Chairman of President Lyndon Johnson's Committee on Hiring the Handicapped. The movie also won Oscars for Best Picture, Actor, Director, Musical Score, and Writer. Butch is played by Hoagy Charmichael, composer of "Stardust." A movie with similar themes is *'Til the End of Time*, with Robert Mitchum and Guy Madison.

Chicken Run

2000, 82 min, G, 7 and up
Dir: Nick Parks. Julia Sawalha, Mel Gibson

PLOT: The stern and angry Mrs. Tweedy (voice of Miranda Richardson) and her brow-beaten (should we say hen-pecked?) husband have bullied their hens into producing eggs, but now they have set up a fierce-looking machine that turns chickens into chicken pies. Ginger (voice of Julia Sawalha) is a smart, brave, loyal chicken who will not leave unless she can take the others with her. When an American circus rooster named Rocky (voice of Mel Gibson) arrives, Ginger gets him to agree to teach the chickens to fly over the fence, so they can find a place where they can live in freedom.

DISCUSSION: Parks is a master at creating a world that is enchantingly believable. The farm seems to be set in the 1950's, and every detail, down to the last nail in the last board on the hen house wall, looks exactly as it should. Though his painstaking process produces only a few seconds of film footage each day, every frame is filled with vivid personalities who seem to be moving in real time, each creating an instantly recognizable character. One look at Mrs. Tweedy's formidable Wellington boots marching into the hen yard for inspection, and we know everything about her. The chickens are highly individual, completely believable, and wildly funny, whether doing Tae-Bo-like exercises for increasing wing power or a celebratory Lindy hop. I admit that my favorite characters are two forager/thief rats who are so completely charming that it is impossible to imagine anyone objecting to their stealing.

The movie also features Parks' special talents for creating deliciously malevolent machines and split-second action sequences. Ginger and Rocky fall into the chicken pie machine for a scene that combines Rube Goldberg complexity of gears and operations with the breath-catching near misses of Indiana Jones.

Warning: this is not a script with jokes that children will necessarily understand. Indeed, given that most of the parents of today's school-age children were born 20 years after the 1950's, there are several jokes parents may not understand, like a pointed reference to the delay in the US entry into World War II and a couple of witty tributes to the classic movie, **The Great Escape**. Although the movie is rated G, it may be too scary or hard to follow for children under 6 or 7. A minor character is killed off-screen and characters are in peril throughout the movie.

This gives families a good opportunity to talk about leadership and teamwork in problem-solving, about Ginger's perseverance in the face of "million to one" odds, and her refusal to escape without her friends.

PROFANITY: None.
NUDITY/SEXUAL REFERENCES: Brief mild humor.

ALCOHOL/DRUG ABUSE: None.
VIOLENCE/SCARINESS: Comic peril. Character killed off-screen.
TOLERANCE/DIVERSITY ISSUES: Strong female characters.
QUESTIONS FOR FAMILIES:

- Why was it hard for Rocky to tell the truth, and even to understand what telling the truth meant? He said, "I didn't lie to them, dollface. I just omitted certain truths," and he told Ginger that if they want the chickens to perform they have to tell them what they want to hear.

- Why did Ginger have a dream of freedom that some of the other chickens could not even imagine? What does it meant to say that "the fences aren't just around the farm—they're up here on your head"?

CONNECTIONS: Families who enjoy this movie will also enjoy Parks' Wallace and Gromit videos: *The Wrong Trousers*, *A Grand Day Out*, and *A Close Shave*.

Gone With the Wind

1939, 222 min, NR, 10 and up
Dir: Victor Fleming. Vivien Leigh, Clark Gable, Leslie Howard, Olivia de Havilland, Hattie MacDaniel
PLOT: Scarlett O'Hara (Vivien Leigh) is the beautiful and headstrong daughter of the owner of a Southern plantation called Tara. She has "the smallest waist in three counties" and dozens of beaux clamoring for her attention. The one she loves is gentle Ashley Wilkes (Leslie Howard). At a party, just as the Civil War is beginning, she finds out he is going to marry his cousin Melanie (Olivia de Havilland). Her fury at this news is witnessed by Rhett Butler (Clark Gable), a dashing, but cynical man who refuses to participate in hypocrisy and speaks very directly, telling Scarlett she is "no lady" and telling the men at the party the South cannot win a war.

Out of pique, Scarlett impulsively agrees to marry Melanie's brother Charles (her sister's beau), who dies just after he enlists. This leaves Scarlett a widow, encumbered to the point of suffocation by the mourning rituals of the era, which restrict her to elaborate black clothes and very limited social activities. She goes to visit Melanie, now married to Ashley, in Atlanta, and meets Rhett again, now a war profiteer, who shocks the community by pledging money for the war effort if she will dance with him. She is delighted to have an excuse to dance. His directness makes her uncomfortable, but also intrigues her, because she has been used to men who are both predictable and easy to control.

Melanie has a baby just as Sherman comes through with his soldiers. Scarlett stays with her, then gets Rhett (staying at a bordello) to take them all back to Tara. She tells Rhett he was right not to join the Confederate army, but he has decided now is the time to join, and leaves her at Tara.

Her mother is dead, her father has had a breakdown, and her sisters are ill. They have no food, and all but two of the slaves have left. Scarlett takes charge, swearing she will never be hungry again. When a Union deserter tries to steal her mother's jewelry, she shoots him, and Melanie helps her bury the body.

The war ends. About to lose Tara, she tries to get the money from Rhett, and when he refuses, she marries Frank Kennedy (her other sister's fiancé), a merchant, to get the money. Frank is killed in a KKK-style raid, and she marries Rhett. She thinks she still wants Ashley, and by the time she realizes it is Rhett she loves, he leaves her, with the most famous exit line in the history of the movies. After he is gone, she reminds herself she will go on and work for what she wants, telling herself "Tomorrow is another day."

DISCUSSION: Considered by many the definitive example of the Hollywood movie, this is by any standard one of the greatest films of all time. It could be and should be viewed from a dozen different perspectives, but it is, above all, a story about adapting to the most challenging circumstances possible.

Interestingly and most importantly, our heroine is not especially brave or smart or considerate. On the contrary, she is completely selfish. She has very little interest or understanding of the world around her or of her own feelings. Yet the movie shows us she has qualities like stubbornness and focus enabling her to survive, while those like Melanie and Ashley (who are thoughtful and honorable) do not. In the first scene, her father tells her that what matters most is Tara, and that becomes her symbol of survival. At the end of the movie, with her emotional life devastated, her first thought is to return there to start over again.

In the first scenes of the movie, we get a glimpse of the South before the Civil War. The lives of the landowners are similar to those of British landed gentry, with even more elaborate standards of gentility, chivalry, elegance, and refinement. Listen to Mammy (Hattie MacDaniel) before the barbecue party, reminding Scarlett of the conventions of the era, from how much it is appropriate for ladies to eat in front of gentlemen to how much skin it is appropriate to expose in the afternoon. All genteel protocol is shattered when the war begins, and shattered again when the illusions about the war as an exercise in chivalry and sportsmanship are relentlessly swept away by the realities of combat with a vastly more powerful adversary. Every belief and assumption the Southerners had about themselves and their future is challenged.

Notice how much of what goes on between Scarlett and others is about power. She and Ashley have little in common; indeed, the qualities she thinks she admires in him are the ones that make her feel contempt for Melanie. Scarlett's primary interest in Ashley seems to be in making sure she can enslave him as she has the Tarleton twins and every other man she knows. In a scene that is even more controversial today than it was when it was filmed, Rhett's willingness to overpower her sexually increases her respect for and interest in him.

Scarlett and Rhett are both free from considerations of honor and duty and therefore able to think in strictly pragmatic terms about survival. The difference is Rhett is always honest with himself and others about what is going on, while Scarlett insists on keeping her illusions about Ashley, until it is too late.

PROFANITY: One "damn" (which was almost excised as too shocking).
NUDITY/SEXUAL REFERENCES: Oblique portrayal of forced sex, character who runs a brothel.
ALCOHOL/DRUG ABUSE: Drinking.
VIOLENCE/SCARINESS: War scenes, including wounded soliders and the burning of Atlanta; Scarlett shoots the Union deserter; Scarlett falls down the stairs and has a miscarriage, accidental death of child and profound grief of parent.
TOLERANCE/DIVERSITY ISSUES: The issue of slavery is raised in subtext.
Period portrayals reflect the racial stereotypes of both the Civil War-era South and the 1930s, when the movie was made. While Mammy is a strong and loyal character, she is childishly won over with a red petticoat, and Prissy is fluttery and incompetent.
QUESTIONS FOR FAMILIES:

• Why were the Southerners so wrong about their ability to win a war with the North?

• Why does Scarlett marry Charles? Why does she marry Frank? Why does she marry Rhett?

• Why is Tara so important to Scarlett?

• Why does Rhett like Scarlett? Why do his feelings about her change?

• What do you think will happen after Scarlett goes back to Tara?

CONNECTIONS: This film, the longtime box office champion, won eight Oscars, including Best Picture, Best Actress, Best Director, Best Screenplay, and Best Supporting Actress (Hattie McDaniel, who beat Olivia de Havilland to become the first black performer to win an Oscar).

Amazingly, director Victor Fleming, the fifth director assigned to the movie, directed **The Wizard of Oz** the same year. With five directors and at least twelve screenwriters, the credit for "authorship" of the movie must go to producer David O. Selznick, whose vision for the film was spelled out meticulously in long memoranda, published in *Memo from David O. Selznick*. A made-for-television movie, *The Scarlett O'Hara War*, is based on the furious efforts in Hollywood by all of the leading actresses (including Bette Davis, Paulette Goddard, Joan Crawford, and Tallulah Bankhead) who wanted this juiciest of parts. *Scarlett*, a television miniseries, continues the story, but with not even a fraction of the quality of the original. Read the original book by Margaret Mitchell instead.

The Great Escape

1963, 168 min, NR, 8 and up
Dir: John Sturges. Steve McQueen, James Garner, Richard Attenborough, James Coburn, Donald Pleasence, David McCallum
PLOT: Toward the end of WWII, the Germans built a special high security prison camp for Allied prisoners with a record of escape attempts. This is the true story of the extraordinary courage and ingenuity of the men imprisoned there, and of their plans for the greatest escape ever.

As the British ranking officer explains, when the camp commandant urges him to relax and "sit out the war as comfortably as possible," his duty is to escape, or, if escape is impossible, to force the enemy to use as many resources as possible to contain them.

Each man contributes his expertise. There are "tunnel kings" to dig the three tunnels, a "forger king" (Donald Pleasence) to forge the papers the soldiers will need when they escape, a "scrounger" (James Garner) to beg, borrow, steal, or obtain through blackmail the materials they need, and others who work as tailors and manufacturers. An American who is something of a loner, Hilts (Steve McQueen) becomes the "cooler king" for his long stints in solitary confinement, as a result of his independent escape attempts. When "Big X" (Richard Attenborough), the British officer who supervises the escape, asks Hilts to go through the tunnel to get information about the area surrounding the camp, and then allow himself to be recaptured so he can let them know what he has found, he refuses.

When his friend is killed trying to escape, his spirit broken by the camp, Hilts changes his mind.

Seventy-five of the prisoners are able to escape before the tunnel is discovered. The Germans track almost all of them down, and fifty are killed, including Big X. It is to "the fifty" that the film is dedicated.

DISCUSSION: As in **Stalag 17** and many other films about prison camp, the prisoners in this story must adapt to the direst of circumstances, and they choose differing approaches. Hilts adapts by working on his own, or with one partner, while others work together on a massive group escape. Ives and Danny begin to unravel under the stress, not so much a "choice" as an involuntary response. Unlike other prison camp movies, this one does not dwell on disputes between prisoners or on the deprivations of the prison camp, which seems almost comfortable. It is about the professionalism, courage, resourcefulness, teamwork, and loyalty of every one of the prisoners.

As in a traditional "heist" film, the story focuses on defining a problem and then solving it. They examine the restrictions imposed by their conditions, change the ones they can, and adapt to the ones they cannot. They must also adapt quickly and calmly when the plan does not go as they expected.

The story gives us an exceptional example of teamwork and loyalty. Note the way the prisoners protect each other. When Danny (Charles Bronson) cannot take it anymore and wants to escape on his own, his friend talks him out of it. When the Forger King goes blind, Big X wants to leave him behind, for his own protection. The Scrounger promises to take care of him.

Point out to kids what factors do and do not go into the prisoners' calculations and strategy. Big X is cautioned not to allow his personal wish for revenge determine the strategy. Pride in the sense of morale is permitted to be considered. When asked, "Have you thought of what it might cost?" he answers, "I've thought of the humiliation if we just tamely submit: knuckle under and crawl." They also consider the risk of failure, to the extent they can. At the end, when the Scrounger asks whether the escape was worth the price, the best the British Commander can do is answer truthfully, "It depends on your point of view."

PROFANITY: None.
NUDITY/SEXUAL REFERENCES: None.
ALCOHOL/DRUG ABUSE: Some drinking; smoking.
VIOLENCE/SCARINESS: Very tense moments; characters in peril and many are killed.

TOLERANCE/DIVERSITY ISSUES: People from a variety of backgrounds and countries work together toward a common goal.
QUESTIONS FOR FAMILIES:

- Why are the experts called "kings"?

- What makes Hilts change his mind about getting the information they want?

- Who was right about taking the Forger out through the tunnel, Big X or the Scrounger?

- Given the results of their action in this story, should officers who have been taken prisoner feel duty-bound to try to escape?

CONNECTIONS: The screenplay was co-written by blockbuster novelist James Clavell (*Tai-Pan*, *Shogun*). His own experiences as a prisoner of war in a Japanese prison camp are the subject of *King Rat*. The outstanding musical score is by Elmer Bernstein (**The Magnificent Seven** and **To Kill a Mockingbird**). Sir Richard Attenborough, who played Big X, later became a director of films such as **Gandhi** and **Shadowlands**. He continues to appear as a performer, and played Dr. Hammond **in Jurassic Park**, and Kris Kringle in the 1994 version of *Miracle on 34th Street*.

Singin' In the Rain

1952, 102 min, NR, 6 and up
Dir: Gene Kelly and Stanley Donen. Gene Kelly, Debbie Reynolds, Donald O'Connor, Jean Hagan
PLOT: Silent movie star Don Lockwood (Gene Kelly) is paired on-screen with Lina Lamont (Jean Hagan), who would like to be paired with him off-screen as well, but Lina's personality is as grating as her squeaky, nasal voice. She is mean, selfish, arrogant, and stupid. Chased by fans following the opening of their latest movie, Don jumps into the car of Kathy Seldon (Debbie Reynolds), who tells him she is a serious actress and not at all interested in the movies. Later, at a party celebrating the new movie, Kathy appears again, jumping out of a cake. Don teases her about her "art," and she throws a pie at him, getting Lina right in the face by mistake. Lina, furious, has Kathy fired.

At the party, the guests are treated to an exhibition of the latest technology, "talking pictures." Everyone present dismisses it as a novelty. When The Jazz Singer becomes a hit, everyone in Hollywood begins to make talkies. Production is halted on the latest Lockwood-Lamont movie, The Dueling Cavalier, while the stars are coached in vocal technique (with a delightful song mocking the exercises; "Moses Supposes"). The movie is a disaster. Test audiences jeer and laugh.

Meanwhile, Don and Kathy have fallen in love. Don, Kathy, and Don's best friend, Cosmo (Donald O'Connor), come up with an idea. They can make it into a musical, The Dancing Cavalier, dubbing Kathy's voice for Lina's. Don resists at first, because it is unfair to Kathy. They persuade him that it will be just this one time, and he goes along.

With Kathy's voice and some musical numbers, the movie is a success. Lina insists that Kathy continue to dub all her movies and, when the audience insists on hearing her sing, Lina forces Kathy to stand backstage so she can perform. Don, Cosmo, and the beleaguered studio head reveal the secret, and Don introduces Kathy to the audience as the real star of the movie.

DISCUSSION: This is often considered the finest musical of all time. Certainly it has it all: classic musical numbers and a witty script, unusually sharp and satiric for a musical comedy, especially one making fun of the industry that produced it. Asked to name the top ten moments in the history of movies, most people would include the title number from this movie, in which Gene Kelly splashes and sings in the rain with what Roger Ebert called "saturated ecstasy." When he swings the umbrella around and around and dances on and off the curb, his "glorious feeling" is contagious. Only in a movie containing that sequence would Donald O'Connor's sensational "Make 'Em Laugh" number be mentioned second. It is a wildly funny pastiche of every possible slapstick gag, done with such energy and skill that it appears as if it is entirely spontaneous.

Screenwriters Betty Comden and Adoph Green, asked to use some of the classic songs by Arthur Freed (later a producer of most of the great MGM musicals) and Nacio Herb Brown, decided to set the movie in the era in which the songs were written, the early talkies. This gave them a chance to use some of the Hollywood folklore of that era, when careers like John Gilbert's were destroyed overnight as audiences found out the stars' voices didn't match their faces. One especially funny scene has the technicians trying to find a way to record Lina's dialogue. When they put the microphone on her dress, all you hear is the sound of her pearls as she rubs them. When they put it lower down, you hear her heartbeat. When they put it near her, her voice fades in and out as she tosses her head.

Note that the cameras are put inside huge boxes. That is authentic, as the cameras of that era were so loud they had to be encased to prevent their own whirring from being recorded.

Don and Cosmo are consummate adaptors. As we see in flashback, they have already switched from vaudeville to movies, and then Cosmo from performer to accompanist to musical director, and Don from stuntman to leading man. Lina resists change and tries to bully her way out of it, but Don, Cosmo, and Kathy all demonstrate resilience and openness to new ideas, and a willingness to be creative in solving problems.

PROFANITY: None.
NUDITY/SEXUAL REFERENCES: None.
ALCOHOL/DRUG ABUSE: None.
VIOLENCE/SCARINESS: None.
TOLERANCE/DIVERSITY ISSUES: None.
QUESTIONS FOR FAMILIES:

• Why does Kathy at first lie about liking the movies?

• Why does Don lie about his background? How is that different from the way that Lina behaves?

• Have there been any new inventions that you have seen that have changed people's jobs a lot?

• What inventions do you use your parents didn't have when they were children? Your grandparents?

CONNECTIONS: The transition from silent movies to talkies was also lampooned in the first play by George S. Kaufman and Moss Hart, *Once in a Lifetime*. A silent star who has become deranged is the centerpiece of *Sunset Boulevard*. When told, "You used to be big in pictures," she says, "I'm still big—it's the pictures that got small." She also says, memorably, that in her day stars didn't need to talk: "We had faces then!"
ACTIVITIES: Children might like to see some of the early silent movies to get an idea of what Hollywood was like in the days depicted in this movie. The films of Charlie Chaplin, Laurel and Hardy, Buster Keaton and Harold Lloyd are still wonderful, and kids will enjoy learning a story can be told without words.

Modern Times

1936, 89 min, NR, b&w, 6 and up
Dir. Charlie Chaplin. Charlie Chaplin, Paulette Goddard

PLOT: This Chaplin classic (he produced, wrote, directed, starred, and composed the music) is about two people struggling with the isolation of the industrial era. Chaplin (simply called "A worker" in the credits) is tightening bolts on an assembly line. He does it so intently that his arms continue to twitch as though he is still tightening when he takes his break. On a break, he smokes in the men's room until the big boss appears on a television screen to tell him to quit stalling and get back to work.

The boss watches a demonstration of a new machine, designed to feed employees while they work, to reduce breaks. Chaplin is selected to try it out. Everything goes wrong in the most deliriously slapstick fashion. He eventually becomes trapped in the huge factory machine itself, stuck in the gears. He comes out a little crazed, tightening everything resembling bolts. He loses his job. A doctor tells him to take it easy and avoid excitement.

Nevertheless, he almost immediately finds excitement by accidentally leading a Communist parade while just trying to return the red flag to the man who dropped it. He is arrested. The prison is not unlike the factory in its regimentation. At lunch, the guards come in "searching for smuggled nose powder." The prisoner who has smuggled it puts it in a salt shaker. When he is taken away, Chaplin sprinkles it on his food and becomes a bit delirious. When he comes upon an attempted escape, he captures the prisoners and releases the guards. Meanwhile, we have met "a gamine," Paulette Goddard, stealing food for herself and other children. Her unemployed father is killed in a street fight, and she and her siblings are taken into state custody, to be sent to an orphanage. Goddard escapes as Chaplin remains "happy in his comfortable cell." However, he is pardoned because of his heroism in the attempted escape, and is given a letter of recommendation to get a job.

After another job disaster, he is "determined to go back to jail," where he was safe and warm. He sees Goddard captured for stealing bread and confesses that it was he who stole it. However, a witness identifies Goddard. He orders a large meal, eats it, then turns himself in as being unable to pay, and happily settles into the police truck on the way back to jail. When Goddard is put in the same truck, they escape together. He takes a job as night watchman in a department store, and they enjoy having the store to themselves. Robbers break in—Chaplin's former colleague at the factory. The next morning, Chaplin is arrested again.

Goddard is waiting for him when he gets out of the police station. She gets a job as a dancer in a nightclub and arranges a job for him as a singing waiter. He is a huge hit (even though he forgets the words to the song and has to make them up). The police come after Goddard, to take her back into the custody of the state. They escape once more, and walk off into the sunset together.

DISCUSSION: We have to remind ourselves how prescient this movie was. To us, it may not be surprising that the boss watches the workers on a screen, but this was before the invention of television and more than a decade before the publication of Orwell's *1984*. Interestingly, it was several years after the invention of the talkies. Chaplin wanted to make a silent movie, and silent this one is, except for a few words, some sound effects, and a gibberish song. Children will adore the slapstick in this movie, especially the scenes where Chaplin tries out the feeding machine and when he experiments with roller skates at the department store. Grown-ups who watch with younger children can read them the title cards and help them follow the story. They can tell older children something about the Depression and the concerns about the dehumanizing effect of technology that are a part of this movie. Point out the use of sheep at the beginning, and then their human equivalents, the crowds of people on their way to work.

PROFANITY: None.
NUDITY/SEXUAL REFERENCES: None.
ALCOHOL/DRUG ABUSE: Cocaine ("nose powder") accidentally ingested by Chaplin.
VIOLENCE/SCARINESS: None.
TOLERANCE/DIVERSITY ISSUES: Use of the term "darkie" in a song.
QUESTIONS FOR FAMILIES:

- Why did the boss want Chaplin to try the feeding machine? What would Frank Gilbreth of **Cheaper By the Dozen** think of the machine?

- Why did Chaplin want to go back to jail? Why didn't Goddard want to go to jail?

- Did Chaplin want you to think that prison was like the factory? Better? How can you tell?

- How did Chaplin and Goddard differ in their reactions to their troubles?

- For high school age: Why was Chaplin arrested for leading the Communist parade? Does that violate the freedom of speech guaranteed by the First Amendment?

CONNECTIONS: Some of the Chaplin shorter movies, like *The Rink* and *The Gold Rush*, are delightful for kids. *City Lights* is a brilliant and touching movie with a darker tone and a more complex and ambiguous ending.

Stalag 17

1953, 120 min, NR, b&w, 12 and up
Dir: Billy Wilder. William Holden, Otto Preminger, Peter Graves
PLOT: As the movie opens, the narrator says the movies he has seen about WWII are about "flyboys" in leather jackets, and do not reflect his own experience as an American prisoner of war in a German stalag (prison camp). This is that story.

Sefton (William Holden) is a cynical loner who bets (successfully) that his fellow prisoners will fail in their attempt to escape. He manages to scrounge or trade for many small luxuries, including a bar of soap and an egg. When the others show their contempt, he says, "So maybe I trade a little sharper. Does that make me a collaborator?" and sums up his philosophy: "This is everybody for himself, dog eat dog...You can be the heroes, the guys with fruit salad on your chest. Me, I'm staying put, and I'm going to make myself as comfortable as I can, and if it takes trading with the enemy to get me some food or a better mattress, that's okay with Sefton."

The other men in his barracks start to suspect him of trading more than cigarettes and silk stockings with the Germans. When Lieutenant Dunbar, a wealthy Bostonian who is in the barracks on his way to the officers' prison camp, is arrested for sabotage, they conclude Sefton told the Germans Dunbar was the one who blew up the train filled with ammunition. They beat Sefton severely. He tells them two people know he is not the one who is telling the Germans their secrets, Sefton himself and the one who is really doing it.

Sefton starts to watch the others, to find the spy, and figures out who it is. What can he do? If he says nothing, the spy will continue to betray the Americans. If he tells the others, the spy will just be sent to another stalag. If they kill the spy, they will be killed as punishment. Sefton finds a way to reveal the identity of the spy. The prisoners use the spy as a decoy so that Dunbar can escape. Sefton insists on being the one to take him, telling the others that the risk of escaping has been outweighed by the chance at a reward from Dunbar's family.
DISCUSSION: This is an exceptionally exciting drama, based on a play by two men who were prisoners in Stalag 17. Holden's superb performance won an Oscar for Best Actor, and the rest of the cast, some of whom were also in the Broadway play, is excellent. This movie provides a good opportunity to talk

about the role of humor, especially "black" or "gallows" humor, in adapting to the harshest circumstances. A former Communist bloc comedian once said that every joke is a "tiny revolution." Here, when all control over their lives is taken from them, the prisoners try to establish some sense of control with jokes and pranks, and again, we see, as W. H. Auden said, "a laugh is less heartless than tears" (see **Sullivan's Travels**).

Examine the other strategies and responses the prisoners had to adapt to their circumstances. Sefton adapted by trying to make whatever small improvements to his life he could, helping him to maintain some sense of power, choice and control. Animal and Harry use dreams to help them feel better; also giving them a sense of control, even if it is only for the future. Joey plays an ocarina and becomes completely withdrawn. Interestingly, the camp commandant, Von Sherbach (Otto Preminger), a ruthless man, is nevertheless also shown as feeling a loss of control, because he has been assigned to the backwater of the war effort. He hopes that identifying Dunbar as the one who blew up the train will bring him to the attention of those who may move him to a position more prestigious.

The narrator says Sefton would fit into one of the Reader's Digest series about the "most unforgettable character." He is interesting because he has none of the redeeming qualities we expect of our heroes. In contrast to Dunbar, who is rich, handsome, charming, unpretentious, modest, and brave, Sefton is selfish, cynical, and hostile. In his last words to the group as he leaves to rescue Dunbar, he says if they should ever run into him after the war, they should pretend they don't know him. When he says he is motivated by the prospect of a reward, we believe him. Heroes are just as complicated as everyone else, possibly more so.

This movie also provides an opportunity to talk about justice and fairness. The evidence was very strongly against Sefton, and his unpleasant personality made him a natural object of hostility and suspicion. Contrast the process for finding Sefton guilty with the process the commandant uses to interrogate Dunbar (who was "guilty").

PROFANITY: None.
NUDITY/SEXUAL REFERENCES: Prisoners make a telescope to spy on the Russian women prisoners, and they often refer to their, long separation from women; Sefton bribes the German guards to let him visit the women; one prisoner keeps insisting "I believe her" when he gets a letter from his wife saying that she found a baby who happens to look just like her.
ALCOHOL/DRUG ABUSE: Prisoners make their own liquor.

VIOLENCE/SCARINESS: Prisoners are shot trying to escape; Sefton is beaten.
TOLERANCE/DIVERSITY ISSUES: Tolerance of individual differences and the overall issue of intolerance as the basis for war.
QUESTIONS FOR FAMILIES:

- Why did Sefton give his egg to Joey?

- Why was Sefton so consumed with his own comforts and privileges?

- Why did the others suspect Sefton?

- How did the prisoners use humor to keep their spirits up? How do the filmmakers use humor to break the tension?

- How can there be "rules" like those of the Geneva Convention in a war? How can those rules be enforced?

CONNECTIONS: Other outstanding movies about prisoners of war include **The Great Escape**. *The Rack* stars Paul Newman as a soldier accused of treason following his release from a Korean prison camp.

BUTCH CASSIDY AND THE SUNDANCE KID

1969, 112 min, PG, 12 and-up
Dir: George Roy Hill. Robert Redford, Paul Newman
PLOT: This superb love letter to Western myths and Western movies is the fictionalized story of two real outlaws, played by Paul Newman and Robert Redford. When their life of robbing banks and trains is no longer possible, due to improved security, they must find a new way to survive.

Like Ringo in **The Gunfighter**, their options are limited by their past transgressions, and they will not be permitted to just say they were sorry and go straight. They go to Bolivia, hoping to be able to return to what they know best, and learn it is hard to rob a bank if you don't speak enough of the language to tell the teller to give you the money. They try to use their expertise as robbers to become security guards, but fail. They use a great deal of energy and ingenuity to escape capture and find a place for themselves, but ultimately they are unable to adapt, and there is no place left for them. The most they can hope for is death with honor according to their terms.
NOTE: There is some profanity, a brief scene with a prostitute, a scene in which it appears a woman is going to be raped at gunpoint (it turns out to be a teasing

prelude to lovemaking by two people who are already intimate), and the usual level of shooting and violence for a Western.

FANTASIA

1940, 120 min, NR, 4 and up
Dir: Ben Sharpsteen.
Considered a failure when it was originally released, this eight-part combination of images and music is now indisputably a classic. Musicologist Deems Taylor explains that there are three kinds of music: music that paints a picture, music that tells a story, and "absolute music," or music for music's sake, and then shows us all three. Highlights include Mickey Mouse as the Sorcerer's Apprentice, whose plan to solve the problem of having to carry water from the well creates more work than it saves. The Nutcracker Suite's forest moves from fall into winter (with the mushrooms dancing to the Chinese Dance); Beethoven's Pastoral Symphony, has characters from Greek mythology celebrating at a festival and seeking shelter from a storm; and in the Dance of the Hours, ostrich and hippo ballerinas dance with gallant (if overburdened) crocodiles.
CONNECTIONS: Play classical and other kinds of music for kids and have them draw their own pictures to illustrate the sounds. Kids might like to read more about the Greek mythological characters. Be sure to see the sequel, *Fantasia 2000*, on an IMAX screen, if possible.

LORD OF THE FLIES

1961, 93 min, NR, b&w, 12 and up
Dir: Peter Brook.
Based on William Golding's award-winning allegorical novel, this is the story of a group of English schoolboys marooned on a remote island. At first, they operate according to the structure they are used to ("Let's make a lot of rules!" shouts one of the boys). Ralph, thoughtful and democratic, is selected as their leader. He plans for the long term, keeping a signal fire going. When no one comes to rescue them, civilization slips further and further away. Jack and his "hunters" take over, becoming more and more savage. They paint themselves and make sacrifices to a mythical "beast," first the heads of the animals they kill for food, and then one of the boys, killed in a wild ceremonial dance. They murder Ralph's last follower, a chubby boy they call Piggy, and they are chasing murderously after Ralph when they are found by rescuers. NOTE: This has some very scary moments, and the overall theme may be particularly troubling for some children and young teens.

CONNECTIONS: Teenagers should read the book, by Nobel Prize-winner William Golding. This movie was remade in 1990, in color, with a glossy, contemporary setting, and the nationality of the boys changed to American. It has some power, but is not as good as the original.

MATILDA

1996, 93 min, PG, 8 and up
Dir: Danny DeVito. Mara Wilson, Danny DeVito, Embeth Davidtz
Danny DeVito directed and stars in this story of a wise little girl (Mara Wilson) who triumphs over dreadful adults. Matilda's hilariously tacky parents (DeVito and his real-life wife, Rhea Perlman) can barely remember Matilda's name and age. They alternately ignore and insult her, insisting she put down her beloved books and watch television, and refuse to allow her to go to school. When they finally do send her to school, the principal, Miss Trunchbull, hates children and enjoys tossing them over the fence like the shot-putter she once was. Matilda discovers she has "powers" (telekinesis) and, with the support of sweet Miss Honey, her teacher, finds a way to live happily ever after.

Parents (and some kids) may be concerned by the comic treatment of abusive behavior. As in *James and the Giant Peach* and some of Dahl's other books, most of the grown-ups are stupid, dishonest, and cruel, genuinely relishing their power over children. Some kids may get upset, but, as with **Home Alone**, many kids find the comic exaggeration reassuring, especially when the child proves less vulnerable than the grown-ups expected. Kids who will enjoy this movie most are those who liked the book-those who are unfamiliar with it should be prepared by parents for what to expect.

DeVito and Perlman made this movie because it was their daughter's favorite book. Dahl's lesson that children can solve their problems by reading and by finding good, trustworthy friends to help them is very worthwhile.
CONNECTIONS: Miss Honey is played by Embeth Davidtz, who appears in **Schindler's List** as the Jewish concentration camp prisoner who fascinates the Nazi commandant.

MR. HULOT'S HOLIDAY

1954, 83 min, NR, b&w, 6 and up
Dir: Jacques Tati. Jacques Tati
This is a gentle slapstick comedy about a man's vacation at the beach. There is no plot to speak of. In a series of elaborate episodes, he creates complete chaos wherever he goes.

This movie requires a bit of patience from viewers who are used to slam-bang, nonstop action, even in comedies. Its charms are worth it. Tati, who directed, cowrote, and stars, is a master of (almost) silent comedy, especially intricate physical comedy. Themes to discuss with kids include their thoughts on Mr. Hulot's reactions when things go wrong, comparing them to other comic actors and fictional characters, from Donald Duck (the ultimate in apoplectic hysteria) to Buster Keaton (the ultimate in Spartan emotionlessness). What makes these reactions funny?

NOTE: It is a French movie, but the opening titles and most of the (very little) dialogue is in English.

SWISS FAMILY ROBINSON

1960, 128 min, NR, 6 and up
Dir: Ken Annahin. John Mills, Dorothy McGuire
This handsome Disney production of the story about the shipwrecked family is a classic family film. John Mills is the optimistic father who assures his wife (Dorothy McGuire) and three sons he will find a way to provide all the comforts of home on the island. The tree house he builds for her is a delight and can still be visited at Walt Disney World.

The family is wonderfully inventive and creative in adapting to life on the island, and the climax has a *Home Alone*-ish set of booby traps for the invading pirates.

NOTE: Though she is spirited and brave, the young woman character is overly stereotyped by today's standards. It is worth discussing with kids how differently she is treated when the Robinsons think she is a boy.

TOPKAPI

1964, 120 min, NR, 10 and up
Dir: Jules Dassin. Melina Mercouri, Maximilian Schell
One of the great pleasures of the perennially popular heist films is the way that the thieves assess and surmount the logistical challenges of the robbery. Elizabeth Lipp (Melina Mercouri) and William Walter (Maximilian Schell) plot to steal a priceless jeweled dagger from a museum in Istanbul called Topkapi. They decide to work with "amateurs," people who have no criminal records, and they assemble a team that includes a strong man, an eccentric inventor, and an inept con artist (Oscar-winning Peter Ustinov). They have to find a way to surmount the extraordinary museum security, which includes a floor alarm sensitive to the slightest pressure.

CONNECTIONS: The 1996 film *Mission: Impossible* borrowed the central heist sequence from this movie, which in turn (and in keeping with the ethos of its hero thieves), stole parts of it from the famous *Rififi*. Since Dassin directed both *Rififi* and *Topkapi*, however, perhaps we can just call it his style. Other classics in this genre include *Oceans 11* and *How to Steal a Million*.

SEE ALSO:
The Diary of Anne Frank Anne and her family must cope with years of confinement as they hide from the Nazis.
Fiddler on the Roof Tevye's family and community must adjust to changing times, first abandoning some of the traditions they have relied on, and then leaving their homes to start a new life.
Mike Mulligan and His Steam Shovel in this classic children's story, Mike's beloved steam shovel is about to be replaced by new technology, but together they find a way to do one last job and find a new way to continue to work together.
The Sound of Music When the Nazis invade Austria, the Von Trapp family must leave the life of wealth and prestige they had known to become a folk-singing group.

6

FAMILIES: FUNCTIONAL AND DYS

"Family faces are magic mirrors. Looking at people who belong to us, we see the past, present, and future. We make discoveries about ourselves."
GAIL LUMET BUCKLEY

Nothing is more fascinating to us than families, our own and others'. Despite what Tolstoy said, every family is different, happy or sad, and the endless variety of approaches to communication, power, anger, and even love is endlessly interesting. Some memorable movies have given us families so vivid we almost feel we belong to them, or they belong to us. Part of what makes them so vivid is many of them are based on real families, the families of the playwrights, novelists, and screenwriters who allow us into their own families, presenting them to us sometimes with pain, but often with forgiveness, and always with insight, and with love.

Our own families are so overwhelming to us, particularly to children, it is especially worthwhile for them to visit with these other families, to help them see their own families in sharper relief. It can help kids with strong, intact families see how other families work well (or badly) together. It can help those dealing with difficult family problems to see movies that show families facing similar problems. Movies can show us the ways different families communicate, argue, compromise, and show love, to make us think about the way we do these things, and how we can do them better.

In movies we meet happy families, families changed by loss, and characters creating their own families. We see families torn apart by greed, jealousy, and lies or by secrets and lack of trust. We see families facing some of the hardest questions of family life as they try to be supportive without being suffocating, to be tolerant without enabling destructive behavior. There are movies that show characters helping family members whose needs can be overwhelming, and movies that show characters loving those they cannot save. We see families grappling with painful issues of betrayal or abuse of power, and with heartbreaking tragedies. Above all, we see families prevailing above overwhelming odds.

While W. C. Fields may refer to his family as "a dismal place, I admit" (*The Bank Dick*), movies more often and more accurately portray them as "that unconquerable fortress" (*Since You Went Away*). The movies in this chapter portray all kinds of families, coping with all kinds of problems, with all kinds of success and failure, all worth visiting.

About a Boy

2002, 101 min, PG-13, 14 and up
Dir: Chris and Paul Weitz. Hugh Grant, Toni Collette, Nicholas Hoult
PLOT: Hugh Grant plays a shallow man appropriately named Will Freeman who believes, contrary to John Donne, that every man is an island. Or at least he believes that that a man can be an island if he tries to, and that if he tries very hard, he can be Ibiza, a highly habitable, even idyllic, self-contained island with no reason ever to leave. Will has enough money from the royalties of his father's Christmas novelty song to pay for a fancy stereo system, espresso maker, and HDTV, and he divides his life into half-hour segments, because he doesn't want to commit to anything much longer than that. Up to his late 30's, he has successfully avoided any emotional entanglements, indeed, he has pretty much avoided any emotion and pretty much any thought, except the thought that his life is pretty much perfect.

In other words, chaos is about to strike, and we will have the pleasure of seeing Will's humiliation and misery as he discovers that Donne probably had it right the first time.

Will has insulated himself so well from romantic emotional entanglements that he decides that the perfect relationship is one with a single mother. They have low expectations and a sympathetic listener can get pretty far with them. So, he pretends to be a single parent himself and makes up a two-year-old child so that he can attend meetings of SPAT (Single Parents Alone Together). A mother in the group brings a friend's twelve-year-old named Marcus (the thankfully unmovie-kid-like Nicholas Hoult) along on a picnic. Marcus is isolated but does not want to be. His single mother is severely depressed and even the outcasts at school think he is too much of a dork to hang out with.

So, with the inability to process other people's reactions and total disregard for his own vulnerability that only a pre-teen could survive, Marcus just shows up at

Will's home every afternoon to watch television and ultimately insists on becoming the closest thing to a friend that Will has ever known.

DISCUSSION: This set-up could easily produce manipulative claptrap from a Hallmark Hall of Fame made-for-TV movie. That's because there is so much appeal in this kind of theme that even a lousy script and poor production values can't completely destroy it. When it is done well, or even very, very well, as it is here, it is one of the most purely, satisfyingly enjoyable films of the year, and a great story about the kinds of families we create for ourselves.

Families should talk about the definition of girlfriend that Will and Marcus discuss and Marcus's idea about the importance of having a back-up. Why does Will watch *Frankenstein*? Does Will create a monster? Families may also want to talk about depression and its causes and treatments.

PROFANITY: Strong language for a PG-13.
NUDITY/SEXUAL REFERENCES: Sexual references and situations.
ALCOHOL/DRUG ABUSE: Will drinks and smokes.
VIOLENCE/SCARINESS: Attempted suicide, tense family scenes.
TOLERANCE/DIVERSITY ISSUES: None.
QUESTIONS FOR FAMILIES:

• How do we decide just how much of an island we want to be?

• Why is it important to Will not to have any relationships?

• Why are the kids in school so mean to Marcus?

• How are Will and Marcus alike and how are they different?

• Is it right for Marcus to believe that it is his responsibility to make his mother feel better? How does Will's relationship with Marcus make him more interested in a relationship with Rachel?

• What kind of grown-up will Marcus be?

• How does helping Marcus change Will's feelings about him?

CONNECTIONS: Families who enjoy this movie will also enjoy *Bridget Jones's Diary*, *Love Actually*, and *Four Weddings and a Funeral* (very mature material). Families with younger children who enjoy this theme should watch Bruce Willis in Disney's delightful *The Kid*.

Captain January

1936, 75 min, NR, b&w, 6 and up
Dir: David Butler. Shirley Temple, Guy Kibbee, Buddy Ebsen
PLOT: Star (Shirley Temple), an orphan, lives with Captain January (Guy Kibbee), a retired sailor who runs a lighthouse. They adore each other, and she loves her life there, with the large community of sailors as her extended family and "Cap" to take care of her and teach her. A meddlesome and jealous woman, Agatha Morgan (Sara Haden), tries to prove that Cap is not a suitable guardian for Star, and that she should be in school, but when Star is tested, her performance is well ahead of her grade level.

When the lighthouse is automated, Cap loses his job, and this gives Miss Morgan another chance to take Star away. To keep her from Miss Morgan, Cap's friend Captain Nazro (Slim Somerville) tracks down Star's wealthy relatives, who come to get her. They do everything they can to make her happy, finally realizing she cannot be happy without the people who have become her real family. They bring Cap, Nazro, and her other special friends to be the crew for their new boat so they can be together.

DISCUSSION: This is one of Shirley Temple's best movies, and it provides an opportunity to discuss some of the most sensitive issues facing some children. Children who are home schooled will appreciate seeing the success of Shirley's home schooling with Cap. Children who are in foster homes or have had to face custody issues may appreciate the opportunity to discuss Shirley's situation as a way of addressing their own.

When Shirley is taken away from Cap, she says, "Why are they taking me away from you? What have I done?" This is a good chance to talk with children about how many kids mistakenly blame themselves for the problems that are created by the grown-ups around them.

Star sings a song about how all that matters is "the right someone to love," and imagines what it would be like to be Cap's nanny. She says that he needs her to take care of him. Children need to know it can be fun to pretend to be the caretaker, but it is the grown-up's responsibility to take care of the child. The movie also depicts the difficulty of finding work, especially after a job has been made obsolete.

NOTE: This is a "happily ever after" movie, and any child whose own situation makes it difficult to watch an ending that ties everything up too neatly may have a hard time with it.

PROFANITY: None.
NUDITY/SEXUAL REFERENCES: None.
ALCOHOL/DRUG ABUSE: None.
VIOLENCE/SCARINESS: Very sad when Star is taken away from Cap.
TOLERANCE/DIVERSITY ISSUES: Miss Morgan is intolerant of Star's unusual home environment.
QUESTIONS FOR FAMILIES:

- Why does Paul try to get Mary to "bend the rules" for Star's test, and why won't she do it?

- How can you tell that Cap and Nazro are friends, even though they insult each other and argue?

- How does Star notice that Cap is sad?

- Nazro does not give Cap two important pieces of information. What are they, and why doesn't he tell Cap?

- Star and Cap both give reasons they are glad to leave the lighthouse. Do you believe them? Why do they do that?

- Nazro says that children "forget quick." Is that right?

CONNECTIONS: Television fans with sharp eyes will recognize Buddy Ebsen (of *The Beverly Hillbillies* and *Barnaby Jones*) as Star's friend Paul, who dances with her to "At the Codfish Ball."
ACTIVITIES: Children might like to visit a lighthouse or a museum exhibit showing the way they used to operate before the automation portrayed in the movie. They might also like to learn something about the opera Shirley pretends to be in, *Lucia di Lammermoor*; the public library may have a recording you can borrow. Cap and Nazro pay pinochle, which children might like to learn. They will enjoy being asked to make up a story, as Star does so well in her test at school.

Cat on a Hot Tin Roof

1958, 108 min, NR, 12 and up
Dir: Richard Brooks. Paul Newman, Elizabeth Taylor, Burl Ives
PLOT: Big Daddy's (Burl Ives) family is celebrating both his sixty-fifth birthday and his medical report, which shows his health problems have proven to be

minor. He has two grown sons, Brick (Paul Newman), an alcoholic former athlete, and Gooper (Jack Carson), who is constantly trying to replace Brick as Big Daddy's favorite. Gooper has five children, and Brick's wife, Maggie (Elizabeth Taylor) knows no matter how much Big Daddy loves Brick, he will not leave Brick his property unless he provides an heir.

Brick is angry at himself and at Maggie, and wants nothing more than to drink until he feels the "click" of peace when he is too drunk to feel anything else. The "odor of mendacity" is too strong for Big Daddy, and all the lies come tumbling down like skeletons out of a closet.

DISCUSSION: This movie, based on Tennessee Williams's play, is about a family that has been damaged more by lies than by greed. They lie to Big Daddy about the results of his medical tests. Brick lies to himself about what really went on with Skipper. Gooper and his wife lie about their feelings for Big Daddy. Maggie lies about being pregnant. It is worth discussing the different kinds of lies and the different motivations behind them, and the impact the truth has on the characters when they are finally confronted with it. Compare this family's method of accomplishing its goals with the methods of other movie families to see which interactions make families stronger and which tear them apart.

PROFANITY: Mild.

NUDITY/SEXUAL REFERENCES: Much of the plot revolves around Maggie's attempts to get Brick to sleep with her so she can get pregnant; reference to homosexuality in the play changed to alleged heterosexual infidelity.

ALCOHOL/DRUG ABUSE: Brick has a drinking problem.

VIOLENCE/SCARINESS: Emotional violence only.

TOLERANCE/DIVERSITY ISSUES: Treatment of women typical of the period.

QUESTIONS FOR FAMILIES:

- Why does Maggie compare herself to a cat on a hot tin roof? What is the roof, and what makes it hot?

- Why won't Brick agree to get Maggie pregnant? Who is he mad at? Why?

- Why does Brick have such contempt for himself? What does Skipper's death have to do with it?

- What makes Brick change his mind?

CONNECTIONS: Compare this family to another classic Southern dysfunctional family, the Hubbards, in **The Little Foxes**. Other Tennessee Williams plays adapted for the screen include **The Glass Menagerie**, *Period of Adjustment*, and *Sweet Bird of Youth*.

ACTIVITIES: Read the play, and you will see that Tennessee Williams wrote two different endings. Take a look at the other ending, and read his comments on it before you decide which one you prefer.

Cheaper by the Dozen

1950, 85 min, NR, b &w, 6 and up
Dir: Walter Lang. Clifton Webb, Myrna Loy, Jeanne Crain, Edgar Buchanan
PLOT: Based on the children's classic about the real-life pioneers of "motion study" (efficiency and ergonomics) and their twelve children, this movie begins with father Frank Gilbreth (Clifton Webb) coming home in 1921 Providence, Rhode Island, and whistling the signal for the children to come running. As the children race in and line up, he greets each one in a way that shows his high standards, affection, and above all his interest and involvement with each of his children. His profession is "motion study," and he applies its principles at home as well as at the factories he advises. Through a variety of inventive games and projects, he teaches the children everything from the multiplication of large numbers to Morse code.

The family is moving to Montclair, New Jersey. Frank and his wife, Lillie (Myrna Loy) make sure all the children get into the huge Pierce Arrow "Foolish Carriage" car and drive off. At the new school, Frank insists the older children come along to help him persuade the principal the middle children should be two grades above their age levels. They don't want to go, but he reminds them "people with inner dignity are never embarrassed." He explains to the principal "I'm not just dropping in." He has set aside the entire morning, and plans to stay until he gets them in the classes he thinks appropriate. As the teachers gather, he demonstrates the efficient technique he developed for taking a bath in just the amount of time it takes to hear one side of the language records he insists the children listen to while they are "unavoidably delayed." They are put in the classes he selected.

The children become ill, and the doctor tells them all but Martha must have their tonsils out. Reluctant at first, Frank becomes excited by the prospect of filming ten tonsil operations, to help him figure out a way to make the operation more efficient. In order to get the doctor to agree, Frank promises to allow the doctor to take his tonsils out as well.

At their beach house, the Morse code and the planets are painted on the walls. The older girls are embarrassed by the old-fashioned bathing suits and hairstyles their father makes them wear. Later, back at home, when the oldest daughter, Anne (Jeanne Crain), starts to date a male cheerleader, Frank insists on going along. "What will he think of me?" "That you're a sensible, well-brought-up girl with sensible parents." When she asks if he trusts her, he says, "Of course I trust you. I trust all my daughters. It's that cheerleader I don't trust." At the school dance, he is popular with the kids. The boy Anne likes tells her boys respect the girls whose parents watch over them carefully.

On the way to achieve his dream of giving two important speeches in Europe, Frank dies suddenly. Lillie asks the children if she can count on them to do what is necessary to keep them together, and they promise to manage things while she goes to give the speeches for him.

DISCUSSION: The dedication of the book on which this movie was based, written by two of the Gilbreth children, reads, "To Father, who had only twelve children, and to Mother, who had twelve only children." That is a perceptive comment about the perspectives these two wonderful people brought to their large family. When the twelfth Gilbreth child is born, Frank and Lillie have a poignant conversation about how they will miss having a baby around. Frank pretends to get sick when the children are so he can be with them, because "all that quiet down there makes me nervous."

Children will be amused by the very old-fashioned swimsuits, and the fact that teenagers in every age argue with their parents about clothes and hair and dating.

The (off-camera) death of Frank Gilbreth is terribly sad. Parents should consider preparing their children ahead of time, and should reassure them (as the narrator does at the end of the movie) the family stayed together and did very well.

PROFANITY: None. Like their real-life counterparts, Frank and Lillie have highly characteristic favorite expletives: "By jingo!" and, "Mercy Maud!"

NUDITY/SEXUAL REFERENCES: None. There is a scene in which the local head of Planned Parenthood, as a joke, is sent to the Gilbreths to ask for their support, and is flustered by their having so many children.

ALCOHOL/DRUG ABUSE: None.

VIOLENCE/SCARINESS: None.

TOLERANCE/DIVERSITY ISSUES: Lillian Gilbreth was a pioneer in her profession, the leading woman industrial engineer in the world, and this is pointed out with great pride at the end of the movie. It is more prominent as a theme in the sequel. Anne's heartthrob has a double standard for women, and explains some girls are all right for fooling around with, but others are the kind he wants to marry.

QUESTIONS FOR FAMILIES:

- Would you like to live in a family of twelve children? What would be the best thing about it? What would be the worst?

- The parents in this family spent most of their time thinking about improving the way everything is done, making it faster and easier. What can you think of that can be improved, at home, at school, or someplace else? What would it take to improve it?

- Why is it important to save time? What do you do with the time you save?

- What do you think about their family councils? If you had one, what would you discuss?

- What does Anne mean when she says she cuts her hair and says she is "doing it for the younger kids"?

CONNECTIONS: The movie version of the sequel features much of the same cast and is equally well done. It shows Lillian Gilbreth's struggles to be successful enough professionally to keep her family together and independent, which requires triumphing over the prejudice against women. Forget about the sitcom-ish 2003 Steve Martin movie of the same name, which has no connection to the book beyond the number of children.

Clifton Webb appeared as a very fussy but effective nanny in *Sitting Pretty*, which inspired two sequels as well as the *Mr. Belvedere* television series. He also appears as the acerbic columnist Waldo Lydecker in the classic romantic thriller *Laura*.

ACTIVITIES: The book and its sequel, *Belles on Their Toes*, are both superb and great fun to read aloud.

Help the children time themselves doing everyday tasks like getting dressed and making a peanut butter and jelly sandwich to see if they can find a "more efficient" way to do them. See if they can imitate Mr. Gilbreth's system for taking a bath.

A Christmas Story

1983, 98 min, PG, 8 and up
Dir: Bob Clark. Melinda Dillon, Darrin McGavin, Peter Billingsley
PLOT: Ralphie (Peter Billingsley) is a nine-year-old boy in 1930s Gary, Indiana, whose entire life is consumed with his one wish: a Red Ryder BB gun for Christmas. All of the adults in his life have the same reaction: "You will shoot your eye out!" He also has to deal with his friends, his family and his teacher, with a seemingly endless wait for his Orphan Annie decoder ring, a nasty bully, and an overworked department store Santa.

His father, "the Old Man" (Darrin McGavin), seems preoccupied with the neighbors' dogs (he hates them), his radio contest prize, a huge lamp in the shape of a lady's fishnet-stocking-clad leg (he loves it), the family's furnace (he engages in fervent combat with it), and the Christmas turkey (he wants it). His mother seems preoccupied with getting his brother to eat and getting the leg-lamp out of the house, but both parents manage to come through for a chaotic but very Merry Christmas.

DISCUSSION: Part of the appeal of this movie, based on the memoirs of humorist Jean Shepard (who narrates), is the authenticity of the period detail, much of which will seem unfamiliar and even bizarre to kids today. What is really engaging is his feel for the timeless details of childhood. Today's kids may not have Ralphie's exquisitely calibrated system of dares and double-dog dares, but they will have some equivalent just as thoroughly understood and immutable in their own schoolyard community. They will have a bully to deal with (and probably the bully's nasty little sidekick as well), something to send in box-tops for, a sibling to be annoyed by, an essay to dream of impressing the teacher with, the adult world to try to figure out, and, most of all, some magic dream of the ultimate Christmas present to hope for beyond all reason.

This is a nice antidote to all those Christmas television specials with perfectly harmonized carols and perfectly wrapped gifts. Because people tend to get so obsessive about every single detail at Christmas, the last scene of this movie, when the family's Christmas dinner is exactly the opposite of what they had planned, is especially sweet. Their reaction, seeing it not as a disappointment but as a delightful and funny adventure to enjoy remembering, is a lesson for all families.

PROFANITY: Some mild epithets and episodes involving a father's and child's use of profanity (not heard). WARNING: A child is punished for swearing by having his mouth washed out with soap.

NUDITY/SEXUAL REFERENCES: Mild, episode of prize lamp in the shape of a woman's leg.
ALCOHOL/DRUG ABUSE: None.
VIOLENCE/SCARINESS: Bully; kids fight; kid touches an icy metal pole with his tongue on a dare and it freezes to the pole.
TOLERANCE/DIVERSITY ISSUES: None.
QUESTIONS FOR FAMILIES:

- What makes people act like bullies? What makes people befriend bullies?

- How will the bully's life change after Ralphie fights him?

- Why does Ralphie's father like the lamp so much? Why does his mother dislike it?

- Why is it hard for Ralphie to talk to his parents about what he wants for Christmas?

- Why is Ralphie so disappointed by the decoder?

- Why is a "triple dog dare" so hard to resist?

CONNECTIONS: A sequel with a different cast but the same director is not as good (*It Runs in My Family*, also known as *My Summer Story*). A third, made for television, is called *Ollie Hopnoodle's Haven of Bliss*.

The Diary of Anne Frank

1959, 170 min, NR, b&w, 12 and up
Dir: George Stevens. Millie Perkins, Joseph Schildkraut, Shelley Winters, Ed Wynn, Richard Beymer
PLOT: In WWII Amsterdam, a young Anne Frank and her family must hide from the Nazis in "the hidden annex." Unimaginable horrors go on outside their tiny sanctuary. Inside, she struggles to understand, coping with both the normal confusions of adolescence and the most abnormal and terrifying circumstances.

The movie begins as Otto Frank (Joseph Schildkraut), Anne's father, returns to the annex after the war, the only one who survived. He finds her diary and begins to read it. Anne (Millie Perkins), her parents, her older sister, Margot (Diane Baker), Mr. and Mrs. Van Daan (Shelley Winters and Lou Jacobi), and their teenage son, Peter (Richard Beymer), are welcomed into the annex by two brave gentile friends. The door to the annex is hidden by a bookcase. The annex is in the attic of a spice factory, and during the day, while employees are working, the families must be absolutely silent. Their friends have only three forged ration cards, so food will be very limited. The families settle in hopefully.

The claustrophobic living conditions, fear of discovery, and lack of food create stress, and the families bicker. Anne teases Peter and quarrels with her mother. Later, they are joined by a dentist, Mr. Dussell (Ed Wynn), who tells them that things have become much worse, and many of the people they know have been taken off to concentration camps. They are almost discovered twice, once by a burglar who breaks into the factory, and once by the police. A radio gives them a connection to what is going on; they hear Hitler speak, and listen to music. They celebrate Hanukkah, and Anne gives everyone small gifts she has made for them. She and Peter become close and, despite the lack of privacy, are able to share their feelings. Just as they are rejoicing that the war is almost over, they are found by the Nazis and sent to concentration camps.

DISCUSSION: This is a faithful and affecting (if long) rendition of Anne Frank's story. Director George Stevens used the actual location, now a museum in Amsterdam, as a model for his set, and re-created every detail for authenticity. In addition to discussions of the Holocaust, this movie raises issues about the way families work together (or don't) in times of dire adversity. Anne's famous statement t, "In spite of everything, I still believe that people are really good at heart" is also worth discussing.

PROFANITY: None.
NUDITY/SEXUAL REFERENCES: Anne and Peter share some chaste kisses. Peter's mother implies more may be going on.
ALCOHOL/DRUG ABUSE: None.
VIOLENCE/SCARINESS: Tension as they are almost discovered; tragic ending.
TOLERANCE/DIVERSITY ISSUES: A theme of the movie.
QUESTIONS FOR FAMILIES:

• The Van Daans each have something that is very important to them: the cat, the food, the coat. Why is that? What does it tell you about each of. them? What does it tell you about the impact of hiding?

• In what ways do the characters behave like anyone living under normal circumstances? In what ways do they behave differently?

• Why is Anne's relationship with her father different from her relationship with her mother?

- What do Anne's Hanukkah gifts tell you about the people she gives them to? About her?

- Is Anne's father like Pollyanna when he tells her that she should be glad there will be no more fights about wearing boots or practicing, and says, "How very fortunate we are, when you think of what is happening outside"?

CONNECTIONS: *Anne Frank Remembered*, an outstanding documentary about Anne and her family, won an Oscar in 1996. *The Attic: The Hiding of Anne Frank* is a made-for-television drama starring Mary Steenburgen as Miep Gies, the woman who hid Anne Frank and her family from the Nazis. It provides a worthwhile opportunity to see the famous story from another perspective, and to consider the character of those who risked their lives to save others.

ACTIVITIES: Anne Frank's diary itself should be read by every teenager. There is a lot of information for people of all ages about the Holocaust. Younger children should read the award-winning book by Lois Lowrey, *Number the Stars*, based on a true story, in which a little girl from Amsterdam helps some Jews escape. Children, and especially teenagers, may like to confide in a diary; remember Anne's saying, "I can shake off everything when I write."

The Grapes of Wrath

1940, 129 min, R, b&w, 12 and up
Dir. John Ford. Henry Fonda, Jane Darwell, John Carradine
PLOT: The classic John Steinbeck novel about dust bowl farmers emigrating from Oklahoma to California became a classic film with Henry Fonda as Tom Joad, and Jane Darwell (in an Oscar-winning performance) as his mother.

Tom returns home, after serving time in prison for manslaughter, to discover his sharecropper family is preparing to leave. They have lost the right to farm the land, so they are setting off to find jobs in California. Ma takes one last moment in their shack of a home to say goodbye, looking in a dim mirror and holding her earrings up to her ears. Then all twelve of them pile into the truck, including Casy, a former minister. On the way, their grandfather dies, and they bury him themselves. The grandmother dies, too, but Ma holds on to her and does not tell anyone until they get to California. Thousands of migrants have arrived for the 800 available jobs. Exploited and even robbed by the bosses, the workers are so desperate they will do anything for any wage. They are too frightened to organize and insist on better treatment.

The bosses have hired thugs who threaten anyone who makes trouble. When one begins shooting at the workers, Tom kills him. Casy takes the blame. Then

Casy is killed, and Tom kills the assailant. The Joads find a government-sponsored work camp with better conditions, but Tom is wanted by the authorities and he cannot stay with them.

He tells his mother farewell: "Well, maybe it's like Casy says. Fella ain't got a soul of his own. Just a little piece of a big soul. One big soul that belongs to everybody…I'll be around in the dark. I'll be everywhere. Wherever you can look, wherever there's a fight, so hungry people can eat, I'll be there. Wherever there's a cop beating up a guy, I'll be there. I'll be there in the way guys yell when they're mad. I'll be there in the way kids laugh when they're hungry, and they know supper's ready, and when people are eatin' the stuff they raised, and livin' in the houses they built, I'll be there, too."

After he leaves, Ma says, "Rich fellers come up. They die. Their kids ain't no good and they die out. But we keep a-comin'. We're the people that live. Can't wipe us out. Can't lick us. We'll go on forever, 'cause we're the people!"

DISCUSSION: This brilliant film shows us a family of enormous dignity and commitment. Although Ma says they are not "the kissin' kind," and they show little emotion (except for Ma's delight in Tom's return from prison), there is clearly a great deal of love in the family.

PROFANITY: None.
NUDITY/SEXUAL REFERENCES: None.
ALCOHOL/DRUG ABUSE: None.
VIOLENCE/SCARINESS: Fighting and shooting.
TOLERANCE/DIVERSITY ISSUES: Class issues.
QUESTIONS FOR FAMILIES:

• Director John Ford was famous for using the landscapes in his movies to help create the mood and tell the story. How did he do that here?

• Casy is often considered to be a Christlike figure. What causes people to make that comparison?

• What do you think about Tom's comment that we all have "a piece of a big soul"? About Ma's comment "the people will go on"?

• What is the life of migrant workers like today? To the extent it has improved, what and who made it better?

CONNECTIONS: John Ford won an Oscar as Best Director. Darwell can be glimpsed as "the bird lady" in **Mary Poppins**. Carradine is the father of actors David, Keith, and Robert Carradine.

ACTIVITIES: Teens should read the book by John Steinbeck. They may also appreciate his books *Of Mice and Men* and *East of Eden*, and the films based on them.

Mask

1985, 120 min, PG-13, high school age (with parental warnings below)
Dir: Peter Bogdanovich. Cher, Eric Stoltz, Sam Elliott
PLOT: This is based on the true story of Rocky Dennis (Eric Stoltz), a teenager with a genetic defect that turned his face into a huge "mask" of bone. As the movie begins, Rocky and his mother, Rusty (Cher), go to his new school, where the principal tells them Rocky cannot enroll. Rusty pulls out a file of paperwork and the name of her "lawyer"; she has been through this many times before. Rocky is enrolled. Then he is examined by a new doctor, who advises him sympathetically he cannot expect to live more than three to six months. Rocky and Rusty have heard that before, too; they tell the doctor Rocky has already outlived all previous predictions.

Rocky does very well in school, and the principal suggests he become a counselor's aide at a summer camp for the blind. There he meets Diana (Laura Dern) and has his first romance. They have a lovely time together, but her parents disapprove of the relationship.

Back at home, Rocky is getting impatient with Rusty. He is disappointed that she is not able to maintain a relationship with former boyfriend Gar (Sam Elliott), and loses patience with her alcohol and drug abuse. For him, she cleans up. Maybe it is because she knows on some level he is nearing the end, and she wants him to die knowing she will be all right.

DISCUSSION: This is not a typical "disease of the week" movie about someone triumphing over adversity. It is a far more complex and moving story about two people who love and care for and about each other. Rusty does not work, lives on the fringes of society, uses drugs and abuses alcohol, and is sexually indiscriminate. Though in other aspects of her life she is completely irresponsible, even dissolute, with Rocky she is the ideal of maternal strength and commitment. Rocky is a source of strength for her, too, acting almost as her parent, trying to help her do better and (mostly) forgiving her when she fails.

The movie has several exceptionally touching moments. Rocky tries to teach Diana about colors by using her other senses, giving her a frozen rock to touch to feel "blue." Rocky peers into a fun house mirror and gets a glimpse of his features, distorted into what they might have been had he been "normal." Moved by Rocky's academic triumph, a tough-looking biker named "Dozer" (short for Bulldozer) reveals the real reason for his silence when he stutters so thickly he can barely get out the words of congratulation. The movie shows us over and over again it is not about an "abnormal" boy in a normal world, but about a real boy in a world where everyone is different. As he says, "I look weird, but otherwise I'm real normal."

Rocky has some interesting ways of coping with his problems. He has his version of Pollyanna's "Glad Game," using happy memories to help him through hard times. His mother, who herself uses drugs, helps him manage his headaches without drugs by "talking them away."

PROFANITY: Yes.
NUDITY/SEXUAL REFERENCES: Yes.
ALCOHOL/DRUG ABUSE: Yes.
VIOLENCE/SCARINESS: None.
TOLERANCE/DIVERSITY ISSUES: Theme of tolerance of difference, including people with disabilities (Diana's parents do not want her to associate with Rocky because of his disability, even though she is disabled herself); people with different lifestyles.
QUESTIONS FOR FAMILIES:

• What do you think of the way Rocky tries to show Diana what colors look like? If you were going to try to explain colors to a blind person, what would you do? What tastes, smells, touches, and sounds would you use to give a blind person the feelings of red, yellow, blue, pink, green?

• Why don't Diana's parents want her to see Rocky? Does that surprise you? How do Rocky and Rusty take care of each other? Give some examples.

• Why is Rusty better at taking care of Rocky than she is at taking care of herself?

• Were you surprised by the tenderness of the bikers? In what ways were they like a family?

• In what ways is it harder for Rocky to resolve his feelings of teenage rebellion than it would be for you?

• What do you think will happen to Rusty after the movie ends?

CONNECTIONS: Families might also like to see actor Eric Stoltz without his "mask," as John Brooke in **Little Women**. Mature high school students may appreciate **The Elephant Man**, another true story of a man with a facial disfigurement who enlarges the understanding and compassion of those who get to know him.

ACTIVITIES: Teenagers who see this movie might like to try helping out in a facility for the handicapped, as Rocky did at the summer camp.

Meet Me in St. Louis

1944, 113 min, NR, 6 and up
Dir: Vincente Minnelli. Judy Garland, Mary Astor, Margaret O'Brien, Lucille Bremer, Leon Ames

PLOT: This episodic story of the Smith family in the St. Louis of 1903 is based on the memoirs of Sally Benson. Its pleasures are in the period detail, the glorious songs (including standards "The Trolley Song" and "Have Yourself a Merry Little Christmas"), and the loving and nostalgic look at a time of innocence and optimism, where a long-distance call was almost as thrilling as having the World's Fair come to your very own city. We see the family over the course of a year, celebrating Halloween and Christmas, riding the ice truck in the summer, and building snowmen in the winter. They face the prospect of having to leave St. Louis so that Mr. Smith can accept a promotion. They wonder whether the older girl's two boyfriends will propose. They treat each other with great loyalty and affectionate tolerance. Then they live happily ever after.

The Smiths' older daughters are Rose (Lucille Bremer) and Esther (Judy Garland). Rose is attracted to Warren Sheffield, and is a bit impatient because he has not proposed. Esther has decided to marry "the boy next door," John Pruitt (Tom Drake), even though they have not yet met. When the girls have a party, their two little sisters (Joan Carroll and Margaret O'Brien as Agnes and Tootie Smith) creep downstairs. Tootie is allowed to do one song with Esther (the cakewalk "Under the Bamboo Tree") before being sent back to bed. Esther asks John to help her turn out the gas lights before he leaves, to have some time alone with him. The next day, he joins her as she and her friends ride on the trolley, and when he catches up with them, she sings "The Trolley Song."

Later, Warren escorts a visiting out-of-town girl (June Lockhart) to another party, and Esther and Rose conspire to fill her dance card with the least appealing partners at the dance. When she is revealed to be so friendly and tactful that she gets Rose and Warren back together, Esther has to take all of her dances. Tootie is heartbroken about moving to New York, and while the rest of the family tries to hide it, they are, too. Mr. Smith gives up, they stay in St. Louis, and when the fair opens, they are there.

DISCUSSION: One of the movie's most evocative scenes is Halloween, celebrated very differently in those days, but like today the one night of the year where children have the power to frighten the grown-ups. Agnes and Tootie dress up in rags and "kill" the people who answer the door by throwing flour at them. Director Minnelli skillfully shows how spooky and at the same time thrilling it is for the girls to be out after dark. When Tootie is successful at "killing" the grouchy neighbor, she is heralded by the other kids, and blissfully announces, "I'm the most horrible! I'm the most horrible!"

This is one of the most loving of all movie families. Everyone in it treats all of the other members with trust and affection, even, when it comes to Tootie, indulgence. They are interested in each other and take each other's concerns seriously, whether it is the seasoning of a sauce or choice of a future spouse. Only the poor father is rather left out. He is not told about the long-distance call, and no one is pleased with his promotion. In a way, that is just a reflection of the family's devotion to him and to the life they have together in St. Louis. The lovely duet he sings with his wife, "You and I," shows it is their relationship that is the foundation of the family.

Minnelli began as an art director and designer, and his use of color is always fresh and fun. There isn't another director in history who would have thought to put Esther in purple gloves for the trolley ride, but once you see it, you can't imagine any other color.

PROFANITY: None.
NUDITY/SEXUAL REFERENCES: None.
ALCOHOL/DRUG ABUSE: Tootie likes to shock people by singing a song that begins, "I was drunk last night, dear Mother…"
VIOLENCE/SCARINESS: None.
TOLERANCE/DIVERSITY ISSUES: None.
QUESTIONS FOR FAMILIES:

• The father in this movie has a hard decision to make about whether he should take the new job, even though his family does not want to move. What are the best reasons for going and what are the best reasons for staying? Who should make the decision? Do you agree with what he decided?

- Why does Tootie knock down her snowmen?

- Why is she proud of being "the most horrible"?

- What is most special about the town you live in?

- Would you like to live back in the time of this movie? What would you like best about living in those days?

CONNECTIONS: Vincente Minnelli was very much in love with Judy Garland when they made this movie (they got married after it was completed), and she never looked more radiant. Judy Garland and Vincente Minnelli were, together and separately, responsible for many of the all-time best movie musicals, including **The Pirate**.

My Big Fat Greek Wedding

2002, 96 min, PG, 10 and up
Dir: Joel Zwick. Nia Vardelos, John Corbett, Lainie Kazan
PLOT: Nia Vardalos plays Toula, the shy, plain daughter of a loving but over-powering Greek family. Her father, Gus (Michael Constantine), can prove that any word originally goes back to a Greek source, even "kimono." Dozens of aunts, uncles, and cousins, who all seem to be named Nick, are constantly involved in the most personal details of each other's lives. In a tradition that goes back to ancient Greek mythology, there is a sense of fate and determinism that leaves Toula feeling that her life has been mapped out for her. Her family believes that Greek girls are here to "marry Greek boys, have Greek babies, and cook a lot of Greek food." In the unlikely event that they do not get married, they are expected to work in the family business, in her case, a Greek restaurant.

Toula dreams of more, and with the help of her mother and her aunt, manages to have Gus thinking that it is his idea to have her go back to school and get another job, in her aunt's travel agency.

This small change means a lot, and Toula begins not just to bloom, but to glow. She attracts the attention of Ian, a handsome teacher (*Sex in the City's* John Corbett). She is a reluctant to have him meet her family, and there are certain cultural adjustments involved, but it all works out and the title event is squarely in the happily-ever-after tradition.

DISCUSSION: The story behind this film is as remarkable as the film itself. Actress/writer Nia Vardalos created a one-woman show about her Greek family and their response when she married a man who wasn't Greek. Tom Hanks and his wife, Rita Wilson (who is Greek) saw the show and decided to make it into a movie with Nia playing herself.

You'll fall in love with Vardalos and her family, too. The family is an irresistible force and she is just plain irresistible.

Vardalos and director Joel Zwick balance the specifics of the Greek-American culture with the transcendent universalities of family dynamics. Vardalos and Corbett have a believable sweetness with each other. The movie is riotously funny but heart-catchingly touching and it will make you want to go back and hug everyone you are related to.

PROFANITY: None.
NUDITY/SEXUAL REFERENCES: Non-graphic sexual situation, but it is clear that Toula and Ian wait until they are really committed before going to bed together.
ALCOHOL/DRUG ABUSE: Characters drink and Ian's parents are introduced to powerful Greek Ouzo.
VIOLENCE/SCARINESS: None.
TOLERANCE/DIVERSITY ISSUES: A theme of the movie
QUESTIONS FOR FAMILIES:

• Why does Toula have a hard time telling her family how she feels?

• How does this family compare to others that you know or have seen in other movies, or to your own?

• Does your family have a combination of ethnic cultures, and what are some of the issues that have come up in meshing them?

CONNECTIONS: Families who enjoy this movie will enjoy some other family cultural clashes in *Moonstruck* (some mature material) and *Flower Drum Song*.

National Velvet

1944, 125 min, NR, 6 and up
Dir: Clarence Brown. Elizabeth Taylor, Mickey Rooney, Anne Revere, Angela Lansbury
PLOT: Mi Taylor (Mickey Rooney) arrives in a small English town and meets Velvet (Elizabeth Taylor) just as she and her sisters have been let out of school for the summer. They like each other immediately, and she is delighted to learn the reason he has come to her town is that he found her mother's name in the address

book belonging to his late father. He does not know what their relationship was, or what he hopes to find from her, but he has no other place to go.

At the dinner, Mi is tentative, not sure himself whether he is looking for a friend or an easy mark. That night, as Mrs. Brown goes over the day's books and puts away the cash from their butcher shop, she and Mr. Brown talk about giving Mi a job. Mr. Brown is reluctant, saying they don't need him, and he seems to have a "sharpness" about him, but she insists. After Velvet tells him he is going to stay, he sneaks back into the house to return their money, which he had stolen.

The horse Velvet loves most is owned by a man who, angry and frustrated at his inability to control it, decides to sell it by lottery. Velvet wins and renames the horse The Pi. He won't pull the butcher shop cart, but he can jump a fence as high as the most treacherous hazard in England's biggest horse race, the Grand National Steeplechase. So Velvet decides he must be in that race, to have a chance to be the very best he can be, the very best there is.

They hire a jockey by mail, but Velvet knows the horse must be ridden by someone who loves him, and would rather not have him race at all than have a jockey who does not believe he can win. Just as Mi is about to volunteer, Velvet decides she will ride The Pi, even if they could have had the best jockey in the world, even if they will get in trouble because girls are not allowed to race. She rides The Pi, and he wins, but they are both disqualified because she is a girl.

They come back home in triumph, knowing they won what was important to them. Though they were not allowed to keep the title or the prize money, all charges have been dropped, and they won't get into trouble for violating the rules. Mr. Brown is excited by all of the offers for appearances and endorsements, but Velvet knows it would not be best for The Pi and it is time to move on. So does Mi, who takes his knapsack and says good-bye to Mr. and Mrs. Brown. When Velvet hears he has left, she asks if she can tell him about his father, who was Mrs. Brown's coach, and how much he meant to her in achieving her dream. Mrs. Brown consents, and Velvet races after him, just catching up to him as the movie ends.

DISCUSSION: National Velvet taps into one of the oldest, deepest dreams, the dream of horses. Every child dreams of controlling these huge, powerful, loyal creatures, of flying over hurdles on their backs, of earning their devotion and of being devoted to them in return.

Then there is the dream of racing, as Velvet says in this movie, until you burst your heart, and then until you burst it again, and then until you burst it twice as much as before, until the two of you explode past the finish line ahead of everyone else.

This is the story of dreams themselves, wise and foolish, big and small, realized and impossible, and about the way all of these dreams change those who are lucky enough to dream them. It is about the importance of faith, Velvet's faith in herself and in The Pi and in her dream, and her family's faith in her and in Mi and the importance of that belief and support in making the dream come true.

Mi says, "You bit off a big piece of dream for yourself, Velvet." Then, in one of the sweetest scenes ever filmed, Mrs. Brown takes out the 100 gold pieces she won for swimming the English Channel and gives them to Velvet. There were a thousand times the family could have used that money, but she was saving it for a dream as big as her own once was. She tells Velvet, "I too believe everyone should have a chance at a breathtaking piece of folly once in his life."

National Velvet is also a rare movie because it deals with what happens after the dream comes true. It sometimes seems half the movies that are made, and well over half of the movies that are made for children, end with the hero or heroine triumphantly standing in the winner's circle, holding the trophy overhead as the music swells and the credits roll.

One of the best insights from this movie is the way that it puts the dream in perspective. After they win the race, Mr. Brown is delighted with all of the offers for appearances and endorsements for Velvet and her horse. Instead of arguing with him, Mrs. Brown asks Velvet how she feels about it. Velvet thinks it might be fun for her, but says she would never put The Pi through all of the foolishness required. Velvet and her friend Mi and those around them take what they have learned from the dream and go on with their lives, something worth discussing in this era when any achievement, good or bad, becomes a miniseries.

Most of all, National Velvet is the story of a loving family. It is very different in many ways from the families the American children of today know. For example, the mother and father are so reserved they call each other "Mr. and Mrs. Brown" until the very last scene. It is a wonderful starting point for a discussion of the ways families of all kinds can teach and support each other.

One of the key themes of the movie is the faith the characters have (and don't have) in themselves and in each other. Mr. Brown is reluctant to accept Mi at first, with good reason. As Mrs. Brown says, it would be surprising for someone who had lived on the streets not to have a "sharpness about him." She persuades Mr. Brown to give him a chance: "What's the meaning of goodness if there isn't a little badness to overcome?" Mi does steal their money, but when he learns of their faith in him, their offer of a job and a place to stay and Velvet's acceptance of him as a friend, he puts it back. Later, when he has a chance to steal much more money from the family, he thinks about it, but decides he can't, because "she trusts me."

Velvet's faith in both Mi and The Pi is at the center of the movie. She accepts them both immediately and irrevocably, though both are mistrusted by others. She does not believe Mi when he says he doesn't like horses, and when he says he is only interested in the race for the money. She knows he feels as passionately for The Pi as she does, though he cannot say it.

Velvet also has faith in the future. She is certain she will win the lottery for the horse she loves. When she tells everyone she will win, a suspicious neighbor suggests she may have cheated by arranging for her father to pick her number in the drawing. She explains she didn't bother with that; she just worked it out with God. Mr. Brown responds to the neighbor's accusation by having him do the drawing, and of course Velvet does win. When the jockey they have hired by mail to ride The Pi in the race shows them he not only does not believe that The Pi can win, he does not even care, Velvet knows that it would be wrong to let him ride her horse. Just like Mi and Velvet herself, The Pi deserves someone who believes in him.

Mr. and Mrs. Brown show their trust by risking letting Mi and their children make mistakes. "She has it in her to do the right thing," Mrs. Brown says of Velvet, and lets her decide how to respond to the offers that come in after she wins the race. Mrs. Brown also lets Velvet run to school after being up all night caring for the horse. When Mr. Brown objects, she reassures him Velvet will be back. It's Saturday, and there is no school. Mrs. Brown let her go because "I like that part of her that wants to go to school after a night caring for the horse."

Mrs. Brown not only lets Mi stay with the family, but she entrusts him to take her 100 gold pieces to London. Mr. Brown is certain he will steal it instead. As the train pulls away, you can see Velvet reflected in the window of the train car. This symbolizes the way the image of Velvet, and her faith in him, stays with Mi, and prevents him from taking the advice of his friends who get him drunk and encourage him to steal the money. As they leave for the race, Velvet says to Mrs. Brown, "You'll be proud of The Pi, mother." Mrs. Brown says, "I want to be proud of you." And she is.

Throughout the movie, Mr. and Mrs. Brown balance a spacious acceptance of their children's passions with a firm set of values and a fairly strict set of rules. Velvet is permitted to pretend to ride in bed only one night a week, and only for fifteen minutes. At his first dinner with the family, Mi is reprimanded sharply by Mr. Brown (Donald Crisp) for feeding the dog at the table ("It will turn him into a beggar," is a pointed comment made to the young man who has arrived at their door and may have some hope of being helped). As we see during the course of the scene, each member of the family, including Mr. Brown, sneaks food to the dog when the others aren't looking.

Similarly, Velvet is constantly reminded by everyone to wear her braces. When Mi does this, on the way to the race, it shows how much he has accepted the family's set of priorities and the responsibility of caring for its members. In this case, though, he lets her take the braces out until the race is over. Like Mr. and Mrs. Brown, he knows when to suspend the rules. Mrs. Brown won't tell Mi how much his father meant to her until he leaves them. As long as he had no faith in himself, that information would be no more than a way to get something from the Brown family. Once he no longer felt "soft and yellow inside," he could accept it as a heritage to build on.

PROFANITY: None.
NUDITY/SEXUAL REFERENCES: None.
ALCOHOL/DRUG ABUSE: Mi gets intoxicated with bad friends, which almost leads him to make the wrong decision and steal the money.
VIOLENCE/SCARINESS: None.
TOLERANCE/DIVERSITY ISSUES: Even though she wins the race, Velvet is deprived of the title and the prize because girls are not eligible to race. No one questions that rule or seems surprised by it; she undertakes the race knowing this will happen. Mr. and Mrs. Brown are equal partners at home and at work, though she is the stronger character.
QUESTIONS FOR FAMILIES:

- Why can't Velvet keep the prize, even though she won?

- Why didn't Mrs. Brown want to tell Mi about his father? What made her decide it was time?

- Why didn't Velvet want to make movies or do any of the other things people asked her to do after she won? What would you do?

- What did Mrs. Brown mean about "goodness not meaning much unless there is a little bit of badness to overcome"?

- What did she mean about everyone's being entitled to a "breathtaking piece of folly"?

CONNECTIONS: Children who watch this movie might like to know there is a real-life story of a little girl's dream behind it. Elizabeth Taylor wanted to play this role as much as Velvet wanted to ride The Pi. She was told she could not have the part because she was too short, and filming was scheduled to start in a few months. She promised to be tall enough by the time filming started, and fate and genes were on her side.

Anne Revere won an Academy Award for her portrayal of Mrs. Brown. She also played strong, wise mothers in many other movies, including, Gentleman's Agreement and Body and Soul. Fans of television's *Murder, She Wrote* will enjoy seeing Angela Lansbury in an early pre Jessica Fletcher role as Velvet's older sister. Thirty-five years after **National Velvet**, Mickey Rooney played an old horse trainer in the second-best movie about a child and a horse, **The Black Stallion**.

The sequel, International Velvet, with Tatum O'Neal (1978), is not very good.

ACTIVITIES: Older children will enjoy the book *National Velvet*, by Enid Bagnold, also the author of **The Chalk Garden**.

Mary Poppins

1964, 1 0 min, G, 6 and up
Dir: Robert Stevenson. Julie Andrews, Dick Van Dyke, Glynis Johns
PLOT: In the London of 1910, the Banks family has a loving, if rather chaotic, household. A nanny has just stormed out, fed up with the "incorrigible" children, Jane and Michael. Mr. Banks (David Tomlinson) writes an ad for a new nanny, and the children compose their own, which he tears up and throws into the fireplace. The pieces fly up the chimney, where they reassemble for Mary Poppins (Julie Andrews), who is sitting on a cloud. The next day, a great wind blows away all of the nannies waiting to be interviewed, as Mary floats down.

She takes the measure of the children and her own ("practically perfect in every way") and slides up the banister. She directs them to clean up the nursery and shows them how to make it into a game. Once it is clean, they go out for a walk and they meet Bert (Dick Van Dyke) drawing chalk pictures on the sidewalk. They hop into the picture and have a lovely time. Mary takes them to see her uncle Arthur (Ed Wynn), who floats up to the ceiling when he laughs, and they find this delightful condition is catching. Later, their father takes them to the bank where he works, and Michael embarrasses him by refusing to deposit his tuppence because he wants to use it to buy crumbs to feed the birds. There is a misunderstanding, and this starts a run on the bank with everyone taking out their money, and Mr. Banks is fired.

Mr. Banks realizes that he has been too rigid and demanding. He invites the children to fly a kite with him. Mrs. Banks realizes that in working for the vote for women, she had neglected the children. Her work done, Mary Poppins says good-bye and floats away.

DISCUSSION: This sumptuous production deserved its many awards (including Oscars for Andrews and for "Chim Chim Cher-ee" as Best Song) and its enormous box office. It is fresh and imaginative, and the performances are outstanding. (Watch the credits carefully to see that Van Dyke also plays the rubber-limbed Mr. Dawes.) The "jolly holiday" sequence, featuring the live-action characters interacting with animated ones, is superb, especially Van Dyke's dance with the penguin waiters.

PROFANITY: None.
NUDITY/SEXUAL REFERENCES: None.
ALCOHOL/DRUG ABUSE: None.
VIOLENCE/SCARINESS: None.
TOLERANCE/DIVERSITY ISSUES: The cause of votes for women is presented as unimportant, even daffy; subtext that parents should spend time with their children instead of working.
QUESTIONS FOR FAMILIES:

• Which of the children's adventures would you like best?

• What do you think of the list of qualifications the children prepare? Why is it different from the one prepared by Mr. Banks?

• How can you make "a spoonful of sugar [to] help the medicine go down" at home?

CONNECTIONS: Julie Andrews starred in another family favorite, **The Sound of Music**. Dick Van Dyke starred in **Bye Bye Birdie**.
ACTIVITIES: Read the four books about Mary Poppins by P. L. Travers, which include many more adventures. Then feed the birds or go fly a kite!

Ordinary People

1980, 123 min, 12 and up
Dir: Robert Redford. Timothy Hutton, Judd Hirsch, Mary Tyler Moore, Donald Sutherland, Elizabeth McGovern, Dinah Manoff

PLOT: Conrad Jarrett (Timothy Hutton) has returned home after four months in a mental hospital. He tried to kill himself following a tragic boating accident with his brother, Buck, who drowned. He is trying to find a way to fit in, both at home and at school. His father, Calvin (Donald Sutherland), tries to reach out to him, but is afraid of saying the wrong thing and is shy about his own emotions. His mother, Beth (Mary Tyler Moore), is uncomfortable with emotions and with anything else that might be "messy" or hard to control.

After some hesitation, Conrad seeks out Dr. Berger (Judd Hirsch), a psychiatrist recommended to him when he left the hospital, telling him he is seeking "control." Berger warns him that control is tough to achieve, but says he will do what he can. He advises Conrad to start from the outside, work on his actions and let the feelings follow.

Conrad begins to reach out to a sympathetic girl at school, Jeannine (Elizabeth McGovern).

He makes contact with Karen (Dinah Manoff), a friend from his hospital stay, who seems to have "control," to be busy with friends and activities and sure of herself. He is devastated when he tries to call her again and hears she has killed herself. He calls Berger in the middle of the night and insists on seeing him. He relinquishes what he thinks of as "control" to confess to Berger and to himself that he can't forgive himself for surviving when his brother died, and he feels guilty and unworthy.

Calvin begins to realize Beth's unwillingness to connect to her own emotions or anyone else's is suffocating the family. They had had the appearance of closeness, but the tragedy revealed how superficial it was. Their relationship unravels quickly, and she leaves as Cal and Conrad begin to share their feelings.

DISCUSSION: This is a movie about emotional honesty, about the courage and emotional vocabulary necessary for the connections and intimacy we need to be able to survive challenges like the tragedy faced by this family. Berger says, "If you can't feel pain, then you're not going to feel anything else, either." The characters represent a wide variety of approaches and abilities to emotional openness and "control." Conrad and Calvin are both groping their way toward a better understanding of themselves and others and the ability to communicate.

Beth does not want to try. She is by no means an ogre. Indeed, it is clear the director and writer of the movie feel sorry for her. She has chosen emptiness she can control rather than "messy" feelings. Beth preferred Buck to Conrad because Buck's easy confidence did not place any emotional demands on her. Conrad says, "I can't talk to her! The way she looks at me! She hates me!" What Conrad feels as rejection is really Beth's fear that his sensitivity and vulnerability will put demands on her she can't or won't be able to respond to. She can't bear the thought she might somehow be responsible for Conrad's pain, while Calvin is willing to confront that issue in order to be able to help Conrad.

Jeannine at first pulls back from Conrad's attempt to connect with her by telling her the truth about himself, but then apologizes. She wants to understand him; it was just that at first she did not know how to respond, so she retreated into the more comfortable and familiar environment of joking around. In contrast, Karen, who seems to have so much "control" and goes to elaborate pains to persuade Conrad she is doing fine, is unable to cope.

Teenagers may know of someone who has attempted suicide. This movie provides an opportunity to discuss what led Conrad and Karen to consider it, how the perspective of a person about his own worth is very different from that of those around him, and what the other options are for people who are deeply depressed.

PROFANITY: Mild.
NUDITY/SEXUAL REFERENCES: Locker-room references.
ALCOHOL/DRUG ABUSE: Beth uses alcohol as an emotional anesthetic.
VIOLENCE/SCARINESS: None.
TOLERANCE/DIVERSITY ISSUES: Anti-Semitic remark by Conrad's grandmother (and lack of objection by Beth) intended to show insularity.
QUESTIONS FOR FAMILIES:

- Why is control so important to Conrad? Is it important to Beth and Calvin, too?

- What do you think of Berger's advice about starting from the outside?

- How does Berger help Conrad? How does Jeannine help him?

- Why does Conrad quit the swim team? Why doesn't he tell his parents?

- How do you feel about Beth? Do you dislike her or feel sorry for her or both? Why is it so hard for her to give her husband and son what they feel they need?

CONNECTIONS: This film received Oscars for Best Picture, Screenplay, and Supporting Actor (Timothy Hutton). It also popularized the lovely "Canon" by Pachelbel. Viewers of TVLand will recognize Mary Tyler Moore from *The Dick Van Dyke Show* and *The Mary Tyler Moore Show*.

Pollyanna

1960, 134 min, NR, 6 and up
Dir: David Swift. Hayley Mills, Jane Wyman, Agnes Moorehead, Adolphe Menjou, Karl Malden, Richard Egan
PLOT: Pollyanna (Hayley Mills) arrives in Harrington to live with her wealthy aunt, Polly Harrington (Jane Wyman), after the death of Pollyanna's missionary parents. Polly is generous with money, buying Pollyanna lots of beautiful clothes, but is reserved and joyless. She uses her influence to run all aspects of the town, even telling the Reverend Ford (Karl Malden) what to preach on Sundays. His fire-and-brimstone sermons make the congregation miserable. Pollyanna's friendliness and her expectation that everyone else will be friendly, too, endear her to everyone from Polly's servants and the Reverend Ford to a cranky invalid (Agnes Moorehead as Mrs. Snow) and the town recluse (Adolphe Menjou as Mr. Pendergast). She teaches her friends "the glad game," finding something to be glad about in any situation.

When the people in the town decide that instead of accepting Polly's charity they will give a bazaar to raise money for a new orphanage, Polly forbids Pollyanna to go. She sneaks out by climbing down a tree and has a wonderful time, but falls on the way back in and is badly hurt. She no longer wants to try to play the glad game, until the whole town shows up to tell her how much she means to them. She leaves for an operation, confident that she will soon be well.

DISCUSSION: This is Disney at its finest, a lavish and gorgeous fantasy of an idyllic American past. Using first-rate actors (including two Oscar-winners) and sumptuous period detail, this movie is a delight for the eyes as well as the spirit.

Pollyanna is best remembered for "the glad game," in which the challenge is to find something to be glad about, no matter how bleak the situation. What really makes her special is the way that she expects the best from everyone, and the transforming effect it has on each person she meets. Pollyanna wears on a chain a quote from Abraham Lincoln: "When you look for the bad in men, expecting to find it, you surely will." She thanks Aunt Polly for her generosity, and the clothes become a gift instead of a duty or a way of establishing position. (Cedric has the same effect on others in *Little Lord Fauntleroy*.)

Pollyanna expects Mrs. Snow and Mr. Pendergast to want to participate in the bazaar, and they do. She quotes her father to the Reverend Ford. He told her that with 826 "happy texts" in the Bible, God must have wanted people to be happy. Pollyanna helps Ford find again not just his own joy in preaching, but also his integrity in preaching what is in his heart and not what Polly Harrington tells him to say. At his next sermon, he tells everyone to enjoy the beautiful day (and to come to the bazaar), and admits, "I should have been looking for the good in you, and I failed, and I apologize."

Many of the mistakes people make in this movie come from trying to protect themselves from hurt. Polly, hurt by her estrangement from Dr. Chilton, relies on her sense of duty. Mrs. Snow, worried about, illness and dependence, tries to blame others and achieves some sense of control (and some attention) with her contrariness. Mr. Pendergast just avoids any contact at all. Pollyanna shows them how to make sure that fear of pain and loss do not prevent opportunities for joy.

Pollyanna, like George Bailey in **It's a Wonderful Life**, gets a rare opportunity to have all she has done recognized and acknowledged by the community. Ask kids who in their community has had a beneficial impact, and how it could be acknowledged.

PROFANITY: None.
NUDITY/SEXUAL REFERENCES: None.
ALCOHOL/DRUG ABUSE: None.
VIOLENCE/SCARINESS: Scary fall from tree.
TOLERANCE/DIVERSITY ISSUES: None.
QUESTIONS FOR FAMILIES:

• Can you play "the glad game"?

• Why do people change when they meet Pollyanna? Who changes the most? How can you tell?

• Why does Mrs. Snow spend so much time thinking about illness and dying? Why does she seem determined not to like anything?

• Why do the people in the town want to raise the money for the orphanage themselves, instead of having Polly give it to them?

• Why does the Reverend apologize?

CONNECTIONS: Hayley Mills received a special Oscar for her appearance in this film, and went on to star in many other Disney movies that have been loved by generations of kids, especially **The Parent Trap** and *The Moon-Spinners*. Her father, distinguished actor John Mills, appeared as the father in **Swiss Family Robinson**, and they appeared together in *The Chalk Garden*. Agnes Moorehead appeared in **Citizen Kane** and is familiar to Nick-at-Nite fans as Endora on

Betwitched. This was the last film appearance of Adolphe Menjou (Mr. Pendergast), a rare departure from his usual dapper and impeccably attired roles.

ACTIVITIES: Pollyanna and Jimmy are enchanted by the way that sunlight through prisms makes rainbows on the walls. Try hanging a few prisms on some of the windows in your house, and watching which times of day make the best rainbows. Read the encyclopedia together to learn why the prisms split the light beam into separate colors. Children may also enjoy the Pollyanna series of books by Eleanor H. Porter, which follow Pollyanna into adulthood.

A River Runs Through It

1992, 123 min, PG, high school age
Dir: Robert Redford. Craig Sheffer, Brad Pitt, Tom Skerritt, Emily Lloyd

PLOT: Writer Norman Maclean's autobiographical story of growing up in Montana with his brother, Paul, begins, "In our family, there was no clear line between religion and fly-fishing." Their Presbyterian minister father taught them their schoolwork, religion and fishing as though they were all one subject. All were strict and thorough. He believed no one who did not know how to fish properly should be permitted to disgrace a fish by catching it. He used a metronome to time their four-count stroke between the positions of ten o'clock and two o'clock.

Norman, though more sober, loved the wild streak in Paul that made him "tougher than any man alive" but feared it would destroy him. While Norman becomes a professor of English literature and falls in love with Jessie Burns (Emily Lloyd), Paul becomes a reporter and gets into trouble drinking and gambling. Norman is called by the police to get Paul out of jail, and ultimately, he is called again when Paul is killed.

DISCUSSION: One of the tragic realizations of growing up is that you can love someone without being able to understand or save them. Like Norman, Jessie has a brother who is self-destructive, though his part of the story is played more for comedy. In today's terms, Jessie's mother would be considered an enabler because she does not impose any limits on her son and does not insist that he recognize the consequences of his behavior.

PROFANITY: Mild.

NUDITY/SEXUAL REFERENCES: Jessie's brother brings a prostitute with him when he goes fishing with Norman and Paul; they fall asleep nude and are sunburned badly.

ALCOHOL/DRUG ABUSE: Paul has a drinking problem; Jessie's brother Neal and a woman become drunk and pass out.

VIOLENCE/SCARINESS: Mostly off-screen.

TOLERANCE/DIVERSITY ISSUES: Paul brings a half-Cheyenne date into a bar that does not permit Indians.

QUESTIONS FOR FAMILIES:

- If you were Norman, what would you have said to Paul? When? Why didn't Norman say those things?

- If you were Jessie, what would you say to Neal?

- Why was it important to have Neal's story in the movie?

- What does Norman mean when he says that his father saw no difference between religion and fly-fishing?

CONNECTIONS: Director Redford addresses the theme of loving families who do not communicate pain well, with one member of the family suffering the consequences, in *Ordinary People* and *Quiz Show*.

A Tree Grows in Brooklyn

1945, 128 min, NR, b&w, 10 and up

Dir: Elia Kazan. Dorothy McGuire, James Dunn, Peggy Ann Garner, Joan Blondell

PLOT: Francie Nolan (Peggy Ann Garner), an imaginative and sensitive girl, lives with her family in a Brooklyn tenement. She adores her father, Johnny (James Dunn), a dreamer with a drinking problem, and respects but resents her down-to-earth mother, Katie (Dorothy McGuire). The family struggles to rise from poverty. Francie and her brother must each read a page aloud every night from the Bible and from Shakespeare, and their parents are intent on their becoming the first family members to graduate from grade school. Francie dreams of going to a better school in a wealthier neighborhood, and her father makes it possible by telling the principal she is moving in with a fictitious wealthy aunt. A teacher there encourages her to pursue her love of writing.

Katie is pregnant again, and decides Francie should leave school. When Johnny dies, Francie is devastated. She is angry with her mother, feeling that her mother did not love Johnny enough, and does not love her enough, either. When her mother has the baby, Francie sees she loves them both, and also perceives

Katie hates having to be practical and "hard." A kind policeman asks permission to court Katie, and Francie knows their life will be easier, and her father and what they shared will be with her always.

DISCUSSION: This family has a great deal of love but a lot of difficulty showing it. Although they clearly love each other, Johnny and Katie have too many shattered expectations to accept tenderness from each other, as we see when he comes home with the food from the party and sees her with her hair down, and when she tries to tell him how much she likes hearing him sing "Annie Laurie."

They have trouble being honest and direct about their circumstances and their feelings. They have to move to a cheaper apartment, but insist to themselves and to everyone else they are doing it to get more sunlight. When Katie decides she wants her sister back in her life, she sends the message via the insurance collector. When Francie tries raising the subject of the school she wants to attend in a roundabout way, Katie tells her to speak more directly. Johnny lets her tell him in her own way and, over Katie's objections, makes it possible for her dream to come true. Francie has a hard time understanding Katie loves her and relies on her, until Katie is in labor and almost does not know what she is saying.

This is a good opportunity to talk about the ways families do (and do not) communicate with each other. Older kids may also want to discuss the impact Johnny's drinking and unreliability had on Katie and why it was different for Francie.

PROFANITY: None.

NUDITY/SEXUAL REFERENCES: Aunt Sissy is involved with many different men, and at one point Katie refuses to let her see the children because she is a bad influence.

ALCOHOL/DRUG ABUSE: Johnny has a serious drinking problem.

VIOLENCE/SCARINESS: Inexplicit scene of Katie in labor may scare younger children, who should be reassured; very sad when Johnny dies.

TOLERANCE/DIVERSITY ISSUES: Issues relating to assimilation, poverty.

QUESTIONS FOR FAMILIES:

- What does the title refer to?

- What did Francie's teacher mean about the difference between imagination and pipe dreams?

- Why did the members of the family have such a hard time talking to each other about what mattered to them?

- Why does the family use the word "sick" to describe Johnny's alcoholism? Why does Johnny seem so sad when Francie talks with him about being "sick"?

- Why was it so important to Kate that the death certificate be changed?

CONNECTIONS: James Dunn won an Oscar for his performance. Joan Blondell appeared as a brassy second lead in a number of early musicals, including *Footlight Parade* and *Gold Diggers of 1933*. Peggy Ann Garner is also lovely as the young *Jane Eyre*.
ACTIVITIES: Students should read the book, by Betty Smith, who based it on her own childhood.

Unstrung Heroes

1995, 93 min, PG, 12 and up
Dir: Diane Keaton. Andie MacDowell, John Turturro, Michael Richards
PLOT: Steven Lidz is the son of Sid (John Turturro), an inventor. He is a distracted man who "believes in documentation" and empirical data. Steven is closer to his warmhearted mother, the emotional center of the family. When she becomes ill, he goes to live with his father's two brothers (Michael Richards and Maury Chaikin), both borderline (and sometimes more than borderline) mentally ill. They are hoarders, with huge piles of newspapers filling every bit of available floor space; paranoid, telling him there are only eight trustworthy people in the world (the other four have been killed); and delusional. Still, they love Steven very much and see in him a strength and ability to be great that he finds very comforting. They rename him "Franz" because they think it suits him better than "Steven."

Franz picks up some of his uncles' peculiarities (singing the "Internationale" in school while the other kids recite the Pledge of Allegiance), but also draws strength from what they tell him. They encourage him to connect to his heritage by studying for his bar mitzvah. His uncles' fascination with objects inspires him to hold on to a bit of his mother by collecting small items that make him feel close to her. When she dies, he retrieves hours of "documentation" (film of experiments and family home movies) from the garbage. He and his father watch them together and, with the uncles, begin to document the family again.
DISCUSSION: Based on the autobiographical novel by sportswriter Franz Lidz (he kept the name his uncles bestowed on him), this is a quietly moving story of a boy growing up in the midst of incomprehensible loss. Perhaps it is the very incomprehensibility of it all that makes his uncles seem understandable by com-

parison. Or perhaps they just have a less frightening way of being impossible to understand. To Steven, they are almost like children, the way they play with the "high-bouncers" from the collection of lost rubber balls that "hold the sounds of the children who played with them." He makes pancakes for them the way his mother made pancakes for him and his sister. He protects them from the landlord who wants to see them evicted. They have time for him, which his parents don't. They have answers for him, which no one else does. They see him as "Franz," and "Franz" is who he decides he wants to be.

This is a movie about loss, but more than that it is a movie about families, and the acceptance of family members who are not always easy to understand. This includes Sid as well as the uncles.

The movie raises the question of faith. Sid is relentlessly scientific and is furious his brothers have encouraged Franz to study Judaism. He tells them "religion is a crutch, only cripples need crutches." Franz's mother, dying, says maybe Franz is right.

Franz's attitude toward his uncles is very sympathetic, even protective. Franz and his friend Ash play a prank on Uncle Danny, slipping him a note sending his paranoia into overdrive. Danny commits himself, and when Franz admits he wrote the note, Danny tells him it is all right, because that made it possible for him to get help.

PROFANITY: None.
NUDITY/SEXUAL REFERENCES: None.
ALCOHOL/DRUG ABUSE: None.
VIOLENCE/SCARINESS: Scariness of mother's illness and death.
TOLERANCE/DIVERSITY ISSUES: Uncle Danny's paranoia has him seeing anti-Semitism everywhere; Steven/Franz studies for his bar mitzvah over his father's objections.
QUESTIONS FOR FAMILIES:

• Why does Steven give up instead of giving his speech?

• Why does Steven decide to go live with his uncles? Why do his parents let him?

• Why do Sid and his brothers have different ideas about religion?

• What does "documentation" mean, and why is it important here?

• What does Sid mean by an "undisciplined mind"?

CONNECTIONS: This was the first feature film directed by actress Diane Keaton (*Annie Hall, Reds, The Godfather,* and many others.).
ACTIVITIES: Older kids, particularly those familiar with Lidz's sportswriting, may want to read the book. Those who are not familiar with the bar mitzvah ceremony may enjoy attending one.

You Can't Take It With You

1938, 127 min, NR, b&w, 8 and up
Dir: Frank Capra. Jimmy Stewart, Jean Arthur, Lionel Barrymore, Ann Miller
PLOT: The Sycamore family, a group of loving and lovable eccentrics presided over by Grandpa (Lionel Barrymore), includes daughter Penny (Spring Byington), who writes lurid plays, and her husband Paul (Samuel S. Hinds), who makes fireworks in the basement with Mr. DePinna (Halliwell Hobbes), the iceman who came by to deliver ice nine years before and just stayed. Mr. Poppin (Donald Meek), who loves to make mechanical toys, has recently joined them. The Sycamores have two daughters. Essie (Ann Miller) loves to dance, and her husband, Ed (Dub Taylor), plays the xylophone. They sell candy to make a little money. The other daughter, Alice (Jean Arthur), is the only one in the family with a job. She works for a banking firm and has fallen in love with the boss's son, Tony Kirby (Jimmy Stewart).

A man from the IRS visits to find out why Grandpa has never paid any taxes. The neighbors are all being evicted because the land is being sold to developers who intend to build a factory. Tony's very elegant and snobbish parents arrive for dinner on the wrong night, descending upon the Sycamore family just as Ed is arrested for enclosing seditious statements in the candy boxes and all the fireworks blow up. Various crises of finance and embarrassment and misunderstanding ensue, but all are straightened out, and everyone lives happily ever after.
DISCUSSION: The well-loved play by George S. Kaufman and Moss Hart is given the Frank Capra treatment, which he himself called "Capra-corn." The entire populist subplot about the land being sold and the appearance of most of the characters in court are the additions of Capra and his screenwriter, Robert Riskin, and they make the film seem a bit dated. Still, children will enjoy the way everyone in the family joyfully pursues his or her own dreams, and the way they all respect and support each other.

Discuss with children the way some characters in the movie do not even seem to notice how eccentric they appear to others, while others notice and enjoy being different, and still others try desperately to appear "normal." Children may have their own ideas about what "normal" means and whether it makes them feel entertained or uncomfortable to be around people who have a different idea of normality. All children feel embarrassed by their families at times, and it is worth paying attention to the way Alice learns, with Tony's help, that her family is not as unacceptable to the "normal" world as she had feared.

PROFANITY: None.
NUDITY/SEXUAL REFERENCES: None.
ALCOHOL/DRUG ABUSE: None.
VIOLENCE/SCARINESS: None.
TOLERANCE/DIVERSITY ISSUES: The two black characters, a maid and her out-of-work boyfriend, are treated with some affection but also with condescension.
QUESTIONS FOR FAMILIES:

• Would you like to live in a family like this one?

• Which family member is most like you?

• Why did Tony tell his parents the wrong night for dinner at the Sycamores'?

• Notice the difference between the way the Sycamores and the Kirbys react when they get arrested. Why?

• What does the title mean?

CONNECTIONS: This movie won Academy Awards for Best Picture and Best Director. Kaufman and Hart were the most successful playwrights of their day, and some of their other plays have been made into movies, too. *George Washington Slept Here*, with Jack Benny and Ann Sheridan, is a very funny story about a family that moves into a ramshackle house. *The Man Who Came to Dinner* is about a nightmare dinner guest who falls and breaks his hip and is stuck in the house long enough to cause complete disruption for everyone. Kaufman was coauthor, with Edna Ferber, of *Stage Door*, about a group of young would-be actresses. It was made into a movie starring Katharine Hepburn and Ginger Rogers, and featuring Ann Miller, Lucille Ball, and Eve Arden. He was also the author of some of the Marx Brothers's most popular movies.
ACTIVITIES: Younger children will enjoy *Weird Parents*, by Audrey Wood, about a boy whose parents are even more outlandish than the Sycamores. Older kids can have fun getting a copy of the play and acting out some of their favorite scenes.

ANNE OF GREEN GABLES

1985, 195 min, NR, 6 and up
Dir: Kevin Sullivan. Colleen Dewhurst, Megan Fallows
L: M. Montgomery's book about the red-haired orphan who found a home on Canada's Prince Edward Island comes to life in this made-for-television production (originally shown in two parts, and followed by sequels), a sheer delight, exceptional in every detail. Colleen Dewhurst is ideally cast as Marilla, the stem farm woman who decides to adopt a boy to help with the chores and ends up with Anne Shirley, a talkative and fanciful girl who is desperate for love. Richard Farnsworth is every bit as good as Marilla's shy brother, Matthew. Megan Fallows is just right as Anne.
CONNECTIONS: An earlier movie, made in 1934, is also very good, though it takes some liberties with the plot. The actress who starred in the title role liked it so much, she changed her name to Anne Shirley.

ARSENIC AND OLD LACE

1944, 118 min, NR, b&w, 12 and up
Dir: Frank Capra. Cary Grant, Raymond Massey, Peter Lorre, Jack Carson
The most hilariously dysfunctional family in the history of the movies, this is a wildly funny black comedy about two darling old ladies who decide to help lonely old gentlemen by killing them with elderberry wine laced with arsenic. What makes it so funny is they are not even the craziest people in the family; in addition to their nephew, Teddy (who thinks he is Teddy Roosevelt, which is pretty handy since he digs the Panama Canal in the basement to give them a place to dispose of the bodies), there is also their nephew Jonathan, a criminal with almost as many dead bodies to his credit as his aunts. In the middle of all of this is their third nephew, Mortimer (Cary Grant), who has just gotten married to the girl next door (Priscilla Lane). In the midst of a wild farce, with lots of slamming of doors (and window seats) and rushing around, there is some wicked satire. Not for all tastes, but irresistibly delectable to many.

AUNTIE MAME

1958, 143 min, NR, 12 and up
Dir: Morton DaCosta. Rosalind Russell, Peggy Cass, Forrest Tucker
Based on the semi-autobiographical Patrick Dennis novel and play, this is the story of a young boy who goes to live with his colorful aunt after his parents' death. Mame (Rosalind Russell) believes "life is a banquet and most poor suckers

are starving to death." She encourages all around her to help themselves to large portions of the banquet.

At first, it seems she will be spending too much time going to parties and buying clothes to pay much attention to her nephew, and her grasp of a child's needs and abilities is dim at best. She turns out to be a loving and devoted guardian and a resilient one as well, after she loses everything in the stock market crash. She suffers an even greater loss when her husband is killed. She questions her abilities as a guardian when Patrick seems bent on achieving the kind of conformity she has always despised. It turns out she has taught him so well that at the end, he lets her take his young son to Europe and teach him about what really matters. NOTE: Mame encourages her secretary to be more outgoing, resulting in an (apparently) out-of-wedlock pregnancy. Lots of drinking. Anti-Semitic characters (over whom Mame triumphs by making it possible for a Jewish family to buy property near them). CONNECTIONS: The movie was remade as a musical (*Mame*) with Lucille Ball.

THE BARRETTS OF WIMPOLE STREET

1934, 110 min, NR, b&w, 12 and up
Dir: Sidney Franklin. Norma Shearer, Fredric March, Charles Laughton
This is the thrilling real-life love story of two of the world's greatest poets, Elizabeth Barrett (Norma Shearer) and Robert Browning (Fredric March). Barrett was confined to bed with a debilitating illness, but the bigger problem was her father, a twisted, bitter man (Charles Laughton) who terrorized and humiliated his grown children and controlled every aspect of their lives, forbidding them to marry or even have close friends. Barrett and Browning first corresponded, and finally she allowed him to call on her, and they fell deeply in love. Barrett's sister, Henrietta, also fell in love with a dashing captain. Both women had to decide whether they would leave everything they had known for love and freedom. CONNECTIONS: The same director remade the film in 1957, with Jennifer Jones, Bill Travers, and John Gielgud as Mr. Barrett, but the original is better.

BENNY & JOON

1993, 98 min, PG, high school age
Dir: Jeremiah Chechick. Aidan Quinn, Mary Stuart Masterson, Johnny Depp
Benny (Aidan Quinn) is devoted to his schizophrenic sister, Joon (Mary Stuart Masterson), and takes care of her lovingly. An eccentric young man named Sam (Johnny Depp) comes to stay with them to help care for Joon. Joon and Sam get

along so well that Benny is able to relax for the first time, and he begins to get friendly with Ruthie (Julianne Moore). When Joon seems to become dependent on Sam, Benny becomes very protective and throws Sam out. The stress causes Joon to have a breakdown, and she is hospitalized. Her doctor encourages Benny to let her make her own decisions about what she wants to do, and she decides to try living with Sam. Although the portrayal of mental illness in this film is sentimental and very unrealistic, the issues it raises about love and letting go are important.

BOYZ N THE HOOD

1991, 107 min, R, mature high school age
Dir: John Singleton. Cuba Gooding, Jr., Laurence Fishburne, Ice Cube
This outstanding debut by John Singleton, who wrote and directed it at the age of twenty-three, is an enormously moving story with one of the great fathers in the history of films, Laurence Fishburne as Furious Styles.

Furious tries to raise his son Tre (Cuba Gooding, Jr.) to be strong and brave in the midst of chaos in a black neighborhood. Tre becomes friends with two brothers who live across the street, tough Doughboy (Ice Cube) and quiet Ricky (Morris Chestnut). Doughboy is sent to prison for seven years and returns devoted to his friends, but bitter and angry.

Ricky, now a promising athlete with a chance for an academic scholarship, is killed by a gang, and both Tre and Doughboy want revenge. Only the intervention of Furious keeps Tre safe, and the movie ends with the admonition, "Keep the Peace." This is a rough movie, far less violent than most urban dramas, but with far more tragic power. NOTE: Strong language, substance abuse, out-of-wedlock pregnancy and violence.

DOMINICK AND EUGENE

1988, 111 min, PG-13, mature high school age
Dir: Robert M. Young. Ray Liotta, Tom Hulce, Jamie Lee Curtis
Dominick (Tom Hulce) and Eugene (Ray Liotta) are twins whose parents are dead. They take care of each other; Dominick takes care of Eugene by working as a garbage man to pay Eugene's way through medical school. Eugene takes care of Dominick, who is mentally impaired. There is a lot of stress involved. Eugene feels overworked and overwhelmed. Dominick worries that Eugene will leave him, especially when Eugene starts to become close to another med student (Jamie Lee Curtis). This is a touching and beautifully performed film capturing the essence of what families are about. NOTE: Theme of child abuse; one child is

badly injured by his father, which prompts memories in both Eugene and Dominick about how Dominick was injured by his own father.

THE GOOFY MOVIE

1995, 78 min, G, 8 and up
Dir: Kevin Lima.
One of the great existential questions of childhood, memorably explored in **Stand By Me**, is, "If Mickey is a mouse, and Pluto is a dog, what is Goofy?" Goofy is in a class (and genus) of his own, as we see in this thoroughly enjoyable film.

At the center of the story is Max, struggling through the torturous insecurity and self-consciousness of adolescence. Like all teens, he is humiliated by his father's goofiness. The movie's great joke is that in this case, his father is not just goofy, he is Goofy, the Goof of all Goofs, the Uber-Goof!

When a prank at school gets Max in trouble, Goofy decides what Max needs is some quality time with his father. So he takes him on a fishing trip, not knowing Max will have to miss his first date with his adored Roxanne, and that in order to get out of the date, Max has lied to Roxanne, telling her his father is taking him to a rock concert. It takes a while (and a run-in with Bigfoot) for Goofy and Max to start talking to each other instead of at each other. They ultimately strengthen their connection and find a satisfying resolution.

Free of the pressures that sometimes smother the big Disney releases, this movie has a refreshingly casual, even insouciant feel, with some sly humor (look fast for a glimpse of Elvis at a remote lunch counter), and it even dares to poke fun at Disney itself. The teen characters are contemporary without the prepackaged feel of other Disney productions and there are lively songs performed by Tevin Campbell.

Although the material in this movie is certainly suitable for all ages, younger children may be uncomfortable with the strain between Max and Goofy. It's a shame the G rating scared off the film's optimal audience, the ten-to-fourteen age group. If you can persuade them to take a look, they will find much to enjoy and identify with, and if parents and kids watch it together, it can inspire some good discussions about parent-child communication.

THE LITTLE FOXES

1941, 116 min, NR, b&w, 12 and up
Dir: William Wyler. Bette Davis, Teresa Wright, Herbert Marshall

This movie, based on the play by Lillian Hellman, presents us with probably the most greedy, vicious, and corrupt of all movie families. Regina (Bette Davis) and her brothers will do anything to get money, and if it means harming each other along the way, so much the better. In order to get the money they need to invest in a new factory, they steal bonds from the safe-deposit box owned by Regina's husband. When he tries to stop them, Regina withholds his medicine so he will die. Ultimately, however, she loses what she most wants: the love and support of her daughter.

CONNECTIONS: To see how these people got the way they were, watch the prequel, *Another Part of the Forest*. Hellman also wrote **The Children's Hour**, which was also filmed as These Three, and the memoir that was the basis for the movie, **Julia**.

LITTLE WOMEN

1994, 118 min, PG, 8 and up
Dir: Gillian Armstrong. Winona Ryder, Susan Sarandon, Christian Bale, Gabriel Byrne, Eric Stoltz, Claire Danes
In this classic Louisa May Alcott story based on her own family, Jo March is Alcott herself, the headstrong but sensitive second daughter of the family, who dreams of being a writer. With her older sister Meg, younger sisters Beth and Amy, and friend Laurie Lawrence, and the guidance of her wise mother and father, she faces the challenges of growing up. The four girls learn patience, compassion and the most meaningful family values. This is an exceptionally good movie for portraying sibling relationships, as the four March girls sometimes squabble but are deeply committed to each other. The story has been filmed four times. This version, produced by Winona Ryder (who plays Jo), has gorgeous period detail and spirited performances by an attractive young cast. The 1933 version, with Katharine Hepburn as Jo, is also exceptional.

ACTIVITIES: Kids should read the book and its sequel, *Little Men*, as well some of Alcott's other classics, like *Eight Cousins* and *An Old Fashioned Girl*. They may also enjoy *Invincible Louisa*, or one of the other biographies of Alcott. If they get to Massachusetts, they can visit her home and find out more about the Alcott girls and their parents, who were the models for the Marches.

LONG DAY'S JOURNEY INTO NIGHT

1962, 136 min, NR, b&w, mature high school age
Dir: Sidney Lumet. Katharine Hepburn, Ralph Richardson, Jason Robards, Dean Stockwell

Based on the family of playwright Eugene O'Neill, this is the searing story of four people who love each other deeply and yet cannot stop causing each other pain. Like O'Neill's father, James Tyrone (Ralph Richardson) is a well-known actor, stuck playing the same part for years just to make money. His wife, Mary (Katharine Hepburn), has just returned from a sanatorium. One son, Jamie (Jason Robards), is an alcoholic, and the other, Edmund (Dean Stockwell), is ailing with tuberculosis. Each of them suffers terribly with a weakness that hurts the others: James's miserliness, Mary's addiction to morphine; Jamie's bitterness, self-loathing, and alcoholism; Edmund's weakness. This is a brilliant portrait of a tortured family, with performances of shattering insight and vulnerability.

MRS. DOUBTFIRE

1993, 125 min, PG-13, 10 and up
Dir: Chris Columbus. Robin Williams, Sally Field
Robin Williams plays Daniel, a loving but irresponsible man whose frustrated wife (Sally Field) asks for a divorce. In order to see his children, he dresses as a woman and applies for a job as their nanny. The movie's strong points are Williams' performance and the devotion of his character to his children. It will be especially reassuring to kids of divorced parents because it makes it clear parents love their children even after divorce, and the parents can find a way to get along with each other even after the marriage ends. Its weak points are a lazy script filled with cheap sitcom humor, often at the expense of Pierce Brosnan, as Field's new beau.
NOTE: I am not a big fan of this movie, so I recommend it only with reservations because of its devoted father and its handling of the issue of divorce, and suggest parents screen it before deciding whether it is appropriate for their children. If it is appropriate as a way to help a child deal with some difficult issues, it may be worthwhile; otherwise, skip it. Some parents will appreciate the positive portrayal of a gay couple. They are presented in such a low-key fashion that it is unlikely to spark any questions for parents who are not comfortable discussing homosexuality. Similarly *Stepmom* has a top-notch cast in a soggy story about children coping with rivalry between their mother and step-mother. It has some mature material, so parents should watch the movie to decide whether it is appropriate for their families.

THE PARENT TRAP

1961, 124 min, NR, 6 and up
Dir: David Swift. Hayley Mills, Brian Keith, Maureen O'Hara

Hayley Mills plays identical twins, separated at birth when their parents divorced, who do not even know of each other's existence. They first discover each other's identity when they meet at summer camp. Initially hostile, they become good friends when they discover they are sisters. They decide to switch places, each going "home" to the parent she hasn't seen. When the parents (Brian Keith and Maureen O'Hara) discover what has happened, they meet to straighten things out, and the girls get them back together, despite the inconvenience of Keith's recent engagement to the social climbing Barnes. NOTE: This might be painful for kids who are dealing with divorce. It also suggests that playing pranks on a prospective stepmother is the way to get parents back together.
CONNECTIONS: The delightful 1998 remake stars Lindsay Lohan who is adorable. Watch for Joanna Barnes, the icky fiancée in the original, as the mother of the icky fiancée in the remake.

RAIN MAN

1988, 140 min, R, mature high school age
Dir: Barry Levinson. Dustin Hoffman, Tom Cruise
Tom Cruise plays Charlie Babbitt, a self-centered young man who is furious to find his wealthy late father left him only a car. The money has been left to a brother he did not even know he had (Raymond, played by Dustin Hoffman), who lives in an institution because he is autistic. Charlie impulsively takes Raymond with him, and as they drive across the country, Charlie moves from irritation to exploitation to understanding and love. Hoffman's Oscar-winning performance as the autistic savant attracted most of the attention, but it is Cruise's painful efforts to uncover his feelings for his brother and his understanding he must do what is best for Raymond and let others take care of him that really matters.

A RAISIN IN THE SUN

1961, 128 min, NR, b&w, 12 and up
Dir: Daniel Petrie. Sidney Poitier, Claudia McNeil
Lorraine Hansberry's classic play, its title taken from a poem by Langston Hughes ("What happens to a dream deferred?…Does it dry up like a raisin in the sun?"), is the story of a black family's debates about what to do with $10,000 in insurance money. The mother (Claudia McNeil) wants to use it to buy a house in a "good" (and all-white) neighborhood and send her daughter to medical school. The grown son (Sidney Poitier) wants to use it to buy a liquor store. Despite setbacks, including an offer by the neighborhood "improvement association" to buy

them out, the family resolves to do whatever is necessary to move into their new home.

SOUNDER

1972, 115 min, G, 8 and up
Dir: Martin Ritt. Paul Winfield, Cecily Tyson
This beautiful film offers a rare depiction of a strong and loving black family, led by Paul Winfield and Cecily Tyson, and is one of the best movie portrayals ever of a family of any color. The members of the family are sharecroppers during the Depression, and times are hard. When the father steals a ham to feed his hungry family, he is sentenced to a year in jail, and the family must bring in the crops without him. The young son is torn between his commitment to his family and his chance to go to an all-black school, where he would have a real opportunity to learn.

Note the beautiful cinematography by John A. Alonzo. Lighting and production design in movies are almost invariably designed for white actors, even in scenes with black characters. In this movie the black actors are photographed beautifully, with loving attention to the rich range of hues of African-American skin tones.

WHAT'S EATING GILBERT GRAPE

1993, 117 min, PG-13, mature high school age
Dir: Lasse Hallstrom. Johnny Depp, Leonardo DiCaprio, Juliette Lewis
Gilbert Grape (Johnny Depp) feels responsible for taking care of everyone, including his loving mother, who is all but incapacitated by her enormous weight; his mentally impaired brother (Leonardo DiCaprio in an astonishingly perceptive and moving performance); the owners of the local grocery store, almost driven out of business by the new supermarket chain; even a lonely housewife, who orders groceries just to get him to come over to have sex. When Becky (Juliette Lewis) and her grandmother stop in town for a few days to repair their trailer, Gilbert gets a glimpse of a world in which he could have something for himself. This quirky movie is not for everyone, but it has become a cult favorite for its odd characters and their deep attachment to each other.
NOTE: Mature themes. Gilbert has an affair with a married woman; Gilbert and Becky have sex; bizarre sexual comments by one character.
CONNECTIONS: Director Hallstrom is also responsible for a perceptive movie about adolescence (with some mature themes), the Swedish **My Life as a Dog**.

YOURS, MINE AND OURS

1968, 111 min, NR, 8 and up
Dir: Melville Shavelson. Henry Fonda, Lucille Ball, Van Johnson
This is no one's idea of a classic, but it is a highly enjoyable comedy on a subject literally close to home for many families. It is inspired by the real-life story of a widower with ten children (Henry Fonda) who marries a widow with eight (Lucille Ball). There is quite an adjustment period, especially after he goes off to sea not knowing she is pregnant with number nineteen, the "ours" in the title. Fonda and Ball are always great fun to watch, and the movie has some genuinely touching moments, especially Fonda explaining to his stepdaughter why she should resist her boyfriend's advances, as he is taking Ball to the hospital to deliver.
CONNECTIONS: You can see Fonda and Ball together twenty-six years earlier in the tragic Damon Runyon story, *The Big Street*.

SEE ALSO:
Bend it Like Beckham A girl from a very traditional Indian family wants to play soccer.
A Christmas Memory A little boy and his elderly cousin form a close family bond in a home where they are neglected by everyone else.
Fiddler on the Roof A strong, loving family must respond to both internal and external pressures, as the daughters insist on marrying the men of their choice, and the mounting prejudice forces the family to leave its home.
The Flamingo Kid A young man is temporarily dazzled by a wealthy and sophisticated man, but ultimately returns to his father and the values he learned at home.
Friendly Persuasion A loving Quaker family must resolve differences and find a way to keep their values while the Civil War comes literally to their doorstep.
Houseboat A widower who barely knew his children, who are hurt by his neglect and the loss of their mother, learn how much they mean to each other, and then almost lose it all again when he falls in love with their housekeeper.
Now, Voyager A woman learns how destructive family members can be, and then, with the help of a gifted therapist and the man who loves her, learns how to protect herself.
The Ramona Series The videos based on this classic series of children's books offer a loving and good-humored portrait of a family dealing with aspects of everyday life, which all children will recognize.

A Thousand Clowns An iconoclastic man learns to conform enough to help him keep custody of the nephew he loves.

Where the Lilies Bloom A young girl shows determination and courage in keeping her family together after the death of her parents.

7

FINDING THE HERO WITHIN

"The greatest obstacle to being heroic is the doubt whether one may not be going to prove one's self a fool; the truest heroism is to resist the doubt; and the profoundest wisdom is to know when it ought to be resisted and when it should be obeyed."
NATHANIEL HAWTHORNE

From Rocky to John Wayne to Indiana Jones to Mr. Smith, we love the movie heroes (mostly white men, unfortunately) who display the courage, intelligence, and persistence we hope lies somewhere within us, too. For that reason, we are especially drawn to the characters who must find the hero within themselves, and the story of the ordinary person thrust into extraordinary circumstances which he at first finds daunting but then masters is one of the most popular and appealing themes of the movies. We get to watch the character evaluate the risks and, more importantly, evaluate himself. We get to see him learn and watch him be transformed as he is tested. We get to think about what makes a hero, and what heroic qualities we can find in ourselves or in the people around us.

We often tend to think of heroism in terms of physical courage and determination, but the movies show us other kinds of heroes as well, heroes with moral courage and unshakable integrity.

The ancient Greek notion of the hero whose destiny is foretold is reflected in some movies directly based on Greek myths and in other myth-based stories. Most often in our movie mythology the hero "has greatness thrust upon him," whether he wants it or not. The more unlikely, the more satisfying it is for us to watch, whether the hero turns out to be a sheep-herding pig, a kid who learns he can take care of himself, a drunken boatman and a prim missionary, a naive new senator, a drunken former gunfighter, or a peaceful mountain man who sets a record for achievement in battle that still stands almost a century later.

372

Very often, the character tries not to be a hero but is then drawn into the conflict. What leads someone to come to that choice? Also, very often, the hero's biggest obstacle is his lack of faith in himself. In some cases, the hero has a flaw he must overcome, or make use of. How do these people develop enough faith in themselves to do what is necessary? How do they change in order to do what they must do, and how does the experience change them?

The most interesting heroes are the ones who are complex enough to be flawed. Oskar Schindler's whole life was one of petty crimes and careless behavior, and yet he risked everything to protect 1,100 Jews while people who had led exemplary lives were participating in the genocide.

These are movies that encourage us to think about the nature of heroism. They remind us the heroic ideal in our hearts and dreams (probably based on some movie) is more complicated and thus more real than we think. There may even be a hero within us.

The African Queen

1951. 103 min, NR, 8 and up
Dir: John Huston. Katharine Hepburn, Humphrey Bogart, Robert Morley
PLOT: Rose Sayer and her brother, Samuel, are English missionaries in 1914 German East Africa. Their rare contact with the outside world is through Charlie Allnut, who delivers their occasional mail on his steam-powered boat, the African Queen. The Germans destroy their village. Samuel is injured and dies, brokenhearted. Charlie offers to take Rose with him.

At first, they are stiffly polite to each other. He respectfully calls her "Miss," and she calls him "Mr. Allnut." She decides they must help fight the Germans by using their explosives to blow up the powerful German gunboat, the Louisa, He becomes angry and frustrated by her insistence on what he sees as a dangerously reckless idea, and she becomes disgusted and furious when he gets drunk. He calls her a "crazy psalm-singing skinny old maid." She pours all his liquor overboard.

He decides she will change her mind when she sees how dangerous the river is, and takes her over the rapids. She is thrilled, telling him that she is "filled with admiration" for his skill, and "I never dreamed any mere physical experience could be so stimulating!"

Charmed by her enthusiasm and praise, he still insists they cannot possibly attack the Louisa. The river is all but impossible to navigate, and a German fort blocks their path. She insists, and as they face challenges together they learn to respect, rely on, and finally love each other. After a tender night together, she asks him, "Mr. Allnut, dear. There's something I must know. What's your first name?"

They make it past the fort and survive bugs, rapids, leeches, and the reeds that strangle the river, finally approaching the Louisa. They are captured and sentenced to death by the captain. Charlie asks for a last request: that they be executed as husband and wife. The captain quickly marries them, and just as they are about to be hung, Charlie's torpedo strapped to the African Queen hits the Louisa, and Mr. and Mrs. Allnut swim to shore together.

DISCUSSION: This is one of the finest and most satisfying of the "two diverse characters must take a journey together and learn to like and respect each other along the way" genre. Rose and Charlie are opposites. Yet they are perfectly suited to each other.

We first see Charlie hideously out of place sipping tea with Rose and Samuel and trying to hide his growling stomach. "Nature, Mr. Allnut, is what we were put in this world to rise above," she tells him later. In another sense, however, Rose and Samuel were out of place in Africa. Ultimately, Rose is not comfortable "rising above" nature, and indeed grows to love it as she gives up some of the strictures of civilization and appreciates the beauty and "stimulation" of the natural world. Charlie learns to appreciate some of the beauties of civilization: to take the challenge and the responsibility of participating in the fight against the Germans, to have a relationship of trust and tenderness.

PROFANITY: None.
NUDITY/SEXUAL REFERENCES: Very mild suggestion that Charlie and Rose sleep together.
ALCOHOL/DRUG ABUSE: Charlie gets drunk; Rose pours all of his liquor into the river.
VIOLENCE/SCARINESS: Destruction of village; characters in peril several times, from nature and from the German sailors.
TOLERANCE/DIVERSITY ISSUES: Class issues.
QUESTIONS FOR FAMILIES:

• What do Samuel's dying words tell you about Rose? What does her reaction tell you?

• How does Rose's experience on the first rapids change the way she feels? How does it change the way Charlie feels about her?

• Why does Charlie decide to go along with her plan to torpedo the Louisa?

- How does each bring out the best in the other?

- What can you tell about Rose from her prayer, asking that God "judge us not for our weakness but for our love, and open the doors of heaven for Charlie and me"?

CONNECTIONS: Humphrey Bogart won a well-deserved Oscar for this performance. Katharine Hepburn, who was also nominated, said her performance was based on director John Huston's suggestion she play Rose as Eleanor Roosevelt. Compare this performance to her appearance in **Pat and Mike** a year later, in which she played a world-class athlete.

The movie is based on a novel of the same name by C. S. Forester, but the romance was added by screenwriters James Agee and John Huston. Adults who enjoy this movie might like to see *White Hunter, Black Heart*, a backstage look at the making of this film, concentrating on John Huston's elephant hunting.

ACTIVITIES: Look at a map of Africa to see where this took place.

Bad Day at Black Rock

1955, 81 min, NR, b&w, 10 and up
Dir: John Sturges. Spencer Tracy, Robert Ryan, Ernest Borgnine, Lee Marvin, Anne Francis, Dean Jagger, Walter Brennan
PLOT: John MacReedy (Spencer Tracy) gets off a train in a tiny, dusty little Western town. It is rare for any stranger to come to the town; it is the first time the train has stopped there in four years. The town residents move from suspicion of the one-armed man in a suit to open hostility when MacReedy enters the local hotel and asks about a local farmer named Komoko. Pete Wirth (John Ericson), the hotel manager, refuses to give him a room, saying they are all booked. When MacReedy takes a key, anyway, a bully named Hector David (Lee Marvin) insists it is his room. MacReedy takes another room.

Hector and most of the rest of the town report to Reno (Robert Ryan). When Reno tells his men to push MacReedy without giving him information, they are happy to oblige. The town doctor (Walter Brennan) tells MacReedy how to get to Komoko's farm, and Liz Wirth (Anne Francis), Pete's sister, rents him a jeep to get there.

MacReedy finds the farm deserted. Coley Trimble (Ernest Borgnine), another of Reno's henchmen, chases MacReedy back to town, driving him off the road and slamming into the jeep with his truck.

MacReedy realizes Reno will never let him get out of town alive. He tries to make a phone call or send a telegram, but Reno has cut him off. When Trimble harasses him at the diner, he refuses to fight, then finally, when Trimble persists, MacReedy devastates him with a karate chop to the neck. That buys him some time, but MacReedy is cornered and he knows it. He persuades Liz Wirth to drive him out of Black Rock. It is a trap. Reno is waiting for them. As Liz runs to Reno, he shoots her; he no longer trusts her to keep his secret. MacReedy puts the jeep's leaking gas into a bottle, stuffs it with his tie, lights it, and throws it at Reno, who is killed.

MacReedy had come to Black Rock to give Komoko the medal his son had been awarded by the U.S. Army for heroism. Komoko's son had saved MacReedy's life before he was killed in battle. Komoko was also dead. Reno and his henchmen killed him at the start of World War II because he was Japanese.

The doctor asks MacReedy if he will leave the medal in Black Rock. MacReedy gives it to him, then puts out the flag so that the train will stop in Black Rock again, for the second time in four years.

DISCUSSION: "A man is as big as what makes him mad." MacReedy says this to Reno in one of this movie's key scenes, and it is a concept children (and parents) should think about. It is also interesting that Reno killed Komoko after he was found ineligible to enlist in the army. His hostility toward Komoko was based on displaced anger and frustration as much as racism.

MacReedy did not choose this battle, but he never turns away from it. A man who had no direction, and no goal beyond the presentation of the medal to Komoko, becomes a man who will not allow Reno and his thugs to win. He is fighting them not just for Komoko, but for himself, and in doing so finds a pride and dignity enabling him to go on.

This is a good movie to use for a discussion of prejudice, not just about race, but also about disabilities.

PROFANITY: None.
NUDITY/SEXUAL REFERENCES: Mild implication that Liz Wirth and Reno are lovers.
ALCOHOL/DRUG ABUSE: Some by the bad guys.
VIOLENCE/SCARINESS: Fighting with cars, guns, and karate.
TOLERANCE/DIVERSITY ISSUES: A theme of the movie is the prejudice against the Japanese leading Reno and his men to kill Mr. Komoko. They also make fun of MacReedy (Hector David says, "You look like you need a hand") because of his disability and, more importantly, they underestimate him. MacReedy may also underestimate himself.

QUESTIONS FOR FAMLILIES:

- What does it mean to say, "A man is only as big as what makes him mad"? Think about a time you got mad. How big was the thing that made you mad? How do you measure?

- The people in the town had different reasons for obeying Reno. What were they?

- How did MacReedy change? What did he learn about himself?

CONNECTIONS: Compare this to **High Noon**, another movie about a lone force for justice. Anne Francis, known to baby boomers for television's *Honey West*, plays opposite Robby the Robot in the science fiction classic *Forbidden Planet*. In both movies, she is the. only woman in the cast.

Interestingly, MacReedy's handicap, so central to the story, was a last minute addition in order to make the character challenging enough to attract Tracy to the role.

The Black Stallion

1979, 118 min, G, 8 and up
Dir: Carroll Ballard. Kelly Reno, Mickey Rooney, Hoyt Axton
PLOT: A young boy named Alec Ramsey (Kelly Reno) is on a ship with his father. Everything seems mysterious to him, the exotic passengers, the high-stakes poker game his father is playing and the wild and beautiful black horse he comforts with sugar cubes. Then the ship is destroyed in a storm, and only Alec and the horse survive. Alec patiently and persistently tames the horse. They are rescued and return to Alec's home. When the horse runs to a farm, Alec meets Henry (Mickey Rooney), a former trainer. They enter the horse in a race against two champions, and he and Alec triumph.
DISCUSSION: Walter Farley's novel was adapted by director Ballard and Francis Ford Coppola's studio into one of the most breathtakingly beautiful and genuinely magical movies ever made. Part of the magic is the movie has the courage to be quiet. There is very little dialogue, and long stretches without a single word. It allows its images to do the work, and the cinematography, by Caleb Deschanel **(The Right Stuff**, *The Natural)*, is a joy for the eye and for the spirit, creating exactly the right atmosphere for what Pauline Kael said "may be the greatest children's movie ever made."

There are some good themes to discuss here, including Henry's views about being a trainer: "It was a lot of work, but it was worth it," and the way Alec's relationship with the horse (and with Henry) help him deal with the loss of his father.

PROFANITY: None.
NUDITY/SEXUAL REFERENCES: None.
ALCOHOL/DRUG ABUSE: None.
VIOLENCE/SCARINESS: Although the movie is rated G, the shipwreck is very scary, and Alec's father (Hoyt Axton) is killed.
TOLERANCE/DIVERSITY ISSUES: None.
QUESTIONS FOR FAMILIES:

• What is the importance of the story Alec's father tells about Alexander the Great and his horse?

• Why does the horse trust Alec?

• Why is it important for Alec to win the race?

• What is the most important lesson Alec learns from Henry?

CONNECTIONS: There is a sequel called The Black Stallion Returns, which is enjoyable, but not nearly as good.

The Boy Who Could Fly

1986, 108 min, PG, 8 and up
Dir: Nick Castle. Lucy Deakins, Jay Underwood, Bonnie Bedelia, Fred Savage, Fred Gwynne, Colleen Dewhurst, Louise Fletcher
PLOT: Milly (Lucy Deakins), her mother, Charlene (Bonnie Bedelia), and her brother, Louis (Fred Savage), move into a new home, still feeling bereft over the loss of the father of the family. Milly sees a mysterious boy (Jay Underwood) on the roof next door. She finds out that his name is Eric, and that he is autistic. He has never spoken, and ever since his parents were killed in a plane crash when he was five, he has apparently thought he was a plane. He lives with his alcoholic uncle, who confides to Milly that Eric really can fly.

Adjustment to the new environment is difficult. Charlene is overwhelmed by the computers at her new job. Louis is terrorized by neighborhood bullies who won't let him ride around the block. Even the dog, Max, is vanquished by the neighborhood Doberman.

At school, Milly befriends Eric, and when an understanding teacher (Colleen Dewhurst) sees that he responds to Milly, she asks her to work with him as a project for school, telling her that he doesn't need a doctor as much as he needs a friend. Milly spends a lot of time with Eric, reading him stories and trying to teach him to understand and not just imitate. He does not speak, but when a ball is thrown at Milly's head, he protects her by catching it.

Milly falls off a bridge on a class trip, and insists that Eric saved her by flying. A psychiatrist (Louise Fletcher) tells her that her mind played tricks, and gently gets her to admit that her father killed himself when he found he had cancer.

Eric is sent to an institution. He somehow escapes, and he and Milly run away from the guards sent to retrieve him. They are chased up to the roof of the high school, where we discover that he really can fly. Eric and Milly float off together, to the astonishment of the entire community. Eric speaks at last, telling Milly he loves her, and flying away forever. She realizes why he had to leave when the scientists and journalists arrive the next day. Eric's influence continues. Charlene masters the computer. Louis triumphs over the bullies. Max even scares away the Doberman. "He made us believe in ourselves again...We're all special. We're all a little like Eric. Maybe we can't soar off into the clouds, but somewhere, deep inside, we can all fly.'"

DISCUSSION: This is a charming fantasy with a lot of heart and outstanding performances by three terrific kids who keep up with some of the finest adult actors in movies. Eric and Milly heal each other by responding to each other. For him, she provides the first reason he has ever had to try to make contact with another person. For her, he provides a reason to feel, and to give to another person, especially important after the loss of her father. In their own ways, Milly and her brother and mother all learn that they can respond to challenges like a hero.

PROFANITY: Mild schoolyard terms.
NUDITY/SEXUAL REFERENCES: None.
ALCOHOL/DRUG ABUSE: Milly and her friend Geneva experiment with liquor. Milly has a bad hangover. Eric's uncle is an alcoholic.
VIOLENCE/SCARINESS: No violence, but some mildly scary moments.
TOLERANCE/DIVERSITY ISSUES: Tolerance of individual differences is a theme of the movie.

QUESTIONS FOR FAMILIES:

• Why was Eric so important to Milly? Why was she so important to him?

• What did Eric teach Milly's family?

• Where do you think he will go next?

• Why did Louis get so upset about his action figures being out in the rain?

CONNECTIONS: Writer-director Nick Castle also directed *The Last Star-fighter*. Bonnie Bedelia, who starred in *Heart Like a Wheel*, is the aunt of former child star Macaulay Culkin. Many of the other performers are better known for television appearances. This was the first movie appearance for Fred Savage, who went on to star in television's *The Wonder Years* and appeared in **The Princess Bride**. Fred Gwynne will be familiar to old-time television fans as Herman Munster, and as Officer Muldoon of *Car 54, Where are You?* Mindy Cohn starred for many years in *The Facts of Life*. If you pay close attention, you will catch a glimpse of future *90210* superstar Jason Priestley as Gary.

ACTIVITIES: This is a fantasy, and is in no way intended to be an accurate portrayal of autism. Kids who want to know more about this mysterious disease may want to read books like *An Anthropologist on Mars*, by Oliver Sacks (of **Awakenings**) and *Not Even Wrong* by Paul Collins. Teenagers will appreciate Dustin Hoffman's Oscar-winning portrayal of an autistic savant in *Rain Man*.

Casablanca

1942, 102 min, NR, b&w, 10 and up
Dir. Michael Curtiz. Humphrey Bogart, Ingrid Bergman, Claude Rains, Paul Henreid
PLOT: Rick (Humphrey Bogart) owns a popular nightclub in Casablanca, in the early days of WWII. France is under the control of the Vichy government, which has close ties to the Nazis, but Casablanca still has an uneasy independence. As a result, people come from all over to try to get exit visas to countries that are still free, and corruption and chaos are pervasive. As the movie opens, the police shoot a man who does not have the proper papers, and refugees negotiate with smugglers for passage to Lisbon, from which one can get to America.

Captain Renault (Claude Rains) of the local police arrives at Rick's with Major Strasser, a Nazi. Strasser is searching for the person who killed two German couriers. Whoever killed them took their papers, including two "letters of transit," which enable the bearer to leave the country without being questioned. Ugarte (Peter Lorre) has the letters and gives them to Rick to hide for him. Ugarte is then captured by the police. Rick makes no effort to protect him, saying, "I stick my neck out for nobody." Strasser is also looking for an escaped Czech named Victor Laszlo (Paul Henreid). Laszlo arrives at Rick's with Ilsa (Ingrid Bergman), planning to meet Ugarte.

Rick and Ilsa knew each other in Paris. They had planned to leave together, before the city fell to the Germans, but at the last minute, Ilsa did not come, and sent a note saying she could never see Rick again. He is angry and bitter, and still so deeply hurt he drinks heavily. When she returns to talk to him, he is drunk and lashes out at her, and she leaves.

The next night, they speak again, and she tells him she is married to Laszlo, and thought he had been killed when she'd first met Rick. She found Laszlo was still alive the day she and Rick were supposed to leave Paris. She loved Rick then, and still loves him. Rick and Renault plan to trap Laszlo by giving him the letters of transit. Then Renault will arrest Laszlo, and Rick and Ilsa will leave together. At the airport, Rick tells Laszlo he must go and Ilsa must go with him. In one of the most famous moments in movies, he tells her "We'll always have Paris." Rick and Renault leave together to join the fight against the Nazis.

DISCUSSION: This is probably the most famous Hollywood movie of all time, certainly the most quoted, and the most frequently cited as the all-time favorite, particularly by men. It is fascinating to read the story of how the film was made. The definitive rebuttal to notions of the "auteur" (director as author) in film, this movie was put together in pieces by many different sources, with script pages completed just moments before the cameras rolled. One reason the performances by Bogart and Bergman, are so subtle and complex is that the actors themselves had no idea how the movie was going to end.

Rick tries to appear cool and amoral. When Renault says he knows Rick ran guns to Ethiopia and fought for the Loyalists in Spain, Rick replies he was well-paid. Renault gently reminds him the other side would have paid him better. In reality, Rick is deeply moral. He will not take any action to protect Ugarte, who does not deserve it, but when a young bride is about to sleep with Renault to get exit visas, he arranges for her husband to "win" at roulette so they can buy the visas instead. Rick is very loyal to Sam, the piano player. When he is able to put Ilsa's actions into a moral context, he forgives her completely and is once again able to "have Paris," to draw on the love they had for one another and the happiness they shared in order to give up all he has to get back into the fight.

Teens may need some of the political and historical context explained to them, especially the meaning of the shot at the end of the Vichy water in the garbage.

PROFANITY: None.
NUDITY/SEXUAL REFERENCES: None.
ALCOHOL/DRUG ABUSE: Much of the action takes place in a bar, Rick drinks when he is unhappy about seeing Ilsa again.
VIOLENCE/SCARINESS: Characters in peril.
TOLERANCE/DIVERSITY ISSUES: Sam, the piano player, is treated with great respect and affection, though Ilsa calls him a "boy."
QUESTIONS FOR FAMILIES:

• Some of the best-remembered lines of this movie indicate the casual corruption of Casablanca. What does it mean to say, "We haven't quite decided if he committed suicide or died trying to escape," or, "I'm shocked to find gambling going on in Casablanca," or, "Round up the usual suspects"?

• What does Rick mean when he says "We'll always have Paris," and that they didn't have it until Lisa came to Casablanca?

• How does knowing Ilsa really loved him change the way Rick looks at the world?

• Was Ilsa right to stay with Laszlo in Paris? Was she right to leave with him to go to Lisbon? Why?

• What do you think Rick and Renault will do next?

CONNECTIONS: This movie won Oscars for Best Picture, Director, and Writer. Almost every frame of this movie is an icon, and it has been endlessly copied and parodied. The Woody Allen movie *Play It Again, Sam* (rated PG, but not for children since the entire plot is about seduction) is an affectionate tribute to Casablanca and other Bogart movies.

Cat Ballou

1965, 96 min, NR, 8 and up
Dir: Elliott Silverstein. Jane Fonda, Lee Marvin, Michael Callan
PLOT: In the days of the Old West, Catherine (Cat) Ballou (Jane Fonda) takes the train home, after graduating from school. She does her best to appear proper,

but hides potboilers about the notorious Kid Shelleen inside her book. On the train, she meets escaping cattle rustler Clay Boone (Michael Callan) and his uncle Jed (Dwayne Hickman). She is attracted to Clay, but not interested in becoming involved with a criminal.

When she gets home and finds out her father (John Marley) is being pressured to give up his land, Cat is angry and upset. Then her father is killed by hired gun Tim Strawn. When the ranch hand, an Indian named Jackson (Tom Nardini), and Clay and Jed are not brave enough to help her fight back, she sends for Kid Shelleen (Lee Marvin).

Kid arrives, a hopeless drunk. They help him pull himself together, and they get their revenge. Cat is captured and sentenced to be hung, but is saved at the last minute by her friends.

DISCUSSION: This cheerful satire of conventional Westerns is a lot of fun, with attractive performers and an Oscar-winning performance by Lee Marvin in the dual roles of Shelleen and Strawn. Stubby Kaye (**Guys and Dolls**) and Nat "King" Cole show up as something between a Greek chorus and medieval minstrels, singing the story as it unfolds. It is good for kids to see a movie with a strong, brave, and resourceful young woman who is an effective and inspiring leader (though they all have crushes on her).

PROFANITY: None.
NUDITY/SEXUAL REFERENCES: None.
ALCOHOL/DRUG ABUSE: Jed is drunk in first scene; Kid Shelleen has a drinking problem, comically portrayed.
VIOLENCE/SCARINESS: Shoot-outs, Cat's father is killed.
TOLERANCE/DIVERSITY ISSUES: Prejudice against Jackson Two-Bears, a Native American.
QUESTIONS FOR FAMILIES:

- Why was Cat so effective at leading Clay, Jed, Kid, and Jackson?

- Do you agree with her decision to take matters into her own hands?

- How does she compare to other Western heroes, such as Shane?

CONNECTIONS: Watch for a character named "Butch Cassidy" in a minor role, four years before Paul Newman and Robert Redford appeared in **Butch Cassidy and the Sundance Kid**, by William Goldman. Marvin appeared more often as the kind of tough guy he parodies in this movie, for example, in **The**

Man Who Shot Liberty Valance. Jed is played by television's *Dobie Gillis*, Dwayne Hickman.

Close Encounters of the Third Kind

1977, 134 min, PG, 8 and up
Dir. Steven Spielberg. Richard Dreyfuss, Melinda Dillon
PLOT: When Roy Neary (Richard Dreyfuss) and Jillian Guiler (Melinda Dillon) "encounter" a UFO, they are compelled to travel to its landing site, Devil's Tower, Wyoming. Jillian is seeking her son, who disappeared with the alien ship, but Roy is strangely drawn to go in a way that is incomprehensible to him. Obsessed with re-creating the monolithic Devil's Tower out of shaving cream, the mashed potatoes on his dinner plate and, finally, out of mud, in a massive sculpture that takes over the living room, Roy drives his family away.
Roy meets Jillian, also drawn to the Devil's Tower in Wyoming. They find that they are not the only ones who feel they have been called there. French scientist Claude Lacombe (Francois Truffaut), a top-secret U.S. government team, and others feeling the same compulsion are there to meet the enormous spacecraft, which returns dozens of humans taken over decades (including Jillian's son). Then the aliens leave the ship, and Roy joins the group boarding the ship in an intergalactic exchange program. In the reissue, which added some new scenes, we get a glimpse of the inside of the spacecraft.
DISCUSSION: This is a thrilling adventure story and a brilliant example of the art and craft of moviemaking. The craft is in the way the story is told. It unfolds with extraordinary power, involving us as much in Roy's inexplicable compulsion as in Jillian's search for her son. The art is in the story itself, the idea not just that "something" is out there, but that it is something wonderful. Watch how Spielberg lets us know that the aliens are friendly. In one of several tributes to Disney, the interplay between the large and small spaceships has a fond, protective, almost maternal quality. This is a device Disney uses over and over, perhaps most memorably with the dancing mushrooms in **Fantasia**. There is something very believable and compelling about the way the aliens use music o communicate, and to teach the people on Earth. They use art as well. Roy's sculptures and Jillian's drawings help the message to reach their conscious minds. Spielberg creates a sense of wonder not just in Jillian's son Barry (Cary Guffey), but in the adult characters and in the viewers, making them children again, with the aliens as the "adults," who reassuringly look and behave like gentle children, giving us a sense of comfort.

PROFANITY: Some.

NUDITY/SEXUAL REFERENCES: None.

ALCOHOL/DRUG ABUSE: None.

VIOLENCE/SCARINESS: The arrival of the spaceships is suspenseful and can be scary. There are tense moments as Roy and Jillian approach Devil's Tower. Smaller children may be scared when Barry is taken by the aliens, and by his mother's distress. Older children may be upset when Roy's family leaves him.

TOLERANCE/DIVERSITY ISSUES: Tolerance on an interplanetary level.

QUESTIONS FOR FAMILIES:

- Why was music a good way for the aliens to communicate with the people on Earth?

- What did the scientist mean when he said it was the first day of school?

- What movie did Roy want his family to see? What does that tell you about him? How does that movie relate to this one? (Hint: listen for a familiar song.)

- Do you think aliens will come to Earth? What will they be like?

- What do you think would happen in a sequel to this movie?

CONNECTIONS: Francois Truffaut was a distinguished French film critic and director (*The 400 Blows, Small Change*).

ACTIVITIES: Kids can draw a picture of what they think the aliens' planet looks like. Do they live in cities? What kinds of inventions do they have that we don't have? Make a model or draw a picture of the planets in our solar system. Go to the library or a museum to get information about space travel. Check out NASA on the World Wide Web at http://www.nasa.gov to get information about the next space mission. Or write to the SETI Institute, 2035 Landings Drive, Mountain View, CA 94043 for the latest research on UFOs and extraterrestrials.

The Court Jester

1951, 101 min, NR, 6 and up

Dir: Norman Panama and Melvin Frank. Danny Kaye, Glynis Johns, Basil Rathbone, Angela Lansbury

PLOT: Hawkins (Danny Kaye) is a follower of the Black Fox, a Robin Hood-style rebel who hopes to put the royal heir on the throne in place of the usurper. Hawkins wishes for more exciting assignments, but is assigned to entertain the troops and care for the heir, a baby with the royal birthmark on his rear. He is in love with Jean (Glynis Johns), a smart, courageous, and tough captain of the rebel forces.

Hawkins disguises himself as Giacomo, the king's new jester, to get access to the palace. He finds himself in the midst of intrigue, hypnotized into wooing the princess (Angela Lansbury) by her lady-in-waiting (Mildred Natwick), and hired by Sir Ravenhurst (Basil Rathbone) to kill those who stand between him and the throne. Jean is captured by the king's soldiers, who have been told to round up the prettiest "wenches" in the kingdom. Hawkins has to do battle with a huge knight named Sir Griswold. Although he has trouble remembering that the pellet with the poison is in the pestle with the vessel, the good guys triumph, and "life could not better be."

DISCUSSION: Pure joy. This is Danny Kaye's best movie, and one of the funniest comedies ever, with a plot that is both exciting and hilarious. The "pestle with the vessel" scene is a classic, but just as good are the scenes in which a snap of the fingers puts Hawkins in and out of his hypnotic state.

It is worth pointing out the scene in which Jean and Hawkins confess their love for one another. He asks shyly if she could love a man who was not a fighter, and she explains that tenderness and kindness are important to her. They are each proud of the other the way they are, almost revolutionary for a movie of that era.

PROFANITY: None.
NUDITY/SEXUAL REFERENCES: None.
ALCOHOL/DRUG ABUSE: None.
VIOLENCE/SCARINESS: Comic battles, jousting match, and sword fights.
TOLERANCE/DIVERSITY ISSUES: Exceptionally active and competent heroine, and a hero who respects her for it.
QUESTIONS FOR FAMILIES:

• How is this movie like The Adventures of Robin Hood and Ivanhoe? How is it different?

• Why did the soldiers cheat on Hawkins's tests for becoming a knight?

• Why did courts have jesters? Whose job is most like that today?

CONNECTIONS: Kids who enjoy this movie will also enjoy some of Danny Kaye's other comedies, especially *The Inspector General* and *Knock on Wood*. Kaye also played the title role in *Hans Christian Andersen*. They might also enjoy seeing him perform with Bing Crosby in *White Christmas* and play the more dramatic role of coronet player Red Nichols in *The Five Pennies*.

Basil Rathbone's performance here, especially in the sword fight, is reminiscent of his appearances in **The Adventures of Robin Hood** and *The Mark of Zorro*. Glynis Johns played Mrs. Banks, the mother, in **Mary Poppins**. Angela Lansbury played Velvet's older sister in **National Velvet** and Mrs. Price in *Bedknobs and Broomsticks*, as well as Jessica Fletcher in television's *Murder, She Wrote*.

Erin Brockovich

2000, 130 min, R, 17 and up
Dir: Stephen Soderbergh. Julia Roberts, Albert Finney, Aaron Eckhart
PLOT: We meet Erin (Julia Roberts) as she is interviewing for a job she is not going to get.
Erin then climbs into her crummy car, which immediately gets slammed into. When she loses her lawsuit against the driver, she forces the lawyer who represented her to give her a job (Albert Finney as Ed Masry). No one wants her there, and no one likes her because she has a big mouth and wears trashy clothes. Still, she is loyal, curious, and tenacious.

She gets interested in a real estate file that includes medical records, and she goes off to investigate. It turns out that the community of Hinkley has been poisoned by hexavent chromium, leaching into the drinking water from a PG&E plant. Erin is able to gain the trust of the community and help Ed put together a case that would win the largest direct claim settlement in American history.
DISCUSSION: Julia Roberts plays Erin as a woman who never stopped believing in herself and yet is deeply touched when others believe in her, too. She understands the way the people in Hinkley feel, mistrustful of lawyers and overwhelmed by the odds. She understands that "people want to tell their stories." She has enough confidence in herself to know that, while she might not have been able to keep her beauty queen promise of ending world hunger, this is a promise she can keep.

She understands, too, that there will be costs. A romance with a loving biker/nanny (George, played by Aaron Eckhart, who makes that combination endearingly believable) and her relationships with her children are threatened by her devotion to the case. In a heartbreaking scene, she is driving back home after a hard day and George tells her that her baby spoke her first word. Erin is overjoyed at the news and devastated to have missed it. The look in her eyes as George tells her all about it is complex, rich, perfect.

Rhere are many "triumph of the underdog" style feel-good moments, like when PG&E's first lawyer, looking like a high school debate club president, tries to bully Erin and Ed, and when Erin uses everything from her cleavage to her baby to get access to the records she needs.

Families who see this movie will want to talk about what Erin found out about herself. They should also talk about the fact that no matter how high the settlement, the fact remains that children and their families were made terribly ill, and no amount of money will make up for that. They may also want to talk about the issue of corporate responsibility. No one at PG&E wanted anyone to get hurt. How do problems like lack of accountability arise?

PROFANITY: Very strong language, the primary reason for the R rating.
NUDITY/SEXUAL REFERENCES: Sexual references and situations. Erin jokes that she got the cooperation of the town's residents by performing sexual favors.
ALCOHOL/DRUG ABUSE: Characters drink and smoke.
VIOLENCE/SCARINESS: Tense and very sad scenes.
TOLERANCE/DIVERSITY ISSUES: A theme of the movie.
QUESTIONS FOR FAMILIES:

• Why can Erin connect with the residents of Hinkley?

• Why is she reluctant to accept help from anyone?

• How can we make sure that we do not judge people based on their appearance?

CONNECTIONS: Families who enjoy this movie will also enjoy Sally Fields' Oscar-winning performance in **Norma Rae**.

The Hustler

1960, 130 min, NR, b&w, 14 and up
Dir: Robert Rossen. Paul Newman, Jackie Gleason, George C. Scott, Piper Laurie
PLOT: "Fast" Eddie Felsen (Paul Newman) is a pool hustler. He and his partner, Charlie, go into pool halls and set up the local players. Eddie pretends to be a pool player who likes to make big bets. When he beats them and takes their money, he makes it look like luck, so they can't tell they have been hustled.

Eddie's dream is to beat the legendary Minnesota Fats (Jackie Gleason), the champion. He challenges him to a contest. At first, Eddie is ahead, but he gets cocky, drinks too much, and is finally worn down by Fats. After more than twenty-four hours, Eddie realizes he can't win. He leaves Charlie the money and the car, and goes off on his own.

Eddie meets Sarah (Piper Laurie), an alcoholic, and moves in with her. When Charlie finds them, Eddie tells him to go. Charlie wants to make enough money to set up his own pool hall. Eddie wants more; he wants to win, and to be a winner.

Angry at himself and the world, Eddie hustles some young punks and shows off, humiliating them. They beat him up and break his thumbs. He has time to reflect, and to grow closer to Sarah. He agrees to go into partnership with Bert Gordon (George C. Scott), a silky gambler who sees everything in terms of dollars. Bert sets up a game with a decadent rich man. In a mirror image of the game with Fats, Eddie loses at first, and then, defying Sarah's appeal to quit, persists, and wins $12,000. At the hotel, Bert and Sarah acknowledge in the tug-of-war for Eddie, Bert has won. Sarah commits suicide.

Bert once told Eddie he needed more than talent to beat Fats. He needed character. Eddie shows he has developed character when he goes back and takes Fats on again. Fats concedes, "I can't beat you." Bert says Eddie owes him his piece of the proceeds, but Eddie refuses. Bert allows him to go, but says he will never be able to play in a big-time pool hall again. That doesn't matter. Eddie has what he wanted.

DISCUSSION: Despite the seedy settings (so evocative they are almost a character in the story), this is almost a traditional morality play about humility and redemption. In the beginning Eddie is, as Fats notes, as fast as his nickname, slick, cocky, superficial. He wants to win for the kick of it. Inside him, there is someone who wants to win for the beauty of the game, and the honor of doing something surpassingly well. He is really not so far removed from Eric Liddell (**Chariots of Fire**), who feels God's pleasure when he runs. Before he can be a real winner, he must get rid of the part of himself that wants to lose and is afraid to take a real risk. For that, he has to experience real loss, the beating, the damage to his thumbs that could have ended his ability to play pool, the loss of Sarah.

As Nietzsche said, "That which does not defeat me makes me stronger." Eddie is strengthened so by these experiences and by what he has learned he can no longer be contained by what had once been his entire world. Bert's threat that he will no longer be able to play big-time pool is meaningless to him. Even if Bert had offered him a fifty-fifty deal, he would not have taken it. That world is too small and self-contained for him now.

Most of the movie takes place in smoky, dingy bars and pool halls. The scenes at the rich man's home in Louisville are just as squalid in their own way. There is only one scene in which Eddie and Sarah are outside together. They are having a picnic. It is in that scene they first reveal the truth about themselves to each other. Sarah confesses the real source of her money (her father) and her limp (polio), contrary to what she has told him before. She then tells him she loves him. Eddie tells her what he barely admitted to himself, the way he loves the game of pool, the way it makes him feel to play it well. Understanding what it means to him is what enables him to begin to go back to it.

The relationship between Eddie and Sarah is a weak part of the movie, mostly because her character is the least well-crafted in the otherwise all-male story. It is hard to feel sympathetic toward her because she thinks so badly of herself. Yet her willingness to love Eddie is what causes him to recognize what is best in himself.

It is also interesting to look at this movie from Fats's perspective. He represents one direction Eddie could take. He could become the new champion and take on every tough kid who wanted to topple him, until one finally would, just as he, himself, toppled his predecessor. This is the theme of **The Gunfighter**, in a life-and-death context.

PROFANITY: None.
NUDITY/SEXUAL REFERENCES: Eddie and Sarah have (off-screen) sex; implication that Bert and Sarah have sex, a factor in her suicide.
ALCOHOL/DRUG ABUSE: A lot of drinking, much of it to excess; smoking.
VIOLENCE/SCARINESS: Eddie is beat up (in shadows); Sarah commits suicide (off-screen).
TOLERANCE/DIVERSITY ISSUES: None.
QUESTIONS FOR FAMILIES:

- People in the movie have different ideas about what makes someone a winner or a loser. What are those ideas? How do they fit with others you have heard about, or with your own?

- What made Eddie different between his two games with Fats?

- Why didn't Sarah want Eddie to keep playing Findlay?

- How do Sarah and Bert represent two different parts of Eddie that fight with each other?

CONNECTIONS: *The Color of Money,* also starring Newman as Eddie Felsen, is a sequel made twenty-six years later by Martin Scorsese (rated R). Felsen becomes a mentor for a young hustler played by Tom Cruise. Both performances are outstanding (Newman won a long-overdue Oscar), but the script is weak, especially in the second half.

The Lord of the Rings Trilogy: Fellowship of the Ring, The Two Towers, Return of the King

2001–2003, PG-13, 12 and up
Dir: Peter Jackson. Elijah Wood, Ian McKellen, Orlando Bloom, Viggo Mortensen, Sean Astin
PLOT: This extraordinary trilogy of movies is that once-to-a-generation, not since *Star Wars,* transcendent reminder of why we tell stories, why we have imagination, and why we must go on quests to test our spirits and heal the world. It is a story that invites us into a fully-realized world with many different civilizations, all so gorgeously and thoroughly imagined that we do not only believe that they each have complete languages, but that they have dictionaries, histories, mythologies, schools, music, and poetry.

Our hero, Frodo Baggins (Elijah Wood), comes from one such culture. He is a Hobbit. He is on a quest to return a powerful ring to the place where it was created, so it can be destroyed. A great wizard called Gandalf has told him that the ring can be the source of great evil. Of course this makes it very sought after by all kinds of scary folks, so Frodo has a lot of adventures ahead of him. He is not the only one who will have to draw on resources he did not know he had to make sure that the ring no longer has the power to destroy.

DISCUSSION: Peter Jackson, who directed and co-wrote the script, has created a movie that seems astonishingly inventive and new and at the same time somehow seems as though it always existed inside us. Every detail, from the tiniest plant to the hugest battle, is exactly, satisfyingly right. The bad guys, all thundering hooves and billowing capes, seem to have come from the core of every nightmare since the world began.

Parents should know that the movie might be overwhelming for younger children who are not familiar with the characters and story. I recommend preparing anyone younger than 12 with some background or encouraging them to read the simpler first story in the series, The Hobbit (about Frodo's uncle, Bilbo). Characters are in severe peril and there are intense battle scenes.

PROFANITY: None.
NUDITY/SEXUAL REFERENCES: None.
ALCOHOL/DRUG ABUSE: Wine.
VIOLENCE/SCARINESS: Intense peril and battle violence, characters killed.
TOLERANCE/DIVERSITY ISSUES: A metaphorical theme of the movie.
QUESTIONS FOR FAMILIES:

- Why is only Frodo immune to the ring's power to corrupt even honorable, wise, and powerful people?

- If "even the smallest person can change the course of the earth," what difference do you think you can make?

- If you were going to form a fellowship for a grand quest, who would you want to be in it?

CONNECTIONS: Families who enjoy this movie should read the books, starting with the prequel, *The Hobbit*, with beautiful illustrations by Michael Hague. The BBC audio version of the books is superb and perfect for a long car trip. Families may want to read more about New Zealand because its extraordinary topography provides the settings for Middle Earth or look at the gorgeously imaginative illustrations by Maxfield Parrish that inspired some of the art direction. They will also enjoy the **Star Wars** movies, *Labyrinth*, and *The Dark Crystal.*

A Night at the Opera

1935, 96 min, NR, b&w, 8 and up
Dir: Sam Wood. The Marx brothers, Kitty Carlisle, Allan Jones, Margaret Dumont
PLOT: Harpo, Chico, and Groucho Marx bring their sublime brand of anarchy to perhaps its most fitting setting in this comic masterpiece. Groucho is (as ever) a fast-talking fortune hunter (this time called Otis P. Driftwood), chasing (as ever) dim dowager Margaret Dumont (this time called Mrs. Claypool).
Mrs. Claypool brings two Italian opera stars to the United States (Kitty Carlisle as sweet Rosa and Walter Woolf King as cruel Rodolfo Laspari) onboard an ocean liner. Talented tenor Riccardo (Allan Jones), who loves Rosa, his manager Fiorello (Chico Marx), and Tomasso (Harpo Marx), Rodolfo's abused dresser, stow away in Driftwood's steamer trunk. They manage to get off the boat disguised as bearded Russian aviators, but are discovered and chased by a New York

detective. When Rosa refuses Rodolfo's romantic advances, she is fired. Tomasso and Fiorello wreak havoc on the opera's performance of Il Trovatore, until Rosa and Riccardo come in and save the show.

DISCUSSION: Many of the Marx brothers' best-loved routines are here, including the wildly funny contract negotiation, as Groucho and Chico try to con each other ("That's what we call a sanity clause." "Oh no, you can't fool me. There ain't no Sanity Clause!"), and the famous stateroom scene, as person after person enters Groucho's closet-sized room on the ship while Harpo manages to stay asleep (and draped over as many women as possible) and Groucho stays philosophical (when the manicurist asks if he wants his nails long or short, he says, "You'd better make them short; it's getting pretty crowded in here."). The movie veers happily from the wildest slapstick (the Marx brothers replace the music for *Il Trovatore* with *Take Me Out to the Ballgame*) to the cleverest wordplay (by George S. Kaufman and Morrie Ryskind), punctuated by musical numbers that range from pleasant to innocuous. Children studying piano may especially enjoy Chico's specialty-playing the piano while his fingers do acrobatics. All children will enjoy learning that the stars were real-life brothers, who performed together for most of their lives.

PROFANITY: None.
NUDITY/SEXUAL REFERENCES: None.
ALCOHOL/DRUG ABUSE: None.
VIOLENCE/SCARINESS: None.
TOLERANCE/DIVERSITY ISSUES: None.
QUESTIONS FOR FAMILIES:

- Why won't Rodolfo sing to the people who came to say good-bye to him?

- The Marx brothers play people who are not very nice in this movie. They steal, they cheat, they lie, and they cause havoc. How does the movie make you like them, anyway?

CONNECTIONS: This was the most commercially successful of the Marx brothers movies, in part because of the very sections that seem most tedious to us now: the serious musical numbers and the romance. Children will enjoy the other Marx brothers movies as well, especially *A Day at the Races* (NOTE: That movie contains some material that seems racist by today's standards, particularly a rather minstrel show-ish musical number), *Duck Soup*, *Horse Feathers*, and *Monkey Business*. Fans of the many movie references in *The Freshman*, with Matthew Broderick and Marlon Brando, may notice that Broderick's fake passport is in the name of Rodolfo Laspari.

The Secret Garden

1993, 101 min, G, 8 and up
Dir: Agnieszka Holland. Maggie Smith, Kate Maberly
PLOT: Mary Lennox is a sour and selfish girl, spoiled by an Indian nanny and neglected by her parents. When Mary's parents are killed, she is sent back to England to live with her uncle, Archibald Craven, a mysterious and lonely man. He rarely returns to his home in Yorkshire, and leaves Mary to the care of Mrs. Medlock, the housekeeper, and Martha, the maid. Both are busy, and Mary has nothing to do but wander around the moors.

One day, Mary finds the key to a secret garden, once the favorite place for her uncle and his wife, whom he adored. After she died, he locked it up and swore no one would go in there again. Mary is determined to find it.

Following the sound of crying she often hears in the night, she finds that there is another child living in the house. It is her uncle's son, Colin. He has been confined to bed all his life and is spoiled and demanding to the point of hysteria. Mary soothes him by telling him about the garden. Later, when he has a tantrum, she is the first person ever to impose limits on his behavior. He tells her that he is afraid he will have a hunched back like his father, and she tells him his back is fine.

Mary finds the garden, and she and Colin and Martha's brother, Dickon, work to bring it back to life. As they do, Mary and Colin get stronger in body and in spirit. When Archibald returns, he meets them in the garden. They run to him, and it is clear that the garden will heal him, too.

DISCUSSION: Every child should read this book and see at least one of the filmed versions. Children respond to Mary Lennox because (at least in the beginning) she is so unlikable, a relief from all the Pollyannas and Cinderellas who are rewarded for their relentlessly sunny characters and good deeds. Then there is the pleasure of meeting Colin, who is even worse, a "young rajah" who has had his every wish granted instantly and is surrounded only by those who live in terror of his hysteria. Mary and Colin are a perfect match for each other, and the scene in which she responds to his tantrum with fury is one of the most satisfying in any children's book—indeed, in any book, as is the scene in which they enter the garden together, a wonderful metaphor for all that is going on inside their spirits.

PROFANITY: None.
NUDITY/SEXUAL REFERENCES: None.
ALCOHOL/DRUG ABUSE: None.
VIOLENCE/SCARINESS: None. (In the 1984 version, we see what happens to the characters and learn that Dickon has been killed in WWI.)
TOLERANCE/DIVERSITY ISSUES: None. (In the BBC version, the domestics are less subservient than they are in the book.)
QUESTIONS FOR FAMILIES:

• How does making friends with the robin change Mary? Why?

• How is her relationship with Ben different from her relationship with Martha? Why is Mary the only one who refuses to do whatever Colin asks? What effect does that have on him?

• How are Mary and Colin alike, and how are they different?

• What do you think will happen after the book ends?

CONNECTIONS: This classic story by Frances Hodgson Burnett has been beautifully filmed four times, and any and all of them are well worth watching. The first, filmed in 1949, stars Margaret O'Brien and Dean Stockwell. Like **The Wizard of Oz**, the early part of the film is in black and white, and then, when they enter the garden, it turns to color. The 1984 version, made for British television is (unsurprisingly) the most authentic, and the Yorkshire accents are a delight. The 1987 version, made for American television, is fine, with Derek Jacobi as Archibald Craven. The 1993 theatrical release has some exquisitely beautiful images, but the first one is the strongest dramatically.
ACTIVITIES: Look up Yorkshire in an atlas or get some travel brochures to see pictures of the moors. Encourage your children to start a garden, even if it consists only of a flowerpot near the kitchen window.

Shipwrecked

1990, 91 min, PG, 6 and up
Dir: Nils Gaup. Gabriel Byrne, Stian Smestad
PLOT: Merrick (Gabriel Byrne) shoots an English naval officer named Howell and assumes his identity. Meanwhile, in Norway, a boy named Hakon (Stian Smestad) is being pushed around by some bullies. He warns them his father will take care of them when he gets back from sea, and they tell him his father owes so

much money, he should never come home. His father does come home, with an injured leg, and with Jens, the man who saved his life. Hakon does not want to go to sea in his place, but when the family risks losing their home, he goes. Jens promises to look after him.

The stern captain tells Hakon, "There is no room for children aboard this ship," and the crew initiates him by hanging him from the mast, but he watches, learns, works hard, and soon fits in well. At the first port, the captain tells him he has passed muster, and can stay on for the entire voyage. They are joined by a new First Mate: Merrick, still passing as Howell. Hakon discovers guns in a crate marked GLASS. Merrick tells him it is a secret. Just as Hakon is about to tell the captain, the captain falls ill, poisoned by one of Merrick's accomplices. The captain dies and is buried at sea. Merrick takes over.

At the next port, a brave young girl named Mary stows away. Hakon discovers her, and brings her food. She teaches him to read, using a book of Coleridge's poetry. When Merrick discovers her, Jens confesses to protect Hakon. Hakon tells Merrick it was his fault, and Merrick orders Jens to whip Hakon. Just then, the ship is struck by lightning and sinks. Hakon is washed up on an island, where he discovers pirate treasure and a newspaper clipping with a drawing of Merrick, leader of the pirates. Hakon knows Merrick will come for the treasure, and sets up elaborate booby traps all over the island. Seeing smoke on another island, he builds a small boat and explores it. He finds Mary and Jens, living with friendly natives. They return to Hakon's island, just before the pirates come to get the treasure. Between the traps and Mary's liberation of the ship, they manage to get away with the treasure and return to Hakon's home in triumph.

DISCUSSION: Neglected on its release, this is an exciting adventure, and a lot of fun to watch. Hakon does a lot of growing up. At the beginning he is a young boy who can only fight bullies by telling them to wait for his father. At the end he is a young man who is confident of his ability to protect himself.

PROFANITY: None.
NUDITY/SEXUAL REFERENCES: Very mild reference to "protecting your valuables" when prostitutes approach the sailors onshore.
ALCOHOL/DRUG ABUSE: Sailors drink ale in a tavern; teasing of Hakon about drinking milk, which he handles very well.
VIOLENCE/SCARINESS: Lead characters in exciting peril several times.
TOLERANCE/DIVERSITY ISSUES: Mary is an especially spirited and resourceful heroine.

QUESTIONS FOR FAMILIES:

- How does Hakon decide whether to tell the captain about the guns he found?

- Why does Jens say it was he who hid Mary?

- Why does Hakon tell the truth?

- Which part of the movie was the scariest? Which part was the funniest?

CONNECTIONS: The booby traps on the island are reminiscent of the invasion of the pirates in **Swiss Family Robinson**, and of course *Home Alone*.

ACTIVITIES: Find Norway on a map and see if you can chart the course Hakon followed. You might also enjoy reading the Coleridge poem Hakon likes, "Kubla Khan." Even if it is hard to follow, the language and rhythms are a pleasure to the ear and tongue. It provides a good beginning for a discussion of dream or ideal places. The "pleasure dome" inhabited by Kane in **Citizen Kane** is named Xanadu, a reference to this poem.

Shrek

2001, 90 min., PG, 8 and up

Dir: Andrew Adamson and Vicky Jenson. Michael Meyers, Eddie Murphy, Cameron Diaz, John Lithgow

PLOT: Shrek is a big, green ogre who lives happily alone in a swamp. But Lord Farquaad of nearby Dulac has a plan for creating the perfect kingdom, and that means getting rid of all of the fairy tale characters and sending them to "a designated resettlement community." Soon, the three blind mice, the three little pigs, the gingerbread man, all the broom-flying witches, Pinocchio, and a talking donkey are all relocated to the swamp. Shrek is furious at the intrusion. He makes a deal with Farquaad, who needs to marry a princess to put the final touch on his kingdom. Shrek will rescue Princess Fiona and bring her to Farquaad, and Farquaad will give Shrek his swamp back.

DISCUSSION: The movie is a marvelous fairy tale, with a thrilling quest and a happily ever after ending. It has the great themes of enduring myths, about believing in yourself, being loved for the person you really are, and good triumphing over evil. It is also a delicious satire, tweaking all of our assumptions about ogres, princesses, rescues, and even fire-breathing dragons. The voice talents of Michael Myers (as the Scottish-burred Shrek), Eddie Murphy (as the talking donkey), Cameron Diaz (as Princess Fiona), and John Lithgow (as Farquaad) are all perfect. The computer animation is breathtaking, like nothing ever done before. The textures are stunning. The glass, fire, clouds, and water seem three-dimensional, and you will feel that the donkey's fur almost brushes your hand. The animation has wonderful warmth and depth, but it also has a great deal of character and wit. The facial expressions and body language are such a treat that the audience can't help thinking that if ogres and donkeys and don't really look like that, they should.

Parents should know that this movie is rated PG, but it is right up at the limit of PG-13, with edgy humor directed at teenagers and adults. It is a shame that Hollywood finds it necessary to include this material in a movie that would be otherwise perfect family fare, but that is the economic reality of this era of movie-making. You can't have a major hit without selling tickets to teenagers, and teenagers will not go without some jokes worth sniggering at. They will be over the heads of most younger children, but parents should be ready for some questions. Parents should also know that it has some potty humor and some gross-out jokes.

PROFANITY: None.
NUDITY/SEXUAL REFERENCES: Some potty humor and double entendres.
ALCOHOL/DRUG ABUSE: None.
VIOLENCE/SCARINESS: Lead characters in exciting peril several times. A bird explodes and its eggs are eaten, and a character loses a leg, but very few others get seriously hurt.
TOLERANCE/DIVERSITY ISSUES: Princess Fiona is brave, loyal, and smart.
QUESTIONS FOR FAMILIES:

- Is it true that Shrek did not care what people thought of him? How can you tell?

- What did it mean to say that ogres are like onions? What does it mean to say that people have layers?

- Who in the movie is judged on his or her looks? By themselves or by others?

- Why does Shrek yell at the donkey when he is really angry about something else?

- Do you agree that "friends forgive each other?"

- Can you look up into the stars and see stories?

CONNECTIONS: Families who enjoy this movie will also enjoy the very funny 2004 sequel and movies like **Ladyhawke** and **The Princess Bride**. Families with younger children will enjoy some of the books by William Steig, who wrote this story. My favorites include *Sylvester and the Magic Pebble*, *Spinky Sulks*, and *Brave Irene*.

Star Wars

1977, 121 min, PG, 6 and up
Dir: George Lucas. Harrison Ford, Alec Guinness, Carrie Fisher, Mark Hamill
PLOT: The movie starts right in the middle of the action, with a battle on a spaceship. Two robots or "droids" escape, the elegant C-3PO and his counterpart, the gurgling and beeping R2D2. They carry a message from Princess Leia to Obi-Wan Kenobi, asking for help. When they arrive at a desert planet, they are bought by Luke Skywalker (Mark Hamill), who is then captured by "sand people" but rescued by Ben Kenobi (Alec Guinness).

Ben gets the message from Princess Leia and tells Luke they must go to help her fight the Empire. He tells Luke that his father was once a great fighter, a Jedi Knight, "the best star pilot in the galaxy and a cunning warrior." Luke says he cannot. Although Luke is restless and eager to explore the universe and had begged his farmer uncle to let him go, he tells Ben, "I can't get involved. I have work to do." He will do as his uncle insisted and stay on the farm another year. Besides, this is not his fight. It all seems very far away.

He returns to the farm to find his aunt and uncle have been killed by Empire warriors trying to capture the droids. He and Kenobi hire Han Solo, a sometime smuggler, to get them to a planet called Alderan. Ben teaches Luke about "the force," a power within and around everyone.

They arrive only to find Alderan has been destroyed. The Empire has a new weapon capable of eliminating whole planets. Luke, Leia, and Han, trapped on this "death star," must first escape, and then find a way to destroy it.
DISCUSSION: George Lucas, who wrote and directed this movie, was deeply influenced by Joseph Campbell's work on myths, and by his love for the great movie classics. This movie is rich in themes from both. The scene in the bar, with all the aliens, is very much like the bar scene in a Western movie. Han Solo resembles the cowboy ideal, the loner with no loyalty to any cause but with his own sense of morality. Even his costume is reminiscent of a cowboy outfit, with boots and a gun holster at the hip.

Han and Luke must both decide whether to join the fight. At first, both are reluctant; in fact, Han leaves. They accept the responsibility, as they must. The concept of "the force" in the movie may be something your children will want to know more about.

PROFANITY: None.
NUDITY/SEXUAL REFERENCES: None.
ALCOHOL/DRUG ABUSE: A sci-fi bar scene.
VIOLENCE/SCARINESS: A lot of comic-book-style fighting. An alien has a limb sliced off. One of the main characters is killed.
TOLERANCE/DIVERSITY ISSUES: Many different species work together well (at least with the good guys). The humans are all white males except for the princess, who is spirited but not a frontline fighter. All of the pilots are males, for example.
QUESTIONS FOR FAMILIES:

• Why does Luke decide to fight the Empire? Why does Han?

• Why does Han leave, and why does he come back?

CONNECTIONS: There are two sequels, *The Empire Strikes Back* and *Return of the Jedi*, both reissued in 1997 with additional scenes and special effects, and both exciting adventures. A new cycle of three movies, set a generation before **Star Wars**, has been a disappointment, but has outstanding visual effects.

The Sword in the Stone

1963, 75 min, G, 4 and up
Dir: Wolfgang Reighterman. Sebastian Cabot, Alan Napier
PLOT: Based on the book by T. H. White, this is the story of the early years of King Arthur. Nicknamed "Wart," the future King Arthur is squire to a knight when he meets Merlin the magician, who promises to take on his education. Merlin turns him into a fish, a bird, and a squirrel to teach him lessons like the importance of brains over brawn. He gets to see this in action when Madame Mim, Merlin's enemy, challenges Merlin to a duel by magic, and, though she cheats, Merlin is able to defeat her.

Wart still has his duties as a squire and, having forgotten the sword for a jousting match, he runs to get it. He sees a sword stuck in a stone and pulls it out, not knowing the legend that whomever will pull the sword out of the stone will be the rightful king. He becomes King Arthur, and listens when Merlin reminds him knowledge is the real power.

DISCUSSION: The King Arthur legend has fascinated people for centuries, and this story about Arthur's childhood has special appeal for children. Aside from the fun of seeing what it is like to be a bird, a squirrel, or a fish, and from having your very own wizard as a teacher, there is the highly satisfying aspect of having one's worth, unappreciated by everyone, affirmed so unequivocally.

PROFANITY: None.
NUDITY/SEXUAL REFERENCES: None.
ALCOHOL/DRUG ABUSE: None.
VIOLENCE/SCARINESS: Wizard fight.
TOLERANCE/DIVERSITY ISSUES: Symbolically, as Wart learns empathy from his experiences.
QUESTIONS FOR FAMILIES:

- What made Arthur the one who could pull the sword out of the stone?

- What did he learn from his adventures with Merlin?

- How will what he learned help him to be a good king?

- How did Madame Mim cheat?

- How did Merlin fight back when she did?

CONNECTIONS: Older kids may like to see *Camelot*, the musical by Lerner and Lowe (of My Fair Lady), to find out some of what happened to Arthur later (WARNING: the focus of that movie is on Guinevere's infidelity with Lancelot.) Mature teenagers might like the rather gory Excalibur, which has some stunning images.
ACTIVITIES: Read aloud T. H. White's *The Sword and the Stone* and *The Story of King Arthur and His Knights*, or the other books about Camelot by Howard Pyle, which also have Pyle's magnificent illustrations.

Who Framed Roger Rabbit?

1989, 109 min, PG, 6 and up
Dir: Robert Zemeckis. Bob Hoskins, Christopher Lloyd, Stubby Kaye
PLOT: In this technical marvel of a movie, human and animated actors interact seamlessly. It begins with a cartoon, lovable Roger Rabbit taking care of adorable Baby Herman, despite every kind of slapstick disaster. Then, as birdies are swimming around Roger's head after a refrigerator crashes down on him, a live-action

director steps in to complain that the script called for stars, and we are in a 1947 Hollywood where "Toons" are real.

A private detective named Eddie (Bob Hoskins) is hired by the head of Roger's studio to get evidence that Roger's gorgeous wife, Jessica, is seeing another man. Eddie does not want the assignment. Once a friend to the Toons, he hates them since one of them killed his brother. He needs the money badly, so Eddie goes to the Ink and Paint nightclub, where Jessica performs, and he takes photos of her playing "patty-cake" (literally) with Marvin Acme (Stubby Kaye), maker of novelties and gags. Roger is distraught when he sees the photographs. It turns out that Jessica is completely faithful to Roger, and that she is caught up in a complex plot to close down Toon Town and Los Angeles's excellent public transportation system to build freeways. Eddie's efforts lead him to Toon Town and then to a warehouse where the real villain is revealed.

DISCUSSION: Children will be delighted with the Toon characters, and with the interaction of the cartoons with the human actors and with the physical world. Eddie's venture into Toon Town is almost as good. The story is fast-paced and exciting, and the slapstick is outstanding.

The human and cartoon characters mix more smoothly than the combination of slapstick and film noir references in this movie. The plot includes murder, corruption, and suspected adultery. The premise that the only possible explanation for the traffic system in Los Angeles is that it was the vision of a sinister madman is funnier for adults than it is for kids. Eddie is not an especially attractive leading character. Still reeling from his brother's murder, he drinks too much and is surly to his clients, to his girlfriend, and to Roger.

PROFANITY: Some mild language (i.e., "wiseass"; "kick you in the—" (balls); "booby" trap; "Is that a rabbit in your pocket...")
NUDITY/SEXUAL REFERENCES: Alleged affair between Jessica and Acme; Jessica is an exaggerated sex symbol.
ALCOHOL/DRUG ABUSE: Eddie has a drinking problem; several scenes in a bar. When Roger drinks alcohol, he has a cartoon-y reaction, turning colors and bouncing around the room.
VIOLENCE/SCARINESS: Some fighting. One Toon killed; one human killed; main characters in peril
TOLERANCE/DIVERSITY ISSUES: The Toons conjure up thoughts of the history of racial discrimination, with the Ink and Paint club reminiscent of nightclubs with white audiences and black performers, and the segregated Toon Town and "otherness" of the Toon characters.

QUESTIONS FOR FAMILIES:

• Why does Eddie blame all the Toons for his brother's death?

• Why is it so hard for him to be nice to anyone?

• Why don't the humans and Toons get along better?

• Would you like to visit Toon Town? What would you do there?

CONNECTIONS: This was a one-time opportunity for cartoon characters from all the studios to join forces, and it is one of the great pleasures in movie history to see them all together. Donald Duck and Daffy Duck perform a hilarious duet at the Ink and Paint club. On his way out the door at Maroon Studios, Eddie brushes by several members from the "cast" of Fantasia. The penguin waiters from **Mary Poppins** show up in another scene, as do Pinocchio, Mickey Mouse, and Woody Woodpecker. The mix of characters and styles works extremely well, and kids will enjoy seeing some of their favorite characters in a different context. Kathleen Turner provided the sultry speaking voice of Jessica Rabbit, but her singing voice was provided by Amy Irving.

ACTIVITIES: A key element of the plot concerns invisible ink. Kids will enjoy making their own or using some from a magic store to write secret messages. Kids lucky enough to go to Walt Disney World or Disneyland will enjoy the Roger Rabbit attractions.

The Witches

1990, 91 min, PG, 8 and up
Dir: Nicolas Roeg. Anjelica Huston, Mai Zetterling, Rowan Atkinson
PLOT: Luke hears about witches from his grandmother (Mai Zetterling). She says they have to wear gloves to hide their clawlike hands and shoes that fit their square feet without toes, and that they are bald and scratch under their wigs. They have a purple gleam in their eyes. They are evil and they steal children, who are never seen again.

Luke's parents are killed, and his grandmother takes him to England. When she is diagnosed with mild diabetes, the doctor advises a vacation, so they go to Cornwall. As it happens, a convention of all the witches in England is staying in the same hotel, posing as the Royal Society for the Prevention of Cruelty to Children. Their leader is slinky, black-clad Eva Ernst (Anjelica Huston). Luke overhears her telling the witches to wipe out all the children in England by turning them into mice, and he watches as she demonstrates by giving a potion to a greedy child named Bruno, transforming him into a mouse. The witches find Luke and, after a chase, capture him and turn him into a mouse. With the help of his grandmother, he steals some of the potion and puts it into the soup to be served to the witches, who are all turned to mice except for Eva's assistant. Luke manages to get Eva's trunkful of money, along with her notebook listing the addresses of all the witches in America, and he and his grandmother plan to go after them.

DISCUSSION: This story has a genuinely twisted flavor that some children will love and others will find disturbing. Luke is exceptionally brave and enjoys being a mouse (in the movie, he is changed back, but in the book, he stays a mouse): Children may be upset not only by the witches, but by the death (off-screen) of Luke's parents, and by his seeming indifference to it.

PROFANITY: None.
NUDITY/SEXUAL REFERENCES: None.
ALCOHOL/DRUG ABUSE: None.
VIOLENCE/SCARINESS: Scary witches; children in peril, including a baby in a carriage pushed down a hill (and rescued); Luke's parents are killed in an (off-screen) accident, which does not seem to bother him too much.
TOLERANCE/DIVERSITY ISSUES: None.
QUESTIONS FOR FAMILIES:

• Do you believe in witches?

• Can you think of other witches in stories or movies? How are they the same? How are they different?

• Is it good for adults to tell children scary stories?

• Why do you think Eva's assistant turns out to be a good witch? Were there any clues that you missed?

CONNECTIONS: Roald Dahl was married to actress Patricia Neal (**The Day the Earth Stood Still**). Huston is the daughter of director John Huston (*The Maltese Falcon*) and the grandaughter of actor Walter Huston (**The Treasure of the Sierra Madre**). Rowan Atkinson is better known as "Mr. Bean," This was the last film worked on by Muppeteer Jim Henson, and his mouse puppets are a marvel.

The Wizard of Oz

1939, 101 min, NR, 6 and up

Dir: Victor Fleming. Judy Garland, Ray Bolger, Bert Lahr, Frank Morgan, Jack Haley, Margaret Hamilton

PLOT: Dorothy Gale (Judy Garland) lives in Kansas with her aunt and uncle and her dog, Toto. Mean Miss Gulch (Margaret Hamilton) swears she will have Toto taken away. Auntie Em and Uncle Henry support Dorothy, but they are too distracted by the coming tornado to pay much attention to her. Dorothy dreams of a place "over the rainbow" where everything is beautiful, "troubles melt like lemon drops," and "the dreams that you dare to dream really do come true." She starts to run away to protect Toto, but is sent back home by the kindly Professor Marvel (Frank Morgan), a traveling fortune-teller.

When the storm arrives, Dorothy is outside the shelter. She goes to her room, where she is hit on the head by a piece of wood torn loose by the wind. The whole house rises, and is carried away by the tornado.

The house lands with a crash, and when Dorothy opens the door, she finds she has landed in the colorful world of Oz (the movie, black and white up to this point, becomes Technicolor). Her house has landed on the Wicked Witch of the East, killing her, and the tiny Munchkins celebrate Dorothy as a great heroine. Their friend Glinda the good witch (Billie Burke) arrives and gives her the Wicked Witch's magic ruby slippers, just as the Wicked Witch of the West (Margaret Hamilton) arrives to take them. The Wicked Witch of the East was her sister. Furious, she swears revenge. Dorothy wants to go home and is told to seek out the Wizard of Oz, who lives in the Emerald City, for help.

On the way to the Emerald City, Dorothy meets a talking Scarecrow (Ray Bolger) who wants a brain, a Tin Woodsman (Jack Haley) who longs for a heart, and a cowardly Lion (Bert Lahr) who wants courage. They all join her to seek the help of the Wizard. At. the Emerald City, the Wizard at first refuses to see them, then finally tells them they must earn their wishes by bringing him the broom of the Wicked Witch of the West. They are captured by the witch's flying monkeys, and just as she is about to kill them, Dorothy douses her with water, trying to protect the Scarecrow from fire, and the witch melts.

They return to the Emerald City only to find that the Wizard cannot help them. He is a fraud, just "the man behind the curtain," whose terrifying displays of smoke and light hide a "humbug" who has no magical powers at all. He is able to show the Scarecrow, Tin Woodsman, and Lion that all along they really did have what they've been seeking, and he promises to take Dorothy back to Kansas in his hot-air balloon.

Toto jumps out of the balloon's basket. Dorothy runs after him and misses the balloon launch. Just as Dorothy despairs of ever going home, Glinda arrives and shows Dorothy that she, too, all along had the means of getting home. Back in Kansas, Dorothy wakes up to find her aunt and uncle, the farmhands, and Professor Marvel (who strongly resemble the Scarecrow, Tin Woodsman, Lion, and Wizard), and tells them that "there's no place like home."

DISCUSSION: This movie is an ideal family film, superb in every aspect, with outstanding art direction, music, and performances. It is still as fresh and engrossing as it was in 1939, and improves with every viewing. If you ever have a chance to see it on a big screen, in a theater with a good sound system, you will enjoy it even more.

It is hard to imagine what it would have been like with the original intended cast, including Shirley Temple as Dorothy and Buddy Ebsen as the Tin Woodsman. Fortunately, 20th Century Fox would not lend its top star. Less fortunately, Ebsen was hospitalized when he inhaled the aluminum dust in the Tin Woodsman's makeup. Judy Garland is a perfect Dorothy, vulnerable, sensitive, and completely believable. On the brink of leaving childhood, her dreams of a place "over the rainbow" are in part a yearning to escape the concerns of adulthood. Jack Haley is a gallant and tender Tim Woodsman.

There is something especially satisfying about the way that the main characters find what they need within themselves. Talk with children about the way that the Scarecrow demonstrates his intelligence, the Tin Woodsman demonstrates his heart, and the Lion demonstrates his courage. Even the humbug Wizard finds that he had the means to go home all the time. Dorothy, who in the first part of the movie runs away from home to try to solve her problems, spends the rest of the movie trying to get back. Even if the story is just a dream (in the book, it is a real adventure), this makes a great deal of emotional sense, a way of working through her inner conflicts.

It is also worth talking about the scene in which Dorothy and her friends disregard the Wizard's plea to "pay no attention to the man behind the curtain" and discover that he is really just an ordinary man. This can be a touchstone or metaphor for many kinds of challenges children face. It can help them recognize that the overpowering figures in their lives (parents, teachers, adults, sports figures) are just imperfect human beings. It can also help them recognize attempts, by themselves as well as by others, to distract people in hopes of hiding our imperfection and vulnerability.

NOTE: There are a number of different scenes in this movie that may be scary for children. Many adults still remember being scared by the flying monkeys or Dorothy looking into the crystal ball and seeing her aunt turn into the witch. Parents should talk to children about the story before seeing the movie, and watch with them to gauge their reactions.

PROFANITY: None.
NUDITY/SEXUAL REFERENCES: None.
ALCOHOL/DRUG ABUSE: None.
VIOLENCE/SCARINESS: Lead characters in peril. Many young children are especially scared by the flying monkeys who guard the Wicked Witch.
TOLERANCE/DIVERSITY ISSUES: Tolerance of individual differences and frailties.
QUESTIONS FOR FAMILIES:

- Why does the Scarecrow think he doesn't have a brain? What does he want to be able to do? Why does the Tin Woodsman think he doesn't have a heart? Why does the Lion think he doesn't have courage?

- How can you see that they do have these things? How does the Wizard show them that they do?

- If Oz is the land "over the rainbow" that Dorothy dreamed of, why does she want to go home?

- Why does the Wizard pretend to have more powers than he really does?

- What does the Wizard mean when he says, "Hearts will never be made practical until they can be made unbreakable"?

CONNECTIONS: Some editions of the video include a fascinating documentary about the making of the film, showing some scenes that were cut, including a musical number called "The Jitterbug." The fourteen Oz books by L. Frank Baum are still loved not only by children but also by adult fans so committed that there is a flourishing Oz society; children who love this movie and read the books may enjoy getting on its mailing list.
Children will enjoy picking out the actors who have double roles in the movie: Margaret Hamilton as Miss Gulch and the Wicked Witch; Ray Bolger as the Scarecrow and Hank; Jack Haley as the Tin Woodsman and Hickory; and Bert Lahr as the Cowardly Lion and Zeke. Watch closely and you will see Frank Mor-

gan in four roles: not just Professor Marvel and the Wizard, but also the guard at the gate of the. Emerald City and the guard at the castle.

You can see the astonishingly limber Ray Bolger in *The Harvey Girls* (again with Judy Garland) and *Babes in Toyland*, and Jack Haley with Shirley Temple in **Poor Little Rich Girl** and *Rebecca of Sunnybrook Farm*. Composer Harold Arlen, who also wrote standards like "Stormy Weather," "That Old Black Magic," and "Accentuate the Positive," was nominated for eleven Academy Awards, but won only once, for "Over the Rainbow."

The Wiz is a black urban version of the same story with a terrific score performed by stars including Michael Jackson, Diana Ross. Contrasting the different interpretations of the story is very worthwhile for kids.

E. T. THE EXTRA-TERRESTRIAL

1982, 115 min, PG, 6 and up
Dir: Steven Spielberg. Henry Thomas, Drew Barrymore
A young boy named Elliott (Henry Thomas) finds an extraterrestrial who has been left behind when his expedition of alien botanists had to depart quickly to avoid detection. He brings E. T. home, finding in their connection a way to begin to heal his sense of loss at his father's absence. E. T. loves Elliott, but begins to weaken in earth's atmosphere and needs to go home. With the help of Elliott and the neighborhood children, he sends a message to his friends. Before they can come for him, he is captured by government scientists. E. T,'s connection with Elliott is so strong, Elliott becomes very ill, too. Both recover, and the children return E. T. to the spaceship, after E. T. reminds Elliott that they will always be together.

This is an outstanding family movie, with themes of loyalty, friendship, trust, and caring. Talk to kids about the way that the adults and the kids see things differently, and have a hard time understanding each other's perspective. One reason is that they don't try to share their feelings with each other). NOTE: Strong language used by kids. This film was justifiably criticized for its almost complete absence of nonwhite characters.

HONEY, I SHRUNK THE KIDS

1989, 93 min, PG, 6 and up
Dir: Joe Johnston. Rick Moranis, Matt Frewer, Marcia Strassman
Another "absentminded professor" style movie from Disney, this one has scientist Rick Moranis inventing a ray that shrinks things. When his children and their friends are accidentally shrunk, they have to find their way back across the yard,

now a terrifying jungle of sky-high blades of grass and monstrous insects. Exciting and fun (though with an absolutely unnecessary concluding joke about French kissing that will be lost on most of the intended audience).

CONNECTIONS: The 1992 sequel, *Honey, I Blew Up the Kid*, has a toddler stomping through Las Vegas like Godzilla. A 1997 straight-to-video release, *Honey, We Shrunk Ourselves*, has the adults getting shrunk, so that their children think they are alone in the house. The plot and dialogue are weak, but sensational special effects make up most of the brief (seventy-five minute) video, especially a roller coaster of a ride in a Hot Wheels car, floating in soap bubbles, and close encounters with a cockroach and a daddy longlegs.

Everyone learns a lesson about the importance of trust and respect for each other, and about what family members really need from one another. Parents will want to talk to kids about what happens when the children, thinking they are alone in the house, have a party that gets out of hand, and when one of the kids decides to rebel by not taking his medicine. There is a nice scene in which a teenage girl tells a boy in no uncertain terms that he may not kiss her without her permission.

HOOSIERS

1986, 114 min, PG, 10 and up
Dir: David Anspaugh. Gene Hackman, Dennis Hopper, Barbara Hershey
In small towns, high school sports can assume transcendent importance. In this story set in the 1950s, a tiny farm community's basketball team becomes the state champion, led by a coach (Gene Hackman) thrown out of college basketball for failure to control his temper. His redemption, and that of his alcoholic assistant (Dennis Hopper), father of one of the players, parallels the effort and triumph of the team. This is an exceptionally moving film, with outstanding performances, and very evocative of the place and time.

INDEPENDENCE DAY

1996, 143 min, PG-13, 10 and up
Dir: Roland Emmerich. Will Smith, Jeff Goldblum, Bill Pullman, Margaret Colin
In this heart-thumping, slam-bang action extravaganza, aliens arrive and blow up the world's major cities. The president (Bill Pullman) and fighter pilots (led by Will Smith) must find a way to fight back. Some kids will find this too intense and scary, but others will want to see it over and over (and over) again. Themes to discuss include behavior in a crisis, honesty, the dilemma faced by the president

in making the choice to use nuclear weapons, and, for film fanatics, finding all of the references to other classic films, from Dr. Strangelove to 2001.

NOTE: The movie was justifiably accused of being sexist. One of the female leads is a stripper. We see her perform, though she remains covered. Her lover resists marrying her because it would hurt his career. Another couple divorced because she was too committed to her career. In addition, parents may be concerned about an unmarried couple that is clearly intimate, and by the tension as the characters are in peril, as well as a massive number of deaths, including two of the main characters.

LABYRINTH

1988, 101 min, PG, 10 and up
Dir: Jim Henson. Jennifer Connelly, David Bowie
An imaginative teenager named Sarah (Jennifer Connelly) impulsively wishes that her fretful baby brother would be taken away by goblins. When her wish comes true, she must go through the labyrinth to the castle of the King of the Goblins (David Bowie) to rescue him.

This is an entertaining adventure, with a clever script and exceptionally imaginative art direction. Like *Alice in Wonderland* and Dorothy in Oz, Sarah finds the power to solve the problem within herself.

CONNECTIONS: This movie was produced by George Lucas (of Star Wars and Raiders of the Lost Ark), written by Terry Jones (of Monty Python), and directed by Jim Henson (of the Muppets).

ACTIVITIES: Kids who like this movie will enjoy looking at the pictures of artist and optical illusionist M. C. Escher, who inspired the set for the final confrontation. You can glimpse a poster of one of drawings in Sarah's bedroom.

LADYHAWKE

1985, 123 min, PG-13, 10 and up
Dir: Richard Donner. Matthew Broderick, Rutger Hauer, Michelle Pfeiffer
Matthew Broderick plays Philippe "the Mouse," a medieval pickpocket, who meets up with an enchanted couple, a knight named Navarre (Rutger Hauer) and his lady love, Isabeau (Michelle Pfeiffer). An evil and jealous bishop has called upon the devil to help him cast a spell on them. Each sunset, Navarre becomes a wolf, and each sunrise, Isabeau becomes a hawk. They travel, "always together, eternally apart," able to glimpse each other for just a brief moment as the sun rises and sets.

Hauer and Pfeiffer are outstanding as the lovers, and except for some jarring rock music the period detail is exceptionally well-handled. Mouse, who has always relied on his wits and his ability to lie and steal, learns about honor (though he does not reform entirely). NOTE: The PG-13 rating is for violence, mostly sword fights.

THE NEVERENDING STORY

1984, 92 min, PG, 6 and up
Dir: Wolfgang Peterson. Noah Hathaway, Barret Oliver, Moses Gunn
Bastian is a boy who runs into a musty old bookstore when he is chased by bullies. He begins to read a huge and ancient book, and is astounded to find that he is part of the story: The beautiful princess of Fantasia is asking for Bastian to give her a name, so her kingdom can be saved. The hero of the story is Atreyu, who must complete a quest to save the kingdom. His courage and power is less important than Bastian's belief and imagination. The characters and effects are wonderfully imaginative and, interestingly, the force they must fight is not a bad guy but Nothingness, a sort of mindlessness and apathy.
CONNECTIONS: There are two sequels (the last one straight-to-video), but they are not nearly as good.

NORMA RAE

1979, 113 min, PG, mature high school age
Dir: Martin Ritt. Sally Field, Ron Liebman, Beau Bridges
Sally Field won an Oscar for her performance as Norma Rae, an uneducated factory worker who finds herself through her efforts to unionize the mill. Based on a true story, this movie shows director Ritt's trademark feel for the South and its people.

Norma Rae is a single mother of two when Reuben, a New York City labor organizer (exceptionally well-played by Ron Liebman), comes to town, looking for a local worker to bring the union's message to the factory floor. She must confront the hostility of the managers, the fear—and worse—the indifference of her fellow workers, and the needs of her family. She must also find the strength and self-respect to allow herself to believe she can make a difference. Once she does, it becomes so important to her that she cannot quit.

Norma Rae and Reuben become very close, and care about each other deeply, but the movie has the courage and the intelligence not to give them any sexual contact (other than a brief nude swim). What matters is that Reuben sees Norma Rae was "too smart to be doing what you're doing to yourself," and she is, indeed, smart enough to understand he is right, and do something about it. NOTE: Some mature themes, including references to extramarital sex and an out-of-wedlock child. Norma Rae's initial lack of self-respect is reflected in her willingness to have casual sex.

CONNECTIONS: Sally Fields won an Oscar for her performance, which some observers felt paralleled her own journey from silly sitcoms to serious drama. The theme song "It Goes Like It Goes," also won an Oscar.

THE PRINCESS DIARIES

2001, min, G, 6 and up
Dir: Garry Marshall. Anne Hathaway, Julie Andrews
Mia Thermopolis (Anne Hathaway) is a shy fifteen-year-old who says, "My expectation in life is to be invisible, and I'm good at it." She dreams of a "foot-popping" kiss from high school hunk Josh Bryant (Erik von Detten) (that's a kiss so good that it makes your foot pop up) and she would like to be able to get up in front of the class to speak without going to pieces. Her sympathetic mother, an artist, her best friend Lily (Heather Matarazzo), and her "baby," a beat-up Mustang she is having repaired, keep her going.

Just before her 16th birthday, she gets a visit from her grandmother (Julie Andrews), whom she has never met. An even bigger surprise is the reason for the visit. It turns out that Mia's grandmother is the queen of Genovia, her late father was the king, and that makes her—a princess! Mia will have to get some fast princess lessons to get ready for the annual ball. That is, if she decides to accept the job, which is not too appealing. As she says to her mother, "Just in case I'm not enough of a freak already, you add a tiara!"

Things get worse when Lily feels deserted and a couple of very public mistakes make Mia feel that she is not up to the job. This would not be a fairy tale if everyone did not live happily ever after, so somehow everyone's wishes come true.

This is a wonderful story about growing up, finding ourselves, and taking chances, with lots of great things for families to talk about afterwards. The queen's head of security (Hector Elizondo in another impeccable performance) quotes Eleanor Roosevelt's famous words, "No one can make you feel inferior without your consent." Mia realizes that the important part of being a princess is not what it does for her, but what it makes it possible for her to do for others. NOTE: Parents should know that Mia drives without a license and manages to escape a ticket using tactics they might find troubling.

THE SANDLOT

1993, 101 min, PG, 6 and up
Dir: David Mickey Evans. Dennis Leary, Karen Allen, James Earl Jones
In the 1960s, a boy whose mother has just remarried moves to a new town and begins to make friends when he joins in a sandlot baseball game. The boy's challenges include developing some baseball skills, trying to achieve a comfortable relationship with his new stepfather (Dennis Leary), and finding a way to triumph over "The Beast" (a junkyard dog) and the bigger, tougher kids who challenge his friends to a game. All are well-handled in this exceptionally perceptive story of growing up. NOTE: Some gross-out moments (which most kids will enjoy). One of the boys pretends to be drowning to get a kiss from a beautiful lifeguard.

SPY KIDS

2001, 88 min, PG, 7 and up
Dir: Robert Rodriguez. Antonio Banderas, Alexa Vega, Alan Cumming, Tony Shaloub
Imagine James Bond crossed with *Willy Wonka and the Chocolate Factory* and you might have an idea the combination of giddy fantasy, exciting adventure, wonderful special effects, and sly comedy in this movie about kids who end up as super spies. Carmen and Juni Cortez (Alexa Vega and Daryl Sabara) are the children of Gregorio (Antonio Banderas) and Ingrid (Carla Gugino), once the cleverest spies in the world, but now loving parents who make a living as consultants. Or so they say. They go off on a mission and get captured.

Carmen and Juni have to rescue their parents, and, while they're at it, the rest of the world, too. First, they have to learn to respect and trust each other. They also have to learn how to use a bunch of gadgets that would leave James Bond, Flash Gordon, Dick Tracy, and even Inspector Gadget green with envy. It is wonderful that instead of ray guns or other destructive devices the kids use fantasy versions of stuff that kids know best. Similarly, instead of scary ninjas or soldiers, most of the bad guys are either thumb-shaped robot creatures who are literally all thumbs or a bunch of robot children whose most menacing aspect is glowing eyes and super strength.

Parents should know that the movie includes a little bit of potty humor (which most kids will find hilarious) and one almost-swear word. Younger children might be frightened by the mutant creatures, but most will find them more silly than scary. Characters are in comic peril and there is a certain amount of head-bonking violence, but no one even gets a scratch except for one villain whose encounter with flames leaves her having a very bad hair day. The movie benefits from featuring strong females and characters and performers from the Latino culture.

Be sure to tell kids that the thumb-robots were inspired by drawings writer/ director Robert Rodriguez did when he was 12, and ask them to come up with some pictures of things they'd like to put into a movie someday. Good topics for family discussion include how to know which secrets to share, the challenges of siblinghood (a two-generation challenge in the Cortez family) and the movie's conclusion that spy work is easy compared to keeping a family together, which is not only more of a challenge, but more important.

CONNECTIONS: The first sequel is also fun, but skip the third in the series, which loses the story in the 3-D special effects.

SEABISCUIT

2003, 141 min, PG-13, 12 and up
Dir: Gary Ross. Jeff Bridges, Tobey Maguire, Chris Cooper
Based on Laura Hillenbrand's best-selling book of the same name, "Seabiscuit" depicts the equine celebrity who came to fame as the too-small, ill-tempered horse who never should have won yet somehow managed to defeat the greatest racehorses of his day. The film places his popularity squarely in the context of the times, tying each race that he won (and indeed those that he lost) to the ability of the working folks of the day to survive the Great Depression and to believe in second chances.

"Red" Pollard (Tobey Maguire) is the too-tall jockey whose family, made destitute during the early days of the Great Depression, gives him to a horse racer who will give him his livelihood by putting him up on his horses. Pollard, full of rage and rapidly becoming too tall for a jockey, picks up any ride he can and prizefights to survive. Charles Howard (a jowly Jeff Bridges) is the bicycle salesman turned successful car dealer realizing the American Dream in the great new markets of the West Coast. When his young son dies in an accident and his wife leaves in despair, he wanders over the border and meets the understanding Marcela (Elizabeth Banks) who gets him riding again and re-engages him in life. With his new wife and desire to own racehorses, Howard seeks out a trainer with a good heart and an understanding of horses, whom he finds in the taciturn, itinerant cowhand, Tom Smith (the ever-mesmerizing Chris Cooper).

Smith tames and heals horses while introducing Howard to the movie's theme: "you don't throw a life away just because it's a little banged up." Smith finds Howard his racehorse when he sees fifteen-hands of angry outcast, Seabiscuit, who has spent the last years losing schooling races to other horses to build up their confidence. On seeing the rearing and biting misfit, most jockeys flee from the scene. However, in a nice shot juxtaposing the antisocial Seabiscuit and the angry Pollard, Smith finds his jockey and the team of people who need and believe in second chances is complete, and our heroes are ready to become champions.

CONNECTIONS: Real-life champion jockey Gary Stevens adds a great deal of class and heart as jockey George Woolf. An earlier movie, *The Story of Seabiscuit*, stars Shirley Temple and the son of the real Seabiscuit playing his father.

THE SOLID GOLD CADILLAC

1956, 99 min, NR, b&w, 10 and up
Dir: Richard Quine. Judy Holliday, Paul Douglas
At the annual shareholders meeting of a company led by corrupt managers and directors, a young woman named Laura Partridge (Judy Holliday) gets up to ask a few questions, starting with what the executives do to earn their enormous salaries. The executives decide to neutralize her by giving her a job. They tell her to communicate with the small shareholders, and they think they'll never hear from her again. Then she goes to Washington to tell the honest former chief executive (Paul Douglas), now a Defense Department official, about her concerns, and they get caught up in a scandal. Meanwhile, the company's management is so incompetent that it drives one of its own divisions out of business. Laura Partridge finds out that anyone who can ask questions can insist on answers.

If you added a couple of zeros to the numbers, this story could have come from today's business section. Funny and romantic, with terrific performances from Holliday and Douglas, this comedy reminds us of the power of asking questions and seeking the truth. The co-author of the play was George S. Kaufman, but the ending feels more like Frank Capra.

CONNECTIONS: The wonderfully gravelly voice performing the narration is George Burns.

SPIRITED AWAY

2002, 132 min, PG, 10 and up
Dir: Hayao Miyazaki. Suzanne Pleshette
A young girl whose parents have been turned into pigs must rescue them with a journey through a wonderland populated by strange and marvelous creatures in this rapturously imaginative animated film. She will have to discover new levels of

courage, determination, empathy, and loyalty within herself to rescue her parents and the friends she makes on her journey.

CONNECTIONS: Families who enjoy this movie will also enjoy *My Neighbor Totoro, Little Nemo: Adventures in Slumberland*, and *Kiki's Delivery Service*.

A TALE OF TWO CITIES

1935, 128 min, NR, b&w, 10 and up
Dir: Jack Conway. Ronald Colman, Reginald Owen, Basil Rathbone
In this Charles Dickens story set during the French Revolution, Ronald Colman plays Sidney Carton, a British lawyer who is disillusioned and detached, settling for the friendship of the woman he loves when she marries another man. He finds meaning by taking the place of her husband, who has been sentenced to die by the guillotine because he is part of the aristocracy. He walks to his death holding the hand of another prisoner, saying, "It is a far, far better thing I do than I have ever done; it is a far, far better rest I go to than I have ever known."

TIME BANDITS

1981, 110 min, PG, 8 and up
Dir: Terry Gilliam. Sean Connery, David Warner
One of the most wildly imaginative and visually entertaining films ever made, this is the story of an English boy whisked through time by six dwarfs who have stolen a map showing the holes in creation. Their plan is to use the holes to go back in time to steal treasure. They visit Agamemnon (Sean Connery), Napoleon (Ian Holm), the Titanic, and Robin Hood (John Cleese), chased by the Supreme Being (God) and by the Evil Genius (the devil). NOTE: The individual episodes are uneven. The director and co-scriptwriter are graduates of Monty Python, and like some of their other work, it lurches from inspired lunacy to lame misfires. The most serious of the latter is the very end, in which the little boy is left alone after his foolish parents are incinerated. This may upset younger children, but those who can handle fairy-tale (or Roald Dahl)-style gore will enjoy it.

WILLIE WONKA AND THE CHOCOLATE FACTORY

1971, 91 min, G, 6 and up
Dir: Mel Stuart. Gene Wilder, Jack Albertson
This is a lavish and colorful musical based on the classic book *Charlie and the Chocolate Factory* by Roald Dahl. Gene Wilder has the title role as the world's most successful (and eccentric) candy-maker. Charlie is the poor but honest boy

who wins one of five golden tickets for a tour of the chocolate factory and brings his beloved grandfather along. The other four winners are obnoxious and spoiled children: a gum-chewer, a television-addict, a glutton, and a selfish rich girl. Each of them is felled by some imaginative catastrophe, leaving Charlie to win the biggest prize of all.

CONNECTIONS: Rock band Veruca Salt is named after one of the characters in this story. Kids who enjoy the movie will want to read Dahl's sequel, *Charlie and the Great Glass Elevator.*

ACTIVITIES: Make some candy from scratch.

SEE ALSO:

All the President's Men Two junior reporters with persistence and determination insist on following the story of a minor burglary to the heart of the Oval Office, despite the skepticism of their editors and colleagues.

The Hunt for Red October A CIA analyst with no field experience risks his career and his life to prove a Soviet submarine captain is seeking asylum in the United States.

Julia A writer is drawn into the resistance effort in pre-WWII Germany by an old friend, and finds within herself unexpected courage and commitment.

A League of Their Own Women given the opportunity to do what they love and excel at (play baseball) find it gives them self-respect and dignity. Their team manager, an alcoholic former player, is inspired by them to help them do their best.

Malcolm X A young man develops a larger vision of life through education and goes on to lead and inspire.

The Red Badge of Courage A young soldier learns courage does not mean lack of fear; it means not letting the fear stop him from doing what needs to be done.

Sergeant York A soldier uses the techniques he learned at home on the farm to capture enemy soldiers.

The Wizard of Oz The characters all learn what they thought they needed was already inside them.

8

UNDERSTANDING EMOTIONS

*"Lord, teach us to take our hearts and look them in the face,
however difficult it might be."*
DOROTHY L. SAYERS

A popular 1997 book, *Emotional Intelligence* by Daniel P. Goleman, makes a compelling argument that "EQ," or emotional intelligence, is a more important predictor of a person's success, both professionally and personally, than what is commonly thought of as "intelligence," meaning mathematical and verbal ability. The stories and the characters in movies provide an ideal vehicle for families to use to develop emotional intelligence through the discussion of feelings and motivations.

First, good movies bring us believable characters in interesting situations, so we get to see the broadest possible range of people facing the broadest possible range of circumstances. Movies can show us variations and extremes of emotion that would take several lifetimes to experience firsthand.

Second, and even more important, is the opportunity movies give us to talk about the most personal and sensitive issues in impersonal terms. It is easier for everyone, and especially for young kids and teenagers, to talk about what is going on with the people on the screen than it is to talk about what is going on inside them. A three-year-old can tell you that Big Bird feels scared and lonely and a teenager can tell you that James Dean feels scared and lonely when it is just too hard to acknowledge or admit those feelings in himself. Talking about the people in the movies will help them develop an emotional vocabulary that will lead them to talk about people in the news, then people they know, and then, if you're lucky, themselves.

Families can learn from the movies how to identify emotions in themselves and in others, developing a valuable approach for dealing with real life issues. Parents watching with very young children can help them by asking questions about what the characters are feeling. Children will learn not to be afraid of feelings like jealousy, anger, and fear; accepting those feelings is the first step to moving beyond them. They will also learn about the power of analogy and making connections, an important starting point for abstract reasoning.

Older kids can learn about some of the more subtle psychological defense mechanisms, like displacement, projection, and denial, as well as about interactions like enabling behavior and about good and, bad ways of resolving arguments.

The best screenwriters have enormous psychological insight. We can see Paula's sense of her value, her sanity, and even her self disintegrating as her husband undermines her sanity in **Gaslight**. Watch Judith Traherne in **Dark Victory** going through Elizabeth Kubler-Ross stages in accepting her terminal illness, long before Kubler-Ross wrote about them. In **Ball of Fire**, a professor of psychology correctly deduces that Sugarpuss O'Shea really wanted to marry Bertram Potts when she "mistakenly" returns the huge diamond from her gangster boyfriend, instead of the ring that Potts gave her, in what we might term a classic "Freudian slip."

In general, movies have not done as well in portraying mental illness and its treatment, though there are some memorable exceptions.

Keep in mind that no matter what else is going on, no matter what the quest is or whether the story is a comedy, musical, adventure, or drama, most movies are really about characters on a psychological journey. At the end, the heroes almost always learn something about themselves or about life, and it often enables them to accomplish some goal or to become close to someone in a way that would not have otherwise been possible.

Dark Victory

1939, 106 min, NR, b&w, 12 and up
Dir: Edmund Goulding. Bette Davis, George Brent, Humphrey Bogart, Geraldine Fitzgerald
PLOT: Judith Traheme (Bette Davis) is an impetuous and headstrong heiress who lives life with furious energy. Her life revolves around parties and horses. She sees Dr. Frederick Steele (George Brent) for her headaches and dizzy spells, and he tells her she has a brain tumor. He operates, and she believes she is cured. Her soul is cured as well, because she and the doctor have fallen in love, and for the first time she feels genuine happiness and peace.

Then she learns Frederick and her friends have kept the truth from her; her prognosis is negative, and she has very little time left. She breaks the engagement, telling Frederick he only wants to marry her out of pity. At first, she returns to her old life, trying to bury her fears and loneliness in a frenzy of parties. She is terribly sad, and when Michael, her stableman (Humphrey Bogart), tells her she should allow herself to see that Frederick really loves her, and take whatever happiness she can, in whatever time she has left, she knows he is right. She marries Frederick, and has blissful months with him on his farm in Vermont before she dies, having had a lifetime of love and happiness in their time together.

DISCUSSION: This classic melodrama is also almost an encyclopedia of emotions. At first, Judith is in denial about her illness and about her feelings. She shows displaced anger when she breaks her engagement to Frederick. Most important to discuss with kids, though, is that she makes the classic mistake of confusing pleasure and happiness. The contrast between her frantic efforts to find distraction through parties ("horses, hats, and food") and fast living, and the peace and joy of her time in Vermont with love and meaningful work (it's her husband's meaningful work, but this was the 1930s) is exceptionally well-portrayed by Davis and by director Goulding, This is one of the most important emotional distinctions for kids to learn, especially teenagers.

PROFANITY: None.

NUDITY/SEXUAL REFERENCES: None.

ALCOHOL/DRUG ABUSE: Judith drinks and smokes too much before she learns what really matters.

VIOLENCE/SCARINESS: No violence, but terminal illness may scare some kids.

TOLERANCE/DIVERSITY ISSUES: Class issues in the relationship of Michael and Judith.

QUESTIONS FOR FAMILIES:

• Why is it so hard for Judith to find happiness, even before she learns she is sick?

• How can you tell she does not understand herself very well?

• Why does she break her engagement with Frederick?

• What does Michael tell her that makes her change her mind?

- Why doesn't she tell Frederick she is close to the end, sending him away instead?

CONNECTIONS: Bette Davis and George Brent made a number of movies together, including *The Great Lie* and *The Old Maid* (also directed by Goulding), *In This Our Life*, and **Jezebel**. Be sure to watch for future president Ronald Reagan as a "member of [her] horsey set."

Gaslight

1944, 114 min, NR, b&w, 10 and up
Dir: George Cuhor. Ingrid Bergman, Charles Boyer, Joseph Cotten, Angela Lansbury
PLOT: Paula Alquist (Ingrid Bergman) falls in love with Gregory Anton (Charles Boyer), a musician, and once they are married, he persuades her to move into the house she lived in as a child, which has been closed since her aunt was murdered there. At first very happy, Paula soon becomes confused and insecure. While Gregory appears to be solicitous and caring, in reality he is cutting her off from all contact with anyone but himself, and making her doubt herself and her sanity. He convinces her she is always losing things, she sees things that are not there, she is unstable and untrustworthy. Every night he leaves to play the piano in an apartment he has rented, and while he is gone the gaslights flicker and she hears mysterious noises from the attic. Gregory persuades her that these are just her delusions.

Just as Paula's fragile hold on reality is about to break, she is visited by Brian Cameron (Joseph Cotten) of Scotland Yard. With his help, she learns Gregory is using an assumed name, he is a thief, and he had known her late aunt, a famous singer. He married Paula just to get into the house, so he can find the missing jewels he could not get the night he murdered Paula's aunt.

Gregory is captured just as he finds the jewels. Brian ties him up and leaves him with Paula while he calls the police. Gregory tries to persuade Paula to cut the ropes and let him go, but she explains she is insane, as he told her, so how could she help anyone? He must admit she has been completely sane all along. She can no longer be manipulated by him. He goes off to jail. Paula and Brian have defeated him.

DISCUSSION: This classic of suspense is a good way to begin a conversation about vulnerability and manipulation. Gregory is almost able to drive Paula mad by making her think she is mad already. By cutting her off from any outside reality, by coolly denying what she sees and hears for herself, by telling her over and over again she is helpless and incompetent, she begins to turn into the person he tells her that she is.

PROFANITY: None.
NUDITY/SEXUAL REFERENCES: None.
ALCOHOL/DRUG ABUSE: None.
VIOLENCE/SCARINESS: Tension and suspense.
TOLERANCE/DIVERSITY ISSUES: None.
QUESTIONS FOR FAMILIES:

- "Gaslighting" someone is now an accepted psychiatric term, based on this movie and its predecessor, the play Angel Street. What do you think it means?

- How does Gregory get Paula to doubt herself?

- How does the director help the viewer get some sense of Paula's feelings of disorientation and doubt?

- Can someone make another person doubt him or herself as Gregory did? Can someone affect other people positively along the same lines, helping them to believe in themselves? How?

CONNECTIONS: Some of the same themes and feelings, in a more contemporary setting, are found in Alfred Hitchcock's Dial M for Murder (1954), with Grace Kelly as the wife whose husband (Ray Milland) plans to murder her, and in Midnight Lace (1960), with Doris Day and Rex Harrison. In Ticket to Heaven (1981), a movie about a bright young man who becomes a member of a religious cult, the techniques of mind control cult leaders use correspond to some of Gregory's tactics for making Paula uncertain about reality.

Bergman won an Oscar for this performance, and the movie also won one for art direction. Angela Lansbury, in her first movie appearance; was nominated for an Oscar for her performance as the insolent maid.

How the Grinch Stole Christmas

2001, 104 min, PG, 6 and up
Dir: Ron Howard. Jim Carrey
This is the Dr. Seuss story about a Christmas-hating Grinch who tries to steal Christmas from the Christmas-loving Whos by taking all of their presents and decorations but learns that Christmas is in their hearts, not under their trees. Jim Carrey and the Grinch were made for each other. In a miracle of costume and

make-up design and an even bigger miracle of acting, Carrey's extraordinarily expressive face and body make the Grinch seem hilarious, touching, and a little scary all at the same time. Newcomer Taylor Momsen, as Cindy Lou Who, is adorable without being sugary. She confesses to having her own doubts about Christmas.

DISCUSSION: Cindy Lou can tell that the Grinch is lonely and hurt, and much less scary than he would like to appear. Just as the Grinch is less grouchy than he would like us to believe, Cindy Lou is less sweet than the Whos want to think they are. It turns out that both of them know more about the Christmas spirit than anyone else in Whoville.

Whoville, as imagined by production designer Michael Corenblith, is the most breathtakingly magical setting since Dorothy landed in Munchkinland. Every detail of the town is perfectly Seuss-ian. The structures suspend the laws of gravity, with no stright lines or right angles. Instead, there are a fantastic series of archways, bridges, stairs and spirals. Whoville clothes and hairstyles echo these shapes and then are topped with candy canes, cups of hot chocolate, and frosted cookies. The narration by Anthony Hopkins is superb.

PROFANITY: None.
NUDITY/SEXUAL REFERENCES: Brief crude humor.
ALCOHOL/DRUG ABUSE: None.
VIOLENCE/SCARINESS: Mild comic peril.
TOLERANCE/DIVERSITY ISSUES: No people of color in Whoville.
QUESTIONS FOR FAMILIES:

- Why is it so easy to forget the simple pleasures of the winter holidays?

- How does it feel to be teased about being different?

- The Grinch often does things that he thinks will make him feel better. Do they work? Do they help him forget his loneliness? Why not? Why doesn't being bad feel as good as you might think?

CONNECTIONS: Families who enjoy this movie should also see the classic animated version, with the unforgettable voice performance of Boris Karloff and the song (briefly reprised in this movie) "You're a Mean One, Mr. Grinch."

Now, Voyager

1942, 117 min, NR b&w, 10 and up
Dir. Irving Rapper. Bette Davis, Paul Henreid, Claude Rains, Gladys Cooper
PLOT: Charlotte Vale (Bette Davis) is the repressed and depressed daughter of an imperious mother (Gladys Cooper), head of a wealthy and socially prominent Boston family. Miserably unhappy and insecure, she spends much of her time in her room, making carved boxes and sneaking forbidden cigarettes. A sympathetic sister-in-law introduces her to Dr. Jaquith (Claude Rains), an understanding psychiatrist. Under his care, at his sanitarium, she begins to develop some sense of herself as worthy, but is still terribly insecure when she departs on a cruise ship for a rest before returning home.

On the ship, she meets Jerry Durrance (Paul Henreid), an architect. At first awkward and self-deprecating, she begins to bloom under his attention, and they fall in love. Jerry is married to a woman whose health is too fragile for him to consider divorce. They say good-bye, and Charlotte returns home. Her mother is as tyrannical as ever, insisting Charlotte must do as she says or she will refuse to support her. Charlotte meets Elliott Livingston (John Loder), a kind businessman who wants to marry her, and her mother approves. But when she sees Jerry again, she knows it is impossible for her to marry Elliott, and turns him down. This so infuriates her mother she has a heart attack and dies.

Overcome with guilt, Charlotte returns to Dr. Jaquith. At the sanitarium, she meets a troubled young girl, Tina, Jerry's daughter. In reaching out to Tina, she finds her own strength and sense of purpose. When Charlotte goes home, Tina moves in with her. Jerry at first wants to take Tina away, thinking it is too much of an imposition, but Charlotte persuades him it is a way for them to be close, telling him, "Don't let's ask for the moon; we have the stars."
DISCUSSION: This movie has a lot of appeal for highly romantic teenagers of both sexes, and for those who are interested in the dynamics and impact of dysfunctional families. Charlotte's mother is completely self-obsessed, consumed with power, incapable of compassion, much less love, for her daughter. As Dr. Jaquith says, "Sometimes tyranny masquerades as mother love." Never hesitating to make it clear Charlotte was unwanted, Mrs. Vale demands Charlotte make up for the burden she inflicted by being born by giving in to her every demand. It is also clear there is no way for Charlotte to be successful in pleasing her mother. Dependent and fearful at the beginning, she has her mother's contempt. As we see at the end, her independence and self-respect are much more threatening to

her mother, who literally cannot survive Charlotte's assertion of her right to her own life.

In one sense, when Charlotte stands up for herself Mrs. Vale as ogre disappears like the Wicked Witch of the West doused with water or the Queen of Hearts when Alice tells her she is only a card. In another sense, Mrs. Vale's attack is the ultimate booby trap for Charlotte, who must then grapple with the guilt she feels for "causing" her mother's death. Both Mrs. Vale and Jerry's off-screen wife assert what F. Scott Fitzgerald called "the tyranny of sickness" or what Dr. Jaquith might call passive-aggressive behavior, using powerlessness as the ultimate method of exercising power. This is a very important form of emotional blackmail to be able to recognize.

The title of the movie is from a line by Walt Whitman that Dr. Jaquith gives to Charlotte: "Now voyager, sail forth to seek and find." Charlotte learns not to be afraid of what she will find, to risk getting hurt, to risk allowing herself to be known, to risk caring about someone else.

It is also worthwhile for kids to see Charlotte must love herself before she is able to love someone else, and just as Jerry's love helps her to bloom, she is able to do the same for Tina. Charlotte tells Jerry, "When you told me you loved me, I was so proud, I could have walked into a den of lions; in fact I did, and the lions didn't hurt me." Just as important, helping Tina is the most enduring "cure" for her sense of being powerless and without purpose, and far better than marrying a man she did not love.

These days, the decision made by Charlotte and Jerry not to stay together seems almost quaint; we tend to think everyone should have both the moon and the stars. Their sense of sacrifice and duty is worth talking about as well.

PROFANITY: None.
NUDITY/SEXUAL REFERENCES: None.
ALCOHOL/DRUG ABUSE: Social drinking; lots of cigarette smoking. Jerry lights two cigarettes, then gives one to Charlotte, a gesture that is highly symbolic and an icon of movie romanticism.
VIOLENCE/SCARINESS: Emotional violence only; Charlotte's mother collapses and dies in the middle of a confrontation.
TOLERANCE/DIVERSITY ISSUES: None.
QUESTIONS FOR FAMILIES:

• Why did Charlotte have such a hard time feeling good about herself?

- Why did Jerry and Charlotte decide not to see each other anymore?

- Why did seeing Jerry make Charlotte change her mind about marrying Elliott?

- What did Charlotte's mother want from Charlotte? Was that fair?

- What should Charlotte have said to her mother?

- Why did helping Tina make Charlotte feel better?

CONNECTIONS: Bette Davis and Claude Rains appeared together two years later in another movie about love, sacrifice, and lessons learned, *Mr. Skeffington*. She plays a self-centered and flighty woman who marries a man she does not love in order to protect her brother, discovering decades later how much she cares for her husband.

SEE ALSO:
All My Sons A mother refuses to acknowledge her son's death in the war (and her husband's complicity) in this example of denial.
All the Way Home A young widow and her son feel many conflicting emotions as they try to cope with their loss.
Ball of Fire A showgirl's Freudian slip reveals that the man she is marrying is not the man she loves.
Snow White Jealousy tortures the queen so badly she is willing to risk everything to destroy Snow White.
The Treasure of the Sierra Madre Dobbs projects his greed and aggression onto his partners.

9

LOSS

"Give sorrow words; the grief that does not speak whispers the o'er fraught heart, and bids it break."
WILLIAM SHAKESPEARE

As parents, we are so anxious to protect our precious children from loss we sometimes make the mistake of making them think we do not recognize or permit those feelings, minimizing the pain they feel at the loss of a favorite toy or beloved pet. However, as Judith Viorst points out in her book *Necessary Losses*, each of us must lose precious connections and beliefs in order to grow. Parents cannot prevent loss, so we must teach children important lessons about how to respond to it.

Viorst also wrote a sensitive children's book, *The Tenth Good Thing About Barney*, about a child coping with the death of a cat. The mourning child's family respects his feelings and helps him to focus on the good things Barney brought and will continue to bring to those who loved him.

If at all possible, it is much better to talk about these issues before a child is confronted with a devastating loss. Films like these can help families begin to raise the subject in a general way, to help kids develop an emotional vocabulary that will be in place if they or anyone they know must experience loss.

All the Way Home

1963, 103 min, NR, b&w, 12 and up
Dir: Alex Segal. Robert Preston, Jean Simmons, Pat Hingle
PLOT: Set in Tennessee in 1815, this quiet, beautiful movie is a story about Jay (Robert Preston) and Mary (Jean Simmons), who are deeply in love, though she disapproves of his drinking, and he thinks she is too rigid in her piety and primness about sex. They are loving parents to their little boy, Rufus, give him com-

fort and guidance, and enjoy him very much. When Jay is killed in an accident, Mary and Rufus must try to make sense of the tragedy and find a way to go on.

DISCUSSION: This quiet, deeply touching movie is based on James Agee's novel *A Death in the Family*, and its adaptation for the theater by Tad Mosel, both awarded the Pulitzer Prize. It is filled with memorable characters and moments of great insight and poignancy. Jay is a warm and wise father. In the first scene, Jay and Rufus enjoy a Charlie Chaplin movie together. As they walk home together, we feel their closeness and the pleasure they feel in spending time with each other. When Rufus is shy in the presence of an elderly relative, Jay gently shows him he can talk to her.

Mary is loving and devoted, but finds it very hard to talk about her feelings, and especially about sex. When Jay tells Mary it is time to let Rufus know they are going to have another baby, all she can manage to say is they are expecting a surprise from heaven. After Jay's death, Mary has to deal with Rufus's grief, as well as her own. She has to find the best of Jay within herself, so she can give that to Rufus.

Children may be especially disconcerted by Mary's reaction to the news of Jay's accident, before she learns he has been killed. She goes through a variety of emotions while she waits with her aunt for news. She laughs over a story Jay had told her, nervously checks the teakettle to see if it has boiled yet, prepares a downstairs room in case he is well enough to be nursed at home, and prays for his life. Discuss with children and teens the way the stress of uncertainty and the unwillingness to believe her husband is dead produce this seemingly contradictory and even uncaring reaction.

PROFANITY: None.

NUDITY/SEXUAL REFERENCES: Although the references are so tame by today's standards, they would hardly qualify for a PG rating, one of the key issues in the movie is the contrast between Jay's openness and Mary's primness. After Jay's death, Mary realizes she has to be able to be for Rufus what Jay would have been, and in the very last scene she puts his hand on her belly and tells him that is where the new baby is growing.

ALCOHOL/DRUG ABUSE: Jay and his brother drink. Mary disapproves, but after she gets the news of Jay's death, she takes a drink.

VIOLENCE/SCARINESS: No violence, but scary (off-screen) death of the father.

TOLERANCE/DIVERSITY ISSUES: Reflecting the era in which the story is set, Rufus tells Jay the big boys teased him by telling him he has a "nigger name."

Jay comforts him, and tells him never to use that word, because it is a hurtful word. The word he uses is "colored." Jay tells Rufus "big boys don't cry."

QUESTIONS FOR FAMILIES:

* What do Mary and Jay disagree on? How can you tell?

* Are those differences part of what makes them attractive to each other?

* Why does Rufus tell the minister and his uncle they can't sit in his father's chair?

* How does Mary become more like Jay after his death? Why?

CONNECTIONS: Robert Preston is the star of **The Music Man**. Jean Simmons appears as Estella in David Lean's version of *Great Expectations* and as Miss Havisham in a later production made for television, and as Sister Sarah in **Guys and Dolls**. Veteran character actor Pat Hingle played the father in **Splendor in the Grass**, and Commissioner Gordon in the Batman movies.

Houseboat

1958, 112 min, NR, 10 and up
Dir: Melville Shavelson. Cary Grant, Sophia Loren
PLOT: Diplomat Tom Winston (Cary Grant) returns to Washington, D.C., following the death of his estranged wife. His three children, David, Robert, and Elizabeth, have been staying with his wife's sister, Caroline (Martha Hyer). They are hurt and resentful. He takes them to an outdoor orchestra concert, and Robert wanders off and meets Cinzia (Sophia Loren), the daughter of a visiting conductor. She has also wandered off, in search of adventure and companionship. When she brings Robert back, Tom sees that Robert likes her, and impulsively offers her a job as a housekeeper. She agrees, because traveling with her father has been boring and lonely.

David causes an accident that destroys their home, so the only place they can live is an old houseboat owned by Angelo, a handyman (Harry Guardino). They settle in there with Cinzia. It turns out she can neither cook nor do laundry, but the children adore her, and Tom warms to her, too. With her help, he reaches out to his children, and they reach out to him.

Caroline tells Tom her marriage is ending, and that she has always loved him. On the way to a country club dance, a tipsy male friend of Caroline's swats Cinzia on her bottom, and she tosses wine in his face. Caroline, annoyed at Tom for sticking up for Cinzia (and jealous), leaves for the dance without him. Tom invites Cinzia to the dance, and she accepts, despite her promise to go fishing with David. At the dance, Tom proposes to Caroline, but then, as he dances with Cinzia, he realizes she is the one he loves, and she loves him, too.

At first, the children are terribly upset and feel betrayed by both of them. Cinzia, unwilling to make them unhappy, runs back to her father, apologizing, "I've learned many things, including how hard it is to be a father." Tom finds her there, but she refuses to go back with him. "Your children are your friends again, and that is the most important thing." He tells her being their friend is not the most important thing; being their father is. They get married. The children, at the last minute, join in.

DISCUSSION: This is a warm, romantic comedy that is exceptionally perceptive and sensitive about the feelings of the children. It does a nice job of showing that David's truculence and petty theft are due to his feelings of vulnerability and loss.

In one scene, Tom at first tries to show David how to fish, then, when David says he feels incompetent, Tom asks him for advice, and they are able to talk for the first time about his mother's death. Tom shows David nothing is ever really lost, and David is able to let Tom know he fears losing Tom, too. After this talk, David feels safer, and confesses to Angelo he took Angelo's knife. (Angelo is very understanding.) Robert's reaction to the loss of his mother is to withdraw, playing mournfully on his harmonica as his only means of expression. Elizabeth reacts by sleeping in her father's room every night, and becomes very upset when she learns will not be possible after he and Cinzia get married.

This is also a rare movie that deals honestly with the issue of children's reaction to remarriage. Even though they love Cinzia, the children do not like sharing her with Tom, or sharing Tom with her. Children who have been in this situation will be grateful for the opportunity to see they are not alone.

PROFANITY: None.
NUDITY/SEXUAL REFERENCES: References to adultery.
ALCOHOL/DRUG ABUSE: A friend drinks too much and behaves badly; jokes about falling off the wagon.
VIOLENCE/SCARINESS: None.
TOLERANCE/DIVERSITY ISSUES: Differences in class and culture.
QUESTIONS FOR FAMILIES:

- How do each of the children show they are hurt and sad? How do each of them show when they are beginning to feel better?

- What can you tell about Caroline's feelings when she gives the dress to Cinzia?

- Why does Cinzia tell Angelo the story about the necklace, and why does it make him leave without her?

- Was Cinzia wrong to leave for the dance when she had promised to go fishing with David?

CONNECTIONS: This movie has two lovely songs, "Almost in Your Arms" (nominated for an Oscar) and "Bing Bang Boom."
ACTIVITIES: Just about every child plays some kind of call and response game like the "Yes Sir, You Sir" game Tom plays with his children. There is one that begins "Who Took the Cookies from the Cookie Jar?" Another one is called "Concentration" and involves a series of claps accompanying the listing of items in selected categories. See if your children know any. If so, play one with them. If not, teach them one. Take them to an outdoor concert, like the one in the movie (the site of the concert in the movie is now the Kennedy Center in Washington, D.C.). Try playing the harmonica.

Lilo and Stitch

2002, 85 min, PG, 7 and up
Dir: Chris Sanders. Ving Rhames, David Ogden Stiers
PLOT: The story opens on some far-away planet with all kinds of monstrous-looking creatures. One of them, a scientist, has been experimenting with genetics, and has created an indestructible destruction machine called 626 in the form of a mischievous-looking little blue guy. The scientist is thrown in jail, but the experiment escapes and races off to a planet they refer to as "E-Arth." So, the scientist and an expert on Earth are sent after him to capture him with a minimum of fuss.
    626 lands in Hawaii and disguises himself as a dog. He is adopted by a tiny little girl named Lilo who is grieving the loss of her parents. She names him Stitch and teaches him that even a creature designed to destroy can learn to create.
DISCUSSION: The story is nothing new, but the Hawaiian location and gorgeous visuals give it a fresh feeling. Instead of the usual wasp-waisted Disney heroines with impossibly big hair, we get attractive but believable-looking Nani, Lilo's sister, who is struggling to grow up quickly so that she can care for Lilo the way her parents did. Lilo's passion for Elvis Presley means that instead of girls looking up at the stars and trilling ballads about their dreams we get a bouncy score of favorites like "Heartbreak Hotel," "Hound Dog," "All Shook Up," and of course, "Blue Hawaii." The score also features Elvis hits "Can't Help Falling in

Love," sung by a chorus of Hawaiian children and "Burning Love" sung by country superstar Wynonna Judd.

Lilo is irresistibly adorable and her relationship with her sister is a believable mixture of affection, resentment, and connection. Both are deeply affected by the loss of their parents and torn between fearing another loss and just wanting to get it over with. Ving Rhames adds just the right note of wry authority to his role as the social worker with a surprising past, and Jason Scott Lee is fine as the friend who would like to be more. There is some very funny dialogue, especially the description of Earth as an endangered species preserve—the endangered species is mosquitos, and humans are just kept around to feed them!

PROFANITY: None.
NUDITY/SEXUAL REFERENCES: None.
ALCOHOL/DRUG ABUSE: None.
VIOLENCE/SCARINESS: Some tense scenes and peril, discussion of loss of parents.
TOLERANCE/DIVERSITY ISSUES: Diverse characters, strong women.
QUESTIONS FOR FAMILIES:

- What do you think about Lilo's definition of a family: "No one gets left behind"?

- Why didn't the other girls want to play with Lilo?

- Are there things that Lilo and Nani could have talked about with each other that would have made them feel better?

- Why didn't Stitch stay the destructive monster he was designed to be?

- Did anything surprise you in the scenes at the end that showed what happened to Lilo and Stitch and Nani?

CONNECTIONS: Learn more about Hawaii and about Elvis!

My Life as a Dog

1987, 103 min, PG, 12 and up
Dir: Lasse Hallstrom. Anton Glanzelius (Swedish with subtitles)
PLOT: Ingemar is a twelve-year-old boy growing up in 1950s Sweden who goes to live with his aunt and uncle in Smaland while his mother is dying of tuberculosis. In the small town of Smaland he meets an assortment of eccentric and

delightful characters who help him adjust to his new life without his mother, brother, and his beloved dog Sickan (he has never known his father).

Ingemar meets an athletic girl who loves to box but who also develops a crush on Ingemar. Berit, the most beautiful woman in town, befriends Ingemar and asks him to chaperon her while she models for the town artist. Ulla and Gunar, his aunt and uncle, adopt Ingemar and help him find family and normalcy during a traumatic period in his life.

DISCUSSION: Told from the perspective of the child, this is an affecting and authentic portrayal of a young boy's attempt to understand the adult world. The director shows us Ingemar's world through a child's eyes, so the smallest events and the largest are presented as equally important. He does not know enough to be able to distinguish ordinary behavior from eccentricity, or to fully understand why a nude model would want a young boy as a chaperon or why a dying man would be so interested in underwear catalogs. His acceptance of everyone he meets is part of his appeal.

Ingemar does not have enough experience of the world to be able to understand what his mother's symptoms mean, or to wonder if she will die. Because no one told him how ill she was, he blames himself for her death. He does not have the opportunity to express his grief, which adds to his feeling of disorientation and his identification with a dog who is circling the globe in a space capsule. The only comfort he (and the audience) have is the sense that his ability to form relationships with the new people in his life will be a source of strength and happiness to him in the future.

PROFANITY: None.

NUDITY/SEXUAL REFERENCES: Brief, nonsexual nudity in an artist's studio; Ingemar's brother tells a bunch of kids how babies are born; girl laments the growth of her breasts, which will make it impossible for her to pass as a boy so that she can participate in sports.

ALCOHOL/DRUG ABUSE: None.

VIOLENCE/SCARINESS: There is some tension when Ingemar and his mother argue and she breaks down crying and tries to hit and push him away.

TOLERANCE/DIVERSITY ISSUES: A girl struggles with limits based on gender.

QUESTIONS FOR FAMILIES:

- Why does Ingemar always say it's important to "compare"? Why do you think Ingemar compares himself to Laika the space dog?

- Why does Ingemar tell us he wishes he told his mom everything? Does he blame himself for not having told her everything?

- Why doesn't anyone tell Ingemar that Sickan is dead? Do you think waiting to tell him made it easier or harder to deal with when he did learn the truth?

Old Yeller

1957, 83 min, G, 8 and up
Dir: Robert Stevenson. Dorothy McGuire, Fess Parker, Tommy Kirk, Kevin Corcoran
PLOT: In 1869 Texas, Jim Coates (Fess Parker) says good-bye to his family as he leaves for three months to sell their cattle. He tells his older son, Travis (Tommy Kirk), to take care of his mother, Katie (Dorothy McGuire), and his younger brother, Arliss (Kevin Corcoran). Travis asks his father to bring him back a horse. His father says what he needs is a dog, but Travis does not want one. "Not a dog in this world like old Belle was."

A stray dog comes to their farm and scares the horse, knocking over Travis and knocking down the fence. Travis throws rocks at the dog, saying, "That dog better not come around here while I got a gun." The dog comes back, and Arliss "claims" him, over Travis's objections. Later, Old Yeller saves Arliss from a bear. Travis admits, "He's a heap more dog than I ever figured him for." Yeller turns out to be an outstanding dog for farming and hunting.

Old Yeller fights a wolf that was about to attack Katie. She insists he be tied up, because the wolf would not have attacked unless he had hydrophobia, and Yeller may have been infected. When Yeller becomes vicious, Travis knows he must shoot him.

Jim returns as Travis and his friend Elsbeth are burying Old Yeller. Jim tells him the loss of Yeller is "not a thing you can forget. Maybe not a thing you want to forget…Now and then, for no good reason a man can figure out, life will just haul off and knock him flat. Slam him agin' the ground so hard, it seems like all his insides is busted. It's not all like that. A lot of it's mighty fine. You can't afford to waste the good part worrying about the bad. That makes it all bad…Sayin' it's one thing and feelin' it's another. I'll tell you a trick that's sometimes a big help. Start looking around for something good to take the place of the bad. As a general rule, you can find it."

Jim has brought the horse Travis wanted, but says, "Reckon you ain't in no shape to take pleasure in him yet." Travis goes back to the house, where he sees

Yeller's pup, and knows that he won't replace Old Yeller, but will be as good a friend as his father was.

DISCUSSION: Jim's talk with Travis is a model of parental wisdom, understanding, and patience. He accepts and validates Travis's feelings completely, and does not try to minimize or talk him out of them. (Contrast that with Elsbeth, who tries to comfort Travis by encouraging him to "come to like the pup.") Instead of telling him what to do, he says, "I'll tell you a trick that's sometimes a big help," letting him decide for himself whether to take the advice and, if he does, letting him decide whether this is one of the times it is a big help or not. By saying Travis is not "in shape to take pleasure from the horse" yet, Jim is again letting him know he respects his feelings of loss and sorrow, and there will be time for him to feel happy about the horse later.

Travis is not just reluctant to adopt Old Yeller at first; he is downright hostile. The reason is his sense of loss over his first dog, Belle. His ability to accept Young Yeller more easily shows how much he has grown up.

This is one of the finest of the early Disney dramas. The fight scenes are exciting, and the family scenes are sensitive and evocative. It is a classic tale of loss, and an excellent way to begin a discussion of those issues.

PROFANITY: None.
NUDITY/SEXUAL REFERENCES: None.
ALCOHOL/DRUG ABUSE: None.
VIOLENCE/SCARINESS: Scary confrontations between Old Yeller and a bear, wild boars, and a wolf.
TOLERANCE/DIVERSITY ISSUES: None.
QUESTIONS FOR FAMILIES:

- Why doesn't Travis want Old Yeller at first? Why doesn't he want the pup?

- How does he hurt Elsbeth's feelings?

- Why does Katie say, "No wonder they didn't want him on no cow drive," about Elsbeth's father?

- Why did Sanderson trade Old Yeller for the toad and a meal?

- Why did Sanderson say, "That's the way a man talks," when Travis told him he was a little scared but would take Sanderson's advice? What made that "manly"?

CONNECTIONS: McGuire, Kirk, and Corcoran appeared together in *Swiss Family Robinson*.

ACTIVITIES: Kids who like animal stories may enjoy the book by Fred Gipson, who cowrote the screenplay.

The Three Lives of Thomasina

1964, 97 min, NR, 8 and up

Dir: Sir Don Chaffey. Patrick McGoohan, Susan Hampshire

PLOT: The story takes place in Scotland in 1912. Mary MacDhui (Karen Dotrice) is a little girl whose mother has died. She loves her cat, Thomasina, more than anything in the world. Her father, Andrew (Patrick McGoohan), a veterinarian, is an ultra-rational man who has trouble communicating and tends to see his animal patients in economic rather than emotional terms. He has a hard time showing Mary how much she means to him, or understanding how much Thomasina means to her. He is unable to cure Thomasina when she is hurt, so he puts her to sleep, a choice that is rational but insensitive.

Mary's friends help her plan a funeral with an enthusiastic chief mourner, who tells her with pride, "I can cry very loud!" They reassure her that the whole town will understand the magnitude of the loss: "Everyone will say, 'There goes the poor widow McDhui a-burying her dear Thomasina, foully done to death, God rest her soul.'"

The funeral is interrupted by Lori MacGregor (Susan Hampshire), a beautiful and mysterious woman who lives in the forest outside the town. She cures animals with herbs and affection and is thought to be a witch. Lori finds Thomasina, who is not dead; she has just used up one of her nine lives. In a fantasy scene set in Cat Heaven, Thomasina is reborn, with no memory of her previous life.

The people in the town begin to bring their sick animals to Lori, upset because Andrew put his daughter's cat to sleep. Mary, pining for Thomasina, glimpses her and runs after her, becoming drenched in a storm. She gets ill, and Andrew, desperate, goes to Lori for help. Lori tells him that his love is what Mary needs. Thomasina appears outside Mary's window, and Andrew brings her inside. Thomasina has brought them all together, and Andrew and Lori get married.

DISCUSSION: Andrew represents the head, and Lori the heart. In the beginning of the story, both are isolated. Thomasina and Mary bring them together. Children may be interested in the way the funeral arrangements are such a comfort to Mary. They also may want to know more about why Andrew had such a problem communicating his feelings. WARNING: Some children may be upset over the notion a cat can die and come back; some who have lost a pet (or a family member) may be upset theirs didn't come back.

PROFANITY: None.
NUDITY/SEXUAL REFERENCES: None.
ALCOHOL/DRUG ABUSE: None.
VIOLENCE/SCARINESS: Sad death.
TOLERANCE/DIVERSITY ISSUES: None.
QUESTIONS FOR FAMILIES:

• What do you think about Mary's decision not to talk to her father? Was that a good way to solve the problem?

• What was her father's reaction? Was that a good way to solve the problem?

• Why is it harder for some people to talk about their feelings than others? Is it ever hard for you to talk about yours?

CONNECTIONS: The children in this movie, Karen Dotrice and Matthew Garber, also appeared in **Mary Poppins**, released the same year, and *The Gnome-Mobile*, released in 1967.

The Yearling

1946, 129 min, NR, 8 and up
Dir. Clarence Brown. Gregory Peck, Jane Wyman, Claude Jarman, Jr.
PLOT: This quiet, thoughtful, visually striking adaptation of the Pulitzer Prize-winning novel by Marjorie Kinnan Rawlings covers a year in the life of the Baxter family, post-Civil War settlers in remote Florida. The focus is on Jody (Claude Jarman, Jr.), aged twelve, a dreamy boy who loves animals and wishes he could have a pet, "something for my own, something to follow me." Pa Baxter (Gregory Peck) is warm and understanding. Ma (Jane Wyman) seems harsh and rigid, but only because she has been so devastated by the loss of three children she feels she has to contain her feelings, and if she allows herself to be vulnerable, she will not be able to stand the pain.

The only other boy Jody knows is a frail boy named Fodderwing, who lives nearby. Jody loves to visit him, to hear his imaginative tales and play with his pets. Over Ma's objections, Pa insists that Jody be allowed to have a young deer as a pet, and Jody goes to Fodderwing to ask him to name the deer. Fodderwing has died, but his father tells Jody he once said that if he had a deer, he would name it Flag, and that is the name Jody chooses. Jody loves Flag, and does every-thing he can to keep him, even building a high fence to keep Flag out of the corn crop, which is essential to the family's livelihood. Flag cannot stop eating the crop and has to be destroyed. Ma shoots him, and then Jody has to put him out of his misery.

Jody runs away, but returns. His father notes approvingly that 'Jody "takes [the loss] for his share and goes on," and tells Ma, "He's done come back differ-ent. He's taken the punishment. He ain't a yearling no more."

DISCUSSION: This is a classic story of loss, not just of a beloved pet but of the innocence and freedom of childhood that Flag symbolizes. Pa says to Jody: "Every man wants life to be a fine thing, and easy. Well, it's fine, son, powerful fine. But it ain't easy. I want life to be easier for you than it was for me.... A man's heart aches seeing his young 'uns face the world knowing they got to have their insides tore out the way his was tore."

All parents want to protect their children this way. Yet, all parents realize hav-ing one's "insides tore out" is a necessary part of growing up, and no one ever learns how to make responsible choices without these painful experiences. Pa tells Jody that life is "gettin', losin', gettin', losin'."

In the last moment of the film, as in the book, the boy and the deer run off together in Jody's imagination. In part, this means Jody's innocence is gone with the deer. It also means a precious part of his spirit, the part that loved the deer so deeply, will be with him always, and will be a part of everything that he does.

PROFANITY: None.
NUDITY/SEXUAL REFERENCES: None.
ALCOHOL/DRUG ABUSE: None.
VIOLENCE/SCARINESS: Bear and dog fight; fistfights; Pa bitten by a snake; deer shot (off-screen).
TOLERANCE/DIVERSITY ISSUES: None.
QUESTIONS FOR FAMILIES:

- Who is "the yearling"?

- What do you think of Pa's strategy for trading his dog for a gun? What did he mean when he later said his words were straight but his intentions were crooked?

- What do Jody's friends Fodderwing and Oliver tell you about him?

- Why was it hard for Ma to show affection? How can you tell?

- How was Jody different when he came back home?

CONNECTIONS: Mature teenagers may be interested in *Cross Creek*, a fictionalized account of Rawlings's life, including the writing of The Yearling and in *Gal Young 'Un*, a film based on one of Rawlings' short stories about an exploitive husband, his wife, and his girlfriend.

ACTIVITIES: Middle-school and high school kids will appreciate the book.

FLY AWAY HOME

1996, 107 minutes, PG, 8 and up

Dir: Carroll Ballard. Anna Paquin, Jeff Daniels, Dana Delaney

Amy, a thirteen-year-old girl from New Zealand (Anna Paquin), wakes up in a hospital bed after an automobile accident to see her father, Tom (Jeff Daniels), whom she barely knows. Her mother was killed in the crash, and she must go back with Tom to his remote farm in Canada. He is an eccentric sculptor and inventor, preoccupied with his work and unsure of how to try to comfort her. Amy does not want to be comforted, and wanders silently through the marshes. When developers illegally mowing down the marsh kill a goose, Amy finds the eggs she left behind, and begins to resolve her loss by mothering the goslings. Since she is the first thing they see when they hatch, they think of her as their mother, following her everywhere, even into the shower. The local authorities insist t their wings be clipped, since without their mother they cannot learn to migrate and will cause problems for the community when they try to fly. Amy and her father will not allow the geese to be harmed.

Tom devises a way for Amy to play the role of "Mother Goose" in teaching the geese to migrate, by learning to fly herself, in an ultra-light plane, and leading them south. With Tom's brother (Terry Kinney) and girlfriend (Dana Delany), they plot a course to a wetland preserve scheduled to be developed unless geese arrive by November 1. As they work together, Amy finds a way to begin to heal her loss of her mother and her relationship with Tom.

This is a thrilling adventure, exquisitely told, by the same director and photographer who made The Black Stallion. Ballard has the patience to let the story tell itself, and the quiet moments are breathtakingly beautiful and heartbreakingly touching. NOTE: There is one profanity in the movie, demanded by the studio, who insisted the movie must have a PG rating so that it would not scare off school-age kids. Of more concern to many parents will be Amy's nose ring, which Tom permits and even appears to encourage.

TRULY, MADLY, DEEPLY

1991, 107 min, NR, 12 and up
Dir: Anthony Minghella. Juliet Stevenson, Alan Rickman
Nina (Juliet Stevenson) is a loving and kind young woman who teaches English as a second language. Her lover, Jamie (Alan Rickman), a musician, has just died, and she is utterly devastated. She is unable to let go of her devotion to him.

One day he reappears, explaining he did not "die properly." She is overjoyed and happily puts up with the quirks of living with a ghost: staying in the apartment as much as possible, ignoring her job and her friends, keeping the apartment stifling hot (since Jamie is perpetually cold), and putting up with Jamie's ghost friends, who want to stay up all night to watch videos.

Nina meets an engaging teacher named Mark (Michael Maloney) and, despite misgivings, agrees to see him again. She is still committed to Jamie. Ultimately, however, she must make a choice between living in the past and going on into the future.

This lovely movie allows itself to be ambiguous about whether Jamie actually appears as a ghost to help Nina accept his death or whether it is just a metaphor for Nina's progress through the stages of grief. All of the performances are beguilingly natural, and Stevenson (who inspired the script) is luminously vulnerable, well worth coming back from the dead for.

CONNECTIONS: Minghella went on to make the Oscar-winning *The English Patient*. Rickman appears as Professor Snape in the Harry Potter movies.

SEE ALSO:
Permanent Record A group of high school kids must come to grips with the suicide of a seemingly happy and successful friend.
Unstrung Heroes A young boy copes with his mother's illness by moving in with two loving but emotionally ill uncles.
Where the Lilies Bloom Fourteen-year-old Mary Call Luther cares for her sisters and brother after their parents die, and learns that may mean breaking a promise to her father.
Where the Red Fern Grows A boy copes with the loss of his beloved dogs.

10

WOMEN WORTH WATCHING

"I long to speak out the intense inspiration that comes from the lives of strong women."
RUTH BENEDICT

Reviving Ophelia, the best-seller by clinical psychologist Mary Pipher, describes how girls often lose confidence as they enter adolescence, based in part on the messages they receive from the media. Certainly, there is a long tradition in the movies (as in the books and folktales that preceded them) of women who achieve success through good grooming and accessorizing, while the males in their lives are saving the world by swashbuckling with dragons, pirates, and each other.

There is no shortage of tough, smart heroines in movies and books about girls under twelve, like Pippi Longstocking, Brave Irene, Amazing Grace, Laura Ingalls Wilder, and Anne of Green Gables. Teenage and adult heroines in books and movies are most often passively good, like Cinderella, whose patient obedience is rewarded when she is given new clothes, and Sleeping Beauty, who literally sleeps while the prince fights the dragon. There are some welcome recent exceptions in books, like *Tatterhood*, edited by Ethel Johnston Phelps; *The King's Equal*, by Katherine Patterson; and *The Outspoken Princess and the Gentle Knight*, edited by Jack Zipes.

Still, little girls and bigger ones see a lot of what I call "makeover movies": In a crucial scene Our Heroine gets a new dress and hairstyle (or just takes off her glasses) and her life changes. Sometimes she transforms herself, as Ella does in **Bells are Ringing**, causing her to have enormous conflicts and self-doubt. More often, she is transformed by someone else. Cinderella's fairy godmother changes her sooty rags to a glamorous gown so she can go to the ball and dazzle the prince. Her modern counterparts are Eliza Doolittle, who, like Cinderella, goes to a ball in borrowed finery (and accent) and dazzles everyone there in **My Fair**

Lady, and **Gigi**, who is actually groomed by her grandmother and great-aunt to be a very elegant prostitute, trained almost like a geisha in manners and skills for pleasing a man.

Over and over, we see the heroines rewarded for being lovely and passive pleasers.

The villains in family movies are equal opportunity, however, and Disney films in particular feature very powerful women as the bad guys. It is hard to find a woman in movies who is both powerful and successful and one of the good guys. A recent guide to "nonviolent, nonsexist" videos included 800 videos, but only 100 of them feature girls or women in central roles, and even most of those have a male character as the lead.

Even more damaging are the constant messages to girls they should be sexually provocative and available. One of the most popular movies among young girls on video is *Grease*, in which a "hopelessly devoted" young woman is able to realize her ultimate goal of getting her boyfriend's attention by dressing and acting like a biker chick. Most troubling, contemporary movies give teenagers no sense there is any hierarchy of sexual contact. The overpowering message is if you like a guy (or want him to like you), you have sex with him. Young women are not portrayed as though they are entitled to establish limits on physical intimacy; there is no sense they have the right to decide a kiss good night is sufficient. Female lead characters in an astonishing number of successful films are prostitutes or strippers. No wonder Ophelia has to be revived!

Girls and boys should watch the classic films because those stories are an important part of our cultural heritage and because they have themes with enduring appeal we can both enjoy and teach our children to try to understand. The challenge is to watch them with a sense of heightened awareness, to learn to decode the hidden messages and to be explicit in our responses to them.

Fortunately, we also have some alternatives to help young women recognize the important satisfactions come from self-respect, love based on trust and respect, and work that makes a contribution. The films of the 1930s gave us a lot of heroines who were strong, smart, independent, and accomplished. Think of the roles played by Katharine Hepburn, Bette Davis, and Rosalind Russell. For some reason, in the late 1940s and especially in the 1950s, most female leads in movies could have stepped out of a "ring around the collar" ad. Even then, we had Doris Day. In the midst of the fluffiest sex comedies she was almost always shown as independent and superbly competent in her work.

These days, some movies still sink into sexist stereotypes, but when they do, they are often criticized for it. More often, they try to have it both ways, with heroines like *Legally Blonde*'s Elle Woods, an adorable sorority girl and Harvard Law School graduate.

We still have a long way to go.

It can help young people understand these issues if you ask children and teens to compare **Cinderella** and **Sleeping Beauty** to more recent heroines of Disney animation. Today's female characters are much more active, curious, independent and intelligent: Look at Ariel in **The Little Mermaid**, Belle in **Beauty and the Beast**, Nala in **The Lion King** (better qualified to lead the lions than Simba), **Pocahontas**, **Mulan**, and Meg in **Hercules**. They may still look like Barbie dolls, but they are not singing to the birds about "Someday My Prince Will Come". They are taking care of themselves and pursuing what they want. In 1998's **Ever After** and 2004's **Ella Enchanted**, we have Cinderellas who make their own magic, and even save the princes.

Make sure boys and girls see some of the movies that give us female characters who want more than a new outfit and hairdo, and who are respected for their abilities and accomplishments. Make sure they also see movies with men and women who share a "marriage of true minds," couples united in the kind of love only possible between people who respect, admire, and trust one another.

Ever After

1998, 129 min, PG, 8 and up
Dir: Andy Tennant. Drew Barrymore, Anjelica Houston
PLOT: Drew Barrymore plays Danielle, the real inspiration for the story of Cinderella. Just as in the classic fairy tale, Danielle lives with her mean step-mother and step-sisters, after the death of her beloved father. They force her to do all the work. She meets the prince, goes to the ball wearing glass slippers, and runs away before midnight. There are some big differences, however. No pumpkin coach, no fairy godmother, and no bibbity-bobbity-boo. This heroine is not meekly obedient. She stays on because she wants to take care of her home and the people who work there, because it makes her feel close to her father, and because she still hopes that somehow she will find approval from the only mother she has ever known.

The step-mother (Anjelica Houston) in her most evil "The Witches" mode, is not going to give it to her. She tells Danielle that she sees her as a pebble in her shoe. All she cares about is making sure that the prince chooses her elder daughter, Marguerite (Megan Dodd), as his bride. She is willing to lie, cheat, and steal to make it happen.

Meanwhile, the Prince (Dougray Scott) is not quite Charming. He appears arrogant, but is really just lonely and aimless. His parents want him to marry the princess of Spain, to cement a strategic alliance, but he wants to fall in love. He meets Danielle when she is in disguise as a courtier, to rescue a family servant sold by her step-mother to pay her debts, and he is very taken by Danielle's passion and intellect.

The stepmother finds out about their relationship, and does her best to thwart it. When the prince finds out that Danielle is not really of noble birth, he is furious, at first. It all ends happily ever after, even without a fairy godmother (though with a little help from Leonardo da Vinci).

DISCUSSION: Sumptuously filmed at medieval castles and chateaux, with gorgeous costumes, this is is a pleasure for the eye as well as the spirit. Danielle is a very modern heroine, smart, brave, honest, and able to save her prince as well as herself, if necessary. The script is clever (though wildly anachronistic in places), and while the accents come and go (and why do French characters speak with English accents, anyway?), the performances are excellent, with particularly engaging turns by Melanie Lynskey as the sympathetic younger step-sister and Judy Parfitt as the queen.

PROFANITY: One brief expletive (removed for video release).
NUDITY/SEXUAL REFERENCES: None.
ALCOHOL/DRUG ABUSE: None.
VIOLENCE/SCARINESS: Action violence, sad death.
TOLERANCE/DIVERSITY ISSUES: A theme of the movie.
QUESTIONS FOR FAMILIES:

• If you were going to rewrite a fairy tale, which one would you pick and how would you change it?

• Why did Danielle stay?

• Do you agree with what happened to Danielle's stepmother?

CONNECTIONS: Everyone should see the more traditional versions of the Cinderella story, especially the wonderful Disney cartoon and the Rogers and Hammerstein musical starring Lesley Anne Warren in the original and Brandy and Whitney Houston in the remake.

Funny Girl

1968, 155 min, G, 8 and up
Dir: William Wyler. Barbra Streisand, Omar Sharif, Walter Pidgeon
PLOT: Based on the real life of Ziegfeld comedy star Fanny Brice (Barbra Streisand), this is the story both of her triumphs as a performer and of her unhappy marriage to gambler Nicky Arnstein (Omar Sharif).

As the movie opens, Fanny is a teenager, passionately committed to becoming a performer. Despite the warnings of her mother's friends that she is not pretty enough to be successful, she believes in herself and her talent and refuses to take "no" for an answer. She is fired during rehearsal in a small vaudeville house but, promising she knows how to roller-skate, is hired again for a dance number on skates. She creates chaos out of the number, but sings a song and is a huge success. That night she meets Arnstein and is fascinated by his sophistication, charm, and good looks.

Soon afterward, she is hired by Florenz Ziegfeld, the greatest producer of the era, to be featured in his new show. They clash when he wants her to sing a song about a bride describing herself as beautiful. At the last minute, on opening night, she decides to turn it into a comic number by making herself appear pregnant. Ziegfeld is furious but concedes it was successful.

Arnstein reappears from time to time without warning, and she falls deeply in love with him, finally leaving the show to join him on an ocean liner to Europe. He makes enough in a poker game to marry her. She is thrilled to be a "Sadie, Sadie, Married Lady" and adores their daughter, Frances. When his winning streak ends, he is upset she is supporting him. Desperate, he tries to make money in a crooked bond deal, but he is discovered and is sent to prison. Fanny remains devoted to him, but when he is released he tells her he cannot stay with her, and they divorce.

DISCUSSION: Barbra Streisand won an Oscar for this, her movie debut (she also starred in the original Broadway production). Her mixture of bravado ("I'm the greatest star/I am by far/but no one knows it") and vulnerability shielded by humor ("You don't have to use leading lady lines on me; I'm a comedian"), both as Brice the performer and as Brice the woman, is captivating.

Contrary to the traditions of the "makeover movie," Brice achieves her dreams without a fairy godmother to give her glamour or teach her how to behave. She stays very much herself, insisting on her right to select her own material and create her own persona onstage. She is not successful in her romantic relationship, however, at least in part due to the same ability to take care of herself, even when part of her wants to be taken care of.

The problem is as much his insecurity as hers. Nick cannot feel comfortable living on her earnings and in her shadow. His self-esteem depends on being able to take care of her, a real problem for a man who makes his living as a gambler. It doesn't matter to him she does not care about his ability to provide for them, and all she is looking for is his love and devotion. Nick and Fanny love each other but cannot stay together. This may be reassuring to children whose parents are apart, because it shows they care about each other, and the problems are between them, and not about their child.

PROFANITY: None.
NUDITY/SEXUAL REFERENCES: Despite the G-rating, there is a PG-level seduction scene, and mild references to non-marital sex; Fanny appears onstage as a pregnant bride (played for comedy).
ALCOHOL/DRUG ABUSE: Social drinking.
VIOLENCE/SCARINESS: Sad, but not scary.
TOLERANCE/DIVERSITY ISSUES: Acceptance of differences (Fanny refers to herself as "a bagel on a plate of onion rolls").
QUESTIONS FOR FAMILIES:

• Why is Fanny so sure of herself as a performer, and so unsure of herself in other parts of her life?

• Was she right to lie to Eddie about being able to roller-skate?

• She promised to do whatever Mr. Ziegfeld told her; why didn't she?

• Why did Fanny care so much for someone who could not be as devoted to her as she was to him?

• Why was it hard for Nick to accept help from her?

CONNECTIONS: *Funny Lady* is a sequel, which is not nearly as good, covering Brice's marriage to impresario Billy Rose, which broke up when he fell in love with a performer in one of his shows. In that movie, she must still deal with her love for Nick Arnstein. Families who enjoy this movie might like to see the real Fanny Brice perform in a skit in *The Ziegfeld Follies of 1946*, a Hollywood version of a Ziegfeld-style revue. That movie also has other treats, including the only dance number ever filmed with both Fred Astaire and Gene Kelly. Children might also like to see Willam Powell's appearance as *The Great Ziegfeld. Ziegfeld Girl* is a glossy and enjoyable backstage soap opera starring Judy Garland, Hedy Lamarr, Jimmy Stewart, and Lana Turner.

Pat and Mike

1952, 95 min, NR, b&w, 8 and up
Dir: George Cukor. Katharine Hepburn, Spencer Tracy, Aldo Ray
PLOT: Pat Pemberton (Katharine Hepburn), a physical education teacher at a small California college, is a superb athlete who is a bit insecure. A widow engaged to Collier Weld, a hearty faculty colleague (William Ching), Pat enjoys competing but fails whenever her fiancé is watching. Mike Conovan (Spencer Tracy), a fast-talking and slightly shady sports promoter, sees her at an amateur golf tournament, asks her to take a bribe to throw the game and, when she refuses, tells her she can make a lot of money by competing professionally.

At first she says no, but later she comes back to him and asks for more information. When he finds out she is not only a superb golfer but an outstanding tennis player and even an expert with a rifle, he takes her on, in addition to his other "properties," a racehorse and Davie Hucko, a punchy boxer (Aldo Ray). She does very well, except when her fiancé is there. As she and Mike get closer, and she becomes more successful, Davie gets jealous. Mike's financial backers want Pat to lose an important golf match. He reminds them he told them from the beginning she was on the level. They take him out to rough him up, but Pat rescues him, using judo. Mike is embarrassed. She finds a way for him to regain his sense of himself as her protector, and they agree to become a romantic team as well as a professional one.

DISCUSSION: This is a delightful and witty love story, and a lot of fun to watch. There are also some thoughtful and insightful moments to make it especially worthwhile. In a very real sense, Pat is looking for a sense of herself and her own worth when she goes to Mike. At some level, she knows the relationship with Collier is not working. Children, who so need their parents to root for them at soccer games or other kinds of competitions, will be interested to see Pat unravels whenever Collier is near. He seems supportive and enthusiastic, but somehow he really sees her as incompetent, and that is what she becomes whenhe is present.

Mike's first observation of Pat is one of the most famous lines in the film. With relish, he says, with his best Brooklyn twist, "Not much meat on her, but what there is, is 'cherse.'" He likes it that she wants to compete honestly. He understands and appreciates her strength, yet, he likes to be the one in charge; he likes to take care of her. He likes to tell her what to eat and to massage her muscle cramps. He is dismayed when she protects him from the thugs who are trying to muscle him into having her intentionally lose the match. A superficial viewing would suggest her finding a way for him to save face by protecting her later is a betrayal of any notion of equality. But what matters is the "five-oh, five-oh" definition of their relationship in the movie's last lines, when she turns the table by asking him his "three questions": "Who made you?" "You did." "Who owns the biggest piece of you?" "You do." "Where will you go if I dump you?" "Down the drain." "And?" "Drag you down with me!"

PROFANITY: None.
NUDITY/SEXUAL REFERENCES: Pat's fiancé is suspicious when he sees Pat and Mike together in an entirely innocent but mildly suggestive situation.
ALCOHOL/DRUG ABUSE: None.
VIOLENCE/SCARINESS: Pat uses judo to subdue three thugs.
TOLERANCE/DIVERSITY ISSUES: The issue of gender equality is implicit throughout the movie.
QUESTIONS FOR FAMILIES:

- Why couldn't Pat play well while Collier was there? How does that show she should not marry him? Why didn't she have the same problem with Mike?

- What does "five-oh, five-oh" mean, and why is it important to Pat and Mike?

- Why didn't Hucko like Pat? What did she do to make him like her?

- How did Mike feel when Pat stopped the men who were trying to beat him up? Why?

- Why did the men want Pat to lose on purpose? Why didn't she want to?

CONNECTIONS: Tracy and Hepburn made nine movies together. The best are **Adam's Rib**, *Woman of the Year*, *Without Love*, and *Desk Set*. This one allows Katharine Hepburn to show off her real-life athletic ability.

If an actor in this movie listed as "Charles Bushowski" looks familiar, that may be because you recognize him from his appearances under another name: Charles Bronson. Look also for Chuck (*The Rifleman*) Connors as a policeman, and Carl "Alfalfa" Sweitzer of *The Little Rascals* as a busboy. Note several of the greatest athletes of the era appear as themselves, including Pancho Gonzales and Babe Didrikson Zaharias.

The Rainmaker

1956, 121 min, NR, 10 and up
Dir: Joseph Anthony. Katharine Hepburn, Burt Lancaster, Lloyd Bridges, Earl Holliman

PLOT: Starbuck (Burt Lancaster) is a traveling salesman with enormous charisma. As the movie opens, he is selling tornado rods, to prevent damage from tornados, but when he is called a con man, he quickly escapes. In the next town, he watches quietly from the shadows and sees Jimmy (Earl Holliman) awkwardly making overtures to Snookie (Yvonne Lime) at a dance held to raise money for damage from a long drought.

Jimmy's sister, Lizzie (Katharine Hepburn), comes home from a visit to her cousins in search of a husband. She didn't find one; at first she hid in her room, and when she came down she made the mistake of letting them know she knew facts like where Madagascar was. Her father and brothers love her, and they say she's just afraid of being beautiful. Lizzie replies, "I'm afraid to think I am when I'm not." She says she wants "to make someone happy...I want him to tell me who he is, and to tell me who I am because I sure don't know." She says this man she dreams of "never has to say thank you because thank you is our whole life together."

Lizzie's father, H. C., her stern, practical brother Noah (Lloyd Bridges), and Jimmy ask File, the new deputy sheriff (Wendell Corey), to dinner, but he refuses, saying, "I don't want to get married." H. C. tells him the town knows he is not a widower but a divorced man whose wife deserted him, and he "needs mending."

Lizzie is at first ashamed to have her family so obviously trying to marry her off, but she, is also terribly disappointed that File turned them down. Starbuck arrives, asking them to hire him to bring rain. Noah is opposed, but Jimmy wants to try it, and H. C. wants to know more about it. Starbuck tells them that "once in your life, you gotta take a chance on a con man."

File arrives. At first he and Lizzie talk, but then, remembering her brother's advice not to "talk too serious," she tries to flirt with him and he gets disgusted with her silly behavior and leaves. Noah tells Lizzie to give up and accept her fate as an old maid. "The sooner you accept it, the sooner you'll stop breaking your heart."

Starbuck does not see her that way. He sees her as "Melisande" and tells her, "Don't let Noah be your looking glass." He kisses her, "because when you said you were pretty, it was true." File comes back, looking for Starbuck. Lizzie and her family persuade File to let him go. Starbuck asks Lizzie to go with him: "Go with me and you'll be so beautiful, you'll light up the world!"

File asks Lizzie to stay. She knows her dream is the life she could have with File. Starbuck gives back the money they gave him, and rides away. When the rain begins, he goes back to get the money, saying to Lizzie, "So long, Beautiful!"

DISCUSSION: This is an excellent counterpoint to the "makeover movie" messages about achieving success in life and love through improvements in appearance and manners. Lizzie has to find herself, her dream, and her own beauty, and only then is able to accept that others find her beautiful. Ironically, it is Starbuck, a professional liar, who tells her the truth: that she has to know her own beauty, and when she finds it for herself, it will be there for others as well. Starbuck gives her the gift of the truth about himself, about his real name, and how he picked the name he wanted to become.

Noah and Jimmy tell Lizzie to behave more like other girls to "get" a man, and she says, "If that is the way a man gets got, I don't want any." She wants to be wanted for who she is, by someone who will be proud she knows where Madagascar is.

Noah is cerebral, practical, even cynical. He tries to persuade Jimmy not to get involved with Snookie and seems to think everything that is not a prudent financial investment is a waste of time. Jimmy is impetuous and emotional. While Noah accuses him of being dumb, his father is closer to the truth when he says Jimmy "always says the smart thing at the dumb time."

Starbuck is full of dreams; he cons himself as much as he cons anyone else, yet he is affected by Lizzie. He even returns the money, until it rains, and he can take credit for it. The rain can be seen as a symbol of the vitality he has brought to Lizzie, and the small piece of integrity she has brought out in him.

File won't let himself dream, because he has been hurt. Yet he has also been a con man in a way, telling the community he is a widower because he does not want them to know the truth. He says, "There's one thing I learned. Be independent! If you don't ask for things, if you don't let on you need things, pretty soon you don't need 'em." He listens when Lizzie says he should not have let his pride keep him from asking his wife to stay, and he proves that by letting her know he needs her.

PROFANITY: None.
NUDITY/SEXUAL REFERENCES: Very oblique references.
ALCOHOL/DRUG ABUSE: None.
VIOLENCE/SCARINESS: None.

TOLERANCE/DIVERSITY ISSUES: Issue of whether a woman can attract a man by being intelligent and telling the truth.
QUESTIONS FOR FAMILIES:

- What do the family's different reactions to Starbuck show us about them?

- Noah tells Jimmy he is dumb, and tells Lizzie she is unattractive and destined to be an old maid. Why? What impact does it have on them?

- Why does Lizzie have to know she is beautiful before she can be beautiful to Starbuck or File?

- What do the drought and rain symbolize?

- Lizzie tells Starbuck "it's no good to live in your dreams," and he replies "It's no good to live outside of them." What does that mean? Which one is right?

CONNECTIONS: The importance of dreams is a theme of many enduring stories. Some, like **The Glass Menagerie** and *The Iceman Cometh*, focus on the destructive impact of using dreams to hide reality. Others show the way dreams illuminate our lives (**Miracle on 34th Street**) and help us to understand reality, even to improve it (**Rocky, Field of Dreams, Lilies of the Field, Rudy, Holiday, Hello, Dolly**). In *Don Quixote*, both aspects of dreams are explored.

Teenagers might like to find out about the use of divining rods or about people like Starbuck who traveled the country selling all kinds of phony cures and spells. Compare this story to **The Music Man**. Starbuck and Professor Harold Hill are similar in many ways, but the movies have very different conclusions. Curiously, the name Starbuck gives Lizzie, "Melisande," is also the name Ella picks for her fictional self in **Bells Are Ringing**. NOTE: Do not confuse this with the 1997 John Grisham movie of the same name.

Mulan

1998, 88 min, G, 6 and up
Dir. Tony Bancroft, Barry Cook. Voices of Miguel Ferrar, Eddie Murphy, Soon-Tek Oh, Donny Osmond, Ming-Na Wen, B.D. Wong
PLOT: This Disney animated feature is based upon the legend of Mulan, a Chinese girl who helps the Chinese army defeat the Mongols. After the Mongols invade, led by Shan-Yu (voice of Miguel Ferrar) every family is called upon to send one man to the army. Although Mulan's father, Fa Zhou (voice of SoonTek Oh) must use a crutch to walk, he is willing to fight for the honor of his family.

Mulan (voice of Ming-Na Wen) disguises herself as a man so that her father will not have to risk his life. The ghosts of her ancestors order a powerful guardian dragon to protect her and bring her home. Instead, a tiny disgraced dragon named Mushu (voice of Eddie Murphy) joins her in the hope he can help her achieve a triumph to bring honor to both of them.

Mulan finds pretending to be a man and meeting the standards of Shang, her tough captain (voice of B.D. Wong) brings her tougher challenges than she imagined. Her determination earns her the respect of the others, and in the midst of battle her quick thinking and courage save the day—instead of shooting her hopelessly outnumbered battalion's last cannon at the enemy, she shoots at a snow-covered mountain, causing an avalanche that blankets them with snow. She then saves Shang from the avalanche.

Nevertheless, when her true gender is revealed, she is left behind. Instead of going home, Mulan and Mushu travel to warn the emperor that Shan-Yu is still alive, and again she saves the day when the Mongols attack.

DISCUSSION: This is one of Disney's best, with gorgeous animation inspired by Chinese paintings, a hilarious performance by Eddie Murphy as Mushu, and a witty, intelligent script transcending the usual formulas. In one nice twist, the macho soldiers who are certain no "girl worth fighting for" would have a mind of her own end up having to dress as women to defeat the Mongols. Captain Shang learns from the wise emperor "the flower that blooms in adversity is the most rare and beautiful of all."

Families will have much to talk about, including the notion of honor, the traditional Chinese view of the ancestors, and the importance of freedom from stereotypes.

PROFANITY: None.

NUDITY/SEXUAL REFERENCES: Male soldiers bathing nude cause Mulan to flee (nothing shown).

ALCOHOL/DRUG ABUSE: None.

VIOLENCE/SCARINESS: Some scary war scenes, death of Shang's father in battle.

TOLERANCE/DIVERSITY ISSUES: A theme of the movie.

QUESTIONS FOR FAMILIES:

• Why did Mulan's father want to join the army despite his bad leg?

• Why was it hard for Mulan to behave the way the matchmaker wanted her to?

- Why was it hard for Shang to accept Mulan's help? Why did he feel differently about her when he found out she was female?

CONNECTIONS: Adults with sharp ears may recognize Donny Osmond singing Shang's songs and June Foray (of *Rocky and Bullwinkle*) as Mulan's outspoken grandmother. Listen carefully when the grandmother sings, though. It's none other than Mari Nixon, who provided the bell-like singing voice for Natalie Wood in **West Side Story**, Deborah Kerr in **The King and I**, and Audrey Hepburn in **My Fair Lady**.

Whale Rider

2003, 101 min, PG-13, 12 and up
Dir: Niki Caro. Keisha Castle-Hughes, Rawiri Paratene, Vicki Houghton
PLOT: This lovely, lyrical fable of a movie is set in the Maori community of New Zealand. According to legend, the Maori came to Whangara when their great leader Paikea led them by riding on a whale. Ever since, the Maori have been led by the descendants of that leader.

The movie begins with the birth of twins, the latest in that line. The boy twin and his mother die. Over the objection of the current leader, Koro (Rawiri Paratene), the girl twin is named Paikaea. Her heartbroken father leaves New Zealand, and Pai is left to be raised by her grandparents.

Koro loves Pai deeply, but he is still bitter about not having a male heir. When she is 12 (an exquisite performance by Keisha Castle-Hughes), Koro assembles the local boys to begin to train them in the traditions of their culture and test them to see which has the courage, skill, wisdom, and leadership. It is clear to her grandmother (Vicki Houghton), to us, and to Pai herself that she has all of those qualities, but Koro, struggling fiercely to maintain the Maori pride and identity against the assaults of the modern world, cannot allow himself to consider such a change.

DISCUSSION: Writer-director Niki Coro perfectly suits the style to the story. The modest buildings in the midst of the starkly beautiful setting conveys the contrast between the timeless culture of the Maori and the ephemeral artifacts of the modern age. Pai's perceptiveness and quiet persistence are always evident, but when she finally speaks from her heart, standing on stage in a school production, wearing traditional garb, she is purely luminous. The movie is not just genuinely lyrical, but, even harder to manage, it is lyrically genuine.

PROFANITY: Brief strong language.
NUDITY/SEXUAL REFERENCES:
ALCOHOL/DRUG ABUSE: Drinking, smoking, brief drug reference.
VIOLENCE/SCARINESS: Some tense family confrontations. The death of a mother and baby in childbirth is very sad. A character is injured, but ultimately recovers.
TOLERANCE/DIVERSITY ISSUES: A theme of the movie
QUESTIONS FOR FAMILIES:

• What are the most important traditions of your family's culture?

• How do we decide which traditions to hold on to and which to change to adapt to changing times?

CONNECTIONS: Families who enjoy this movie will also enjoy "The Secret of Roan Inish," "Into the West," and "Island of the Blue Dolphins." They should also find out more about the Maori culture.

THE BEST LITTLE GIRL IN THE WORLD

1981, 100 min, NR, 12 and up
Dir: Sam O'Steen. Jennifer Jason Leigh, Charles Durning, Eva Marie Saint
This "disease of the week" television movie about anorexia nervosa rises well above the average due to the performances of Jennifer Jason Leigh as the lead, Charles Durning and Eva Marie Saint as her parents, and Jason Miller as her therapist. Treatment of anorexia has made some progress since 1981, but the movie may still be a way of helping some girls recognize and understand eating disorders, which raise issues of a fear of growing up, of overwhelming images of the "perfect" body, and of a misplaced sense of control.

A DOLL'S HOUSE

1973, 105 min, G, 12 and up
Dir: Patrick Garland. Claire Bloom, Anthony Hopkins
Nora is a "doll-wife," adored by her husband and children but treated like a cherished pet. She needs money to save her husband's life, and so in a shrewd and daring act, she commits forgery. Although she pays it back, her husband finds out about it. He cannot forgive her, not because she lied, but because she acted independently, and because she protected him. He is willing to go on as they were

before, but she has found she needs to be treated as a person, not a doll, and so she leaves, slamming the door.

CONNECTIONS: Another movie version of this play was also released in 1973, directed by Joseph Losey, and starring Jane Fonda and David Warner. It is also rated G, but is most suitable for ages twelve and up.

Writer/director Nora Ephron (*Sleepless in Seattle*, *When Harry Met Sally*) was named after the leading character in this drama by her screenwriter parents.

ACTIVITIES: Teens who enjoy this may like to read or see some of Ibsen's other plays, including *Hedda Gabler*, about a woman who destroys herself when she is not able to manipulate others to give her the power and control she desperately craves, *Ghosts*, about the destructive power of secrets and overly restrictive social conventions, and *An Enemy of the People*, about a doctor who tells the truth about the dangers of the city's supposedly healthy waters, the foundation of the city's economy.

ELLA ENCHANTED

2004, 95 min, PG, 8 and up
Dir: Tommy O'Haver. Anne Hathaway, Hugh Dancy
Why did Cinderella do whatever her evil step-mother and step-sisters told her to? According to author Gail Carson Levine, it's because a well-meaning but careless fairy named Lucinda (Viveca A. Fox), tried to give a gift to Ella (Anne Hathaway) when she was born, and cast a spell so she would always be obedient. That meant that whenever Ella was given a direct order, she had to do whatever she was told. Literally. This is an inconvenience in a loving household but becomes downright dangerous when Ella's mother dies and her father marries nasty Dame Olga (Joanna Lumley). It becomes downright deadly when an evil usurper orders Ella to commit murder.

Ella's journey to find a way to break the spell has its own dangers as she meets up with elves, ogres, giants, fairies, and of course a very charming prince (Hugh Dancy).

Like Shrek, this is a fairy tale with some broad (and occasionally crude) humor and winking references to modern times. Ella's support for the rights of ogres, giants, and elves (including an elf who wants to be a lawyer despite rules that require all elves to be entertainers) shows us her heart and spirit and gives her something to discuss with the prince beyond who should rescue whom and his latest appearance in Medieval Teen magazine.

The movie works so hard to be entertaining that it can feel a little hyper-charged at times, cluttered with too many talented performers with too little to do. The production design helps maintain the sense of magic, with storybook castles and forests. Hathaway is so radiantly lovable that she could make an ATM withdrawal feel like a fairy tale. When Ella is ordered to entertain the guests at a giant's wedding celebration, she breaks into Queen's "Somebody to Love" and dances across the tabletop with such joyous gusto that even Freddie Mercury would approve. Dancy makes the prince more than the usual arm candy/swordsman and the way they learn to trust and respect each other enough to stop fighting the attraction they feel is unexpectedly tender.

NOTE: The movie has some crude language ("bite me" "cute butt") and social drinking. It is supposed to be humorous when a character gets tipsy and has a drinking problem. There is violence, including fighting, knives, and swordplay and characters are in peril. A character is hit in the crotch in a slapstick fight. In a more serious fight, it appears that a character is killed, but it turns out not to be the case. Ella's mother becomes ill and dies. Ella is ordered to shoplift and due to the curse, must obey. An ogre's pants reveal the top of his butt crack.

Families who see this movie should talk about what it was that made it possible for Ella to break the curse? What did she have to learn or feel to make that happen? They may want to talk about the theme of discrimination and segregation in the story. What creates prejudice? Part of the fun of the movie, and explored in more detail in the book, is the way that the literal meaning of the words in direct orders to Ella have unexpected results. Families should talk about the way that the way listeners hear words can mean something different from what the speaker intends.

Families will enjoy Gail Carson Levine's superb book and might also want to read—or write—some other modern takes on fairy tales.

MY BRILLIANT CAREER

1979, 101 min, G, 10 and up
Dir: Gillian Armstrong. Judy Davis, Sam Neill
This movie is based on the autobiography of Miles Franklin, a girl from the Australian outback, who wrote the book when she was only sixteen. Judy Davis is brilliant as Franklin, whose independent spirit and sense of her own worth cannot be squelched by the suffocating conventions of the Victorian era. She is clearly attracted to handsome Harry Beecham (Sam Neill), but when he finally proposes, clearly loving her for what she loves most about herself, she cannot accept. What she wants from life cannot be found in the life he offers.

MY GIRL

1991, 102 min, PG, 12 and up
Dir: Howard Zieff. Anna Chlumsky, Dan Ayhroyd, Jamie Lee Curtis
This uneven story about a young girl trying to understand loss stars the talented and appealing Anna Chlumsky as Vada, the sensitive daughter of a loving but distant mortician father (Dan Aykroyd). The loss of her mother just after she was born, her grandmother's fading memory, the embalming facilities in the basement, and the prospect of growing up all leave her anxious, even worried that she herself is going to die. She has to deal with some major changes, including a romance for her father with kindhearted Shelly (Jamie Lee Curtis), her first period, and the death of her closest friend, played by Home Alone's Macaulay Culkin. Vada finds strength in herself and in her ability as a writer.
CONNECTIONS: A sequel, *My Girl 2*, features much of the same cast, as Vada goes to visit her uncle and searches for information about her late mother. Vada is not just sensitive; she is smart and brave. Both movies are set in the 1970s, which can give parents a chance to point out some of the cultural touchstones of that era. NOTE: Both movies have some mature material. Parents should screen the films before showing them to young teens.

SMOOTH TALK

1985, 92 min, PG-13, mature high school age
Dir: Joyce Chopra. Laura Dern, Treat Williams
Based on a story by Joyce Carol Oates, this is an exceptionally vivid portrayal of the restlessness (and risks) of adolescence. Laura Dern is outstanding as Connie, caught up in the small rebellions and obsessions (especially self-obsession) of a fifteen-year-old, bickering with her mother, sniping at her sister and, daringly, experimenting with her sexual power as she cruises through the mall with her friends. Things get sickeningly out of control when the signals she has been sending out are received by a much older man, disturbingly named "A. Friend" (Teat Willams), and she has none of the sense of self necessary to send him away. NOTE: This movie may provide a good opportunity for discussing important issues, but it deals with sexuality in a way that may be upsetting for teenagers (and their parents), and should be viewed by parents before deciding whether to show it to teens.

THE TAMING OF THE SHREW

1967, 126 min, NR, 10 and up
Dir: Franco Zeffirelli. Elizabeth Taylor, Richard Burton, Michael York
Shakespeare's play about the wild woman tamed by an even wilder man stars then-married wild couple Elizabeth Taylor and Richard Burton, enjoying themselves enormously. Burton plays Petruchio, who comes "to live it wealthily in Padua," saying he will marry any woman as long as she brings a fortune. This is very convenient for his friends, both of whom want to marry the beautiful Bianca, because Bianca's wealthy father has said she may not marry until someone marries her sister Katherina, also known as "Kate the cursed" for her temper. Petruchio agrees to marry Kate for her fortune. Once he meets Kate, he sees she is both beautiful and witty, and that her temper stems from feeling misunderstood and unloved. He marries her quickly, and then "tames" her by showing her an excess of attention. When Petruchio and Kate return for a visit, they amaze the community with her docility, both hugely enjoying the joke.

Though sometimes criticized as a feminist nightmare (the idea of "taming" connotes mastering an animal), it is perfectly possible to view this play as quite the contrary, and the range of interpretations are well worth family discussion. NOTE: In Shakespeare's play, the entire story is a "play within a play," put on as a part of a prank designed to confuse a homeless man into thinking he is a nobleman. What does this tell us about Shakespeare's view of the story?
CONNECTIONS: Watch *Kiss Me Kate* the brilliant musical about a warring couple starring in an adaptation of Shakespeare's play.

WILD HEARTS CAN'T BE BROKEN

1991, 88 min, G, 8 and up
Dir: Steve Miner. Gabrielle Anwar, Cliff Robertson, Michael Schoeffling
In the 1930s, one of the top tourist attractions in the country was a girl who dove into water mounted on a horse, in Atlantic City. That girl was Sonora Webster, and what the audience did not know was that she was blind as the result of an accident in one of her first dives. This movie is based on the real story of Sonora (Gabrielle Anwar), a plucky teenager who leaves home during the Depression and shows independence, persistence, and courage in following her dream.

SEE ALSO:

Adam's Rib Katharine Hepburn plays a feminist lawyer married to a man who respects and admires her intelligence and courage, even when they are on opposite sides in the courtroom.

Annie Oakley Contrary to the popular conception, fueled by Irving Berlin's Annie Get Your Gun, this version of the story accurately shows that Oakley's husband, fellow sharpshooter Frank Butler, was her most enthusiastic supporter.

Born Yesterday Judy Holliday plays a woman who learns she has a fine mind and an honest heart, and she can get more satisfaction from relying on them than she did in relying on her looks and ability to attract men.

Cat Ballou Jane Fonda plays a young woman of courage and determination in the Old West. When her father is killed by crooks who want their land, she takes charge.

The Journey of Natty Gann A young girl travels across the country to join her father.

Julia Two strong, independent women, friends since childhood, demonstrate commitment and loyalty as one helps the other in her fight against the Nazis.

A League of Their Own Based on a true story, this movie about women baseball players shows their spirit, skill, and teamwork, and the pleasure it gave them to be able to use them.

Mean Girls A new student has to learn to navigate the social intricacies of high school.

The Nasty Girl The heroine of this real-life story will not be dissuaded from her search for the truth about her town's culpability for Nazi war crimes, no matter what the cost.

National Velvet Velvet disguises herself as a boy to enter the Grand National Steeplechase with her beloved horse, and together they give everything they have to win.

The Solid Gold Cadillac A woman finds that asking honest questions and insisting on honest answers leads to the overthrow of corrupt managers.

Where the Lilies Bloom A young girl keeps her family together after her father dies.

11

SCHOOL DAYS

"Have you learn'd lessons only of those who admired you,
and were tender with you, and stood aside for you?
"Have you not learn'd great lessons from those who reject you, and brace themselves
against you? or who treat you with contempt, or dispute the passage with you?"
WALT WHITMAN

Schools, like the Old West, provide a basic point of reference for almost any kind of story. They are arenas where an infinite number of stories and characters reside, a natural setting for drama or comedy, even for a musical or a thriller. We all go to school and we all have many of our formative experiences there.

In our first venture outside of our families, we enter school, learning not just reading and writing and arithmetic but equally important lessons about the larger world. We learn about rules, explicit (hang your coat in your cubby, raise your hand before you speak, take turns on the swings) and implicit (kids who bring peanut butter sandwiches never get anyone to trade with them, kids who can cross the monkey bars without falling are cooler than ones who can't, takeovers only for interference). We have our first confrontations with bureaucracy. We eat whatever that gloppy mess is that the ladies with the hair nets give us every Tuesday. Teachers wield enormous power over our lives. Sometimes they make us miserable. If we are very, very lucky, over the course of our school years, we have some who inspire us so much their words live inside us forever.

Movies throughout this book draw on school as a setting. Some movies use schools as a microcosm of society, with firmly established hierarchies that have their own highly individualized criteria for determining status and power. This can be played as comedy (as in **The Lawrenceville Stories**) or drama (**The Chocolate War**). Some use school simply as the setting for a coming-of-age story, focusing almost exclusively on the students, with very little time in the classroom and no adult major characters. There are many school movies that focus on a teacher who changes the students' lives, whose life is changed by teaching, or both.

Occasionally, we also see a teacher with a malevolent influence or horrible schools with cruel teachers. But books, plays, and movies are all written by writers, all of whom at some time in their lives fell in love with words, and all of whom have some teacher they want to thank (as in **The Corn Is Green** for example), and movies give us a chance to be inspired by those who inspired them the most.

Dead Poets Society

1989, 128 min, PG, 12 and up
Dir: Peter Weir. Robin Williams, Ethan Hawke, Robert Sean Leonard 12 and up
PLOT: Welton is an exclusive boys' prep school, dedicated to "Tradition, Discipline, Honor, and Excellence." The boys' parents, arriving for the new term, are equally demanding, reminding their boys of the importance of academic success and encouraging conformity.

A new teacher named Keating (Robin Williams) takes a different approach with his boys. He urges them to "seize the day," make the most of their youth and energy, and express themselves as individuals through poetry and language. When he attended Welton, Keating was a founder of the "Dead Poets Society," a group dedicated to Thoreau's aim to "suck the very marrow out of life."

The boys take Keating's lessons to heart. They reestablish the society and, breaking out of the mold the school has formed for them, commit themselves to goals that mean something more important to them than achieving good grades. Knox Overstreet (Josh Charles) writes poetry to a beautiful girl; Neil (Robert Sean Leonard) auditions for a play and, forging his father's signature on the permission slip, accepts a lead part. Keating's words also have an effect on a nervous Todd Anderson (Ethan Hawke), who lives in the twin shadows of a successful older brother and out-of-touch parents.

The school authorities try to stamp out the boys' self-expression. The headmaster seeks to root out the Dead Poets Society and find out who put the boys up to it. The boys break ranks and admit it was Keating.

Neil, meanwhile, glories in a highly successful portrayal of Puck in *A Midsummer Night's Dream*. His father is furious and wants to remove his son from Welton, send him to a military school, and groom him for Harvard and medical school as planned. Neil, despairing he will never be allowed to do what he wants, commits suicide.

The Welton authorities blame Keating and the Dead Poets Society. Keating is fired, but some of his students have learned to seize the day.

DISCUSSION: Keating's challenge is subtler than that of the teachers in **Stand and Deliver** or **The Blackboard Jungle**. His students are at the other end of the economic spectrum, with more material goods than they know what to do with. Like the barrio and ghetto students, they have a kind of complacency that Keating must overcome. His challenge is to get them to accept the responsibility of thinking for themselves.

Despite Williams's magnetic and inspiring performance, the weakness of this plot makes this a hard movie for many grown-ups to take. Still, it is a popular and moving film for teenagers and provides a good opportunity for discussing important issues.

Keating challenges the boys to think for themselves instead of blindly accepting the system and values presented to them by the school and their parents. He asks why poetry was invented and brushes aside the expected "blue book" answers for one that goes straight to the boys' hearts: "To woo women." This is meaningful because it is refreshingly honest and direct, and because it connects them with the "dead poets," who they now understand had precisely the same feelings as the boys themselves.

Though awkwardly and melodramatically handled, the film raises the issue of conflict between a parent's goals and ideas about what is best for a child and the child's own dreams. When do parents cross the line between using their experience and judgment about what is in a child's best interests and losing sight of the child as an individual with his own talents and goals? It is also a chance to talk about Neil's decision to commit suicide, and why he felt he had no other alternatives.

Keating makes learning exciting. He orders his boys to tear up an introduction to poetry in their textbook that seeks to explain the value of Shakespeare by resorting to a mathematical graph. Instead, he teaches them to explore the vitality of language. He teaches his students to become thinking human beings, not robots, to challenge assumptions, to ask questions.

Keating teaches there is nothing wrong in being a doctor or a lawyer, but it is wrong for anyone to commit himself to any career without the music and passion of language in his soul.

At the end, Keating is fired, one boy whom he has inspired lies dead, and another is expelled. Yet Keating has left something of lasting value and that boys have learned, in the words of Drummond in **Inherit the Wind**, to think about what they think about.

PROFANITY: Mild.

NUDITY/SEXUAL REFERENCES: Mild.

ALCOHOL/DRUG ABUSE: Drinking at a party; Knox gets drunk, boys smoke pipes.

VIOLENCE/SCARINESS: Boy punished by being paddled, Neil commits suicide (off-camera).

TOLERANCE/DIVERSITY ISSUES: Tolerance of individual differences is a theme of the movie. The student body is all white males.

QUESTIONS FOR FAMILIES:

- What is the meaning of carpe diem and why does Keating tell the boys it is important?

- Why is Todd Anderson so nervous about coming to Welton? Why does he find it hard to join the Dead Poets Society? Why is he unable to complete the poetry assignment?

- How does Keating turn the boys into "free thinkers"?

- How is Knox eventually able to win over Chris?

- Why are some of the boys willing to accuse Keating of inciting them to misbehavior?

CONNECTIONS: Weir is also the director of *Witness*, *Master and Commander*, *The Truman Show*, and *The Year of Living Dangerously*.

ACTIVITIES: Form a Dead Poets Society and spend an hour every month reading aloud, starting with some of the poetry from this movie. Have each member of the family bring a poem, and hold the meetings at different times and places: midnight in the attic, dawn in the kitchen.

Drumline

2002, 118 min, PG-13, 12 and up

Dir: Charles Stone III. Nick Cannon, Orlando Jones, Zoe Saldana, GQ

PLOT: Devon (*Nickelodeon*'s Nick Cannon) is a spirited kid who wins a full scholarship to college for his drum playing. The school, the fictitious Atlanta A&T, has a world-class marching band that hasn't won the big competition sponsored by BET television, and the school's president has put a lot of pressure on the bandmaster Dr. Lee, (Orlando Jones) to do whatever it takes to beat cross-town rival (and real-life marching band champs), Morris Brown College. Lee believes that his job is to teach his students about music and about character, even at the cost of losing. At the center of this argument is Devon, whose flashy style and buoyant self-confidence put him at odds with the band's most sacred commitment: "one band, one sound."

We first see Devon at his high school graduation, adding a few unscripted licks to a drum performance, thanking his mother, and then before going to his party, stopping by to confront his father with grace and dignity, letting him know that he has managed to achieve success even without his help or support. We see that Devon is talented, confident, and headstrong, but that he is also acutely aware of his struggle to achieve all he has so far and of the challenges ahead as he leaves home for the first time.

He arrives at A&T to find something like boot camp. The student director of the "drumline," Sean (Leonard Roberts) is the drill sergeant, and he and Devon are like two rams getting ready to head-butt each other in a battle for dominance. Devon also has to learn that his bravado won't get him very far with Laila (Zoe Saldana), the pretty upper-classman who leads the band's dancers. Devon has to pay the price for some mistakes, from not reading to the end of the rule-book to having lied on his application. He learns that "one band, one sound" is about more than the music.

DISCUSSION: John Philip Sousa and all of the Music Man's 76 Trombones never dreamed that marching bands could be this cool. Farewell to the nerdy reputation for "band camp." "Drumline" makes marching bands as soul-stirring as raise-the-roof gospel and more irresistibly, foot-stompingly, hip-hoppily thrilling than any video currently playing on MTV.

It's a simple story, but very winningly told.

The movie is about more than music, too. The band numbers themselves would be more than worth the price of admission, but the story and the characters hold their own. The story may be an old one, but the details of this unexplored world make it seem fresh and the very appealing performers make it seem real. Orlando Jones is one of the most talented comic actors in movies today, but in this decidedly un-comic role he manages to make Dr. Lee seem dedicated and principled without being priggish or inflexible. Cannon is outstanding, making us believe in Devon's talent and charm. Cannon makes Devon confident and vulnerable at the same time, and lets us see Devon's growth subtly and naturally.

PROFANITY: Some very strong language.

NUDITY/SEXUAL REFERENCES: Moderate sexual references, including comparison of playing an instrument to making love, "virgin" used as an insult. Laila makes it clear that she is interested in a boyfriend, not a brief encounter.

ALCOHOL/DRUG ABUSE: Mild references.

VIOLENCE/SCARINESS: None.

TOLERANCE/DIVERSITY ISSUES: A theme of the movie; the one white student in the band is at first looked at with suspicion, but later accepted warmly.

QUESTIONS FOR FAMILIES:

- What conflicts does Dr. Lee face as he tries to do what is best for the band. What does he decide is most important, and when, and why?

- Why was it important to show Devon's confrontation with his father? How did that relationship affect his relationships with strong characters like Sean and Dr. Lee?

- What is it about Devon that Laila is drawn to? Why?

- What can you tell from the scene where each of the section leaders explains why that instrument is the most important? What does "one band, one sound" mean?

- Why does Dr. Lee think that honor and discipline are more important than talent?

CONNECTIONS: Families who enjoy this movie will enjoy *Fame*. Mature viewers should see Spike Lee's outstanding film based on his experiences at a traditionally black college, *School Daze*. Families should try to see some marching bands and compare the different styles.

Harry Potter and the Sorcerer's Stone

2001, 152 min, PG, 10 and up

Dir: Chris Columbus. Maggie Smith, Richard Harris, Daniel Radcliffe

PLOT: Harry (Daniel Radcliffe) is the orphan who lives with the odious Durs-leys, his aunt, uncle, and cousin. They make him sleep in a closet under the stairs and never show him any attention or affection. On his 11th birthday, he receives a mysterious letter, but his uncle destroys it before he can read it. Letters keep coming, and the Dursleys take Harry to a remote lighthouse to keep him from getting them. Finally one is delivered to the lighthouse in the very large person of

Hagrid, a huge, bearded man with a weakness for scary-looking creatures. It turns out that the letters were coming from Hogwarts, a boarding school for young witches and wizards, and Harry is expected for the fall term.

Hagrid takes Harry to buy his school supplies in Diagon Alley, a small corner of London that like so much of the magic world exists near but apart from the world of the muggles (non-magical humans). We are thus treated to one of the most imaginative and engaging settings ever committed to film, mixing the London of Dickens and Peter Pan with sheer, bewitching fantasy. A winding street that looks like it is hundreds of years old holds a bank run by gnomes, a store where the wand picks the wizard, and a pub filled with an assortment of curious characters.

Then it's off to the train station, where the Hogwarts Express leaves from Track 9 ¾. On the train, Harry meets his future best friends, Ron (Rupert Grint) and Hermione (Emma Watson) and gets to try delicacies like chocolate frogs (they really hop) and Bertie Bott's Everyflavor Beans (and they do mean every flavor).

Then things really get exciting. Hogwarts is in many ways just like every other school, but with classes in potions and "defense against the dark arts," a sport called Quidditch (a sort of flying soccer/basketball), a mysterious trap door guarded by a three-headed dog named Fluffy, a baby dragon named Norbert, some information about Harry's family and history, and some important lessons in loyalty and courage.

DISCUSSION: The settings manage to be sensationally imaginative and yet at the same time so clearly believable and lived-in and just plain right that you'll think you could find them yourself, if you could get to Track 9 ¾. Richard Harris turns in his all-time best performance as headmaster Albus Dumbledore, Maggie Smith (whose on-screen teaching roles extend from **The Prime of Miss Jean Brodie** to *Sister Act*) brings just the right tone of dry asperity to Professor McGonagall, and Robbie Coltrane is a giant with a heart to match as Hagrid (for me, the most astounding special effect of all was the understated way the movie made him look as though he was 10 feet tall). Alan Rickman provides shivers as potions master Professor Snape. The kids are mostly just called upon to look either astonished or resolute.

PROFANITY: Mild schoolyard language.
NUDITY/SEXUAL REFERENCES: None.
ALCOHOL/DRUG ABUSE: None.
VIOLENCE/SCARINESS: Intense peril for a PG, tense and gross moments.

TOLERANCE/DIVERSITY ISSUES: A metaphorical theme of the movie, increasingly emphasized as the series progresses. Strong and capable female characters but no significant minority characters.

QUESTIONS FOR FAMILIES:

- What made the books so popular with children all over the world?

- Why did Dumbledore leave Harry with the Dursleys?

- Why did Harry decide not to be friends with Draco?

- Harry showed both good and bad judgment—when? How can you tell?

- What do you think are some of the other flavors in Everyflavor Beans?

CONNECTIONS: Families will enjoy all of the Harry Potter books and the movie sequels, *Harry Potter and the Chamber of Secrets* and *Harry Potter and the Prisoner of Azkaban*. The director of the third movie, Alfonso Cuarón, directed **A Little Princess**.

The King and I

1956, 133 min, NR, 8 and up
Dir: Walter Lang. Yul Brynner, Deborah Kerr, Rita Moreno
PLOT: British Anna Leonowens (Deborah Kerr) and her son, Louis, arrive in Siam in the mid 1800s. She has accepted a position as teacher for the children of the king (Yul Brynner). She is frightened and unsure, far from home in a place that seems very exotic. She tells her son that whenever she feels afraid she "whistles a happy tune" so no one will suspect, and so she fools herself into thinking she isn't afraid.

She meets the king and is upset to find that contrary to his promise in the letter offering the position, he does not plan to give her a house of her own but wants her to live at the palace. She is ready to leave, but when she meets the children, she is utterly charmed by them and agrees to stay.

Anna becomes friendly with the king's first wife, Lady Thiang (Terry Saunders), mother of the heir to the throne, Prince Chulalongkom. She enjoys "getting to know" the children and their mothers, from the king's vast harem. Anna and the king find each other's cultures "a puzzlement," but grow to respect each other. She finds a special friend in Tuptim, who was delivered to the king as a "gift" and longs to be with the man she loves.

The king is devoted to the traditions of his country, but is also passionately interested in bringing the best of the modem Western world to his people. When British diplomats arrive, Anna helps the king show them Siam need not be colonized. Tuptim, who organized the entertainment, puts on a production of *Uncle Tom's Cabin* to make the point that the king should not have slaves. The king is furious, even more so when he finds she has run away with her lover. He starts to whip her. But the traditions and modern concepts of "civilization" battle within him until he is stricken. He dies, Anna by his side, as the prince decrees the changes he will make for the country's future.

DISCUSSION: The king is eager to embrace scientific advances, but has a hard time defining himself and his role in a manner consistent with the cultural traditions of his country. Those traditions place a huge burden on him by making him, at least in the eyes of his subjects, infallible. When confronted with too much conflict between his heart and his mind, he cannot bear it, and dies almost literally of a broken heart.

There is also the more personal issue of pride. As Anna points out, when Tuptim runs away, his pride is hurt, not his heart. This provides a chance to talk about the difference between the kind of pride that means you feel good about what you have accomplished and who you are and the kind of pride making you worry too much about how you appear to others.

In the letter he writes to Anna as he is dying, the king says he thinks most often of those who insisted he be his best self.

Talk to young people about the way the music helps to tell the story. See what they can tell about each of the children as they come in to greet their father, and what they learn from the way he greets them.

PROFANITY: None.

NUDITY/SEXUAL REFERENCES: The king has a harem, including slaves like Tuptim. Wives wear hoop skirts for the dinner with the British, but when they bow, Anna sees (off-camera) they are not wearing underwear.

ALCOHOL/DRUG ABUSE: None.

VIOLENCE/SCARINESS: Tuptim is brought back to be beaten; the king's illness and death.

TOLERANCEIDIVERSITY ISSUES: A theme of the movie.

QUESTIONS FOR FAMILIES:

• Why does "whistling a happy tune" make Anna feel less afraid? What do you do when you need to feel less afraid?

- In what ways does the king want to keep his traditions? In what ways does he want to change? What kinds of changes are the hardest?

- Why does the king think that Lincoln is doing the right thing in freeing the slaves, while being unable to connect Lincoln's actions to the situation in his own country?

- What can you tell about the king and Anna by the way she keeps her head no lower than his?

- How is Chulalongkom different from his father?

CONNECTIONS: A nonmusical film of the story, *Anna and the King of Siam*, is also very good. Anna is played by Irene Dunne, and the king is played by Rex Harrison, a long way from his roles as Henry Higgins in **My Fair Lady** and as *Dr. Doolittle*. Children are not likely to enjoy Harriet Beecher Stowe's *Uncle Tom's Cabin*, but they may like to know more about Stowe's life, and about the story of her book and the role it played in educating Americans about the tragedy of slavery. Discuss the way that Tuptim adapted this very American story to Siamese traditions of storytelling.

Yul Brynner won an Oscar for his performance as the king, the role for which he is best remembered. You can also see him in **The Magnificent Seven**. Deborah Kerr appeared in many outstanding films, playing a governess in **The Chalk Garden** and *The Innocents*, and appearing as the sympathetic wife of a teacher in **Tea and Sympathy**. Rita Moreno, who plays Tuptim, appeared as Anita in **West Side Story**.

ACTIVITIES: Look up Siam (now Thailand) on a map and read about it, and about the reigns of Mongkut and Chulalongkom in an encyclopedia. You may be able to find instructions for making Thai shadow-puppets, a terrific craft for children.

The Miracle Worker

1962, 108 min, NR, b&w, 10 and up
Dir: Arthur Penn. Anne Bancroft, Patty Duke
PLOT: Helen Keller, blind and deaf from an illness she had as a toddler, is treated more as a pet than as a child by her family. She has no knowledge or understanding, and just grabs whatever she wants and breaks whatever she doesn't want. Her parents hire Annie Sullivan, once blind herself, to be her teacher, though Helen's father and brother have no hope Helen will ever learn

anything, and her mother is too tenderhearted to support any attempt to impose any rules on Helen.

Sullivan begins by teaching Helen basics like insisting she eat only from her own plate. She also teaches Helen finger spelling, using her hands to spell out the names of everything Helen touches. Helen learns to imitate the finger motions, but does not connect them to anything. "Obedience without understanding is a blindness, too—is that all I wished on her?" Sullivan asks. Before Helen can learn language, she must understand there is such a thing as language.

Sullivan gets permission to take Helen to live in a small building on the Kellers' property so she can uphold consistent standards without being undermined by the family. They have some fierce battles, but make enough progress to move back into the house. Once home again, Helen reverts to her wild ways. After one chaotic meal, Sullivan grabs her and forces her to the pump, to fill the pitcher of water she knocked over. As Helen feels the water rush over one hand, Sullivan finger spells "water" into the other. Suddenly, Helen understands. A word she heard as a baby comes back to her, and she knows that "w-a-t-e-r" spells water. She runs all over, asking for the names of everything. As the movie ends, it is clear that Sullivan has opened the world to her.

DISCUSSION: This outstanding movie is based on the true story of two of the great figures of American history, Helen Keller and Anne Sullivan Macy. Keep in mind the title refers to Sullivan; when the playwright-screenwriter William Gibson is asked about "the movie about Helen Keller," he says, "If it were about her, it would be called 'The Miracle Work-ee.'" Helen Keller was a woman of astonishing achievement, but all of it was made possible by her teacher.

Talk to kids about how people learn, about the importance of language and the challenges of teaching children with disabilities. Discuss the different ways the main characters felt about Helen and how that affected their ability to teach her.

PROFANITY: None.
NUDITY/SEXUAL REFERENCES: None.
ALCOHOl/DRUG ABUSE: None.
VIOLENCE/SCARINESS: Helen's tantrums.
TOLERANCE/DIVERSITY ISSUES: A theme of the movie, as applied to the disabled.

QUESTIONS FOR FAMILIES:

- Why did Helen's father and brother think she could not learn? Why did Annie Sullivan think she could?

- Why was it hard for Helen's mother to help her?

- Why is it important to be taught by someone who believes in you?

CONNECTIONS: The movie was remade for television, with Duke playing Annie Sullivan.

ACTIVITIES: Kids can read one of the many biographies of Helen Keller, and *The Story of My Life*, her autobiography. Most dictionaries include a diagram of finger spelling. Children can have a lot of fun learning to finger spell and sending messages to each other. Let them experiment walking around the house blind-folded, watching television with the sound off, or trying to understand someone speaking a language they don't know, to give them an idea of the challenges faced by people with disabilities.

My Bodyguard

198 97 min, PG, 10 and up
Dir: Tony Bill. Ruth Gordon, Martin Mull, Chris Makepeace, Adam Baldwin, Joan Cusack

PLOT: Fifteen-year-old Cliff (Chris Makepeace) lives in Chicago's elegant Ambassador East Hotel with his kind but harried father, the hotel manager (Martin Mull), and his loving but dotty grandmother (Ruth Gordon). On Cliff's first day in a new high school, he offends the school bully, Moody (Matt Dillon). When Cliff refuses to pay protection money, Moody and his friends harass him relentlessly.

Cliff has another classmate, huge, silent, and mysterious Ricky Linderman (Adam Baldwin); there are rumors Ricky killed a kid and raped a teacher. Cliff asks Ricky to be his bodyguard. At first he refuses. Ricky is clearly someone who does not want to have any kind of relationship with anyone. When he finds Cliff stuck in a locker, he agrees, and there is a supremely satisfying scene where Cliff springs his new bodyguard on Moody, to the cheers of his new friends.

Cliff, exulting, wants to make friends with Ricky, but Ricky refuses. Cliff asks a sympathetic teacher for advice, and learns Ricky's brother accidentally killed himself with a gun, and Ricky was the one who found him. Cliff follows Ricky, and gradually earns his trust. Together they find the missing piece of the motorbike Ricky is rebuilding. Then Moody returns, with his own bodyguard, and Cliff and Ricky must both find a way to fight back.

DISCUSSION: Just as life becomes the most confusing, as everyone around us seems to be at a different stage of development, and we seem to be at several different stages ourselves, we are confronted with problems our parents can't solve for us. This movie beautifully catches that moment. Without telling Cliff, his well-meaning father calls the school principal after Moody chases him on the first day of school. Cliff already knows this is not the answer, and sure enough, the next day, the principal calls them both in, tells Moody not to make jokes like that again, and tells Cliff not to be so quick to "cry wolf."

Cliff is nervous about talking to Ricky, but he knows he would rather pay to hire someone than pay extortion, so he approaches him. Cliff correctly sees the problem is not the risk of physical injury as much as the risk of losing his self-respect. At the end of the movie, when Ricky has vanquished Moody's "bodyguard," Ricky insists Cliff fight Moody himself; he understands the real problem, too.

Also well-handled is the way that Cliff gains Ricky's confidence, and the way this allows Ricky to tell the truth about the accident that killed his brother, which in turn allows him to begin to heal at last. When Ricky pulls away from Cliff's grandmother's efforts to read his future in his palm to hide the scars on his wrist, she says to him quietly, "Open up, Ricky. You're among friends." The subplot at the hotel, about an ambitious employee who plots to get the manager's job, does not work as well as the rest of the movie, but it does provide a nice counterpoint; the employee is a menace in Cliff's father's life as Moody is in Cliff's.

PROFANITY: Mild.
NUDITY/SEXUAL REFERENCES: Cliff and his father use a telescope to gaze at women in lingerie. Cliff's grandmother flirts (sometimes outrageously) with just about everyone and is referred to as always "picking up men." Cliff's father has a conversation with some mild innuendo with a woman guest leaving the hotel.
ALCOHOL/DRUG ABUSE: Ricky smokes (but not after he makes friends with Cliff). The grandmother has a drinking problem and gets tipsy.
VIOLENCE/SCARINESS: The bullies engage in menacing behavior, but there is little violence until the fistfights at the end.
TOLERANCE/DIVERSITY ISSUES: All of the main characters are white. Gender roles are fairly standard—female teacher, male principal, etc.

QUESTIONS FOR FAMILIES:

- How does Cliff know he does not have to be scared of Ricky?

- Why are there untrue rumors about Ricky?

- What makes people act like bullies?

- Do some of the kids admire Moody for his behavior? How can you tell?

CONNECTIONS: Veteran actress Ruth Gordon, an Oscar-winner for *Rosemary's Baby*, was also an accomplished screenwriter and playwright and, with her husband, Garson Kanin, wrote Tracy and Hepburn classics **Adam's Rib** and **Pat and Mike**. Fans of television's *Fernwood 2-Night* and *Roseanne* will recognize Martin Mull. Joan Cusack plays Cliff's friend Shelley.

The Prime of Miss Jean Brodie

1969, 116 min, PG, high schoolers
Dir: Ronald Neame. Maggie Smith, Pamela Franklin
PLOT: Miss Jean Brodie (Maggie Smith) is a strong-willed and unconventional teacher at the Marcia Blaine School for Girls in Scotland in 1932. She tells her students, "I am in the business of putting old heads on young shoulders, and all of my students are the creme de la creme. Give me a girl of an impressionable age, and she is mine for life." She tells them, too, she is giving them her "prime," that they are her life's work.

She teaches a small group of "impressionable" students whom she has selected to be her special followers, who must do big and important things. The girls, dazzled by her vibrant and independent spirit, are enthralled by her. Miss Brodie encourages foolish Mary McGregor to run away to fight on the side of the fascists in the Spanish Civil War, and she is killed when her train is blown up by rebel troops. Miss Brodie has determined Jenny will be the romantic beauty and plans to make this happen by having her be seduced by Miss Brodie's own former lover, art teacher Teddy Lloyd. Sandy (Pamela Franklin), the brightest of the girls, decides to "put a stop to" her. Sandy deliberately has an affair with Teddy Lloyd both to spite Miss Brodie's plans and to compete with her, and she is hurt badly when she sees, in Teddy's portrait of her, that it is still Jean Brodie whom he cares for. Sandy "puts a stop" to her at last by giving the headmistress the ammunition she needs to fire Miss Brodie.

DISCUSSION: Maggie Smith won an Oscar for her performance as Jean Brodie, brilliantly showing the fascinating as well as the foolish aspects of the character. As children begin to look beyond their parents for inspiration and validation, it is worthwhile for them to think about how easily they can be manipulated or simply misdirected. Some of Miss Brodie's students loved her because she was the only one who thought they were special. Mary McGregor died trying to live up to that image. Sandy knows Mary was special, but not for the reasons Miss Brodie thought.

Miss Brodie projected herself and her dreams onto her students. Even Sandy was a victim. She did not develop or pursue her own dreams (any more than Teddy pursued her instead of Jean Brodie); everything she did was more about Miss Brodie than it was about herself.

PROFANITY: None.
NUDITY/SEXUAL REFERENCES: The girls compose a letter as they imagine Miss Brodie would send to her beau, including, "allow me, in conclusion, to congratulate you warmly on your sexual intercourse as well as your singing." Miss Brodie hopes Jenny will have a number of interesting lovers, and all but acts as a procurer to arrange (unsuccessfully) for Teddy to be her first. There is a brief nude scene when Teddy paints Sandy's picture.
ALCOHOL/DRUG ABUSE: None.
VIOLENCE/SCARINESS: None (Mary is killed off-screen).
TOLERANCE/DIVERSITY ISSUES: None.
QUESTIONS FOR FAMILIES:

- In what ways is Miss Brodie good for her students? In what ways is she bad for them?

- What about her makes it possible for her to be such a strong influence on them? What about each of them makes this possible?

- How does Miss Brodie try to have her students live the lives she cannot or will not live herself?

- How does Sandy "put a stop" to her? Why is she the only one who can do it?

CONNECTIONS: The novel by Muriel Spark is well worth reading. Maggie Smith also appears in **A Room With a View**, playing a very different character, and in the **Harry Potter** movies, playing a very different kind of teacher. Fans of public television's *Upstairs, Downstairs* may recognize Gordon Jenkins as Hudson, the butler.

ACTIVITIES: Teenagers may want to learn something about the Spanish Civil War to understand why Sandy objected to Miss Brodie's support of the fascists (in a small way, she was something of a fascist herself, which may explain her enthusiasm for them). *To Die in Madrid* is a documentary about the conflict. Another documentary, *The Good Fight*, focuses on the Americans who fought the fascists.

School of Rock

2003, 108 min, PG-13, 10 and up
Dir: Richard Linklater. Jack Black, Joan Cusack
PLOT: Jack Black plays Dewey Finn, a musician who doesn't just live for rock. He barely acknowledges that there is anything else. That is why he is astonished when he is fired by his band and when his best friend Ned (screenwriter Mike White) tells him that if he does not start paying rent, he will have to move out. Ned was once a rocker with a group called Maggots of Death, but now he is a substitute teacher with a girlfriend and tells Dewey it is time to grow up.

So, when Dewey intercepts a call from Principal Mullins (Joan Cusack) offering Ned a substitute teacher position for fifth graders at a posh prep school, he accepts and shows up pretending to be Ned.

Of course he thinks he will just snooze through the classes and of course his students will be appalled (but also a little bit thrilled) by his sense of anarchy. When he tears down the neatly lettered class list of stars and demerits, they are stunned. They look around as though waiting for lightning to strike, a sort of ultimate demerit. The fifth graders are just young enough to trust their teacher and just old enough to be enthralled when he tells them that their secret new project will be to spend the entire school day creating a rock band. Once he assures them that this will impress the admissions office at Harvard, they are all on board.

Soon, everyone in the class is a part of the band, with guitar wizard Zach, back-up singers, roadies, groupies, and a stylist. The kids learn something about the history of rock, something about music, and quite a bit about expressing themselves. Dewey learns something about what it really means to be part of a band.

DISCUSSION: Like the music he loves, Dewey is loud, immature, messy, self-absorbed, passionate, incapable of complying with any authority, rule, or attempt at civilization, and just about irresistible. Dewey's love for the music is so pure and so complete that it is impossible for him to imagine that everyone might not support him.

This is by far the most accessible and conventional film from director Richard Linklater (*Waking Life, Dazed and Confused*) and Mike White (*The Good Girl*) neither of whom are known for heartwarming, feel-good movies. Still, that is what this is, a sort of **To Sir With Love** crossed with *Spinal Tap*. Black is enormously entertaining and the kids are terrific. So is the music!

PROFANITY: Brief strong language.
NUDITY/SEXUAL REFERENCES:
ALCOHOL/DRUG ABUSE: Alcohol abuse, drug references. Character loosens up when she gets tipsy.
VIOLENCE/SCARINESS:
TOLERANCE/DIVERSITY ISSUES:
QUESTIONS FOR FAMILIES:

• In the movie, Dewey and the children tell a terrible lie. What should be the consequence?

• Why is music so important to him? What does it allow him to express?

• What is the most important thing he learned from the kids, and what is the most important thing they learned from him?

CONNECTIONS: Mature audiences who enjoy this movie will also enjoy *The Commitments* and *Spnal Tap* and they will enjoy Black's performance as a devoted music fan in *High Fidelity*.

For information about Black's own rock band, Tenacious D, check http://www.tenaciousd.com. Families might also like to see some very different movies about music teachers who touch the lives of students, like *Music of the Heart* and *Mr. Holland's Opus*. They will also enjoy a very different story about a music teacher who begins by being a con man, **The Music Man**.

THE BLACKBOARD JUNGLE

1955, 101 min, NR, b&w, 12 and up
Dir: Richard Brooks. Glenn Ford, Vic Morrow, Sidney Poitier
This movie shocked audiences when it came out, but audiences were more sensitive and vulnerable back then. Just to put things in perspective, it was considered shocking the musical score included rock and roll (*Rock Around the Clock*), the

first Hollywood release to do so. Glenn Ford plays the teacher who is confronted by a group of tough juvenile delinquents, including Vic Morrow and Sidney Poitier. The movie ends a little more positively than the book, but does not pretend to suggest a teacher can reach more than a few of these kids.

THE BROWNING VERSION

1951, 90 min, NR, b&w, mature high school age
Dir: Anthony Asquith. Michael Redgrave
As a British prep school classics professor (Michael Redgrave) is forced to retire due to ill health, he is overcome by his failure to achieve any connection to his bitter, unfaithful wife or to his bored students. He is able to gather the courage to acknowledge his failure and establish some sense of dignity and accountability following two unexpected expressions of support, from a student he has been tutoring and from his wife's lover. Redgrave is heartbreaking.
CONNECTIONS: The 1994 remake (rated R for language and sexual references) is uneven, but Albert Finney is superb.

CONRACK

1974, 107 min, PG, 12 and up
Dir: Martin Ritt. Jon Voight, Paul Winfield, Hume Cronyn
Before he wrote the books that became The Prince of Tides and The Great Santini, Pat Conroy spent a year teaching the children on an island off the coast of South Carolina. This movie is based on his memoir of that year (Conrack is what the kids called him). Jon Voight plays Conrack, who is horrified at the indifference and racism of the local school authorities and who, with more energy than strategy, does his best to help the children learn. Paul Winfield is terrific as a recluse who becomes his friend, and Hume Cronyn is smoothly wicked as a bigoted school administrator.
CONNECTIONS: A new movie based on Conroy's book is currently in production.

GOODBYE. MR CHIPS

1939, 118 min, NR, b&w, 10 and up
Dir: Sam Wood. Robert Donat, Greer Garson
The story of a shy schoolmaster based on the sentimental novella by James Hilton (Lost Horizon) stars Oscar-winner Robert Donat. At first, he is so worried about losing control of the students he is overly strict and humorless. When he falls in

love with the warm and understanding Katherine (Greer Garson, in her film debut), she encourages him to allow his compassion and affection for the boys to show. After her death in childbirth, he devotes his life to the boys, coming back from retirement when the younger teachers leave to fight in World War I, and staying on into his eighties, to provide tea and tutoring to "his boys." CONNEC-TIONS: Families who enjoy this movie will also enjoy *To Serve Them All My Days*.

THE LAWRENCEVILLE STORIES

1988, 3 hour-long episodes, NR, 8 and up
Dir: Allan A. Goldstein. Zach Galligan, Nicholas Rowe, Stephen Baldwin, Dave Foley
Owen Johnson's classic stories of life at a turn-of-the-century boys' school have been turned into a completely delightful three-part miniseries produced for the Disney Channel and available on video. Zach Galligan and Nicholas Rowe are superb as the two boys competing for status according to rules that are arcane and inexplicable but somehow completely understood and accepted by every boy and teacher, with the possible exception of one boy from a wealthy family dubbed, in the school's tradition of evocative nicknames, "The Uncooked Beefsteak." High-lights include "Hungry" Smeed's great pancake record, and the headmaster's sub-lime plan for letting the punishment fit the crime after an especially outrageous prank. The production values are gorgeous, with sumptuous period detail.
CONNECTIONS: Future stars Stephen Baldwin (*The Usual Suspects*) and Dave Foley (television's *Kids in the Hall* and *NewsRadio*) appear as two of the students, known as "Gutter Pup" and "Old Ironsides." The headmaster is played by Edward Hermann (*The Gilmore Girls*).
ACTIVITIES: The books were also filmed as *The Happy Years*, with Dean Stock-well, and are still delightful to read (or read aloud). Author Johnson insisted all of the details were based on actual experience, even the nicknames.

MEAN GIRLS

2004, 97 min, PG-13, 14 and up
Dir: Mark S. Waters. Lindsay Lohan, Tina Fey
The best of a recent flurry of "alpha girl" movies, this one has an exceptionally clever premise. Cady (Lindsay Lohan) arrives in Evanston, Illinois after growing up in Africa with her zoologist parents who taught her at home. So everything about the high school experience is completely new to her, and she ends up as something of a zoologist herself. She brings an outsider's perspective to the social

interactions of the suburban teenager, drawing a social network map based on the seating selections in the school cafeteria. She compares the teenagers to African animals, seeing mall as though it was a watering hole in the savannah. She learns about the difference between "animal world" and "girl world." In girl world, she decides, you have to be sneaky.

Cady finds herself having a hard time understanding the social norms in the school. "I had never lived in a world where adults didn't trust me," she says. The approach that had always worked for her in the past—assuming that everyone was sincere and meant what they said—turns out to be inadequate. No wonder Cady is happiest in math class, where everything makes sense.

Cady is befriended by two kids who are very comfortable being different. She is also drawn to the queen of "the Plastics," the aptly named Regina (Rachel McAdams). When her friends assign her to infiltrate the Plastics, she is filled with loathing but also with longing. Their plots to humiliate her backfire. Regina is such an undisputed style-setter that when they vandalize her shirt everyone else just adopts it as the latest fad. Cady's real friends feel betrayed by what Cady has to do to make Regina think she is on her side. Even Cady starts to wonder whose side she is on, admitting that "I could hate [Regina] but I still wanted her to like me."

Screenwriter Fey, who also appears as a sympathetic teacher, has a good sense of how girls like Regina operate to establish their domination, appearing to be sweet and supportive but in reality being competitive, duplicitous and manipulative, and always surrounding themselves with people who will add to their power and not challenge them.

There is much that is fresh and sharp in this movie. It has an uncertain hold on its plot and ends up pulling some of its punches and throwing in teen comedy cliches we have seen endlessly in dozens of movies that all blur together. NOTE: The movie has crude humor, sexual references, underage drinking, and comic violence. There is a prank involving a pregnancy test. A strength of the movie is its positive portrayal of diverse characters, including disabled, gay, and minority students.

STAND AND DELIVER

1987, 105 min, PG, 12 and up
Dir: Ramon Menendez. Edward James Olmos, Andy Garcia
Edward James Olmos was nominated for an Oscar for his performance as Jaime Escalante, a real-life businessman who got a group of east Los Angeles barrio students so excited about calculus that every one of them passed a brutally difficult

college-level exam. He does such a good job of showing the students any dream is possible if they work hard and respect themselves. Everyone who watches will begin to wonder whether there isn't something they should be studying instead of watching a movie. NOTE: Harsh language.

CONNECTIONS: There is an entire genre of movies about idealistic teachers reaching out to cynical students despite being mired down in bureaucracy: *The Principal*, *Teachers*, *Lean on Me*, *Dangerous Minds*, among others. The genre is spoofed in the intermittently funny *High School High*.

TEA AND SYMPATHY

1956, 122 min, NR, high school age
Dir: Vincente Minnelli. Deborah Kerr, John Kerr
It is dated now, but this story of a boy unsure of his masculinity who is given "tea and sympathy" by the understanding wife of his housemaster still provides a good opportunity for a discussion of growing up. John Kerr plays a sensitive teenager who becomes something of a Rorschach test for the fears others project onto him. He is not gay (and the movie completely shies away from what would happen if he were), but he is different in a way that makes the other boys and the hearty housemaster uncomfortable. He tries to prove his manhood by visiting a prostitute, but when he is unable to go through with it, it only makes him feel more humiliated and inadequate. Deborah Kerr (no relation) plays the housemaster's wife, who gives him a loving introduction to adult sexuality, asking only that "in the future, when you talk about this—and you will—be kind."

She also understands her husband's revulsion masks his fears about himself. Like the boys he leads, he has retreated within limited notions of masculinity to give himself a safe place to operate from, a place no one can question. Most teenagers go through this stage while they are learning about what it means to be a man or a woman. The movie can give parents a chance to talk to teens about the temptation to prove one's adulthood or sexuality (or, for girls in particular, to show sympathy) by having sex.

CONNECTIONS; John Kerr appears as Lieutenant Cable in *South Pacific*, and Deborah Kerr stars in **The King and I**, *King Solomon's Mines*, and *The Chalk Garden*.

UP THE DOWN STAIRCASE

1967, 124 min, NR, mature high schoolers
Dir: Robert Mulligan. Sandy Dennis, Jean Stapleton

This Alice In Wonderland-like saga is based on the best-seller by Bel Kaufman. Sandy Dennis plays the idealistic teacher assigned to an inner-city school. She dreams of conducting classes on Chaucer but finds herself mired in a swamp of absurd administrative minutiae and overwhelmed by the needs of her students. The director of **To Kill a Mockingbird**, the playwright of **All the Way Home**, and a group of untrained teenage actors give the movie an authentic feeling, and Dennis conveys the sensitivity and humor enabling her to touch the students and, far more difficult, allow them to touch her. NOTE: This movie has frank language and discussions of unwed pregnancy and suicide.

CONNECTIONS: See also **To Sir, With Love**, released the same year. Kaufman was the granddaughter of Sholem Aleichem, author of the stories that were the basis for Fiddler on the Roof.

SEE ALSO:

The Chocolate War A struggle for power between an ambitious teacher and a manipulative student focuses on the school's annual chocolate sale.

Educating Rita A tired, bored university professor is inspired by the enthusiasm for learning and the lively mind of his student.

Lucas A bright and sensitive kid with a crush on an older girl tries desperately to be the person he thinks she is looking for.

School Ties A poor Jewish student enters a stuffy WASP-y prep school on an athletic scholarship and encounters prejudice and dishonesty, but also loyalty and friendship.

To Sir, With Love A teacher assigned to a rowdy and rebellious group of students teaches them about respect for each other and themselves, and learns a great deal in the process about himself.

PARENTAL CONCERNS ABOUT PERENNIALLLY POPULAR TEEN MOVIES

Several movies about high school kids pose some real problems for parents. While they are interesting, engaging films with good performances and an appealing authenticity, and they raise issues well worth exploring with teenagers, they also include behavior presented without any kind of consequences, which will give parents some real problems. I strongly encourage parents who are considering these movies to watch them first, and then, if they decide the movies are appropriate, to watch them with the kids, not to provide the kind of running commentary that will have kids running from the room, but to watch their reactions and make yourself available for discussion.

THE BREAKFAST CLUB

1985, 97 min, R, high school age
Dir: John Hughes. Molly Ringwald, Anthony Michael Hall, Judd Nelson, Emilio Estevez, Ally Sheedy
Five very different kids are stuck in an all-day detention (called "the breakfast club"). They start the day ranging from indifference to hostility, but end up turning the day into something like group therapy. Adults will find no surprises, but teens will find it moving and true to their own experience. NOTE: The R rating is for strong language. Some parents will wince at the "makeover moment" in which a sullen girl is transformed with a little makeup.

CLUELESS

1995, 97 min, PG-13, mature high school age
Dir: Amy Heckerling. Alicia Silverstone, Paul Rudd
A smash success, this very funny satire loosely based on Jane Austen's Emma is hugely popular with kids. Alicia Silverstone plays a pampered teen who tries to run other people's lives, only to discover she first needs to work on her own. NOTE: Silverstone's sensational performance, the exceptionally funny script, and the core values all make it worth watching, but parents should be warned substance abuse and sex are both treated casually to the point of nihilism. Parents, particularly of kids under fifteen, should watch it before making a decision whether to permit their kids to see it.

FAME

1980, 134 min, R, mature high school age
Dir: Alan Parker. Irene Cara, Anne Meara, Barry Miller
Students at New York City's High School for Performing Arts go through adolescent drama and melodrama, but they do it while they are singing and dancing to an Oscar-winning score. Teens will relate to the anxiety and identity crises of the attractive and talented leads as they reconcile their dreams of fame with the reality of hard work, rejection, and growing up. NOTE: The R rating is for rough language, an out-of-wedlock pregnancy, brief nudity as a girl takes off her shirt for a man who promised to help her in show business, and a gay character.

PRETTY IN PINK

1986, 96 min, PG-13, mature high school age
Dir: Howard Deutch. Molly Ringwald, Andrew McCarthy, James Spader, Annie Potts, Harry Dean Stanton
This time, Molly Ringwald plays Andie, a creative and self-sufficient girl from the wrong side of the tracks who falls for Blane, a rich kid played by Andrew McCarthy, in this John Hughes production that has some sensitive moments and authentic insights. McCarthy's character is very attracted to Andie but breaks a date with her due to pressure from his bored and snobbish best friend (James Spader), who is bitter over being rejected by Andie. Andie also has a best friend, the quirky but funny and loyal Ducky (Jon Cryer), who is trying to figure out a way to let her know he loves her. (In the original script, they ended up together, but test audiences wanted Andie to end up with Blane so it was changed.)

SIXTEEN CANDLES

1984, 93 min, PG (but probably PG-13 or even and R by today's standards), high school age
Dir: John Hughes. Molly Ringwald, Anthony Michael Hall
Molly Ringwald is sensational as Samantha, whose sixteenth birthday is forgotten by her family in the flurry of preparations over her sister's wedding. Worse than that, the gorgeous senior she adores (Michael Schoeffling) never notices her, and a geeky freshman (Anthony Michael Hall) asks for her underpants.

This movie includes some exceptionally insightful material about being a teenager, and it is hugely popular, but my recommendation has some serious reservations. Among my concerns: insensitivity to the point of racism in the portrayal of an Asian character (his name, Long Duk Dong, gives some idea of the level of humor), insensitive portrayals of the grandparents and the sister's fiancé, and extremely irresponsible treatment of alcohol, drugs, and sex (for example, the Geek not only sells peeks at Samantha's underpants to his friends, but also has sex with the senior's dreamboat girlfriend when they are both so blitzed they don't know what they are doing and her only reaction afterward is that it was sweet).

SOME KIND OF WONDERFUL

1987, 93 min, PG-13, mature high school age
Dir: Howard Deutch. Mary Stuart Masterson, Eric Stoltz, Lea Thompson
Kind of a gender-reverse of Pretty in Pink, this one has Mary Stuart Masterson as Watts, the tomboy who knows she is better for her friend Keith Nelson (Eric

Stoltz) than Amanda Jones (Lea Thompson), the glamour girl he dreams of. There is some nice interaction between Keith and his father (John Ashton), who doesn't want anything to get in the way of his son's college education, and between close and supportive friends Keith and and Watts.

12

IT'S TOUGH TO BE A TEENAGER

*"The day the child realizes that all adults are imperfect,
he becomes an adolescent; the day he forgives them, he becomes an adult; the day he
forgives himself, he becomes wise."*
ALDEN NOWLAN

Poor teens. Their hormones go into overdrive, and their bodies start to change so fast they feel like strangers to themselves. They realize their parents really do not have all the answers, and even if they do, it will destroy the teen's fragile but terribly important sense of independence to ask their parents for help. In a way, the teen years are a replay of the terrible twos. Toddlers show breathtaking courage and resilience in learning to stand, pulling themselves up, crashing down, then, astonishingly, starting over again and again, and putting everything they have into it in a way no adult could ever think of trying. Teens do the same on an emotional level, experiencing mood swings, rejection, and humiliation far past what any adult could tolerate, and yet they still pick themselves up and go on. Just as an infant can withstand a body temperature that would kill an adult, teenagers experience a range of feelings on a daily basis that might be considered evidence of psychosis in an adult.

Their poor parents. Just as our precious darlings confront the really scary issues, the ones with possibly permanent consequences, they don't want to listen anymore. At least not to us. They want to get their answers from their friends, of course, but for those really sensitive issues too painful to talk about, they read magazines and books, they listen to music, and they watch movies. Sometimes, if parents and teens watch together, they can find a way to talk about the issues faced by the characters that is a lot easier than talking about them in more personal terms.

Many parents find themselves withdrawing from their children at this stage because it is so difficult to deal with them, rationalizing this is what the teens want. Teens do not want less attention, they just want different attention. They want your time and interest, but they want a lot less of your telling them what to do. They need your approval more than they need your advice.

The important thing is for parents not to take teenage angst personally, and not to give up. Remember that they really do need your support. They barely know themselves anymore, and they need you to reflect back to them what you see as strong and positive. Somewhere inside that moody, self-centered person who won't get out of the shower is your precious baby (the one who always said he/she loved you the most in the world forever and ever). Even more amazing, somewhere in there is the fine, responsible, and loving adult who will be your greatest joy.

The discoveries, the changes, and the miseries of the teen years make such a powerful impression that there are many fine films with sensitive portrayals of this part of life. They can help convey to kids the uncertainty and pain they experience is not just normal; it is universal, and it is all for a purpose. They can help remind parents how real the pain of these years can be, in fact, must be, to enable them to achieve maturity.

One of the most important struggles for teens is the attempt to define what it means to be a man or a woman. Movies, of course, establish the icons of manhood and womanhood; if you ask anyone to define those terms, it is almost inevitable that within thirty seconds there will be a reference to John Wayne or Marilyn Monroe. These two icons come to mind because they represent extremes, of course, and that is why it is important for families to discuss their own views on this very complex issue. John Wayne often played men who kept all of their emotions inside. His characters demonstrated manhood through physical courage and power. Marilyn Monroe often played women who were soft-hearted and not very bright. Her power was achieved through her beauty, vulnerability, and sexuality. It is worthwhile making sure teens and preteens see some of the exceptions: movie heroes and heroines who show some emotional vulnerability along with physical and intellectual power.

Even watching movies about teenagers can feel overwhelming to an adult, as we see teens struggle with the excruciating mortification of that stage of life. For kids it can seem validating, whether the characters are struggling with problems like a jealous boyfriend, a crush, leaving for college, a school bully, death of a sibling, suicide of a friend, racism, establishing independence, or handling sexual feelings and values. Many movies about teens deal with the passionate need for acceptance. Occasionally we see a teenager who confronts worldwide problems like the threat of nuclear war. Other important themes and conflicts faced by teenagers are explored in the movies discussed in the School and Women Worth Watching chapters.

One theme present in nearly every movie about teens is parents who do not understand or support them. **Rebel Without a Cause** is one classic example, and **Romeo and Juliet** is an even more classic example. This feeling of being misunderstood reflects one of the most conflicted but important aspects of the developmental stage of adolescence. As much as teens long to be understood, the importance of separating from their parents makes them prefer, on another level, to be if not misunderstood, then at least ununderstood a little, to give them the breathing room they need to decide who they are and what they want. These movies can help families recognize and understand this process, and maybe talk about it.

American Graffiti

1973, 110 min, PG, 12 and up
Dir: George Lucas. Richard Dreyfus, Ron Howard, Paul Le Mat, Charles Martin Smith
PLOT: The movie takes place on a single night in 1962, immediately before two good friends, Curt (Richard Dreyfus) and Steve (Ron Howard), are about to leave for college. Curt and Steve are facing enormous changes and they are both scared and excited. Although the film is nostalgic in tone (based on the memories of director George Lucas), it is clear the country is on the brink of enormous (and tumultuous) changes, too.

Most of the episodic plot centers on kids driving around and interacting with each other. Curt and Steve stop by the high school dance. Curt's sister, Laurie, is Steve's girlfriend, and is very concerned about losing him when he goes away.

Steve tells his friend Terry "the Toad" (Charles Martin Smith) that he can use Steve's car when he goes to college, and Terry spends the night driving around, feeling powerful and exciting. He meets Debbie (Candy Clark), a pretty, if slightly dimwitted, girl, and is thrilled when she agrees to ride with him. Then the car gets stolen, and he has a frantic time getting it back.

The boys have another friend, John Milner (Paul Le Mat), who is a hotrod champion. When he tries to get some pretty girls to ride with him, they send a bratty thirteen-year-old (Mackenzie Phillips) to get in his car instead. John gets challenged by a tough guy named Bob (Harrison Ford). Laurie, angry with Steve, agrees to ride with Bob in the race.

Curt spends the night in search of a mysterious blonde (Suzanne Somers), who whispered "I love you" to him from her car. He finally goes to see Wolfman Jack, the DJ all the kids listen to, to ask for help.

John wins the race, but Bob's car crashes. Steve realizes he cannot leave Laurie, and promises to stay and attend the community college. Curt finally leaves, his radio on his lap as the plane takes off. He listens until the sound disappears in static.

DISCUSSION: This brilliant and highly influential film, filled with soon-to-be stars, provides a good opportunity for talking about some of the feelings teenagers have as they move into adulthood. Curt is deeply conflicted between his big dreams and his fear of leaving home. It is Steve who discovers he is not ready to leave. Although he tries to break his ties to home by telling Laurie he plans to date other people and giving his car to Terry, when Laurie is almost killed in the drag race he sees how much he cares for her. Thoughtful older teens may like to speculate about the symbolism of the mysterious blonde in the white Thunderbird, and the guidance from Wolfman Jack.

PROFANITY: Some.
NUDITY/SEXUAL REFERENCES: Some.
ALCOHOL/DRUG ABUSE: Some alcohol, Terry gets an adult to buy liquor for him to drink with Debbie.
VIOLENCE/SCARINESS: Hot-rod race; car thieves.
TOLERANCE/DIVERSITY ISSUES: Carol says she is not allowed to listen to Wolfman Jack because he is black (he isn't).
QUESTIONS FOR FAMILIES:

• Why is Curt so ambivalent about leaving?

• What does Curt's ex-girlfriend's teasing tell you about him?

• Why is Laurie afraid to let Steve go?

• Why does Laurie ride with Bob? Who is she hurting?

• Why does the movie end by telling you what happens to those characters in the future?

CONNECTIONS: Don't waste time on the sequel, *More American Graffiti*, with a different director, which is not nearly as good. This movie is a good place to find many future stars in small roles, including Harrison Ford, who went on to star in the director's next movie, **Star Wars**.

ACTIVITIES: The sound track includes some of the greatest hits of the era. Listen to some other music by some of the artists, and see if teens can trace the influence of those artists on some of their favorite performers.

Bend it Like Beckham

2002, 112 min, PG-13, 15 and up
Dir: Gurinder Chadha. Parminder K. Nagra, Kiera Knightley, Jonathan Rhys-Meyers

PLOT: Jess (Parminder K. Nagra) is a young woman from an Indian Sikh family awaiting her college entry exam results in the suburbs of London. She is the obedient daughter of tradition-minded parents who have mapped her life's flight path from law degree to Indian husband to perfecting her ability to cook 'aloo gobi'. They have have reluctantly tolerated her love for soccer playing by turning a blind eye to her practices in the park with her best friend, Tony (Ameet Chana).

Jess' life is about to change as her older sister, Pinky (Archie Panjabi), launches the family into a tizzy of wedding preparations. Since Pinky is soon to leave the house, it is time, think their parents, that Jess settle down, give up soccer for studies and find a serious Indian boyfriend. Just as her parents are telling Jess to stop playing soccer, she is offered the opportunity to take her playing to the next level. Jess is spotted playing in the park by Jules (Keira Knightley) a kindred spirit who is a founding member of the all-women's soccer club, the Hounslow Harriers. The Harriers, independent young women completely dedicated to their sport, represent everything that Jess would like to be in the world beyond the loving community of her family. What follows are the first rebellious steps into adulthood for the otherwise model teen, Jess, as she gains confidence and independence on the field, while gently stepping out of her parent's protective boundaries.

DISCUSSION: This cheerful little story is about second generation Indian families in England striving to maintain traditions that kids, more British than Indian, find increasingly irrelevant. However, families from any cultural background will appreciate the central conflict between tradition and dreams that may lie outside tradition's borders. Even if the answers seem a bit pat, it is nice to think that complicated relationships and challenges can be resolved with the proper communications and the ability to make nice, round chappatis.

Some of the characters are two-dimensional and played for humor, including Jules' super-feminine English mum (Juliet Stevenson) who frets about her daughter's tomboy "sportiness" and Jess' mother (Shaheen Khan) who is more concerned about Jess' cooking abilities than her happiness. Bollywood superstar Anupam Kher brings a great deal of sensitivity and depth to the role of the father.

PROFANITY: Some strong language.
NUDITY/SEXUAL REFERENCES: Sexual references, including locker room boasting, engaged couple having sex, gay character, characters mistakenly thought to be gay.
ALCOHOL/DRUG ABUSE: Social drinking.
VIOLENCE/SCARINESS: Tense family scenes.
TOLERANCE/DIVERSITY ISSUES: A theme of the movie.
QUESTIONS FOR FAMILIES:

• Why does Jess feel she cannot talk to her family about her love of sports?

• How does her father's cricket experience impact his view of Jess' soccer playing?

• What might be the common bond between Irish Joe and Indian Jess?

CONNECTIONS: Families who enjoy this movie might like to see **My Big Fat Greek Wedding**, which shares a similarly ebullient approach to cultural differences. Director Chadha's *What's Cooking* is a warm, touching, and very funny story about four families from different cultures preparing for Thanksgiving. Those who enjoyed the South Asian elements of this movie will enjoy *Monsoon Wedding*, a lovely tableau of an Indian family preparing for a celebration (mature material). For those interested in the soccer theme, *The Cup* is a lighthearted look at a Buddhist monastery where the young novices are intent on watching the World Cup.

Breaking Away

1979, 100 min, PG, 12 and up
Dir: Peter Yates. Dennis Quaid, Dennis Christopher, Daniel Stern, Paul Dooley
PLOT: Four friends just out of high school are enjoying the summer and thinking about their future. They live in Bloomington, Indiana, home of Indiana University, and consider themselves "cutters," the name the college students gave to the town kids a generation before, when most of the local men worked for the local quarry. Dave (Dennis Christopher) has tested well enough to go to college, but spends all his time racing his bicycle and trying to emulate his heroes, the

Italian bicycle racing team, about to arrive in Bloomington on tour. Mike (Dennis Quaid) believes his year as quarterback of the high school football team will be the highlight of his life, and is bitter and resentful of the college students. Cyril (Daniel Stem), lanky and sardonic, says his father is always grateful when Cyril fails, so he can show how understanding he is. Moocher (Jackie Earl Haley) is the only one with adult responsibilities and a steady girlfriend.

Dave's mother is sympathetic about his obsessions with Italy and bicycles, but his father is embarrassed and impatient. Dave tells a pretty coed named Katherine (Robyn Douglass) he is an Italian exchange student, and she is charmed by him. When the university for the first time invites local teams to participate in their annual "Little 500" bicycle race, Dave's friends want to enter. Although it is supposed to be a relay race, they figure that Dave can ride the entire fifty miles and still beat the college teams. At first Dave refuses because he does not want Katherine to find out the truth about him. When he is disillusioned by a race with his Italian idols and by his father's used-car lot sales policies, he tells Katherine the truth and agrees to race.

Dave is hurt in the race, all four of the friends end up participating, and Dave is able to lead them to finish in first place. He has developed enough of a sense of who he is to move on, and he starts college, where he meets a pretty exchange student—from France.

DISCUSSION: This is a movie about friendship, about establishing identity, and about growing up. The friends stick together and support each other as they struggle in different ways with adulthood. Just out of high school, they sense their youth is ending, while each fall a new generation of students begins at the university. Mike says, "These college kids out here, they're never going to get old. There'll always be new ones coming along." Each spring, they see a new generation leave to go on to better things while they stay behind. "At sixteen, they call it sweet sixteen. At eighteen, you get to drink, to vote, to see dirty movies. What the hell do you get to do when you are nineteen?" He hates to think "maybe they are better than us."

Dave, on the other hand, is thrilled by the thought his heroes are "better than us." His heart is broken when the Italians cheat in a race, pushing him off the track. When he learns later his father won't return a dissatisfied customer's money, he cries, "Everybody cheats. I just didn't know." Yet, somehow finding this out helps him tell Katherine the truth, and accept himself the way he is. That is what enables him to take the risk of moving on, going to college, and becoming more than a "cutter."

PROFANITY: Some.

NUDITY/SEXUAL REFERENCES: Mild. Dave's mother becomes pregnant.

ALCOHOL/DRUG ABUSE: Some alcohol use and smoking.

VIOLENCE/SCARINESS: Cyril is beat up by Katherine's boyfriend. Moment of scariness when one of the boys tricks the others by pretending to be trapped under water.

TOLERANCE/DIVERSITY ISSUES: Class issues.

QUESTIONS FOR FAMILIES:

• Why would the kids in a college town feel the way these kids do about the students? Why would the students feel the way they do about the town kids?

• What does Cyril mean when he says his failure is like a gift for his father? Does that relate to his saying he "lost all interest in life"?

• Why does Dave's father say, "You're not a cutter. I'm a cutter"? What does that tell Dave?

• What do you think of Dave's father's refusal to return the money to the dissatisfied customer? Do you agree "everybody cheats"? How did Dave react? Why?

• How does what Dave sees lead him to tell Katherine the truth and take the chance on going to college?

• Why is Dave's mother's passport so important to her?

CONNECTIONS: This movie won an Oscar for Best Screenplay. The most poignant town-gown confrontation in the movies is the scene in the fast-food place in Spike Lee's *School Daze*. This is most definitely not for children (and not for some adults), but the movie, which Lee says is based on his own college experience, is an important and insightful look at issues of identity for all races.

ACTIVITIES: This may inspire you to go on a family bike ride. It may also inspire you to watch a bicycle race or read up on some of the famous teams Dave admires. If you can, visit a quarry to learn more about how stone is cut to be used in buildings. If that is not convenient, you can take the kids for a walk to look at the materials used in some of the buildings near your house, and talk about where they come from, and what the advantages and disadvantages are of each kind of material.

Parents might also want to take their children for a walk through a local university campus, and even attend an event there. Talking about how Dave pursues his interest in bicycle racing and Italy may give kids some ideas on how to expand their own interest in a particular subject.

Bye Bye Birdie

1961, 112 min, NR 8 and up
Dir: George Sidney. Dick Van Dyke, Janet Leigh, Ann-Margret, Maureen Stapleton, Paul Lynde.
PLOT: In this musical satire of 1950s popular culture and suburban life, America's most popular rock singer, Conrad Birdie (Jesse Pearson), like Elvis, has been drafted. Albert Peterson (Dick Van Dyke) is unable to tell his mother he wants to be a biochemist and not a songwriter. His longtime fiancée, Rosie DeLeon (Janet Leigh), arranges for Birdie to sing Albert's song "One Last Kiss" on The Ed Sullivan Show before he leaves for boot camp. He will sing it to a member of his fan club, picked at random. This will give Albert the success he needs in order to please his mother, enabling him to quit songwriting.

The fan picked at random is Kim McAfee (Ann-Margret), a teenager who has just agreed to go steady with Hugo (Bobby Rydell). Everyone ends up at the McAfee home, including Albert's overbearing mother. As Albert obtains the cooperation of Kim's father (Paul Lynde) and others by promising them they will be on The Ed Sullivan Show, Hugo becomes more and more jealous, Rosie becomes frustrated and impatient, Kim dyes her hair, and Albert's invention, a pill making animals (and people) speed up their activity, comes in very handy when Birdie's number is bumped to make time for a Soviet ballet.

DISCUSSION: It is fun for kids to get this glimpse (even though idealized and exaggerated) of how teenagers in the past behaved, how they felt about big issues like rock stars, going steady, and growing up. Like *Grease*, this musical starts with a song amusingly depicting the different reactions of the boys and girls to the news of a romance. In this case, it is the announcement of Kim and Hugo going steady. Teenagers may be interested in why the reactions of the boys and girls were different, and whether the same distinctions are made today.

Kim sings about how lovely it is to be a woman (as she dresses in sloppy old clothes) and airily informs her parents she is going to start calling them by their first names. The call from Rosie about her selection as the girl to be kissed goodbye by Conrad Birdie has her calling for "Mommy" again. Albert has a huge problem in declaring independence from his mother. Children will react differently to this, based on their own development; younger children may be reassured he still behaves with the obedience of a child, but teenagers will think he should have established his own identity long before. Fortunately, this is a musical comedy, and when that moment comes, Albert's mother is as ready for it as he is.

In the song "Kids" Kim's father and Albert's mother sing about "what's the matter with kids today." It is possible to draw some parallels to the way parents think about children now, and the conflicts you had with your own parents, and the conflicts they had with theirs.

It may be worth discussing what Kim and Rosie do when they are upset with the men in their lives. Both react by going off with other men (for some extraordinary dance numbers). Whether out of impatience or an attempt to make Hugo and Albert jealous, it is risky and manipulative behavior. (This is even more true in the original play.)

PROFANITY: None.

NUDITY/SEXUAL REFERENCES: Rosie and Kim admit to each other that they are both "good girls." Rosie appears in a bra.

ALCOHOL/DRUG ABUSE: Birdie drinks beer. Rosie and Albert go to a roadhouse. The speed-up pill, although a whimsical idea, is less charming in light of current issues of drug abuse.

VIOLENCE/SCARINESS: None.

TOLERANCE/DIVERSITY ISSUES: Rosie is Hispanic without any ethnic characteristics; everyone else is white and Anglo.

QUESTIONS FOR FAMILIES:

• One of the interesting things about this movie is the way so many people end up agreeing to do things they don't want to. Why does Hugo agree to let Kim kiss Conrad? Why does her father agree?

• Why does Kim call her mother "Doris"? Why does she change back to "Mommy"?

• What do you think of the song "Kids"? Is it as relevant today as it was when the movie was made?

• Why do Kim and Rosie decide to go off to dance with people other than their boyfriends? Does it accomplish what they intended?

• Does Albert pay too much attention to his mother? What makes you think so? What would you do if you were Albert?

CONNECTIONS: This plot is reminiscent of *The Man Who Came to Dinner*, the Kaufman and Hart comedy about the ruin brought on to a 1940s family when a media celebrity stays at their home, and the 2004 comedy *Win a Date With Tad Hamilton!* about a small-town girl who wins a date with a movie star. Janet Leigh, who appears here in a black wig, is perhaps most famous for her shower scene in *Psycho*. Dick Van Dyke, repeating his role in the Broadway production, also appears in **Mary Poppins**.

ACTIVITIES: Students might like to listen to some of Elvis Presley's hit records or look at some of the publicity about his induction into the army and talk about which star might have that kind of impact today.

The Flamingo Kid

1984, 98 min, PG-13, high school age
Dir: Garry Marshall. Matt Dillon, Richard Crenna

PLOT: On a hot early summer day in Brooklyn in 1963, Jeffrey (Matt Dillon) is talking to his friends when some old friends who have moved out of the neighborhood come by to invite him to play cards at their country club on Long Island. The El Flamingo Club is a dazzling contrast to hot, sweaty Brooklyn, everything sleek and spotless. Jeffrey is self-conscious, but impressed. His friends are delighted when he helps them win their gin game. He is delighted when he is offered a job parking cars at the club.

His father, Arthur (Hector Elizondo), however, is not delighted. He had arranged for Jeffrey to work as an office boy in an engineering firm. He finally agrees to let Jeffrey work at the El Flamingo.

At the club, Jeffrey sees Phil Brody (Richard Crenna), a car dealer and the champion player in the high-stakes gin game. Invited to dinner by Carla (Janet Jones), Brody's niece from California, Jeffrey is awkward but in awe of Phil, who treats him with easy charm and arranges for him to be promoted to cabaña boy.

Jeffrey admires Phil, and Phil enjoys being admired. He gives Jeffrey advice on everything from playing gin to what to wear to what Jeffrey should do for a career. Phil has an answer for everything, and all of the answers appeal to Jeffrey. "The salesmen of the world make the money." "God put certain people on this earth to give you money, and your responsibility in life is to go out there and get it."

Jeffrey goes home, repeating Phil's views, and his father is furious, especially when Jeffrey says "college is overrated," and he may not attend. When Arthur responds by saying he is the boss, Jeffrey says he has decided not to go to college. Jeffrey and his friends go to a racetrack, and his friend Fortune loses his college money. Afterward, they go to a restaurant and get into a fight with some other kids. They are arrested, and Arthur has to bail them out. "In Brooklyn, you go to school. In Long Island, you go to jail. From now on, you stay in Brooklyn." Jeffrey argues his friends know how to have a good time, and their family could live on Long Island if Arthur was willing to spend the money instead of saving every penny.

Arthur hits Jeffrey. Later, he apologizes. "Something you ought to know about your father, Jeffrey. Fast things bother him," he explains. Jeffrey likes fast things, and he moves out. When he tells Phil he is ready for the job he promised at the car dealership, Phil offers him a job as a stock boy. On the last day of the season, Jeffrey realizes Phil has been cheating at gin. One of the opposing team members becomes ill and Jeffrey offers to play against Phil. The game goes so long, it overlaps with the Labor Day dance. They double the stakes, and Jeffrey wins. Phil is a bad loser. When he realizes Jeffrey knows the truth, Phil offers Jeffrey a sales job. Jeffrey responds by telling Phil's friends Phil cheated. Jeffrey gives the money he won to his friend Fortune, to replace his losses at the racetrack. Then he joins his family for dinner at their favorite restaurant.

DISCUSSION: While there are a number of caveats, due to language and other concerns, this movie raises some valuable issues for family discussion. At the club, Jeffrey sees a different way of life for the first time. At first, he is impressed by Phil, by his house, his car, his clothes, his smoothness, his view that "money is the name of the game, and if you can make it easy, make it easy." He is ready to put aside the values he learned from his father. He finds out not just Phil is dishonest, but he is dishonest with his friends, and even with himself. Phil assumes everyone is either like him or stupid.

On Jeffrey's last night with Carla, he tells her how ships going out to sea sail back and forth between two lights to "box" (set) their compasses, before venturing into the ocean. This is a lovely metaphor for what Jeffrey does in this movie, as he sets his own moral compass by comparing Phil and his father.

PROFANITY: About a dozen four-letter words, including all of the most popular ones.
NUDITY/SEXUAL REFERENCES: There are some PG shots of Jeffrey and Carla spending the night together (bare backs and legs). One of the country club members asks if she can put his tip in Jeffrey's pocket, and he agrees. When he says, "You missed my pocket again, Mrs. Unger," she replies, "I like to miss it." She compliments him on his "behind." Reference to "jacking off."
ALCOHOL/DRUG ABUSE: Some alcohol.

VIOLENCE/SCARINESS: Fight in a restaurant. Arthur hits Jeffrey.

TOLERANCE/DIVERSITY ISSUES: Jeffrey's friend Fortune is black. No issue is made of this in any way (unless you consider it's stereotypical to have him going to college on a basketball scholarship). There are negative homosexual references, not to anyone in particular, just as general insults. The movie also raises class issues. Phil's wife is a snob.

QUESTIONS FOR FAMILIES:

• Why does Jeffrey like Phil at first? What is it about Phil that he likes? How can you tell Jeffrey likes Phil?

• What makes Jeffrey change his mind?

• Why does Carla like Jeffrey?

• What does Arthur mean when he says he is afraid of fast things?

• What is the importance of the explanation about boxing the compass?

CONNECTIONS: Watch carefully as Richard Crenna tries out his new remote control and you will see him click by a quick glimpse of his younger self as Luke on television's *The Real McCoys*. Before that, he appeared as Walter Denton on the radio and television versions of *Our Miss Brooks*. Athlete Janet Jones, who plays Carla, is the real-life wife of hockey legend Wayne Gretsky. Bronson Pinchot, who appears in a small part, became well known for his appearances in the *Beverly Hills Cop* movies, and played Balki on the television show *Perfect Strangers*.

The movie includes some of the finest songs of the era, well-used to comment on the story and characters, including, "Walk Right In," "Stand By Me," "Money (It's What I Want)," "South Street," "He's So Fine," and "It's All Right."

ACTIVITIES: Teach the students to play gin or poker. Take them to a swim club, and let them compare it to the El Flamingo Club.

Jezebel

1938, 103 min, NR, b&w, 10 and up
Dir: William Wyler. Bette Davis, Henry Fonda
PLOT: Julie Marsden (Bette Davis) is a spoiled Southern belle in pre-Civil War New Orleans. She does not hesitate to pull Preston Dillard, her fiance (Henry Fonda), out of a business meeting to consult on a clothing purchase, and uses sulking and petulance to get her way. She decides to punish Pres for failure to

devote his complete attention to her by doing something shocking—wearing a scarlet dress to the Olympus Ball, where by tradition unmarried ladies always wear white.

When she gets to the ball, however, she is embarrassed and asks to leave. Pres insists on dancing with her. The two of them waltz around the empty dance floor, watched by everyone there, and then he takes her home. He breaks off their engagement and moves north. She insists he will come back to her. Three years later, he returns, and she puts on a white dress to greet him with an apology, but he is married to Amy, a northern lady. Devastated, Julie manages to get Buck Cantrell (George Brent), another suitor, to challenge Pres to a duel, and, when Pres's brother takes his place, Buck is killed.

Julie's guardian refuses to have anything to do with her anymore, comparing Julie to Jezebel in the Bible. Pres gets yellow fever in an epidemic, and the patients are evacuated. Julie persuades Amy to let her go nurse him, to redeem herself, risking her own life by exposure to the disease. She promises if he gets well, she will bring him back to Amy.

DISCUSSION: This is a great movie for teenagers because it is an entertaining depiction of the kind of immature behavior people engage in when they are just trying out the complications of adult relationships, particularly romantic ones. Julie's spoiled and selfish actions have nothing to do with intimacy; on the contrary, they are all about power, and power in a very superficial sense at that. She wants Pres completely within her control. She could have that from Buck, but is not interested, because he is not enough of a challenge. Julie is only attracted to men she cannot control, yet she cannot be happy unless she is in control—a collision course with disaster.

It is important to recognize Julie makes decisions that seem as though they will make her feel better, but they never do. She backs herself into a corner with the red dress, leaving herself no graceful way out. When she gets to the ball, she finds she really did not want to shock people as much as she'd thought she did. Of course the ultimate consequence of her decision is losing Pres for good.

Compare Julie to Scarlett O'Hara in **Gone With the Wind** (some people consider this film a consolation prize to Bette Davis for not being cast as Scarlett). Both manipulate men rather than attempt genuine intimacy, and both end up losing the men they really want.

Teens may be interested in considering how much of Julie's frustration and manipulation might stem from the highly restricted forms of power women had in both the era depicted and the era in which the movie was made. If Julie could have attended her own business meetings, would she have wanted to make Pres leave his? It is also worth looking at the way Bette Davis resolved some of the problems she faced in her career, challenging the studio system's control of actors. Ultimately, the issues she raised ended up in the Supreme Court, resulting in a decision giving actors much more freedom to choose their own projects.

PROFANITY: None.
NUDITY/SEXUAL REFERENCES: None.
ALCOHOL/DRUG ABUSE: None.
VIOLENCE/SCARINESS: None.
TOLERANCE/DIVERSITY ISSUES: Depiction of blacks typical of the era.
QUESTIONS FOR FAMILIES:

- Why was Julie so spoiled? Do you think she was a "Jezebel"?

- What should Pres have done about the red dress?

- Could Julie and Pres have ever been happy together?

CONNECTIONS: Both Bette Davis and Fay Bainter won Oscars for their performances. The "red" dress used in the movie was, in reality, a deep rust color, for a more effective contrast on black-and-white film. A movie with an even more jealous, insecure, and destructive heroine is *Leave Her to Heaven*.
ACTIVITIES: Look up Jezebel in the Bible to see why Julie's aunt made the comparison. Read *Here We Are* and *The Sexes* by Dorothy Parker, for exquisite renditions of similarly manipulative women who are (at least temporarily) more successful; read some of her other short stories for what happens after the men in the lives of women like this get frustrated or bored by that treatment. Read a famous short poem called *The Glove and the Lions*, by Leigh Hunt, about a lady who drops her glove among the lions at a sporting event, knowing the count who loves her will risk his life to get it back for her. He gets it back, then throws it in her face, while the king notes approvingly, "'No love,' quoth he, 'but vanity, sets love a task like that.'"

The Learning Tree

1969, 107 min, PG, high school age
Dir. Gordon Parks. Kyle Johnson, Dana Elcar, Estelle Evans
PLOT: Photographer-filmmaker Gordon Parks produced, wrote, directed, and even scored this movie, based on his autobiographical novel about coming of age in a black family in 1920s rural Kansas. Like **The Wizard of Oz**, that other great

novel of Kansas, it begins with a twister that causes great disruption. Like that other great American autobiographical novel, *Tom Sawyer*, this is the story of two boys, one from a loving family, the other the son of an abusive alcoholic father, and of a murder involving them both.

Fourteen-year-old Newt Winger comes from a family that is comfortable, respected, and principled. When Newt and his friends steal some apples, the owner, Mr. Kiner, comes after them with a whip. He catches up to Marcus (Alex Clarke), who beats Kiner badly. Newt and his mother, Sarah (Estelle Evans), visit Kiner in the hospital, and Newt promises to work for no pay to make up for what happened. Marcus is charged and sent to a reformatory, where he is cruelly beaten, and becomes even more hostile, especially toward Newt.

Newt, in the meantime, has his first girlfriend, Arcella Jefferson (Mira Waters). Chauncey Cavenaugh, son of the judge for whom Sarah keeps house, sees Newt and Arcella and invites them for a Coke. The waiter refuses to serve them, insisting they take the Cokes and leave. Later, Newt sees Arcella get in Chauncey's car. She will not see Newt anymore and won't tell him what the problem is. She is pregnant; Chauncey is the father. She and her family leave town.

Marcus is released from the reformatory. He fights Newt at a fair, but Newt wins. Newt sees Marcus's father, Booker, kill Kiner. A white man named Silas is charged. Newt is afraid to tell the truth because he fears reprisals against the black community. He cannot see Silas wrongly convicted, so he testifies about what he saw. When the crowd in the courtroom shouts, "Kill the nigger," Booker runs out of the room and kills himself. Marcus comes after Newt with a gun. Newt subdues him, and he runs. The sheriff shoots him. He offers Newt a ride home, and Newt says, "I can make it by myself."

DISCUSSION: In addition to the classic coming-of-age themes of confronting death and losing innocence, this movie adds issues of racism and tolerance by both blacks and whites. By some standards, there is much in the town that is very progressive, despite segregation. Sarah does not hesitate to tell the (racist) white sheriff to watch his tongue when he tells her (correctly) her son is in trouble. She speaks very openly and directly to the judge, and even more directly to his son. The black Wingers and the white Kiners are mutually respectful and genuinely friendly. The same is true of their relationship with the white doctor. The judge tells the crowd in the courtroom they executed Booker by their reaction to Newt's testimony, and it was Newt's fear of just this kind of racist reaction that made him hesitate about telling the truth.

This makes the racism that does exist stand out more sharply. As the principal admits, black students are not allowed on the school teams or at the dances. When Newt complains to his teacher about his grade, she says it is a waste of time for black students to go to college. He argues, and she takes him to the principal's office. The principal sides with Newt but asks Newt to remember the teacher is a victim, too, and Newt can't change all the rules he would like to. He will speak to the teacher, but Newt must always treat her with "the highest respect."

When Newt asks his uncle Rob why white people "do so many awful things," Rob explains, since he is blind, he just looks at people as individuals. "I don't figure his color into it; I figure his deed." This ties in with Sarah's advice to Newt that their community is like a tree, with some of the fruit good and some bad. (This should be a "learning tree" for him.) The movie is evenhanded in its portrayal of both good and bad in blacks and whites. Most important, it is a fine portrait of a fine family.

Note that the way people express themselves indicates something about what they think and about their relationships. It is revealing to notice who gets to use first names, for example. It is also worthwhile discussing what the community's responsibility should have been to Marcus. Sarah tells the judge it is not Marcus's fault he behaves so badly, and the judge says, "I can't send the father to the reformatory for something the son did."

PROFANITY: Reference to "I hear you ain't got no cherry no more" after, (off-screen) sexual encounter; racial epithets.
NUDITY/SEXUAL REFERENCES: Nudity at a swimming hole; out-of-wedlock pregnancy; nude couple in bed; scenes in a whorehouse.
ALCOHOL/DRUG ABUSE: Booker abuses alcohol.
VIOLENCE/SCARINESS: Fights; one character is beaten to death; two are shot; one commits suicide (off-camera); scary nightmare of bringing dead body up from under the water; death of Newt's mother.
TOLERANCE/DIVERSITY ISSUES: One of the themes of the movie.
QUESTIONS FOR FAMILIES:

- What do you think about the scene in the restaurant? If you were Chauncy, what would you do? If you were Newt or Arcella, what would you do?

- Why didn't Arcella want to be with Newt anymore? Why did her family leave town?

- What do you think about what the judge said about Arcella to Sarah?

- Why does Newt say, after Sarah's death, he is not afraid anymore?

- How does Newt's brother help him?

CONNECTIONS: **The Learning Tree** was among the first twenty-five films included in the Library of Congress's National Film Registry as "culturally, historically, or esthetically significant." Parks' background as one of Life Magazine's greatest photographers is evident in this film's exceptional visual flair. Parks' later movies were the "blaxploitation" hits, *Shaft* and its sequel, *Shaft's Big Score*, featuring a powerful black hero who battles racist cops and criminals and romances many women along the way.

Lucas

1986, 100 min, PG-13, high schoolers
Dir: David Seltzer. Corey Haim, Kern Green, Charlie Sheen, Winona Ryder
PLOT: Lucas (Corey Haim) is a very bright fourteen-year-old, in high school with older kids. He is confident enough to approach Maggie (Kerri Green), a pretty girl who is new in town and vulnerable because of her parents' recent divorce. They become close friends. On the first day of school, Lucas is humiliatingly carried up onstage by a football player named Bruno during a rally. He manages to turn it to his advantage by making fun of the coach, but he is embarrassed. That night, at a movie with Maggie, Bruno harasses him again, but the captain of the team, Cappie (Charlie Sheen), intervenes. Cappie likes Lucas and owes him a lot because Lucas helped Cappie with his schoolwork when he was sick.

Lucas is heartbroken when Cappie and Maggie are attracted to each other. He is barely aware of Rina (Winona Ryder), who likes him very much. He decides to go out for the football team, even though he had always been contemptuous of the "superficiality" of football, and even though he is about one-third the size of the other players. When the coach refuses to let him play, he threatens a lawsuit. In the locker room, Cappie is not able to save him, when, responding to taunts about his masculinity, Lucas bravely lashes back. The other players rub deep-heating ointment on his genitals, then throw him outside wearing nothing but a towel. Even though Maggie is there, all he can do is run for the drinking fountain and jump in.

The principal forbids him to play. At a big game, when the team is losing badly, he persuades the coach to put him in. He is hurt, and Cappie, Maggie, and Rina go to the hospital with him. Rina tells the others Lucas does not live in the mansion he told Maggie was his home. That is where he works as a gardener's assistant. He lives in a trailer park, with an alcoholic father.

Lucas returns to school, not sure how he will be received. Bruno is standing near his locker, waiting for him. So are Rina, Cappie, and Maggie. He opens his locker to find a football jacket with his name on it. As he tries it on, the students applaud.

DISCUSSION: This is an exceptionally intelligent and sensitive movie about an exceptionally intelligent and sensitive kid, based in part on the memories of writer-director David Seltzer. It evokes the emotions of high school: terror, exhilaration, the breathtaking swings from confidence to self-doubt.

Lucas is fascinated by insects, especially the locusts who take seventeen years to mature and emerge from their cocoons. He is impatient to emerge from his cocoon, to grow into the feelings he has for Maggie, to be seen by others the way he sees himself inside. His lies about his parents, and his devastation when Maggie and Cappie become involved show despite his ability to handle Bruno's harassment and his courage in confronting the coach and insisting on playing football, he is very vulnerable.

Departing from the usual formulas, this movie has the intelligence to make Cappie a thoughtful, funny, caring person (very well-portrayed by Charlie Sheen), and the courage not to have Lucas win the football game. Kids who see this may want to talk about why Lucas is attracted to Maggie and why he does not perceive Rina is attracted to him. Older kids may be interested in talking about the way some big, tough, physically mature boys like Bruno are threatened by small, brainy kids like Lucas because of their developing and uncertain notions of masculinity and sexual power.

PROFANITY: Strong language, especially in the locker-room scene, is the reason for the PG-13 rating.
NUDITY/SEXUAL REFERENCES: Typical adolescent talk about who has "done it"; behavior is comparatively circumspect, however.
ALCOHOL/DRUG ABUSE: None.
VIOLENCE/SCARINESS: Lucas is assaulted with deep-heating ointment in the locker room and injured when he is tackled on the football field.
TOLERANCE/DIVERSITY ISSUES: Tolerance of individual differences is a theme of the movie.
QUESTIONS FOR FAMILIES:

• Why does Lucas describe his parents the way he does?

- What does it show when Maggie is honest about her parents and their problems?

- How does Lucas turn the situation to his own advantage when he is pulled up onstage?

- Should Maggie not have gone out with Cappie? What are the obligations of friends like Maggie and Cappie in this situation?

- What kind of grown-up do you think Lucas will become?

CONNECTIONS: This was the first movie for gifted actress Winona Ryder, who went on to play sensitive teenagers in a number of films, including *Beetlejuice*, *Mermaids*, and **Little Women**.

Rebel Without a Cause

1955, 110 min, NR, 12 and up
Dir: Nicholas Ray. James Dean, Natalie Wood, Sal Mineo, Jim Bachus
PLOT: Teenager Jim Stark (James Dean), new in town, is picked up by the police for being drunk. At the police station, he sees two other teens, Judy (Natalie Wood), who has been walking around miserably, feeling rejected by her father, and Plato (Sal Mineo), neglected by his parents, brought in for killing some puppies. Jim's parents and grandmother come to pick him up, but they are too caught up in their own bickering to listen to him. Judy's mother comes for her, and Plato is picked up by his housekeeper. Only Ray, the understanding policeman, listens, and he encourages Jim to come talk to him at any time.

The next morning is Jim's first day at his new high school. He tries to talk to Judy, but she rejects him harshly and goes off with Buzz, her tough boyfriend, and his punk cronies. At a field trip to the local planetarium, Buzz challenges Jim to a knife fight. Jim wins, and Buzz challenges him to a "chickie run" with stolen cars that night at eight o'clock. Jim tries to get advice from his father, asking what he should do when something very dangerous is "a matter of honor"? His father's response is patronizing and ineffectual. Jim is disappointed: "I want answers now. I'm not interested in what I'll understand ten years from now."

At the "chickie run," Jim asks, "Why do we do this?" and Buzz answers, "We gotta do something." Jim jumps out of the car just before it goes off the cliff, but Buzz's sleeve gets caught, and he cannot get out in time. He is killed. Jim goes home and asks his parents for help. His mother wants to move, as she always does when there is any trouble. They tell Jim not to go to the police, to stay out of it.

Jim is desperate. He asks his father to stand up for him, wanting him to show some kind of support. When he sees none, Jim is disgusted and shoves his father aside.

He goes to the police station alone. Buzz's friends, brought in for questioning, see him and want to stop him from telling what happened. When Jim discovers Ray is not there, he leaves, and sees Judy. Together, they go to an abandoned mansion near the planetarium and have some happy moments, pretending they are safe and grown up, in their own home, away from all their troubles. Plato arrives with a gun. He wants to protect them.

For a moment, they make up a family, Jim and Judy as the parents, Plato as the child they cover tenderly when he falls asleep. Judy and Jim realize they care deeply for each other. She is happy to have found "a man who can be gentle and sweet and someone who doesn't run away when you want him."

Buzz's friends arrive. Plato panics when he wakes up and doesn't see Jim and Judy, and feels abandoned again. When the police arrive, he shoots one of the policemen and runs to the planetarium. Jim and Judy go in after him, and Jim calms him down and takes the bullets from his gun. The police think Plato is going to fire the gun again, so they shoot him and he is killed. Jim sobs in his father's arms as his father assures him, "You did everything a man could," and promises, "I'll try to be as strong as you want me to be." Jim and Judy reach out for each other as the movie ends, just twenty-four hours after it began.

DISCUSSION: This is the ultimate classic of teenage angst, and an excellent movie for families to watch together to talk about some of the feelings parents and their children have during these years.

A generation later, James Dean is still the teenage icon, partly because he died a few months after this film was released, and so remains frozen in time, but partly because his performance in this film had and has such resonance for teenagers and for everyone else who feels unsure and angry, and unsure of why they feel angry. The title says it all: Jim is a rebel without the ability to put into words what he is rebelling against. Even teenagers like those in the 1960s, who found causes for their rebellions, identify with Jim's feelings of frustration and loneliness as they begin to establish their own identities and take responsibility for their own choices.

As Judy's mother says, this is "that age when nothing seems to fit." Judy feels rejected by her father. He, in turn, feels rejected by her simply because she is growing up. He is uncomfortable with her as she becomes a woman, and has no way to relate to her except to call her a tramp when she wears makeup or slap her away when she tries to kiss him.

Jim, like most teenagers, looks for extremes of gender definition and identification while he is sorting out what it all really means. He is humiliated by his father's submission to his mother's insults and even says he wishes his father would hit her. He hates to see his father wearing an apron and bringing up dinner on a tray for his wife. This seems emasculating to him. Perhaps one reason he feels such a need to prove his courage and "honor" is his conflict about his own feelings of tenderness and vulnerability. In the very first scene, drunk and lying on the ground, he gently covers a little mechanical bear as though it were a child.

At the police station, Jim asks if he can keep the toy. He is gentle with Plato, offering him his jacket in the police station and at the planetarium, and Judy tells him how important that is to her. He is everything to Plato he wishes his father could be for him, "standing up" for him with the police, promising to take care of everything.

He cannot take care of everything, and Plato is killed. He learns, tragically, a little of what it is like to be a parent, and has to give up the idea forever (as all teenagers must) that parents are all-powerful. His father learns something, too: that he can draw on his strength, as his son did; and they can be strong for each other.

It is interesting that the sympathetic policeman is named Ray, like the director, underscoring that character's representation of the director's perspective. Note that Jim asks both Ray and his father to put limits on him. Parents should talk with their kids about why Jim is afraid he cannot limit himself. Most importantly, they should talk about why the parents and kids in this movie find it so hard to communicate.

PROFANITY: None.
NUDITY/SEXUAL REFERENCES: None.
ALCOHOL/DRUG ABUSE: Teens smoke and drink.
VIOLENCE/SCARINESS: Characters are in peril; Buzz is killed in "chickie run"; Plato shoots at two people and is himself shot and killed.
TOLERANCE/DIVERSITY ISSUES: None.
QUESTIONS FOR FAMILIES:

• What does the title mean?

• Judy says, "You shouldn't believe what I say when I'm with the rest of the kids." What does that mean? Why does she say things with the others that she is uncomfortable about?

- What do we learn from Buzz's "we gotta do something" answer about why they do the "chickie run"?

- What does Judy discover when she says "All the time I've been looking for someone to love me, and now I love somebody"?

- What does it imply when Jim wears a jacket and tie in some scenes and a T-shirt and windbreaker in others?

CONNECTIONS: Dean starred in only two other movies, and he is riveting in both: *Giant*, an epic saga of Texas oil and cattlemen, and *East of Eden*, from the John Steinbeck novel of two brothers who are rivals for their father's affections. Goon is played by Dennis Hopper, who starred in *Easy Rider* and played memorable villains in *Blue Velvet* (for adults only) and *Waterworld*. Jim's father is played by Jim Backus, best known for his more humorous television appearances, as Mr. Howell on *Gilligan's Island* and as the voice of Mr. Magoo. Ed Platt, who plays Ray, the sympathetic cop, also played the Chief, Maxwell Smart's choleric boss on television's *Get Smart*. Judy's father is played by William Hopper, son of Hedda Hopper, who was Paul Drake on television's *Perry Mason*.

Say Anything

1989, 100 min, PG-13, high school age
Dir: Cameron Crowe. John Cusack, Ione Skye, John Mahoney
PLOT: Lloyd Dobler (John Cusack) is an engagingly aimless high school graduate who likes junk food and kick-boxing. Courageously, he sets his heart on Diane Court (Ione Skye), the most beautiful and brilliant girl in school, described as a brain "trapped inside the body of a game show hostess." Lloyd has no conventional "smooth" talk, but his free-association "say anything" style, good humor, and obvious genuineness make her laugh. She agrees to let him take her to a graduation party, and they have a good time together.

Diane and her father, James (John Mahoney), are very close, and he assures her they can always "say anything" to each other. When Diane wins a prestigious fellowship to study in England, he tells her it is everything they have ever worked for. One problem is Diane's fear of flying. The other problem is her growing attachment to Lloyd.

Though she tries not to become too involved, Diane becomes closer to Lloyd. Her father feels she is drifting away from him. Diane and Lloyd make love, a gentle, intimate experience, and she immediately tells her father about it. Finally,

James forces Diane to choose, and she chooses her father over Lloyd. She tells Lloyd she just wants to be friends.

Her father's love, which has always bordered on the obsessive, has also developed into the criminal. His nursing home is investigated for tax fraud. James has been taking money from the residents to spend on Diane. Diane is shattered. She returns to Lloyd for support. She cannot bring herself to visit her father in jail, so she sends Lloyd to see him with a letter. In an exceptionally sweet final scene, Lloyd and a terrified Diane are on the plane to England.

DISCUSSION: In this movie, the guy who appears to be aimless and incapable of achieving anything turns out to have a stronger moral code than James and to be more in control of his life than Diane. Diane may have an outstanding record, but she has missed out on making friends. Lloyd has excellent relationships with his sister and her son and with a number of friends. He is the one reliable enough to be the "key master" to make sure no one leaves the party too drunk to drive. When he wavers about taking a stand with Diane, his friend reminds him not to be "a guy," but to be "a man." He is even willing to mediate the relationship between Diane and her father.

Lloyd waits for his future to come to him. As he says, "I don't want to sell anything, buy anything, or process anything as a career. I don't want to sell anything bought or processed, or buy anything sold or processed, or process anything sold, bought, or processed, or repair anything sold, bought, or processed. You know, as a career, I don't want to do that." He knows he wants to be with Diane, and he is willing to do whatever it takes to make that possible. Lloyd is ready to make his own choices and make his own mistakes. Diane, by contrast, has always had all her choices made, for her.

The strength of Lloyd's relationship with Diane is also contrasted with the disastrous teenage relationships of his friends, especially Cory's broken heart over Joe. In a memorable scene, Lloyd's buddies offer him (terrible) advice on how to treat women, and he responds, "I got a question. If you guys know so much about women, how come you're here at, like, the Gas 'n' Sip on a Saturday night completely alone drinking beers with no women anywhere?" "Conscious choice, man" is their funny but unconvincing reply.

Diane's father, desperate for her to succeed, is too overprotective and too involved with her. He has made her dependent. She is only able to flourish in Lloyd's company. She appreciates Lloyd's thoughtfulness in guiding her around some broken glass and his willingness to help her become more independent by teaching her to drive. Yet, she is still not ready to be on her own. She needs Lloyd to deliver her message to her father, and to comfort her as the plane takes off for England.

PROFANITY: Mild expletives.
NUDITY/SEXUAL REFERENCES: Diane and Lloyd make love in the back of a car, an overwhelming and intimate experience for both of them. She goes home afterward and tells her father about it, pleased she can "say anything" to him.
ALCOHOL/DRUG ABUSE: Liberal drinking at high school party with a couple of students actively drunk. Lloyd is responsible for making sure everyone gets home safely.
VIOLENCE/SCARINESS: None.
TOLERANCE/DIVERSITY ISSUES: None.
QUESTIONS FOR FAMILIES:

- Why would a girl as successful and ambitious as Diane like Lloyd?

- If all James does is try to do what is best for his daughter, how does this go wrong?

- Lloyd has a lot of friends. What makes him so likable?

- What will happen to Lloyd and Diane? Why do you think so?

CONNECTIONS: Ione Skye, the daughter of 1960s pop star Donovan, appeared in another story about a young man who flounders through his attraction to her, *The Rachel Papers* (deservedly rated R), based on the novel by Martin Amis. Cusack stars in **The Sure Thing** and *The Journey of Natty Gann*, and provides the voice of Dimitri in *Anastasia*. Mahoney appears on television's *Frasier*.

Splendor in the Grass

Dir: Elia Kazan. Warren Beatty, Natalie Wood, Pat Hingle
PLOT: In this classic of repressed teenage sexuality set in the 1920s, Bud (Warren Beatty) and Deanie (Natalie Wood) are high school students who are newly in love and breathless with desire, physical and emotional. Deanie's parents are unable to give her any guidance. They make her feel ashamed of her feelings. Her mother says, "Your father never laid a hand on me until we were married and then I just gave in because a wife has to. A woman doesn't enjoy these things the way a man does. She just lets her husband come near her in order to have children." Bud's father, Ace (Pat Hingle), tells Bud there are two kinds of girls,

"good" and "bad," and the "bad" ones are fair game. This apparently applies to Bud's sister, whose reputation has been "ruined" by having sex and has come home from college in disgrace. At a party, she drinks too much and has sex with a group of men.

Deanie will not have sex with Bud, and they break up. Both suffer break-downs. His is moral; he has sex with another girl, known to be "easy." Hers is emotional; overcome with despair and self-loathing, Deanie has a breakdown and becomes a patient at a mental hospital. Ace will not permit Bud to go to agricultural college and insists he go to Yale. When the stock market crashes, Ace is wiped out and kills himself. Bud leaves college.

When Deanie comes home from the hospital, her mother does not want her to see Bud. Deanie's father tells her how to find him, and, with some friends, Deanie drives out to the shack where Bud lives with his wife.

Deanie and Bud speak, briefly, achieving some resolution, enabling them to go on, if not as they had once hoped, at least grateful for what they have had. Deanie remembers the words of the Wordsworth poem she learned in school: "Though nothing can bring back the hour/Of splendor in the grass, of glory in the flower/We will grieve not, rather find/Strength in what remains behind."

DISCUSSION: This movie was immensely controversial for its frankness when it was first released. (A brief glimpse of nudity as Deanie ran from the bathtub was cut from the final print.) Most teenagers face a different set of issues today, but they are presented with no less hypocrisy or more reassurance than the messages to kids like Bud and Deanie. Instead of being told sexual feelings are nonexistent or evidence of being "bad," today's teenagers often get the message they are "bad" or lacking if they do not feel ready to engage in sexual activity freely almost as soon as they enter high school. The issues of honesty in communicating about sexuality and the overwhelming confusion of teenage passion remain important and valid, and this movie can provide a good opening for a talk about what has changed and how teenagers feel about the decisions and the consequences Bud and Deanie face in this movie.

PROFANITY: Mild.
NUDITY/SEXUAL REFERENCES: Sexuality is a theme of the movie.
ALCOHOL/DRUG ABUSE: Bud's sister gets drunk.
VIOLENCE/SCARINESS: Bud's sister is sexually assaulted.
TOLERANCE/DIVERSITY ISSUES: Some class issues.

QUESTIONS FOR FAMILIES:

- Why does Ace make a distinction between "good" and "bad" girls? Do people make that distinction today? What makes a girl "bad"?

- Is anyone honest with Bud and Deanie?

- What do Bud and Deanie mean when they say they don't think about happiness anymore?

- Why did Deanie refuse to have sex with Bud? Why did Bud refuse to have sex with Deanie? What should two people think about before they make the decision to have sex?

CONNECTIONS: In another classic movie of teenage sexual repression, *A Summer Place*, Sandra Dee and Troy Donahue do have sex, and she becomes pregnant. Dee's mother is repressed to the point of hysteria, but her father, who has left his wife to be reunited with the woman he loved when they were teenagers, is sympathetic and supportive, all to lush and unforgettable theme music by Max Steiner.

William Inge (who appears as the minister) won an Oscar for Best Screenplay. He also wrote *Picnic*, **Bus Stop**, and *The Dark at the Top of the Stairs*, all about vulnerable people who must struggle to find intimacy and happiness, themes that are especially appealing to sensitive teens.

Stand By Me

1986, 87 min, PG, 10 and up
Dir: Rob Reiner. River Phoenix, Wil Wheaton, Corey Feldman, Jerry O'Connell, Richard Dreyfus, Kiefer Sutherland
PLOT: Four twelve-year-old boys hear of a dead body out in the woods and they agree to go on an overnight hike to find it so they can be on the news. They come back having learned a lot about themselves and about what it takes to be independent and brave. The friends are tough Chris Chambers (River Phoenix), sensitive Gordon LaChance (Wil Wheaton), Teddy DuChamp (Corey Feldman), and Vern Tessio (Jerry O'Connell). The plot focuses on the relationship between Chris and Gordon, who are very different but support and learn from each other.

The movie follows the boys as they leave their small town in Oregon for an overnight hike along the tracks to where the dead body is said to be. The movie sets up the inevitable confrontation at the train tracks where the body is located between the young friends and their older brothers who originally knew the location of the body. The confrontation proves to be nonviolent but tense.

DISCUSSION: This movie is based on a novella by Stephen King called The Body, but it is by no means a horror movie. It is an especially wellcrafted "road picture," with four friends learning about life and each other as they travel together. Each of the characters is appealing, but most appealing of all is the loyalty and trust they share.

PROFANITY: Schoolyard language.
NUDITY/SEXUAL REFERENCES: Minor.
ALCOHOL/DRUG ABUSE: The older brothers of the boys abuse alcohol, drink and drive, and smoke.
VIOLENCE/SCARINESS: Characters in peril; a dead body; some fistfights.
TOLERANCE/DIVERSITY ISSUES: Class issues.
QUESTIONS FOR FAMILIES:

- Why does Chris cry when he tells the milk money story even if he did take it? Do you think it is fair for him to feel disappointed by the teacher, and by what other people expect of him?

- Why do you think Gordon's dad is so uncaring toward him?

- How are Gordon and Chris alike?

- Why is Teddy destined for failure?

- Do you think you will look back at your friends when you are grown up the way the narrator does in this story?

CONNECTIONS: Kiefer Sutherland, son of Donald Sutherland (**Ordinary People**), stars in television's *24*. Author Stephen King is better known for his scary stories that were the basis for movies including *The Shining* and *Misery*.

The World of Henry Orient

1964, 104 min, NR, 12 and up
Din George Roy Hill. Peter Sellers, Tippi Walker, Merrie Spaeth, Angela Lansbury, Tom Bosley, Phyllis Thaxter, Paula Prentiss
PLOT: Valerie Boyd (Tippi Walker) and Marian "Gil" Gilbert (Merrie Spaeth) become good friends after they meet at a posh New York prep school for girls. Valerie is the child of wealthy parents who travel most of the time and send her

gifts like a mink coat. Gil lives with her mother (Phyllis Thaxter) and her mother's friend "Boothy" (Bibi Osterwald) in a modest home.

The girls see pianist Henry Orient (Peter Sellers) with Stella (Paula Prentiss), a married lady friend, in Central Park. Stella is attracted to Henry but panicked about being discovered by her husband. Val develops a huge adolescent crush on Henry, and the girls begin following him around, researching his career and establishing elaborate silly rituals for pledging their devotion. Stella is close to hysterics, thinking they are employed by her husband to report on her.

Val's parents, Isabel (Angela Lansbury) and Frank (Tom Bosley), return to New York. Isabel is annoyed to hear of Val's escapades. When she meets Henry herself, though, she is attracted to him, and they sleep together. Frank can no longer ignore Isabel's infidelities and, more importantly, her neglect of Val. He leaves Isabel, taking Val with him to Europe. When she comes back for a visit with Gil, they excitedly talk about boys.

DISCUSSION: This is an appealing and believable story of two girls who are at that stage where they are not quite ready to enter into real relationships with real boys, so they "practice" the emotions of romance by fixating on an unattainable object. The two girls who play Val and Gil are wonderfully natural, and the film makes New York City look as invitingly enchanting as the land of Oz.

Even though Gil's parents are not together, she has a warm and loving family with her mother and Boothy. Val's more extravagent behavior reflects a neediness and self-doubt stemming from the neglect by her parents.

PROFANITY: None.
NUDITY/SEXUAL REFERENCES: Henry's prolonged attempt to seduce Stella; Henry and Isabel have a one-night stand; in the last scene, Val brags about kissing a boy whose name she didn't know.
ALCOHOL/DRUG ABUSE: Social drinking.
VIOLENCE/SCARINESS: None.
TOLERANCE/DIVERSITY ISSUES: None.
QUESTIONS FOR FAMILIES:

• Why does Val pick Henry Orient to have a crush on?

• What do Stella and Isabel see in him?

• What makes Frank decide to leave Isabel? How did his talk with Gil's mother play a role?

• Does the movie do a good job of showing how friends behave? What parts seemed real to you and what parts didn't?

CONNECTIONS: This movie was written by longtime screenwriter Nunnally Johnson (*The Grapes of Wrath*), based on a semi-autobiographical novel written by his daughter. Famed society band leader Peter Duchin plays Joe Byrd. The score, by legendary composer Elmer Bernstein (**The Magnificent Seven**) and Ken Lauber, is superb.

THE CHALK GARDEN

1964, 104 min, NR, 14 and up
Dir: Ronald Neame. Hayley Mills, Deborah Kerr
Hayley Mills plays Laurel, a troubled teenager who lives with her eccentric grandmother, Mrs. St. Maugham (Dame Edith Evans). Miss Madrigal (Deborah Kerr), a mysterious woman with no references, is hired to be Laurel's governess. While Mrs. St. Maugham encourages Laurel's wild and manipulative behavior, Miss Madrigal realizes Laurel is acting out because she is desperately unhappy, and if she does not find a home with someone who loves her enough to impose limits, it will be like planting flowers in a chalk garden. She must confront her own tragic experiences to make it possible for Laurel to return to her mother. The sensitive portrayal of a girl's reaction to her feelings of hurt and abandonment and the performances by all of the actors are exceptional.
CONNECTIONS: Maitland the butler is played by John Mills (Swiss Family Robinson), Hayley's real-life father. The movie is based on a play by Enid Bagnold, who also wrote **National Velvet**.

GIDGET

1959, 95 min, NR, 10 and up
Dir: Paul Wendkos. Sandra Dee, Cliff Robertson, James Darren
The original movie in the series about the surfing teenager is dated in the details, but the themes are eternal. Francie Lawrence (Sandra Dee) wants to please her loving but overprotective parents, but she also wants to grow up. She wants to be a part of the group of boys she admires on the beach, who dub her "Gidget" for "girl midget." Moondoggie (James Darren), already a part of the group, is also struggling to find himself. His parents want him to go to college, but he is drawn to the life of the Big Kahuna (Cliff Robertson), who has given up his career as a pilot to become a surfer bum.

In this gentle romantic comedy, Gidget and Moondoggie try to find themselves and learn some lessons about how much to compromise and about the consequences of choices. Even the Big Kahuna learns something about the importance of self-respect.

Kids might like to know the original novel about Gidget was based on the real-life experiences of the author's daughter. The sequels (with other actresses in the title role) and television series are moderately entertaining. Parents might want to discuss Gidget's imperishable innocence, almost absurd by today's standards.

CONNECTIONS: You can see the real Gidget in the terrific 2003 documentary about surfing, *Step Into Liquid*.

GOOD WILL HUNTING

1997, 126 min, R, mature high school age
Dir: Gus Van Sant. Matt Damon, Robin Williams, Ben Afflech, Minnie Driver
Mature teens will appreciate this story, written by its appealing young stars, about a brilliant young man with a troubled past. Will (Matt Damon), who grew up as an abused foster child in tough South Boston, works as a janitor at MIT. When he solves advanced math problems that stump the students, a professor searches for him, only to find he is in jail for having hit a policeman. The professor promises he will work with Will and will get him some psychiatric help. Will manages to scare off a string of therapists, so the math professor seeks out his estranged college friend, Sean (Robin Williams), a therapist. Like Will, the survivor of a tough Southie upbringing, and, like Will, still struggling with his own loss, Sean is able to help Will realize he is not betraying his friends by using his gifts to enlarge his world. Will falls in love with Harvard premed student Skylar (Minnie Driver). She and Sean teach him the walls he has built to protect himself from pain are no longer needed, and are getting in his way. NOTE: Very strong all-but-incessant profanity and very explicit sexual references.

GREGORY'S GIRL

1981, 91 min, PG; 12 and up
Dir: Bill Forsyth. Gordon John Sinclair, Dee Hepburn
Gregory (Gordon John Sinclair) is a gangling but amiable Scottish teenager who is mildly befuddled by just about everything, especially Dorothy (Dee Hepburn), who takes his place on the soccer team. In contrast, the girls he knows, including his ten-year-old sister, seem to understand everything in this sweet, endearing comedy with a great deal of insight and affection for its characters.

THE MANHATTAN PROJECT

1986, 117 min, PG-13, 12 and up
Dir: Marshall Brickman. Christopher Collett, Cynthia Nixon
Paul Stephens (Christopher Collett) is a very bright kid with an exceptional talent for science. His mother (Jill Eikenberry) begins to date a scientist from a nearby research lab (John Lithgow), and Paul grows suspicious about what the lab is researching. He decides that he can make his point about the ethical dilemma posed by nuclear weapons (and, not incidentally, prove something to all of the people who underestimated him) by stealing plutonium from the lab to make a nuclear weapon for his science fair project, with the help of a friend from school who wants to be a journalist (Cynthia Nixon). This is a rare movie that does a convincing job of portraying smart people. The characters and performances are exceptional.
CONNECTIONS: Writer-director Marshall Brickman has been a collaborator with Woody Allen, and shared an Oscar for the screenplay of *Annie Hall*. Television viewers will recognize John Mahoney from *Frasier*, John Lithgow from *Third Rock from the Sun*, Cynthia Nixon from *Sex in the City*, and Jill Eikenberry from *L.A. Law*.

PERMANENT RECORD

1988, 91 min, PG-13, high school age
Dir: Marisa Silver. Keanu Reeves, Kathy Baker
A high school senior who seems to have everything commits suicide, leaving his friends groping for clues about what was really going on inside him, and how they can put their own lives back together. Keanu Reeves plays his best friend, an underachiever who must learn in some important way he has achieved more than his friend ever can simply by being willing to continue to face whatever challenges life holds.

The reactions of the school administration will be of special interest to kids. The understanding principal knows the students need to have a ceremony to pay some tribute to their friend, but his supervisor forbids it, saying it will somehow make suicide seem more glamorous. Kids may also want to discuss the way the friend who seems to be far less accomplished in reality has a core of loyalty and strength that even he had not suspected. NOTE: Rough language, alcohol and drug use by teenagers, mature themes. The boy who commits suicide has a passionless sexual relationship with a girl, with the agreement they never ask questions of each other or share their feelings.

POWDER

1995, 111 min, PG-13, high school age
Dir: Victor Salva. Sean Patrick Flanery, Mary Steenburgen, Jeff Goldblum
Powder (Sean Patrick Flanery) was born when his mother was struck by lightning. He was abandoned by his father as a freak because he had no skin pigmentation or hair. He stayed on his grandparents' farm, having no contact with the outside world, until their deaths, when a kind social worker (Mary Steenburgen) finds him. She discovers he has extraordinary intellectual gifts and has memorized hundreds of books. She puts him in an institution for disturbed cildren, where he astounds the bullies with his ability to give objects a powerful electric charge.

The rest of the film consists of a number of scenes in which Powder astonishes everyone with his extraordinary gifts, which include telepathy and telekinesis. While most of the locals resent and fear him, a few (including Jeff Goldblum as a science teacher) are awestruck. Ultimately, even these friends cannot protect Powder, but he finds a way to unite his energy with the powerful forces all around us.

This movie has much more appeal for teens, who will identify with the sensitive hero's inability to find a place for himself in an insensitive world, than it has for parents, who will find the plot too pedestrian for an allegory and too awkwardly constructed to garner much sympathy.

WARNING: Parents should know one reason this film did not succeed in theatrical release was the controversy over its director-screenwriter, who served time in prison for molesting a young boy who appeared in one of his earlier films. Viewed through that lens, parts of the movie seem a bit creepy, and teens who have heard of this issue may want to discuss the life of the artist in interpreting a work of art and whether it is appropriate to boycott the film.

CONNECTIONS: Characters with special perception abilities who feel misunderstood by those around them are particularly appealing to teenagers, because they identify most with characters who feel isolated and unappreciated. Other films with this theme include *Phenomenon* and *Charley*, films about gifted and lonely people who make those around them feel both inspired and threatened. Mature teens might also want to compare these films to *Being There* (PG, but some strong sexual references), the story of a retarded man, isolated all his life, who is perceived by politicians as brilliant when he states what he thinks in the simplest terms.

ROMEO AND JULIET

1968, 138 min, PG, 12 and up
Dir: Franco Zeffirelli. Olivia Hussey, Leonard Whiting
Shakespeare's play about the "star-cross'd lovers" is the ultimate tale of misunderstood teenagers. In this lush and romantic version, with the memorable Nino Rota score, the title characters are played by real teens Olivia Hussey and Leonard Whiting, only fifteen and seventeen when the movie was made.
CONNECTIONS: *William Shakespeare's Romeo & Juliet*, released in 1996, is a dazzling MTV-style staging of the play, retaining much of the original dialogue but setting it in contemporary Venice, California. Leonardo DiCaprio and Clare Danes play the lead roles, and John Leguizamo is an electrifying Tybalt.

WHERE THE BOYS ARE

1960, 99 min, NR, 12 and up
Dir: Henry Levin. Paula Prentiss, Jim Hutton
Four young women leave their snow-covered college for spring vacation in Florida's Fort Lauderdale, because that's "where the boys are." This movie is very dated in its treatment of women (Paula Prentiss famously declares all she wants is to become a "walking, talking, baby machine," and at least three of the women seem to believe finding a husband is all that matters), but its treatment of the pressures women feel to have sex holds up surprisingly well.

Intellectually, Dolores Hart believes it is not wrong to have sex before marriage, but she refuses handsome (and very rich) George Hamilton, and he respects her for it. Yvette Mimieux falls for a line from a boy who uses her and then passes her on to a friend. When she is the victim of what today would be called date-rape, she is so devastated she walks out onto the highway in a daze and is hit by a car. Far more damaging is her loss of self-respect. Families with teenagers, especially teenage girls, can watch this together to talk about what has changed and what hasn't.
CONNECTIONS: Ignore the 1984 remake, which is dreadful.

SEE ALSO:
Mask in this true story, a teenager with a severe facial disfigurement finds acceptance and a way to make a contribution to those he loves.
My Bodyguard A teenager facing a bully at school must find a way to keep both his self-respect and his lunch money.

The Sure Thing A college student who is promised a "sure thing" (a beautiful girl guaranteed to have sex with him) finds his developing relationship with a prickly classmate becomes even more important to him.

Tex A high school student being cared for by his older brother learns to take care of himself.

13

MAKING LIFE CHOICES

"Be neither chided nor flattered out of your position of perpetual inquiry. Neither dog-matize nor accept another's dogmatism. Why should you renounce your right to traverse the star-lit deserts of truth for the premature comforts of an acre, house and barn? Truth also has its roof, bed and board."
RALPH WALDO EMERSON

Movies provide a wonderful opportunity to talk about choices: how they are presented, how to make them. Even very young children can appreciate Robert Frost's "The Road Not Taken" and talk about how the characters in movies think about which road to take, what they consider and how much weight they give to each factor.

Sigmund Freud said the most important elements of a healthy life are "love and work." The movies in this chapter feature characters who must make important choices about the direction of both aspects of their lives, especially about evaluating their priorities and their tolerance for risk. Over and over we see people examining their options, often discovering what they want is not what they thought they wanted. As La Rochefoucauld said, "Before we set our hearts too much on anything, let us examine how happy are those who already possess it."

In some movies, characters have explicitly devoted their lives to a goal they must reconsider once they are close to attaining it. Usually, for men, the goal is money and power. In **7 Faces of Dr. Lao**, a greedy and unethical man is close to realizing his dream of economic domination of a community. In **Local Hero**, a man who measures his success by his job title and his possessions is about to succeed in an important business deal. In **I Love You Again** and in **The Music Man** a con man is about to close a successful swindle when something makes them change direction.

Most often for women in movies, the goal is usually represented through marriage (often to a wealthy and powerful man). She defines herself by the choice of a husband. In **I Know Where I'm Going!** a determined young woman is close to achieving her life's dream of marriage to a wealthy and powerful man, just, as in **Ball of Fire** a showgirl is about to marry a wealthy and powerful gangster. **In His Girl Friday** a woman reporter is about to leave journalism to marry a man who sells insurance. In **The Philadelphia Story** a wealthy, upper-class woman is about to marry a man who worked for her family's business. In **A Room With a View** a young woman is about to marry a rather prim but wealthy gentleman. In all of these films, the women choose men who love them for what is important to them about themselves instead. We do see men being kept by wealthy women in **An Affair to Remember, An American in Paris** and **Breakfast at Tiffany's**, but they are all artistic (and one of them is Cary Grant), which somehow seems to make them less dishonorable.

A young woman makes an important choice about her professional life, with no romantic context, in **Up the Down Staircase**. She decides to stay with the inner-city students who need her most instead of leaving for the rarefied environment of a private school. A male teacher makes a similar choice in **To Sir, With Love**, giving up his earlier plans to be an engineer. Preston Sturges, who loved to turn convention on its head, gave us a completely different approach in **Sullivan's Travels**, in which a wealthy and successful Hollywood director tries hard to do something more "meaningful" only to discover he was already making an important contribution.

Each of these characters is confronted with a situation or with some knowledge (particularly self-knowledge) leading them to a different choice. In most of these movies, the character realizes money and power are less important than love, and they want to be loved by someone who sees in them what they want seen, whether it is a side of them they have been reluctant to show or a kind of emotional honesty they have not been aware of themselves. In some, they end up alone, but happier.

These movies often provide early indications of the main character's dissatisfaction with the choices he or she has made establishing a foundation for the satisfying conclusion of changing direction. This is worth discussion in the family, for two reasons. The first is to help understand motivation, foreshadowing, and narrative structure, and develop interpretive skills and an understanding of context, all crucial in understanding literature (and in getting through high school English). The second is to develop sensitivity to indicators of motivation in ourselves and those around us. The only way to make sense of the plot of **I Love You Again** is to understand at some level in his days as a con man, Larry really wanted a middleclass existence, and could find no other way to get there but to develop amnesia (this kind of emotional truth is one reason this is among the best of all screwball comedies). This same idea is explicit in **The Music Man**, when Harold Hill confides he wishes he could really lead a band. In **Lili**, we see an even clearer example, as Paul expresses his tender and vulnerable side only through the puppets.

Some movies show us characters who do not appear to have thought much about their choices. In **Awakenings**, Dr. Sayer's research position is discontinued, and he is thrust into a job treating patients. For that very reason, he brings a freshness of perspective to the chronic ward the other doctors do not. His exposure to the patients on that ward causes him to rethink the choices that have left him isolated. Another movie with Robin Williams, **Dead Poets Society**, shows us a teacher who inspires his entire class to rethink their complacent resignation about the direction of their lives and seize the day.

Movies also show us the consequences of choices, sometimes difficult or even wrong ones. Movies can show us how people make choices, and what the consequences of those choices are, but they can also remind us we can learn from our mistakes, and go on to do better.

Awakenings

1991, 121 min, PG-13, 10 and up
Dir: Penny Marshall. Robin Williams, Robert De Niro, Penelope Ann Miller, Julie Kavner
PLOT: Malcolm Sayer, a shy neurologist (Robin Williams), is assigned to work with patients for the first time after his research funding is cut off. His patients, all but catatonic, are in a ward called "the garden" because their only treatment consists of "watering and feeding." Ever since an epidemic of encephalitis ("sleeping sickness") decades before, they have not spoken or appeared to understand anything going on around them. Everyone else has given up hope, but Sayer, approaching them as a researcher, notices they are capable of reflex reactions, and believes new medication used for patients with Parkinson's disease may help these patients, too. Over the objections of the doctors in charge, he gets permission to try it on one patient, Leonard Lowe (Robert De Niro).

At first, there is no reaction, but soon Leonard "awakens." His transformation is so thrilling that Malcolm is easily able to get permission and funding to treat the other patients. They, too, awaken, some more fully than others. A onetime musician does not speak, but plays the piano. Some of them are horrified at the time they have lost, but most are giddy with the pleasures of being alive. Malcolm takes Leonard outside, and Leonard's embrace of everything around him contrasts sharply with the inhibitions of Malcolm, who hesitates to try anything but his work and cannot even bring himself to have a cup of coffee with a friendly nurse (Julie Kavner).

Leonard becomes impatient to experience more. He develops a warm friendship with the daughter of another patient in the hospital (Penelope Ann Miller). He asks for permission to leave the hospital on his own. He becomes hyperactive, angry, and ridden with tics. The medication's side effects begin to overwhelm him. Malcolm sees that he is losing Leonard, and the other patients know this regression must soon happen to them, too.

Soon, all of them are returned to their previous state of catatonia, the only evidence of their brief awakening the greater respect and affection they receive from the staff, and their impact on Malcolm, who heeds Leonard's call to life by reaching out to the nurse.

DISCUSSION: This movie is based on the book of the same name by neurologist Oliver Sacks, who was the basis for the character Malcolm Sayer. It is a powerful and moving story, brilliantly acted and directed. Like Malcolm, we can all use a reminder to appreciate the pleasures of being alive, including the pleasures requiring us to take risks.

PROFANITY: A few expletives.
NUDITY/SEXUAL REFERENCES: None.
ALCOHOL/DRUG ABUSE: None.
VIOLENCE/SCARINESS: Sad, but not scary.
TOLERANCE/DIVERSITY ISSUES: Theme of respecting the humanity of those who are different.
QUESTIONS FOR FAMILIES:

- What does the neurologist mean when he says, "Because the implications of that would be unthinkable"? Why would he prefer to believe the patients are not aware of what is going on?

- Were you surprised by the way any of the patients reacted to being "awakened"? Which reaction was most like the way you think you might feel?

- Why is it hard for Malcolm to interact with other people?

- How does Leonard change the way Malcolm behaves?

- Why does the staff treat the patients differently after the awakening, even when they go back to the way they were?

CONNECTIONS: Compare this movie to Thornton Wilder's play *Our Town*, especially Emily's speech after her death, about what she misses and what she wants the living to be aware of. Similar themes are raised in *Charley* with Cliff Robertson's Oscar-winning performance. Scriptwriter Steven Zaillian also wrote the screenplay for **Schindler's List** and wrote and directed **Searching for Bobby Fischer**.

ACTIVITIES: Teens will enjoy reading the Sacks book, and some of his others, especially *The Man Who Mistook His Wife for a Hat* and *An Anthropologist on Mars*, with astonishing and compassionate descriptions of some of his neurology patients.

Ball of Fire

1941, 111 min, NR, b&w, 8 and up
Dir. Howard Hawks. Gary Cooper, Barbara Stanwyck, Dana Andrews
PLOT: In this modem version of Snow White and the Seven Dwarfs, eight professors are writing an encyclopedia, funded by a bequest. They all live together, cared for by a grumpy housekeeper, and work together in one large room. As the movie opens, they have been working for seven years and have only reached the letter "S." All are unmarried (one is a widower) and all are elderly, except for Professor Bertram Potts (Gary Cooper), a scholar of English literature and language. When the garbage man comes by to ask for help in answering a radio quiz, Potts listens to his speech and is appalled to find that his article on slang, based on scholarly papers, is years out of date. So, for the first time in seven years, he ventures out into the world, taking notes on everything he hears, and inviting the most colorful speakers he meets back to the house for further study.
Among his subjects is the dazzling Sugarpuss O'Shea (Barbara Stanwyck), whom he spots performing in a nightclub and invites back to the house. She turns him down. Then she has to stay out of sight while her mobster boyfriend, Joe Lilac (Dana Andrews), is under investigation, and she decides the professor will provide the perfect hideout. She shows up on his doorstep and insists on moving in.
He brings chaos to the professors, but also fun and music. Potts falls in love with her and proposes. Lilac proposes, too (via his henchmen), as a handy way of making sure she won't be able to testify against him. Pretending that she is taking him to meet her family, she gets the professors to drive her to Lilac. But when she changes her mind and refuses to marry Lilac, the professors are taken hostage and must escape and rescue her, using their expertise in almost every subject, including physics, anatomy, geography, and psychology.

DISCUSSION: This movie is sheer delight, with one of the wittiest scripts ever, cowritten by Billy Wilder, the screenwriter-director of **Some Like It Hot** and *Sunset Boulevard.* It is astonishing to think that a movie so knowing about American English was written by Wilder, who first came to the United States as an adult to escape the Nazis. The movie includes my all-time favorite line of dialogue: When told her sore throat shows "a slight rosiness," Sugarpuss answers, "It's as red as The Daily Worker, and just as sore!" It must be watched more than once to get all of the jokes and references.

Kids will enjoy the way Sugarpuss disrupts the lives of the professors, and the way that the professors use their expertise (and a book on boxing) to rescue Sugarpuss. Older kids might be interested in the disagreement between Potts and Oddly about the best way to show love for a woman, and by the psychological validity of Magenbruch's conclusion that Sugarpuss didn't want to marry Lilac because she sent back the wrong ring.

PROFANITY: None.
NUDITY/SEXUAL REFERENCES: None.
ALCOHOL/DRUG ABUSE: None.
VIOLENCE/SCARINESS: Characters in peril, but nothing scary.
TOLERANCE/DIVERSITY ISSUES: None.
QUESTIONS FOR FAMILIES:

• Why do people use slang? Where does slang come from?

• What slang words do you like best?

• What can you tell about someone by what kind of slang words he or she uses?

CONNECTIONS: The professors are played by some of Hollywood's finest character actors, including S. Z. "Cuddles" Sakall and Henry Travers (Clarence the angel in **It's a Wonderful Life**). Drummer Gene Krupa makes a memorable appearance playing "Matchstick Boogie."

The movie was remade by the same director as *A Song Is Born,* a musical starring Danny Kaye and Virginia Mayo.
ACTIVITIES: Of course the slang is very outdated today, dating back half a century. Ask kids to imagine what would catch Potts's ear if he went out today. Where would he go? Compare Potts to Professor Higgins in **My Fair Lady**, who could locate someone by hearing their speech. Note that Potts listened to many different groups of people to get examples of different kinds of slang.

Professor Potts would be delighted to see the Random House Dictionary of American Slang, by J. E. Lightner. Lightner's schedule would also delight Potts; at this writing, only the dictionary's first two volumes have been published (four years apart), listing slang words through the letter "0."

Breakfast at Tiffany's

1961, 119 min, NR, 12 and up
Dir: Blake Edwards. Audrey Hepburn, George Peppard, Mickey Rooney
PLOT: Paul Varjack (George Peppard), a writer who is being supported by a wealthy woman (Patricia Neal), is intrigued by his downstairs neighbor, Holly Golightly (Audrey Hepburn). Holly is an enchanting combination of breathtaking elegance, glossy Manhattan sophistication, and an engaging willingness to confide in Paul because she says he reminds her of her brother Fred. Still, she doesn't really tell him anything about herself except that she likes to go to Tiffany's when she has "the mean reds" and needs to be surrounded by something comforting. She has a very active social life, but no particular job, and she picks up money in a number of odd ways from men, the oddest being getting paid to visit an elderly mob figure in Sing Sing prison once a month.

A man seems to be following Paul, but when Paul confronts him it turns out he was following Holly. He explains he was once Holly's husband, and he took care of Holly and Fred when their parents died and married her when she was fifteen. He has come to take her back home to rural Texas. She tells him she is a "wild thing" and cannot be kept in a cage, and sends him home alone.

Holly's plan is to marry a wealthy man so she can take care of Fred when he gets out of the army. She is almost successful in becoming engaged to a millionaire, but he is unsettled when it turns out she has unknowingly been carrying messages back and forth in her visits to Sing Sing. Paul comforts her when her brother is killed, and he realizes he has fallen in love with her. She will not admit to loving him, and he accuses her of being afraid to let herself become too close to anyone, even her cat. She realizes she wants to be with someone she can really love and runs after him and the cat in the pouring rain.
DISCUSSION: Holly says, "I can't think of anything I've never done," and, "I'm used to being top banana in the shock department." This might sound tawdry from most people, but she manages to make it seem as though she found it all a delicious adventure. She tries hard to protect herself from her feelings, categorizing all the men she considers possible partners for her as "rats and super rats," planning to marry a man she does not love, refusing to give Cat a real name, trying to create a world for herself that is a perpetual Tiffany's, where "nothing bad

could happen to you," but it does not work. Holly's carelessness about forgetting her keys and imposing on others to get in, about her apartment decor and about Cat, and about her means of support all hide a core of pragmatic resolve, as we see in Doc Golightly's story about her, and by her devotion to Fred. They also hide her vulnerability, as though she feels if she does not float above her emotions she will give way entirely. She does give way entirely when Fred is killed, an outpouring of real emotion scaring away the man she is cultivating.

Paul understands this because it parallels his own experience. He once cared about writing, but as the movie opens he has given up any notion of personal or artistic integrity to allow himself to be kept by a wealthy woman. Her grotesque and excessive decoration of his apartment makes him just another ornament for her collection. His relationship with her is his way of protecting himself from taking the risk of feeling deeply, as an artist or as a man. Paul and Holly understand each other, and that understanding makes them ashamed of the hypocrisy of their lives.

Holly describes "the mean reds" as "suddenly you're afraid, and you don't know what you're afraid of." Everyone has this feeling from time to time, but it resonates particularly with teenagers, who experience more volatile and complex emotions than any they have known before, and who tend to conclude since these emotions are new to them, they have never been felt before. This movie provides a good opportunity to talk about those feelings and about strategies for handling them.

Parents should note that on their day in New York City together, Paul and Holly steal two masks from a dime store for fun. Although it is probably not a good idea to make heavy-handed references to this as a moral failure, in discussions with teenagers, parents may want to voice their concerns.

PROFANITY: None.
NUDITY/SEXUAL REFERENCES: Very subtle references to the fact that Holly is practically a paid escort.
ALCOHOL/DRUG ABUSE: Drinking and smoking; characters get drunk.
VIOLENCE/SCARINESS: Some mild suspense; Holly's hysteria when she receives the telegram about her brother may be scary.
TOLERANCE/DIVERSITY ISSUES: Mickey Rooney plays a Japanese man in an exaggerated style that is very insensitive by today's standards.

QUESTIONS FOR FAMILIES:

- Have you ever felt "the mean reds"? Why does Tiffany's make Holly feel better when she feels that way? What makes you feel better?

- Why did Holly marry Doc? Why did she leave him?

- What makes Paul decide to break up with the woman he refers to as "2-E"?

- What did Holly's friend mean when he called Holly a "real phony"?

CONNECTIONS: The young boys in **To Kill a Mockingbird** and **A Christmas Memory** are based on the childhood of author Truman Capote. "Moon River," one of the most memorable songs in the history of the movies, was written around Hepburn's sweet, but limited, range and won the Oscar for Best Song.

Blake Edwards enjoyed making the party scene in this movie so much he went on to make an entire movie about a crazy party called, not surprisingly, *The Party*. It is not as good as some of his other movies, including this one, **The Great Race**, *The Pink Panther*, and (for mature teenagers only) *Days of Wine and Roses*, and *Victor/Victoria*.

ACTIVITIES: Visit Tiffany's. The novella, by Truman Capote, is worth reading for mature teenagers, but in the book Paul is gay, and Holly does not have the elegance and class that Hepburn brought to the role or the Hollywood happy ending of the movie.

Bringing Up Baby

1938, 103 min, b&w, N, 6 and up
Dir: Howard Hawks. Cary Grant, Katharine Hepburn
PLOT: Shy paleontologist David Huxley (Cary Grant) is hoping for three things: a rare dinosaur bone fossil, a million-dollar research grant, and his marriage to colleague Miss Swallow. Madcap heiress Susan Vance (Katharine Hepburn), instantly smitten with David when he objects to her playing his golf ball and driving off in his car, manages to disrupt his life completely when she asks him to help her transport a leopard named "Baby" to her aunt's estate in Connecticut. Complications include Susan's dog, George, taking the irreplaceable bone fossil to bury somewhere, serenading the leopard to get him down from a neighbor's roof, being thrown in jail, confusing Baby with a vicious circus leopard, and the destruction of an entire dinosaur skeleton. David does not ultimately get the mil-

lion dollars (it turns out that Susan's aunt was the prospective donor), but Susan does, so everyone lives happily ever after, including Baby.

DISCUSSION: Bringing Up Baby is generally considered to be the ultimate example of the screwball comedy, which reached its apex in the 1930s. These movies featured outlandish plots (most often featuring wealthy people subjected to utter chaos) carried out at breakneck speed with a lot of witty repartee and romantic tension.

PROFANITY: None.

NUDITY/SEXUAL REFERENCES: When asked by Aunt Elizabeth what he is doing in a feathery negligee, David explodes, "I just went gay all of a sudden!" which is likely to be interpreted differently by today's audiences than it was when the film was released.

ALCOHOL/DRUG ABUSE: None.

VIOLENCE/SCARINESS: None.

TOLERANCF/DIVERSITY ISSUES: None.

QUESTIONS FOR FAMILIES:

• What is it that Susan likes so much about David? Why, ultimately, does he like her?

• Would you like to meet someone like Susan?

CONNECTIONS: Grant and Hepburn made three other films together. Two are also classic: **The Philadelphia Story** and **Holiday**. The third, *Sylvia Scarlett*, is an odd little movie (though with an enthusiastic cult following) about a group of performers that has Hepburn dressed as a boy through most of it. Other classic screwball comedies include *My Man Godfrey*, *Nothing Sacred*, **It Happened One Night**, *The Palm Beach Story*, and Peter Bogdanovich's attempted update, **What's Up, Doc?** For very thoughtful and serious essays on **Bringing Up Baby** and some of the other screwball classics, see *The Pursuit of Happiness*, by Stanley Cavell.

ACTIVITIES: Kids who enjoy this kind of comedy might enjoy some of the stories by P. G. Wodehouse, like "Uncle Fred Flits By," which portray the same kind of deliriously joyful anarchy. This movie may inspire them to take a look at dinosaur skeletons' in a museum, though there is no such thing as an "intercostal clavicle."

The Enchanted Cottage

1945, 92 min, b&w, 10 and up
Dir: John Cromwell. Dorothy McGuire, Robert Young, Mildred Natwich, Herbert Marshall
PLOT: Mrs. Minnett (Mildred Natwick), a widow, owns a small cottage that she rents out to honeymooning couples. Some people believe there is a magic about the house that keeps the couples safe and happy. Laura (Dorothy McGuire) is a plain girl who comes to work in the house because she responds to its special feeling. Oliver (Robert Young), rich and careless, comes to see the house and reserves it for his honeymoon. Before he can be married, he is called off to war and seriously injured. He comes to the cottage alone and bitter, to retreat from the world. Wanting to shield himself from his family and his former fiancee, he impulsively proposes to Laura, who accepts but does not tell him that she loves him. He is so self-absorbed that he does not even wonder why she agrees.

After the wedding, they go back to the cottage, embarrassed and uncomfortable. Then the cottage works its enchantment, and they realize that they have become beautiful and whole, and deeply in love. They live in blissful happiness, confiding only in Mrs. Minnett and their blind friend. When Oliver's family arrives, they cannot see the transformation. Oliver and Laura are crushed, until they realize that the enchantment was love, and that it would always make them beautiful to one another.

DISCUSSION: Like the magic in the story, this movie is only for believers, but there are many cynics who have a special affection for what can only be called its enchantment. As Antoine de Saint-Exupery says in The Little Prince, "It is only with the heart that one can see rightly; what is essential is invisible to the eye." Many will not have the patience for this story, but others will find it one of their favorite films.

PROFANITY: None.
NUDITY/SEXUAL REFERENCES: None.
ALCOHOL/DRUG ABUSE: None.
VIOLENCE/SCARINESS: None.
TOLERANCE/DIVERSITY ISSUES: Blind character is treated very respectfully; overall issue of tolerance of differences of appearance, ability, and class.
QUESTIONS FOR FAMILIES:

• How do the writer and director help the viewer believe in the magic that Oliver and Laura feel?

- Why doesn't Oliver want to see his family?

- Do people in love see each other differently than others see them? Can you think of other movies or books where this happens?

CONNECTIONS: Dorothy McGuire, who is highly unsuccessful in her attempt to appear unattractive in this movie, was Kathy in **Gentleman's Agreement** and played the mothers in **Swiss Family Robinson** and **A Summer Place**. Following a successful career as a leading man in the movies, Robert Young turned to television as the star of *Father Knows Best* and *Marcus Welby, M.D.*

Hello, Dolly!

1969, 146 min, G, 6 and up
Dir: Gene Kelly. Barbra Streisand, Walter Matthau, Michael Crawford, Tommy Tune
PLOT: Dolly Levi (Barbra Streisand) is a matchmaker in turn-of-the-century Yonkers, outside of New York. She is hired by Horace Vandergelder (Walter Matthau) to find him a wife. He also hires her to take his niece Ermengarde (Joyce Ames) to New York City, to encourage her to forget about marrying her artist beau, Ambrose (long-legged Tommy Tune). Instead, Dolly makes matches for his two clerks (Michael Crawford and Danny Lockin), advises them on how to get promotions from Horace, and helps Ermengarde get permission to marry Ambrose. Finally, after a series of intricate maneuvers, Dolly makes a match for herself, with Horace.
DISCUSSION: This is one of the last of the big-time, old-fashioned musicals, with lavish production values and a dozen hummable tunes. The very slight story is bolstered by terrific singing and dancing-staged by two masters of the genre: Gene Kelly, who directed, and Michael Kidd, who choreographed. The elaborate sets, costumes, and musical numbers make this movie a treat for the eyes and ears.

Dolly is almost a magical figure, with business cards for every purpose. When she tells Ermengarde and Ambrose they can earn the money they need by winning the dance contest at Harmonia Gardens, she produces one that says ARTISTS TAUGHT TO DANCE. With all the confidence it takes to transform the lives of everyone around her, she still hesitates when it comes to herself. She still mourns her late husband, Ephraim, but she wants more out of life "Before the Parade Passes By." Yet when Horace finally proposes, she waits for a sign of Ephraim's approval. What she gets is a sign that Horace has the qualities she is looking for: that, as she suspected all along, his gruff exterior conceals a warm heart and a wish to help others.

PROFANITY: None.
NUDITY/SEXUAL REFERENCES: None.
ALCOHOL/DRUG ABUSE: None.
VIOLENCE/SCARINESS: None.
TOLERANCE/DIVERSITY ISSUES: None.
QUESTIONS FOR FAMILIES:

• Why doesn't Dolly just tell Horace the truth about what she thinks is right for him and for Ermengarde?

• How does she help the people in the movie to think differently about themselves, and how does that help them change?

• What does Dolly mean when she sings "Before the Parade Passes By"?

• When the young couples sing "We've Got Elegance," do they really think they are fancy?

• What would you do if you were Barnaby and Cornelius at the Harmonia Gardens?

• What is the difference between Dolly's view of money and Horace's view?

CONNECTIONS: Michael Crawford went on from male ingénue parts (*A Funny Thing Happened on the Way to the Forum*) to star in the title role of *Phantom of the Opera*. This story, originally a German play, has been produced in a number of forms, including *The Matchmaker*, a nonmusical play written by Thornton Wilder (of *Our Town*), filmed with Shirley Booth, and most recently redone by avant-garde playwright Tom Stoppard, from the perspective of the two clerks, as *On the Razzle*.
ACTIVITIES: Take the kids to a parade, preferably one where they can march along. They might also enjoy making some hats inspired by the spectacular creations in the movie.

I Know Where I'm Going!

1945, 91 min, NR, b&w, 10 and up
Dir. Michael Powell and Emeric Pressburger. Wendy Hiller, Roger Livesey

PLOT: As a baby, as a five-year-old, as a schoolgirl, and as a young woman, Joan Webster (Wendy Hiller) always knows exactly what she wants. Whether it is "real silk stockings" instead of synthetic ones, or dinner in an elegant restaurant instead of an evening at the movies, she insists on getting it. As the movie begins, she tells her father she is about to marry one of the richest men in England, and she is leaving that night for his island off the coast of Scotland. At each step of the trip, one of her fiancé's employees is there to make sure things go smoothly, but once she gets to Scotland the fog is so thick, she cannot take the boat to the island. That night she wishes for a wind to blow away the fog, and the next morning she awakens to discover she has been too successful—the wind is so strong no boats can get to the island.

Stuck where she is, she meets some of the people from the community, including Torquil MacNeil (Roger Livesey), a naval officer home on leave. "People are very poor around here," she comments to Catriona, a local woman who is a close friend of Torquil's. "Not poor, they just haven't got any money." "Same thing." "No, it isn't."

While waiting for the wind to die down, Joan has a chance to see something of the life she would have as the wife of Sir Robert Bellinger. She meets his bridge-playing friends and hears of his plans to install a swimming pool on the Kiloran estate he is renting. (It turns out he is renting it from Torquil, who is the Laird of Kiloran.) She visits a castle where Torquil's ancestors lived, and where it is said that any Laird of Kiloran who goes inside will be cursed. She goes to the sixtieth wedding anniversary party of a local couple, still very much in love.

Even though it is still not safe to take the boats out, she is desperate to leave, telling Torquil, "I'm not safe here…I'm on the brink of losing everything I've ever wanted since I could want anything." She pays a young man to take her out in the boat, and Torquil goes along. The boat almost sinks, and she loses the bridal gown she had planned to be married in. When it is finally safe to go, Joan and Torquil say good-bye. He asks her to have the bagpipes play for him someday, and she asks him for a kiss. They part, but she returns with three bagpipe players and joins him in the castle, where it turns out the curse provides any Laird of Kiloran who enters will never leave it a free man. "He shall be chained to a woman until the end of his days and he shall die in his chains."

DISCUSSION: Like **I Love You Again**, this movie falls into the category of "the life I didn't know I wanted." Joan thinks she knows what she wants and where she is going, but she is given the gift of a chance to see the alternatives. She learns while the people from the community miss having money, there are other things they care about more. She learns she can fall in love with someone who is going in a very different direction from her ideas of "where I'm going."

This movie provides a good starting point for a discussion of how we make decisions about what we want out of life, how we pursue those goals, and what we do when we are presented either with obstacles or with new information. It is a good starting point for a discussion of what is important, and how we determine what is important to us.

PROFANITY: None.
NUDITY/SEXUAL REFERENCES: None.
ALCOHOL/DRUG ABUSE: Drinking at a party.
VIOLENCE/SCARINESS: Reference to curse; stories of women whose infidelity leads to disaster; near shipwreck.
TOLERANCE/DIVERSITY ISSUES: None.
QUESTIONS FOR FAMILIES:

• The title of this movie is taken from a famous old folk song. Why did the film-makers choose it? Why did they insist on an exclamation point at the end of the title?

• Does Joan know where she is going? When does she know? Where is she going?

• What makes Joan change her mind? What do you think her life will be like?

• What is the meaning of the "terrible curse"?

CONNECTIONS: The little girl who seems so much more mature than her parents is played by then-child actress Petula Clark, who became a pop star in the 1960s ("Downtown") and appeared in the musical version of *Goodbye, Mr. Chips*.
ACTIVITIES: The bagpipe plays an important role in this movie. Children might enjoy hearing more bagpipe music, especially if they can see it performed live. Look up the Hebrides, where this movie takes place, in an atlas or encyclopedia. Find out if your area has any legends like the ones described in the movie.

I Love You Again

1940, 99 min, NR, b&w, 8 and up
Dir: W. S. Van Dyke. William Powell, Myrna Loy

PLOT: Prissy, stingy Larry Wilson (William Powell) bores everyone aboard ship on his way back to the United States from a business trip. When Ryan, a fellow passenger, falls overboard, Larry is accidentally knocked overboard trying to save him. Hit on the head, he comes to as George Carey, a smooth con man whose last memory is of a train ride nine years before, when someone stole the money he was taking to bet on a fight. He has no recollection of his life as Larry, in a small town called Habersville. When he finds "Larry's" bankbook with a substantial balance, he and Ryan decide to visit Habersville to get as much of it as they can.

At the dock, they are met by Larry's wife, Kay (Myrna Loy). Carey is smitten with her, but she has come to get him to agree to a divorce. They go back to Habersville together, where Carey and Ryan plan an elaborate swindle, with the help of Carey's former partner, Duke. Constantly confronted with people and questions he cannot remember, Carey manages to fake his way through, even on a hilarious hike with a Scout-like troop of boys. Kay begins to warm to him and, when she finds out the truth from Ryan, she remains loyal. Carey tries to call off the swindle and, when that does not work, resolves everything with his last con job, happily looking forward to staying in Habersville with Kay.

DISCUSSION: Powell and Loy appeared in more films together than any screen couple since the silent movies, and this delightful romantic comedy is one of their best films. Carey's horror as he finds out more and more about his life as "Larry" is balanced by Powell with smooth maneuvering to keep everyone from finding out he can't remember anything about his life in Habersville. Loy is, as always, "the perfect wife," witty, wise and loyal. She sees the essence of the truth and is adorably charmed by it.

Amnesia of this kind occurs only in the movies and in soap operas. Even though it makes no sense medically, it does make sense dramatically. When Carey was hit on the head in a robbery nine years before, he became Larry, the boring businessman. It had to be because, on some level, a part of him wanted a "respectable life." At the end, he is neither Carey nor Larry, but a synthesis of both, ready to stay in Habersville with Kay and live happily ever after. Kay's motives are also justified. She married a bore like Larry because, as she says, she saw something exciting behind his eyes. She was the only one who glimpsed Carey inside of the stiff and proper Larry. She also sees the best in Carey. When she says he is noble and honest, she turns out to be right.

PROFANITY: None.
NUDITY/SEXUAL REFERENCES: None

ALCOHOL/DRUG ABUSE: Carey drinks (before he gets hit on the head, his refusal to drink is a signal of his prissiness); Kay gets tipsy.
VIOLENCE/SCARINESS: A couple of punches.
TOLERANCE/DIVERSITY ISSUES: None.
QUESTIONS FOR FAMILIES:

- What does Carey do to convince everyone he is Larry, and he remembers his life in Habersville?

- When he is closest to being found out, how does he handle it?

- How does he con Duke into letting him out of the swindle?

- What do you think will happen after Duke leaves with the money?

- Will Carey be at all like Larry in the future? How?

CONNECTIONS: As in **The Music Man**, this is a story about a con man who comes to a small town and is redeemed by love. Another movie with a funny scene involving a counterfeit Scout leader is *It's a Wonderful World*, with Jimmy Stewart and Claudette Colbert, and also directed by W. S. Van Dyke. A romantic drama about amnesia is **Random Harvest** in which Greer Garson marries Ronald Colman, who has forgotten his past, and loses him when he remembers it.

All of the Powell and Loy movies are a pleasure to watch, especially the Thin Man series and *Libeled Lady*. Harkspur, Jr., is played by Carl "Alfalfa" Switzer of *Our Gang*.

It Happened One Night

1934, 105 min, NR, b&w, 8 and up
Dir: Frank Capra. Clark Gable, Claudette Colbert
PLOT: Ellie Andrews (Claudette Colbert), a sheltered heiress, is furious with her industrialist father (Walter Connelly). She impetuously married an aviator named King Westley, and her father brought her home and carried her off on his yacht. She jumps overboard, swims ashore, and gets a bus ticket to get back to Westley.

On that bus is Peter Warne (Clark Gable), a hard-boiled reporter who has just been fired for drinking on the job. They annoy each other immediately. He discovers who she is and knows he has the story of a lifetime. Without letting her know that he has guessed her identity, he resolves to stay with her so he can write about whatever she does.

A storm makes the road impassable. Without much money, Peter and Ellie are forced to share a cabin at an "auto camp" (predecessor to motels in the days before interstate highways). He hangs a blanket between their sides of the room, calling it "the wall of Jericho," assuring her that "I have no trumpet." The next morning, detectives come to the cabin looking for Ellie, and Peter is charmed by her quick thinking and imagination as she pretends to be his squabbling wife. She is not the spoiled brat he imagined, just rebelling against an overprotected life.

When one of the other bus riders recognizes Ellie, they realize they will have to leave. Peter tries to teach her to hitchhike, but Ellie has her own method, which works even better. They fall in love. Through a misunderstanding, each thinks the other has left. So she goes back home, and her chastened father promises her a real wedding to Westley. The day of the wedding, Peter shows up to get reimbursed for the $39.60 he spent on Ellie. Andrews, realizing that Ellie and Peter really love each other, escorts her down the aisle at the wedding, urging her to make a break and run off with Peter. In the last scene, Ellie and Peter are back at the auto camp, and the walls of Jericho are tumbling down.

DISCUSSION: This is an exemplar of the "road picture," in which two people who don't like each other much have to get someplace together and through their adventures develop respect (and usually fall in love). In Capra's autobiography he notes that he and the screenwriter made a crucial change to the story (which originally appeared in a magazine as "Night Bus"). In that story, the rich girl was spoiled. Capra knew that the audience and Peter both had to sympathize with her, so they made her someone whose zest for life and adventure was so strong, she felt smothered by her wealth. The scene in which she explains that she had never been allowed to do anything for herself does away with any feeling of envy or resentment the audience (or Peter) might feel.

PROFANITY: None.
NUDITY/SEXUAL REFERENCES: Mild spiciness of "wall of Jericho"; in the famous hitchhiking scene, Ellie gets a car to stop by raising her skirt to show off her pretty calf, which would send an entirely unacceptable message today.
ALCOHOL/DRUG ABUSE: Peter is fired for drunkenness.
VIOLENCE/SCARINESS: None.
TOLERANCE/DIVERSITY ISSUES: Class issues (prejudice against the upper class).

QUESTIONS FOR FAMILIES:

- What makes Peter and Ellie change their minds about each other?

- If it happened today, what would be different?

- Why did Ellie and her father have a hard time communicating with each other?

CONNECTIONS: Neither of the stars was enthusiastic about this film. MGM wanted tp punish Clark Gable for being uncooperative and so loaned him to Columbia to make this movie. Several top female stars turned down the script, and Claudette Colbert said she would appear only if they doubled her usual salary. It went on to become the first movie to win all five top Academy Awards: Best Picture, Director, Actress, Actor, and Screenplay (the only others so honored were *The Silence of the Lambs* and *One Flew Over the Cuckoo's Nest*).

This movie established a standard for "screwball comedy," which has been imitated constantly but seldom matched. A crisis ensued in the underwear industry when Gable removed his shirt and audiences saw that he wasn't wearing an undershirt. Millions of men abandoned theirs in imitation. A book called *The Runaway Bride* uses the image of Ellie's change of heart as she walks down the aisle as the symbol of one of the most enduring themes in movies.

Lili

1953, 87 min, G, 6 and up
Dir: Charles Walters. Leslie Caron, Mel Ferrar, Jean Pierre Aumont, Kurt Kaszner, Zsa Zsa Gabor
PLOT: Lili (Leslie Caron), a French orphan, is dazzled by a handsome carnival magician named Marcus (Jean Pierre Aumont) when he is friendly to her, and she follows him back to the carnival. She gets a job as a waitress there, but is fired for spending too much time watching his act. Lonely and sad, she thinks of suicide, but a puppet called Carrot Top calls out to her kindly, and she starts to talk to him and the other puppets: Golo, the simple giant who is shy with girls; Marguerite, the vain beauty; and Renaldo, the sly, crafty fox.
Paul (Mel Ferrar), the puppeteer, a bitter, angry man, offers her a job in the act. His assistant, Yacov (Kurt Kaszner), explains he had once been a great dancer but was wounded in the war. Paul, drunk, refers to himself as "half man, half mountebank."

Audiences love Lili's conversations with the puppets because she is so sincere, and the show is very successful. She spends the money she makes on foolish games and knickknacks, and Paul angrily asks if there isn't something she really wants. At the show, the puppets gently ask the same thing, and we see Paul's face as he has the puppets tell Lili what she wants is to be loved, and he cares for her.

Marcus gets an offer from a hotel and leaves the carnival. It turns out he was secretly married to his assistant (Zsa Zsa Gabor). When Lili runs after Marcus to give him the ring he dropped in her trailer, Paul thinks she is running after him because she loves him, and he slaps her.

Paul is offered a wonderful opportunity to take his act to Paris. Asked by the producers if Lili is a superb actress or if he is a Svengali, he says, "She's like a little bell giving off a pure sound no matter how you strike it, because she is in herself so good and true and pure." When he finds they did not know he had been crippled, he is deeply moved. He has succeeded in transcending his disability and no longer sees himself as less than a complete man.

Lili has decided to leave. She tells Marcus, "I've been living in a dream like a little girl, not seeing what I didn't want to see," and sometimes a person outgrows dreams like a girl outgrows her dresses.

As she leaves, Carrot Top calls her back again, and asks to go with her. As each of the puppets tells her how much they care, we see Paul speaking through them. At first very touched, she thrusts back the curtain to see Paul. All he can do is speak harshly to her about the new offer, and she thinks he has been pretending to be nice to her just to get her to stay with the show. He tells her that the puppets are the parts of him he cannot show any other way. She runs away. On the road, she dreams of dancing with the puppets, each one transforming itself into Paul. Understanding all of the characters she loves are really him, she runs back to him.

DISCUSSION: This is a charming story with a lovely theme song, simply told but with a great deal of psychological insight. Lili believes what she sees on the surface. She believes the shopkeeper who offers her a job, but it turns out he is just making a pass at her. She believes Marcus's easy charm and small tricks. She believes Paul is unfeeling. That same naiveté is what makes her interaction with the puppets so endearingly believable. As she says, she always forgets they are not real. Just as Paul can only open up through them, she only opens up to them.

Paul is attracted to Lili because she is such a contrast to him. She is direct, honest, completely clear about her feelings. His leg is not as crippled as his heart. He has closed himself off, and yet his spirit needs to express itself; he needs to relate to people. So he does it through the puppets, and through them he has a freedom he could not otherwise have. When the act becomes successful, he can for the first time since his injury begin to develop the self-confidence he needs to be able to open himself up to a relationship without going through the puppets as his intermediaries.

PROFANITY: None.
NUDITY/SEXUAL REFERENCES: G-rated references to infidelity, seduction.
ALCOHOL/DRUG ABUSE: Paul gets drunk.
VIOLENCE/SCARINESS: Paul slaps Lili.
TOLERANCE/DIVERSITY ISSUES: Coming to terms with disability.
QUESTIONS FOR FAMILIES:

- Why is it easier for Paul to say what he is thinking through the puppets?

- What does he mean when he says, "I am the puppets"?

- What does Lili mean when she says people outgrow dreams?

- Why is it so important to Paul that the men who made him the offer didn't know he had a limp?

CONNECTIONS: The story for this movie was by Paul Gallico, who was inspired by Burr Tillstrom and his charming television show *Kukla, Fran and Ollie*, which is still available on video. Gallico was a prolific writer who enjoyed writing in a variety of genres, and films made from his work include, **Pride of the Yankees**, **The Three Lives of Thomasina**, and *The Poseidon Adventure*.
ACTIVITIES: Put on a puppet show. Let the kids try to make puppets that express different parts of themselves or behave in ways they cannot.

Local Hero

1983, 111 min, PG, 12 and up
Dir: Bill Forsyth. Peter Riegert, Burt Lancaster
PLOT: McIntyre (Peter Riegert) is an ambitious executive with Knox Oil & Gas, based in Houston, Texas. He is dispatched by Happer (Burt Lancaster), the company's eccentric billionaire chief executive, to a remote corner of Scotland to acquire a fishing village named Ferness and the land surrounding it for an oil refinery and storage facility.

McIntyre, all business, arrives in Ferness with Danny Oldsen (Peter Capaldi), a Knox employee from Scotland. At first, McIntyre finds it hard to adjust to the pace of Ferness. Gordon Urquhart (Denis Lawson), the local innkeeper and resident accountant, tells him to enjoy the area for a couple of days before they open negotiations. Gordon tells the villagers about the offer from Knox. They are delighted at the prospect of being bought out and begin to debate the relative merits of a Rolls-Royce over a Maserati. The only hitch to finalizing the deal is Ben, a reclusive beachcomber who lives in a shack by the shore. He owns several miles of beach and refuses to sell.

Meanwhile, McIntyre sheds his hurried Houston style and comes to enjoy the tranquil rhythms of the village. In a whiskey-induced moment, he tells Urquhart that he wants them to swap jobs. Following Happer's order to "watch the sky," he is dazzled by the aurora borealis, the northern lights, and calls Happer to report.

Happer arrives from Houston. He establishes an instant rapport with Ben and decides instead of the refinery, he will create an observatory and marine laboratory called the Happer Institute. McIntyre is sent back to Texas to organize the changes and returns to Houston, deeply missing the charm and character of his brief Highland life.

DISCUSSION: McIntyre's life in Houston is cluttered but empty. He resorts to phoning colleagues seated ten yards away to see if they are free for lunch. He cares a great deal about material things. In Ferness, his expensive watch falls into the water, and he doesn't miss it. He learns to enjoy collecting shells and examining the night sky.

In a poignant final shot we see McIntyre calling the village's pay phone. It rings and rings, but no one answers. The suggestion is tacit that while the village has invaded McIntyre's soul, he has not had a similar impact in return. McIntyre represented a fleeting interest in lives that run to slower rhythms.

The film is to be noted less for its messages or themes than its magnificent cast of quirky, delightfully observed characters and gorgeous location photography. There is a touch of magic in the story, with a marine biologist who seems to be part mermaid, and a deus ex machina happy ending for most of the characters.

NOTE: This movie has the feel of a fairy tale, but there are some odd moments that may bother some kids. Happer hires a "therapist" for a bizarre "abuse therapy." Danny saves a rabbit that is then cooked and served to Danny and McIntyre by Gordon. The very un-Hollywood resolution, with McIntyre back in Texas by himself, should prompt some discussion of what young viewers think may happen to him.

PROFANITY: Mild.
NUDITY/SEXUAL REFERENCES: Gordon and his wife have frequent (off-screen) sex; McIntyre uses a mild epithet when he is angry at his former girl-friend.
ALCOHOL/DRUG ABUSE: A great deal of social drinking; McIntyre gets drunk.
VIOLENCE/SCARINESS: None.
TOLERANCE/DIVERSITY ISSUES: Tolerance of individual differences.
QUESTIONS FOR FAMILIES:

- What does McIntyre list as the requirements for an excellent life in Houston? Do the villagers agree with him, since all but Ben are anxious to sell?

- Why does the girl with the punk outfit say she likes McIntyre?

- Why didn't Ben want to sell?

- Why, when McIntyre calls the village pay phone at the end of the film, does no one answer?

CONNECTIONS: Forsyth is also the director of the wonderful **Gregory's Girl**.
ACTIVITIES: Find Scotland on a map. Visit a marine study facility like the one they plan to build in Ferness.

The Music Man

1962, 151 min, NR, 6 and up
Dir: Morton Da Costa. Robert Preston, Shirley Jones, Buddy Hackett, Ronny Howard, Hermione Gingold, Paul Ford
PLOT: "Professor" Harold Hill (Robert Preston) is a con man posing as, a sales-man of band instruments and uniforms. He happens upon River City, a small town in Iowa. As the citizens explain in song, Iowa is a place of stubborn people who keep to themselves unless someone needs help. Hill happens upon an old friend, Marcellus Washburn (Buddy Hackett), and is ready to run his favorite scam. He plans to sell the town on the idea of a boys' band, with himself as leader, get them to order instruments and uniforms, and skip town with the money. Marcellus tells him a bit about the town and its people, and especially about the town librarian and music teacher, Marian Paroo (Shirley Jones).

Marian lives with her mother (Pert Kelton) and her little brother, Winthrop (Ronny Howard), a shy boy with a lisp, who deeply mourns his late father. In her own way, Marian, like Winthrop, is still grieving, and finds it hard to allow herself to become close to anyone. This is especially difficult because she is the subject of some gossip in the town. She has the job as librarian because an elderly man, a friend of her father's, bequeathed the library building to the town, but left the books to her, to ensure she would have permanent employment. This has caused some speculation about their relationship. The ladies in the town also think the books she recommends (including the Rubaiyat of Omar Khayyam and the novels of Balzac) are improper. Despite her mother's attempts to encourage her to be friendlier, Marian is very skeptical about Harold's motives and his credentials. He is able to dazzle the town (with the famous patter song "Trouble," offering the band as an alternative to the decadence of the town's new pool parlor), but she vows to check his credentials.

The town gets caught up in the notion of the band. Harold's charm and smooth promises enrapture everyone from the town council (he transforms them from four squabbling politicians into a harmonizing barbershop quartet) to the teenage boy all the others look up to (Harold challenges him to invent an apparatus for holding the music so that the piccolo player can read it and encourages his romance with the mayor's daughter). Harold even charms Winthrop, who is at last excited and happy about something. Harold tells all the parents their children are wonderfully gifted and the band will make them stars. Meanwhile, Harold's attention to Marian is becoming more than just a way to help him get the money. Despite evidence that he does not have the credentials he claims, and her certainty he is not what he pretends to be, she finds herself softening toward him and protecting him.

Because of her, he stays too long, and he is arrested. As he says, "For the first time, I got my foot caught in the door." Somehow, the boys force a few sounds out of the instruments, enough for their proud parents. Harold stays on. It turns out that all along, deep inside, what he really wanted was to lead a band.

DISCUSSION: Robert Preston brought his award-winning performance as Harold Hill on Broadway to the screen in this impeccable production, perfect in every detail. In addition to the glorious production, with some of the most gorgeous music and dancing ever filmed, there is a fine story with appealing characters. Marian learns about the importance of dreams from Harold, and he learns about the importance of responsibility from her.

Harold has made a life out of other people's dreams, creating them and then spoiling them. He gives people an image of themselves as important and creative, and it is clear this is what he loves about what he does, not stealing the money from them. Marian has faith in Harold. It is not the blind faith of the rest of the town, the people who see the seventy-six trombones he sings about. She sees what is good inside him, the real way he affects people like Winthrop, the way he affects her. (She sings, "There were bells on the hills, but I never heard them ringing, oh, I never heard them at all, 'til there was you.") When Marian sees Harold and is willing to love him in spite of his past, he is for the first time able to move on from the notion of himself as a thief and a liar. Each finds the core of the other, allowing both of them to heal and take the risk necessary to make their dreams come true. For him, the risk is prison and disgrace. For her, the risk is the kind of hurt she felt when her father died, the risk we all take in loving someone. Because this is a musical, they live happily ever after.

PROFANITY: None.
NUDITY/SEXUAL REFERENCES: Very oblique speculation by the "Pick a Little, Talk a Little" ladies and by Harold and Marcellus about why the elderly gentleman donated the library building to the city but left the books to Marian; also, criticism of the raciness of the books she recommends; Harold's song about the "Sadder But Wiser Girl for Me" describes (in G-rated terms) his preference for women with some sexual experience.
ALCOHOL/DRUG ABUSE: None.
VIOLENCE/SCARINESS: None.
TOLERANCE/DIVERSITY ISSUES: None.
QUESTIONS FOR FAMILIES:

- Why is Winthrop so shy? What makes him change?

- How does Harold change people's minds? Is that good or bad?

- How does the music help to tell the story? Listen to the songs "Seventy-six Trombones" and "Good Night, My Someone" again. They are very much alike, as you can tell when they are sung together. What did the composer want that to tell you about the people who sing them?

- Why were the parents worried about their children playing pool? What do parents worry about today?

- How is Marian's library like yours? Do you know your librarian? Do people in your town ever argue about what books should be in the library?

CONNECTIONS: This movie shows some of the most talented people of their time at the top of their form. Shirley Jones appeared in many musicals, including

Oklahoma! and *Carousel*, always exquisitely lovely in voice and appearance. She also won an Oscar for her dramatic role as a prostitute in *Elmer Gantry*. Of course, she was the mother in television's musical comedy series, *The Partridge Family*.

Robert Preston had more luck in theater than in movies finding movie roles that gave him a chance to show all he could do. Every one of his film appearances is worth watching, including *The Last Starfighter* and **All the Way Home**. Choreographer Oona White also did the sensational dance numbers in **Bye Bye Birdie**. Composer Meredith Wilson never again came close to the glorious score for **The Music Man**, but he produced some nice songs for *The Unsinkable Molly Brown*.

Ninotchka

1939, 101 min, NR, b&w, 10 and up
Dir: Ernst Lubitsch. Greta Garbo, Melvyn Douglas
PLOT: Three Soviet bureaucrats arrive in Paris to sell some jewels so they can buy tractors. The former Grand Duchess Swana (Ina Claire), who lives in Paris, is outraged because they were her jewels confiscated during the Russian Revolution. Her beau, Count Leon (Melvyn Douglas), goes to court on her behalf, seeking return of the jewels. More importantly, he goes to the three Russians and plies them with wine, food, and fun to distract them from their mission.

The Soviets respond by sending a stem and severe senior official, Lena Yakushova (Greta Garbo), to straighten things out. Leon, who calls her by the nickname "Ninotchka," is unsuccessful in persuading her to enjoy the pleasures of Paris. Finally, he tries vainly to make her laugh. She is unmoved by even his best jokes, but when he falls over in his chair, she laughs uproariously. From then on, she warms to the pleasures of Paris and the charms of Leon. She dons an elegant little hat and a glamorous gown. She drinks champagne until she is tipsy.

Swana gets the jewels from a hotel employee sympathetic to the exiled Russian nobility. She tells Ninotchka she will give them back if Ninotchka will leave Paris (and Leon) immediately. Given her duty to the Soviet Union, Ninotchka has no choice. Soon, based on the success of their mission, the same three men are dispatched to Constantinople to sell furs, and soon Leon has corrupted them again and Ninotchka is sent to straighten things out. This time Leon is waiting for her, so they can stay together forever.
DISCUSSION: Kids will need some introduction to the issues behind this enchanting romantic comedy. A few words about the state of the Soviet Union following the Revolution and the different ideas of the Communists and the capitalists will prepare them.

The movie is really not about politics; it is about romance, and being open to the pleasures of life. Leon learns as much about this as Ninotchka does. Before she arrives, he is in what looks more like a business partnership than a love affair with Swana. He does not introduce the Soviets to food, drink, and girls in order to teach them about having a good time, but in a calculated attempt to profit. Ninotchka makes an emotionally honest man out of him as he makes an emotionally honest woman out of her. Note that as much as Ninotchka loves Leon, she will not compromise on her duty to her country. She completes her mission, even though she knows it may mean she will never see him again.

In a way, the story is the obverse of **Born Yesterday** and **My Fair Lady**. The women in those stories grow by using their intellect; Ninotchka grows by using her emotions.

Ernst Lubitsch was the master of the sophisticated romantic comedy. Close observers of his films notice he often uses doors to tell the story. An example in this film is the way the count's successful corruption of the Soviet emissaries is shown through a succession of delightful treats being delivered to them through the doors of their hotel suite.

PROFANITY: None.
NUDITY/SEXUAL REFERENCES: An intimate relationship between Swana and Leon is implied.
ALCOHOL/DRUG ABUSE: Festive drinking; Ninotchka gets tipsy on champagne.
VIOLENCE/SCARINESS: None.
TOLERANCE/DIVERSITY ISSUES: Ninotchka is a high-ranking and highly respected official.
QUESTIONS FOR FAMILIES:

• If they had gone to court, who would have won the jewels? What is the best argument for each side?

• What does Swana try to do when she sees Ninotchka at the nightclub?

• What would you say the "moral" of this little romantic comedy is?

CONNECTIONS: This movie had one of the most famous ad slogans of all time: "Garbo Laughs." The mysterious dramatic actress had not made a comedy before. Director Ernst Lubitsch reported when he was considering her for the part, he asked her if she could laugh, and she said she would let him know, and then came back the next day to say she could, and proceeded to show him. *Silk Stockings* is a musical version of this story, with songs by Cole Porter. An odd update made in 1956 with Katharine Hepburn and Bob Hope(!) is called *The Iron Petticoat*.

Compare this movie to **Ball of Fire** by the same screenwriting team, another story of an intellectual who is taught to appreciate the more frivolous pleasures of life.

ACTIVITIES: Older children may want to read more about this era in Soviet history, or find out about the fall of the U.S.S.R. and the current efforts of the former Soviet states at capitalism and democracy.

The Quiet Man

1952, 129 min, NR, 8 and up
Dir: John Ford. John Wayne, Maureen O'Hara, Barry Fitzgerald
PLOT: Tall American Sean Thornton (John Wayne) arrives in Innisfree, a small, beautiful Irish village, and meets Michaeleen Flynn (Barry Fitzgerald), who drives him into town. Something of a busybody, Michaeleen is very curious and is delighted to find that Sean was born in Innisfree, and that he has come back to buy back his family home and settle there. Over the objections of "Squire" Will Danaher (Victor McLaglen), a huge fiery man, Sean buys the cottage, called White O'Morning, from the Widow Tillane (Mildred Natwick), a wealthy woman who owns the adjoining property, and settles in.

Sean sees Will's sister, Mary Kate Danaher (Maureen O'Hara), out in a field and is immediately struck by her. Sean finds her in his cottage, "being neighborly" by cleaning it for him, and he grabs her and kisses her. He sees her again at church. He approaches her as he would approach an American girl, but finds out the customs are different in Ireland, and if he wants to court Mary Kate, he must do it according to quaint, old-fashioned rules, with the permission of her brother. Will's objections to their courtship are overcome by Father Lonergan (Ward Bond) and others, who persuade Will that he must allow Mary Kate to marry in order to be able himself to marry the Widow Tillane. He grudgingly consents, and allows them to proceed under the eye of a chaperon, none other than Michaeleen, who reminds them, "The proprieties must be observed." They drive off with Michaeleen, sitting on opposite sides of a wagon, but they get off the wagon and run away together, and as they are drenched by a sudden rainstorm, they cannot wait for "the proprieties" any longer, and they kiss.

At the wedding, Will finds out he has been tricked, and the Widow Tillane does not want her acquiescence to marry him taken for granted. He is furious. He refuses to give Mary Kate her dowry or the fine furniture she inherited from her mother. Sean does not care, and cannot understand why it is important to Mary Kate. All he wants is her. Far from being reassured by this, Mary Kate is hurt. She feels that her things and her dowry are part of who she is and part of what she brings to the marriage, and that if Sean cared about her he would fight for them. They sleep apart.

The next morning, their friends arrive with the furniture. They have "persuaded" Will to give it to her. He still won't give her the dowry. Although they love each other deeply, Sean and Mary Kate cannot resolve the problem. Mary Kate is ashamed of herself and ashamed of Sean, and goes to the train station, planning to leave him. He follows her and drags her back to a confrontation with Will, telling Will if he will not pay the dowry, he must take her back. Will gives them the money, and together, they burn it. Mary Kate smiles with delight and tells Sean she will go home and prepare supper for him.

Will and Sean then enter into an epic fistfight, which takes them all the way through the town as crowds gather to watch, cheer, and bet on the outcome. Finally, bruised, drunk, and happy, they arrive at White O'Morning for supper, Will bawling happily, "Bless all in this house."

DISCUSSION: Some critics have claimed this is an antifeminist movie, but that is a very superficial perspective. The furniture and money are important to Mary Kate because she wants to enter the relationship as an equal. She believes without them she will be to Sean what she was in Will's house, just someone to do the work. She says, "Until I've got my dowry safe about me, I'm no married woman. I'm the servant I've always been, without anything of my own!" It is just as important to Sean to let her know all he cares about is his love for her, and that alone is enough to make her an equal partner. For this reason, burning the money, which might otherwise seem foolishly wasteful, was a way for them each to win a victory.

Sean also has to conquer his fear of fighting, which requires him to open up emotionally. As "Trouper Thorn," a professional boxer in the United States, he accidentally killed an opponent in the ring. This left him afraid to let go. In the fights with Will and Mary Kate he learns he can let go physically and emotionally and strengthen his relationships. Notice how Sean and Mary Kate seem to affect even the weather as they fall in love. Gusty winds and torrential rain reflect the emotions they are feeling for each other.

PROFANITY: None.

NUDITY/SEXUAL REFERENCES: References (fairly subtle) to the fact that Mary Kate and Sean do not sleep together following their wedding. Seeing a broken bed frame following the wedding night, Michaeleen, says, "Impetuous! Homeric!"

ALCOHOL/DRUG ABUSE: A lot of drinking in pubs; references to Michaeleen's "terrible thirst"; drunkenness.

VIOLENCE/SCARINESS: Fistfight. (Flashback to Sean's professional boxing career, in which he accidentally killed another boxer, which is the reason he is reluctant to fight in Ireland.) References to ability of married couples to hit each other.

TOLERANCE/DIVERSITY ISSUES: Some prejudice against Sean as an American and an outsider. Very nice depiction of religious tolerance, as the Catholic priest tells his parishioners to pretend they are congregants of the Protestant minister, so he can impress his bishop with how many members he has in his congregation. Brief references to a (nonviolent) IRA. By today's standards, the scene where Sean drags Mary Kate quite forcibly from the train to her brother's house (and where a woman from the village hands him a stick to "beat the lovely lady with") and Michaeleen tells Mary Kate not to hit Sean until they are married, when he will be entitled to hit her back, are quite sexist, but the essence of the story shows Mary Kate and Sean are equals in the marriage.

QUESTIONS FOR FAMILIES:

- Sean and Mary Kate loved each other very much, but had a hard time understanding each other. Why was Mary Kate's dowry so important to her? How did Sean show he understood that?

- Why did they burn the money? Was that a good way to solve the problem of the dowry for both of them?

- How did Sean's friends persuade Mary Kate's brother to let Sean marry her? Was that fair?

- Why did Sean and Will like each other better after fighting each other?

CONNECTIONS: Ford won an Oscar for Best Director.

One of the highlights of **E.T.** is the scene in which E. T. is in Eliot's house alone, watching *The Quiet Man* on television. We see his connection to Eliot; E. T. sees Sean kiss Mary Kate as the wind rushes through the cottage, and Eliot, at school, grabs a classmate and gives her a kiss.

Maureen O'Hara, born in Ireland, was never more ravishing than here on her home ground, shot in magnificent Technicolor. She and Wayne made four other films together, including *Rio Grande*, also directed by Ford. She also plays the mother in **Miracle on 34th Street** and **The Parent Trap**.

This was quite a family affair. The Reverend Cyril Playfair is played by character actor Arthur Shields, in real life the brother of Barry Fitzgerald (Michaeleen). Francis Ford, who plays the man who gets off his deathbed to watch the fight, is the older brother of director John Ford. Wayne's four children and two of O'Hara's brothers also appear in the movie.

A Room With a View

1985, 115 min, NR, 10 and up
Dir: James Ivory. Helena Bonham Carter, Maggie Smith, Julian Sands, Daniel Day-Lewis

PLOT: Lucy Honeychurch (Helena Bonham Carter) arrives in Italy with her straitlaced aunt Charlotte (Maggie Smith). Disappointed at not getting the room with a view they had been promised when making their reservations at the inn, they are not sure whether it is proper to accept the offer of Mr. Emerson (Denholm Elliot) and his son George (Julian Sands), staying at the same inn, to switch rooms so they may have a view after all. Reassured by the clergyman, Mr. Beebe (Simon Callow), they agree.

Later, out in the countryside, George impetuously kisses Lucy, and her aunt, horrified, whisks her back to England. There, Lucy is engaged to Cecil, a prissy man who likes Lucy's "freshness" and "subtlety" and kisses her lightly only after asking her permission. Mr. Beebe says, "If Miss Honeychurch ever takes to live as she plays (the piano), it will be very exciting both for us and for her." He clearly does not think the engagement to Cecil is evidence that she has.

The Emersons move into a cottage near the Honeychurch family, invited by Cecil, who does not realize Lucy knows them. Lucy is distressed, partly because she wanted two elderly ladies she met in Italy to live there, and partly because having George so near is disturbing to her. She does her best to resist her attraction to him and to the passionate reality he offers, but ultimately breaks the engagement to Cecil, marries George, and returns with him to the room with a view.

DISCUSSION: Lush natural settings have a powerful effect on fictional characters, especially those in love or wanting to fall in love. In Shakespeare, lovers go to the woods to straighten things out. In the British literature of the nineteenth and early twentieth century, they often go to Italy, which represents freedom from repression, with Enchanted April and this film as prime examples. The wheat field where George kisses Lucy is in sharp contrast to the manicured lawns of the Honeychurch home, as the precise and cerebral Cecil is in contrast to the passionate George.

This is a movie about having the courage to face one's feelings, and to risk intimacy, fully knowing and being known by another person. George never hesitates to take that risk. Cecil, sensitively played by Daniel Day Lewis as a full character and not a caricature of a fop, has feelings but will never be able to "take to live as (he) plays." Clearly, he does care deeply for Lucy, but he does not have the passionate nature to respond to hers fully, as George does. As George says, Cecil "is the sort who can't know anyone intimately, least of all a woman." Cecil wants Lucy as an ornament, perhaps to enjoy her passionate nature by proxy, not realizing his own proximity is likely to stifle it. George wants Lucy "to have ideas and thoughts and feelings, even when I hold you in my arms."

PROFANITY: None.
NUDITY/SEXUAL REFERENCES: Brief nude scenes as the men go swimming (and as they run when the women approach); overall theme of the importance of sensuality.
ALCOHOL/DRUG ABUSE: None.
VIOLENCE/SCARINESS: None.
TOLERANCE/DIVERSITY ISSUES: None.
QUESTIONS FOR FAMILIES:

- Mr. Emerson refers to a "Yes! a Yes! a Yes" at the "side of the Everlasting Why." What does this mean?

- What leads Lucy to break her engagement to Cecil? What leads her to accept her feelings for George?

- What is the meaning of the title?

CONNECTIONS: Some of the themes of this movie are reminiscent of movies like **I Know Where I'm Going!**, **Born Yesterday**, *Sabrina*, **Breakfast at Tiffany's**, **It Happened One Night**, and others in which the leading lady ends up marrying someone other than the man she'd planned to marry, choosing true love and intimacy over comfort and a relationship that seemed safer.
ACTIVITIES: Teenagers might enjoy the book by E. M. Forster, and some of his other books, including *Howards End*.

7 Faces of Dr. Lao

1964, 101 min, NR, 6 and up
Dir: George Pal. Barbara Eden, Arthur O'Connell, Tony Randall
PLOT: Along a dusty western trail, an elderly Chinese man on a donkey stops beside a rough wooden sign that says "Abalone" to light his pipe with his thumb, which spouts fire like a lighter. He is Dr. Lao and he says he has a traveling circus, though all anyone can see is his donkey and a small fish in a bowl.

Lao arrives just as a wealthy man named Stark (Arthur O'Connell) is trying to buy the whole town. He warns the citizens in a town meeting that the water supply is at risk and that they must sell quickly or risk losing everything. Most are inclined to go along with him, except for Ed Cunningham, the newspaper editor (John Ericson), and Angela Benedict, the town librarian (Barbara Eden). Only Stark knows that the town will become more valuable soon when the railroad is built nearby.

Just as the town is debating Stark's offer, the circus opens. The "performers" (all played by Randall) are Merlin the Magician, Medusa, Pan, the Abominable Snowman, and the blind fortuneteller, Apollonius. Each has a lesson for someone in the town. Ultimately, the circus teaches them all the importance of staying in Abalone, and Lao goes on to his next performance.

DISCUSSION: The classic characters are all here: the idealistic newspaper editor, the lovely widowed librarian who thinks she cannot love again, the foolish middle-aged flirt, the overbearing loudmouth, and of course the avaricious villain, who brags that he bets on weakness and never loses. That works well in this story, which mixes myth and fantasy. The loudmouth is turned to stone by looking at Medusa (and when turned back by Merlin, her personality is sweetened). The librarian's heart is awakened by Pan, who changes to resemble the editor who loves her. Stark has a delightful conversation with a rattlesnake whose resemblance to him is more than physical. The low-key approach lets the children notice for themselves that Dr. Lao really is all of the characters himself. Other issues: The librarian's son begs to go with Dr. Lao, and some children may be upset when he cries at the end because Dr. Lao has left without him (even though he has left him a gift).

PROFANITY: None.
NUDITY/SEXUAL REFERENCES: In a very mild scene, Pan's music and dancing excite the librarian, who loosens up considerably.

ALCOHOL/DRUG ABUSE: Lao smokes a pipe, Stark smokes a cigar, and there is a stereotypical "town drunk."

VIOLENCE/SCARINESS: Very mild. Thugs smash the newspaper office; they are later vanquished by the Loch Ness monster.

TOLERANCE/DIVERSITY ISSUES: Today the casting of Caucasian Tony Randall as an Asian would probably cause controversy. It is not inconsistent, though, with the character's ability to transform himself into many shapes and personas. As one of the characters notices, even when he is appearing as Dr. Lao, his English shifts from fluent to pidgin depending on the circumstances.

QUESTIONS FOR FAMILIES:

• What does it mean when Dr. Lao tells Mike that "All the world's a circus"?

• If you went to that circus, what would you want to see?

• If it came to your town, who would you want to learn something from it?

CONNECTIONS: Pal was a pioneer of special effects, before the days of computers. His other films include **tom thumb** and *When Worlds Collide*.

The Sound of Music

1965, 174 min, NR, 6 and up
Dir: Robert Wise. Julie Andrews, Christopher Plummer
PLOT: This beloved musical is the fictionalized story of Maria von Trapp (Julie Andrews). It is an outstanding family film, filled with glorious music ("Do Re Mi", "My Favorite Things", "Edelweiss", "So Long, Farewell"), a romantic real-life love story, a courageous moral choice, and a heart-stopping escape.

As a postulant, Maria is "not a credit to the Abbey." While she means well, she is constantly in trouble. The wise Mother Abbess sends her away to be the governess for the seven children of a stem widower, Captain von Trapp. Obedient to their disciplinarian father, the children are uncooperative with Maria until she wins them over with her own high spirits, as well as her kindness. She also shares her love of music and her joy in the beauty around them, and they become devoted to one another.

The captain's friend Max (Richard Hadyn) hears the children sing and wants them to perform at the local festival. The captain refuses, thinking it is foolish and inappropriate. Meanwhile, the captain is considering marriage to a titled and wealthy woman, and his oldest daughter, Leisel, is beginning a romance with

Rolfe. As the Nazis threaten control of Austria, the captain knows his military skill and experience will lead them to him. He knows they will ask him to join them, and they will not accept a negative answer.

Maria, realizing she has fallen in love with the captain, runs back to the Abbey. The Mother Abbess counsels her to follow her heart, and she returns to the children. The captain realizes he loves Maria, and they are married in the Abbey. They return from their honeymoon to find that an invitation to join the Nazi Navy is waiting.

Max has put the children on the festival program, hoping the captain would relent. He forbids them to participate and makes plans to escape. When the Nazis arrive to stop him, he explains they are just on their way to perform at the festival. The Nazis escort them to the festival, where they win first prize and use their encore number to camouflage their escape. On their way out of Austria, they are betrayed by Rolfe, now a Nazi, but they are protected by the nuns in the Abbey, and they leave for Switzerland, over Maria's beloved mountains.

DISCUSSION: A number of people in this movie must make important choices when they face challenges that are completely unexpected. Maria and the captain both thought they had established what their lives would be like. Maria planned to be a nun and live in the Abbey all her life. Maria's unexpected challenge comes from within herself. She is lucky to have the wise Mother Abbess help her examine her heart to learn she is better suited for a life outside the Abbey. The Captain expected to continue with the life he had, a loving but stern father to his children and a respected aristocrat and military leader. His family had always lived in Austria, and he expected his children and grandchildren would live there, too.

The captain is used to being in control. It may be that his regimental approach to the children is as much prompted by a need to feel in greater control following the loss of his wife as it is by his military training. His original inclination to marry the baroness seems to be led by his head rather than his heart; it feels more like an alliance than a romance. Then he finds he cannot resist Maria's warm and loving heart.

Just as all of this is happening, every aspect of the life they had known in Austria is challenged by the Nazis. Unlike his friends, the captain does not have the option of making a slight accommodation to the Nazis. He must fight for them if he wants to keep his home. He gives up every material possession he has to get away, preserving freedom for himself and his family.

Everyone in Austria has to make a choice when the Nazis arrive. Rolfe becomes so committed to the Nazis he is willing to betray the young woman he cared for. Even the nuns in the Abbey must make a choice. They decide to protect the Von Trapps and impede the Nazis, risking their own freedom.

Children, especially young children, will need to be introduced to some background information to understand what these choices involved and what the risks were. It is also worthwhile to discuss with them the sweet song the captain sings to Maria, telling her he must have done something good in his past to deserve her love and the happiness she has given him.

PROFANITY: None.
NUDITY/SEXUAL REFERENCES: None.
ALCOHOL/DRUG ABUSE: None.
VIOLENCE/SCARINESS: Tension as the family escapes.
TOLERANCE/DIVERSITY ISSUES: None.
QUESTIONS FOR FAMILIES:

• Why does Maria have a problem fitting in at the Abbey?

• What does the captain learn from Maria?

• The same people, wrote the song about "My Favorite Things" in "Sound of Music" and "Whistle a Happy Tune" in The King and I. How are they alike? (Think about when it is that Maria sings the song.) If you were going to write the song, what would be on your list of favorite things?

• What is the difference in the way the captain, Max, and Rolfe each react to the Nazis?

• What does the song "Climb Every Mountain" mean?

CONNECTIONS: Sister Sophia is played by Marni Nixon, a rare onscreen appearance by the off-screen singing voice from **My Fair Lady**, **West Side Story**, and **The King and I**.
ACTIVITIES: Kids who enjoy this movie can read more about the real life family in one of the books written by Maria von Trapp, and can visit the family's lodge in Stowe, Vermont. Find Austria, Germany, and Switzerland on a map but do not try to trace the family's escape route. If they had climbed over the mountains they took in the movie, they would have ended up in Germany.

Tuck Everlasting

2002, 88 min, PG, 8 and up
Dir: Jay Russell. William Hurt, Alexis Bledel, Sissy Spacek, Jonathan Jackson
PLOT: Winnie Foster (Alexis Bledel) has a proud and proper mother (Amy Irving) who laces her into a tight corset, fences her inside manicured lawns, and pins her inside dozens of rules intended to demonstrate refinement and superiority.

Winnie's days stretch bleakly and endlessly until her mother tells her that she is going to be sent away to an even more restrictive environment, a very strict finishing school. Winnie goes outside the fence and the perfectly landscaped grounds of the house to run into the untamed woods, not knowing if she is running away from something or to something.

She gets lost. Then she sees a boy (Jonathan Jackson as Jesse), drinking from a secret spring. he and his brother kidnap her and take her to their family's hidden cabin. They treat her with an odd mixture of hospitality and intimidation, making it clear that she is not free to go. Her prim lessons in manners have given her no way to respond but acquiescence. she is drawn to Jesse and comes to love her life with the Tucks and with their sense of timelessness.

DISCUSSION: In the Tuck home, there is no time. Or, there is too much time, which turns out to be pretty much the same thing. They drank from the secret spring not realizing that its water had special power. Then they slowly began to realize that they can never be hurt or killed. They will never grow older. They will stay as they are forever.

More unsettling, though, is another growing realization, that this one difference moves them so far from the core reality of human existence that they can no longer have anything in common with other people. Indeed, they present such a challenge to the most fundamental assumptions that people are either terrified or overcome with greed. The Tucks must do anything necessary to make sure no one knows their secret. Angus Tuck (William Hurt) tells Winnie that he feels like a rock by the side of a stream, life rushing past him. For her own reasons, she feels that way, too.

PROFANITY: None.
NUDITY/SEXUAL REFERENCES: Mild romantic encounters, including a swim in underwear.
ALCOHOL/DRUG ABUSE: None.
VIOLENCE/SCARINESS: Peril, murder.
TOLERANCE/DIVERSITY ISSUES: None.

QUESTIONS FOR FAMILIES:

- What would you do if you had the choice presented to Winnie?

- Compare the movie to the book. Why make Winnie a teenager in the movie when she is only 10 in the book? How does that change the story?

CONNECTIONS: Families who enjoy this movie will enjoy the book and other books by the same author, *Bub* or *The Very Best Thing* or my favorite, *The Search for Delicious*. They might like to compare this movie to the earlier filmed version.

AN AFFAIR TO REMEMBER

1957, 115 min, NR, 10 and up
Dir: Leo McCarey. Cary Grant, Deborah Kerr
This schmaltzy classic, immortalized in Sleepless in Seattle, is about two people (Cary Grant and Deborah Kerr), both more or less "kept" by wealthy lovers, who meet on an ocean voyage and fall deeply in love. In order to prove themselves worthy of these feelings, they make a commitment to separate for six months, to support themselves through their work to see if they are both really willing to live that way together. When she is seriously injured on her way to meet him (at the top of the Empire State Building), he believes she has decided she is not willing. He is deeply hurt, but his feelings for her have made it impossible for him to return to his old life. Fast-forward through the part with the singing kids and linger over the classic weepy ending, when he discovers the real reason she was not there to meet him.
CONNECTIONS: The original version, *Love Affair*, by the same director, stars Irene Dunne and Charles Boyer, and is just as good, but stay away from the 1994 remake with Warren Beatty and Annette Bening.

CROUCHING TIGER, HIDDEN DRAGON

2000, 120 min, PG-13, 14 and up
Dir: Ang Lee. Chow Yun-Fat, Michelle Yeoh
This ravishing fairy tale/epic is the story of two sets of star-crossed lovers who face enormous obstacles, within themselves as well as those imposed by the outside world. It is a thrilling adventure saga that includes a magical 400-year-old sword called "Green Destiny," a warrior who must avenge the murder of his master, a handsome bandit, the spoiled daughter of a high-ranking official who dreams of the freedom to do what she wants, and the bitter villain who wants to

destroy them all. It is dazzling, with breathtaking landscapes, gorgeous costumes, and magnificent cello music played by Yo Yo Ma. It also has, unquestionably, the most brilliantly staged fight scenes ever put on film. Dirrector Ang Lee has described this movie as "**Sense and Sensibility** with kick-boxing," and that is indeed very apt. As in Jane Austen's novel and his screen adaptation, this is the story of two women, one led too much by her heart, one led too much by her head, and of the men they love. Families who see this movie should talk about how we balance our heads and our hearts to forge lives that are grounded in honor and in love.

The story is told with great subtlety and power, giving it the quality of a myth or a collective dream. NOTE: The movie features many beautifully choreo-graphed martial arts battles. Most are bloodless, but one character is killed when a blade is hurtled into his forehead. Major characters are killed, and one death could be interpreted as suicide. Although the women in the movie are treated with complete equality and are equal to or superior to the men in judgment and combat, one female character expresses bitterness that she was not permitted to train as a warrior. There is brief mild language.

A HARD DAY'S NIGHT

1964, 85 min, NR, b&w, 8 and up
Dir: Richard Lester. The Beatles
The documentary style of this movie masks its tight construction, clever script, and sublime anarchy second only to the Marx brothers. A surrealistic day in the life of the most overwhelmingly popular rock group of all time, it portrays the Beatles sympathetically. Like the heroine of It Happened One Night, they are constantly told what to do and are smothered by all they have, while Paul's "clean" grandfather causes most of the trouble. Musical numbers include "Can't Buy Me Love" and "Should Have Known Better." Themes for discussion include the nature of fads and the problems created by success.
CONNECTIONS: See also *Help!* (more like a comedy with music, while this is more like a musical with comedy). Kids twelve and up might enjoy *I Wanna Hold Your Hand*, about teens overcome by Beatlemania, or *That Thing You Do*, written and directed by Tom Hanks, the story of a 1960s Erie, Pennsylvania, rock group that has an unexpected hit song.

HIS GIRL FRIDAY

1940, 92 min, NR, b&w, 10 and up
Dir: Howard Hawks. Cary Grant, Rosalind Russell

The Front Page, by Ben Hecht and Charles MacArthur, is a raucous romp based on the authors' experiences as reporters in the days when major cities had a dozen different newspapers competing with each other. There are a couple of good movies by that name, but in this version there is a crucial difference: the star reporter, Hildy Johnson, is played by a woman (Rosalind Russell), and the editor, Walter Burns (Cary Grant), is her ex-husband. So, his interest in keeping her at the newspaper is romantic as well as professional.

When Hildy tells Walter she is about to be married again (to a mild-mannered insurance salesman, played by Ralph Bellamy), and that she plans to move to Albany with him, Bums does everything he can to obstruct their departure. Walter persuades Hildy to cover one last story, the execution of Earl Williams, a mild-mannered man who accidentally killed a policeman. When Earl escapes, Hildy wants to make sure her paper gets the exclusive.

This is a fast and funny movie, with some barbed portrayals of reporters and government officials. Director Hawks said he wanted to make this movie the fastest ever, and the dialogue spills all over itself as all of the characters talk at the same time. NOTE: A reference to the political difficulty of the murder of a "colored" policeman is insensitive by today's standards.
CONNECTIONS: Listen for Grant's reference to "Archie Leach." That's his real name.

IT'S ALWAYS FAIR WEATHER

1955, 102 min, NR, 8 and up
Dir: Gene Kelly and Stanley Donen. Gene Kelly, Michael Kidd, Dan Dailey
At the end of WWII, three army buddies (Kelly, Dan Dailey, and, in a rare appearance before the camera, choreographer Michael Kidd) promise to meet in ten years to catch up with each other. Ten years later, none of them has done what he'd dreamed of. Kelly is a two-bit hustler whose only asset is the management contract of a boxer he won in a card game. Dailey, who'd dreamed of being an artist, is a dyspeptic advertising executive. Kidd, who'd dreamed of having an elegant restaurant, has a burger joint. At first, they can barely remember their friendship. When they team up to defend Kelly from some crooked fight promoters, and each finds something to be proud of in himself and the others.

If at all possible, see this one in a theater or in a letter-Box format, as it makes sensational use of the wide screen, especially in the number where they dance with garbage can lids on their feet. There is also a spectacular number with Kelly on roller skates. Cyd Charisse, as the brilliant and beautiful executive, sings a song with the names of all of the heavyweight champions! Screenwriters Betty

Comden and Adolph Green put some real bite into the script, especially in dealing with television, then the movies' greatest nemesis. Themes for discussion include friendship and loyalty, the role of advertising, finding self-respect.

KISS ME KATE

1953, 109 min, NR, 6 and up
Dir: George Sidney. Howard Keel, Kathryn Grayson, Ann Miller
A musical version of *The Taming of the Shrew* stars two formerly married actors in this witty and energetic musical featuring the songs of Cole Porter. Howard Keel and Katherine Grayson are at their very best as the immature (but highly tuneful) couple, and Ann Miller is sensational as the brassy tap dancer cast as Bianca. James Whitmore and Keenan Wynn play small-time hoods who advise Keel to "Brush Up Your Shakespeare," and Carol Haney and Bob Fosse are on hand for some sensational dancing. Everyone learns something about being honest with themselves and others about what they really want.
CONNECTIONS: The movie was originally filmed in 3-D, which is why the characters keep throwing things at the screen!

SABRINA

1954, 113 min, NR, b&w, 10 and up
Dir: Billy Wilder. Audrey Hepburn, Humphrey Bogart, William Holden
Audrey Hepburn is incandescent in this story of the dreamy, impractical chauffeur's daughter who falls in love with the playboy son of a millionaire (William Holden). Sent to Paris to get over him, she returns more in love than ever, but now so soigne that he is utterly dazzled by her. When his businessman older brother (Humphrey Bogart) tries to distract her, he finds that he is the one becoming distracted.
CONNECTIONS: Avoid the 1995 remake.

SEARCHING FOR BOBBY FISCHER

1993, 111 min, PG, 8 and up
Dir: Steven Zaillian. Joe Montegna, Ben Kingsley, Joan Allen, Laurence Fisburne
Brilliantly written, directed, and performed, this movie is based on the true story of chess prodigy Josh Waitzkin (played by real-life chess champion Max Pomeranc), his sportswriter father (Joe Mantegna), wise mother (Joan Allen), chess master tutor (Ben Kingsley as Bruce Pandolfini), and street-player friend (Laurence Fishburne). Josh's parents must find a way to support his interest, challenge his

extraordinary ability, and make sure that he has as normal a childhood as possible. Should you teach a child to be single-mindedly competitive, if that is what it takes to be a champion? Can you relish a child's achievements without confusing them with your own? Even parents whose children are not prodigies will identify with Josh's father as he tells Josh's teacher that his son is better at chess than he will ever be at anything. The movie gets the details just right (one of the most authentically messy family dwellings in the movies) and each of the performances is quietly magnificent.

SENSE AND SENSIBILITY

1995, 135 min, PG, 10 and up
Dir: Ang Lee. Emma Thompson, Kate Winslet, Hugh Grant, Alan Rickman
Based on Jane Austen's first published novel, this is the story of two sisters, one representing "sense" (rationality) and one "sensibility" (emotion). Each falls in love, and each must struggle with the limitations of trying to conduct herself exclusively according to one of those extremes. One (Emma Thompson, who also wrote the Oscar-winning screenplay) almost loses her chance at happiness from an excess of prudence, and the other (Kate Winslet) almost loses her reputation and self-respect from an excess of romantic ardor. When the man she thinks she loves turns out to be unworthy of her admiration, she is shattered. She finds contrary to her "sensibility," it is possible to love again, and the heart and the head can work together to achieve love.

SHADOWLANDS

1993, 130 min, PG, high schoolers
Dir: Richard Attenborough. Anthony Hopkins, Deborah Winger
Anthony Hopkins plays author C. S. Lewis (whom teens may know best from the Narnia series), a man very sure of his faith and of his life alone until he meets joy Gresham (Debra Winger), an American poet. He cannot allow himself to admit his feelings for her until it is almost too late; she is diagnosed with terminal cancer. Through his love for her, he finds a deeper faith and understanding of himself. It is through his own experience of love that he begins to achieve a more profound understanding of God.
CONNECTIONS: An excellent earlier version of this story, made for the BBC with Joss Ackland and Claire Bloom, is also available.

THE SHOP AROUND THE CORNER

1940, 97 min, NR, b&w, 10 and up
Dir: Ernst Lubitsch. Jimmy Stewart, Margaret Sullavan
The employees in a Budapest leather goods shop run by Hugo (Frank Morgan) work closely together and get along well, albeit a few rough spots. Alfred (Jimmy Stewart) is used to being Hugo's favorite, and he is disconcerted when Hugo hires Klara (Margaret Sullavan). Alfred and Klara dislike each other, not realizing that each is the other's secret pen pal. As pen pals, they share their feelings and fall deeply in love. As coworkers, it takes more time for them to appreciate each other. NOTE: Hugo finds that his wife is having an affair with one of his clerks, and tries to kill himself.
CONNECTIONS: The musical remake starring Judy Garland is *In the Good Old Summertime*. There was also a Broadway musical called *She Loves Me*, and *You've Got Mail*, with Tom Hanks and Meg Ryan courting via email. Hugo is played by Frank Morgan, who plays the title role in The Wizard of Oz.

TOY STORY 2

1999, 92 min, PG, 7 and up
Dirs: Ash Brannon, John Lasseter, Lee Unkrich. Tom Hanks, Tim Allen
Woody (again voiced by Tom Hanks) is stolen by Al (voice of Wayne Knight) an evil toy store owner, who recognizes Woody as a valuable collectable. With Woody to complete the full set of toys from a 1950's television show (deliciously re-created), Al can sell them all to a toy museum in Tokyo. Woody is delighted to find out his origin and value, and to meet up with "Woody's Roundup" co-stars Jessie (voice of Joan Cusack), Stinky Pete (voice of Kelsey Grammer), and his faithful steed Bullseye. They tell him that he will be better off in the museum than waiting for Andy to outgrow him, and he starts to think they may be right. Meanwhile, Woody's friends from Andy's house have organized a rescue mission led by Buzz Lightyear (again voiced by Tim Allen). After a series of hilarious and breathtaking adventures, they arrive to rescue a Woody who is not sure he wants to be rescued.

It is enormously valuable to think about the issue Woody must face. Should he have a brief but satisfying life as the beloved friend of a child who will eventually grow up and leave him bereft? As Jessie says with some bitterness, "Do you expect Andy to take you on his honeymoon?" Or should he remain perfectly preserved and perpetually honored as a museum exhibit? Ultimately, Woody concludes that "I can't stop Andy from growing up, but I would not miss it for the world." Buzz agrees: "Life is only worth living if you're being loved by a kid." This is an enormously satisfying and meaningful point for children and parents, especially as we face the holiday season avalanche of ads and gifts. Just as it is important for the toy, it is important for the child to love and respect the few toys that are really precious and think about what it is that makes them so special. As The Little Prince says, "It is the time you have wasted on the rose that makes it so important."

CONNECTIONS: The original *Toy Story* is also a delight.

SEE ALSO:

Holiday All three leading characters are faced with a choice between a life of comfort and status and a life of adventure and meaning.

Pat and Mike A superb but insecure athlete finds that she wants something more than a quiet life in a college town with a fiancé who does not have confidence in her.

The Philadelphia Story An heiress about to marry a "man of the people" discovers spirit, intelligence, and understanding can be found in the upper classes as well as the lower.

Sullivan's Travels A successful movie director wants to make serious films, until he finds out it is comedy that provides the greatest benefit to those in need.

THE MOVIE MOM'S GUIDE FOR FAMILY VIEWING

- Watching television and movies is a treat, not a right. It's a good idea to make sure that it comes only after homework, chores, other kinds of play, and family time. Make sure there is some quiet time each day as well. The spirit is nourished by silence. All too often, we try to drown out our unsettled or lonely feelings in noise, instead of allowing them to resolve themselves. Just as important, the best and most meaningful family communication flourishes only in quiet.

- Plan with your child what he or she is going to watch. You might say something like, "We should have time for one hour of television today" or "Let's get a video to watch on Sunday afternoon." Then look at the newspaper or television guide listing together or look through a movie guide like this one to see the options and pick which ones you think are worthwhile. Try to avoid the "let's see if there's anything on television" channel surf, which has a tendency to be numbing rather than engaging or relaxing. Distract the kids with crayons or toys; not television and videos. The Washington-based Center for Media Education estimates that preschoolers watch four hours of television a day. Most educators think that anything over two hours at that age takes too much time away from the important "work" of playing, learning to interact with others, learning to amuse themselves, and developing their imaginations. School-age kids should spend even less time with television.

- Turn the television off when the program or video is over, unless there is something else you planned to watch on next. This discourages the idea that we "watch television" instead of watching particular programs.

- Watch with the kids whenever possible, and comment on what you see. Encourage them to comment, too. "What do you think he will do next?" "She looks sad. I think they hurt her feelings." "He's having a hard time feeling good about himself, isn't he?" "If you were that kid, what would you do?" "If someone said that to you, how would you feel?"

- Look for positive role models for girls. Children's shows produced for commercial networks tend to ignore girls. Producers are asked for shows with "boy appeal," because the numbers show that girls will watch shows produced for boys, but boys won't watch shows produced for girls. There is a lot of what I call "the Smurfette syndrome," a reference to the once-popular cartoon show that featured 99 highly varied male characters and one girl character, whose sole and defining characteristic was that she was a female. Whether you have daughters or sons, help them to be sensitive to these concerns, asking questions like, "Do you think it's fair that there are no girls on that team?" "How come only the boys get to go on that adventure?" and commenting positively on good female role models: "She's brave!" "That's what I call persistence!"

- Be alert for issues of race, religion, ethnicity, and class. The media tends to feature Dick and Jane, Ozzie and Harriet suburban families, where Dad works and Mom stays home and does housework and everyone is white and Christian. Non-whites are often portrayed condescendingly or stereotypically. Make sure your children know that there are many different kinds of families, and many different kinds of homes. Make an effort to be sure they see diverse families in what they watch.

- Set a good example. Don't let the kids see you veg out in front of the television, aimlessly clicking the remote. Don't tell them not to talk to you so you can watch some sitcom. Do let them see you reading, and enjoying what you read.

- Don't ever let anyone—parent, grandparent, sibling or friend—tell a child that a program or video he or she wants to watch is "too babyish." Respect children's interest and affection for the shows they like, and their need to return to old comforts.

- Make sure that children understand the difference between programs and commercials. Saturday morning cartoon commercials are particularly troublesome, with a sort of hip-hop precocity that shows grade-school kids acting like hyperactive mini-teenagers.

- If you find that you have made a mistake and taken your children to a film that you find inappropriate, leave the theater. You can get your money back. You also communicate an important lesson to your children about your commitment to protecting them, and about their right to speak up when they are unhappy. The same is true, of course, for a video or DVD you have brought home.

- Do not be shy about setting television limits with babysitters, friends' parents, or grandparents. Never leave your children with anyone without being clear about your rules.

- Be careful with tie-ins, especially cartoons based on movie characters. Just because a Saturday morning cartoon like "Beetlejuice" or "The Mask" or some fast food gizmo is geared for children does not mean that the associated movie is appropriate for them as well.

- Use movies as a starting point for developing interests. Go to the library to check out a book or video relating to what you have seen. Read the newspaper for stories relating to what you have seen. Make a craft project inspired by the show. ("Can you draw Mickey carrying the buckets of water?" "Let's try to find where Indiana Jones went on a map.")

- When in doubt, turn it off. Remember that there is no reason to watch any video unless you genuinely feel it is the best use of your child's time.

- Every month or so, try a "television diet" day without any television at all, and use the extra time for special family activities.

- When an older sibling is watching a video that is not appropriate for a younger child, make sure the younger child has an appealing alternative. It's a good time for you to do something special together, even if it is just sorting laundry or setting the table.

- Establish strict limits on viewing, but try not to use limits as a punishment, unless the offense relates to television itself (watching without permission, for example) or time management ("If you don't finish cleaning up by 3:00, you won't have time to watch the movie.") This reinforces the message that we make decisions about television and videos based only on the merits of the shows.

- Let them know why you like (or don't like) particular shows. Try not to say that something is "too old" for them, as this will just make them more interested in seeing what it is about. Sometimes it works better to say (truthfully) that it is "too stupid." Compare it to food; some shows are like healthful food, some are like candy, some are like poison. Model good television behavior yourself. Don't keep it on as background noise. Don't watch anything you don't want them to see if they are around (you'd be amazed and appalled at what a three-year-old can pick up.)

- No television in a child's bedroom, unless he or she is sick in bed. It is not only isolating, but it makes establishing limits impossible.

- Never, never, never have the television on during family meals. That is your most precious time to share the day's experiences, challenges, and thoughts, and to let children know how important they are to you. The same goes for rides in the car, minivan, or RV.

For information and permission write to Nell Minow at moviemom@
moviemom.com

Index